Characters in Fictional Worlds

Revisionen
Grundbegriffe der Literaturtheorie

Herausgegeben
von

Fotis Jannidis
Gerhard Lauer
Matías Martínez
Simone Winko

3

De Gruyter

Characters in Fictional Worlds

Understanding Imaginary Beings in Literature, Film, and Other Media

Edited by

Jens Eder
Fotis Jannidis
Ralf Schneider

De Gruyter

ISBN 978-3-11-048606-3
e-ISBN 978-3-11-023242-4

Library of Congress Cataloging-in-Publication Data

Characters in fictional worlds : understanding imaginary beings in literature, film, and other media / edited by Jens Eder, Fotis Jannidis, Ralf Schneider.
  p. cm. − (Revisionen. Grundbegriffe der Literaturtheorie ; 3)
Includes bibliographical references.
ISBN 978-3-11-023241-7 (acid-free paper)
  1. Characters and characteristics in mass media.   2. Fictitious characters.
3. Influence (Literary, artistic, etc.)   I. Eder, Jens.   II. Jannidis, Fotis.
III. Schneider, Ralf, 1966−
  P96.C43C47   2010
  809'.927−dc22

2010037621

Bibliographic information published by the Deutsche Nationalbibliothek

The Deutsche Nationalbibliothek lists this publication in the Deutsche Nationalbibliografie; detailed bibliographic data are available in the Internet at http://dnb.d-nb.de.

© 2010 Walter de Gruyter GmbH & Co. KG, Berlin/New York

Printing: Hubert & Co. GmbH & Co. KG, Göttingen
∞ Printed on acid-free paper
Printed in Germany
www.degruyter.com

Preface

Most of the contributions to this volume are based on papers presented and discussed at the conference »Characters in Fictional Worlds: Interdisciplinary Perspectives«, which was held at the Centre for Interdisciplinary Research (Zentrum für interdisziplinäre Forschung, ZIF) of the University of Bielefeld, Germany, 28 February – 2 March 2007. We would like to thank the Centre for the funding and the organization of the conference. A number of contributions were added to the topics of the conference to complement the present collection. The volume has been a long time in the making – we are very grateful to all contributors for joining this project and for their patience.

Our heartfelt thanks go to Marcus Willand for the editorial work on this project. Without his indefatigable support, care, and patience this volume would not have been printed. Sarah Böhmer, Mareike Brandt, Daniel Bund, Anne Diekjobst, Sebastian Eberle, Christian Maintz and Maike Reinerth joined forces with him, and we would like to express our gratitude to them, too.

Some of the chapters were translated into English, for which we thank the translators, Wolfram Karl Köck, Alison Rosemary Köck and Michael Pätzold. Thanks are also due to Wallace Bond Love for last-minute language support.

The editors

Content

Introduction

JENS EDER / FOTIS JANNIDIS / RALF SCHNEIDER
Characters in Fictional Worlds. An Introduction 3

I General Topics

HENRIETTE HEIDBRINK
Fictional Characters in Literary and Media Studies. A Survey
of the Research 67

MARIA E. REICHER
The Ontology of Fictional Characters 111

PATRICK COLM HOGAN
Characters and Their Plots 134

II Characters and Characterisation in Different Media

ALAN PALMER
Social Minds in *Persuasion* 157

JONATHAN CULPEPER / DAN MCINTYRE
Activity Types and Characterisation in Dramatic Discourse 176

SIMONE WINKO
On the Constitution of Characters in Poetry 208

MURRAY SMITH
Engaging Characters: Further Reflections 232

JOHANNES RIIS
Implications of Paradoxical Film Characters for Our Models
and Conceptualizations 259

JÖRG SCHWEINITZ
Stereotypes and the Narratological Analysis of Film Characters 276

CHRISTIAN HUCK / JENS KIEFER / CARSTEN SCHINKO
A ›Bizarre Love Triangle‹. Pop Clips, Figures of Address and
the Listening Spectator 290

FREDERIK LUIS ALDAMA
Characters in Comic Books 318

HENRIETTE C. VAN VUGT / JOHAN F. HOORN /
ELLY A. KONIJN
Modeling Human-Character Interactions in Virtual Space 329

III Characters and Their Audiences

RICHARD J. GERRIG
A Moment-by-Moment Perspective on Readers' Experiences
of Characters 357

CATHERINE EMMOTT / ANTHONY J. SANFORD /
MARC ALEXANDER
Scenarios, Characters' Roles and Plot Status. Readers'
Assumptions and Writers' Manipulations of Assumptions
in Narrative Texts 377

URI MARGOLIN
From Predicates to People like Us. Kinds of Readerly
Engagement with Literary Characters 400

KATJA MELLMANN
Objects of ›Empathy‹. Characters (and Other Such Things)
as Psycho-Poetic Effects 416

DAVID C. GILES
Parasocial Relationships 442

IV Characters, Culture, Identity

MARGRIT TRÖHLER
Multiple Protagonist Films. A Transcultural Everyday Practice 459

RUTH FLORACK
Ethnic Stereotypes as Elements of Character Formation 478

MARION GYMNICH
The Gender(ing) of Fictional Characters 506

V Transtextual and Transmedial Characters

BRIAN RICHARDSON
Transtextual Characters 527

WERNER WUNDERLICH
Cenerentola Risen from the Ashes. From Fairy-Tale Heroine
to Opera Figure 542

Bibliography

JENS EDER / FOTIS JANNIDIS / RALF SCHNEIDER
Characters in Fictional Worlds. A Basic Bibliography 571

Introduction

JENS EDER / FOTIS JANNIDIS / RALF SCHNEIDER

Characters in Fictional Worlds
An Introduction

1 Questions of Character Analysis and Theories of Character

Most kinds of fiction centrally feature characters – from ad hoc bedtime stories to the most complex works of art. Some characters are known to millions of people, such as Anna Karenina or Lara Croft, Ulysses or James Bond, Mickey Mouse or R2-D2. The aim of this volume is to present a survey of the varieties of international and interdisciplinary research on characters in fictional worlds in different media. That such a survey does not exist to date is perhaps due to the gaps between the disciplines, but perhaps also to the apparent normality and ubiquity of characters: We encounter them every day, and they are so familiar a phenomenon that they do not seem to require closer inspection. Yet another reason could be that once they are subject to closer scrutiny, characters prove to be highly complex objects in a number of ways. They remind one of real persons, but at the same time they seem to consist of mediated signs only. They are ›there‹ but they do not appear to exist in reality – we do not meet them on the streets, after all. They do exert an influence on us, but we cannot interact with them directly. They are incredibly versatile, they change over time and appear in different forms in different media. The introduction to Ronald B. DeWaal's Sherlock Holmes bibliography gives an impression of this:

> This bibliography is a comprehensive record of the appearances in books, periodicals and newspapers of the Sacred Writings or Canonical tales (fifty-six short stories and four novels), the Apocrypha and the manuscripts written by Sir Arthur Conan Doyle between 1886 and 1927, together with the translations of these tales into sixty-three languages, plus Braille and shorthand, the writings about the Writings or higher criticism, writings about Sherlockians and their societies, memorials and memorabilia, games, puzzles and quizzes, phonograph records, audio and video tapes, compact discs, laser discs, ballets, films, musicals, operettas, oratorios, plays, radio and television programs, parodies and pastiches, children's books, cartoons, comics, and a multitude

of other items – from advertisements to wine – that have accumulated throughout the world on the two most famous characters in literature.[1]

Terminology already posits a problem for a general or comparative approach that wants to examine (maybe even equally ›famous‹) characters across those media: We have to subsume readers, hearers, viewers, users, and players under the heading of ›recipients‹, and books, paintings, radio plays, films, video games, etc. under the heading of ›texts‹.[2] (Coming from literature and moving image studies, the authors of this introduction are aware of their limited disciplinary perspectives in trying to give a general survey of the field.)

Moreover, in any media, characters confront those who are concerned with them – creators, audiences, critics and commentators – with numerous questions. These questions can be clustered into three groups concerning the analysis and interpretation of characters.

1. In the production phase of a media product, authors, filmmakers and other media producers are mainly confronted with the question of how characters can be crafted in a way that allows them to evoke certain thoughts, feelings and lasting effects in the target audience. Sir Arthur Conan Doyle had to invent Holmes in the first place, screenwriters had to adapt him, casting agents had to cast an actor for the role, etc.
2. The interpretation of a work of fiction confronts critics and scholars with the question of how characters can be understood, interpreted and experienced, and by which stylistic devices they are shaped.
3. Studies in the fields of cultural theory and sociology consider characters as signs of empirical production and reception processes embedded in their socio-cultural contexts in different historical periods and (sub-)cultures. The master sleuth Holmes, for instance, has been read in connection with the socio-cultural developments of a modern, industrialised society.

Each of these three fields of inquiry – production, interpretation and cultural analysis – has prompted scholars to find answers and develop

---

1 De Waal: Holmes <http://special.lib.umn.edu/rare/ush/ush.html#Introduction> (Jul. 21st, 2008).
2 When we use the term ›text‹ in this introduction, we include literature, everyday language, film – and, indeed, all other utterances in which characters may occur. Following Mosbach: Bildermenschen – Menschenbilder, p. 73, we might define text to mean ›complex, coherent utterances based on signs, which are contained in a media format, and, in their totality, communicative and culturally coded‹ (German original: ›komplexe, aber formal begrenzte, kohärente und [als Ganze] kommunikative, kulturell kodierte Zeichenäußerungen‹; on film as text, see montage/av: Film als Text, and Hickethier: Film- und Fernsehanalyse, pp. 23–25.

theories. For the first two thousand years of the debate, the first set of questions was tackled mainly by practitioners – dramatists and directors, artists and media producers – with a view to practical concerns. It was only in the 19th century that a more theoretical, descriptive and systematic analysis of characters was developed in various disciplines of scholarship, such as literary studies, theatre studies, and later in film and media studies, communication studies, the history of art, philosophy and psychology. Each of these disciplines has produced diverse rival theories on which we can only cast a passing glance in this introduction (for a more detailed survey of the research, see the contribution by Henriette Heidbrink in this volume).

Simplifying matters for the purposes of clarity, we can point to four dominant paradigms that reach across disciplines but have different tenets, emphases and methods.

1. *Hermeneutic* approaches view characters dominantly as representations of human beings and emphasise the necessity of taking into consideration the specific historical and cultural background of the characters and their creators.
2. *Psychoanalytic* approaches concentrate on the psyche of both characters and recipients. They aim at explaining the inner life of characters, as well as the reactions of viewers, users, and readers with the help of psycho-dynamic models of personality (e.g., those developed by Freud and Lacan).
3. *Structuralist* and *semiotic* approaches in contrast highlight the very difference between characters and human beings, focussing on the construction of characters and the role of the (linguistic, visual, auditive or audio-visual) text. They frequently regard characters themselves as sets of signifiers and textual structures.
4. *Cognitive* theories, which have been established since the 1980s, centre on modelling in detail the cognitive and affective operations of information processing. In these approaches, characters are regarded as text-based constructs of the human mind, whose analysis requires both models of understanding text and models of the human psyche.

The rivalry between these approaches in various disciplines and regions has contributed to the fragmentation of character theory and the co-existence of viewpoints. The interdisciplinary and international survey we envisage with this volume may help to remedy the situation. Most contributors to this book have done extensive research in the field, and are thus able to present their own established approaches and theoretical results. We are hoping that this will facilitate a dialogue between different positions. The essays are roughly clustered into five groups: (1) general topics (the research on characters, their ontology, and their relation to narrative plots); (2) characters and characterisation in different media (prose fiction, drama, poetry, feature films, pop clips, comics, the internet);[3] (3) recipients' cognitive and affective responses to characters (from understanding to empathy and aesthetic evaluation); (4) relations of characters to identity and culture (stereotyping, gender); and finally, (5) characters that cross the borders of single texts or media. Clearly, this clustering is far from being comprehensive. It is only giving a first orientation and is not supposed to draw rigid lines. Many essays deal with several topics and could have been located in a different group as well.

This introduction is intended to help to situate the contributions in a more general context. We hope that our footnotes and references serve as links for the readers, pointing to essays that deal in more detail with topics we can only briefly mention here. Keeping our considerations on a rather abstract level and leaving out extensive examples and historical case studies, we start with some fundamentals: the definition and ontology of characters, their relations to real people and to the media they are represented in. We then turn to action and character constellations as two important contexts of individual characters in fictional worlds. On that basis, we examine somewhat more specifically how characters are re-identified and characterised in different media. From a more global perspective, characters can then be associated with recurring types and media genres, as well as with certain functions they fulfill and meanings they convey. Finally, we conclude with some thoughts on how recipients respond to characters and what kinds of lasting effects characters may have.

2 Definition and Ontology of Character

How we define *character* is relevant not only with regard to theoretical questions, but also in quite practical terms, for the definition influences how we analyse characters: If we regard Sherlock Holmes as a person-like being, we are likely to focus on his personality traits; if we see him as a sign, we will concentrate on the textual structures of his presentation; if we think of him as a mental construct, the psychological processes of his recipients will move centre stage, and so on. Each of these approaches, and some others, have been explicated in detail, and we can only gesture

---

3 Unfortunately, we did not succeed in including further important art forms and media like painting or TV.

towards them here.⁴ Little explanation can be found in the etymology of the term, and the languages differ to boot. The English term ›character‹ goes back to Greek *charaktér*, ›a stamping tool‹, meaning, in a figural sense, the stamp of personality, that which is unique to a human being.⁵ The French and Italian terms – *personnage* and *personaggio*, respectively – point to Latin *persona*, i.e. the mask through which the sound of the voice of an actor is heard. The German *Figur* in turn has its roots in the Latin *figura*, and suggests a form that contrasts with a background.

In spite of the differences, in all of these languages characters are most frequently defined as fictive persons⁶ or fictional analoga to human beings.⁷ Such definitions are in accordance with the intuition that we resort to knowledge about real people when we try to understand fictional characters. Definitions of this type, however, are not entirely unproblematic: they are too vague as far as the ontological status of fictive beings is concerned, they are restricted to anthropomorphous characters and exclude, e.g., animal characters, aliens, monsters and robots. This raises two questions. First, there is the basic question of the ontology of characters: What kind of object are they? Second, there is the question of their specificity: What is the difference between them and other objects of the same kind?

The ontology of characters has been discussed most widely in philosophy and in literary scholarship.⁸ One position, according to which characters are regarded as component parts of fictional worlds, has been particularly prominent in this context. Fictional worlds are in turn explained in the scholarly discourses of *fictional worlds theories* and the philosophical *possible worlds theories*.⁹ Within this framework, a fictional world is conceived of as a system of non-real but possible states, or as a constellation, created by the text, of objects, individuals, space, time,

---

4 For more detailed discussions of the definition and ontology of characters, see Eder: Fiktionstheorie; Jannidis: Figur, chap. 5 and 6; as well as the references in the subsequent footnotes.
5 See the entry in the Oxford English Dictionary.
6 E.g. Wilpert: Figur, p. 298.
7 E.g. Smith: Characters, p. 17.
8 For introductions to the debate in the discourse of philosophy, see Proudfoot: Fictional Entities; Howell: Fiction; Lamarque: Fictional Entities. The discussion in literary theory can be found in Rimmon-Kenan: Narrative Fiction, pp. 31–34, Margolin: Individuals and Margolin: Characters.
9 See Margolin: Individuals; Eco: Lector; Ryan: Worlds, Possible Worlds Theory; Doležel: Heterocosmica; Pavel: Fictional Worlds; Ronen: Possible Worlds; Buckland: Digital Dinosaurs. Cf. also the helpful surveys in Martinez / Scheffel: Erzähltheorie, pp. 123–134, and Surkamp: Narratologie.

events, regularities, etc.[10] Upon closer inspection, however, it becomes apparent that the character problem is not fully solved by referring to fictional or possible worlds, for their very status has itself been disputed.[11] Models of fictional or possible worlds do allow for an integration of characters into the larger structure of the world presented in, or created by, the text, but they do not manage to clarify the ontology of characters convincingly, because fictional or possible worlds are subject to ontological problems themselves. What is more, the scholarly discourse on characters is much older and more varied than that on fictional worlds. Therefore, it makes sense to start from the perspective of character proper.

There are four major positions on the ontological status of characters, and they are highly controversial:

1. Semiotic theories consider characters to be signs or structures of fictional texts.[12]
2. Cognitive approaches assume that characters are representations of imaginary beings in the minds of the audience.[13]
3. Some philosophers believe that characters are abstract objects beyond material reality.[14]
4. Other philosophers contend that characters do not exist at all.[15]

As we mentioned above, each of these positions has its own far-reaching implications for the analysis of characters. Each definition thus entails a particular perspective and a particular method.

This is not the place to deal with the pros and cons of the various positions in detail, not least because the authors of this introduction are not unanimous in their theoretical stance: Ralf Schneider conceives of

---

10 See, e.g., Doležel: Heterocosmica, pp. 16–23; Ryan: Narrative, p. 91.
11 For a survey of philosophical positions on the ontology of possible worlds, see Melia: Possible Worlds.
12 Branigan: Point of View, p. 12 (›surface feature of discourse‹); Wulff: Charakter, p. 1 [French ed.: 32]; see also Jannidis' criticism of (post-) structuralist varieties of this position (Figur, chap. 5).
13 For psychological approaches in literary theory, see Grabes: Personen; Schneider: Grundriß; Culpeper: Characterization; Gerrig / Allbritton: Construction, and the criticism in Jannidis: Figur, pp. 177–184. No comparably detailed version of this theory has been put forward in the area of film studies, but it is implied in many approaches, such as Bordwell: Cognition; Ohler: Filmpsychologie; Grodal: Film Genres, or Persson: Understanding Cinema.
14 See Thomasson: Fictional Characters, and Reicher: Metaphysik; see also Howell: Fiction, and Lamarque: Fictional Entities.
15 Künne: Abstrakte Gegenstände, pp. 291–322; Currie: Characters; see also Proudfoot: Fictional Entities; Howell: Fiction; Lamarque: Fictional Entities.

characters as mental constructs, as in position 2 above, whereas Fotis Jannidis and Jens Eder stand for different versions of position 3, maintaining that characters are abstract objects; another variety of this thesis can be found in Maria Reicher's contribution to this volume.¹⁶ Despite such differences, we share a number of convictions. The philosophic-semantic view that characters do not exist is jeopardised by the fact that it requires extremely complicated logical re-formulations of quite straightforward utterances about characters: every sentence about a character would have to be translated into a sentence about the text – we would not be talking about Sherlock Holmes at all, but about the books and films in which he appears. Some hold the view that characters are signs, mere words or a paradigm of traits described by words. A well-known example of this approach is Roland Barthes's *S/Z* (1970) in which one of the codes, ›voices‹, substitutes for person, understood as the web of semes attached to a proper name. In this view, a character is not to be taken for anything like a person, yet on closer examination these semes correspond to traditional character traits. Moreover, the reduction of characters to words poses many practical problems in literary and media criticism. In addition to that, every aspect of meaning of the term ›sign‹ leads to counterintuitive consequences when applied to characters: characters simply cannot be reduced to *signifiants* or *signifiés* or relations between them, because each of these aspects would imply that one character is always restricted to the one text to which it belongs, as part of the overall set of signs. It is, however, a well-known fact that characters can appear in a number of texts, as the example of Holmes and Watson clearly shows.

Given this situation, the series of essays by Uri Margolin, by combining elements of structuralism, reception theory and the theory of fictional worlds, proved to be a breakthrough. For Margolin, characters are first and foremost elements of the constructed narrative world: ›character‹, he claims, ›is a general semiotic element, independent of any particular verbal expression and ontologically different from it‹.¹⁷ If, in a similar vein, we consider characters to be elements of fictional worlds, which exist either as subjective mental entities or as inter-subjective communicative constructs, the question is what differentiates them from the other elements of the text. To what extent is Sherlock Holmes different from his pipe, the Thames or a lifelike Sherlock Holmes wax figure? This

---

16 See Schneider: Grundriß and Literary Character; Jannidis: Figur, chap. 5; Eder: Fiktionstheorie; Reicher (in this volume).
17 Margolin: Characterisation, p. 7.

question has been addressed by referring to some closely connected criteria that a character fulfills, including being animate, having an intentional mind (in the phenomenological sense), being able to act, being humanlike and having person status.[18] Some of these criteria, however, prove to be too broad or too narrow: the criterion of being animate would on the one hand include the earthworm in the possession of an angler that Holmes identifies as a clue as a character; on the other hand, it would exclude inanimate characters, such as robots. Anthropomorphism and person status would exclude many well-known characters such as Lassie or the extraterrestrial plant Audrey II (*The Little Shop of Horrors*). In contrast to these criteria, the ability to act and to have an inner life (of whatever quality) appear to be more plausible. In addition to that, an element of the text is more likely to be regarded as a character if it is a particular, recognisable entity, not an indistinct part of a mass (of beings).

At the prototypical core of the concept of character, then, is a recognisable fictional being, to which the ability to think and act is ascribed. Individual characters can deviate from this prototype in a variety of ways and to various degrees. Models in advertisements, for instance, can be hard to identify (criterion of recognisability); a character can be a reference to historical persons, such as Napoleon in historical novels and feature films (criterion of fictionality); some cannot use their bodies to act, such as the invalid Johnny in *Johnny Got His Gun* (criterion of being able to act); others are even dead from the beginning of the story, such as Harry in Hitchcock's *The Trouble with Harry* (criterion of being animate). In addition to that, Uri Margolin has pointed out that not all characters exist within the main level of the fictional world at all. He reminds us that characters can have various modes of existence: they can be factual, counterfactual, hypothetical, conditional, or purely subjective.[19] At the end of the mind game movie *Fight Club*, for instance, Tyler Durden (Brad Pitt) turns out to be the hallucinated alter ego of the nameless narrator-protagonist (Edward Norton), who suffers from a split personality syndrome. Cases like this highlight the relevance of some further questions: What is the relationship between characters and real persons?

---

18 Eder: Fiktionstheorie, pp. 55–59.
19 Margolin: Characters, p. 375.

3 Characters and People

If we conceive of characters as beings in fictional worlds, to which the audience ascribes intentionality or action, we must ask what precisely the difference between characters and real persons is. The differences concern especially the textual construction and fictional representation of characters, their ontological incompleteness, and, in connection with that, the difference between the audience's knowledge about characters on the one hand and about persons on the other.[20] Obviously, the reception of characters is quite different from the direct encounter with real persons: Readers, listeners, or viewers focus on media texts, activate media knowledge and communication rules, they cannot interact with the represented persons but can think about their meaning, as well as about causes and effects, and they can shift their attention from the level of what is represented (Sherlock Holmes) to the level of presentation (the words of the book, the actor's performance). The symbolism and the communicative mediation of characters mark fundamental differences to the observation of persons in reality. In addition to that, the texts that construct characters are *fictional*. Real persons can of course also be represented in (non-fictional) texts, such as biographies or the news, but they do not owe their existence to these texts.

This consideration is connected with the ontological incompleteness of characters. Objects in the real world have certain properties. If such objects are mentioned in a *non*-fictional text, all persons involved in the communication process will assume that even those properties of the object which the text does not name and specify explicitly are still accessible in principle. This is even true in circumstances where there is a lack of sources, so that the evidence cannot be provided. If, for instance, the colour of Napoleon's hair had not been mentioned in any of the contemporary texts about him, we would still assume that his hair was of a certain colour, and that this colour could still be found out, through the discovery of hitherto unknown sources, an exhumation, etc.

The situation appears to be entirely different in the case of characters in fictional worlds. If the medium that constitutes them provides no information on a certain property, this property is simply lacking in the fictional world – there is a gap, as it were, in that world. The recipient has

---

20 The term ›knowledge‹ is used in a wide sense here, including also erroneous beliefs, pre-conscious dispositions, procedural or implicit knowledge, kinds of embodied cognition, etc. The incompleteness of fictional characters has been discussed extensively in analytical philosophy; see Eaton: Character; Crittenden: Fictional Characters; Lamarque: How to Create.

no opportunity to fill this gap in a way that would allow him to consider it an item of reliable knowledge. We simply cannot know how many children Lady Macbeth had, or if Sherlock Holmes has a birthmark on his back – to mention two cases in point which have been discussed extensively. There is, of course, nothing that would stop the recipient from contributing such pieces of knowledge, and each individual reading, viewing, etc. is likely to differ from all other readings with regard to the unmentioned details the recipient *imagines* in the process, but on the level of the fictional universe the text creates, the information will remain unavailable.

Things get more complicated because the above formulation that ›the medium which constitutes a character provides information‹ is admittedly vague. In the most straightforward case, the colour of a character's hair is simply mentioned explicitly (in the language-based media genres) or shown (in the visual media genres). The case is less clear if a text presents this piece of information implicitly rather than explicitly (see below for a further discussion of this distinction). A character may, for instance, be presented as a typical Frisian, or a typical Italian from the south of Italy – in both cases, information on the colour of the hair is implied. The question here is to what extent the perception of persons feeds into – or ought to feed into – the perception of characters. As has become clear, knowledge that comes from outside the text plays a crucial role in many cases when a character's behaviour is to be understood adequately. Therefore, if we want to understand the text, film, etc. in its historical context, we need to find out about the psychological and anthropological knowledge that was available to the author and her or his contemporaries. This process, however, is quite different from the way we approach persons, for in a historically adequate interpretation it only makes sense to fill in information that would have been available in the context of the text's original production and reception. If we read, for instance, a historical report about the symptoms of an unknown disease, we may of course say that according to today's knowledge, it is likely that this or that particular disease is meant; in the case of a fictional text, this procedure would be anachronistic and meaningless: If the disease is unknown in the fictional world and its context, the lack of information cannot be remedied. Whether or not one wants to admit such potentially anachronistic readings depends to some degree on the theoretical background one chooses: On the one hand, it has been an established practice, e.g. in psychoanalytical interpretations, to find prove of the symptoms described by psychoanalysis in texts that precede the development of the discipline itself by a few hundred years (consider, for instance, Freud's famous analysis of the Oedipus myth in Shakespeare's *Hamlet*); on the other hand, in the context of Foucault's discourse theory it makes sense to regard the moment in which a phenomenon – say, an illness – is first described as the one in which the discourse brings forth the phenomenon in social reality, so that an *a posteriori* interpretation of a phenomenon of a previous epoch raises a number of epistemological and ideological questions. What is more, we not only make use of our knowledge about persons in understanding characters, but also our knowledge about character types, genres and the protagonists they typically feature, and the rules of specific fictional worlds: The utterance ›I want to see the sun‹ can be understood adequately in rather different ways, depending on whether it comes from a human being or a vampire.

Does this mean that characters are indefinitely changeable concepts which can only be understood in the context of particular contemporary knowledge about persons and characters? The answer is that in principle they are, but in spite of all this flexibility there seems to be a core set of properties, a common denominator that all presentations of characters share. This prototypical core or ›base type‹ – or basic structure of mental character models – is constituted by only very few and rather general properties, which seem to be anthropological givens of the perception of human (and humanlike) beings: In contrast to objects, characters have mental states, such as perceptions, thoughts, feelings, and aims. Accordingly, characters have both an outer appearance and an inner state of the psyche that is not visible from the outside. This definition of the base type is supported by recent research on person perception in early childhood.[21] Assumptions about stable features or traits appear to be essential for most characters, too, so that it makes sense to include this aspect in the definition of the basic type as well. Other approaches also include the sociality of characters as a fundamental component beside corporeality and inner states.[22] The relationship between a character and its environment may presuppose body and mind, but further particular qualities emerge from social interaction, e.g., social roles. In all three areas of the general structure of characters – corporeality, psyche, and sociality – the features that characters are ascribed can be either stable (static) or changeable (dynamic).

Even if this base type may be the same across cultures, it can only provide a very general framework. How this frame is filled will depend to a major extent, and perhaps entirely, on the respective cultural context,

---

[21] On the base type, see Jannidis: Figur, pp. 185–195, with further references to the relevant research; cf. also Tomasello et al.: Understanding.
[22] Eder: Figur, pp. 173–185.

which is subject to historical change. The constitution of characters from textual information and cultural knowledge is based on character schemata. This concept refers to expectations of regular connections that exist between two or more pieces of information. Such expectations direct the inferences of the audience: If one piece of information is given in the text, the schema allows the reader or viewer to fill in the second bit. Such schemata include such everyday items of knowledge as the fact that the consumption of alcohol will lead to intoxication.

The sources of such processes of inferencing consist of, on the one hand, knowledge about the actual world, especially the social world.[23] On the other hand, there is media knowledge and narrative knowledge about fictional worlds in general, and about the rules of the narrated world in particular.[24] Social knowledge includes person schemata; images of human nature; social categories; prototypes and stereotypes; knowledge of patterns of social interaction; groups and roles; folk psychology and sociology; the dynamics of social cognition; attribution and the interpretation of behaviour (e.g., the so-called fundamental attribution error); the knowledge of prototypical persons and last, but not least, the self-image of the reader/viewer/user. Media knowledge, on the other hand, includes an awareness of a text's communication processes and fictionality; an awareness that is guided by the rules and aims of communication as well as media-specific knowledge of genres, modes of narrative, character types, dramaturgical functions, aesthetic conventions, star images, contexts of production, intertextual references, and individual popular characters (e.g., Sherlock Holmes as a pattern of later detectives).

The entirety of the character schemata formulated by, or implied in, a text, constitutes its ›text-internal anthropology‹.[25] Of central importance in this context are traditional configurations such as the book-keeper, the melancholic, the extrovert, the beau, the vamp, etc. Such character types can emerge from a variety of sources: the knowledge of the specific kind of narrated world, the knowledge about fictional worlds in general, and

---

[23] On accounts of social perception or social cognition, see for instance Zebrowitz: Social Perception; Lavine / Borgida / Rudman: Social Cognition.

[24] On the interaction between different kinds of social and media knowledge, see Ohler: Filmpsychologie; Eder: Figur, pp. 162–248.

[25] Titzmann: Psychoanalytisches Wissen, p. 184. Titzmann correctly points out that terms like ›psychology‹ and ›anthropology‹ ought not to be taken literally, because neither should we project the concepts formulated by the specialist disciplines back onto the text and its context, nor should we overestimate the coherence of such bits of knowledge.

the knowledge about the actual world, including the habitus of social groups. We will say more on such character types below.

In view of the abundance of knowledge about people and characters in every society, it seems unlikely that there should still be gaps left in the fictional world. Even information missing from the text could be filled in from these knowledge stores. We should not forget, however, that fictional worlds are not autonomous worlds; rather, they emerge from processes of communication with their own particular rhetorical structure. Some aspects of the presentation of characters may be part of aesthetic structures that reach beyond the characters. Most importantly, characters themselves can be signs in a number of ways: they can be instances of exemplary behaviour, they can be symbols or in other ways representative of feelings, attitudes, problems and the like. In addition to that, characters are an important part of the emotional structure of literary texts, films, etc. They influence the feelings, moods and emotions of the audience to a considerable degree (see the remarks on ›Functions and Effects of Characters‹ in this introduction). In accordance with the complexity of the rhetorical structures, the reader or viewer may of course consider the number of Lady Macbeth's children. Many of the questions of this kind, however, will look irrelevant, for the aesthetic structure sketched here will determine the quality and quantity of the import of contemporary knowledge.

The differences between characters and real persons come to the fore if we systematically consider the ways we understand and talk about them. Theories of reception stress the fact that we understand characters on several levels:[26] Viewers, readers, listeners or users do not only grasp a character's corporeality, mind, and sociality in the (fictional) world. They are building on those processes to understand the character's meanings as sign or symbol, and to reflect on the character's connections to its creators, textual structures, ludic functions, etc. The latter processes diverge from the social perception of real persons, and it would be unusual (to say the least) to think about human beings in those ways. Moreover, and in accordance with the different levels of reception, the readers' or viewers' meta-fictional discourse about characters (e.g., talking about them after leaving the cinema) contains sentences of different logico-semantical structure:[27] While the statement ›Holmes is a detective‹ stays safely in the boundaries of the fictional world and might also be

---

[26] E.g., Persson: Understanding Cinema.
[27] Künne: Abstrakte Gegenstände, pp. 295–296, and Currie: Characters, are proposing different logical transcriptions of such sentences.

uttered by another character, sentences like ›Holmes stands for human reason‹, ›Holmes was invented by Sir Arthur Conan Doyle‹, or ›Holmes is more perceptive than any other fictional or real detectives‹ transcend the fictional world in different ways, connecting it with reality. But again, we usually do not talk about real persons in those ways.

Several theories have given accounts of that. Phelan has proposed the description of characters as participating in a mimetic sphere (due to the character's traits), a thematic sphere (as a representative of an idea or of a class of people), and a synthetic sphere (the material out of which the character is made).[28] In a similar way, but starting from a triangulation of several theories, Eder distinguishes between analysing characters (a) as artifacts (how are they represented, and what are their textual structures?); (b) as fictional beings (what features do they possess in the fictional world?); (c) as symbols (what do they stand for?); and (d) as symptoms (why are they the way they are, and what are their effects?).[29] According to that distinction, we perceive real persons as inhabitants of a world (the actual one), but we do not perceive them as artifacts, symbols or symptoms. This also indicates a crucial difference between emotional reactions to characters and to real humans: We not only emotionally react to characters as fictional beings, but also react to their (brilliant or clumsy) representation, to the (often controversial) meanings they impart, to the intentions of their makers (e.g., propagandistic ones), or to the supposed effects they may have (e.g., on minors). Those kinds of reactions in turn may influence the feelings we have for the fictional being (see the section on ›Recipients' Reactions and Relations to Characters‹ in this volume).[30]

Distinguishing between different aspects of analysing characters might also be helpful in understanding their media specificity, intertextuality, and transmediality. It seems plausible that characters which are represented in different media (like Holmes) may – or even have to – retain their core properties as fictional beings and symbols (e.g., in many film adaptations, Holmes is still a detective standing for human reason), while their metafictional properties as artifacts and symptoms usually change (in film, for instance, Holmes is represented by images of actors). The next section elaborates on such questions.

---

28 Phelan: Reading.
29 Eder: Figur.
30 For a reformulation and elaboration of this model in terms of semantics and pragmatics see Uri Margolin's contribution to this volume. Margolin has been one of the first to argue for considering characters' different aspects as non-actual individuals in fictional worlds, as thematic elements, as topical entities of discourse, and as artificial constructs.

4 Trans-medial and Media Specific Aspects of Character

The section on defining character (above) has shown that characters are entities in fictional worlds which are brought forth through signs, but are not identical with those signs. Most characters in modern societies are not created in face-to-face narrations, but with the help of media, such as books, comics, theatre, film, TV, the radio, or computer games. The way they are created is therefore subject to the conditions of the respective media – an aspect systematically dealt with in a forthcoming anthology by Rainer Leschke and Henriette Heidbrink.[31] Some aspects of characters and their presentation are the same across the media, while others are media specific. In what follows, we will first deal with the media specific aspects and then turn to the trans-medial ones. If we want to understand the relationship between characters and the media, we need to define the contested term ›media‹ first. Following Siegfried J. Schmidt, ›medium‹ can be seen as a compound term which comprises four components: (1) instruments of semiotic communication, such as natural languages and images; (2) media technologies used by the producer and the recipient, such as print or television technology; (3) the institutionalisation of the media-technological dispositives, for instance by publishing houses, TV stations, cinemas, etc; and (4) the individual media products, such as books, newspapers or TV spots.[32] Schmidt refers to the systemic constellation of these factors as a ›medium‹, while other authors apply the term to the individual components. In any case, the function of media is to transmit, with the help of signs, certain experiences of a perceptual, cognitive, emotional and bodily kind.[33]

Schmidt's definition of the term ›media‹ points to fundamental factors that contribute to the media specific forms of the production and reception of characters: media sign systems, technologies and institutions. The options for the production of character implied in this can be further differentiated with the help of Marie-Laure Ryan's narratological categories, which can be applied to characters in different media.[34] First,

---

31 Heidbrink / Leschke: Formen.
32 The original quotation reads: »(1) semiotische Kommunikationsinstrumente [z.B. natürliche Sprachen oder Bilder], (2) die jeweilige Medientechnologie auf Produzenten- wie auf Rezipientenseite [z.B. Druck- oder Fernsehtechnologien], (3) die sozialsystemi- sche Institutionalisierung der medientechnischen Dispositive [etwa durch Verlage, Fernsehsender, Kinos etc.] sowie (4) die jeweiligen Medienangebote wie z.B. Bücher, Zeitschriften oder Fernsehspots« Schmidt: Medienkulturwissenschaft, pp. 351–369.
33 Cf. also Vogel: Medien, p. 292.
34 Ryan: Media, pp. 282–292.

the media can be differentiated according to their spatio-temporal extension: the radio play creates characters in a specified time slot, but without positing a particular space; photo-novellas in contrast are spatially specific, but not temporally (you can look at the characters as long as you wish); other media, including the cinema or the theatre, develop characters over a specific time and space. Second, certain kinetic properties of media and their characters are connected with the spatio-temporal ones: characters in paintings are static; characters in computer games are dynamic. The third aspect refers to the semiotic code of character representation, and the sense of the recipients affected: On the one hand, there is language as a »code which speaks to the mind through the conventional meaning of its signs«, while on the other there are some »sensory modes of expression, such as sounds and pictures, which convey meaning without relying on a fixed semantic content«.[35] Because of this, characters develop varying degrees of sensory presence or distance, concreteness or abstraction. Fourth, if several codes and sensory channels are combined, they are related to each other in varying states of priority – music, for instance is more significant in the creation of character in the opera than in drama in general. The fifth differentiation deals with the technological support and materiality of signs: television allows for live broadcasts of theatre figures, while cinema does not. Finally, the cultural role and methods of production/distribution is, according to Ryan, a pragmatic differentiation: Individual media fulfil a range of functions within the system of the media, and they follow rather practical conventions: The production of a feature film is more expensive than, say, the production of a novel, and the economic considerations this entails frequently influence the creation of characters.

These differentiations can be illustrated briefly using the example of Guy Ritchie's action movie *Sherlock Holmes* (2009). The cinematic representation of Holmes deviates from that of Doyles' narratives in a number of ways: In the film, Holmes is not represented by printed words but by moving images and sound, which gives him a sensory specificity that at the same time diminishes the range of individual imaginations by the recipients. The film employs specific visual and auditory strategies of characterisation, including the acting of Robert Downey Jr., the dynamic montage and the urging music. Close-ups invite the study of Holmes' facial expression, while long shots place him in his London surroundings. Holmes' actions are slotted into a precise temporal dramaturgy, and despite the ironical mode of narration, the impression that the character is

---

35 Ibid., p. 291.

mediated through a narrator recedes into the background. This action-oriented version of Holmes, which emphasises the bodily rather than the mental capacities of the sleuth, owes much to economic constraints. However, some similarities to the literary or dramatic representations of Holmes do remain: as in novels and short stories, Holmes in the movie is characterised through various, changing perspectives, times and places; as in theatre performances, he is represented by an actor and addresses the senses of the spectators in a finite temporal sequence. In none of these media, however, is the audience in control of the character or interact with him – ludic elements that are characteristic of computer games.

In view of such basic differences the question arises to what extent we may still speak of the same character here. It is frequently the case that characters are distributed via numerous texts, media and cultures over time.[36] But is the character the same in all of these cases? Is the hero of Ritchie's action movie identical with Doyle's Holmes? Or did Doyle himself perhaps create different Holmes characters in his various stories?[37] Characters can be presented across the media, and in principle, any character can appear in any medium. Their appearances in various media products may differ according to their qualities as artifact, symbol or symptom (i.e., their crafted-ness, their meaning, and their references to reality), but it will still be the same character as long as the core features of the fictional being remain the same. There are, however, kinds of characters or character types that are specific to one medium and therefore difficult to transfer. Computer game characters such as Pacman who fulfil a predominantly ludic function and possess only few traits would appear fairly uninteresting in other media – who would want to read a novel about Pacman? In contrast to this, characters like Holmes are present in various media; they are at the centre of transmedial storytelling.[38] This is not only the case with media adaptations of individual

---

36 See Werner Wunderlich's contribution to this volume, in which he demonstrates this with the example of Cenerentola, providing ample material.

37 The contributions by Brian Richardson and Maria Reicher to this volume deal with questions of trans-textual and trans-medial identity of characters. According to Richardson, truly trans-textual characters are legitimised through the author of the original character, and they are congruent with it in terms of traits. Reicher offers an explanation for this kind of continuity of traits, differentiating between two ways of approaching the character: when experts interpret a character, they refer to a ›maximal character‹, possessing a multitude of detailed traits; normal recipients, in contrast, tend to speak about ›sub-maximal‹ characters with fewer differentiated traits. A reference to the diegetic core elements of a character in the sense of a ›sub-maximal character‹ will suffice to establish trans-textual identity.

38 Jenkins: Culture.

works, as e.g. literary adaptations, but even more so with the protagonists of the major entertainment franchises (including James Bond, Lara Croft, Harry Potter, or the characters from the *Lord of the Rings*), and even characters from advertisements (Ronald McDonald) or the personae created by successful comedians (Sacha Baron Cohen's Borat). Such trans-medial characters occur in a dense network of stories, games and other entertainment products, giving them coherence, and in many cases also their name. They can be found in the media cultures of many countries and exist, beyond the original fictional world, in marketing, merchandising, fan fiction, news reports and recipients' conversations.

The trans-medial presence of characters reaches its peak when characters are not even created through one original text in one medium, but amalgamated from sources in various media. Henry Jenkins, in his discussion of ›synergistic storytelling‹ emphasises that certain dispositions in the characters ›The Kid‹ and Niobe in *The Matrix Reloaded* can only be understood if the corresponding short films and computer games from the context of the film are known.[39] We are only able to hint at the complex questions connected with the media specificity, intertextuality and trans-mediality of characters – serious scholarly investigation of them has only just begun.

5 Character and Action

For a long time, theories of prose fiction, theatre and film have played character and action off against each other, and they have tended to give the preference to action. One of the oldest theoretical statements on character reflects on the relation of character and action in this way: »for tragedy is not a representation of men but of a piece of action [...]. Moreover, you could not have a tragedy without action, but you can have one without character-study«.[40] What Aristotle said in relation to tragedy became the origin of a school of thought which claims that in order to understand a character in a fictional world, one need only analyse its role in the action.[41] The most common labels for character in use since Greek antiquity refer in fact to the role, or function, of a character in the action of a narrative: ›Protagonist‹ refers to the main character of a narrative or a play, and ›antagonist‹ to its main opponent. In modern literary theory, the

---

39 Jenkins: Culture, pp. 103–110.
40 Aristotle: Poetics, 1450a.
41 Pfister: Drama, p. 220.

approach that reduced characters to mere functions in the action was put on a new foundation, especially in the plot theories of structuralism and in actant models.[42] In a ground-breaking corpus study of the Russian folktale, Vladimir Propp[43] analysed a hundred Russian fairy tales, constructing a sequence of 31 functions which he attributed to seven areas of action or types of character: opponent; donor; helper; princess and her father; dispatcher; hero; false hero. Greimas[44] generalised this approach with his actant model in which all narrative characters are regarded as expressions of an underlying narrative grammar composed of six actants ordered into pairs: the hero (also *sujet*) and his search for an object; the sender and the receiver; the hero's helper and the opponent. Each actant is not necessarily realised in one single character, since one character may perform more than one role, and one role may be distributed among several characters. Schank's concept of story skeletons also starts from the idea that stories have an underlying structure, but in his model there are many such structures and therefore many different roles for actors, e.g. the story of a divorce using the story skeleton ›betrayal‹ with the two actors: the betrayer and the betrayed.[45]

The models presented here stand in contrast to a number of approaches in drama theory and in practical film theory.[46] The changing number of potential positions that characters can have surrounding the core constellation of protagonist and antagonist indicates that such models are to some extent contingent, except for the core itself. If we wish to explicate which of them lends itself best to the analysis of functional roles, their theoretical foundations and their practical applicability would have to come under close scrutiny and be compared accordingly. Whether one takes as one's starting point the syntax of the language (see Greimas), analogies to mental problem solving processes (as do the developers of *Dramatica*), or Jung's theory of archetypes – none of the theoretical bases is in itself unproblematic. In spite of the differences between the models, they all contain similar core functions. This suggests that these at least can be found in typical and wide-spread types of narration.

The claim that the action of a narrative is more important than the characters must, in any case, remain ambiguous as long as it remains

---

42 Chatman: Story, pp. 108ff.; Koch: Menschendarstellung.
43 Propp: Theory.
44 Greimas: Structural Semantics.
45 See Schank: Story, chap. 6.
46 See Asmuth: Dramenanalyse, pp. 99ff.; Pfister: Drama, pp. 234ff.; Dramatica 1999).

unspecified what ›action‹ is supposed to mean. The term action can refer, in order of increasing specificity, to the following items:

1. The entire set of events in a story, including events which are not set in motion by characters but by chance, nature, etc. Included in this definition are also events in which characters are neither involved as agents nor affected in any other way, e.g., a sunrise that only the audience watches.
2. The overall activities of the characters, including the consequences of these activities. This definition also includes the mental processes in the minds of characters. Many modernist novels, with their focus on the inner life of characters, present little action in terms of physical activity and changes of situation, but much action in terms of the characters' psychological processes. Virginia Woolf summed up this tendency of the modernist novel to ›turn within‹ in her programmatic plea for a representation of the ›truth‹ of human existence beyond surface action, and even beyond the seeming logic of a plot: »Let us record the atoms as they fall upon the mind in the order in which they fall, let us trace the pattern, however disconnected and incoherent in appearance, which each sight or incident scores upon the consciousness«.[47]
3. Only the intentional behaviour of the characters, their speech and action. Some media genres favour narratives that focus on such behaviour, either because they profit from the spectacular, such as the adventure story, the war movie and a good number of computer games; or because the very intentionality is the point of the narrative, as is the case in the mystery, crime and detective story – the ›whodunit‹ usually includes the question why someone committed a crime.
4. Only the physical activities of characters, *excluding* their speech acts. Although there will be few examples of fictional worlds in which characters move and do things without ever speaking, some media genres heavily rely on action as a means of characterisation and narration, as can be seen in the suggestion of many screenwriting manuals to tell the story by action rather than by dialogue.

The action of a story in the sense of item 1 may not be constituted exclusively by *characters'* actions in the sense of items 2 to 4, but in most cases, such actions will account for the major part of the story: Stories are always stories of and about someone, and they narrate the activities of anthropomorphous characters as a rule.[48] Character, in contrast, can in

---

47 Woolf: Common, p. 190.
48 See Eder: Dramaturgie, pp. 78–82.

principle be presented without any action, as is the case in portraits, descriptions or sculptures. Even in the temporal media, such as film, some minor characters are characterised not by action but, for example, by a physiognomy that hints at the features of personality. At least in some media and some phases in the narration of fictional worlds, then, characters can be independent of action (in every sense), which is not true the other way round. There are also features of characters that are independent of action, and action-oriented approaches tend to overlook these aspects. They fail to capture the audience's understanding and experiencing of the fictional world, which is frequently focused on the characters. It is particularly in the cinema that a character has »a palpable autonomy that seems to make action subordinate to his/her prior existence«,[49] and a similar statement can of course be made for theatre. Features of characters that are independent of action may influence not only the audience's empathy, but also determine the thematic focus of a text, as well as its ethics and rhetoric. Therefore, if the action-oriented perspective is not complemented by one that focuses on character, central aspects of fictional worlds are overlooked.

With reference to the dramaturgical functions of characters in the plot, we can differentiate between two approaches. The traditional approaches have tended to employ a genre- and period-specific vocabulary for action roles. Examples that come to mind are the allegorical stock characters of the morality play (everyman, vice, folly, etc.), confidant and intriguer in traditional drama, the libertine and the fop in English Restoration comedy, or villain, sidekick, and henchman in the popular media of the 20th century. Other approaches have looked at characters' functions in more generalised ways. In an influential work, Campbell, for instance, described what he called the ›monomyth‹, using a term coined by James Joyce. A monomyth is an abstraction of numerous mythological and religious stories marking the stages of the hero's way: separation/departure; the trials and victories of initiation; return and reintegration into society.[50] According to Campbell, who bases his argument on Freud's and especially on Jung's version of psychoanalysis, the monomyth is universal and can be found in stories, myths, and legends all over the world. The tradition of universalist approaches has continued until today. For instance, Vogler has applied Campbell's approach to the structure of Hollywood films and has been influential in the screen trade.[51] From a

---

49 Bordwell: Cognition, pp. 183–198.
50 Campbell: Hero, p. 36
51 See Vogler: Journey.

more theoretically founded perspective, Patrick Colm Hogan argues that identifiable universal patterns of story-telling and emplotment are generated by a restricted set of human emotions across time and space.[52]

Although many of the approaches to plot have focused on the action rather than the characters, as we have seen, there are at least some approaches in the bewildering diversity of plot theories,[53] which have emphasised the connections rather than the distinction between character and action. E.M. Forster coined the wide-spread definition of plot as the causal and logical connections which exist between the actions of the characters in a story, and which underlie the temporal sequence in which the story is presented. In this vein, we may look at the ›and‹ in ›character and action‹ as signifying a connection rather than a separation. The logic of the story then automatically implies the logic of the character's intentions and hopes as to future events. Consequently, in order to understand the story, the reader or viewer needs to understand the wishes, plans and motivations of the characters. Among the approaches to plot that pay attention to the wish-world of the characters and the mental projection of potential, non-actual actions by the audience are those put forward by Bremond[54] and the more elaborated formulation in terms of possible worlds theory by Ryan.[55] Furthermore, Palmer expands the perspective to include the ›social mind in action‹.[56]

The ›motivation‹ of characters constitutes the interface between characters and action. The term motivation usually refers to a part of the psyche, the inner life and personality traits: the entirety of psychical processes that initiate, maintain and regulate behaviour. This definition includes aims, wishes, feelings and drives.[57] We explain the actions of characters by ascribing them such motivations, and we expect certain actions once we know their motivations. This is why motivation tends to be the motor and the centre of a story, transmits its theme and presents a significant influence on emotional reactions. It is important both for narrating characters and for interpreting them. Thus, even a rather formulaic narrative that has traditionally been analysed in terms of characters' plot functions requires at least one character's motivation in order to set the action in motion. Consider, for instance, heroic epics

---

52 Hogan: Mind; see also Hogan's contribution to this volume.
53 Dannenberg: Plot.
54 Bremond: Logic, pp. 387–411.
55 See Ryan: Worlds.
56 Palmer: Minds; see also his contribution in this volume.
57 On the psychological definition of 'motivation', see the relevant sections in Gerrig / Zimbardo: Psychology, chap. 11.

centering around a quest plot, which can be found in Western narratives from *Beowulf* to *The Lord of the Rings*. If the aim of saving the community from an external or internal threat were not an important element in the value system of the hero, he would never venture out to face the dangers; there is either the fear of disturbances to the community (and, conversely, the wish to keep disturbances away); also, he must hope for some reward for his deeds, whether the acknowledgement of the community, the love of a lady, or riches. Values, aims, wishes, hopes and fears therefore propel the action of the hero, and they invite a psychological reading of the character at the same time. Most modern narratives deal with *problems* that motivate the characters' actions. The plotting of mainstream films, for instance, follows the aims of their protagonists, who are involved in exciting problem-solving processes.[58] Motivation is a precondition also in other forms of narration: Episodic narratives deal with the momentary problems of several characters; character studies focus on unconscious needs of persons on a quest, and even characters who do not even try to fulfill their wishes produce actions on a small scale to which we ascribe motivation. Even when surreal narratives and films, such as *Un chien andalou*, prevent us from reconstructing motivations, they generate their potential to provoke from the fact that apparently we cannot help but look for motivations.

Motivations in many cases are the core of the personality of fictional beings, particularly in their interaction with other characters, so that the basic motivations of characters are a major element of their evaluation and interpretation. Once we turn to understanding narratives on the basis of characters' motivations, it is helpful to differentiate between various kinds and aspects of motivation. Concepts from psychology, philosophy, drama theory and theories of fictional worlds can contribute to a more refined definition of motivation.[59] Motivations differ according to whether they are localised in the person itself or in its environment, whether they are egotistic or altruistic, whether the person is aware of and willing or able to reflect on them, how stable and influential they are, and whether they are consistent or contradictory. To take an example: Is a murder that Holmes investigates explained by a momentary impulse, the personality of the murderer, the external situation or determined by previous events? Is it a planned homicide by a hired killer or an act of madness? Did the doer pursue the plan for a long time? Did he kill for his own advantage or because he wanted to protect others? Did he have any scruples, did he

---

58 Eder: Dramaturgie.
59 Stückrath: Literatur; Eder: Figur, pp. 428–463.

engage in an inner moral battle or is he evil to the core, as for instance Holmes' arch rival Professor Moriarty? Motivation is, finally, an important factor in the constellation of characters, which places individual characters in a network of relationships.

6 Character Constellations

Characters do not tend to appear on their own in narratives. In most cases they are part of a constellation of at least two, and frequently many more, characters. This constellation puts all the characters of a fictional world in relation to each other. The traditional classifications of characters that go back to antiquity are already based on the notion that characters are related to each other: The term ›protagonist‹, derived from the term for the first player in the classical Greek tragedy, classifies a character in terms of his function in the action, as does the opposite term, ›antagonist‹. Other terms point in the same direction: minor character, opponent, parallel or foil character – all view characters as in some way related to other characters.

An average 19th century English novel presents some two dozens of interrelated characters, a novel by Charles Dickens easily goes up to fifty or more, and in films like *Ghandi* or a TV series like *Six Feet Under*, these systems of relationships comprise up to several hundred speaking parts. A character constellation is, however, more than the mere sum of all the characters. Its structure is determined by all relationships between the characters: relations of importance, correspondences and contrasts of properties and functions, interaction and communication, conflict and agreement, mutual seeing and listening to, wishes and desires, power and value systems, narration and being narrated, perspective and participation.[60]

This is why the character constellation of a text is an abstraction. One way of reconstructing it is by looking at the changing configurations in the scenes (scenes in drama, chapters or sequences in novels, sequences or shots in film, etc.) in which certain characters are present at the same time. The dynamics of the character relationships can be approached via the succession of scenic configurations. The configuration profile of a theatre performance, a film or an episode highlights, for instance, which

---

60 On character constellations see Platz-Waury: Figurenkonstellation, pp. 591f.; Pfister: Drama; Tröhler: Hierarchien, pp. 20–27.

characters appear, and when and how many times they do, with which other characters they appear together and with which they don't.

Having said that, there are of course numerous examples in which the quantitative analysis of only the configuration misses the point of the text. Who would doubt, for instance, that the love relationship in Shakespeare's *Romeo and Juliet* is the central interest of the play? They appear together on the stage, however, in only four of the scenes, and some of these encounters are rather short. Another example is Graham Swift's novel *Last Orders* (1996), in which four elderly friends go on a journey together in order to bring the ashes of their deceased friend, Jack Dodds, to the sea and disperse them there, according to his will. During the journey, the individual memories produce a kaleidoscopic view of Jack and his various relationships to each of the four friends plus a large number of other characters. The character constellation of this novel thus includes a range of configurations that are ›only‹ remembered, in addition to the ones that occur in the main story time. What is more important in these cases is the qualitative analysis of the relationships and the properties of the characters. To some extent, then, character constellations can be mental constructs invited by the text but not necessarily projected there by the configurations. Such qualitative aspects as slight contrasts between two (or more characters), whether they have scenic appearances together or not, are particularly useful for highlighting the individuality of each of them and pointing to the thematic focus of the text.[61]

The concept of the character constellation is an important tool for the analysis and interpretation of media products and works of art. It has proved particularly useful in the analysis of novels, TV series or transmedial narrative universes that contain complex social networks. With the help of constellation analysis, various kinds of relationships can be investigated, including their social relationships (conflicts and bonds), their values and norms (moral and otherwise), their diegetic and aesthetic similarities and differences (parallel and foil characters), the hierarchies of relevance (main vs. minor characters), and their dramaturgical and thematic functions.[62] The analysis of those aspects is closely connected to questions of ideology, politics, and understanding texts as indicators of collective dispositions, problems, wishes and fears in a certain time and culture.[63]

---

61 In their contribution in this volume Emmott / Sanford / Alexander distinguish between principal characters and scenario-dependent characters.
62 Eder: Figur, pp. 464–520.
63 For instance, Margrit Tröhler connects the proliferation of multi-protagonist films in recent years with increased cultural skepticism about heroes and a greater willingkess

7 Identifying Characters

Some media texts and works of art such as paintings, sculptures or one-act plays display characters in a temporally continuous, unified or even static representation. In most narratives however, characters are presented in separate sequences interrupted by parts in which they do not appear. The question is how a character is recognised in each of the sequences, and how the individual representations are related to each other. This point is even more acute if these representations occur in different media formats or texts: if, for instance, a drawing of Holmes illustrates a novel, or if we identify Holmes across several novels or serial instalments.[64]

The fact that in real life humans ascribe a spatio-temporal continuity to bodies and assume that persons continue to exist even if they cannot be seen or heard anymore, is a precondition for this ability to identify characters. Fictional worlds constructed in the media can rely on our willingness to keep the characters existent if they are not shown or mentioned. For this to happen, each individual medium needs to establish the link between the initial presentation of a character and the subsequent occurrences. Obviously, the way characters are presented differs across various forms of media. In purely language-based texts nothing acquires an existence of its own if it is not explicitly mentioned. The link between one presentation of a character and the next will differ according to the technique of mentioning. Usually, the link is established by a stable referent, whether in the form of a name (Holmes) or a repeated description (›my friend‹ – as Sherlock Holmes is sometimes called by the narrator Watson). The mention or presentation of objects, especially articles of clothing, can have the same effect of supporting the identity of the character referred to.

Scenes play a major role in the process of identity construction within individual media texts. Literary and audiovisual narratives can, following Catherine Emmott, be understood as sequences of scenes or situational frames, of which only one is active at a particular point in the narration.[65] Scenes integrate spatio-temporal aspects with events and information

---

to consider multiple perspectives on complex modern worlds. See Tröhler: Welten; also her contribution to this book.

64 See Maria Elisabeth Reicher's contribution on the ontology of characters and Brian Richardson's chapter on transtextual characters in this volume.

65 See Emmott: Comprehension, and the contribution by Catherine Emmott, Anthony J. Sanford and Marc Alexander in this volume; cf. also the reformulation of this approach in Jannidis: Figur, pp. 109–149, which contains a more detailed discussion of the various aspects of identifying characters.

about the characters. Links to previous character representations in scenes follow special rules; in a scene in which two female and one male character are present, the personal pronoun ›he‹ will suffice to refer to one of the characters unequivocally. Identifying characters with the help of (anaphoric) references in language-based texts can be described systematically as follows. References to characters can be direct or indirect. Direct references include the use of names, definitive descriptions (e.g., ›the boy‹, ›the visitor‹) and personal pronouns.[66] Indirect references can be made by the presentation of direct character speech without any introductory fomulae, the description of actions that do not refer to any one character directly (›a hand grabbed‹) or the use of the passive voice (›the window was opened‹). The first reference to a character can be termed the ›introduction‹; if reference to the character is made in a subsequent frame, we speak of ›identification‹.[67] We can differentiate between normal, false, impeded, and deferred identifications. A ›false identification‹ occurs when a previously mentioned character is identified but it turns out later that some other character was in fact being referred to. An ›impeded identification‹ does not refer unequivocally to any specific character, and a clear reference to the character or characters is never given in the text, while in the case of ›deferred identification‹ the recipient is ultimately able to establish the identity of an equivocally presented character. Deferred identification can further be broken down into an overt form in which the recipient knows that he is kept in the dark and a covert form in which he does not.[68]

In purely auditory media like the radio play, voice, typical sounds or musical leitmotifs are added to the above list of linguistic linking devices. In purely visual media, such as comics or the silent movie, identification is usually (i.e., except for intertitles or captions) established by the similarity or identity of the visual appearance of a character, which is created through the bodies, and especially the faces, presented by the actor, or the drawing or animation.[69] In silent movies, characters are three-dimensional entities, many of whose outer attributes (looks, beauty, dress, age, gender) are immediately apparent, while other features such as names, traits, social position and relationships only emerge in the course of the film, if at all. Sound film and other audiovisual media (video games, internet clips) combine stills, moving images, spoken and written language, sound and

---

66 Margolin: Literary Narrative, p. 374.
67 In film studies, Murray Smith uses the term ›re-identification‹ to distinguish it from ›identification *with*‹ characters. See Smith: Characters, pp. 110–116.
68 Jannidis: Figur, chap. 4 and 6, based on Emmott: Comprehension.
69 Smith: Characters, pp. 110–141 on the re-identification of characters in film.

music, and can therefore also combine different techniques of identification. Rick Blaine in *Casablanca*, for instance, is first introduced by linguistic means, for his name appears on the lettering on his café, and other characters talk about him. This will arouse the audience's curiosity and make them expect his first appearance, which happens, however, only ten minutes after the film has started. The combination of language and image is established in this scene by having Rick write his name on a cheque and by having the camera pan on the upper part of his body after a cut. As in the case of Rick Blaine, the identification of characters in film, and also in music videos, is frequently predetermined by additional contextual cues. This not only concerns the text itself, but also certain para-texts. All cues which are apt to activate social and narrative knowledge in certain communicative contexts (pre-release information, advertising, paratexts, etc.) play a role in identifying characters, and they can also contribute to characterisation (see the following section).[70] When characters are represented by actors or pop stars who have had appearances in other media products, a complex network of identifications emerges.[71] Characters in film can even be re-identified when they are presented by different actors with entirely different looks, as is the case in Todd Solondz' *Palindrome*.[72] The narrative context is of great importance for establishing continuity here. A character that has been introduced by the text and identified by a recipient is attributed properties in the course of the reception. This is the area of characterisation, which we will discuss in the next section.

8 Characterisation

Until recently, characterisation was understood to mean the ascription of mainly psychological or social traits to a character by the text.[73] In fact, however, texts ascribe all manner of properties to characters, including physiological and locative ones. Thus, the term ›characterisation‹ can refer to different phenomena, not all of which are distinguished from each other clearly enough in common usage. In many cases, the term is used when a person is ascribed a certain number of stable properties. These

---

70 Eder: Figur, pp. 326–254.
71 On characters and stars in the music video, see the contribution by Christian Huck, Jens Kiefer and Carsten Schinko in this volume.
72 See the contribution of Johannes Riis in this volume for a discussion of this phenomenon.
73 E.g. Chatman: Story.

properties tend to be character traits, as for example in ›he was shy and anxious‹. Many languages have a rich stock of words for such character traits at their disposal.⁷⁴ This dimension of the term ›characterisation‹ includes statements about the outer appearance of a character. These can be rather unspecific – ›his beauty attracted men and women alike‹ – and perhaps in some way related to character traits, but they can also refer to certain specific physical markers, such as a high forehead. Whether such remarks are decoded to refer to character traits depends on the cultural contexts: In the 19th century, the popular pseudo-sciences of physiognomy and phrenology provided a code system for creating and understanding literary character via the descriptions of the shape of the head, nose, chin, mouth, etc.⁷⁵

In a broader sense, the term characterisation is frequently used to refer to information about habitual actions, the circumstances of a person and his or her social relationships: e.g., ›he lived a very secluded life‹, ›his flat was furnished in a plain style‹, ›the family doctor was his only friend‹. Such pieces of information tend to be indirect characterisations: they invite the recipient to look for a character trait that motivates the action, the circumstances or the relationships. Usually, however, more information comes in to play, for one piece of information may also hint at other motivations: A shy person may be homeless and ashamed, and somebody may be living a secluded life because they suffer from paranoia.

The broadest definition of characterisation includes all information associated with a character in a text. In addition to the usages already listed, this includes information about time, place, actions, and events connected to the character. In many cases, this is contingent information that does not hint at stable character traits. Part of this information can of course be understood to contribute to the narrative identity of the character – comparable to other operations of identity construction. It even makes sense to use this broadest sense of characterisation, simply because it is not easy to decide where to draw the line between information that is characterising and information that is not, and because the question arises whether we would not have to regard all information as contributing to narrative identity. The word ›character‹ in ›characterisation‹ puts the emphasis on a specific mental entity that is imagined as stable (e.g., ›he is a difficult person‹). In this sense, only statements about

---

74 Allport and Odbert found nearly 18.000 English words for character traits, and since then there has been considerable further research on that topic. Cf. John: Taxonomy, pp. 66–100.
75 For example, Lavater's physiognomy was very successful and influential; Graham: Lavaters' Essays.

character traits ought to count as characterisations. Having said that, there is the danger that one particular conception of character/personality, which may be culturally specific, forms the basis of all characterisations. Therefore, even if we would argue for a very broad definition of characterisation, we have to acknowledge that the usage of the term in the second sense is more common, both in everyday language and in literary scholarship. In any case, whoever uses the term in whatever sense ought to be aware of the implications.

Characterisation (in the wide sense) can then be defined as the process of connecting information with a figure in a text so as to provide a character in the fictional world with a certain property, or properties, concerning body, mind, behaviour, or relations to the (social) environment. From the perspective of reception, this distribution of information about a character corresponds to processes of understanding the character: Textual cues or signs activate inferences based on different kinds of knowledge about reality as well as about media and communication.[76] In the language-based media, characterisation works by directly and verbally ascribing to characters certain traits which are not visible from the outside, particularly psychological traits. Indirect characterisation also ascribes traits directly in words, or it reports actions which may hint at invisible states and properties. This includes all manners of activity, from habitual movements to the description of actions a character performs in his or her working life, down to the report of habitual movements or gait. In addition to that, when characters are focalizers, their mind style, i.e. habits of reasoning and of formulating thoughts in the mind, may hint at traits.

Literary scholarship has introduced the differentiation of modes of characterization, some of which are media-specific, while others are not. As early as the 19th century, literary critics spoke of the difference between direct and indirect characterisation. Scherer,[77] for instance, differentiates between direct presentation, which involves the explicit naming of the traits (»Ich zähle die Eigenschaften auf, die jemand besitzt«) on the one hand, and indirect presentation, in which the traits, and the entire personality of a character or a person need to be guessed from words, opinions and actions, on the other (»bei welcher man aus Worten, Gesinnungen, Thaten gewisse Eigenschaften und so den ganzen Charakter errathen lässt«). He argues that writers in his day prefer the

---

[76] Cf. also Jannidis chap. 6; Schneider: Grundriß, pp. 80–90; Eder: Figur: pp. 69–107; 168–232; 326–372.
[77] Scherer: Poetik, pp. 156–157.

indirect mode to the direct one, which is used in historiography, and sometimes in the novel. The indirect mode, according to Scherer, is both more skilled (»kunstvoll«) and closer to life, because this is the way we infer personality traits of other human beings. This technique of having the audience guess (»die Technik des Errathenlassens«) relies on the activity of the audience (»Selbstthätigkeit des Publicums«), whose interest can be increased by precisely this strategy.[78]

To conceptualize direct and indirect characterization as a binary opposition, however, is less convincing than meets the eye. All of the above characterisation strategies in both the language-based and the visual and audiovisual media may *appear* more or less direct to the recipients, and in many cases it is all but impossible to define which is the case: If a character in a novel is described as ›plain‹, it will to some extent depend on the specific cultural and social milieu of the character – and the reader's knowledge of its conventions – whether this verbal ascription is directly understood to refer to a certain disposition or not. In a similar vein, can the close-up of a care-worn face in a film still be called ›indirect‹? So it is probably more accurate to view direct vs. indirect as a continuum; characterisation can then be described as more or less direct.

Another important differentiation is that between altero-characterisation and self-characterisation, for information about characters can be provided by agencies other than the character (the narrator, for instance, or other characters in the same fictional world), or the character may ascribe properties to him- or herself. Other characters may pass on perfectly reliable information about the character in question, and there is no reason to assume that each and every altero-characterisation is entirely wrong simply because characters' perspectives happen to be naturally restricted by subjectivity. The other characters, however, may also pursue their own aims and motivations in the social interaction when they make a characterising statement. Such statements can therefore reveal their own value systems, so that every explicit altero-characterisation can also be read as an indirect self-characterisation of the utterer. Moreover, characterisation is not always reliable. Some textually explicit ascriptions of properties to a character may turn out to be invalid, as when this information comes from an unreliable narrator or fellow-character. Explicit ascriptions may also turn out to be hypothetical or purely subjective.

The crucial issue in the process of characterisation is thus what information, especially of a psychological nature, a recipient is able to

---

78 Ibid., pp. 156f.

associate with any character as a member of the fictional world and where this information comes from. There are at least three sources of such information: (a) textually explicit ascription of properties to a character, whether in altero-characterisation or in self-characterisation; (b) inferences that can be drawn from textual cues (e.g. ›she smiled nervously‹); (c) inferences based on information which is not associated with the character by the text itself but through reference to historically and culturally variable real-world conventions (e.g. when the appearance of a room reveals something about the person living there or the weather expresses the feelings of the protagonist).[79]

Most inferences can be understood in terms of abductions. Abduction is a more heuristic form of reasoning than deduction and induction.[80] Abductive reasoning infers the case from the result and the rule: (1) Socrates is mortal. -- *(2) All humans are mortal.* -- (3) Socrates is human. Such reasoning is not obligatory; if ›Socrates‹ is the name of a dog, (1) and (2) are still valid, but (3) is false. The inference is therefore based mostly on likelihood and it is part of a heuristic which produces well-founded assumptions rather than certified knowledge in the best case. The question in each case is whether the right rule was used for the phenomenon, i.e., the observed result. If we understand inferences in terms of abductions, the fundamental role of character models and of the character encyclopedia as rules becomes obvious: (1) is given in the text, but (2) is usually only presupposed by it and has to be supplied. Characterisation can therefore be re-conceptualised as a process to which both the text and the recipient contribute (see below).

Another key issue concerns the limits and underlying rules of such inferences when they are applied to fictional beings. Ryan, noting that recipients tend to assume that a fictional world resembles the real world unless explicitly stated otherwise, adopts the philosopher David Lewis's ›principle of minimal departure‹.[81] In a thorough criticism of this and similar hypotheses, Walton points out that this would make an infinite number of inferences possible, and he comes to the conclusion:

> There is no particular reason why anyone's beliefs about the real world should come into play. As far as implications are concerned, simple conventions to the effect that whenever such and such is fictional, so and so is as well, serve nicely […].[82]

---

79 For a systematic description of such inferences employed in characterisation, cf. Margolin: Characterization.
80 Keller: Theory, chap. 9, based on Peirce.
81 Ryan: Fiction.
82 Walton: Mimesis, p. 166.

This approach, in turn, increases the number of conventions without necessity and without providing any convincing argument as to how recipients go about accessing these conventions, apart from drawing on their real-world knowledge, despite the fact that many conventions apply only to fictional worlds. Even so, this does not invalidate Walton's criticism, which can probably be refuted only by including another element: the fact that characters are constitutive of fictional worlds which are not self-contained, but communicated. Recipients' assumptions about what is relevant in the process of communication determine the scope and validity of inferences.[83] Conan Doyle's readers may of course infer that Holmes' chin is stubbly when he does not shave; that his bodily functions are comparable to those of Watson, and, indeed, the reader; that he wears underwear under his characteristic garments – but both agents in the communication process, Doyle and his readers, appear to follow a tacit understanding that these points are unlikely to be what the story is about.

The presentation of characters is a dynamic process, as is the construction of characters in the recipient's mind. Schneider,[84] building on concepts developed by Gerrig & Allbritton,[85] has proposed a model for describing the psychological or cognitive dynamics that come into play here, based on the ›top-down‹ and ›bottom-up‹ processes observed during empirical studies on reading comprehension. The processing of information in the top-down mode involves the activation of a knowledge structure, such as a schema or a category, stored in long-term memory; this structure is initially triggered by a piece of textual information and will then guide the further processing as long as possible. Bottom-up information processing, in contrast, involves the successive accumulation of textual information in working memory, where it is kept accessible until it can be connected with prior knowledge or turned into a category or schema itself. In understanding a character in a fictional world, the recipient builds a mental model of the character into which all characterising information is integrated. Depending on the quality and quantity of the information on the character presented in the text on the one hand, and the availability of knowledge structures of the recipient on the other, the mental model construction can proceed in either of two ways: A top-down process occurs in the application of a category to a character, by slotting the information given in the text into this category, while a bottom-up process results from the successive integration of information

---

83 See Sperber / Wilson: Relevance.
84 Schneider: Grundriß; Schneider: Theory.
85 Gerrig / Allbritton: Construction.

on a character, which will lead to an individualised representation. At the beginning of a character presentation, textual cues may trigger various types of categorisation: social types (›the teacher‹, ›the widow‹); literary or media types (the hero in a *Bildungsroman*); text-specific types (characters that do not change throughout the story and are introduced in a way that evokes precisely that expectation). The mind, following a principle of parsimony, will tend to slot as many characters into such categories as possible. Successful top-down processing, however, depends on the availability of knowledge structures, and the varieties of types just mentioned involve different types of knowledge that feed into the processing: social knowledge and categories from folk psychology; literary or media knowledge, especially narrative knowledge (of genres with their typical character constellations, character types, actants, and characters' narrative functions, etc.).[86] While producers of characters can use categorisation cues for efficient characterisation, on the side of the recipient the categorised mental model is felt to be complete at a fairly early stage.

In contrast to the top-down processing that takes place in these forms of categorisation, bottom-up processing occurs when the recipient is unable to integrate the given information into an existing category, resulting in a personalised mental model of the character. This is frequently reached by producers of characters through the distribution of characterising information over the text rather than providing it initially, by presenting many pieces of information that do not easily fall into any one category – or both. Personalised characters can of course also be members of a category, but this is not the focus of their description. Reading a text, watching a film, or using other narrative media involves building up either categorised or personalised character models, and the type of processing elicited accounts for different experiences: Characters that can be personalised tend to trigger more emotional involvement and more tolerance for change and development (they are therefore comparable to what is called a ›round‹ and ›dynamic‹ character in structuralist approaches). Categorised characters, in contrast, tend to be the reliable representatives of a property, and are likely to attract increased attention only when information is presented that does not fit the category, for this will make the recipient aware of his or her previously unconscious inferencing. Generally, information encountered in the text

---

[86] See Ohler: Filmpsychologie; Eder: Figur, pp. 168–248; see also the sections on ›Characters and People‹, ›Character and Action‹ and ›Character and Genre‹ in this introduction.

subsequent to the categorisation or personalisation may change their status and possibly decategorise or depersonalise those characters.

The role of names in interpreting characters may be taken as an example for the functioning of characterisation devices, because it has been treated repeatedly, resulting in different ways of classifying name usage.[87] Telling names occur in many guises: there are names that quite overtly hint at individual characteristic qualities, features or habits (e.g. allegorical figures, or Mrs. Malaprop in Richard Brinsley Sheridan's comedy *The Rivals*, 1775). In the tradition of Western literature, characters' names have often referred to figures from the Bible, so that the characters in question have inherited more complex sets of properties, both in the sense of psychological dispositions and their function in the story – Mary and Ruth, Thomas and Stephen are names of characters that can be found in a large number of novels of the 18th and 19th centuries, when authors could still count on their recipients' knowledge of the sacred texts. Telling names are characterisation devices that appear on a graded scale between the two poles of direct characterisation on the one hand, and indirect characterisation on the other: If a name closely follows the label for a property – as it has for instance been formulated in folk psychology – the name functions as a direct characterisation. In contrast to that, many characters have names that acquire a characterising function only in the course of the text, when the actions and properties of the character turn out to be reflected by its name. In accordance with the reception-oriented approach sketched above, the most likely effect of a directly characterising telling name is that the recipient constructs a mental model of the character based on this quality from the moment when the character is first mentioned. The model is then likely to be activated top-down in the further information processing. Whether or not the model is kept stable as a categorised one, and whether the one quality remains the only one in focus, depends on the further interaction between textual information and the recipient's activation of knowledge. Some texts use a telling name to elicit an expectation only to frustrate that expectation later on.

In theatre and audiovisual media, names are also a common device, but more importantly, characterisation is intimately connected to casting and acting. The casting of an actor or actress for a role will determine not only what the character looks like, how he or she speaks and moves (stature, facial expression, gestures, body language, proxemics, etc.) These outer attributes also provide hints to further properties, such as age, gender, ethnicity, character and social milieu. A close analysis of the performance

---

87 See e.g. Lamping: Name; Birus: Vorschlag.

of actors and actresses, i.e. the individual way in which they execute body movements, speech acts and actions is therefore of central importance for an understanding of theatrical and audiovisual characterisation.[88] On a general level, various forms of over- or underacting in comparison with real-life repertoires of expression are as important as the differentiation between a self-referential autonomous performance (as for instance in musicals) and a more unobtrusive integrated performance,[89] which shapes different acting styles, as for instance the repertoire style or method-acting.[90] If the actors are well-known, audiences can activate knowledge about star images and role biographies.[91]

The different media all make use of many further specific techniques of characterisation, for instance camerawork, production design, sound design, music, and editing in audiovisual media; styles of painting; or styles of drawing in cartoons. Our cursory remarks in this section can only give a vague impression of the multifarious forms of characterisation, many of which also rely on the recipients' knowledge of certain character types.

9 Character Types

The term ›character types‹ is used here to refer to a fixed set of character traits, in the sense of a *gestalt*, which feature repeatedly in certain media products which belong to at least one specific cultural milieu and its recipients' collective knowledge. Common examples of such types include the mad scientist, the altruistic nurse who works herself to exhaustion, the femme fatale, the schemer at court, the trickster, etc. Such character types frequently occur as parts of larger social constellations, so that they are related to each other. In many comedies, for instance, we find the jealous but slightly stupid old cuckold in combination with a significantly younger wife and her young and daring lover. Such constellations also account for typical action sequences (see the section on ›Character Constellations‹).

In the literature on the subject, a number of specific terms are used for characters types, including ›archetype‹ for types of trans-historical and trans-cultural distribution, and ›stereotype‹ for the ideological and derogative typification of social groups.[92] Two aspects of such types must be differentiated: the prototypical constellation of character traits within

---

88 See Fischer-Lichte: Semiotik; Dyer: Stars; Naremore: Acting.
89 Maltby / Craven: Hollywood, pp. 249–257.
90 Dyer: Stars, pp. 136ff.
91 Ibid., pp. 127ff.
92 Eder: Figur, pp. 375–381.

the fictional world on the one hand, and the typical representation of the character on the aesthetic level on the other. The two aspects can coincide, but this is not necessarily always the case: Social stereotypes may lurk behind an extraordinary and formally complex representation. Two common assumptions about character types are false anyway: the assumption that they always possess only few traits and the assumption that they never change in the course of the story.[93] A typified character can possess a quite complex system of traits and be represented in much detail, as in the case of Molière's imaginary invalid (*Le Malade imaginaire*). It is not the simplicity of a character, but the degree to which it agrees with established schemata which turns it into a type. Typified characters can also change, though they tend to change in a typical way: The cuckold tends to realize he has been duped in the last scene in a comedy of manners, and – with enervating regularity – the typified career woman of many romantic comedies is overwhelmed towards the end by the insight that marriage and household are her best choice, after all.

In the history of media fictions, it was a matter of course for a long time that the construction of fictional characters would revert to types. This even increased the plausibility of character presentation and supported claims of mimetic authenticity.[94] This attitude changed radically in the course of the 18th century, when the concept of individuality gained central importance.[95] Since then, character types have been rejected for being non-realistic, at least in the areas of so-called high culture. The ideal of a representation of individuality has been approached by using constellations of traits that stand in apparent contrast to each other, or of which some are surprising to find in combination with the others.[96] A character construction of such complexity, however, is in most cases possible only for very few characters in one work, and even these characters tend to be innovative variations of well-known types.[97]

There are various sources for character types. Some of them are without a doubt based on everyday social types that a society develops and that can be studied as stereotypes by social psychology. Age, gender,

---

93 This is the opinion of Dyer: Images, pp. 12ff.
94 See Ruth Florack's contribution in this volume where she discusses how the use of common knowledge condensed in national and ethnic stereotypes contributed to the plausibility of the poetic fiction.
95 Luhmann: Individuum, pp. 149–258.
96 See the famous definition of round characters by Forster: Aspects.
97 Shorter texts, for example poems, rely on using types and typified character constellations; cf. Simone Winko's contribution in this volume which discusses characters in poetry.

origin and social status have been central aspect of such stereotyping since Aristotle – there is a line of tradition that formulates and discusses such types which goes back to antiquity. The ›Characters‹ of Theophrastus, and its extended 17th-century revision by La Bruyère, are the most well-known examples. Another source is the store of fictional media representations of characters that exist in a society.[98] Such stock media characters – which turn into stock characters partly through frequent use in widespread fictions – in many cases owe their existence to some very influential works or genre contexts. The character of the hard-boiled detective, for instance, acquired its popularity in US-Amerian film of the 1930s and 40s through the iconic representation in *The Maltese Falcon*. Upon closer inspection, some character types prove to be typical for specific genres; Sherlock Holmes, e.g., is not only a figure in a range of media representations located in Victorian England, the type also turned into a blueprint of a large number of detectives in all periods and locations (see the section on ›Character and Genre‹).[99] Since the representation of characters relies heavily on such types, a lot of research has been done in the field, whether on types in one particular medium or in transmedial fictional worlds like *Star Trek* or *Sherlock Holmes*. The questions to what extent the creation of types is influenced by media specific features, or whether there are certain media specific types, have received significantly less attention.[100]

The fictional media representations are part of the overall media representations of a culture, and as such they absorb social stereotypes of gender, national character or the habitus of certain professions. Due to the pressure to be innovative, the fictional representations modify the stereotypes and feed them back into the circulation of social patterns. It is therefore hard to overemphasise the contribution of fictional media to the distribution and modification of such auto- and hetero-stereotypes.

To be sure, there is a whole range of stereotypes which a particular society regards as purely fictional, but there is also a large area in between the fictional and the non-fictional representations involved in the creation of social types. This is the reason why they play a major role in the creation and distribution of ideologies. As a consequence, clichés, including anti-Semitic ones, gender-images or national stereotypes, have

---

[98] See Schweinitz: Stereotypes (in this volume).
[99] As is well-known, Sherlock Holmes is based to a large extent on Edgar Allen Poe's Dupin. See also the contribution by Wunderlich in this volume, who sketches the process of Cinderella's typification.
[100] See the section on ›Transmedial and Media Specific Aspects of Character‹.

come under severe criticism.[101] If transmitted via direct characterisation, such stereotypes are easy to identify. If the characterisation is indirect, however, things are more complicated, because very few hints in the text will suffice to evoke the entire stereotype; in other words the reader will apply his or her knowledge based on small prompts from the text.[102] This works fine as long as the reader has the necessary knowledge. Without it character representations can appear more harmless if the text does not directly address but only indirectly evokes the evaluations implied in the stereotype, which can only be traced if the work is systematically checked against the relevant historical sources.[103] On the other hand, characters can have an unsettling effect in the context of later cultural knowledge. The character Veitel Itzig in Gustav Freytag's novel *Debit and Credit*, who is the antagonist of the hero, Anton Wohlfahrt, and presented in a very negative light, appears as a concentration of anti-Semitic clichés today; if we analyse the historical constellation at the moment of writing, however, it is at least debatable whether it has to be understood that way.[104]

The placement and connection of typified characters in the context of character constellations and action is of utmost importance for the analysis of media products. The position of the individualised protagonist or hero is frequently filled by a character that can be associated with a dominant group in society. (In the classical Hollywood movie, for instance, they tend to be white male Americans between 20 and 50 years of age.) In contrast, stereotyped members of social groups which are marginalised or treated as enemies in that society tend to be represented as antagonists, and mostly as (comic or evil) minor characters.[105] It depends on the position of a media genre in the cultural discourses of a society and the intention of the producers to criticise social structures whether such ideological tendencies can be found or their opposites. In the English novel since the Victorian period, for instance, we find larger numbers of characters who are marginalised and ostracised in terms of established patterns of social stereotyping (dissenters, fallen women, bankrupts,

---

101 See the essay by Marion Gymnich in this volume for a discussion of gender stereotypes and its counterpart by Ruth Florack on national and ethnic stereotypes. For an introduction to this topic in the area of US-American film, cf. Benshoff / Griffin: America.
102 Empirical research shows that readers make mental representations of the situation represented in the text and have assumptions about the participants based on their knowledge; authors use this sometimes to mislead readers; cf. the article by Emmott, Sanford and Alexander in this volume.
103 Jannidis / Lauer: Antisemitismus, pp. 103–119.
104 See the discussion in Matoni: Juden, pp. 107–116.
105 Eder: Figur, pp. 519–520 provides a checklist for the analysis of social stereotypes.

criminals, etc.), but who are nevertheless the individualised protagonists. The novels frequently follow the didactic impulse of pleading for acceptance of such persons. Whether or not a social group is stereotyped or even discriminated against in a media product also depends on the entire scope of character presentations in the work, i.e., whether there are individualised representatives of the group beside the typified ones in the character constellation.

A historical reconstruction of stereotypes, their central features and the scope of strategies with which they can be evoked turns out to be an intricate business. One of the reasons is the referencing function of characters: They can exemplify general tendencies, including assumptions about particular social groups, but in most cases it requires laborious historical reconstruction to find out which of the many parallel features of a particular character is meant to be the one that is exemplary. The Prince in Lessing's drama *Emilia Galotti*, for instance, can be regarded as a representative of the bad ruler, for he is distracted from his duties of good rule by his private feelings; but he can also be seen as a representative of a ruling class who uses their privileges for the satisfaction of their personal wishes and desires. In the first case the Prince exemplifies the ruler who misbehaves in the office granted him by a divine law; in the second case, he exemplifies the injustice of the feudal system. In retrospect, we can identify both cases as types from our modern perspective, but only the first was known to Lessing's contemporary audience.

10 Character and Genre

The production and reception of characters, as well as their cultural relevance, depend to a considerable degree on the media genres in which they appear. A genre is best conceived of as a mental schema in the minds of producers and recipients.[106] A schema contains skeleton structures of information with slots to be filled by specific instantiations of the general pattern. Genre schemata in literature, film and other media environments combine typical plot elements, and sometimes settings, with typical types and/or functions of character. Any of the classical Hollywood genres,[107] for instance, seems to involve certain character types: cowboys in the Western, singers in musicals, soldiers in the war movie, monsters in the

---

106 Fishelov: Structure; see also the above remarks on Schank's story model approach.
107 On the selection of those genres see Neale: Genre, p. 51.

horror movie, aliens in the science fiction film, gangsters in the crime movie, detectives in the detective film, and so on.

The occurrence of one typical element of a genre will then trigger a complex set of expectations concerning the kind of characters to appear, the situations they encounter, the themes they are likely to be confronted with, their conception as flat or round, or static or dynamic, and typical constellations with other characters. Moreover, genres are connected to prototypical kinds of appropriate emotions; this not only concerns comedy, horror, or thriller but also less obvious cases (e.g., specific forms of empathy in melodrama).[108]

Genre markers that trigger character-related expectations are frequently present already in the title of the media product (the name of the character in many cases *is* the title or at least part of it). Sometimes they appear in the description (or, in audiovisual media, the presentation) of a setting or the outer appearance as well as verbal and non-verbal actions of a character in the very first scene of a narrative.

Traditional literary genres have established some character patterns that can still be found in numerous narratives today. Thus, the *Bildungsroman*, or novel of development, to mention one prominent and particularly long-lived example, contains a protagonist growing up from childhood to adolescence and adulthood, usually in a succession of stages which imply changes of place, one or more mentor figures helping him along his way, characters who put obstacles in his way, and love partners who either distract the protagonist from following his own route or support him in his development. Here, it becomes apparent that there is some overlap between genre theory, plot theory and the actant models described above, since characters in some genres typically fulfil certain functions. For instance, the quest plot – one of the time-honoured patterns in the Western narrative tradition – feeds into the *Bildungsroman*, and it also features protagonist/helper and protagonist/antagonist constellations. The difference between the approaches is that theories of basic plot patterns and actants tend to be rather general, whereas approaches to media genres are more sensitive to the *particular* factors that shape the qualities of the media products in that genre or sub-genre: A theory of media genres would have to take into account not only the signs systems used, but also the specific physical materiality of the media products, which always depends on the particular historical stage of technological development, and the reading or viewing habits of the consumers (see also the above remarks on media specific aspects of characters in section

---

108 See Grodal: Moving Pictures.

›Trans-medial and Media Specific Aspects of Character‹). This of course holds for all fictional worlds, not only those mediated in the more recent, audiovisual media: The *Bildungsroman* emerged in a particular historical moment, making use of the conditions of a book-market that had developed on the basis of the 18th-century developments in printing technology, and catered to the intellectual, ideological and emotional needs of a middle-class readership in newly-formed consumer societies of the late 18th and early 19th centuries.

Although every recognisable genre is likely to contain such typical characters and character constellations, some genres are more formulaic than others in raising expectations as to the appearance of a specific character in specific plot lines and circumstances, such as the Gothic novel and its filmic equivalent, the horror movie, where the villain/victim constellation is a generic requirement. The detective story, with Sherlock Holmes as an early example, is another case in point, and the Western movie is also a popular formulaic text with characters that are subject to heavy genre constraints.[109] Part of the success of popular genres and the typical characters they feature appears to rely on their very expectability. However, the history of fictional worlds in the various media would look fairly bleak if it were a history of endless repetitions and reinforcements of formulaic patterns, and if characters were merely instantiations of precisely what readers already expect. Rather, genres ought to be regarded as flexible frameworks within which a considerable amount of deviation from prototypicality is possible: not only do some texts create blends between two ore more generic traditions,[110] which will result in the occurrence of unexpected character varieties. What is more, much variation in the representation of characters and their effects on readers and viewers results from deviations from the established generic norms. These may be turned upside down, as for instance in the case of the novel of negative development, where the hero fails to establish his position in society, or modified, as in the female novel of development, which casts a critical look at the different conditions of development for women, or the *Bildungsroman* featuring two protagonists, which tend to be contrasted in terms of the motivation and success of their development, etc. Within the context of genre theory, then, characters need to be analysed both with regard to their genre-dependence and the degree to which they depart from the underlying genre schema.

---

[109] On genre theory, see Fowler: Kinds, and cf. Neale: Genre, pp. 133–149.
[110] Sinding / Genera / Perloff: Postmodern; cf. the remarks about the pervasiveness of hybridity in Hollywood cinema in Neale: Genre, pp. 248–251.

While the above considerations (as well as research in general) have been focusing on narrative genres in literature and film, many of them can be applied also to other genres, formats, or categories of different media, for instance, the genres of TV series (e.g., hospital drama, sitcom, telenovela), comics (e.g., cartoon, graphic novel, shojo manga), or video games (e.g., adventure, artificial life, shooter, educational).[111] But there is still a lot to be done in describing the specifics of those genres and their typical characters.

11 Functions and Meanings of Characters

As we have pointed out several times, characters can be seen as entities in a fictional world. However, this should not be understood to mean that characters are self-contained, on the contrary: They are devices in the communication of meaning and serve purposes beyond the fictional world as well. Individual characters are embedded in numerous contexts. As fictional beings they stand in the context of the fictional world and its events; as artifacts, they must be seen in the context of stylistic and dramaturgical strategies; as symbols, in the context of themes and networks of signification; as symptoms, in the context of the reality of production and reception. More specifically, characters fill positions and roles in larger webs of relations, such as structures of communication and narration; constellations of characters; situations, plots, themes; and effects of an aesthetic, emotional, rhetorical or ideological kind. They cause part of the overall effect of a text or work, fulfill certain functions, are intended to serve specific purposes.[112]

Very generally, characters contribute to the functions of the media texts they are part of, as for instance entertainment, artistic appreciation, education, information, distribution of ideologies, or advertising. Some of their functions are media-specific: In novels or feature films, they serve primarily narrative purposes, whereas in board games or video games their ludic purposes seem to be more important, for the player must be able to perform certain moves with them.

---

111 See Creeber / Miller / Tulloch: Television Genres; Wolf: Genre, pp. 113–137.
112 We need to differentiate here between the functions of individual character-related pieces of information (e.g., the fact that Holmes smokes a pipe) and the functions of the entire character (Holmes as the protagonist). For different models of the functions or motivation of textual information, see Jannidis: Figur, pp. 221–229 and Bordwell: Narration.

In previous sections, we have addressed a number of more specific character functions, including actant roles and certain generic functions. There are many more, for instance in evoking impressions of realism, establishing inter- and transtextual relations, and eliciting aesthetic or emotional effects. We would like to focus here on the construction of meaning. In many artworks and media products, it is not action that is the organizing principle, but a theme or an idea, and the characters in these texts are determined by that theme or idea. An extreme example is personification, i.e. the representation of an abstract principle such as justice as a character, as found in allegorical literature or film. Other examples are certain dialogue novels or art films, where the characters' role is to propound philosophical ideas. But even the most life-like characters in a realistic novel or movie can often also be described in light of their place in a thematic progression. It has to be added that audiences do not only draw conclusions as to the overall meanings from individual characters, but mostly from character constellations. With the help of a comparison of characters with similar or contrasting properties and attitudes, the various aspects of, and perspectives on, the thematic scope of a media text can be explored.

More generally, a variety of meanings can be associated with characters, be represented or transmitted by them:[113] thematic statements or questions; human properties, problems, virtues and vices (e.g., the evil); abstract ideas or intangible phenomena (e.g., personifications of death); latent meanings in a psychoanalytical sense (suppressed wishes or fears); membership in social groups and roles, as well as archetypes; references to real persons (in the case of key characters) or to characters of the artistic tradition (in the case of intertextual characters). These types of character-related meaning can in turn serve a variety of purposes: They establish connections to reality and the life of the audience; they condense complex contexts and make them tangible; they express indirectly what would be difficult or inefficient to express directly, including taboos, surpressed thoughts, or the quality of individual experience; they stimulate processes of creativity and association in the reception and they contribute to the arousal of emotions. The topics of narratives and other artworks tend to be linked to the properties, values, conflicts, needs, weaknesses or developments of characters; conversely, characters give relevance and unity to stories or artworks as a whole. Moreover, they are one of their most important sources of recipients' responses.

---

113 Eder: Figur, pp. 518–538.

12 Recipients' Reactions and Relations to Characters

Our cognitive and affective responses to characters are manifold. Between art and entertainment, we engage with fictional humans, animals, and fantastic creatures of all sorts. Nevertheless, our different kinds of reactions are often lumped together under global notions like ›identification‹, ›sympathy‹, or ›empathy‹. This clearly is too reductive. Usually, we do not identify with the dog Lassie, sympathise with the sinister Professor Moriarty, or empathise with monsters we kill playing a shooter game. We react not only to sympathetic protagonists, but also to their antipathetic adversaries or to minor characters; our reactions shift between the various inhabitants of a fictional world.

Moreover, even if we engage with single sympathetic characters, we do not have to ›identify‹ with them in any sense of the word.[114] For instance, if ›identification‹ is understood as a relation to characters who are similar to the recipient, it is clear that recipients also develop feelings for characters who drastically differ from themselves. The differences in age, gender, class and nationality do not prevent today's teenage girls from developing sympathy for Sherlock Holmes. Neither do they only have to react to characters as role models, a concept of identification frequently used in the context of classroom teaching of literature or film. Because of those kinds of difficulties, recent theories have replaced ›identification‹ with more encompassing umbrella terms like ›engagement‹, ›involvement‹ or ›parasocial interaction‹.[115]

Whatever label we use, modeling our reactions to characters confronts us with challenges concerning historical changes, cultural differences, the

---

114 There are older models of identification, based on Freud or Lacan, for example Holland: Dynamics, p. 262–280. More recent models, some of which are based on empirical research, integrate empirical findings and media analysis, e.g. Oatley / Gholamain: Emotions, pp. 263–281. The concept of ›identification‹ has been discussed widely and controversely in approaches based on psychoanalysis (e.g., Aumont / Bergala / Marie / Vernet: Aesthetics, pp. 200–236; Cowie: Woman, pp. 72–122; Friedberg: Denial, pp. 36–45; van Beneden: Viewer); hermeneutics (Jauß: Erfahrung, pp. 244–292); or philosophy, psychology, and cognitive sciences (e.g., Schneider: Grundriß, pp. 103ff.; Carroll: Philosophy, pp. 261–270; Smith: Characters; Neill: Empathy, pp. 175–194; Plantinga: Scene, pp. 183–199; Tan: Emotion).
115 For a survey and discussion of some influential theories, see Anz: Turn, Schneider, Grundriß, pp. 99–134, and Eder: Figur, pp. 561–686. Several contributions in this volume deal with affective involvement or engagement, especially the contributions of Margolin; Mellmann; Smith; and van Vugt / Hoorn / Konijn in this volume; see also Giles: Interaction. Comprehensive accounts of character engagement in film are Smith: Characters; and Plantinga: Viewers.

various media, and most fundamentally, the general relation between media texts and their reception. On the one hand, theoretical models may be used to reconstruct reactions intended by their creators (or suggested by intersubjective structures of the text). On the other hand, they might be used to form hypotheses about actual experiences of particular audiences. Moreover, those models can direct attention to different sources of data: the text itself with its potential to generate certain responses; information about production and reception (e.g., criticism, interviews, etc.); or experimental studies (e.g., measurements of brain activity). From these possible sets of data two directions of investigation are usually taken. Either the text serves as a starting point to formulate hypotheses about (intended) reactions in the audience, or certain reactions are observed in the audience and explained by referring to the text. Often, both ways of investigation are combined.

But any theoretical model of reactions to characters will need conceptual frameworks accounting for (1) the recipients' possible reactions, (2) the relevant textual structures, and (3) the connections between the two.[116] The core competencies for each of these areas of research are to be found in different disciplines: (1) in psychology and philosophy of mind, emotion, and embodiment; (2) in literary, image and media studies; and (3) in a vast range of sciences and humanities from biology to sociology and cultural studies. The connections between text and reception may be established by referring to semantic analysis, rules of communication, and the diverse bodily and mental dispositions of recipients and creators: their biological and anthropological reaction tendencies; socio-cultural rules and norms; their collective beliefs, wishes, fears, or values of a certain time; and finally, their individual experiences.

This of course raises the question how culture-specific affective reactions to characters are. Is there such a thing as a universal set of emotions? How strongly do recipients feel bound to follow the cultural codes of emotional response? Some situations would appear to be fairly universal in the emotions they evoke, such as the suffering of a child (pity, perhaps coupled with a feeling of helplessness). Of course, the affective experiences that occur in the process of engaging with characters cannot be reduced to such straightforward situations, but include the entire range of the subtlest responses, from *Schadenfreude* to hopeful expectation, which open up considerable space between the culturally expectable emotional response and the individual feeling.

---

116 Eder: Reactions, pp. 271–289.

The different media also tend to evoke different kinds of reactions and relations to characters. For instance, literary characters emerge from the readers' imagination, while characters in paintings, comics, film and TV can be visually or acoustically perceived and may influence their viewers' bodily reactions more directly. This applies even more to characters in computer games that are controlled by their players. And the viewers of long-running TV series often build quite intense parasocial relations with their favourite characters.[117] Each of those media specific possibilities will also give rise to different kinds of affective reactions.

What is more, historical changes in any of those media need to be acknowledged. For instance, the presentation of literary characters before 1800 pursues a significantly different aim from that of the post-1800 period. Much literature before 1800 aims more at creating an attitude of admiration than it does at immersing the recipient in the situation of the character. Comparably, the early ›cinema of attractions‹ until 1906 let the viewers rather watch spectacular characters from a distant observer's position, in contrast to the later ›cinema of narrative integration‹ that introduces various techniques to bring the viewers close to their protagonists and to make them share their point of view.[118] Thus, not only the aims of character presentation change over time but also the means used to reach those aims.

Diverse theoretical approaches have tried to tackle those challenges, but nearly all of them have focused on one of the various media. We can only briefly mention some main lines of research here. In film theory, research has been dominated for a long time by psychoanalytical approaches explaining viewers' reactions to characters with concepts of ›identification‹, ›transference‹ or ›object relations‹ as well as by ›desire‹, ›pleasure‹, ›voyeurism‹, ›sadism‹, and the like.[119] In strong opposition, positions relying on analytical philosophy have rather been pointing at the moral evaluation of characters leading to sympathy or antipathy.[120] Recently, scholars in cognitive as well as phenomenological theories, some of them informed by psychology or the neurosciences, have developed more intricate accounts of character engagement by distinguishing different dimensions, levels, and types of viewer responses and their

---

117 See Vorderer: Fernsehen.
118 On the historical shift from ›attraction‹ to ›narrative integration‹ in film see Gunning: Cinema.
119 For an overview see Allen: Film; Aumont / Bergala / Marie / Vernet: Aesthetics; for a more recent and complex approach, see Cowie: Woman.
120 E.g., Carroll: Philosophy, pp. 245–290.

functional correlates in film structure.[121] However, an exchange between those different approaches and other, related research (e.g., in communication studies)[122] has only just begun. Eder has recently tried to integrate positions from several disciplines into a model of engagement which focuses on film, but which with some modifications may be applied also to literary characters.[123] In order to apply it to static media like paintings or interactive media like video games, however, significant changes to this model seem to be necessary. The characters of different media have quite different potentials in evoking affective responses. In video games, the characters' interactive and ludic aspects are of crucial importance: they can be moved by their players, moving them in turn.[124] In contrast, the static characters in paintings seem to elicit specific feelings in their beholders exactly because they are ›frozen‹ in certain movements, postures and gestures; some scholars try to describe such impact in neuro-scientific terms.[125]

To understand our reactions to characters, it is important to take into account that those reactions do not only concern the characters as inhabitants of their fictional worlds.[126] We can also aesthetically evaluate the representation of characters as artifacts, for instance, criticise their stereotypical form or appreciate the elegance of their development. We can ponder over more abstract meanings that are embodied by them, for instance, over the meanings of Death in Bergman's *The Seventh Seal*. And we can react to communicative aims and possible effects associated with characters, for instance, be distraught by realising how the protagonist of Veit Harlan's Nazi film *Jud Süß* (1940) was used as a propagandistic tool with terrible impact during the Holocaust. This example shows also that many, but not all of our actual responses are prefigured by the text or intended by its creators.

---

[121] E.g., Smith: Characters; Plantinga / Smith: Views; Grodal: Film, pp. 115–28; Tan: Emotion; Zillmann: Creation, pp. 164–79; Carroll: Philosophy, pp. 245–90; Plantinga: Viewers.

[122] Theories of parasocial interaction describe how people interact with characters and persons represented in media. E.g., Giles: Interaction, pp. 279–304, and his contribution to this volume; Hartmann / Klimmt / Schramm: Interactions, pp. 291–313.

[123] Eder: Figur, 561–706. For a short discussion of the literary research on identification cf. Jannidis: Figur, pp. 229–236; for a different approach based on evolutionary psychology cf. Mellmann: Empathy (in this volume).

[124] See Frome: Reality, pp. 12–25; Thon: Perspective.

[125] Freedberg: Power

[126] See the distinction between reactions to characters as fictional beings, artifacts, symbols, and symptoms in Eder: Figur, chap. 4. For a discussion of Eder's model and a different approach see Margolin: Engagement (in this volume).

This is also true of the evaluation of characters as media artifacts, which is based on historically and culturally variable measures of aesthetic appreciation. Depending on the standards commonly accepted in a community of recipients, evaluation will take into account the originality of character conception or a character's intertextuality, e.g. as an innovative variation of an established type (the presentation of Sherlock Holmes in *Without a Clue* (1988), in which Watson is the true leader of the team). A character's intermediality can also play an important role. This is the case when characters are recognised to be manifestations of a particular type (see section on ›Character Types‹).

Obviously, those different kinds of reactions have to be distinguished analytically, but they are closely connected in the actual experience. For instance, in theatre or film the real-world persona or star image of a well-known actor may influence the character's function as a role model. Conflicting evaluations may result from this, if the actor plays a perpetrator, whose actions and values are supposed to be rejected on the grounds of common moral codes, but if the actor invites admiration at the same time. Marlon Brando's appearance as Don Vito Corleone in *The Godfather* may be a case in point.

If we concentrate on responses to characters as fictional beings (leaving out their effects as artifacts, bearers of meaning, and socio-cultural factors), their specific forms of representation still play a fundamental role. This is quite obvious if we consider the impact of narration and focalisation: Our attitudes towards a character are influenced by her being commented on by a reliable narrator or being part of an unreliable narrative. On a more concrete level, reactions to characters are (often subliminally) guided by the expressive use of presentational devices, for example the use of language or the verbal presentation of emotions, using phonetic, rhythmic, metrical, syntactical, lexical, figurative, rhetorical, and narrative devices, including free indirect discourse and comparable strategies,[127] or the expressive use of cinematic devices like mise-en-scène, camera work, sound design, editing, and music.[128] In theatre, film and to some extent also in computer games (their filmed scenes and voices) the actor cast for the role is an important factor.

The textual presentation of characters establishes specific relations towards them, leading to different degrees of closeness or distance in several respects: spatio-temporal proximity, understanding and perspec-

---

127 Winko: Gefühle.
128 See the description of how these devices play a significant role in eliciting ›synesthetic affects‹ in Plantinga: Viewers, pp. 140–168.

tive-taking, familiarity and similarity, interaction, and affective engagement.[129] For instance, we accompany characters in their experiences and perceive the same situations and their possibilities. We feel spatially close to characters (audiovisual close-ups or their equivalent in literary descriptions) or are synchronised with them in our experience of time (e.g., by slow motion, fragmented narration, or extended descriptions of environments). We understand the inner and social life of characters well or not so well. We compare ourselves with characters and develop the feeling that they are familiar to us, resemble us, or are completely different. We place them in our in-groups or out-groups, project our wishes onto them or even have the impression that they interact with us (especially in video games).

If we want to systematically understand our reactions to characters, it is of crucial importance that all of them are reactions from a certain *perspective*, guided by the text. This has been discussed by many theorists in connection with concepts like identification, empathy, imagination, point of view, or focalisation.[130] In analysis we can ascribe to characters on the one hand, and to recipients on the other, a range of mental experiences which are directed to certain aspects of the fictional world, such as another character, an event, or an idea. This relation of actual and fictional minds to certain objects may be called (mental) perspective.[131] Drawing on the work of Berys Gaut with slight modifications,[132] we can distinguish between at least four aspects of perspective: (1) perceptual/imaginative, e.g. seeing, hearing; dreaming; (2) epistemic/doxastic, e.g. knowing, believing; (3) evaluative/conative, e.g. judging, evaluating; having aims and plans; and (4) affective, e.g. having emotions, moods, and feelings.

In each aspect, the perspectives of recipients and characters can be more or less similar or divergent. A recipient may just know the character's perspective, but may herself have a completely different one. But she can also share or even actively take the character's perspective in certain respects. In literary texts for example, a transfer of perspective is invited by various modes of the representation of consciousness, including free indirect discourse and interior monologue. Some media provide access to many aspects of perspective just described to degrees

---

129 Eder: Ways, pp. 68–80.
130 E.g., Grodal: Film, pp. 115–28; Neill: Empathy, pp. 175–94; Persson: Cinema; Plantinga: Scene, pp. 183–199; Ryan: Narrative. A classical formulation of ›focalisation‹ is Genette: Discourse, pp. 189–194. See also the contributions of Mellmann: Empathy, and Smith: Reflections (both articles in this volume).
131 Eder: Figur, pp. 579–646.
132 Gaut: Identification, pp. 200–216.

hardly found in social interaction. This is certainly true for prose fiction. When E.M. Forster spoke of the way readers relate to literary characters and why they are so attractive to readers, what he said appears to point precisely in this direction:

> [P]eople in a novel can be understood completely by the reader, if the novelist wishes; their inner as well as their outer life can be exposed. And this is why they seem more definite than characters in history, or even our friends [...].[133]

The media differ in their potentials to allow their recipients access to certain kinds of the characters' experiences. For instance, in audiovisual media, a transfer of perceptual or imaginative experiences can be affected through subjective shots or mindscreen,[134] while language is exceptionally apt to convey more abstract thoughts. Whichever technique is used to render the contents of focalisation, there is good reason to assume that in general, recipients relate to characters more intensely if they are focalisers. As a consequence of such kinds of focalisation, we experience characters from different positions, for instance, as distanced observers or participant empathisers.

The relations of perspective between characters and their audiences are crucial in understanding the complex phenomenon of affective engagement. Artworks or media texts direct our affective reactions by focusing our attention on certain features of the characters and their situations. Those ›textually pre-focused‹ features[135] serve as triggers eliciting feelings, moods, and emotions. Our resulting involvement takes various forms that can be systematically distinguished by two criteria: First, we can differentiate between reactions to the characters themselves – their bodily, psychological, social, and behavioural features – and reactions to their situations. And second, our reactions range from feeling *for* a character (sympathy/antipathy) to feeling *with* a character (empathy).[136] Both dimensions open up not a strict opposition but a continuum of responses: We focus *more or less* on the character or her situation, and our feelings are *more or less* similar to or different from hers.

Reactions to the characters themselves can take the form of intersubjective, subjective, and empathic appraisal. They involve a huge number of affect-triggering properties, among them especially bodily, mental, or social capabilities and disorders; beauty, disease and death; group

---

133 Forster: Aspects, p. 57.
134 Kawin: Mindscreen.
135 Carroll: Philosophy, pp. 261–270.
136 This distinction is discussed also in Smith: Characters, and Smith: Reflections (in this volume).

membership, positions of power and status; egoistic or altruistic motives; pro-social or anti-social actions as well as the emotions of the characters themselves. In empathic appraisals we share or approximate the feelings of the characters in different ways, many of them connected to the characters' situations (see below). In subjective appraisals we appraise characters according to individual concerns and react with directly self-related feelings, such as fear of a monster or desire for a character that appeals to us erotically. In intersubjective appraisals we evaluate the characters' features by collectively accepted criteria (e.g., morality or aesthetics) and react with corresponding feelings (e.g., appreciation). This includes the possibility of pleasure from characters resisting or violating collective norms.

When reading a novel or watching a film, we often assume an external observer's perspective on the characters: We accompany Sherlock Holmes and Watson through space and time and learn more or less about their adventures, experiences, and their inner life, and feel for them in ways that diverge from their own feelings. Those feelings *for* characters are based on (often pre-conscious) forms of appraisal according to historically, culturally and individually variable measures of value, but also according to biological schemata. An evaluative stance toward a character creates such emotional responses as sympathy, admiration or repulsion. Those feelings are influenced by further factors like the implicit comparison between the recipients and the protagonist, already described by Aristotle.

In many cases, our attention and appraisal are directed not only at the characters themselves but at the *situations* that they experience or that concern their interests. The forms of appraisal mentioned above are the foundation for our developing durable dispositions of sympathy or antipathy for characters as well as for siding with or against them in situations involving their interests. We hope that Holmes discovers the perpetrator, we fear for him in his fight with Moriarty. Usually, the emotional siding with protagonists and against antagonists develops into longer emotional episodes.

Our responses to the situations, actions and events involving the characters and their interests again take various forms. They may follow social norms or even be altruistic, but they may also be of a sadistic or voyeuristic kind. First, the situations themselves can trigger general, historical, and cultural schemata for ›natural‹ or ›usual‹ feelings, for instance, towards murder or passionate love. Second, we may focus on the characters' affective reactions to the situation. Characters' feelings and emotions may be explicitly expressed by words or body language (e.g., crying), but they may also be only implicitly suggested (e.g., by events not directly related to the characters but ›externalising‹ their affects, like a storm reflecting the agitated state of a protagonist). When a character covers a fight against tears behind an expressionless face, we can react to that from a distant observer's perspective informed by social rules of ›appropriateness‹.

But any of our intersubjective or self-related appraisals of characters, their situations and emotions may also be combined or mixed with *empathetic feelings*: with kinds of simulation, perspective-taking, or empathy that approximate the characters affects.[137] Such feeling *with* a character may develop out of the mental simulation of depicted actions and expressions, by ›somatic empathy‹, ›affective mimicry‹ or ›emotional contagion‹.[138] For instance, a character's facial expression of deep sadness may cause the recipient to respond from an observer's perspective (typically with pity), but may also activate similar feelings of sadness. A film character's exuberant dance may cause the viewer to be amused about such childishness, but also to tap his feet. To what extent such simulations actually occur has been discussed extensively: Proponents see support for their position in the discovery of mirror neurons,[139] while opponents claim that this aspect plays a limited role if any at all.[140] In any case, mental simulation seems to be only one of several ways to share a character's feelings. This can also be caused by the character and the audience simultaneously startling at a sudden noise; by both reacting to the affordances of depicted situations (desiring the beautiful person or the glass of cold beer); or if the recipients project their own feelings about an event onto the character.

The recipients' responses to characters are the basis of further processes of discussion, elaboration, evaluation, negotiation, imitation etc., leading to medium-term and long-term *effects* concerning cognition, emotion, and behavior. Memories of characters linger in the recipients' minds; characters are thought and talked about, and they influence readers, listeners, viewers, and players. The question what effects characters have on recipients is of decisive importance in several

---

[137] The term ›empathy‹ has been understood in very different ways, ranging from feeling with a character (having similar feelings) to feeling for her (e.g., having pity while she is sad). E.g., cf. Feshbach: Fernsehen; Smith: Characters; Smith: Imagining; Smith: Gangsters; Neill: Empathy; Plantinga: Scene, pp. 183–199; Wulff: Empathie, pp. 136–160; Zillmann: Empathy, pp. 135–168 (here, the term refers to – partly – sharing a character's feelings).
[138] See Smith: Characters, pp. 98–102; Brinckmann: Empathie, pp. 111–120; Grodal: Film, pp. 115–128.
[139] Lauer: Spiegelneuronen, pp. 137–163; Grodal: Film, pp. 115–128.
[140] Carroll: Philosophy, pp. 261–270; Mellmann, who models the recipient's response on the basis of evolutionary psychology in her contribution in this anthology.

discourses beyond individual media use: It looms large in media production, economy, legislation, and pedagogy; in psychotherapy; in cultural studies, communication studies, theories of media impact and social stereotyping; and in the criticism of ideologies and progaganda. Such approaches may focus their interest on particular effects of characters on individual recipients, but they may also investigate collective effects on groups or entire societies. Their conclusions – which consider a character in terms of, for instance, an ideal or orientation, a counter-idea, an opinion leader, an identification device, a role model, someone who offers experience by proxy, or a parasocial interaction partner – all imply models of recipients and effects that need to be made explicit in the analysis of characters.[141]

That the effects of characters on audiences are highly complex is due to the multifactor dynamics of reception and subsequent processes. Most theories of media effects nowadays no longer posit strong or weak effects in a generalized way, but they assume that media take effect selectively on recipients who are active and interact with each other.[142] If we apply this assumption to the field of fictional characters, we can only say that ›some of them take effect on some recipients under certain conditions at particular times‹.[143] It is therefore necessary to consider each case individually instead of starting with generalisations.

The individual effects can in turn rarely be found in the area of immediate and profound changes in attitudes, opinions or behaviour. More often, they will work in the sense of subtle suggestions, priming, framing, agenda setting, and the cultivation and shaping of memory.[144] These kinds of effect are shaped by the way in which recipients engage with characters actively and by how they discuss them among each other. Generally, a large number of comparable characters, which recur in diverse media texts, seem to exert the most wide-spread and strongest influence on audiences. For instance, there is evidence that TV users considerably overestimate the real number of rich persons, criminals, detectives, doctors and lawyers, because they appear in TV programs with high frequency (whereas women, senior citizens and minorities are underrepresented).[145]

---

141 See Eder: Figur, pp. 538–557.
142 See Brosius 2003: Medienwirkung, p. 133; Leffelsend / Mauch / Hannover: Mediennutzung.
143 A phrase borrowed from Brosius: Medienwirkung, p. 133, who describes media effects in general.
144 Ibid., pp. 136–140; Staiger: Media.
145 Brosius: Medienwirkung, p. 139; Gerbner: Casting.

In this manner, characters contribute to the support or criticism of ideals or concepts of reality, and they are highly influential in the construction and dissemination of social stereotypes.[146] Characters can initiate learning, support the spread of information, the development of opinions and images of humankind or the status quo in a society; they can provide the building blocks of identity formation, invite mimicry, remedy social deficits or prevent social activities. Sometimes their effects are problematic: The *Werther* effect, propaganda movies like *Jud Süß*, public criticism of scandalous books like *Ulysses*, or films like *A Clockwork Orange* and the corresponding copycat crimes – all of these demonstrate how influential characters can be.

To single out an especially important aspect, recent decades have seen a growing interest in the social construction of identities – national identities, gender identities, etc. Analysis of character representation and formation plays an important part in any interpretation interested in identity construction in media, but up to now those engaged in identity analysis have neglected research on character in narratology or media studies; at the same time, narrative analysis has mostly ignored the recent or historical case studies carried out on identity construction by specialists of cultural studies or sociology.

In those and other fields of discussion, analysis of characters and their effects needs to make explicit, or indeed question, implicit or intuitive assumptions by referring to the aspects of character discussed in this introduction and in the following contributions of this book. This is also true for the closely connected (and still neglected) issue of evaluation in literary texts, films and other media products. There are many ways a text can influence evaluative stances of its recipients, and much systematic and historical work in this area remains to be done. Probably, the answers to those kinds of general questions often have a transmedial as well as a media-specific part. The core of certain stereotypes, for example, seems not to be bound to a specific medium, but certain aspects of some stereotypes seem to be determined by their presentation in specific media.

These and many other questions that we were able only to touch upon can be discussed nowadays because some of the old questions, such as those concerning the relation between text and action, the ontology of character, or the mechanisms of characterisation, have found not final answers but answers complex enough to build on, in a way that does justice to the richness of the phenomenon of character. ›There is no research on character‹ – this is an often repeated claim found in many

---

146 Bar-Tal / Teichman: Stereotypes.

articles and monographs. We hope that our outline has shown not only that this claim is wrong, but that the research is multifaceted and theoretically challenging. We also hope to have provided a possible explanation for the longevity of this erroneous topos: the complexity of the subject. Very different disciplines and traditions have contributed to throwing light on it, but it is obvious that a lot of research still has to be done. We hope that this volume helps outline the field and its most pressing problems.

References

Allen, Richard: Psychoanalytic Film Theory. In: Toby Miller / Robert Stam (Eds.). A Companion to Film Theory. Malden 1999, pp. 123–145.
Anz, Thomas: Emotional Turn? Beobachtungen zur Gefühlsforschung. In: Literaturkritik 8/12 (2006). <http://www.literaturkritik.de/public/rezension.php?rez_id=10267> (Jul. 21st, 2009).
Aristotle in 23 Volumes. Vol. 23: The Poetics. Tr. W. H. Fyfe. London 1932.
Asmuth, Bernhard: Einführung in die Dramenanalyse. 5th edn. Stuttgart / Weimar 1997.
Aumont, Jacques / Alain Bergala / Michel Marie / Marc Vernet: Aesthetics of Film. Austin 1992.
Bar-Tal, Daniel / Jona Teichman (Eds): Stereotypes and Prejudice in Conflict. Representations of Arabs in Israel. New York 2005.
Beneden, Peter van: Viewer ›Identification‹ with Characters in Television and Fiction Film. Nov. 1998. <http://www.aber.ac.uk/media/Students/pjv9801.html> (Oct. 24th, 2001).
Benshoff, Harry M. / Sean Griffin: America on Film. Representing Race, Class, Gender, and Sexuality at the Movies. Malden, MA et al. 2004.
Birus, Hendrik: Vorschlag zu einer Typologie literarischer Namen. In: Zeitschrift für Literaturwissenschaft und Linguistik 17 (1987), pp. 38–51.
Bordwell, David: Cognition and Comprehension. Viewing and Forgetting in »Mildred Pierce«. In: Journal of Dramatic Theory and Criticism 6/2 (1992), pp. 183–198.
Bordwell, David: Narration in the Fiction Film. London 1985.
Branigan, Edward: Point of View in the Cinema. A Theory of Narrativity and Subjectivity in Classical Film. Berlin 1984.
Bremond, Claude: The Logic of Narrative Possibilities. In: New Literary History 11 (1980), pp. 387–411.
Brinckmann, Christine Noll: Somatische Empathie bei Hitchcock. Eine Skizze. In: Heinz B. Heller / Karl Prümm / Birgit Peulings (Eds.): Der Körper im Bild. Schauspielen – Darstellen – Erscheinen. Marburg 1999, pp. 111–120.
Brosius, Hans-Bernd: Medienwirkung. In: H.-B. B. / Günther Bentele / Otfried Jarren (Eds.): Öffentliche Kommunikation. Opladen 2003, pp. 129–148.
Buckland, Warren: Between Science Fact and Science Fiction: Spielberg's Digital Dinosaurs, Possible Worlds, and the New Aesthetic Realism. In: Screen 40/2 (1999), pp. 177–192.
Campbell, Joseph: The Hero with a Thousand Faces. New York [1949] 1990.
Carroll, Noël: A Philosophy of Mass Art. Oxford / New York 1998.

Chatman, Seymour: Story and Discourse. Narrative Structure in Fiction and Film. Ithaca / London 1978.
Cowie, Elizabeth: Representing the Woman. Cinema and Psychoanalysis. Minneapolis, MN 1997.
Creeber, Glen / Toby Miller / John Tulloch (Eds.): The Television Genre Book. 2nd edn. London 2008.
Crittenden, Charles: Fictional Characters and Logical Completeness. In: Poetics 11 (1982), pp. 331–344.
Culpeper, Jonathan: A Cognitive Approach to Characterization. Katherina in Shakespeare's »The Taming of the Shrew«. In: Language and Literature 9/4 (2000), pp. 291–316.
Currie, Gregory: The Characters of Fiction. In: G.C.: The Nature of Fiction. Cambridge et al. 1990, pp. 127–181.
Dannenberg, Hilary: Plot. In: David Herman / Manfred Jahn / Marie-Laure Ryan (Eds.): Routledge Encyclopedia of Narrative Theory. London / New York 2005, pp. 435–39.
de Waal, Ronald B: The Universal Sherlock Holmes. 1994. <http://special.lib.umn.edu/rare/ush/ush.html#Introduction> (Jul. 21st, 2008).
Doležel, Lubomír: Heterocosmica. Fiction and Possible Worlds. Baltimore, MD / London 1998.
Dramatica Pro 4.0: Elektronic »Theory Book« of the Screenwriting Program. Concept: Phillips, Melanie Anne / Huntley, Chris. Developers: Hindley, Kevin. Distributor: Screenplay Systems Inc., 1999.
Dyer, Richard: Stars. New Edition with a Supplementary Chapter and a Bibliography by Paul McDonald. London 1999.
Dyer, Richard: The Matter of Images: Essays on Representations. London / New York 1993.
Eaton, Marcia M.: On Being a Character. In: British Journal of Aesthetics 16 (1976), pp. 24–31.
Eco, Umberto: Lector in Fabula. Die Mitarbeit der Interpretation in erzählenden Texten. 3rd edn. München 1993.
Eder, Jens: Analysing Affective Reactions to Films. Towards an Integrative Model. In: SPIEL 22/2 (2003), pp. 271–289.
Eder, Jens: Die Figur im Film. Grundlagen der Figurenanalyse. Marburg 2008.
Eder, Jens: Dramaturgie des populären Films. Drehbuchpraxis und Filmtheorie. Hamburg 1999.
Eder, Jens: Was sind Figuren? Ein Beitrag zur interdisziplinären Fiktionstheorie. Paderborn 2008 (E-Book).
Eder, Jens: Ways of Being Close to Characters. In: Film Studies 8 (2006), pp. 68–80.
Emmott, Catherine: Narrative Comprehension. A Discourse Perspective. Oxford 1997.
Feshbach, Norma Deitch: Fernsehen und Empathie bei Kindern. In: Jo Groebel / Peter Winterhoff-Spurk (Eds.): Empirische Medienpsychologie. München 1989, pp. 76–89.
Fischer-Lichte, Erika: Semiotik des Theaters. Eine Einführung, vol. 1: Das System der theatralischen Zeichen. Tübingen 1983.
Fishelov, David: The Structure of Generic Categories: Some Cognitive Aspects. In: Journal of Literary Semantics 24 (1995), pp. 117–126.
Forster, Edward M.: Aspects of the Novel [1927]. San Diego et al. 1985.
Fowler, Alastair. Kinds of Literature. An Introduction to the Theory of Genres and Modes, Cambdridge, Mass., 1982.
Freedberg, David: The Power of Images. Studies in the History and Theory of Response. Chicago, IL 1989.

Friedberg, Anne: A Denial of Difference. Theories of Cinematic Identification. In: E. Anne Kaplan (Ed.): Psychoanalysis and Cinema. London / New York 1990, pp. 36–45.
Frome, Jonathan: Reality, Representation, and Emotions aross Media. In: Film Studies 8 (2006), pp. 12–25.
Gaut, Berys: Identification and Emotion in Narrative Film. In: Carl Plantinga / Greg Smith (Eds.): Passionate Views. Film, Cognition, and Emotion. Baltimore, MD / London 1999, pp. 200–216.
Gemoll, Wilhelm: Griechisch-deutsches Schul- und Handwörterbuch. München / Wien 1954.
Genette, Gérard: Narrative Discourse. An Essay in Method. Trans. by Jane E. Lewin. Itahaca, NY 1980.
Gerbner, George: Casting and Fate. Women and Minorities on Television Drama, Game Shows, and News. In: Ed Hollander / Coen van der Linden / Paul Rutten (Eds.): Communication, Culture, Community. Houten 1995, pp. 125–135.
Gerrig, Richard J. / David W. Allbritton: The Construction of Literary Character. A View from Cognitive Psychology. In: Style 24/3 (1990), pp. 380–391.
Giles, David C.: Parasocial Interaction. A Review of the Literature and a Model for Future Research. In: Media Psychology 4/3 (2002), pp. 279–304.
Grabes, Herbert: Wie aus Sätzen Personen werden. Über die Erforschung literarischer Figuren. In: Poetica 10 (1978), pp. 405–428.
Graham, John: Lavater's Essays on Physiognomy: A Study in The History of Ideas. Bern et al. 1979.
Greimas, Algirdas Julien: Structural Semantics: An Attempt at a Method. Lincoln [1966] 1983.
Grodal, Torben: Film, Character Simulation, and Emotion. In: Jörg Frieß / Britta Hartmann / Eggo Müller (Eds.): »Nicht allein das Laufbild auf der Leinwand...« Strukturen des Films als Erlebnispotentiale. Berlin 2001, pp. 115–128.
Grodal, Torben: Moving Pictures. A New Theory of Film Genres, Feelings, and Cognition. 2nd edn. Oxford 1999.
Gunning, Tom: The Cinema of Attraction. Early Film, its Spectator and the Avant-Garde. In: Wide Angle 8/3&4 (1986), S.63–70.
Hartmann, Tilo / Christoph Klimmt / Holger Schramm: Parasocial Interactions and Relationships. In: Jennings Bryant / Peter Vorderer (Eds.): Psychology of Entertainment. Mahwah, NJ 2006, pp. 291–313.
Heidbrink, Henriette / Rainer Leschke: Formen der Figur. Figurenkonzepte in Künsten und Medien. Konstanz 2010. (forthcoming)
Hickethier, Knut: Film- und Fernsehanalyse. 3rd edn. Stuttgart 2001.
Hogan, Patrick Colm: The Mind and Its Stories: Narrative Universals and Human Emotion. Cambridge 2003.
Holland, Norman N.: The Dynamics of Literary Response. Oxford / New York 1968.
Howell, Robert: Fiction, Semantics of. In: Edward Craig (Ed.): Routledge Encyclopedia of Philosophy. London / New York 1998, pp. 659–663.
Jannidis, Fotis / Gerhard Lauer: »Bei meinem alten Baruch ist der Pferdefuß rausgekommen«. Antisemitismus und Figurenzeichnung in »Der Stechlin«. In: Konrad Ehlich (Ed.): Fontane und die Fremde, Fontane und Europa. Freiburg. 2002, pp. 103–119.
Jannidis, Fotis: Figur und Person. Beitrag zu einer historischen Narratologie. Berlin 2004.
Jauß, Hans Robert: Ästhetische Erfahrung und literarische Hermeneutik. Frankfurt/M. 1982.
Jenkins, Henry: Convergence Culture. Where Old and New Media Collide. New York 2006.

John, O. P.: The Big Five Factor Taxonomy. Dimensions of Personality in the Natural Language and in Questionnaires. In: L. A. Pervin (Ed.): Handbook of Personality. Theory and Research. New York 1990, pp. 66–100.
Kawin, Bruce F.: Mindscreen. Bergman, Godard, and First-Person Film. Princeton, NJ 1978.
Keller, Rudi: A Theory of Linguistic Signs. Oxford 1998.
Koch, Thomas: Literarische Menschendarstellung. Studien zu ihrer Theorie und Praxis. Tübingen 1991.
Künne, Wolfgang: Abstrakte Gegenstände. Semantik und Ontologie. Frankfurt/M. 1983.
Lamarque, Peter: Fictional Entities. In: Edward Craig (Ed.): Routledge Encyclopedia of Philosophy. London / New York 1998, pp. 663–666.
Lamarque, Peter: How to Create a Fictional Character. In: Berys Gaut / Paisley Livingston (Eds.): The Creation of Art. New Essays in Philosophical Aesthetics. Cambridge 2003, pp. 33–51.
Lamping, Dieter: Der Name in der Erzählung. Zur Poetik des Personennamens. Bonn 1983.
Lauer, Gerhard: Spiegelneuronen. Über den Grund des Wohlgefallens an der Nachahmung. In: Karl Eibl / Katja Mellmann / Rüdiger Zymner (Eds.): Im Rücken der Kulturen. Paderborn 2007, pp. 137–163.
Lavine, H. / E. Borgida / L.A. Rudman: Social Cognition. In: V.S. Ramachandran (Ed.): Encyclopedia of Human Behavior, vol. IV. San Diego, CA 1994, pp. 213–223.
Leffelsend, S. / M. Mauch / B. Hannover: Mediennutzung und Medienwirkung. In: Peter Vorderer / R. Mangold / G. Bente (Eds.): Lehrbuch der Medienpsychologie. Göttingen 2004, pp. 51–71.
Luhmann, Niklas: Individuum, Individualität, Individualismus. In: N.L.: Gesellschaftsstruktur und Semantik, vol. 3. Frankfurt a.M. 1993, pp. 149–258.
Maltby, Richard / Ian Craven: Hollywood Cinema. Oxford / Cambridge, MA 1995.
Margolin, Uri: Characterisation in Narrative: Some Theoretical Prolegomena. In: Neophilologus 67 (1983), pp. 1–14.
Margolin, Uri: Characters in Literary Narrative: Representation and Signification. In: Semiotica 106/3&4 (1995), pp. 374–357.
Margolin, Uri: Individuals in Narrative Worlds: An Ontological Perspective. In: Poetics Today 11/4 (1990), pp. 843–871.
Margolin, Uri: The What, the When, and the How of Being a Character in Literary Narrative. In: Style 24/3 (1990), pp. 453–468.
Martinez, Matias / Michael Scheffel: Einführung in die Erzähltheorie. München 1999.
Matoni, Jürgen: Die Juden in Gustav Freytags Werken. In: Oberschlesisches Jahrbuch 8 (1992), Berlin, pp. 107–116.
Melia, Joseph: Possible Worlds. In: Edward Craig et al. (Eds.): Routledge Encyclopedia of Philosophy. Online Edition: <http://www.rep.routledge.com/philosophy/articles/entry/N/N088/N088SECT1.html> (March 3rd, 2010).
Mosbach, Doris: Bildermenschen-Menschenbilder. Exotische Menschen als Zeichen in der neueren deutschen Printwerbung. Berlin 1999.
Naremore, James: Acting in the Cinema. Berkeley et al. 1988.
Neale, Steve: Genre and Hollywood. London / New York 2000.
Neill, Alex: Empathy and (Film) Fiction. In: David Bordwell / Noël Carroll (Eds.): Post-Theory. Reconstructing Film Studies. Madison, WI / London 1996, pp. 175–194.
Oatley, K. / M. Gholamain: Emotions and Identification. Connections between Readers and Fiction. In: M. Hjort / S. Laver (Eds.): Emotion and the Arts. Oxford / New York 1997, pp. 263–281.

Ohler, Peter: Kognitive Filmpsychologie. Verarbeitung und mentale Repräsentation narrativer Filme. Münster 1994.
Palmer, Alan: Fictional Minds. Lincoln, NE 2004.
Pavel, Thomas: Fictional Worlds. Cambridge, MA 1986.
Perloff, Marjorie (Ed.): Postmodern Genres. Norman, 1989.
Persson, Per: Understanding Cinema. A Psychological Theory of Moving Imagery. Cambridge / New York 2003.
Pfister, Manfred: Das Drama. München 1988.
Phelan, James: Reading People, Reading Plots. Character, Progression, and the Interpretation of Narrative. Chicago u.a. 1989.
Plantinga, Carl / Greg Smith (Eds.): Passionate Views. Film, Cognition, and Emotion. Baltimore, MD / London 1999.
Plantinga, Carl: Moving Viewers. American Film and the Spectator's Experience. Berkley, CA 2009.
Plantinga, Carl: The Scene of Empathy and the Human Face on Film. In: C. P. / Greg Smith (Eds.): Passionate Views. Film, Cognition, and Emotion. Baltimore, MD / London 1999, pp. 183–199.
Platz-Waury, Elke: Figurenkonstellation. In: Klaus Weimar et al. (Eds.): Reallexikon der deutschen Literaturwissenschaft, vol. 1. Berlin / New York 1997, pp. 591–593.
Propp, Vladimir: Theory and History of Folklore. Minneapolis [1928] 1984.
Proudfoot, Diane: Fictional Entities. In: David E. Cooper (Ed.): A Companion to Aesthetics. Oxford / Cambridge, MA 1992, pp. 152–155.
Reicher, Maria E.: Zur Metaphysik der Kunst. Eine logisch-ontologische Untersuchung des Werkbegriffs. Graz 1998.
Rimmon-Kenan, Shlomith: Narrative Fiction. Contemporary Poetics. 6th edn. London 1996, pp. 31–34.
Ronen, Ruth: Possible Worlds in Literary Theory. Cambridge et al. 1994.
Ryan, Marie Laure: Fiction, Non-Factuals and the Principle of Minimal Departure. In: Poetics 9 (1980), pp. 403–422.
Ryan, Marie-Laure: Media and Narrative. In: David Herman / Manfred Jahn / Marie-Laure Ryan (Eds.): Routledge Encyclopedia of Narrative Theory. London / New York 2005, pp. 282–292.
Ryan, Marie-Laure: Narrative as Virtual Reality. Immersion and Interactivity in Literature and Electronic Media. Baltimore, MD 2001.
Ryan, Marie-Laure: Possible Worlds, Artificial Intelligence, and Narrative Theory. Bloomington, IN / Indianapolis, IN 1991.
Schank, Roger C.: Tell me a Story. Evanston, IL 1995.
Scherer, Wilhelm: Poetik [1888]. München 1977.
Schmidt, Siegfried J.: Medienkulturwissenschaft. In: Ansgar Nünning / Vera Nünning (Eds.): Konzepte der Kulturwissenschaften. Stuttgart / Weimar 2003, pp. 351–369.
Schneider, Ralf: Grundriß zur kognitiven Theorie der Figurenrezeption am Beispiel des viktorianischen Romans. Tübingen 2000.
Schneider, Ralf: Toward a Cognitive Theory of Literary Character. The Dynamics of Mental-Model Construction. In: Style 35 (2001), pp. 607–640.
Sinding, Michael. Genera Mixta. Conceptual Blending and Mixed Genres in Ulysses. In: New Literary History 36 (2005), pp. 589–619.
Smith, Murray: Engaging Characters. Fiction, Emotion, and the Cinema. Oxford 1995.
Smith, Murray: Gangsters, Cannibals, Aesthetes, or Apparently Perverse Allegiances. In: Carl Plantinga / Greg Smith (Eds.): Passionate Views. Film, Cognition, and Emotion. Baltimore, MD / London 1999, pp. 217–238.

Smith, Murray: Imagining from the Inside. In: Richard Allen / Murray Smith (Eds.): Film Theory and Philosophy. Oxford / New York 1997, pp. 412–430.
Sperber, Dan / Deirdre Wilson: Relevance: Communication and Cognition. Oxford 1986.
Staiger, Janet: Media Reception Studies. London / New York 2005.
Stückrath, Jörn: Wovon eigentlich handelt die epische und dramatische Literatur? Kritik und Rekonstruktion der Begriffe ›Figur‹ und ›Geschehen‹. In: Hartmut Eggert / Ulrich Profitlich / Klaus R. Scherpe (Eds.): Geschichte als Literatur. Formen und Grenzen der Repräsentation von Vergangenheit. Stuttgart 1990, pp. 284–295.
Surkamp, Carola: Narratologie und ›possible-worlds theory‹: Narrative Texte als alternative Welten. In: Ansgar Nünning / Vera Nünning (Eds.): Neue Ansätze in der Erzähltheorie. Trier 2002, pp. 153–184.
Tan, Ed S.: Emotion and the Structure of Narrative Film. Film as an Emotion Machine. Mahwah, NJ 1996.
Thomasson, Amie L.: Speaking of Fictional Characters. In: Dialectica 57/2 (2003), pp. 207–226.
Thon, Jan-Noël: Perspective in Contemporary Computer Games. In: Peter Hühn / Wolf Schmid / Jörg Schönert (Hg.): Point of View, Perspective, and Focalization. Modeling Mediation in Narration. Berlin: de Gruyter 2009, pp. 279–299.
Titzmann, Michael: Psychoanalytisches Wissen und literarische Darstellungsformen des Unbewußten in der Frühen Moderne. In: Thomas Anz (Ed.): Psychoanalyse in der modernen Literatur. Kooperation und Konkurrenz. Würzburg 1999, pp. 183–217.
Tomasello, Michael / Carpenter, M. / Call, J. / Behne, T. / Moll, H.: Understanding and Sharing Intentions: The Origins of Cultural Cognition. In: Behavioral and Brain Sciences 28 (2005), p. 675–735.
Tröhler, Margrit: Hierarchien und Figurenkonstellationen. In: Britta Hartmann / Eggo Müller (Ed.): 7. Film- und Fernsehwissenschaftliches Kolloquium / Potsdam 1994. Berlin 1995, pp. 20–27.
Tröhler, Margrit: Offene Welten ohne Helden. Plurale Figurenkonstellationen im Film. Marburg 2007.
van Beneden, Peter: Viewer ›Identification‹ with Characters in Television and Fiction Film. Nov. 1998. <http://www.aber.ac.uk/media/Students/pjv9801.html> (Oct. 24th, 2001).
Vogel, Matthias: Medien der Vernunft. Eine Theorie des Geistes und der Rationalität auf Grundlage der Medien. Frankfurt/M. 2001.
Vogler, Christopher: The Writer's Journey. Mythic Structures for Storytellers and Screenwriters. Studio City (CA) 1992.
von Wilpert, Gero: Figur. In: G.v.W.: Sachwörterbuch der Literatur. Stuttgart 1989, p. 298.
Vorderer, Peter (Ed.): Fernsehen als ›Beziehungskiste‹. Parasoziale Beziehungen und Interaktionen mit TV–Personen. Opladen 1996.
Walton, Kendall: Mimesis as Make-Believe. Cambridge 1990.
Whittock, Trevor: Metaphor and Film. Cambridge 1990.
Winko, Simone: Kodierte Gefühle. Berlin 2003.
Wolf, Mark J.P.: Genre and the Video Game. In: M.J.P.W. (Ed.): The Medium of the Video Game. Austin 2001, pp. 113–137.
Woolf, Virginia: The Common Reader [1927], London 1968.
Wulff, Hans J.: Attribution, Konsistenz, Charakter. Probleme der Wahrnehmung abgebildeter Personen. In: montage/av 15/2 (2006), pp. 45–62 (first pub. in French as: La perception des personnages de film. In: Iris. Revue de théorie de l'image et du son 24 (1997), pp. 15–32).
Wulff, Hans J.: Empathie als Dimension des Filmverstehens. In: montage/av 12/1 (2003), pp. 136–160.

Zebrowitz, Leslie: Social Perception. Buckingham 1990.
Zillmann, Dolf: Cinematic Creation of Emotion. In: Joseph D. Anderson / Barbara Fisher-Anderson (Eds.): Moving Image Theory. Ecological Considerations. Carbondale, IL 2005, pp. 164–179.
Zillmann, Dolf: Empathy. Affect from Bearing Witness to the Emotions of Others. In: D. Z. / Jennings Bryant (Eds.): Responding to the Screen. Reception and Reaction Processes. Hillsdale, NJ 1991, pp. 135–168.
Zimbardo, Philip G. / Richard J. Gerrig: Psychology and Life. 17th edition. Upper Saddle River (NJ) 2004.

Filmo- and Mediography

»A Clockwork Orange«. Germany 1949, D: Veit Harlan, S: Veit Harlan, Ludwig Metzger (novel by Lion Feuchtwanger).
»Borat: Cultural Learnings of America for Make Benefit Glorious Nation of Kazakhstan«. USA 2006, D: Larry Charles, S: Sacha Baron Cohen, Anthony Hines, Peter Baynham, DanMazer.
»Casablanca«. USA 1942, D: Michael Curtiz, S: Julius Epstein, Philip Epstein, Howard Koch.
»Det Sjunde Inseglet (The Seventh Seal)«. Schweden 1957, D: Ingmar Bergman, S: Ingmar Bergman.
»Fight Club«. USA 1999, D: David Fincher, S: Jim Uhls (novel by Chuck Palahniuk).
»Gandhi«. UK/ India 1982, D: Richard Attenborough, S: John Briley.
»Johnny Got His Gun«. USA 1971, D: Dalton Trumbo, S: Dalton Trumbo.
»Jud Süß«. Germany 1940 D: Veit Harlan, S: Veit Harlan, Ludwig Metzger.
»Matrix Reloaded«. USA / Australia 2003, D: Andy Wachowski, Larry Wachowski, S: Andy Wachowski, Larry Wachowski.
»Palindromes«. USA 2004, D: Todd Solondz, S : Todd Solondz.
»Sherlock Holmes«. USA / Germany 2009, D: Guy Ritchie, S: M. R. Johnson /A. Peckham / S. Kinberg (characters by Arthur Conan Doyle).
»Six Feet Under«. USA, HBO 2001–2005, Showrunner: Alan Ball.
»The Godfather«. USA 1972, D: Francis Ford Coppola, S: Francis Ford Coppola, Mario Puzo, Robert Towne (novel by Mario Puzo).
»The Little Shop of Horrors«. USA 1986, D: Frank Oz, S: Charles B. Griffith.
»The Maltese Falcon«. USA 1941, D: John Huston, S: John Huston (novel by Dashiell Hammett).
»The Trouble with Harry«. USA 1955, D: Alfred Hitchcock, S: John Michael Hayes.
»Un Chien Andalou«. France 1929, D: Luis Bunuel, S : Salvador Dali, Luis Bunuel.
»Without a Clue«. UK 1988, D: Thom Eberhardt, S: Gary Murphy, Larry Strawther.

(D = director, S = screenplay by)

I General Topics

HENRIETTE HEIDBRINK

Fictional Characters in Literary and Media Studies
A Survey of the Research

Fictional characters exhibit a certain ambivalence that makes them delicate to catch: On the one hand they are seamlessly integrated into the work they appear in; on the other hand they seem to be easily unhinged from their medial context and therefore possess a certain autonomy. Characters are suited to be seen as *quasi-autonomous phenomena*: not whole works, not single signs but mostly showing sufficient cohesion to be considered as somewhat independent fictional entities.

So far nobody has devised a theory that is meant to cover fictional characters exhaustively. It has repeatedly been claimed that the diversity and complexity of the phenomenon makes it difficult to expect a fully satisfactory result.[1] With regard to the chronological course of the research on characters it has to be stated that a very large variety of single articles has been published.[2] Along with this dispersion goes the fact that problems keep being reintroduced over again and manifold solutions presented.[3] But especially since the 1990s increasingly more monographies have been written, which might be considered an effect of the enhanced inter- and transdisciplinary research endeavors within cultural, literary, and media studies.[4] When looking at the allocation by nationalities one has to

---

1 Cf. Frow: Spectacle, p. 227; Eder: Figur, p. 14; Nieragden: Figurendarstellung, p. 15; Jannidis: Figur, pp. 4ff, pp. 19f.
2 Cf. Rosenberg: Character; Jannidis: Figur, pp. 1ff; Eder: Figur, pp. 39ff.
3 Cf. Jannidis: Figur, p. 2.
4 Eder: Figur; Fokkema: Postmodern; Jannidis: Figur; Klevjer: Avatar; Koch: Menschendarstellung; Leschke / Heidbrink: Formen der Figur; Michaels: Phantom; Nieragden: Figurendarstellung; Palmer: Fictional Minds; Phelan: Reading; Schneider: Grundriß; Sheldon: Character; Smith: Engaging Characters; Tomasi: Il personaggio; Tröhler: Offene Welten. See also Margolin's article about character in *The Cambridge*

assert that the Anglo-Saxon research tradition comprises by far the main share of the debate around characters, especially character-typologies.⁵ Blüher states that in contrast to cinema, the research of the filmic figure in France has been lying idle; as exceptions she names the approaches of Vernet, Gardies, and Brenez.⁶ Lately, we have seen German-speaking scholars catching up with the production of monographs that exclusively deal with characters in different types of media.⁷ Some of these extensive works on characters also give a detailed survey of the past research.⁸

The term ›character‹ is often intermingled with closely related but different concepts of which I shall only briefly sketch a few here in advance to avoid confusion:⁹ In the following, fictive characters will be separated from real persons or human beings, although they often seem to be perceived by the audience in analogous ways.¹⁰ They are not to be confused with actors or stars, whose bodily features, charisma, and performance are essential for the embodiment and representation of the character.¹¹ And within film and media games they also need to be

---

Companion to Narrative (Margolin: Character, pp. 66–79) and Jannidis' contribution to the same topic in the *Handbook of Narratology* (Jannidis: Character, pp. 14–29).

5   Cf. Jannidis: Figur, pp. 3f, p. 102.
6   Blüher: Ansätze, p. 61.
7   Cf. Koch: Menschendarstellung; Leschke / Heidbrink: Formen der Figur; Schneider: Grundriß; Jannidis: Figur; Eder: Figur; Tröhler: Offene Welten.
8   Eder works his way historically and systematically through a manifold of different positions, cp: Eder: Figur pp. 39–60. Jannidis extracts six narratological aspects and finally opens out into a look at characters as aggregated phenomena, cf. Jannidis: Figur pp. 2f. A rather historical approach that focuses rhetorical and poetical aspects is made by Koch: Menschendarstellung. Schneider, who aims at a cognitive model, mentions the development of theoretical approaches that refer to receptional and empirical questions, cf. Schneider pp. 15f. See also Jannidis in Hühn et al.: Handbook and Margolin in Herman: Companion.
9   Cf. Eder (2007, p. 79) who delineates characters from real persons, the individual personality [in German: *Charakter*, HH], actors, stars, star-images, roles, functions, and actants.
10 Cf. Chatman: Story / Discourse, pp. 126ff. On the relation of ›character‹ and ›person‹ in the dramatics see Pfister: Drama, pp. 221f. For details on the ›person schema‹ in film theory see Smith: Engaging Characters, pp. 20ff. On the periphery of humanness see Grodal: Moving Pictures, pp. 106ff.
11 Actors and Stars *represent* characters but they *are not* the characters. Cf. Vernet: Personnage, p. 177. On the star-phenomena cf. Morin: Les Stars; Patalas: Sozialgeschichte; Dyer: Stars; Gardies: L'acteur; Faulstich / Korte: Star; Lowry / Korte: Filmstar.

delimited from concepts like ›subjectivity‹, ›point of view‹,[12] the player, the first-person-experience, and the avatar.[13]

First of all, fictional characters have to be created. The normative and prescriptive proposals that deal with the question how characters should be formed have a long tradition that goes back to the ancient world: Aristotle formulated in his *Poetic* (approx. 335 B.C.) certain rules that regulated how a hero was supposed to be. He held the view that the heroes of tragedies should imitate men slightly better than average, whereas in comedies the heroes should be geared to men worse than average.[14] Theophrast, a scholar of the former, sketched descriptions of characters (approx. 319 B.C.) with their typical flaws and failings,[15] and Horaz argued in his *De arte poetica* (14 B.C.) above all for the coherence of the character regarding content and style.[16] Especially the antique opuses of Aristotle and Horaz kept their impact until the 18th century. They were later followed by the theoretical notions of dramatists and literary scholars such as Johann Christoph Gottsched, who specified the rules to create successful characters regarding the representation of virtues and effects in his work *Versuch einer critischen Dichtkunst* (1730). These positions are united by the idea to establish normative directions in order to regulate the creation of characters – mostly with quite explicit ideas about preferred receptional effects.[17] The normative poetics were strictly in line with specific intentions and differed in relation to the historical, social, and ethic background of the particular author.[18] Within the course of scholarly observation, these prescriptive approaches – most notably since the end of the 19th century – lost ground against descriptive endeavors that are geared to scientific benchmarks like objectivity, neutrality, and systematic-

---

12 Cf. Branigan: Point of View.
13 Salen and Zimmerman conceptualize the ›player consciousness‹ as a threefold: ›character in a simulated world‹, ›player in a game‹, and ›person in a larger social setting‹ (Salen / Zimmerman: Rules, p. 454). On the ›avatar‹ see Klevjer: Avatar.
14 Cf. Chatman: Story / Discourse, pp. 108ff.
15 Cf. Koch: Menschendarstellung, pp. 88–99; Eder: Figur, pp. 42f; Smeed: Theophrastan ›character‹.
16 Cf. Koch: Menschendarstellung, pp. 32ff; Eder: Figur, p. 43.
17 For the 19th century cf. Freytag: Technik, pp. 215–277; Spielhagen: Beiträge, pp. 67–100.
18 See for instance Friedrich Schiller's speech »Die Schaubühne als eine moralische Anstalt betrachtet« (June 26th, 1784) or Lessing's claim against Gottsched's »Ständeklausel« in *Hamburgische Dramaturgie* (1958). Furthermore, cf. Brecht: Kurze Beschreibung; Lukács: Physiognomie, pp. 151–196.

ity.[19] From their beginning the codes of character-production were closely tied to their implications for the reception.[20]

Today the popular manuals of Lajos Egri (1942), Linda Seger (1990), Christopher Vogler (1992), and Robert McKee (1997)[21] deal with the intricacies of creating characters. These manuals picture characters mainly in analogy to humanlike beings with a ›consistent core‹ and therefore carry out techniques and formulas that are supposed to guide authors to achieve the required successes.[22] Creativity techniques are meant to enhance the fantasy and imaginative potential of the author in order to form ›someone‹ individual, original, authentic, exciting, and fascinating.[23]

In the following I want to look at some crucial points of the research that has been done on fictional characters. I will focus on narrative media products. Since most of the research applies to literature and film, these two media will be central. My general intention is to compare different theoretical approaches in terms of their central concepts, terms, and distinctions. Towards the end I will take a close look on the trans- and intermedial perspective.

---

19 But the former can still be found: Thomas Docherty's book *Reading (absent) character* for instance is inspired by neostructuralist and deconstructivist ideas and aims at the liberation of the reader from his or her repressed self. Docherty: Reading, p. 86. On Docherty cf. Koch: Menschendarstellung, pp. 240ff. On the suppression of subjectivity via character see also Cixous: Character.

20 Thomas Koch, who traces the roots of character-design, states that any characterization is located in the context of author and reader and therefore combines technical and stylistic shares always with a strategic dimension (cf. Koch: Menschendarstellung, p. 10). As Koch convincingly shows, the refinement of different character-rhetorics has changed over time but still tends to oscillate between characters' mimetic qualities to human beings and their functionality within the media product (ibid., pp. 302ff). See also Jannidis: Individuum.

21 Egri: Art; Seger: Creating; Vogler: Writer's Journey (published on the basis of Campbell's book *A Practical Guide to The Hero With a Thousand Faces*, 1949); McKee: Story.

22 Cf. Seger: Creating, pp. 29ff. According to Seger, the semblance of personal depth and complexity can be achieved by implementing paradox attributes to a character (cf. Seger: Creating, pp. 32ff). Another example is the psychoanalytically inspired idea of a ›true character‹ (McKee: Story, p. 101) *behind* a façade that has to be *revealed* along with the progression of the narration (ibid., p. 103). For further details cf. Eder: Figur, pp. 163f.

23 McKee advises script-authors to fall in love with their characters (cf. Mckee: Story, p. 384); a similar view was advanced by Bayley: Characters.

1 The Emergence of Central Questions

Before the end of the 1970s the academic references to fictional characters were in general rather normative, less focused, less systematic; in sum: rather singular and parenthetic projects referred to larger scaled entities like literature,[24] poetics,[25] aesthetics,[26] novels,[27] or fiction.[28] A set time-cut at the starting point of the 1980s does not at all deny that before this date important articles were published and single works were written that by now have become classics.[29] Especially in the 1960s and 1970s one can find monographies,[30] articles,[31] and increasing references towards the side of reception that, in retrospective,[32] had a great influence on the debate. A variety of positions was documented by an issue titled »Changing Views of Character« that was published by the journal *New Literary History* in 1974.[33] But primarily the publications of Chatman, Grabes, Rimmon-Kenan and Margolin in 1978 and 1983 covered the relevant theoretical ground and led to a boost of publications in the following decades up untill today:[34]
In the third and fifth chapter of her book *Narrative Fiction: Contemporary Poetics* Shlomith Rimmon-Kenan addressed two dichotomies concerning the ›mode of existence of character‹: ›people or words‹ and ›being or doing‹.[35] They are followed by the topic of the ›reconstruction‹ of

---

24 Löwenthal: Literature.
25 E.g. Gottsched: Versuch, Lessing: Dramaturgie.
26 Hegel: Vorlesungen, pp. 138ff, pp. 260ff; Wenger: Introduction.
27 Spielhagen: Beiträge.
28 James: Art.
29 For instance: Forster: Aspects, pp. 43–98; James: Art; Harvey: Character; Propp: Morphologie.
30 Walcutt: Man's; Harvey: Character; Gillie: Character.
31 Barthes: Introduction; Price: Other Self, People; Ewen: Theory; Greimas: Struktur, Les Actants; Todorov: Narrative Men; Chatman: Story / Discourse; Grabes: Sätze; Weinsheimer: Theory.
32 Schmidt: Literaturwissenschaft; Iser: Akt; Groeben: Rezeptionsforschung; Jauß: Erfahrung.
33 Cf. Bayley, Cixous, Ferrara, Ingarden, Jauß; two years later, a documentation of a panel-discussion on characters was published by Spilka: Character. Also released in 1974 Greimas: Actants.
34 The attention steadily shifted from literature towards film. David Bordwell for instance drew a picture of identification as confinement to character knowledge (Bordwell: Narration, p. 65). The studies of computer or video games in the mid-1980s were not far enough developed to conceptualize their characters.
35 Rimmon-Kenan: Fiction, pp. 31, 34.

characters from the text.³⁶ Ever since, these dichotomies and questions have been a constant focus of examination of fictional characters:
1. The notion of a character naturally seems to be connected to concepts of *humanlikeness*, although they seem to be made of rather abstract *medial material* like words, images and sounds.
2. Different characters seem to be of different importance to the plot in respect to their *acts* and *functions*.
3. Characters seem to be constructed by a link between the observed *material* and the thereby elicited *reception processes* and *effects*.

In general all three points refer to a continuum between ›abstraction‹ and ›concretion‹, whereas the first pole stands for the <u>medial</u> material, the text, the signs, or the structures of the <u>medial</u> product and the second pole stands for the character that is *via reception* perceived as a humanlike entity with a coherent self including an individual personality.

In this first chapter I will refer to the first point by the dichotomy ›signs vs. persons‹, of which ›enrichment vs. deflation‹ and ›individual vs. type‹ are common subdistinctions. I will refer to the second point by dealing with the dichotomy ›being vs. action / function‹. The second chapter aims at more specific questions that ask for theoretical aspects like the definition, ontology, elements, analytical categories, construction, typologies, and functionality, narrativity and synthesis of characters. The discussion of the third point refers to the relation between ›medial material vs. mental representation‹; it will be dealt with in the third chapter with reference to the actual inter- and transmedial debates. The article will be closed with a general outline of current tendencies in the research of characters.

1.1 Coming Alive!? – Signs vs. Persons

> [...] the concept [of character; HH] is both ontologically and methodologically ambivalent; and any attempt to resolve this ambivalence by thinking character either as merely the analogue of a person or as merely a textual function avoids coming to terms with the full complexity of the problem.³⁷

The debate around ›signs‹ and ›persons‹ addresses the gap between the *medial constructedness* of characters and the receptive processes that lead to

---

36 Ibid., pp. 36ff.
37 Frow: Spectacle, p. 227.

the *mental construction* of a character.³⁸ There is a long ongoing debate between ›humanistic‹ positions on the one hand that deal with characters on a mixed basis of phenomenology,³⁹ hermeneutics and textual analysis, and on the other hand so-called formalists, structuralists and semoticians that hold the view that characters should be addressed as signs,⁴⁰ semantic components (›semes‹),⁴¹ ›bundles of differentiations‹ / paradigms,⁴² words, sentences, or more generally, textuality.⁴³

From the mid-1960s on, structuralists and semioticians began to dwell on the linguistic *construction* of the character and fought against any synthetical notion of characters. They strongly voted against any understanding of characters as human beings and intentionally depreciated any psychological or moral examinations that circle around keywords like ›personality‹, ›individuality‹, ›originality‹, ›deepness‹, ›authenticity‹ and the like.⁴⁴ Furthermore, no autonomy was granted to characters beyond the text – as signs or structures they were inextricably wrapped in the media material: »In semiotic criticism, characters dissolve«.⁴⁵ In contrast, their opponents attested to characters even »[…] a greater measure of coherence […] than we expect of actual people […]« and warned against »the rather puritanical fear of character«.⁴⁶

To illustrate the changing facettes of this debate, we shall move along some classical positions that can be located within the continuum that is characterized by the dichotomies of ›humanlikeness vs. abstraction‹ and ›enrichment⁴⁷ / individual vs. deflation / type‹:⁴⁸ E.M. Forster, in 1927,

---

38 For a detailed overview of the debate around the continuum of ›humanlikeness vs. abstracion‹ see Jannidis: Figur, pp. 153ff; Hochman: Character, pp. 13–27.
39 Cf. Bradley: Tragedy; Knights: Children; Britton: Bradley; Chatman: Story / Discourse, pp. 134ff.
40 »[…] as a sign, character has an immediate presence in the text« (Fokkema: Postmodern, p. 44).
41 Barthes: S/Z, p. 74.
42 Lotman: Structures, p. 251.
43 »Whereas in mimetic theories (i.e. theories which consider literature as, in some sense, an imitation of reality) characters are equated with people, in semiotic theories they dissolve into textuality« (Rimmon-Kenan: Fiction, p. 33).
44 Amongst others, cf. Propp: Morphologie; Robbe-Grillet: Nouveau, pp. 31ff; Barthes: Introduction, S/Z; Greimas: Erzählaktanten; Culler: Structuralist Poetics, p. 230; Hamon: Statut Sémiologique; Chatman: Story / Discourse, pp. 107–145; Weinsheimer: Theory; Rimmon-Kenan: Fiction, pp. 29–42, 59–70.
45 Weinsheimer: Theory, p. 195.
46 Price: Logic, p. 373, p. 377.
47 »Or, among more modern narratives, the reticences of Hemingway and Robbe-Grillet are obvious examples of ›enrichments by silence‹« (Chatman: Story / Discourse, p. 133).

was less concerned with *degrees* of humanlikeness but drew a clear distinction between ›homo sapiens‹ and ›homo fictus‹.⁴⁹ He explained the difference in two ways: First *thematically* by comparing the five »main facts in human life […]: birth, food, sleep, love and death« and secondly from a *formal* point of view concerned with the criteria of transparency and explicability of characters:⁵⁰ They are »explicable, and we get from this a reality of a kind we can never get in real life«.⁵¹ Forster's famous distinction of ›flat‹ and ›round‹ characters alludes to the ›homo fictus‹ and suggests that the impression that one gets of a character depends on the given *amount* of character-attributes,⁵² although the currency of these attributes (ideas, factors, qualities) is not further specified;⁵³ neither does he explain *how* the attributes have to be related in order to create the tragic or comic effects he mentions.⁵⁴ While the ›flat‹ character can yet be resembled by one single trait, Forster states about the ›round‹ character that we can even »[…] know more about him than we can know about any of our fellow creatures«.⁵⁵

Forster's flat-round-distinction made its career: Christian N. Wenger referred to it in 1935 by developing six analytical foci that were meant to refine the view on characters. His foci appear abstract: ›organization‹, ›unity / consistency‹, ›completeness‹, ›condition‹ (dynamic / static), ›duration‹, and ›modus of manifestation‹ – but they are still geared to humanlikeness.⁵⁶ Only the »modus of manifestation« tends towards a closer analysis of the medial material.

Instead of searching for revealing categories of analysis, Marvin Mudrick traced the characters that are said to appear ›individual‹ through

---

48 Cf. Gardies 1980, pp. 81ff. Fishelov – with reference to Forster (1927), Harvey (1965), Hochman (1985) – sees a ›basic tension‹ between ›type‹ and ›individual‹ that manifests itself in every character (Fishelov: Types, p. 422). Historically speaking ›types‹ are displaced by ›characters‹ (Jannidis: Individuum, p. 1).
49 Forster: Aspects, pp. 54f; cf. Hochman: Character, pp. 59–85; Koch: Menschendarstellung, pp. 135f.
50 Forster: Aspects, p. 47.
51 Ibid., p 61.
52 Ibid., pp. 65, 71; for a critical evaluation see Rimmon-Kenan: Fiction, pp. 40f.
53 Forster implies an additive logic: the more ideas, qualities, or factors mark a character, the more it moves towards the round (cf. ibid., p. 65).
54 Cf. ibid., pp. 70ff.
55 Ibid., p. 55.
56 Cf. Jannidis: Figur, pp. 87f.; Koch: Menschendarstellung, p. 123; concerning the focus of duration (›durée‹) cf. ibid., p. 180. Concerning the ›completeness‹ he distinguishes ›symbols‹, ›types‹ and ›individuals‹ and while the first two represent certain matters or qualities, the third ones ›come alive‹ (Wenger: Introduction, p. 623).

the *history* of literature: »In nineteenth-century fiction, the image of the individual personality emerges for the first time as an identifying feature of a literary genre [the novel; HH]«.⁵⁷ Regarding the relation of character and event, Mudrick also differentiates between a *purist* argument and a *realistic* argument.⁵⁸ The first comes close to the request of the structurally oriented literary critics who point out that »[…] any effort to *extract* them [the characters; HH] from their context and to discuss them as if they are real human beings is a sentimental misunderstanding […]«.⁵⁹ The second comes close to mimetic approaches and argues that »[…] characters acquire […] a kind of *independence* from the events in which they live, and that they can be usefully discussed at some distance from their context«.⁶⁰ Therefore the poles of the continuum can be expanded by adding context-independence (by realism) to the ›humanlikeness‹-pole and by adding context-dependence (by purism) to the ›abstraction‹-pole.

Let us move on to the structuralist-semiotic branch that is amongst others represented by Roland Barthes, who in 1966 stated that characters »[…] can be neither described nor classified in terms of ›persons‹ […]«.⁶¹ In 1970 he metaphorically refers to the term ›enrichment‹:

> From a critical point of view it is likewise wrong to suppress the character or to fetch it out of the paper in order to make a psychological character (that is possibly equipped with motives) out of it; character and discourse are complices to each other.⁶²

Another classical structuralist concept has been lined out by the Russian semiotician Jurij Lotman. He works with a double term that corresponds to what we here call fictional character: He defines »persona«, with reference to Propp as ›an intersection of structural functions‹ (similar to Barthes's ›agent‹)⁶³ and ›character‹ (similar to the humanists' notion of ›person‹) that refers to that »[…] human essence which, in a culture of a given type, appears as the only possible norm of behavior, in an artistic

---

57 Mudrick: Character, p. 213; cf. ibid., p. 211. Jannidis locates ›subjectivity‹ and ›individuality‹ as constituting categories already in the period of Storm and Stress (cf. Jannidis: Individuum, p. 1).
58 On this distinction, see Rimmon-Kenan: Fiction, pp. 32f.
59 Mudrick: Character, p. 211, italics added.
60 Cf. ibid. Later Mudrick even states: »In its supreme instances, it [fiction; HH] accomplishes a vision of history more comprehensive than recorded history […]« (Mudrick: Character, p. 218).
61 Barthes: Analysis, p. 105.
62 Barthes: S/Z, p. 184: »D'un point de vue critique, il es donc aussi faux de supprimer le personnage que de le faire sortir du papier pour en faire un personnage psychologique (doté de mobiles possibles) […]« (all trans. by H.H.).
63 Lotman: Structures, p. 240.

text is realized, as a definite set of possibilities only partially realized within its limits«.[64] The »character« of the persona« (personality of the agent) can be compiled by ›a very specific list of differential features«.[65] The clou of this double-term consists in the amalgamation of the abstract concept of the ›persona‹ (agent) with the notion of the ›character‹ (person), enriched via *human essence*.

> The hero's behavior is always unpredictable, first because his character is constructed, not as a previously known possibility, but as a paradigm, a set of possibilities unified on the level of the conceptual structure and variational on the level of the text.[66]

Yet the US-American structuralist and narratologist Seymour Chatman was convinced that the equation of characters with »mere words« was wrong.[67] Referring to Barthes (1970), however, he developed another concept that was inspired by the idea of a »paradigm« – with slight differences at first sight but major theoretical consequences at the second: He defined the fictive character as a ›*paradigm of traits*‹ that changes with the development of the text.[68] With the substitution of the term ›semes‹ by the term ›traits‹ Chatman emphasized their psychological quality and refered explicitly to the personal qualities of the character. Thereby he opened the discussion for further psychological conceptualizations:

> For narrative purposes, then, a trait may be said to be a narrative adjective out of the *vernacular* labeling a *personal quality* of a character, as it persists over part or whole of the story (its ›domain‹). [...] Thus the *traits* exist at the *story level*: indeed, the whole *discourse* is expressedly designed to prompt their emergence in the *reader's consciousness*.[69]

Chatman's work had farther reaching consequences for theories on characters because he inaugurated the distinction between the story realm, where the ›traits exist‹ and the mental processes that are in fact elicited by the discourse but gain a certain independence: »[...] we must *infer* these traits to understand the narrative, and *comprehending* readers do so«.[70] With this distinction, methodological questions arose: How are discourse and

---

64 Ibid., p. 252.
65 Ibid., p. 254.
66 Lotman: Structures, p. 255. See also: »Thus at the foundation of the text construction lies a semantic structure and actions which always represent an attempt to surmount it« (ibid., p. 239).
67 Chatman: Story / Discourse, p. 118.
68 Ibid., pp. 126ff. Cf. Schneider: Grundriß, p. 27.
69 Chatman: Story / Discourse, p. 125 (emphasis by HH.).
70 Ibid., p. 125 (emphasis by HH.).

story related by the reader's consciousness? How do readers *infer* and *comprehend*?[71]

Consequently, the debate was not concerned any more with voting for ›people‹ or ›words‹ but with the challenge to explain how the neverending options of the media arrangements of signs were able to trigger different shades of character-impressions.[72] Five years later, in 1983, Rimmon-Kenan and the Canadian scholar of comparative literature, Uri Margolin, asked in connection with Chatman (1978) *how* characters are reconstructed from the text.[73] Both dealt with the ›people-or-words-question‹ and Rimmon-Kenan stated:

> [...] that the two extreme positions can be thought of as relating to different aspects of narrative fiction. In the *text* characters are *nodes in the verbal design*; in the *story* they are – by definition – non (or pre-) verbal abstractions, *constructs*. Although these constructs are by no means human beings in the literal sense of the word, they are extracted from their textuality. Similarly, in the text, characters are inextricable from the rest of the design, whereas in the story they are extracted from their textuality.[74]

While Rimmon-Kenan, in the wake of the flat-round-distinction of E. M. Forster, asked for the ›degree of ›fullness‹‹,[75] Margolin explicated a continuum »from actant to character as person«, that shows »an increasing humanization and enrichment [...]«.[76] Rimmon-Kenan, making reference to Joseph Ewen, distinguished three axes to classify characters in terms of the *story*: ›complexity‹ (one or more traits), ›development‹ (static vs. dynamic), and ›penetration into the inner life‹ (the availability and details of information that refers to outer or inner states).[77] Searching for the rules that regulate the inferences drawn due to the *text*, she defined the character as a ›network of character-traits‹[78] and distinguished two basic types of textual indicators of characters: ›direct definition‹ and ›indirect representation‹.[79]

---

71 Cf. Grabes's article from the same year, Grabes: Sätze.
72 Weinsheimer for instance still argued against any ›personal surplus‹ of characters beyond the text in 1979, insisting they were nothing more than segments of a closed text, cf. Weinsheimer: Emma.
73 Rimmon-Kenan: Fiction, p. 36.
74 Ibid., p. 33; italics added. Chatman's ›discourse‹ comes close to Rimmon-Kenan's ›text‹. Culler defines characters as ›nodes in the verbal structure‹ (Culler: Structuralist Poetics, p. 231).
75 Cf. Rimmon-Kenan: Fiction, p. 40.
76 Margolin: Characterization, p. 3.
77 Cf. Rimmon-Kenan: Fiction, pp. 40ff.
78 Ibid., p. 59.
79 Cf. Ibid., pp. 59–70.

Margolin was convinced that ›readers [...] *do* create characters from text‹ and the data handling finally leads to a ›macro-semantic unit‹.[80] He defined the character as »[...] *narrative agent* (= NA), that is, an individual capable of fulfilling the argument position in the propositional form DO (X), which is the *sine qua non* of all narrative and drama«.[81] Margolin refined the model of receptional processes by distinguishing the primary ›characterization‹ – the ›ascription of individual properties‹ – and the secondary ›character building‹ that »consists of a succession of individual acts of characterization, together with second order activities of continual patterning and re-patterning of the properties obtained in these acts, until a coherent constellation of mental attributes has been arrived at«.[82] Again, this had important consequences on the deflation-enrichment-continuum because it finally leads to the conviction that the functions a character might fulfill do not necessarily determine its ›personal‹ enrichment – nor vice versa:

> The relation role / actant and person is therefore completely indeterminate in narrative contexts, and no universal selection restrictions on the combinability of type of actant / role and personal features / model can be stated. On the other hand, in the narrative surface one never encounters bare actants / roles. They are always individuated in some degree, so that the NA fulfilling them possesses at least some personological features.[83]

In fact it seems rather impossible to that time to find a position concerning fictional characters that does not take up a stance on the closeness or distance of character to impressions of humanlikeness, individuality or personality: Steven Cohan's approach is theoretically located between mimetic, gestalt-theoretic, and poststructuralist conceptions. He was convinced that ›character does point to a human referent [...]‹.[84] Martin Price clearly voted for a hermeneutical focus on the character as the »illusion of a person« that is foremost thematically oriented.[85] And Thomas Docherty affirmed these positions by negation and asked for a reading against the grain that was supposed to be antihumanistic and anti-mimetic but still circulates around the idea of ›self / non-self‹ and its subjectivity: »Another way of putting this might be to say

---

80 Margolin: Characterization, p. 1.
81 Ibid.
82 Ibid., p. 4.
83 Ibid., p. 3.
84 Cohan: Figures, p. 8.
85 Price: Forms, pp. 37ff.

that we replace the notion of the self with that of the subject, a subjectivity which always eludes objectification«.[86]

To sum up the preliminary results: So far, we have to deal with a phenomenon called ›character‹ that is elicited by media signs (that in combination build certain structures) and potentially sticks out of the text and transcends it. Therefore a character might be considered as a *figuration of signs* that is able to elicit an idea within the spectator that under certain conditions tends to ›tip over‹ and appear *human- or personlike*. Consequently, *both* sides of the central continuum are worth looking at. However, everything that is supposed to transcend the text's semiotic basis is hard to determine as intersubjectively valid. But one can look for techniques that are likely to elicit these effects.

1.2 Coming Apart!? – Being vs. Action / Function

While the dichotomy of ›signs vs. persons‹ was concerned with the potential of characters to transcend the media product that elicited their mental presentation in the first place, the interest – mainly due to structuralist and formalist interventions – was turned towards the dichotomy of ›being vs. action / function‹.[87] Within the 1960s they increasingly focused on the character as agent and denied its psychological qualities in favor of its actions and plot-oriented functions.[88] The transcending qualities of the character had to be ignored in order to reveal its functional substance. Further questions arose when other forces applied for a major impact on the narration: the ›event‹, ›happening‹, or ›incident‹. Thus a third dichotomy poses the question: Who determines whom? How do events, actions, characters / agents relate to single events, to the plot, or to the whole narration?

Aristotle is famous for favoring the plot and thereby the function of a character by its acts (*pratton*) over the personality of the characters (*ethos*).[89] Classical positions that refer to this distinction were developed in the typologies of Edward Muir (1928) or Wolfgang Kayser (1948) – the

---

86 Docherty: Reading, p. 85.
87 Cf. Koch: Menschendarstellung, pp. 150f; Jannidis: Figur, p. 108; Eder: Figur, pp. 15ff.
88 In 1988 Manfred Pfister postulated a dialectical relation between the categories ›character‹ and ›action‹. According to him, besides Aristotle, Johann Christoph Gottsched, and Bertolt Brecht had also voted for the primacy of action while the opposite position was defined by Gotthold Ephraim Lessing, Jakob Michael Reinhold Lenz, and Johann Wolfgang von Goethe (cf. Pfister: Drama, p. 220).
89 Aristotle: Poetik 21; Chapter 6.

former distinguished the ›novel of action‹ from the ›novel of character‹, and the latter between ›Geschehnisroman‹, ›Figurenroman‹, (and ›Raumroman‹).[90] Marvin Mudrick (1961) postulated a reciprocal relation regarding the complexity of ›event‹ and ›character‹:

> Yet, in the work of fiction, a character lives in and is an aspect of events; and events have their own internal cause, duration, magnitude, and consequence. The events of a work of fiction may be linear and unresonant: simply and clearly motivated, of sufficient duration and magnitude to gratify expectation and sustain interest, with clear and simple consequences. [...] Narrative – which is the action of a work of fiction considered exclusively as a sequence of events – is complex and resonant in direct proportion to the complexity of the individual lives whose natures it suggests.[91]

Mudrick gave no proof for his thesis though, and the relation of the complexity of action, events and characters does not necessarily seem to be determined in this way. A clearer definition of complexity would be needed for further examination. Claims of this type were common though; Ferrara presumes:

> In fiction the character is used as the structuring element: the objects and the events of fiction exist – in one way or another – because of the character and, in fact, it is only in relation to it that they possess those qualities of coherence and plausibility which make them meaningful and comprehensible.[92]

In the 1920s the Russian structuralist and morphologist Vladimir Propp (1928) was concerned with different ›spheres of action‹.[93] The idea behind his project of comparing the event-chains of a hundred Russian fairy tales was to deduce the irreducible basic elements (functions). He extracted 31 invariant functions that he merged to seven circles of action which were in turn assigned to specific roles or actants, such as ›the hero‹, ›the helper‹, or ›the donor‹.

On the basis of Propp's and Souriau's works the French structuralist Algirdas Julien Greimas introduced his ›actantial scheme‹.[94] Along with the

---

90 Muir: Structure, pp. 7–40; Kayser: Kunstwerk, pp. 359–361. These considerations find their predecessors in the normative theories of the novel, for instance in Friedrich von Blanckenburg's *Versuch über den Roman* of 1774 (cf. Koch: Menschendarstellung, p. 150).
91 Mudrick: Character, p. 214.
92 Ferrara: Theory, p. 252.
93 Lotman – with reference to Propp – defines character as ›an intersection of structural functions‹ (Lotman: Structure, p. 240).
94 Souriau: Situations, pp. 83–112. Cf. Greimas: Struktur, Les actants, Actant / Acteur. Many other authors have referred to the model, e.g. Bremond, Gardies, Hamon, Jameson, Todorov. For a critique on the ›actant model‹ see Jannidis who argues that inner dimensions of characters and diffuse lines of action are missed by the analytical questions that can be generated by the model (cf. Jannidis: Figur, pp. 100ff). See also

distinction between ›actant‹ and ›acteur‹ this concept led to a complex model of abstract descriptions. He established a double view on the narrative surface where concrete ›acteurs‹ carry out the action while in the subfont a limited number, namely six, ›actants‹ (sender, receiver, subject, object, helper, and opponent) provide the general classes out of which any ›acteur‹ can be formed.[95]

Barthes tried different modes to grasp the problems related to characters: In 1966 he criticized the structural positions of Tomachevski, Propp, Bremond, Todorov, and Greimas that defined the character (›personnage‹) functionally »[...] par sa participation à une sphère d'actions [...]«.[96] He stated that »[l]a veritable difficulté posée par la classification des personnages est la place (et donc l'existence) du *sujet* dans toute matrice actantielle, quelle qu'en soit la formule«.[97] His search for (the location of) the ›subject‹ in literature, in language,[98] in a narrative, as the hero, or »une classe privilégiée d'acteurs«, or ›deux adversaries‹ is the quest for one point that is in some way central.[99] Thus, especially in the modern novel, this central point can become quite diffuse due to the central features of modernism: formal fragmentation, the multiplicity of perspectives, and new forms of character-construction.[100] In 1960 Barthes wanted to capture the character with the very categories of the person, not in a psychological sense, but in a grammatical one.[101] Four years later, in *S/Z* (1970), he approaches the problem once again but with a different definition:

Margolin: Individuals, p. 845; Rimmon-Kenan: Fiction, pp. 34f; Eder: Figur, pp. 49f, pp. 225f.

95 Other approaches also referred to typologies of functions: André Gardies differentiates four character-components: actant, role, character, actor and the entirety of these components (Gardies: Le récit, pp. 59–63; cf. Blüher: Ansätze). Unfortunately the relations and interactions between these components remain unclear. Francesco Casetti and Federico di Chio refer to three structures of the character: ›persona‹ (person), ›ruolo‹ (role) und ›attante‹ (actant). Further distinctions: flat / round, active / passive. (Casetti / di Chio: Analisi, pp. 170–181).

96 Barthes: Analyse, p. 17. [»Most important, it must be stressed again, is the definition of the character according to participation in a sphere of actions [...]« (Barthes 1984, 107)].

97 Ibid., p. 18. [»The real difficulty posed by the classification of characters is the place (and hence the existence) of the subject in any actantial matrix, whatever its formulation« (Barthes 1984, 108)].

98 Ibid., p. 16.

99 Ibid., p. 18. [›a privileged class of actors‹ or ›two adversaries‹ (Barthes 1984, 108)].

100 »The contemplation of character is the predominant pleasure in modern art narrative« (Chatman: Story / Discourse, p. 113).

101 Cf. Barthes: Analyse, p. 18.

> The character is a product of combination: [...]; this complexity determines the ›personality‹ of the character, which is as combinatory as the taste of food or the bouquet of a wine.[102]

And expectedly, different distinctions follow: Barthes separates the ›personnage‹, from the ›figure‹ and the ›je‹: The character (figure) is thereby understood as a kind of literary foil that is detached from the personnage and – particularly in modern literature – exposed to a high degree of ambiguity.[103]

> As character the person can oscillate between two roles, without that oscillation making any sense, because it resides beyond biographical time (beyond chronology): the symbolic structure is completely reversible: one can read it in all directions.[104]

In contrast to Barthes' focus on the relation of character and its personality, Jurij Lotman's ›plot functions‹ deal with the mediation between certain elements of the plot:[105]

> The type of world picture, the type of plot and the type of persona are all dependent on each other. Thus we have established that among personae, among the heroes of numerous artistic and non-artistic texts who are provided with human names and human appearances, we can distinguish two groups: agents, and the conditions and circumstances of the action.[106]

Certain narrative settings are supposed to motivate certain acts or call for certain types of action and agents, but the exact rules of the interaction between the hero and the semantically and topologically structured textual environment remain unclear. Notably, according to Lotman the »*personification* of plot functions depends on the nature of the semantic classification« and »both groups of plot functions« need to be ›*humanized*‹ by a »special type of comprehending the world«.[107] Thus in spite of all structural ambitions he does not explain *how* this special type of comprehension works but the well-known reference to humaneness is kept.

---

102 Barthes: S/Z, p. 74: »Le personnage est donc un produit combinatoire [...]; cette complexité détermine la ›*personnalité*‹ du personnage, tout aussi combinatoire que la saveur d'un mets ou le bouquet d'un vin« (emphasis by H.H.).
103 Jannidis remarks that the protagonist can be seen as a collective term for a deep structure similar to Greimas's actants (cf. Jannidis: Figur, p. 120).
104 Barthes: S/Z, p. 74: »Comme figure, le personnage peut osciller entre deux rôles, sans que cette oscillation ait aucun sens, car elle a lieu hors du temps biographique (hors de la chronologie): la structure symbolique est entièrement réversible: on peut lire dans tous les sens«.
105 Cf. Lotman: Structure, p. 240.
106 Ibid., p. 243.
107 Ibid.

Another important contribution was made in 1971 by Tzvetan Todorov who opposed Henry James' famous diction by stating:[108] »Character is not always [...] the determination of incident, nor does every narrative consist of ›the illustration of character‹«.[109] His discrimination between ›psychological‹ and ›a-psychological‹ narratives illustrated that character and action are two *intermingled* concepts that within differently shaped narrations take different orders of precedence.

> A character trait is not simply the cause of an action, nor simply its effect: it is both at once, just as action is.[110]

Todorov called a narration ›psychological‹ when the action »is *transitive* with regard to its subject« and he called a narration ›a-psychological‹ when »action is important in itself and not as an indication of this or that character trait«.[111] This revealed that the pleasure that is triggered by the consumption of medial products – be they narrative, ludic, experimental or of other types – is by far not exclusively focused on the plot-drive. Todorov consequently distinguished between a ›psychological causality‹ (»a by-product a psychological cause-and-effect coupling«) and the ›causality of events or actions‹.[112] He saw them as different but related layers, whose relation is established by the interpretation processes of the audience. Thus a functional analysis of the character does not have to be geared to the plot and might miss important attributes that determine the type of the narration. The distinction of Todorov pointed to the fact that reception of narrations often comes very close to social observations that focus on the characters' actions and reactions and combines them with various processes of inference-drawing and attribution.

The discursive intervention of Todorov provides a good example of the fact that some normative debates recede through the influence of other disciplines. In this case the possible hierarchies of character, action, and plot become of minor importance in favor of the relation of more or less psychologically saturated characters with regard to certain *types* of plots that again are very likely to include certain types of events. And these

---

108 Henry James wrote in 1884: »What is character but the determination of incident? What is incident but the illustration of character? What is either a picture or a novel that is *not* of character?« (James: Art, p. 34).
109 Todorov: Narrative-Men, p. 70.
110 Ibid., p. 68.
111 Ibid., p. 67; Cf. Rimmon-Kenan: Fiction, pp. 35f.
112 Cf. Todorov: Narrative-Men, p. 69.

relationships in turn have shaped typical genre patterns.[113] Seven years later, in 1978 Chatman stated that »[...] where chief interest falls is a matter of the changing taste of authors and their publics«.[114]

> There seems no self-evident reason to argue the primacy of action as a source of traits, nor for that matter the other way around. Is the distinction between agent and character really necessary? Let us argue that plot and character are equally important and escape the awkwardness for explaining how and when character (*ethos*) traits are ›added‹ to agents.[115]

Instead he claimed that there exists a »[...] fundamental difference between events and traits«.[116] Theoretically speaking, he incorporated psychological saturation by aligning adjectives with narrative traits and defining them as *personal qualities*.[117]

A different contribution to the ›character-action-continuum‹ was made by the literary scholar Jörn Stückrath. He was rather interested in an analysis that was able to grasp the content-relations of different narrations. He proposed an analysis of story-lines that focuses on the wishes and purposes of characters in relation to the conflict-laden developments and final outcomes.[118] This kind of elementary analysis of actions applies to a level of meaning where many tasks of basic comprehension have already taken place and thereby exposes the character to forms of social observation and comparison.[119]

As can be seen, the observation of characters depends on the question what is being observed: It makes a great difference to capture them as humanlike persons, signs, structures, or functions, respectively, because each concept is based on different entities and theoretical premises that are incomparable: the physicalness and conduct of Rick Blaine,[120] »la systématique d'un lieu (transitoire) du texte«,[121] the barometer and the piano of *Mme Aubain*,[122] the character as lever for moral orientation,[123] the

---

[113] For further details on the relationship between genre, characters, actions, and events see Grodal: Moving Pictures.
[114] Chatman: Story / Discourse, p. 113.
[115] Ibid., p. 110.
[116] Ibid., pp. 126ff.
[117] Ibid., pp. 125.
[118] Cf. Stückrath: Entwurf.
[119] Cf. Stückrath: Figur / Geschehen, pp. 288f.
[120] Cf. Eder: Figur, pp. 266ff.
[121] Barthes: S/Z, p. 101.
[122] Chatman, referring to Barthes, discusses *Mme Aubain's* piano in Flaubert's *Un Coeur Simple* as index for her bourgeoisie and her barometer as a »useless« luxury of narration (cf. Chatman: Story / Discourse, p. 144).
[123] Cf. Smith: Engaging Characters, pp. 187–227; cf. Carroll: Suspense.

face of *Jeff* in *Rear Window* (1945)[124] – all these observations start from different levels of semiotic aggregation, focus on different types of inferences and are based on different types of logical foundations. So what exactly would be the point of a theory of the fictional character?

2 The Question of Theory Revisited

A theory, in the broadest sense, builds a model or draws a set of descriptive and explanatory propositions that claim a systematic relation to a defined object of interest. Therefore first steps mostly include a *description* or a *definition* of the object and further *terms* and *distinctions* that build on this basis in order to explain the *functional integration* of the object within given *contexts*. The research on characters displays these issues by repeatedly asking what characters are (ontology),[125] how they can be defined (definition), what they are made of (components / elements / segments), how they are constructed (construction / characterization), what functions they fulfil within different media contexts (e.g. theatre / film / prose fiction), and how to explain the coherence-effect that characters reveal (synthesis). In the following I want to address the mentioned issues by tracing selected classical positions in the field of character-research.[126]

2.1 Elements, Segments, and Components

The selection of ›elements‹ that are in someway observable is in the majority of the cases the first step that is taken. Thus, if anyone wants to grasp the character as some kind of more or less defined entity, the question arises, which elements, components, attributes, or features belong to it. While many early approaches proceeded intuitively hermeneutically, things changed with the rise of formalism, structuralism and semiotics. The proponents of these approaches were eager to focus

---

124 Plantinga: Scene, pp. 241f.
125 The ontological perspective on characters must not necessarily imply that characters *exist*. Instead it shall give an account of the multiple ways that can refer to character-like entities.
126 Recent publications have outlined in detail a great variety of existing positions: An extensive discussion of ontological questions and options to define ›character‹ can be found in Eder: Figur, p. 61; Jannidis: Figur pp. 151–195; Margolin: Introducing and Margolin: Individuals.

on structures, codes and functions that were to be grasped systematically with an explicit terminology and meant to guarantee a higher degree of intersubjective understanding.[127]

Concerning the struggle with elements, Roland Barthes in 1970 suggested the proper name as a cohesion device:

> When identical semes repeatedly cross the same proper name and appear to establish themselves there, a character emerges.[128]

But once relevant entities and cohesive factors are made out, their relations among one another have to be explicated: questions of order, hierarchy, segmentation, and stability have to be answered. Hence, others referred to his suggestion but pointed implicitly to its weakness:[129] »The unity created by repetition, similarity, contrast, and implication may, of course, be a *unity in diversity* […]«.[130] As already outlined, Chatman explicitly psychologized Barthes's mere linguistic concept of semes but was confronted with the same problems: »The ineffability of round characters results in a part from the large range and diversity or even discrepancy among traits«.[131] But being aware of the changes within the development of the character via the text, he integrated the traits into the course of the plot:

> The paradigmatic view of characters sees the set of traits, metaphorically, as a vertical assemblage intersecting the syntagmatic chain of events that comprise the plot.[132]

Lotman aimed to grasp the fictive agent structurally by looking for segments that it would apply to:

> The mutual superimposition of these binary segmentations creates bundles of differentiation. These bundles are identified with personae and become characters. The character of a persona is a set of all the binary oppositions *between him and other personae* (other groups) as given in the text, the sum of his inclusions in groups of other personae; in other words, it is a set of *differential features*. Thus character is a paradigm.[133]

---

127 Cf. Todorov: Erbe des Formalismus.
128 Barthes: S/Z, p. 74: »Lorsque des sèmes identiques traversent à plusieurs reprises le même nom propre et semblent s'y fixer, il naît un personnage«; pp. 101ff.
129 Cf. Rimmon-Kenan: Fiction, pp. 39f; cf. Chatman: Story / Discourse, pp. 126, 131.
130 Rimmon-Kenan: Fiction, p. 40; italics added. For further thoughts on the concept of the proper name that combines the philosophical (eg. philosophy of language and modal logic of Saul Kripke) and cognitive approach of Possible Worlds-Theory, see Margolin: Naming. He defines the name as a »label of a mental file we keep of someone«.
131 Chatman: Story / Discourse, p. 133.
132 Ibid., p. 127.
133 Lotman: Structures, p. 251.

But his underlying concept of segmentation remains problematic, because he fails to clarify the primal entities: As segments of theatre he lists incommensurable kinds like ›scenes‹ and ›entrances‹, and concerning film he mentions ›borders of the screenplay‹ and the ›shot‹.[134]

Uri Margolin defined character as an element of the fictional (possible) world that comes into being through the reception of the media material.[135] In contrast to Chatman's psychologically based distinction between ›real-person traits‹ and ›fictional-character traits‹ Margolin clearly separated the fictional character from persons and claimed that it was dedicated to a different sphere, namely the ›fictional‹ or ›possible world‹.[136] Thus the character becomes the product of inferences that a spectator draws *because of* the displayed and observed media material; it is not an immediate result from signs or the text itself any more.

> [...] ›character‹ or ›person‹ in narrative will be understood as designating a human or human-like individual, existing in some possible world, and capable of fulfilling the argument position in the propositional form DO(X) – that is, a Narrative Agent (=NA), to whom inner states, mental properties (traits, features) or complexes of such properties (personality models) can be ascribed on the basis of textual data.[137]

2.2 Construction / Characterization

Consequently, the focus turned towards the *construction of characters* as they are represented via the media material and therefore appear as beings of a fictional world *due to reception*. Margolin points to the fact that reception is a dynamic endeavor, but the complete coverage of all attributes and its synthesis is possible only in the retrospective view. The clear separation of the reader's reality, the media material, and the character as part of the *fictional* world, has important consequences: The described processes of ›characterization‹ and ›character building‹ are now meant to mediate between the text and the emerging mental construct of the recipient.[138] Margolin's thoughts dwell on the potentials of the manifold textual cues

---

134 Ibid., p. 250. Notably: »[...] the close-up is not a relevant feature«; it is synonymous to verbal descriptions of the type »to gaze in horror« or »to look attentively« [...]« (ibid., pp. 250f).
135 Maître: Literature, Doležel: Heterocosmica.
136 Chatman: Story / Discourse, p. 126, p. 138.
137 Margolin: Doer / Deed, p. 205
138 Cf. Margolin: Characterization, p. 4.

that directly and indirectly point to the attributes of the character, including: psychic states, physicalness, settings, and actions.[139]

Margolin intended to find the »rules of inference governing the reader's transition from statements about the acts, appearance, and setting of a NA [narrative agent; HH] to CSs [characterization statements; HH] about him«.[140] Notably these are based on natural, not formal logic and are supposed to constitute a semiotic code.[141] In contrast to the semiotic codes of Barthes or Eco, it consists »of life-world and literary subsets or components« and consequently its use bears different, namely hermeneutical, qualities:[142] The transition processes it governs involve several intermediary stages, »different, equally justified characterizations [...], each based on a different code«.[143] Consequently one has to reckon with the divergence of psychological inferences.

> Human acts are not immediate, elementary data to be identified and described per se but hypothetical, complex constructs posited by the reader from narrative data about the doings of NAs, after these data have been interpreted for their cultural and social significance. Acts must be identified, categorized and typified before they can serve as a basis for the characterization of their agents.[144]

Margolin tried to remedy the problem that all inferences are »already interpretation-laden« by reverting to frames, symbolic and literary codes and scripts, without satisfactorily solving the problem, though.[145] The »standard cultural significance / status to certain phrases or gestures« might in polysemic cases,[146] as Margolin admits himself, »not be adequate for a full decoding«.[147]

Aleid Fokkema, in her examination of characters of postmodern novels, claimed that they are constructed by different codes.[148] With

---

139 Cf. Margolin: Doer / Deed, p. 208.
140 Ibid., p. 207.
141 Cf. Ibid. For critical thoughts on the rise and fall of semiotic ›code models‹ in the 1960s and 1970s cf. Jannidis: Figur, pp. 45ff.
142 Margolin: Doer / Deed, p. 208. Barthes' ›code‹ mediates between author and reader (cf. Barthes: Analysis, pp. 110ff). For a critique on the imprecise reconstruction of indirect characterizations on the basis of Barthes' code model cf. Jannidis: Figur, pp. 157ff.
143 Ibid., p. 209.
144 Ibid., pp. 208f.
145 Cf. ibid., pp. 209f.
146 Ibid., p. 210.
147 Ibid.
148 For a critical notion see Schneider, who argues that the semiotic approach of Fokkema is rather interested in the codes of the text than in the processes that occur in the reader (cf. Schneider: Grundriß, p. 28).

reference to Ferdinand de Saussure and Umberto Eco, she sees the character as a code-based sign of the ›expression plane‹ that relates to one or several elements of the ›content plane‹. She distinguishes amongst others the *logical Code* that is supposed to guarantee the consistency of character-information, the *biological and the psychological Code* that put characters in a close relation to biological and psychological conventions; these codes allege that characters have a body and an ›inner life‹.[149] The problem with these codes lies in the fact that the relation between the two planes cannot be clearly defined.

> The sign of character [...] develops a combination and recombination of elements from the expression plane and the content plane. [...] New elements from the expression plane will be linked to the content plane, and add up to earlier processes of signification. The text generates a complex character sign.[150]

A similar approach that tries to grasp characters categorically consists in the examination of textual (or audiovisual) propositions. In 1995 the literary scholar Göran Nieragden developed a narratological model as a basis for the analysis of characters, subsequent to his mentor, Helmut Bonheim.[151] He started from the examination of textual propositions (›Speech acts‹) in order to find categories for all given information that refer to characters: comments, dialogues, descriptions and the alike. In contrast to Margolin's ›characterization‹ his attempt dispensed with an interdisciplinary theoretical framework. The same holds true for Anke-Marie Lohmeier (1996) who applied a large variety of analytical aspects, mainly from literary studies, to film. She imported her categories of character-analysis from Pfister.[152] Both attempts are very helpful and reveal their productivity when is comes to the detailed observation of the media material. They, however, face difficulties because they produce large amounts of analytic results without offering models or strategies to evaluate and order this knowledge.

2.3 Typologies und Taxonomies

Another common way of dealing with characters was and is to build typologies and taxonomies that are burdened with the same problem,

---

149 Cf. Fokkema: Postmodern, pp. 73ff.
150 Ibid., pp. 44f.
151 Bonheim: Literary Systematics.
152 Lohmeier: Theorie, pp. 270ff. The title is somewhat deceptive, because Lohmeier mainly refers to the semiotics of Eco.

namely the missing systematic relations between the chosen categories. Northrop Frye's cyclical typology of protagonists was based on his analysis of literature that brings literary epochs in line with specific forms:[153] mythic, romantic, high mimetic, low mimetic, and ironic. Each category sets the protagonist in a different relation to society. Leo Löwenthal and Charles Child Walcutt saw characters as literary indicators for historical circumstances. They were created by an author and could be traced as reflections of their time.[154]

William Harvey (1965) outlined the relation of *action* and *character* by his typology of four kinds of characters: the »protagonists« and the ›background figures‹ of which he accentuates the ›ficelle‹, and the ›card‹ – that are distinguished by their different influence concerning the action and the development of conflict. The ›ficelle‹ is more individualized than other characters and possesses a specific function, while the ›card‹ is a static character with rather exceptional traits. The criteria of the distinction consist in their relation to the plot, concerning their integration and function as well as the elaborateness and dynamics of the character-conception.[155]

Baruch Hochman's taxonomy (1985) contains eight categories that »[...] described aspects of characters in literature [...]« and »[...] allow us to conceptualize the images we form of such characters as we ›liberate‹ them from the text within which they figure«.[156] His categories referred to the character as an analogon to real humans, the amount of attributes that belong to a character as well as their relations. His terminology indeed became more abstract but a systematic development of categories was still missing.[157]

David Fishelov (1990) strove for a systematic connection to Forster's distinction of round and flat characters.[158] Via the differentiation of a ›textual level‹ (*discourse / Darstellung*) and a ›constructed level‹ (*histoire / fiktionale Welt / Dargestelltes*) he reached a matrix that in fact still referred to ›humaneness‹ (types vs. individuals) but had the advantage of being sensitive to different strategies of character-construction that in turn regulate the impression of characters.

---

153 Frye: Anatomy.
154 Walcutt: Mask; Löwenthal: Literature.
155 Harvey's distinctions where again integrated by Hochman: Character, pp. 87f.
156 Hochman: Character, p. 89.
157 For an elaborated commentary and critique on Hochmann's approach cf. Janndis 2004, pp. 94ff. See also Fishelov: Types, pp. 423ff.
158 Fishelov: Types.

2.4 Analytical Categories

Yet another type of approach consists in the development of analytical categories and perspectives on the object of interest. A great variety of proposals can be found which usually resort to previous works. The theoretical shortcoming commonly lies in the fact that the analytical categories are simply added without any underlying systematic order. These forms of multidimensional analyses have the advantage of being open for further suggestions but they also suffer from a certain amount of arbitrariness. Taylor and Tröhler (1999) for instance refer to the character as a ›conglomerate of facets‹ (»Facetten-Konglomerat«)[159] that can be described in different ways: attributive, dynamic, and differential. The character is defined along a paradigmatic and a syntagmatic axis through the film, and ought always to be analyzed in relation to the social context of the film.[160]

Manfred Pfister developed various categories for the observation and analysis of characters in drama: dramatis personae (»Personal«), constellation, configuration, complexity, scale, duration, conception (including static / dynamic, one- and multi-dimensional, open / closed, (trans-) psychological), as well as different forms of characterization.[161] Pfister first defines the character ex negativo and separates it from real persons by emphasizing their fragmentation and the various options of their creation; he then turns to the positive side:

> In contrast, the dramatic character can be defined in positive terms as the sum of its structural functions regarding the change or stabilization of the situation, and the personality (in the neutral sense of the identity of a character) can be defined as the sum of correspondence and contrast relations towards the other characters of the text.[162]

Pfister's definition might sound convincing due to its high degree of abstraction but it is not really handy when it comes to practical analysis,

---

[159] Taylor / Tröhler: Facetten, pp. 149f.
[160] Ibid., p. 149. Gardies differenciates two axes of character conception: ›L'axe d'attribution‹ and ›L'axe de difference‹ (Gardies: Le récit, pp. 56ff).
[161] Cf. Pfister: Drama, pp. 221–264.
[162] Pfister: Drama, p. 224: »Positiv ist dagegen die dramatische Figur zu definieren als die Summe ihrer strukturellen Funktionen der Situationsveränderung und der Situationsstabilisierung, und der Charakter (im neutralen Sinn der Identität) einer Figur als die Summe der Korrespondenz- und Kontrastrelationen zu den anderen Figuren des Textes«.

mainly because of the large quantity and wide range of character-attributes and character-relations that are often incomparable.[163]

James Phelan (1989) was concerned with ›a double focus on character and progression‹.[164] He differentiated between *synthetic* (the artificial component), *mimetic* (characters as images of real people) *and thematic* (the implied significance)[165] aspects of characters whereby these aspects can alternatively be brought to front.[166] He also separated ›dimensions‹ from ›functions‹ and stated that »[...] dimensions are converted into functions by the *progression* of the work«.[167] By emphasizing the *dynamics* of any narration he overcomes the rather static structuralistic view and turns towards a kind of rhetorical analysis that aims at the text as communicative device.[168]

2.5 Characters in Theatre and Film

Notably the switch to a different medium – for instance from the mainly narrative text of the novel to dramatic texts but also theatrical representations – entails the option to observe other types of semiosis: images, theatrical performance, and spectacle provide again new theoretical accesses than linguistic structures made of words. Hence within the media field of drama and theatre Erika Fischer-Lichte in the 1980s established a substantial semiotic approach in the domain of theatre studies.[169] She was convinced that analysis and interpretation emerged from the interaction of the dramatic text, production, the presence and physicalness of the actors

---

163 His analogy to a chess game is not able to live up to expectations either, because narrative characters are geared to other ›rules‹, namely dramaturgical ones, than chess-tokens that are to obey to the rules of the game.
164 Phelan: Reading, ix. Cf. Jannidis: Figur, pp. 228ff; Eder: Figur, p. 126.
165 Phelan: Reading, pp. 2f. Phelans distinctions come close to three of Eder's four analytic categories: characters as artefacts, as fictive beings, and as symbols (cf. Eder: Figur, p. 131).
166 Cf. ibid., p. 3.
167 Ibid., p. 9. Unfortunately Phelan's terminology is partially blurred by circular relations: the distinction between the ›dimension‹ and the ›function‹-distinction is based on the ›attribute‹ which is already part of the definition of the ›dimension‹ and of the ›function‹ (cf. ibid.).
168 Phelan elaborates his approach in 2005 when he distinguishes between different rhetorical functions and different types of character narration. Besides, he discusses possible ethical implications of narrative communication with regard to characters. Cf. Phelan 2005: Living.
169 Fischer-Lichte: Semiotik, pp. 31–131.

in actu (»Tätigkeit«) as well as the staging and their appearance (»Erscheinung«): »Theatre presupposes the a priori of the body«.[170] After the first appearance of a character, the process of the play is accompanied by a constant accumulation of different kinds of signs. In contrast to theories of characters in printed literature the semiotic basis changes significantly when the bodily appearance of characters comes into play. The theoretical challenge differs slightly within the semiotic paradigm; one typical reaction is the addition of further codes that in turn refer to other types of signs than linguistic ones:

> The spectator then relates the linguistic, paralinguistic, physical (facial expression and gestures), and proxemic signs that are generated by the actor to this identity, which has been tentatively established.[171]

Richard Dyer (1979) also based his examination of film characters on semiotics, analyzing the acting, staging and filmic devices. But he also integrated *extrafilmic* aspects that referred to the actors as social phenomena, as star-personas and thereby included information about their star-images and their private lives. When references appear that *exceed* the basis of the media work, the analytical basis is again changed. Through the integration of discourses that leave the fixed media product, the amount of information offered and thus ›additional meanings‹ becomes unlimited. A similar approach – with reference to Dyer – was undertaken by Dario Tomasi (1988) who was particularly interested in the significant elements and structures of the character that traverse different dimensions of signs. He dwelled on the constellation of the character within the intra- and extranarrative discourses and added structural observations in order to compile the ›meaning‹ of the filmic character:[172]

> To analyze a cinematic character means to become aware of its articulations on different levels [...], from the story, to the speech of the actors, [...], to the narration, and the film. Only in consideration of all these elements can we ascertain the meaning of the cinematic character.[173]

---

170 Ibid., p. 98. »Theater geht vom Apriori des Leibes aus [...]«.
171 Ibid.: »Auf diese vorläufig beigelegte Identität bezieht nun der Zuschauer die anderen vom Schauspieler hervorgebrachten Zeichen, die linguistischen, und paralinguistischen, die mimischen, gestischen und proxemischen«.
172 Cf. Tomasi: Personaggio, p. 174.
173 Ibid., p. 173: »Analizzare un personaggio cinematografico vorrà dire dunque tener conto dei diversi livelli su cui esso si articola, da quello della storia [...], il discorso dell'attore [...], quello del racconto [...] e quello del film [...]. Solo tenendo conto di tutti questi elementi si potrà arrivare a determinare il significato del personaggio cinematografico«.

2.6 Character and Narration: Focalization and Subjectivity

Others again saw the character as an agency with a great impact on the formal construction of a narration. Gérard Genette tied the voice of the narrator to the characters of a narration: With his three ›types of focalization‹ he ascertains the relation of the knowledge of the narrator with regard to the characters.[174] And Edward Branigan (1984) turned towards character via the construction of *subjectivity* in films and defined »[…] narration in the visual arts as a positioning of the viewer with respect to a production of space, and subjectivity as a production of space attributed to a character«.[175]

> Subjectivity, then, may be conceived as a specific instance or level of narration where the telling is *attributed to* a character in the narrative and received by us *as if* we were in the situation of a character.[176]

The criterion that Branigan names for subjectivity is the united reference of the ›six units of representation‹:[177] origin, vision, time, frame, object, and mind.[178] Consequently one reaches the character by the analysis of diegesis which is provided by the film as »the implied spatial, temporal, and causal system of a character – a collection of sense data«.[179]

2.7 Problems of Synthesis

As can be easily seen, there are many options to define signs, features, entities, certain aspects, perspectives, or categories to observe characters in order to establish at best a reliable ground for any further analytical steps. Once these decisions are made, another problem seems to arise, namely the question of synthesis: How are the detected elements or the analytical results kept together? Therefore, within the theories about characters concepts of ›unity‹, ›coherence‹, and ›cohesion‹ are repeatedly at stake.[180] These come in different kinds. Koch, for instance, referred to rhetorical coherence:

---

174 Cf. Genette: Person.
175 Branigan: Point, p. 64.
176 Ibid., p. 73.
177 Ibid., pp. 61ff.
178 Ibid., p. 75.
179 Ibid., p. 35.
180 Within the debate on the so-called ›post-modern‹ film it is a commonplace to describe characters as disjointed, split, and predominantly fragmented. In doing so the term

The inner *aptum* reveals itself firstly as a coherence between different attributes of a character within one type and secondly as a coherence between *ethos* and *pathos* on the one hand, and their manifestation in speech, gesture, and facial expression on the other side.[181]

Cohan (1983) alluded to approaches of gestalt theory (Gurwitsch), phenomenology (Husserl) and the aesthetics of reception (Iser) in order to locate the imaginative construction of the character. »For it is here [in the crucial space between the text and its reader; HH] that the coherence of character as a virtual existent comes into play«.[182] Hochman again implied that the impression of gestalt, wholeness and cohesion does not only depend on the *amount* of the given information but on the *order* and *arrangement* in close relationship to already existent knowledge, experience, sensibility, sensitivity, and the esthesia of the recipient regarding the »Gestalt«. He stated

> [...] that the generation of character rests in large part on prior typifications. The implication is that in literature as in science, figures and other patterns are not generated by direct observation and combination of particulars – that is, that they are formed not inductively and inferentially, but rather by deduction from prototypes and patterns.[183]

The common conception refers to the coherence that is supposedly caused by the ›human identity‹, as Hochman puts it: »What links characters in literature to people in life, as we fabricate them in our consciousness, is the integral unity of our conception of people and of how they operate«.[184] Actual theories are aware of the fact that the impression of coherence is evoked by the interaction of the reader with the medial material. Jannidis puts it as follows:

›fragmentation‹ stands for the impression that emerges during the viewer's reception and interpretation process, when a film or a character is structured in a certain manner. For details on different »strategies of fragmentation« cf. Heidbrink: Summen.
181 Koch: Menschendarstellung, p. 37: »Das innere *aptum* stellt sich also einmal dar als Kohärenz zwischen verschiedenen Charaktereigenschaften innerhalb eines Typenbildes und zum Zweiten als Kohärenz zwischen *ethos* und *pathos* auf der einen Seite und ihrer Manifestation in Rede, Gestik und Mimik auf der anderen«.
182 Cohan: Figures, p. 9.
183 Hochman: Character, p. 112.
184 Ibid., p. 36.

> The identity of the character is not to be understood as ontological or semantic but in relation to communication [...] The character [...] is not a textual entity but a conceptual identity that is generated by the text [...].[185]

To sum up: When we turn to the multiple answers of the question ›What is a character?‹ we get different answers that are closely related to the disciplines they stem from;[186] the range of offers runs from ›nonexistence‹ through to structures,[187] signs, trait-clusters, agents, rhetoric effects, plot-functions, humanlike persons, mental representations, imaginative beings, inhabitants of a fictional / possible world – and combinations of these positions. We are repeatedly confronted with similar results that often metaphorically blur the relations between text and mental constructs, when asking for the location of the character. They typical shift between the media material and the recipient's mind.[188] Remarkably two interventions advanced the situation: Firstly, Chatman's hint that it is advantageous to understand the character as a part of the ›story‹ by introducing Tzvetan Todorov's differentiation of ›*histoire*‹ *(what)* and ›*discourse*‹ *(how)*.[189] And secondly, the emergence of the possible-worlds-discourse:[190] Margolin defines the character as a part of the *fictional world* that is brought to being by the medial material. The act of ›representation‹ thereby establishes this world *via* semiosis. This *fictional* world is treated as an *existent* world and, very importantly: it is *dependent* but distinguishable from the semiosis that forgoes it.[191]

3. Moving together: Trans- and Intermedial Impacts

Since paradigms always superimpose and interfere with each other in many ways, it is hard to say when the interdisciplinary influences exactly found their way into the debates around characters. In the 1960s and

---

185 Jannidis: Figur, p. 147: »»Identität der Figur‹ ist nicht ontologisch oder semantisch zu verstehen, sondern lediglich kommunikationsabhängig: [...] Die Figur [...] ist keine sprachliche Einheit, sondern eine sprachlich erzeugte konzeptuelle Einheit [...]«.
186 Cf. Eder: Figur, pp. 65f.
187 Cf. Rimmon-Kenan: Fiction, pp. 29f; cf. Currie: Nature of Fiction, pp. 127–181.
188 Cf. Barthes: Analysis, p. 109; Cohan: Figures, p. 27; Frow: Spectacle, pp. 246ff.
189 Chatman: Story / Discourse, p. 125. Cf. Todorov: Catégories. For details see Jannidis: Figur, pp. 163f.
190 Cf. Doležel: Heterocosmica; Margolin: Individuals, Constitution; Ronen: Possible Worlds; Pavel: Fictional Worlds; Ryan Possible Worlds.
191 Cf. Margolin: Introducing; Margolin: Reference. For further details on the independency of the fictional world system, see Ronen: Possible Worlds, p. 12.

1970s the structurally and semiotically based positions started their counter influence on phenomenologically and hermeneutically saturated approaches; and with a slight changeover also poststructuralist positions formed their impact on the discourse on characters.[192] The strict structurally oriented paradigms began to open up in the 1980s and integrated the fruitful knowledge that led away from the text towards reception. In doing so the first attempts of the aesthetics of reception were confronted with the serious influence of the cognitive perspective that significantly increased during the 1980s.[193]

3.1 Coming Along!? – Mediality and Mental Representation

In 1978 the German anglist Herbert Grabes published an article that by now can sure be counted among the classics within the research on characters. In *Poetica* no. 10, he explained how persons emerge from the literary sentences and thereby showed that the *process-quality* of the reception makes an important contribution to the analysis of characters. With his very successful attempt he shed a light on (social-)psychological factors that are involved in the process of creating fictional characters.[194] Since then the influence from disciplines that are directly focused on the human-being like psychology, anthropology, but also sociology has become increasingly important. As a result of the contribution of Grabes to the research on characters the main features are pointed out: Reception is a dynamic, highly individual, complex, selective, and time-bound process in which the recipient is actively engaged. Not all attributes are

---

[192] Cixous: Character; Docherty: Reading. Psychological impacts were present in form of references to psychoanalytical concepts of Freud, Lacan, and Jung. Jung's archetypes influenced Propp and Vogler. Lacan's concept of suture is to be found in the works of Heath and Vernet, and the overarching concept of ›identification‹ inspired several scholars (e.g. Jauss: Levels).

[193] Cf. Jauß: Levels; Iser: Akt. Relevant contributions that merged interdisciplinary efforts are the works of Gardner: The Mind's; Bordwell: Narration. For overviews see Currie: Image; Ibsch: Cognitive Turn.

[194] The theoretical development can be traced if one compares Cohan's article, that locates the character-construction »[...] into an imaginative space located in our heads« (Cohan: Figures, p. 27) and Schneider's book on cognitive character-construction that appoints ›the consciousness of the recipient as the place where illusions emerge‹ (Schneider: Grundriß, p. 30: ›das Bewußtsein des Rezipienten als Ort der Illusionsbildung‹) – within significantly different theoretical frameworks.

observed equally, and there are certain rules to be named that govern this process despite its singularities.[195]

Together with the impact of the cognitive sciences came the growing and spreading field of narratology.[196] Subsequent to the advances that the ›aesthetics of reception‹ had made,[197] the engagement and involvement of the recipient with the media product was conceptualized as a form of interaction or communication. Thereby the crux of the matter always consists in the systematic observation of the material in combination with a grammar that regulates the inferences that are most likely drawn by different spectators.

3.2 Current Problems, Aims & Concerns

Within the last 15 years there have been increasingly attempts to conjoin different perspectives with the corresponding terminologies in order to grasp the phenomenon of the character in a more satisfying sense. This is achieved by combining on the one hand refined modes of material-observation – be it in structuralist, formalist, semiotic, phenomenological, or hermeneutical terms – with psychologically (mainly cognitive and emotional approaches; also social psychology), anthropologically, and socially based approaches.[198] In the following I will briefly sketch some characteristics of the contemporary research on characters:

---

[195] Evident examples are the ›primacy‹ and the ›recency effect‹ (cf. Grabes: Sätze, p. 418; Schneider: Grundriß, p. 30; Eder: Figur, pp. 212, 237, 362). See also the examination of complexity, causality, ›category- and person-based expectations‹, and immersion of the character by Gerrig and Albritton (Construction); for evaluation and critique cf. Schneider: Grundriß, p. 31. For further empirical research on characters cf. Jannidis: Zu anthropologischen Aspekten, pp. 158f., footnote 10.

[196] The strong emergence of narratology together with ludology within the game studies mark expedient steps in the evolutionary growth of mediascientific theories. Cf. Nünning: Grenzüberschreitungen, Narratologie; Aarseth: Genre Trouble; Eskelinen: Towards. For a systematic argumentation that deploys the threefold of ›narration‹, ›game‹, and ›experiment‹ as basic categories of media sciences, see Venus: Masken.

[197] Iser: Leser; Fish: Text. Philippe Hamon (Hamon: statut sémiologique) and Marc Vernet (Vernet: personnage) see characters as ›effects of the text‹ that are constructed via the interaction of text and recipient (cf. Blüher: Ansätze; Tomasi: Personaggio: pp. 6f). Likewise Cohan: Figures.

[198] Hermeneutics and phenomenology are often blamed for not having developed a satisfying theoretical framework to explicate the conclusions they draw (cf. Leschke: Verstehen; Jahraus: Literaturtheorie, pp. 246–268, 338–364; Bordwell: Making Meaning).

1. At first sight, and very generally, theoretical *adequacy, accuracy*, and the *precision* of systematic descriptions, in both a terminological and a historical sense, become more and more important. Normative quarrels are increasingly turned into the challenge for the best explanation and different types of questions are separated: The equipment of a character with attributes must not be confused any more with the question as to the function it serves in the plot; both questions are worth being asked.

2. *Ontological questions* are solved in a rather practical and comparative manner.[199] This leads to abstract models that are built within the communicative involvement with the narrative fiction. Jannidis defines the character as a prototypically organized concept that is generated by the text (cp. Jannidis: Figur, 193). Whereby the structural basis of this prototypical concept is called ›Basistypus‹, or base type.[200] The latter is *not* the character itself and it is *not* generated by the text but an anthropological cognition-pattern.[201] According to Eder characters exist as abstract objects that are elicited by communication and are part of an objective social reality.[202] He defines the *character itself* – with reference to Amie L. Thomasson – as an ›abstract object‹ like laws, theories or works of art.

3. Together with the manifold imports from psychology goes the fact that the *human being* remains the *dominant reference*.[203] Consequently the deflation-enrichment-continuum remains its validity for the debate and various production strategies and kinds of material formations are discussed to describe fictional characters that appear more or less humanlike.[204]

4. The actual approaches focus in the main on either the establishment of a *(mental) model* or of the formulation of preferably insightful and far-reaching *analytical categories*.[205] With a focus on receptive processes

---

199 Cf. Jannidis: Figur, pp. 151ff.
200 Orig.: »[…] textgeneriertes, prototypisch organisiertes Konzept […]« (Jannidis: Figur, p. 193).
201 For Details on the ›basistypus‹ cf. Jannidis: Figur, p. 170, pp. 185ff.
202 Eder distinguishes the *character itself*, the medial *presentation / display* of a character, and the *mental representations* by the recipient, cf. Eder: Figur, p. 67 and pp. 68f.
203 Anthropomorphous schemata play a major role in the reception of media narratives. Cf. Bordwell: Narration; Eder: Figur; Grodal: Moving Pictures; Hogan: Cognitive Science; Jannidis: Individuum; Persson: Understanding; Schneider: Grundriß; Smith: Engaging Characters.
204 Notably Culpeper points to the fact that his model for characterization ›can accommodate a scale of humanisation for characters‹ (Culpeper: Language, p. 38) and therewith is able to distinguish between rather humanised and rather allegorical characters.
205 For details on models of characters and their structure cf. Eder: Figur, pp. 168ff.

Schneider outlines the difference between the modification and the revision of character-models.[206] Jannidis' ›base type‹ integrates the minimal structure of character-information that is necessary to identify a character-like entity and can be grasped by distinguishing the ›denomination‹ and »attribution of character-information«.[207] It includes three categories of information: (1) the capability of acting, (2) the marking of in- and outside, and (3) the difference between temporarily and rather stable inner conditions.[208]

5. Questions concerning the methods of the observation and analysis of textual material and different types of *inference-drawing* receive a large amount of attention. The analytic strategies – that are rooted in formalistic, structuralistic and semiotic traditions – are steadily refined in order to closely explore the media material. One is less concerned with the extraction of semiotic elements like single words, traits, or semes but rather deals with reasonable structures that can be found on different levels of interpretive aggregation: Narratology serves as a common theoretical basis that provides extricable entities and partitions of media products. There is also a notable tendency towards the observation of patterns, forms, and shapes that lead to salient areas of media products.[209] These salient areas in turn call for a higher degree of attention and trigger the urge of the audience to make meaning.[210] Furthermore any examination of the media material is linked to the subsequent processes that are likely to happen during the receptive process. Culpeper for instance, who is concerned with ›the process of characterization‹, does not restrict his view on textual propositions but asks »how we form *impressions* of characters in our minds [...]«,[211] thereby using a term that goes back to the research on impression formation in social psychology.

6. The recent theories of fictional characters are mostly embedded in theoretical frameworks that refer to *communicative* and *receptive processes*.[212]

---

206 Cf. Schneider: Grundriß, pp. 167f.
207 Cf. Jannidis: Erzähltheorie, p. 20.
208 Ibid., pp. 126f.
209 See for instance the ›foregrounding theory‹ that has its precursors in Russian Formalism and the Prague School and was further on developed by Jakobson and Leech in the 1960s and 1970s (cf. Cuplpeper: Language, pp. 129ff).
210 Cf. Culpeper on linguistic approaches like research on ›language attitudes‹ and ›speech styles‹ (ibid., pp. 143ff).
211 Ibid., p. 2.
212 Cf. Schneider: Grundriß, pp. 15ff; cf. Culpeper's ›model for characterization‹ (Culpeper: Literature, pp. 34ff, Culpeper: cognitive approach); cf. Jannidis: Figur, pp. 15–83.

Jannidis integrates the reception of characters in a three-layer model of literary communication and develops categories for a narratological analysis of characters that describe systematic correlations within the literary communication by procedural knowledge. Eder refers to characters as ›communicative constructs‹ that rise through different communicative formations and open out into imaginations that notably feature an intersubjectively shared common denominator.[213] Schneider grounds his theory on a constructivist basis and conceptualizes the understanding of narrative text as the processing of information; ›understanding‹ is not to be confused with the transfer of a certain meaning by the text though but as the constitution of a cognitive-emotional construct.[214] Reception is a time-bound process that includes the selective perception of the media material and the complex processing of different types of mediated information. Models of character-reception are multi-layered and describe basic perceptions,[215] the saturation of the perceived by the recipient's knowledge, memories, associations that finally lead to a mental representation of the character. The mental models stay flexible and might change due to further receptions, new discoveries of information, and up-following interpretations.

7. The *application* and *combination* of different theories, concepts, and approaches becomes one of the major endeavors that rule these new academic projects.[216] Since characters traverse distinct ›layers‹ or ›dimensions‹, the respective analyses apply to different fields of theoretical reflection. The main challenge thereby lies in the fact that an intermedial theory of characters needs a combination of theoretical approaches that simultaneously have to deal with media specifity.[217] It has to integrate the domains of media production, the adequate observation of the media material, and assertions on the processes of reception and communica-

---

213 For further explanations on Eder's terms »collective intentionality« (›kollektive Intentionalität‹; cf. Eder: Figur, p. 71) and ›communicative imagination-games‹ (›kommunikative Imaginationsspiele‹; cf. Eder: Figur, pp. 131f). Jannidis states that the immense amount of information about characters is reduced by the reader's communicative competences that were achieved by literary experience through socialisation (cf. Jannidis: Figur, p. 18).
214 Schneider: Grundriß, pp. 15ff.
215 Culpeper: Inferring Characters, Language; Eder: Figur, pp. 101, 138.
216 These include aesthetics, narratology, ludology, linguistics, semiotics, theories of perception and comprehension, social / folk / cognitive psychology, neurophysiology, sociology, evolutionary theory, anthropology, ethnology, etc.
217 Cf. Wulff: Charaktersynthese, pp. 43ff.

tion. A salient issue is the closely-drawn analogy towards every day life[218] that serves for a theoretical basis and draws its inferences on folk psychological grounds.[219] It is argued that characters can trigger processes of evaluation in the recipient that are similar to the ones when meeting a real person.[220] On the other hand there are obviously differences between everyday life and literary or cinematic perception that limit the analogy between real persons and fictive characters.[221]

Via the observation of narrative structures, namely on a high level of aggregation of single elements, one can extract entities that can be applied to psychologically based terminologies. Torben Grodal (1997) for instance developed a complex filmtheoretical approach that combines the observation of filmic (narratological) structures, with research results from psychology, neurophysiology, evolutionary theory, and anthropology. Thus he closely linked the observation of the material to cognitive, emotional, and sensual processes that were likely to take place during reception. He developed distinctions that turned out to be effective devices to analyze the basic structures in mass media products.[222] What is repeatedly shown is the *high degree of mutual interpenetration* between the impression of a character and its actions, conduct, and behavior with regard to the plot.[223] Thus the extractions of structures and entities that can be tied to theories of social and personality psychology are highly

---

[218] Cf. Schneider: Grundriß, p. 21. For differences between the perception of real persons and fictive characters in different media cf. Forster: Aspects, pp. 43–79; Chatman: Story / Discourse, p. 126; Hochmann: Character, pp. 59–85; Persson: Understanding; Eder: Figur, pp. 220ff.

[219] Cf. Davies / Stone: Folk Psychology; Gordon: Folk Psychology; Goldman: Interpretation; Malle: How People; Smith: Engaging Characters, p. 17.

[220] For the discussion of affective solicitousness, empathy, and closeness / distance to characters see amongst others: Brütsch: Kinogefühle; Bartsch / Eder / Fahlenbrach: Audiovisuelle Emotionen; Eder: Wege, Imaginative Nähe, Being close; Grodal: Film; Plantinga / Smith: Passionate Views; Smith: Engaging Characters; Tan: Emotion; Vaage: Empathy, Empathic Film Spectator. On the reception of the face see: Plantinga: Scene; Noll Brinckmann: Kamera.

[221] See for instance the simulationist account of imagination held by Gregory Currie (cf. Currie: Image, pp. 152ff).

[222] For instance Gordal's opposition of ›automatic / schematic‹ versus ›flexible‹ human conduct, cf. Grodal: Moving Pictures, p. 108. For different kinds of perceptions and affective transactions of characters that are based upon ›distal‹ and ›proximal‹ attention locations, cf. ibid., pp. 130ff. See also the ›fundamental attribution error‹ by Gerrig / Albritton: Construction.

[223] Grodal distinguishes telic and paratelic action; the former is goal-directed and the latter is not goal-directed and rather repetitious (cf. Grodal: Moving Pictures, pp. 61f, see also pp. 108f).

beneficial. Culpeper states: »Characterization clearly needs a model that can cope with social aspects«.[224] It is no surprise that within these contexts models of action undergo a renaissance because they are needed to make the act-structures comparable.[225]

8. Lastly, *intermediality* and *media specifity* come to the fore. Characters are – especially because of the accelerating media-convergence – intertwined in various functional relations and they transcend the former relation of the narratively saturated concept of the ›plot‹. In ludic contexts or in the manifold portal worlds of the web (e.g. *Second Life*) they possess the ability to fulfill various duties that are not necessarily related to a plot within narrative structures.[226] With the diminishing of intermedial boundaries new phenomena, e.g. intermedial character-hybrids, come along: The game-version of *Lara Croft* surely shares many features with the film-, the comic-, and the novel-version but they also differ from each other in many ways when it comes to specifying their factor of humanness, their functionalities within the narrative plot, for the ludic goals, or the modalities of character-bonding. A flexible framework that aims to produce an integrating view on the manifold formal and functional changes that characters are able to undergo is introduced in terms of a ›morphological view‹ on characters.[227] The morphological gaze concentrates on relative contrasts, for instance between *narrative* vs. *ludic* characters and it searches for character features that are likely to reveal the impression of game-likeness or narrativity.[228] It conceptualizes the character as intermedial concept that undergoes certain accommodations and transformations in order to enter new media-constellations.

Consequently nowadays the theoretical requirements to grasp fictional characters are rising again due to the fast developments in the creation of media products. Characters indeed emerge within a certain work but they

---

224 Culpeper: Inferring Character, p. 28.
225 Venus (Team Spirit, pp. 308ff) and Sorg (Games of Death, pp. 355ff) link their character-observations to Kenneth Burke's »pentad of key terms« (Burke: Grammar of Motives, pp. xvff). For different ›parameters of action‹ see Herman (Story Logic, pp. 61ff) who refers to Burke and Nicholas Rescher (Aspects of Action) and Margolin (Doer / Deed, p. 208).
226 As an example, we may take the character *Jorda* from *ICO* who has her share in the narrative, because she takes the female part in the romance between *Ico* and her, and at the same time has her ludic aspects because she functions as a ›handicap‹ that increeases the degree of difficulty for the player avatar *Ico* when it comes to meeting the challenges of the game (cf. Heidbrink / Sorg: Dazwischen).
227 Leschke / Heidbrink: Formen der Figur.
228 It might ask for the difference between a narrative ›character‹ and a ›token‹ or ›gaming piece‹.

are very likely to be unhitched as autonomous entities and transferred to a different media context. They do not only appear on stage, in literary and filmic works, and in computer games, they can also be found in cartoons, comics, commercials, music-clips, and hypertexts. This again has consequences for the reception perspective: The advanced viewing skills of highly differentiated audiences command a rich reservoir of media specific experiences. Additionally they are familiar with subversive, ironic, and spectacular strategies and bring along reception-modes that partially depart from dominant identificational shares and put new emphasis on terms like ›immersion‹ and ›interaction‹. Finally, fictional characters as important parts of single media-products make a significant difference when it comes to the competition for attention. As quasi-autonomous entities they rather seem to accelerate their flotation through the flow of massmedial communication. Consequently, as plurivalent phenomena, they remain a theoretical challenge – quite delicate to catch.

References

Aristotle: Poetik. Ed. by Manfred Fuhrmann. Stuttgart 1982.
Aarseth, Espen: Genre Trouble. Narrativism and the Art of Simulation. In: Noah Wardrip-Fruin, Noah / Pat Harrigan (Eds.): First Person. New Media as Story, Performance, and Game. Cambridge 2004, pp. 45–55.
Bartsch, Anne / Jens Eder / Kathrin Fahlenbrach (Eds.): Audiovisuelle Emotionen. Emotionsdarstellung und Emotionsvermittlungdurch audiovisuelle Medienangebote. Köln 2007.
Barthes, Roland: Introduction à l'analyse structurale des récits. In: Communications 8 (1966), pp. 1–27.
Barthes, Roland: S/Z. Paris 1970.
Barthes, Roland: An Introduction to the Structural Analysis of Narrative. In: Stephen Heath (Ed.): Image – Music – Text. New York 1984, pp. 79–124.
Barthes, Roland: S/Z. Frankfurt/M. 1987.
Bayley, John: The Characters of Love. A Study in the Literature of Personality. London 1962.
Blüher, Dominique: Französische Ansätze zur Analyse der filmischen Figur – André Gardies, Marc Vernet, Nicole Brenez. In: Heinz B. Heller (Ed.): Der Körper im Bild: Schauspielen – Darstellen – Erscheinen. Marburg 1999, pp. 61–70.
Bonheim, Helmut: Literary Systematics. Cambridge 1990.
Bordwell, David: Narration in the Fiction Film. Wisconsin 1985.
Bordwell, David: Making Meaning: Inference and Rhetoric in the Interpretation of Cinema. Cambridge 1989.
Bradley, Andrew C.: Shakespearean Tragedy. Lectures on »Hamlet«, »Othello«, »King Lear«, »Macbeth«. London:1937.
Branigan, Edward: Point of View in the Cinema. A Theory of Narration and Subjectivity in Classical Film. New York 1984.

Brecht, Bertolt: Kurze Beschreibung einer neuen Technik der Schauspielkunst, die einen Verfremdungseffekt hervorbringt. In: Idem: Gesammelte Werke. Ed. with Elisabeth Hauptmann. Bd. 15. Frankfurt/M. 1967, pp. 341–357.
Brinckmann, Christine Noël: Die anthropomorphe Kamera und andere Schriften zur filmischen Narration. (Zürcher Filmstudien 3) Zürich 1997.
Britton, John: A. C. Bradley and those Children of Lady Macbeth. In: Shakespeare Quarterly 12/3 (1961), pp. 349–351.
Brütsch, Matthias / Hediger, Vinzenz / Keitz, Ursula von et al. (Eds.): Kinogefühle. Emotionalität und Film. Marburg 2005.
Campbell, Joseph: The Hero with a Thousand Faces. Novato 1949.
Carroll, Noël: The Paradox of Suspense. In: Peter Vorderer / Hans J. Wulff / Mike Friedrichsen (Eds.): Suspense. Conceptualizations, Theoretical Analyses, and Empirical Explorations. Mahwah 1996, pp. 71–92.
Casetti, Francesco / Federico di Chio: Analisi del Film. Mailand 1994 [¹1990].
Chatman, Seymour: Story and Discourse: Narrative Structure in Story and Film. Ithaca 1978.
Cixous, Hélène: The Character of ›Character‹. In: New Literary History. 5 (1974), pp. 383–402.
Cohan, Steven: Figures Beyond the Text: A Theory of Readable Character in the Novel. Novel 17.1 (1983), pp. 5–27.
Culler, Jonathan: Structuralist Poetics: Structuralism, Linguistics, and the Study of Literature. Ithaca 1975.
Culpeper, Jonathan: Inferring Character from Texts: Attribution Theory and Foregrounding Theory. In: Poetics 23/5 (1996), pp. 335–361.
Culpeper, Jonathan: A Cognitive Approach to Characterization. Katherina in Shakespeare's »The Taming of the Shrew«. In: Language and Literature. 9/4 (2000), pp. 291–316.
Culpeper, Jonathan: Language and Characterization: People in Plays and other Texts. Edinburgh 2001.
Currie, Gregory: The Nature of Fiction. Cambridge 1990.
Currie, Gregory: Image and Mind: Film, Philosophy and Cognitive Science. New York 1995.
Davies, Martin / Tony Stone: Folk Psychology and Mental Simulation. In: Anthony O'Hear (Ed.): Contemporary Issues in the Philosophy of Mind. Cambridge 1998, pp. 53–82.
Docherty, Thomas: Reading (Absent) Character: Towards a Theory of Characterization in Fiction. Oxford 1983.
Doležel, Lubomír: Heterocosmica. Fiction and Possible Worlds. Baltimore 1998.
Dyer, Richard. Stars. London 1979.
Eder, Jens: Die Wege der Gefühle. Ein integratives Modell der Anteilnahme an Filmfiguren. In: Matthias Brütsch / Vinzenz Hediger / Ursula von Keitz et al. (Eds.): Kinogefühle. Emotion und Film. Marburg 2005, pp. 225–242.
Eder, Jens: Imaginative Nähe zu Figuren. In: Montage / av. 15/2 (2006), pp.135–160.
Eder, Jens: Ways of Being Close to Characters. In: Film Studies: An International Review 8 (2006), pp. 68–80.
Eder, Jens. Die Figur im Film. Grundlagen der Figurenanalyse. Marburg 2008.
Egri, Lajos: The Art of Dramatic Writing. New York 1946 [¹1942, How to Write a Play].
Eskelinen, Markku: Towards Computer Game Studies. In: Noah Wardrip-Fruin / Pat Harrigan (Eds.): First Person. New Media as Story, Performance, and Game. Cambridge MA, London 2004, pp. 36–44.

Ewen, Joseph: The Theory of Character in Narrative Fiction. In: Hasifrut 3 (1971), pp. 1–30.
Faulstich, Werner / Korte, Helmut (Eds.): Der Star. Geschichte, Rezeption, Bedeutung. München 1997.
Ferrara, Fernando: Theory and Model for the Structural Analysis of Fiction. In: New Literary History 5/2 (1974), pp. 245–268.
Fischer-Lichte, Erika: Semiotik des Theaters. Eine Einführung. Bd. 1: Das System der theatralischen Zeichen. Tübingen 1983.
Fish, Stanley: Is There a Text in This Class. The Authority of Interpretive Communities. Cambridge 1980.
Fishelov, David: Types of Character, Characteristics of Types. In: Style 24/3 (1990), pp. 422–439.
Fokkema, Aleid: Postmodern Characters. A Study of Characterization in British and American Postmodern Fiction. Amsterdam 1991.
Forster, Edward Morgan: Aspects of the Novel. London 1963 [^{1}1927].
Freytag, Gustav: Die Technik des Dramas. In: Idem: Gesammelte Werke Bd. 14. Darmstadt 1965 [^{1}1863].
Frow, John: Spectacle Binding. On Character. In: Poetics Today 7/2 (1986), pp. 227–249.
Frye, Northrop: Anatomy of Criticism. Princeton 1957.
Gardies, André: L'ácteur dans le système textuel du film. In: Francois Baby / André Gaudreault (Eds.): Cinéma et recit. Québec 1980, pp. 77–109.
Gardies, André: Le récit filmique. Paris 1993, pp. 53–68.
Gardner, Howard: The Mind's New Science: A History of the Cognitive Revolution. New York 1985.
Genette, Gérard (dt 1994) [^{1}1972]: Person. In: Idem: Die Erzählung. München 1994, pp. 174–181.
Gerrig, Richard G. / David W. Allbritton: The Construction of Literary Character: A View from Cognitive Psychology. In: Style 24/3 (1990), pp. 380–391.
Gillie, Christopher: Character in English Literature. London 1965.
Goldman, Alvin I.: Interpretation Psychologized. In: Martin Davies / Tony Stone (Eds.): Folk Psychology. The Theory of Mind Debate. Oxford 1995, pp. 74–99.
Gordon, Robert M.: Folk Psychology as Simulation. In: Martin Davies / Tony Stone (Eds.): Folk Psychology. The Theory of Mind Debate. Oxford 1995, pp. 60–73.
Gottsched, Johann Christoph: Versuch einer Critischen Dichtkunst. Leipzig 1730.
Grabes, Herbert: Wie aus Sätzen Personen werden: Über die Erforschung Literarischer Figuren. In: Poetica 10 (1978), pp. 405–428.
Greimas, Algirdas J.: Die Struktur der Erzählaktanten. Versuch eines generativen Ansatzes. In: Ihwe, Jens (Ed.): Linguistik und Literaturwissenschaft, Vol. 3, Frankfurt/M. 1972, pp. 218–238.
Greimas, Algirdas J.: Les actants, les acteurs et les figures. In: Claude Chabrol (Ed.): Sémiotique narrative et textuelle. Paris 1973, pp. 161–176.
Greimas, Algirdas J.: Actant / Actor. In: Algirdas Greimas / J. Courtés: Semiotics and Language. An Analytical Dictionary. Bloomington 1982, pp. 5–8.
Grodal, Torben: Moving Pictures: A New Theory of Film Genres, Feelings and Cognition. Oxford 1997.
Grodal, Torben: Film, Character Simulation and Emotion. In: Jörg Frieß / Britta Hartmann / Eggo Müller (Eds.): Nicht allein das Laufbild auf der Leinwand... Strukturen des Films als Erlebnispotenziale. Berlin 2001, pp. 115–128.
Groeben, Norbert: Rezeptionsforschung als empirische Literaturwissenschaft: Paradigma- durch Methodendiskussion an Untersuchungsbeispielen. Kronberg 1977.

Hamon, Philippe: Pour un statut sémiologique du personnage. In: Roland Barthes et al. (Eds.): Poétique du récit. Paris 1977, pp. 115–180.

Harvey, William James: Character and the Novel. London 1965.

Heath, Stephen: Body, Voice. In: Stephen Heath: Questions of Cinema. London 1981, pp. 176–193.

Hegel, Wilhelm Friedrich: Vorlesungen über Ästhetik: 3 Die Poesie. Ed. by Rüdiger Bubner. Stuttgart 1984 [^{1}1842].

Heidbrink, Henriette: Das Summen der Teile. Über die Fragmentierung von Film und Figur. In: Jens Schröter / Gregor Schwering (ed.). Navigationen. Zeitschrift für Medien- und Kulturwissenschaften. 1/2. Marburg 2005, pp. 163–195.

Heidbrink, Henriette / Jürgen Sorg: Dazwischen. Zur Mesodimension der Medien. In: Ingo Köster / Kai Schubert (Eds.): Medien in Raum und Zeit. Maßverhältnisse des Medialen. Bielefeld 2009, pp. 81–101.

Herman, David: Story Logic. Problems and Possibilities of Narratives. Lincoln: 2004.

Hochman, Baruch: Character in Literature. Ithaca 1985.

Hogan, Patrick Colm: Cognitive Science, Literature, and the Arts. A Guide for Humanists. New York 2003.

Ibsch, Elrud: The Cognitive Turn in Narratology. In: Poetics Today 11/2 (1990), pp. 411–418.

Iser, Wolfgang: Der implizite Leser. Kommunikationsformen des Romans von Bunyan bis Becket. München 1972.

Iser, Wolfgang: Der Akt des Lesens: Theorie ästhetischer Wirkung. München 1976.

Jahraus, Oliver: Literaturtheorie: Theoretische und methodische Grundlagen der Literaturwissenschaft. Tübingen 2004.

James, Henry: The Art of Fiction. New York 1948 [^{1}1884].

Jannidis, Fotis: ›Individuum est ineffabile‹. Zur Veränderung der Individualitätssemantik im 18. Jahrhundert und ihrer Auswirkung auf die Figurenkonzeption im Roman. In: Aufklärung 9/2 (1996), pp. 77–110.

Jannidis, Fotis: Figur und Person. Beitrag zu einer historischen Narratologie. Berlin, New York 2004.

Jannidis, Fotis: Zu anthropologischen Aspekten der Figur. In: Rüdiger Zymner / Manfred Engel (Eds.): Anthropologie der Literatur. Paderborn 2004, pp. 155–172.

Jannidis, Fotis: Zur Erzähltheorie der Figur. Alte Probleme und neue Lösungen. In: Der Deutschunterricht 57/2 (2005), pp. 19–29.

Jannidis, Fotis: Character. In: Peter Hühn / John Pier / Wolf Schmid / Jörg Schönert (Eds.): Handbook of Narratology. Berlin 2009, pp. 14–29.

Jauß, Hans Robert: Ästhetische Erfahrung und literarische Hermeneutik, Frankfurt/M. 1977 [^{1}1971].

Jauß, Hans Robert: Levels of Identification of Hero and Audience. In: New Literary History. 5/2 (1974), pp. 283–317.

Kayser, Wolfgang: Das sprachliche Kunstwerk. Bern ^{15}1971 [^{1}1948].

Klevjer, Rune: What is the Avatar? Fiction and Embodiment in Avatar-Based Singleplayer Computer Games. Dissertation, University of Bergen, submitted 14 July 2006.

Knights, Lionel C.: How many Children had Lady Macbeth? An Essay in the Theory and Practice of Shakespeare Criticism. New York 1973 [^{1}1933].

Koch, Thomas: Literarische Menschendarstellung, Studien zu ihrer Theorie und Praxis. Tübingen 1991.

Leschke, Rainer: Verstehen und Interpretieren. In: Karlheinz Barck et al. (Eds.): Ästhetische Grundbegriffe. Historisches Wörterbuch in sieben Bänden, Bd. 6, Tanz – Zeitalter / Epoche, Stuttgart 2005, pp. 330–367.

Leschke, Rainer / Henriette Heidbrink (Ed.). Formen der Figur. Figurenkonzepte in Künsten und Medien. Konstanz 2010.
Lessing, Gotthold Ephraim: Hamburgische Dramaturgie. Stuttgart 1958 [¹1767].
Löwenthal, Leo: Literature and the Image of Man. Oxford 1986 [Part I ¹1956, Part II ¹1971].
Lohmeier, Anke-Marie. Hermeneutische Theorie des Films. Tübingen 1996.
Lotman, Jurij M.: The Structure of the Artistic Text. Michigan 1977 [¹1971].
Lowry, Stephen / Helmut Korte: Der Filmstar. Brigitte Bardot, James Dean, Götz George, Heinz Rühmann, Romy Schneider, Hanna Schygulla und neuere Stars. Stuttgart 2000.
Lukács, Georg: Die intellektuelle Physiognomie des künstlerischen Gestaltens. In: Idem: Probleme des Realismus. Werke. Bd. 4. München 1971 [¹1936].
Maître, Doreen. Literature and Possible Worlds. London 1983.
Malle, Bertram F.: How People Explain Behavior: A New Theoretical Framework. In: Personality and Social Psychology Review 3/1 (1999), pp. 23–48.
Margolin, Uri: Characterization in Narrative: Some Theoretical Prolegomena. In: Neophilologus 67 (1983), pp. 1–14.
Margolin, Uri: The Doer and the Deed: Action as a Basis for Characterization in Narrative. Poetics Today. 7/2 (1986), pp. 205–225.
Margolin, Uri: Introducing and Sustaining Characters in Literary Narrative. A Cet of Conditions. In: Style 21 (1987), pp. 107–124.
Margolin, Uri: Individuals in Narrative Worlds: An Ontological Perspective. In: Poetics Today 11/4 (1990), pp. 843–871.
Margolin, Uri: Reference, Coreference, Referring, and the Dual Structure of Literary Narrative. In: Poetics Today 12/3 (1991), pp. 517–542.
Margolin, Uri: Characters in Literary Narrative: Representation and Signification. In: Semiotica 106, 3/4 (1995), pp. 373–392.
Margolin, Uri: The Constitution of Story Worlds: Fictional and / or otherwise. In: Semiotica 131, 3/4 (2000), pp. 327–357.
Margolin, Uri: Character. In: David Herman (Ed.): Cambridge Companion to Narrative. Cambridge 2007, pp. 66–79.
McKee, Robert: Story. Substance, Style, and the Principles of Screenwriting. New York 1999 [¹1997].
Michaels, Loyd: The Phantom of the Cinema. Character in Modern Film. New York 1998.
Morin, Edgar: Les Stars, Paris 1957.
Mudrick, Marvin: Character and Event in Fiction, Yale Review 50 (1961), pp. 202–218.
Muir, Edwin: The Structure of the Novel. London 1979 [¹1928].
Nieragden, Göran: Figurendarstellung im Roman. Eine Narratologische Systematik am Beispiel von David Lodges »Changing Places« und Ian McEwans »The Child in Time«. Trier 1995.
Nünning, Ansgar / Vera Nünning: Von der strukturalistischen Narratologie zur »postklassischen« Erzähltheorie. Ein Überblick über neue Ansätze und Entwicklungstendenzen. In: Idem (Ed.): Neue Ansätze in der Erzähltheorie. Trier: 2002, pp. 1–34.
Nünning, Ansgar / Vera Nünning: Produktive Grenzüberschreitungen: transgenerische, intermediale und interdisziplinäre Ansätze in der Erzähltheorie. In: Idem (Ed.): Erzähltheorie transgenerisch, intermedial, interdisziplinär. Trier 2002, pp. 1–22.
Palmer, Alan: Fictional Minds. Lincoln 2004.
Patalas, Enno: Sozialgeschichte der Stars. Hamburg 1963.
Pavel, Thomas: Fictional Worlds. Cambridge 1986.
Persson, Per: Understanding Cinema. Cambridge 1993.

Phelan, James: Reading People, Reading Plots. Character, Progression, and the Interpretation of Narrative. Chicago 1989.
Phelan, James: Living To Tell About It: A Rhetoric and Ethics Of Character Narration. New York 2005.
Plantinga, Carl / Smith, Greg (Eds.): Passionate Views. Film, Cognition and Emotion. Baltimore 1999.
Plantinga, Carl: The Scene of Empathy and the Human Face on Film. In: Carl Plantinga / Greg M. Smith (Eds.): Passionate Views: Film, Cognition, and Emotion. Baltimore 1999, pp. 239–255.
Price, Martin: The Other Self. Thoughts About Character in the Novel. In: Maynard Mack / Ian Gregor (Eds.): Imagined Worlds. London 1968, pp. 279–299.
Price, Martin: People of the Book. In: Critical Inquiry 1 (1975), pp. 605–622.
Price, Martin: Forms of Life. Character and Moral Imagination in the Novel. New Haven 1983.
Propp, Vladimir: Morphologie des Märchens. Frankfurt/M. 1975 [¹1928].
Rescher, Nicholas: Aspects of Action. In: Idem: The Logic of Decision and Action. Pittsburgh 1967, pp. 215–219.
Rimmon-Kenan, Shlomith: Narrative Fiction. Contemporary Poetics. London 1983.
Robbe-Grillet, Alain: Pour un Nouveau Roman. Paris 1963.
Ronen, Ruth: Possible Worlds in Literary Theory. Cambridge 1994.
Rosenberg, Brian: Character in Fiction 1900–1980. In: Bulletin of Bibliography 40/4 (1983), pp. 200–205.
Ryan, Marie-Laure: Possible Worlds, Artificial Intelligence, and Narrative Theory. Bloomington 1991.
Salen, Katie / Eric Zimmerman: Rules of Play. Game Design Fundamentals. Cambridge 2004.
Seger, Linda: Creating Unforgettable Characters. New York: 1990.
Sheldon, Lee. Character Development and Storytelling for Games. Boston 2004.
Schmidt, Siegfried J.: Literaturwissenschaft als argumentierende Wissenschaft. München 1975.
Schneider, Ralf: Grundriß zur kognitiven Theorie der Figurenrezeption am Beispiel des viktorianischen Romans. Tübingen 2000.
Sorg, Jürgen: Enter the Games of Death. Zu Form, Rezeption und Funktion der Kampfhandlung im Martial Arts Film. In: Rainer Leschke / Jochen Venus (Eds.): Spielformen im Spielfilm. Zur Medienmorphologie des Kinos nach der Postmoderne. Bielefeld 2007, pp. 331–366.
Smeed, John William: The Theophrastan ›Character‹. The History of a Literary Genre. Oxford 1985.
Smith, Murray: Engaging Characters. Fiction, Emotion, and the Cinema. Oxford 1995.
Souriau, Étienne: Les deux cent mille situations dramatiques. Paris 1950.
Spielhagen, Friedrich: Beiträge zur Theorie und Technik des Romans. Göttingen 1967 [¹1883].
Stückrath, Jörn: Entwurf eines Kategoriensystems zur Analyse epischer Figuren und Handlungen – Am Beispiel von Sarah Kirschs Erzählung »Blitz aus heiterem Himmel«. In: Bettina Hurrelmann / Maria Kublitz / Brigitte Röttger (eds.): Man müsste ein Mann sein…? Interpretationen und Kontroversen zu Geschlechtertausch-Geschichten in der Frauenliteratur. Düsseldorf 1987, pp 83–103.
Stückrath, Jörn: Wovon eigentlich handelt die epische und dramatische Literatur? Kritik und Rekonstruktion der Begriffe ›Figur‹ und ›Geschehen‹. In: Hartmut Eggert / Ulrich

Profitlich / Klaus R. Scherpe (eds.): Geschichte als Literatur. Formen und Grenzen der Repräsentation von Vergangenheit. Stuttgart 1990, pp. 284–295.

Tan, Ed S.: Emotion and the Structure of Narrative Film. Film as an Emotion Machine. Mahwah 1996.

Taylor, Henry M. / Margrit Tröhler: Zu ein paar Facetten der menschlichen Figur im Spielfilm. In: Heinz B. Heller (Ed.): Der Körper im Bild: Schauspielen – Darstellen – Erscheinen. Marburg 1999, pp. 137–151.

Thomasson, Amie L.: Speaking of Fictional Characters. In: Dialectica 57/2 (2003): pp. 207–226.

Todorov, Tzvetan: Les catégories du récit littéraire. In: Communications 8 (1966), pp. 125–151.

Todorov, Tzvetan: Narrative-Men. In: Idem. The poetics of prose. Ithaca 1977 [^{1}1971], pp. 66–79.

Todorov, Tzvetan: Das methodologische Erbe des Formalismus. In: Jens Ihwe (Ed.): Literaturwissenschaft und Linguistik II/1. Frankfurt/M. 1971, pp. 17–40.

Tomasi, Dario: Il Personaggio. Cinema e Racconto. Turin 1988.

Tröhler, Margrit: Offene Welten ohne Helden. Plurale Figurenkonstellationen im Film. Marburg 2007.

Vaage, Margarethe Bruun: Empathy and the Episodic Structure of Engagement in Fiction Film. In: Joseph D. Anderson / Barbara Fisher Anderson (Eds.): Narration and Spectatorship in Moving Images. Newcastle, pp. 186–203.

Vaage, Margarethe Bruun: The Empathic Film Spectator in Analytic Philosophy and Naturalized Phenomenology. In: Film and Philosophy 10 (2006), pp. 21–38.

Venus, Jochen: Teamspirit. Zur Morphologie der Gruppenfigur. In: Rainer Leschke / Jochen Venus (Eds.): Spielformen im Spielfilm. Zur Medienmorphologie des Kinos nach der Postmoderne. Bielefeld 2007, pp. 299–327.

Venus, Jochen: Masken der Semiose. Zur Semiotik und Morphologie der Medien. Berlin 2010 [forthcoming].

Vernet, Marc: Le personnage de film. In: Iris, 7 (1986), pp. 81–110.

Vogler, Christopher: The Writer's Journey: Mythic Structure for Writers. Studio City 1998.

Walcutt, Charles Child: Man's Changing Mask: Modes and Methods of Characterizations in Fiction. Minneapolis 1966.

Weinsheimer, Joel: Theory of Character. Emma. In: Poetics Today 1 (1979), pp. 185–211.

Wenger, Christian N.: An Introduction to the Aesthetics of Literary Portraiture. In: Publications of the Modern Language Association of America 50 (1935), pp. 615–629.

Wulff, Hans J.: Charaktersynthese und Paraperson. Das Rollenverständnis der gespielten Fiktion. In: Peter Vorderer (Ed.): Fernsehen als ›Beziehungskiste‹. Parasoziale Beziehungen und Interaktionen mit TV-Personen. Opladen 1996, pp. 29–48.

MARIA E. REICHER

The Ontology of Fictional Characters

1 Introduction

From the perspective of philosophical semantics, fictional characters (or, rather, discourse about them) raise the following puzzle: It is an empirical fact that people utter sentences which seem to be declarative sentences about fictional characters, sentences like ›Pegasus is a winged horse‹, ›Lieutenant Columbo owns a Peugeot 403‹ or ›Lisa Simpson is smarter than her brother Bart‹. Moreover, it seems that people who utter sentences of this kind claim truth for what they say; and, thirdly, some of these sentences seem to be true (or, to put it more carefully, at least they seem to be closer to the truth than others). Thus, it seems to be true that Pegasus is a winged horse (instead of, say, a winged camel), that Lieutenant Columbo owns a Peugeot 403 (instead of, say, a Renault) and that Lisa Simpson is smarter than her brother Bart (instead of the other way around). These data, however, seem to be in conflict with some fundamental and widely (though not universally) accepted logical principles. One of these may be called the ›predication principle‹, which may be stated as follows:

> (PP) If a predication (that is, a sentence which consists of a subject term followed by a predicate term) is true, then there exists an object which is denoted by the subject term.

If PP is applied to the above-mentioned example, we get: If ›Columbo owns a Peugeot 403‹ is true, then there exists an object which is denoted by the subject term ›Columbo‹. But one might argue that, as a matter of fact, Columbo does not exist, since ›he‹ is a fictional character.[1] It will not

---

1 Later in this paper, I will argue that fictional characters are not the sort of objects that may have a sex, literally speaking. Therefore, the use of male (or female) personal pronouns is, strictly speaking, false and potentially misleading. Therefore, I will sometimes use the neutral ›it‹ instead of ›he‹ or ›she‹, and where I use the male and

do, of course, to identify Columbo with Peter Falk, the actor who plays ›his‹ role. For (as I assume) Peter Falk does not own a Peugeot 403, and even if he did, many other things that seem to be true of Columbo would not be true of him. If the sentence ›Columbo owns a Peugeot 403‹ has a subject at all, then it is Lieutenant Columbo, not the actor Peter Falk. Briefly put, the problem is this: ›Columbo owns a Peugeot 403‹ is true. ›Columbo owns a Peugeot 403‹ implies that Columbo exists. But Lieutenant Columbo does not exist.

Philosophers and logicians have proposed various solutions for this problem.[2] Some have proposed to distinguish between ›mere being‹ on the one hand and ›existence‹ on the other and claimed that *there are* fictional characters, although they do not *exist*.[3] The basic idea behind this view is that there are various ›modes of being‹, existence being only one of them, such that *there are* things that do *not exist*. Proponents of such a modes of being distinction usually consider existence to be the strongest kind of being, relying on the intuition that there are, as it were, *degrees of reality*. Modes of being distinctions are applied not only to fictitious objects but to other metaphysically contentious objects (in particular to abstract objects) as well. Their proponents share the intuition that there are objects which lack full reality, while it cannot be denied that they are *something*. Thus, modes of being distinctions seem to be, in general, a way of attenuating ontological commitments without abandoning them altogether. To the problem under discussion here, they may be applied as follows: Since not everything exists, the predication principle must be revised as follows:

(PP*) If a predication is true, then *there is* an object which is denoted by the subject term.

According to (PP*), ›Columbo owns a Peugeot 403‹ does not imply that there exists an object which is denoted by the subject term ›Columbo‹, but only that *there is* an object which is denoted by the subject term ›Columbo‹. The latter is consistent with the empirical fact that Columbo does not exist; and thus the problem does not arise.

Unfortunately, however, modes of being distinctions are notoriously unclear: If their proponents try to explicate them at all, they typically do so

---

female pronouns (thereby following the standard conventions of discourse about fictional objects), I will occasionally put them under quotation marks to remind the reader that they should not be taken literally.

2   For a survey of the philosophical debate on fictitious characters see Woods / Alward: Logic; also Voltolini: Ficta, and Brock: Fictionalism.
3   See, e.g., Parsons: Analysis.

in terms of categorical differences. It is said, for instance, that existence is the mode of being of ordinary material and mental objects (and only of those). This gives rise to the suspicion that modes of being distinctions may be reduced to category distinctions, that is, that there are no different kinds of being but just different kinds of object (as Quine, among others, famously argued).

Instead of revising the predication principle, some have proposed to give up the predication principle altogether.[4] To reject the predication principle is to claim that there are cases where a predication (i.e., a sentence of the form ›a is F‹) is true and ›a exists‹ (or ›There is a‹) is not true. Even in the revised version of PP*, the predication principle claims a strong connection between the truth of sentences and the furniture of the world. To deny the predication principle is to deny this connection. Rejection of the predication principle provides a simple solution to the problem of fictitious characters, since, if neither PP nor PP* holds, ›Columbo owns a Peugeot 403‹ does neither imply that Columbo exists nor that *there is* something that is denoted by the term ›Columbo‹. However, the predication principle is strongly supported by common-sense intuitions. In the big majority of cases, it would seem bizarre to claim that a is F and to deny in the same breath that a exists (or, at least, has being).

Others claim that sentences ›about‹ fictional characters are not (at least not always) real declarative sentences. That is, people do not (at least not always) claim truth for their utterances ›about‹ fictional characters, and (more importantly) utterances of this kind are neither true nor false but lack truth values altogether. Rather, it is argued, people who utter sentences like ›Columbo owns a Peugeot 403‹ are engaged in a ›game of make-belief‹, that is, they act as if they take a fictional work as non-fiction. According to this view, when we talk about fictitious characters, we are like actors on a stage: We pretend to make claims about things we (make-believedly) believe to exist, but we do not really do so. When we utter ›Columbo owns a Peugeot 403‹ we pretend to make a claim about a person named ›Columbo‹, just as an actor on a stage pretends to stab the (pretended) king or pretends to demand freedom of speech from an (alleged) ruler.[5] If the sentence ›Columbo owns a Peugeot 403‹ lacks a truth value, then neither PP nor PP* may be applied to it; and thus the problem of fictitious objects does not arise.

---

4   See, e.g., Jackson: Commitment.
5   See Walton: Fictions.

Although this strategy has some plausibility for a particular kind of utterances about fictitious objects, it utterly fails with respect to others. Consider, for instance, the sentence ›The character Columbo has been created by Richard Levinson and William Link‹. Evidently, such an utterance cannot be part of a game of make-believe in which we pretend to hold the Columbo series to be a documentary. Obviously, the sentence ›The character Columbo has been created by Richard Levinson and William Link‹ is a serious declarative utterance for which we claim truth. According to PP, it implies that Columbo exists. Thus, the make-believe strategy does not resolve the problem.

Still others try to avoid the problem by claiming that sentences like ›Columbo owns a Peugeot 403‹ are not really sentences about fictional characters, but sentences about, e.g., movies,stories, thoughts and imaginations of authors and/or readers.[6]

Finally, some philosophers accept what is for others either a plain empirical falsehood or even a *contradictio in adiecto*, namely that *there are fictional objects*, or, in other words, *that fictional objects exist*.[7] I belong to this last group. In what follows, I give a brief sketch of what one might call ›a realist ontology of fictional characters‹. But in advance, I shall say a couple of things about the relationship between fictional characters on the one hand and fictional works and stories on the other.

2 Are Fictional Characters Something Over and Above Stories?

In a certain sense, fictional characters are ›parts‹ of fictional works and fictional stories. Therefore, it seems reasonable to assume that the ontology of works and stories may shed some light on the ontology of characters. So, what kinds of objects are stories and works?

Both stories and works are particular kinds of *abstract objects* which I call ›*types*‹. To say of an object that it is ›abstract‹ is to say that it is neither material nor mental, and that is to say that it is not perceivable by the senses, located in space or something ›in the mind‹ of a particular subject.

The claim that fictional characters are abstract objects may be, at first glance, more plausible for characters of ›literary‹ fiction than it is for characters of movies and TV series. One might object that it seems that we can *perceive* the fictional character Columbo when watching an episode of the TV series. But this is not true. When we watch *Columbo*, we do not

---

6   See, e.g., Ryle: Objects.
7   See, e.g., van Inwagen: Creatures; Thomasson: Fiction; Voltolini: Ficta; Eder: Figuren.

perceive a fictional character but pictures of an actor who embodies a fictional character. It seems that, in principle, one and the same character may be embodied by different actors. Moreover, it seems that one and the same character may occur in a movie (embodied by an actor) and in a strip cartoon and/or in a novel.

The category of types is a particular category of abstract objects that is, in the philosophical tradition, called the category of ›universals‹. A universal is, roughly, an abstract object which may be *instantiated* in more than one concrete particular. Standard (though not unproblematic) examples of types are words and letters: One and the same word-type may be instantiated many times.

A story, as I use the term, is a type of a series of states of affairs and/or events. That is, a story is an abstract object that can be instantiated, in principle (unless it is logically inconsistent), by concrete states of affairs and/or events. True stories are (or, rather, have been) instantiated; fictional stories usually have never been instantiated.

What a fictional work is cannot be answered in such a concise way, for there are a large variety of different kinds of fictional works: literary works (novels, short stories etc.), film works, paintings, musical works, strip cartoons, dramatic works etc. However, despite of all of their important and interesting differences, there are some very general features that all these works have in common. In every fictional work one may distinguish the following three elements:

1. The element of the represented world: that is, the represented states of affairs, events, characters, places, things etc. (the ›story‹, in a wide sense).
2. The ›mode of presentation‹ element: that is the way the represented world is presented to the reader or viewer etc., i.e., the particular words, sounds, pictures, gestures etc. used by the author and the particular way the author uses them.
3. The element of the intended experiences: that is, those experiences (sensual, cognitive and/or emotional) which the author intends his ›audience‹ (in a wide sense, including readers) to have, as a result of the reception of the mode of presentation element.

Thus, works are distinguished from stories, and this seems to be adequate, since it seems that, in principle, one and the same story may be a component of two or more different works. Think, for instance, about the film version of a dramatic work: Surely, in such a case the works are different, although the story may be the same in each work.

The mode of presentation element is distinguished from the element of the represented world, since it seems that one and the same fictional world may be represented in different ways. Finally, the element of the represented world is distinguished from the element of the intended experiences, since it seems possible, in principle, that different authors may intend different experiences in their audience by representing one and the same fictional world.

Each of the three elements is best considered to be a type. The mode of presentation element is a type of a series of words and/or pictures and/or sounds etc. That is, it may be multiply instantiated in concrete (material) books, film copies, performances etc. The element of the represented world is a type of (a complex and/or series of) states of affairs, events, characters etc. That is, it may be instantiated (in principle) in concrete states of affairs, events, persons etc. The element of the intended experiences is a type of (a complex and/or series of) sensual, cognitive and/or emotional experiences. That is, it may be multiply instantiated in concrete sensual and/or cognitive and/or emotional experiences of distinct readers or viewers.

In principle, fictional characters could be instantiated (just like the represented world of fictional works as a whole), although, in reality, they seldom are. Note that Peter Falk is not an instantiation of the character Columbo. For (among many other things) Peter Falk earns his living as an actor, while an instantiation of Columbo would have to earn his living as a police officer. Neither are the film frames of the Columbo series instantiations of the character Columbo. An instantiation of the character Columbo would have to be a police officer, not a frame (or a set of frames) of an actor who plays a police officer. An instantiation of Columbo would be a person who owns a Peugeot 403, who usually wears an old, crumpled raincoat, etc.

Fictional works and stories as well as fictional characters are *contingent* objects. That is, they do not exist necessarily. Rather, they owe their existence to particular (human) activities through which they are *created*.

Since fictional characters are parts of works and stories, one might suspect that characters may be ›reduced to‹ works and/or stories, i.e., that they are nothing ›over and above‹ the works and/or stories of which they are parts. If this were true, talk about ›characters‹ would be just a ›facon de parler‹, which would be, strictly speaking, erroneous. Strictly speaking, then, there were no such things as ›characters‹, but only works and/or stories.

However, *prima facie*, this is not true. Characters seem to be creations in their own right. First of all, it seems to be possible, in principle, to create a character without creating something that could be called ›a story‹ in the usual sense.[8] It may be that the character Columbo has been created

---

8 Patrick Hogan supports this claim when he writes that »perhaps the most straightforward way of particularizing most prototypical events is by particularizing

before the first episode of the *Columbo* series has been written. It may be that the authors decided in advance to write their stories ›around‹ a character that is determined as being an extraordinarily astute Lieutenant, an unusually successful crime investigator whose appearance is, in sharp contrast to his mental abilities, a bit shabby, who owns an old Peugeot 403, etc.

Second, it seems that one and the same character may not only occur in different works but even in different stories. This is particularly apparent in the case of sequels and series, but one might also think of cases like Faust or Don Juan.

Thus, if the concept of a character is supposed to be interesting and fruitful, it is to be construed in such a way that it is possible for one and the same character to occur in different works and in different stories. Otherwise, the concept of a character threatens to become redundant, to be reducible, in principle, to the concept of a work or at least to the concept of a story. I shall assume, for the rest of this paper, that characters are creations in their own right.

3 Fictional Characters as Incompletely Determined Objects

I have claimed that Lieutenant Columbo is, literally speaking, not a person but an abstract object. But how can an abstract object own a car, smoke cigars, love chili, etc.? – Literally speaking, Columbo, the character, cannot do these things. Yet, there is a close connection between the character Columbo and the properties of owning a Peugeot 403, smoking cigars, etc. These properties seem to be constitutive for Columbo's identity (in contrast to, say, being a womanizer, smoking a pipe, being an airplane pilot).

To solve this problem, I distinguish two kinds of predicates of fictional characters. I call them ›internal predicates‹ and ›external predicates‹, respectively. An internal predicate of a fictional character is a predicate that applies to the character ›in a story‹ or ›according to a story‹, to use two familiar locutions. An external predicate of a fictional character is a predicate that applies *directly* to it, i.e., not ›in a story‹ but without any such proviso. ›Owns a Peugeot 403‹, ›smokes cigars‹, ›loves chili‹, etc. are internal predicates of the character Columbo. External predicates of Columbo are, for instance, ›has been created by Richard Levinson and

---

prototypical characters« (see Hogan: Characters (in this volume); for more on Hogan's theory of prototypes and particularizing see note 10 below).

William Link‹, ›has been embodied by Peter Falk‹, ›occurs in more than 60 episodes of a TV series‹.

To distinguish these two kinds of predicates, I use the following terminology: If a predicate ›is F‹ is an *internal* predicate of a character c, I say: ›c is *determined as* being F‹. If a predicate ›is F‹ is an *external* predicate of a character c, I say simply: ›c *is* F‹. Thus, we may say: The character Columbo *is determined as* owning a Peugeot 403, as smoking cigars, and as loving chili; and ›he‹ *has been created by* Levinson and Link, *has been embodied by* Peter Falk and *occurs* in more than 60 episodes of a TV series.

Obviously, ›c is determined as being F‹ does not imply ›c is F‹, and vice versa. That Columbo *is determined as owning a Peugeot* does not imply that he *owns* a Peugeot (he does not and he cannot, since he is not the sort of object that can own a car). On the other hand, that Columbo *has been created by* Levinson and Link does not imply that *he is determined as having been created by* Levinson and Link. Actually, it is not the case that Columbo is determined as having been created by Levinson and Link: Levinson and Link are not even part of the respective stories; and even if two scriptwriters named ›Levinson‹ and ›Link‹ would occur in one of the stories, it would hardly be the case that in this story they are the ›creators‹ of Columbo.

The distinction between internal and external predicates (or something analogous to it) is an essential ingredient of any realist ontology of fictional characters. So, there is a kernel of truth in the claim that Columbo does not exist. The truth is that there is, literally speaking, no *person* who is called ›Lieutenant Columbo‹, who owns a Peugeot 403 and has all the other features that Columbo in the series has. All that there is (or exists) is a fictional character that *is determined as being* a person who owns a Peugeot 403 etc.

For sake of convenience, I will take the liberty to move freely back and forth between talk of predicates and talk of properties. This can be done because the main points can be made both in terms of predicates and in terms of properties. Here is an explicit formulation (a little translation manual, if you like) of the relation between the predicate terminology and the property terminology:

> If a character c is determined as F, then c exemplifies (i.e., has) the property of being F as an internal property (i.e., c exemplifies the property of being F according to a story); and vice versa.

> If a character c is F, then c exemplifies the property of being F as an external property; and vice versa.

One of the most salient features of fictional characters is their so-called ›incompleteness‹. Characters are, in a certain sense, never completely determined. That is to say, for every character c, there is at least one internal predicate ›is determined as F‹ such that it is not true that *c* is determined as F *and* it is not true that *c* is determined as *non*-F. For instance, it is not true (to my knowledge) that Columbo is determined as being born in May. But neither is it true that Columbo is determined as not being born in May (although, surely, Columbo is determined as either being born in May or not being born in May). Surely, Columbo is determined as having been born on a particular day, but it is not determined which day this was. The character Columbo, as one might say, is not determined with respect to his birthday. There are many other things with respect to which Columbo is not determined: It is (to my knowledge) not determined whether Columbo still has his appendix or not; it is not determined how many girlfriends he had before he met his wife; and so forth. In this sense, most fictional characters are highly incomplete.[9]

Incompleteness is a core feature not exclusively of fictional characters but of types of all kinds. Fictional works as well as fictional stories are incompletely determined too. For instance, the story of Patrick Süskind's novel *Das Parfum* is determined as being such that a young man called ›Jean-Baptiste Grenouille‹ left Paris on a sunny day in May 1756. But it is not determined at which day exactly this happened, what the exact temperatures were in Paris on this day, what the colour of Grenouille's shirt was, etc.[10]

To sum up, characters are contingently (but actually) existing incompletely determined abstract objects. It seems, however, that (in most cases at least) characters can be considered to be parts of other contingently existing incompletely determined abstract objects, namely of *works* (literary

---

[9] Perhaps it should be noted that this conception of incompleteness is not identical with the ›openness‹ of what is called ›personalized mental models of characters‹ in cognitive character reception theory (see Schneider: Grundriß, and Schneider: Cognitive). While the latter concept concerns a disposition of recipients to process further information for the construction of a mental model of a character (i.e., the recipients do not understand the character as a fixed stereotype), the former concerns an ontological feature of the characters themselves.

[10] Patrick Colm Hogan's ›prototypes‹ (prototypical stories, e.g., the prototype *love story*) are incomplete objects in the sense explicated here. (See Hogan: Characters.) However, Hogan's ›particularized prototypes‹ (i.e., particular stories, e.g., *Romeo and Juliet*) are incomplete objects as well, although they are less incomplete than the prototypes of which they are particularizations. As Hogan rightly observes, particular stories, story prototypes and narrative structures in between (e.g., sub-genres) may be brought in a hierarchical order, or, as I would put it: incompleteness comes in degrees. By means of ›particularization‹ one may get less incomplete stories from more incomplete ones. ›Prototypes‹ are *types of types*. The same sort of hierarchy is to be found among characters (see section 5.4 below).

works, film works, cartoons, etc.) and *stories*; and it seems that one and the same fictional character may be part of distinct works and stories. This leads to the problem of identity conditions for fictional characters.

4 Problems of Identity of Fictional Characters

One may distinguish (at least) three kinds of identity questions concerning fictional characters:

(i) questions concerning identity within a work or story;

(iia) questions concerning identity across different works or stories, and

(iib) questions concerning identity across different episodes of a series (or across an original work and a sequel of it).

4.1 Identity Within a Story

In order to see the first problem more clearly, imagine a novel whose story consists of two strands: The first strand describes the life of an average man from the morning until the evening.[11] Let's call this character Mr. Doe. The second strand describes the life of a criminal during the night. Let's call this character Jack. Let's assume that the author of the novel does not make it explicit whether Mr. Doe is identical with Jack or not. The text allows for both interpretations. Is the character Mr. Doe identical with the character Jack? Is there a justified answer to this question? Is this a reasonable question at all?

I think that questions of this sort make sense and that, in principle, there can be justified answers to them (though, in some cases, it may be impossible to determine definitely which answer is the right one). But I think that this is not a problem of identity in the narrower sense. Rather, it is a special case of the more general problem of which internal properties a character has in a given story.

This is a serious and complex problem. Does a character have those properties that are explicitly ascribed to it in the story? Surely, many of a character's properties are explicitly ascribed to it in the story, but not all of them are. Many of a character's predicates may be logically implied by

---

11 My talk of ›descriptions of a character in a novel‹ is not to be taken literally but merely as a convenient *façon de parler*. Authors do not *describe* characters by means of their utterances but *create* them.

those predicates that are applied to it in the story. Many others may be ›conventionally implied‹, as it were.

The concept of conventional implication can be explicated as follows: That a predicate ›is G‹ is conventionally implied by another predicate ›is F‹ means, roughly, that it is part of the shared background beliefs of the audience that, under usual circumstances, every object that is F is also G. For instance, if a character is determined as a human being, it is conventionally implied that it is determined as being born by a woman, as having a heart and a liver, as having a normal human metabolism, etc. (unless there are explicit hints to the contrary). But conventional implication is a vague thing, and it may be subject to historical changes. If in a fictional text from the 17th century a character is described as being a tall and most beautiful woman, what does this (conventionally) imply? Probably, being tall as well as being beautiful meant something different in the 17th century than it means today. Shall we say that the character has those internal properties that were conventionally implied by the text at the time of its origin or those that are conventionally implied by the time of its actual reading?

Perhaps some would like to argue that a character might have internal properties which are neither explicitly ascribed to it in the story nor logically or conventionally implied (unless the concept of conventional implication is made extremely broad). For instance, the fact that Sherlock Holmes (in the stories) shares his apartment with another man and that he shows very little interest in women may be interpreted as a hint that Holmes has a homosexual leaning, although one would hardly say that this is conventionally implied by the text of the stories.

Thus, that a property is explicitly ascribed to a character in the story is not a necessary condition for the character having this property as an internal property. But it is neither a sufficient condition. For what if the narrator (or any other source of information) is unreliable? For instance, what we know (or believe to know) about Columbo's biography is mostly due to remarks Columbo himself makes in various episodes of the series. But Columbo is unreliable in this respect. Quite probably, sometimes he makes up details of his life in order to promote confidence and intimacy to get suspects and witnesses to talk.

If a character's internal properties are not fully and unambiguously determined by what is explicitly said and/or shown and what is (logically and conventionally) implied by that which is explicitly said and/or shown, then what determines a character's internal properties? – Roughly, two kinds of accounts suggest themselves. One might suppose that a character's internal properties are determined by the author's intentions, or, alternatively, one might say that a character's internal properties are determined by cognitive processes within particular readers or viewers.

I strongly tend to an author-centred view on this matter, because, first of all, I'd like to take serious the familiar idea that authors are the creators of their characters (as well as of stories and works), and, second, I'd like to take serious the view (which is at the heart of what has been said so far) that characters are *objective* entities (just like stories and works), i.e., something that can be grasped, in principle, by distinct subjects at distinct occasions.

This is not to say that the author's intentions *alone* determine a character's internal properties. It is only to say that author's intentions rather than actual cognitive processes within readers and/or viewers etc. are relevant for a character's internal properties.[12]

This does not rule out, of course, that a reader or viewer imagines or interprets a given character in a very particular and subjective way, that distinct readers or viewers imagine or interpret the same character in different ways or that one and the same reader imagines or interprets the same character differently at different occasions.

However, to blur the distinction between a character's creation on the one hand and its interpretation/reception on the other entails that it does not make sense to say that an interpretation is right or wrong (in an epistemic sense). But a theory of characters should provide an account for the truth that, for instance, a viewer who interprets Columbo as a naive person has *misinterpreted* the character in question.

I do not wish to deny that readers or viewers, in principle, may create their own characters on the basis of (or inspired by) characters given through fictional works. Yet I think that this is not the standard case, for there is more to the creation of a character than the mere experience of a series of spontaneous associations, ›inner pictures‹, and the like. The creation of a character (just as the creation of stories and works) involves, among other things, conscious *decisions*.

I will not dig any further into this problem here. Let us suppose, for what follows, that we have sufficiently reliable means to determine, by and large, which properties a given character has in a given story and let us return to the problem of identity across stories and the problem of identity across different episodes of a series.[13]

---

[12] For a defence of author intentionalism from the point of view of literary theory see Jannidis: Figur.

[13] This does not rule out that there are undecidable cases. Indeed, an author may even deliberately leave it undecided whether Mr. Doe is identical with Jack or not.

4.2 Problems of Character Identity Across Works, Episodes, and Stories

First of all, one might ask whether the problem of identity across different episodes of a series (or original works and sequels) and their respective stories is really distinct from the problem of identity across different works, or whether the former is just a special case of the latter. The answer on this depends on whether one considers episodes of a series as parts of a more complex work or as independent works. I think that there is a good reason to consider episodes as parts of a more complex work (I will say something about it towards the end of this paper). Yet, *prima facie*, the two problems seem to be similar in various respects.

4.3 The Problem of Character Identity Across Works with Identical Stories

Undoubtedly, the novel *Gone with the Wind* is not the same work as the movie *Gone with the Wind*. Yet, *prima facie*, Scarlett O'Hara, the heroine of the novel *Gone with the Wind*, is identical with Scarlett O'Hara, the heroine of the movie *Gone with the Wind*. But one might conceivably argue that the novel heroine has certain properties which the movie heroine doesn't have, and vice versa. This would be true at any rate, if one takes into account what one could call ›representational properties‹. Representational properties of a character are those properties that make it the case that the character is presented to us (i.e., described, pictured etc.) in a certain way, i.e., for instance, by means of certain words or by means of certain pictures etc. Thus, Columbo's appearance, for instance, may be represented by means of a description in English words or by means of a drawing or a photograph etc. Representational properties are, of course, *external* properties.

Whether the story of the novel *Gone with the Wind* is identical with the story of the movie *Gone with the Wind* is a question that does not need to be settled here. An answer to it would require both theoretical considerations about identity criteria for stories and an empirical investigation (a careful comparison of the novel and the movie, on the basis of certain identity criteria). Probably, it would turn out that the story of the novel and the story of the movie are not strictly identical, but only ›overlap‹ to a large degree.[14] But surely there may be cases of distinct works with

---

14 I will say more on this relation of ›overlapping‹ below, although not with respect to stories but with respect to characters, but the relation is the same in both cases.

identical stories. Think, for instance, about a performance of a dramatic work and a recording of it for television, where the TV version shows the actions on the stage from different angles, using different focal lengths, making use of various kinds of cutting techniques. Surely, the TV version is a work in its own right, distinct from the performance on the stage, with distinct aesthetic qualities. Yet the story of the one work will be (most probably at least) identical with the story of the other. Or think of strip comics and animated cartoons for another kind of example for (possibly) distinct works with identical stories. Thus, it seems to be possible that one and the same character may occur in different works with identical stories; and this is *prima facie* problematic, since characters from different works typically have not exactly the same properties. Usually, they differ in some of their external properties.

4.4 Problems of Character Identity Across Distinct Stories

As already indicated above, one might doubt whether Scarlett O'Hara, the movie heroine, has really exactly the same *internal* properties as Scarlett O'Hara, the novel heroine. Most probably, there are details of Scarlett O'Hara's feelings and thoughts described in the novel which are not represented in the movie; and, on the other hand, probably there are details of Scarlett O'Hara's appearance represented on the movie screen which are not described in the novel. So how can one say that the movie character is identical with the novel character?

The problem of character identity across different stories is particularly pressing for archetypical characters like Faust and Don Juan, which occur in many distinct stories that are not related in the same direct way as a novel and its film version or an original and its sequel. Yet, *prima facie*, there is something like character identity across distinct Faust stories. But how is this possible? In some stories, Faust is a magician, in others he is a scholar; in some stories, he goes to hell, in others he is saved by God's grace. What makes it the case (if it is the case) that Christopher Marlowe's Doctor Faustus is identical with Goethe's Faust?

4.5 The Sequel and Series Problem

It seems natural to say that characters of series may undergo certain changes. They may ›grow older‹, for instance. But they may also undergo more essential changes. Thus, a character that is determined as being a rebellious girl in episode 1 may turn into a wholly conformist wife and mother in episode 25. *Prima facie*, the character in episode 1 is identical with the character in episode 25. But is it really? How can a character undergo changes at all?

5 Towards a Solution of Some Identity Problems of Fictional Characters

5.1 ›Internalism‹

It seems clear that internal properties play a crucial role for the identity conditions of fictional characters. That is, for a character's identity, it is relevant which properties it has ›in the story‹. The question is to which extent external properties (in particular ›representational‹ and ›historical‹ properties) play a role too. What I call ›historical‹ properties are properties that are expressed by means of predicates like ›has been created by so-and-so‹, ›has been inspired by so-and-so‹, ›occurs in this-and-this story‹ etc.

I propose to rely exclusively on internal predicates for the formulation of identity conditions of characters. The reason for this decision is that it would lead to *prima facie* implausible consequences to take into account representational and historical predicates as well. If representational properties were relevant for a character's identity, a character of a novel could never be identical to a character of a movie – which seems to be *prima facie* wrong (the heroine of the novel *Gone with the Wind* seems to be identical to the heroine of the movie *Gone with the Wind*).

The case of film versions of novels is particularly perspicuous, but I think that an analogous reasoning holds true for characters that occur in different works of the same medium. For instance, the character King Kong of the film from 1933 surely differs in his representational properties from the character King Kong of the remake from 2005. (Among many other things, the King Kong from 1933 is represented by means of black and white pictures while the King Kong from 2005 is represented by means of coloured pictures.) Yet I would like to say that the character King Kong is the same in both works.

Therefore, I propose the following formulation of identity conditions for characters:

(I_1) A character c_1 is identical with a character c_2 if, and only if: For every F: If c_1 is determined as being F, then c_2 is determined as being F, and vice versa.

If reference to works or stories is built in, we get the following formulation:

(I$_2$) A character c_1 of a work w_1 (a story s_1) is identical with a character c_2 of a work w_2 (a story s_2) if, and only if: For every F: If c_1 is determined as being F in w_1 (s_1), then c_2 is determined as being F in w_2 (s_2), and vice versa.

Perhaps it should be noted here that (I$_1$) and (I$_2$), respectively, are attempts to provide identity *conditions*, not identity *criteria* for characters. The task of identity conditions is to clarify *what it means to say* that a certain x and a certain y are identical. The task of identity criteria is to provide *means which allow us to determine* whether a certain x is identical with a certain y or not. Although (I$_1$) and (I$_2$) provide some hints of how to determine whether a character x and a character y are identical (since they tells us, implicitly, that we must not look at representational and historical properties), they do not provide the means to settle the question as to which internal properties a given character exactly has.

Since, according to (I$_1$) and (I$_2$), representational predicates are irrelevant to a character's identity, the obvious representational differences between the Scarlett from the novel and the Scarlett from the movie do not hinder us to say that the novel character is identical with the movie character (if we assume for the moment that the story of the novel is identical with the story of the movie). Thus, the problem of character identity across works with identical stories is resolved.

5.2 Essential versus Inessential Internal Properties?

(I$_1$) and (I$_2$) have the advantage of stating *strict* identity conditions, that is, they allow, in principle, to decide unambiguously in every case whether a character c_1 from a work w_1 or a story s_1 is identical with a character c_2 from a work w_2 or story s_2. However, the disadvantage of (I$_1$) and (I$_2$) is that they seem to make character identity across stories impossible. For even the slightest changes in a story unavoidably change the internal properties of each of its characters. Scarlett O'Hara, for instance, in *Gone with the Wind*, makes a dress from a green velvet curtain. Thus, this character is determined as making a dress from a green velvet curtain. Now, suppose, in a remake of the movie, Scarlett makes (in the very same situation) a dress from a blue velvet curtain. According to (I$_2$), because of this minor change alone, the Scarlett from the original would not be identical with the Scarlett from the remake. The same effect would result from minor abridgements and/or additions, minor changes in other characters or in the environment. For, according to (I$_2$), a character that is determined as falling in love with a person who has green eyes cannot be identical with a character who is determined as falling in love with a person who has blue eyes, a character that is determined as living in a room with flowered wallpaper cannot be identical with a character that is determined as living in a room with striped wallpaper, and so forth.

Analogous considerations hold, of course, for characters which occur in stories with more salient differences. According to (I_2), a Faust character that goes to hell in a story s_1 cannot be identical with a Faust character that is saved by God's grace in a story s_2, for the former is determined as going to hell (and not as being saved by God's grace), while the latter is determined as being saved by God's grace (and not as going to hell).

This strikes me as an undesirable consequence. As mentioned above, a theoretically fruitful concept of a fictional character should be such that it is not ruled out *a priori* that one and the same character may occur not only in different works but also in different stories. Otherwise, the concept of a character would become redundant; it could be reduced to the concept of a story.

So, obviously, (I_1) and (I_2) do not resolve the problem of character identity across distinct stories (rather to the contrary). As a way out, one might propose to distinguish *essential* from *inessential* internal properties. Thus one might say that a character c_1 of a story s_1 is identical with a character c_2 of a story s_2 if, and only if, c_1 and c_2 have exactly the same essential internal properties. Accordingly, one could argue that going to hell and being saved by God's grace, respectively, do not belong to Faust's essential internal properties. Thus, a character that goes to hell in one story may well be identical with a character that is saved by God's grace in another story.

The tricky question is, of course, which of a character's internal properties are supposed to be essential and which are not. What is the ›essence‹ of a character? The distinction between ›essential‹ (or ›necessary‹) and ›inessential‹ (or ›contingent‹) properties is a big metaphysical burden. I am afraid that it is impossible to draw a sharp line between a character's essential properties on the one hand and its inessential properties on the other without arbitrariness. Is it, for instance, an essential feature of Columbo that ›he‹ is determined as smoking cigars? Couldn't it be that, in a new episode, Columbo quits smoking? Would we, say, then, that it is not the same character anymore? – Probably not, given that Columbo's other familiar features remain unchanged. But what if, at the same time, Columbo changes his outfit and his car, makes regular use of his gun, flirts with young girls, and resolves his cases by means of high-tech equipment and violent methods of interrogation? Probably, in this case, many would say that this is not the same character anymore. But where exactly is the boundary where Columbo ceases to be Columbo? It seems impossible to answer this question in a non-arbitrary way. But the metaphysical concept of ›essence‹ does not allow for arbitrariness. Therefore, it seems that the distinction between essential and inessential properties must be dropped altogether.

5.3 Loose Identity Conditions?

As an alternative way out, one might propose to give up the search for strict identity conditions altogether and go with ›loose‹ identity conditions instead. Loose identity conditions might be formulated in something like the following way:

(I$_3$) A character c_1 of a story s_1 is identical with a character c_2 of a story s_2 if, and only if, c_1 and c_2 have essential parts in common.

(I$_3$) raises two questions: 1. What is a ›part‹ of a character in the first place? 2. Under what conditions is it the case that a character c_1 has ›essential parts‹ in common with a character c_2?

Here is an answer to the first question: I say that a character c_1 may be composed of other characters c_2, c_3, etc., where c_2, c_3, etc. are less determinate than c_1. In other words, the characters c_2, c_3, etc. are parts of c_1. Assume the character Columbo has exactly the following internal properties: being an extremely astute crime investigator, living in Los Angeles, usually wearing an old, crumpled raincoat, smoking cheap cigars, driving an old Peugeot 403, and being married. (Assume that Columbo does not have any further internal properties.) Let's call this character C_1, for short. Now, the following characters are parts of C_1:

C_2: The character that is determined as being an extremely astute crime investigator (and has no other internal properties).

C_3: The character that is determined as living in Los Angeles (and has no other internal properties).

C_4: The character that is determined as usually wearing an old crumpled raincoat (and has no other internal properties).

And so forth.

Character C_4, for instance, is not identical with character C_1, in just the same sense in which a leg of a chair is not identical with the chair as a whole. To every complex character c_1 (i.e., every character that has more than one internal property), there is a set of less complex characters c_2, c_3, … which are parts of c_1. Some of these less complex characters have just one internal property, others may have more (given that c_1 has more than two internal properties), but at any rate the number of each of these internal properties is smaller than the number of c_1's internal properties.

Thus, if c_1 has exactly 10 internal properties, there are exactly 10 less complex characters which are parts of c_1 such that each of them has exactly one internal property; and every character which is a (real) part of c_1 has at most 9 internal properties.

The concept of a part of a character seems to be sufficiently exact. Let me, thus, now turn to the second question raised by (I₃): Under what conditions, exactly, is it the case that a character c_1 has ›essential parts‹ in common with a character c_2? Unfortunately, there does not seem to be an answer to this question. It seems impossible to determine in general how many (and which kinds of) internal properties constitute what one might call the ›core‹ of a character. It seems that a question of this sort can be answered at most for particular cases, and even for those only more or less *ad hoc*. It seems that there is no such thing, in general, as a firm ›core‹ of a character.

Thus, one might come to the conclusion that characters are ›vague objects‹. The concept of ›vague objects‹ is much discussed in contemporary philosophy. *Clouds* are standard examples of vague objects: Clouds are accumulations of H_2O molecules. Yet H_2O molecules occur also outside clouds. Many H_2O molecules in the atmosphere clearly belong to a cloud, many others clearly do not belong to a cloud. But there are always some H_2O molecules which neither clearly belong to a cloud nor clearly fail to belong to a cloud. Clouds do not have sharp boundaries. Or, in other words, for some H_2O molecules, the question whether a particular molecule belongs to a cloud cannot be answered without arbitrariness.

From the point of view of a (scientific) philosopher, vagueness of all kinds tends to be an outrage, in particular the vagueness of objects, for not only does it offend our sense for exactness and clarity – it may even throw out widely accepted basic principles of logic.

5.4 Maximal and Sub-Maximal Characters

However, I think that characters are not really vague objects. The impression to the contrary is a result of the fact that our names for fictional characters are ambiguous. We need to distinguish what I call, for want of better terms, a ›maximal character‹ from what I call a ›sub-maximal character‹. A maximal character is a character that has all those properties as internal properties that it exemplifies according to a given story. A sub-maximal character is a character that has a *subset* of these properties as internal properties. Note that a maximal character is not a completely determined object; characters are *never* completely determined.

A sub-maximal character is sub-maximal relative to another character. Every sub-maximal character is a (real) part of some maximal character.

When a literature specialist says that in the 17th century there were many plays about Faust, most of them influenced by Christopher Marlowe's play, probably he refers with the name ›Faust‹ to a character that is a sub-maximal character with respect to (i.e., a part of) the maximal Faust character of Marlowe's play. Probably, the literature specialist is able to make explicit, exactly, which are the internal properties of the sub-maximal character he had in mind. Other users of the name ›Faust‹ may not be able to do this. But this is nothing peculiar to the reference to fictional characters: We often use names (successfully) without being able to give identifying descriptions of the objects referred to.

It is well possible that different competent users of the name ›Faust‹ use the name to denote distinct sub-maximal characters (i.e., sub-maximal characters with not exactly the same internal properties). Different users may use the name to refer to sub-maximal characters which are parts of distinct maximal characters (i.e., characters from distinct stories). Thus, one user may use ›Faust‹ to refer to a character that is part of Marlowe's Faust, while another may use it to refer to a character that is part of Goethe's Faust. Furthermore, different users of the name ›Faust‹ may refer to different parts of one and the same maximal character. The different sub-maximal characters referred to by one and the same name may overlap each other, or it may be that one includes the other. It is possible, in principle, that between two sub-maximal characters which are parts of the same maximal character there is no overlap and no inclusion (i.e., that they do not have a single internal property in common). But probably such cases are rare exceptions. Usually, there should be a certain amount of agreement among competent users of ›fictitious names‹ (i.e., names of fictional objects).

Thus, Faust is not a vague object. If anything is vague at all, then it is the meaning of the name ›Faust‹; it is vague in the sense that different users (or the same users at different occasions) use the name to refer to distinct characters and that sometimes it may not be completely clear to which one. It is used either to refer to a maximal character of any of the Faust stories or to some (real) part of any of these characters.

The concept of a sub-maximal character allows us to resolve the problem of identity across distinct stories without abandonment of the strict conditions (I_1) and (I_2). Those characters that can be identical across distinct stories are, of course, sub-maximal characters only. It is impossible that a maximal character from a story s_1 has exactly the same internal properties as a maximal character from a distinct story s_2. But it is well possible that a sub-maximal character from a story s_1 has exactly the same internal properties as a sub-maximal character from a story s_2.

5.5 Episodes, Sequels and the Problem of Change

If one treats sequels and episodes of series as separated stories, there is no particular series and sequel problem left. One can say, then, for instance, that there is a certain sub-maximal character which occurs in each episode of the *Columbo* series, and that would be it.

However, I propose to consider episodes of a series and sequels as parts of one large story, because this allows accounting for the *prima facie* truth that a character may *change* in the course of a series. Literally speaking, a character cannot change at all (according to the account I have proposed in this paper). This holds for maximal characters as well as for sub-maximal characters. A character's identity is defined by a particular set of internal properties; change one of them and you will have a distinct character. The new character may overlap to a considerable degree with the original one, but overlapping is not the same thing as identity. Moreover, even if there is a causal connection between the original and the new character (such that the new character has been developed out of the original one), the new character is not identical with the original one, just as the motorcar is not identical with the carriage, although the two types of vehicles have a lot of properties in common and the one has been developed out of the other.

Yet it seems to be true, in some sense, that Columbo (and not just Peter Falk) has grown older in the course of the series, that his hair (and not just Peter Falk's) has turned grey, etc. How can this be? – The answer is that fictional characters may change *within stories* (but only there). In most (if not in all) stories time goes by. Therefore, internal properties of characters are, strictly speaking, ›time relative‹. Thus, Columbo does not just have the internal property of having dark hair or the property of having grey hair but rather the internal property of having dark hair during a certain period of his life and grey hair during another period of his life. One of the reasons why, in most cases, we ignore the time relativity of internal properties of characters may be that the sub-maximal characters to which we usually refer by means of fictitious names are often quite ›stable‹ (i.e., they remain, by and large, unchanged).

According to my proposal, sequels and episodes of a series are to be treated like chapters of a novel: That the descriptions given of a character in chapter two are different from those given in chapter one, does, of course, not imply that the character from chapter one cannot be identical with the character in chapter two. Rather, it is the same character that is described ›from different angles‹, as it were. Therefore, it is possible to ›enrich‹ a character, to make it less indeterminate, in the course of a novel as well as in the course of a series.

6 Summary

I have outlined a realist ontology of fictional characters, according to which a fictional character is an incompletely determined contingent abstract object that can be instantiated in ›real‹ persons (unless it has contradictory internal properties). At the heart of this ontology lies the distinction between internal and external properties of characters. Internal properties are those that a character has ›in the story‹, whereas external properties are, among others, representational and historical properties. I have argued that characters are something over and above stories and works, such that one and the same character may occur in distinct works and distinct stories. This raises questions of character identity across works and stories. I have proposed and defended strictly ›internalist‹ identity conditions, according to which character identity rests exclusively on a character's internal properties. There is strict character identity across works with identical stories for characters in distinct works with identical stories (e.g., a performance of a drama and a film version of it), since in this case the internal properties of the characters in both works are strictly identical. In order to account for character identity across distinct stories, I have introduced the concepts of maximal and sub-maximal characters. A maximal character c_1 is determined by all of those internal properties that it has ›in a given story‹. A sub-maximal character c_2 relative to c_1 has a subset of the set of c_1's internal properties. The proposed solution for the problem of character identity across distinct stories is thus as follows: A maximal character of a story s_1 cannot be identical to a maximal character of a distinct story s_2. Yet, a sub-maximal character of s_1 may be identical to a sub-maximal character of s_2.*

---

* Work on a previous version of this paper was supported by the Austrian Fonds zur Förderung der wissenschaftlichen Forschung (FWF), project P19471-G15.

References

Brock, Stuart: Fictionalism about Fictional Characters. In: Noûs 36 (2002), pp. 1–21.
Eder, Jens: Was sind Figuren? Ein Beitrag zur interdisziplinären Fiktionstheorie. Paderborn 2008.
Hogan, Patrick Colm: Characters and Their Plots. In this volume.
Jackson, Frank: Ontological Commitment and Paraphrase. In: Philosophy 55 (1980), pp. 303–315.
Jannidis, Fotis: Figur und Person. Beitrag zu einer historischen Narratologie. Berlin 2004.
Parsons, Terence: A Meinongian Analysis of Fictional Objects. In: Grazer Philosophische Studien 1 (1975), pp. 73–86.
Ryle, Gilbert: Symposium: Imaginary Objects. In: Proceedings of the Aristotelian Society, supp. vol. 12 (1933), pp. 18–43.
Schneider, Ralf: Grundriß zur kognitiven Figurenkonzeption am Beispiel des viktorianischen Romans. Tübingen 2000.
Schneider, Ralf: Toward a Cognitive Theory of Literary Character: The Dynamics of Mental-Model Construction. In: Style 35/4 (2001), pp. 607–640.
Thomasson, Amie L.: Fiction and Metaphysics. Cambridge 1999.
van Inwagen, Peter: Creatures of Fiction. In: American Philosphical Quarterly 14 (1977), pp. 299–308.
Voltolini, Alberto: How Ficta Follow Fiction. A Syncretistic Account of Fictional Objects. Dordrecht 2006.
Walton, Kendall: Fearing Fictions. In: Journal of Philosophy 75 (1978), pp. 5–27.
Woods, John / Peter Alward: The Logic of Fiction. In: Dov M. Gabbay and Franz Guenthner (eds.): Handbook of Philosophical Logic. Volume 11. 2nd edn. Dordrecht 2004, pp. 241–316.

PATRICK COLM HOGAN

Characters and Their Plots

1 Introduction

Stories involve both events and characters. I imagine that, for most people, such a claim is neither controversial nor interesting. The controversial and interesting issues begin to arise when we ask about the relation between the plots and the persons that enact them. Aristotle famously ranked action above agent in importance for the emotional impact of tragedy. At the same time, his ethical criteria necessarily made reference to the tragic hero's moral qualities, for such a character should not be ›eminently good and just‹ but also not driven by ›vice or depravity‹.[1] In contrast, Henry James stressed the origin of novels in character – yet even for James, the crucial compositional issue was a matter of ›drama‹,[2] an answer to the question, ›what will [these characters] DO?‹.[3]

The inter-relation of plots and characters is complicated by the fact that neither is wholly individual and unique. Both fall into patterns. For example, as to plots, there are horror stories, adventure stories, love stories. Moreover, the patterns in plots are related to the patterns in characters. A love story has lovers. A ghost story has a ghost (or at least characters who think there is a ghost). More technically, genres (e.g., love story) imply roles or character functions (e.g., lovers).

Of course, stories are more than genres and characters are more than roles. While not wholly and uniquely particular, stories and characters are necessarily more specific than the patterns they instantiate. This leads us to perhaps the most interesting question in the relation between plot and character – how do they inter-relate at the level of particularity?

In order to examine this question, it is valuable to begin with genre – for, again, plot and character are mutually implicated at this level. One way

---

1   Aristotle: Poetics, p. 45.
2   James: Portrait, p. 16.
3   Ibid., p. 14, emphasis in original.

of exploring this issue would involve attention to cultural or even personal specificity – the genres found in Bollywood cinema since economic liberalization in 1990, or the (micro-) genres of a particular writer (say, Shakespeare). These are valuable projects. However, these genres are themselves variants on cross-cultural and trans-historical patterns. The Bollywood romantic comedy and the Shakespearean romantic comedy are different. But they share romantic patterns found in other times and places as well. It is these universal patterns – and the still broader structures shared across universal genres – that should be most fundamental in any account of the relation between plots and characters.

In the following pages, I will consider the ways in which stories are particularized through the specification of characters and plots. In order to examine this topic, I will first outline important cross-cultural patterns, then take up two cognitive processes that turn general structures into particular stories. I will conclude with a brief illustration of these points by reference to Shakespeare's *Hamlet*.

2 Narrative Universals and Prototypicality

Three narrative patterns recur prominently across cultures and across historical periods.[4] These are romantic, heroic, and sacrificial tragi-comedy. Very briefly, the romantic plot involves two people who fall in love, but whose union is blocked by some representative of social order, typically a parent. In the full version, the lovers are separated, sometimes with suggestions of death, but are ultimately joined. The heroic plot has two components. The first includes the usurpation of legitimate social leadership (often by a relative of the rightful leader), the exile of the rightful leader, and the ultimate restoration of that leader. The second treats a threat against the home society by some alien force. Commonly, the displaced leader is restored in the course of defending the home society against the alien threat. Finally, the sacrificial plot comprises a communal violation of some norm (e.g., a divine precept), social devastation (often famine or epidemic) resulting from that violation, a sacrifice (often an innocent person's death), and the resulting restoration of normalcy.[5]

---

4 See Hogan: Mind.
5 In *Affective Narratology*, I have argued that there are other recurring genres as well. However, they are not as prominent as these three. I will leave them aside in the present discussion.

These patterns are best characterized as prototypes in that they are not defined by necessary and sufficient conditions, but by a sort of graded match between instances and general structures. Just as certain birds (e.g., robins) are more prototypical, more ›bird-like‹, than others (e.g., ostriches), certain stories are more prototypical, more ›story-like‹ than others. Moreover, like bird prototypes, story prototypes vary with context. A prototypical bird on the seashore (e.g., a seagull) is different from a prototypical bird in a suburban yard (e.g., a robin). Similarly, a prototypical story in the context of personal life (e.g., a romantic tragi-comedy or love story) is different from a prototypical story in the context of political life (e.g., a heroic tragi-comedy or war story).[6]

Beyond these prototypes, there are still more general patterns. Thus the three prototypes themselves have what we might call ›schematic‹ structures in common. Moreover, above even this schematic structure, we may ultimately be able to articulate some sort of definition that encompasses not only prototypical stories, but stories of any sort. In this way, it is possible to distinguish several (partially discrete) levels of abstraction in our conception of stories.

Clearly, a hierarchy of this sort must be found not only above the level of prototypes, but below the level of prototypes as well. This lower hierarchy includes, for example, sub-genres and ways of extending prototypes that vary according to cultural tendencies or historical periods. Most importantly, the sub-prototypical strata extend down to the level of actual stories – tales, plays, novels, epics, and so forth. Indeed, once one has isolated general structures shared by stories – whether within or across cultures and time periods – one necessarily encounters the question of just

---

[6] Since some readers have misunderstood my point here, I should note that I am not claiming that all stories conform to one of these prototypes. Indeed, it is clear that stories often do not conform to any of these prototypes. Not all birds are robins or seagulls – even in a suburban yard or at the seashore. Similarly, not all stories are romantic, heroic, or sacrificial. However, unlike birds, stories are produced by the human mind. As a result, we have a strong tendency to produce stories guided by these prototypes – just as we have a strong tendency to think of prototypical birds. This tendency becomes increasingly pronounced as the storytelling becomes less bound by actual experiences and particular interests shared by speaker and addressee. In other words, the orienting and structuring effects of prototypes increase as we move from the sorts of ephemeral reports that occupy much of our daily personal interactions (›Well, son, what happened at soccer practice today?‹) to stories that are shared by large social groups and endure across time (e.g., *Romeo and Juliet* or *Abhijñānaśākuntalam*). On the other hand, the tendency is not an absolute rule. Narratives recounted in personal interaction are often oriented and structured by these prototypes (e.g., when people talk about their ›love life‹) and a number of enduring, socially prized works are not. The crucial point is that these prototypes recur – and, indeed, have a prominent place – in unrelated narrative traditions.

how the abstract structures become particulars. For example, how does the romantic prototype become *Romeo and Juliet*.

The process of producing particulars from general patterns is clearly a cognitive process, a process that occurs in the mind of one or more authors. (Of course, particularization involves the influence of many other people, even when there is only one author.) That process may be understood in terms of ›development principles‹,[7] principles that apply to prototypes, etc., to ›develop‹ these bare structures into full particulars. (We will consider such principles in the following sections.)

Though narrative prototypes are primarily a matter of plot, they are inseparable from character in the minimal sense of agency or purposive human action. Specifically, the prototypical plots are themselves explicable by reference to prototypical happiness goals. These goals vary with context (e.g., personal or social/political). Their pursuit by characters marks the basic trajectory of prototypical narratives. For example, the prototype of happiness in a personal context seems to be romantic union.[8] Thus an agent pursuing romantic union with a beloved defines the basic trajectory of one prototypical form of narrative – romantic tragi-comedy. Plot-related considerations determine that there must be some obstacle to the lovers' union. However, here too character enters, for that obstacle is commonly a matter of willful interference – the intervention of some social authority (such as a parent) or a rival.

Other aspects of the prototypical plot are connected with scene. The inhibition of the lovers' union is commonly connected with a physical separation. That physical separation is most often a matter of imprisonment and/or exile. But this too is inseparable from character, at least in the minimal sense of agency. In stories, as in life, scene is not simply a backdrop for events. It is defined and organized, first of all, by an agent's desires and actions. Scenes are places where characters act in certain ways, places that they seek or that they flee. A town, for example, is first of all one's home or an alien place; it is a space where one can do certain things and not others.

In short, general narrative structures, prominently prototypes, set out a causal sequence of events or event types. But these events imply specific character functions. They also entail certain scene types, which are themselves inseparable from character functions. Needless to say, all three components of a prototype (event sequences, characters, and scenes) are developed in the articulation of a particular story. In what follows, I will consider some of the ways in which this is done. However, while

---

7   See Hogan: Narrative.
8   See Hogan: Mind, pp. 94–97 and citations.

recognizing the importance of all three, I will lay special emphasis on character. This is because the particularization of events appears to be disproportionately affected by the particularization of character.

Again, the transformation of general structures into particular works may be best understood by reference to ›development principles‹. More exactly the production of a particular story involves at least three components. The first component is the hierarchy of previously existing structures – from particular stories up through schemas and definitions, but with prototypes having particular salience and thus cognitive importance. The second component is a set of development principles which apply to the previously existing structures. The third component is a set of evaluation principles which apply to the product that results from the application of development principles to general structures.

I will speak of these as if they constitute three compositional stages. However, this is only for ease of exposition and clarity of causal attribution. In fact, they continually interact and alter each other. Suppose I am writing a romantic story, perhaps a story based to some extent on my own experience. I begin with the romantic prototype, along with relevant exempla or instances (e.g., *Romeo and Juliet* or, to take a case from popular fiction, *Titanic*) – and, indeed, a range of other, relevant prototypes, subprototypes, and so on. I begin with these structures in two senses. First, they are there before my particular romantic experiences. Second, they are there as I begin to reflect on those experiences in order to write the story. In both cases, the romantic prototype (along with the other structures) helps to select features from my experience, place them in causal relations with one another, relate them to possible outcomes, sharpen emotional continuities and contrasts, etc. But, at the same time, my experience begins to particularize the prototype. As a result of this specification, the precise configuration of my cognition – its particular complex of selecting, organizing, and orienting structures – changes. For example, some instances become more prominent (thus the modeling function of *Romeo and Juliet* or *Titanic* may decline and be replaced by, say, Wong Kar-wai's much less prototypical *In the Mood for Love*).[9] These instances may even

---

9 Wong's film takes up most elements of the love triangle version of the romantic plot. However, it manipulates these elements in ways that go against their more common usage. For example, the lover is often exiled before being reunited with the beloved on a return home. Moreover, that reunion is often connected with a larger, familial reunion, sometimes involving the couple's children. The end of Wong's film involves the lover returning from exile to his former home. The beloved is, in fact, there – but in another apartment. Because she is in another apartment, the two do not meet. Moreover, the beloved is there with her child, but it is not the child of the lover. The close connection with the more prototypical ending serves to enhance the effect of

assume greater importance than the prototype. In addition, the relative significance of other prototypes and sub-prototypes will change.[10] Similarly, I may begin to focus on particular, recurring motifs that are separable from prototypes (e.g., the motif of the journey away from home and the return home) – and so forth. Moreover, as this is going on, I am continually evaluating what I write, what I have written, and what I anticipate as the result of what I am writing and have written. My negative evaluation of a passage or scene may lead me to revise what I have done, or it may lead me to plan certain corrections later in the story. For example, I may feel that I am beginning to make my heroine too unsympathetic. I may then change some of what I have written, or I may include more sympathy-fostering moments later on. In short, the components are in continual interaction and mutual modification. Moreover, there are many such components, including components that are quite idiosyncratic. Nonetheless, it is valuable to separate types of components for ease of exposition and to focus on recurring patterns (e.g., narrative prototypes) to achieve greater explanatory breadth. That is what I will do in the following sections.

3 Development Principles

We may distinguish two sorts of development principles. First, there are principles that serve to alter the basic prototype or its representation. We

---

this ending. Though it is not precisely prototypical, it remains structured by reference to the prototype. This is the sort of effect that might serve as an important model for a new writer if Wong's film becomes a particularly salient instance. It is worth remarking in this context that the ending of Wong's film is a good example of the way in which the production of a narrative involves a simultaneous process of reception (for a fuller discussion of this, see Hogan: Interpretation, pp. 163–180). When Wong was writing this script, he simultaneously experienced it as a reader (and when he was directing, he simultaneously experienced the events as an audience member). I have no reason to believe that he thought self-consciously about prototypical and non-prototypical endings. However, when he felt that this ending was ›right‹, he was, in all likelihood, tacitly bringing into play his prototype-based expectations about the ending of a romantic narrative. He was experiencing the ending in relation to those expectations, in much the same way as many other viewers would. That receptive experience is what allowed him to judge that the ending was right.

10 For example, certain schemas for ›activity types‹ (such as going on a date) will enter locally, but crucially, as the story develops. On the nature and operation of activity types, see Culpeper / McIntyre: Activity Types (in this volume). Though I will not be discussing such schemas, they play a significant role throughout narrative particularization. Moreover, it seems likely that they follow the same general principle of being specified by character and scene.

may refer to these as ›alteration principles‹. Second, there are principles that serve to make the abstract prototypes concrete. We may refer to these as ›specification principles‹.

As just noted, alteration principles may bear on the prototype itself or the representation of the prototype, the way the prototype is presented to an audience. Thus I would include discourse manipulation here – including, for example, the re-ordering of story events. Suppose I begin a film with the wedding of the loving couple. I cut to the best man talking to one of the bridesmaids. He sighs and exclaims, ›Thank God! I thought it would never happen!‹ The dewy-eyed bridesmaid inquires innocently, ›But why not?‹ The best man then explains the wacky and tumultuous sequence of events that led to the wedding – the unlikely meeting of the couple, their initial alienation, their growing affection, the sinister interference of money-grubbing relatives and the doltish intervention of buffoonish rivals with strangely large overbites, the traffic-jams, the car chases, the disheartening fiasco with the wedding cake, the loss and recovery of the wedding ring, and a strange series of mix-ups involving identical twins and a police officer posing as a prostitute. Framing the tale with this dialogue is a simple discursive change that follows an ›alteration principle‹. The general form of this discourse alteration principle might be something along the following lines: ›Place an emotionally significant outcome before its causal explanation‹. It would commonly be combined with a meta-principle to the following effect: ›Motivate any discursive departures from story/discourse parallelism‹.

Discourse manipulations bear on all the main components of a story, not only events. For example, temporal alteration in character appears when an important fact about a character – a fact that both explains and contextualizes his or her action – is concealed from the reader until the end of the story. A principle here might be something along the following lines, ›Withhold explanatory information about a character – prominently including identity information‹. This is, in turn, qualified by another meta-principle, ›Supply adequate story information so that a reader is not disoriented‹.

Other alteration principles include the multiplication or deletion of prototype elements and the insertion of non-prototype elements. The multiplication of events with slight variations is perhaps the most obvious. This practice is probably most familiar from oral tales.[11] We also find it in canonical literature – as in Lear's triple division of his kingdom and triple test of his daughters' love. *King Lear* is particularly apt to our concerns, for it shows that the variation is inseparable from differences in the characters

---

11 See Rubin: Memory, p. 30 and citations for examples.

involved (itself a matter of specification). The first and second tests and divisions are very similar, due to the near indistinguishability of the characters, Goneril and Regan. The third test and division are, however, distinctive. This is due to the character of Cordelia. In effect, we see the same abstract structure ›run‹ or processed three times, with different characters determining the differences in the resulting episodes.

Ellipsis (the deletion of prototype elements) may be less common in standard forms of storytelling, but it is a sometimes obtrusive feature of Modernist and Postmodern storytelling, in which crucial narrative information may simply be absent. In many cases, that absence is balanced by a more intensive development of some limited segment of the story – often through character focus and elaboration, as when Robbe-Grillet dwells on the mental state of a jealous lover in *La Jalousie*.

Another development principle involves the insertion of elements – most obviously events or characters – that are not part of the initial prototype. In some cases, these elements are drawn from other prototypes. For example, the separation of lovers in a romantic plot may be connected with a war, drawn from the heroic plot, and their reunion may be facilitated by the suffering or death of a scapegoat figure, drawn from the sacrificial plot. In other cases, the elements are not components of other prototypes. Rather, they are ›free motifs‹, narrative elements that may be introduced anywhere. Examples of this would include such events as the investigation of a secret or the undertaking of a journey and such characters as an investigator, suppliant, clown, or sage.

Indeed, not only may any plot include an investigator, any character may take on the (›free motivic‹) role of an investigator. This brings us to another set of alteration principles – the fusion and subdivision of elements. These principles apply almost entirely to characters. As a number of writers have noted,[12] for a given set of character functions, one character may fulfill one or more than one function and one function may be fulfilled by one or more than one character. For example, in the sacrificial plot, there is a sin that leads to communal devastation. That devastation can be reversed only by a sacrifice. The facts of sin and sacrifice entail two character functions – the sinner and the sacrificial victim. There is also, commonly, a deity responsible for the punishing devastation and the subsequent forgiveness. The ›sinner‹ may be one character (e.g., a group leader) or many (e.g., an entire community). The sacrificial victim may be the same as the sinner or may be different. The Judeo-Christian story of the fall gives us two sinners (Adam and Eve) and a sacrificial victim (Jesus) who is different from the sinners – but who is

---

12 E.g. Propp: Morphology, pp. 79–83.

the same as a (split) deity, an unusual and obviously emotionally effective variant. In *Oedipus the King*, Oedipus fuses the (sacrificial prototype) roles of sinner and sacrificial victim – as well as the free motivic role of investigator. (His story also manifests the discursive alteration principle of identity concealment.)

While alteration principles are certainly important, they only vary what is given in the prototypes themselves. They do not give us particular stories. Indeed, they become substantial only insofar as they operate on prototypes that are elaborated in concrete detail. This is where specification principles enter.

Specification principles begin with event types and character functions, as well as broad divisions of scene (e.g., home place vs. alien place). All three abstract structures must be specified. However, I do not believe that the specification operates equally in all three cases. Authors may and often do particularize events without reference to characters. For example, an author may decide to write a heroic plot treating a nuclear war before he or she has determined anything about character. However, perhaps the most straightforward way of particularizing most prototypical events is by particularizing prototypical characters (and scenes). What makes *Romeo and Juliet* different from *Abhijñānaśākuntalam*? In many ways, it is the characters and their circumstances. Romeo is highly passionate, prone to rashness. Moreover, he lives in a society peopled by feuding patriarchs and hotheaded youths. These are the characters who hinder his love. His helper is a scheming friar. Duṣyanta, in contrast, is a cultivated gentleman, somewhat inclined to melancholy, and skilled in arts of leisure, such as painting. His society is peopled by jealous wives and choleric sages. These are the characters who hinder his love. The helper function is taken up by a lazy and self-indulgent priest. In many ways, the differences in the narrative follow from these differences in character.

Of course, it is possible that these authors began with the plot events and worked back to the character traits. Moreover, in some cases, that is undoubtedly what happens. However, our ordinary processes of imagining the world involve projecting events based on our understanding people with their intentions, goals, and dispositions. Even when we first think about some major event, such as war, our imagination of unfolding subsequent scenarios is based on how individuals – with their personalities, virtues and vices, intellect, and so on – would behave. Thus we think, how would Kim Jong Il react if George Bush ordered an invasion of North Korea? In other words, we do not ordinarily start out imagining some situation, then working backward to agency. We do not usually think, ›Let's imagine that North Korea invades South Korea. What sort of North Korean leader might undertake such an invasion?‹ The reasons for our agent-based imagination are obvious for evolutionary reasons – or perhaps for simple reasons of learning in childhood. Most of the time, it is far more functional in the real world to think in this way. Of course, that does not mean that it is more functional in the creation of verbal art and fictional narratives. But there is no reason to believe that we follow one principle in our ordinary imaginative lives – which is to say, our ordinary imagination of narratives that relate hypothetical situations to real world possibilities – and another principle in our imagination of literary narratives.[13]

As I have already noted, character specification begins with character functions. Character specification affects two things. First, it details and expands the character's motivations, feelings, decisions, and actions. Second, it alters and intensifies the reader's response to the character – including the reader's understanding of, feelings about, and evaluation of the character.

More exactly, it is a commonplace in current cognitive theory that we all understand other people through our ›theory of mind‹, our sense of other people as having distinct beliefs, experiences, motives, and so forth. There are two common ways of interpreting our responses to others, insofar as these are based on our theory of mind. One is the ›theory theory‹. According to this account, we draw conclusions about other people's ideas, experiences, feelings, and so forth, based on inferential principles. The other way of understanding theory of mind is called ›simulation theory‹. According to this account, we imagine ourselves in the place of the other person and ›simulate‹ his or her responses.[14] I see no reason to choose between the two. It seems clear that, in fact, we sometimes draw conclusions based on inferential principles and at other times we imagine ourselves in the place of the other person and simulate

---

13 I am speaking here, most importantly, of hypothetical stories. The situation is different with stories that come to us from the past and that we see as determined by facts. In the case of actual events – as recounted in history or biography – our tendency is the opposite. In those cases, we are much more likely to know about and feel constrained by particular event sequences. As a result, we are more likely to try to work from the events to the characters (e.g., we may try to infer aspects of Nixon's character from his foreign and domestic policies, his involvement in Watergate, and so on). On the other hand, the more our stories are constrained by actual events, the less prototypical they tend to be as stories (though, as Hayden White has shown, they are not unaffected by standard plot structures). As they become more hypothetical (e.g., in historical or biographical fiction), this tendency almost certainly diminishes. In any event, had I been discussing the emplotment of history rather than verbal art, I would have treated the place of character differently. But, of course, in that case, narrative development operates rather differently across the board.
14 For a discussion of this distinction, see Gazzaniga: Brain, pp. 173–178.

his or her responses. Both processes seem to be involved in the creation and reception of characters. On the other hand, while the two processes undoubtedly interact extensively and are most often inseparable in practice, it is worth distinguishing between them theoretically. This is important as the two strategies do not always have the same emotional, evaluative, and other consequences.

Again, prototypes give us character functions – sinners, scapegoats, lovers, rivals, and so on. Alteration principles may divide or fuse these, or add to the list. Specification principles operate on these functions to produce characters to whom we may respond as persons. The first step in this specification involves a fundamental division in types of character. This division is determined by our two fundamental sorts of response to persons – theoretical inference and simulation. Simulation is distinct from empathy (i.e., one can simulate someone else's thoughts without sharing their feelings). However, simulation is a necessary component of empathy that is sustained beyond immediate experiential responses (e.g., a pang of fear on hearing someone scream in fear). Thus lack of empathy is related to lack of simulation. For example, our empathy is inhibited with respect to members of out-groups.[15] This is presumably due in part to a diminished inclination to simulate their experiences and feelings. Put very simply, in responding to an in-group member – when that in-group membership is salient – we are likely to use a combination of simulation and inference in our ›theory of mind‹ responses to that person. Perhaps there is even some weighting toward simulation. In any case, the simulation tends to foster a more sustained empathy. In contrast, we may be less likely to simulate the attitudes, experiences, decisions of out-group members. One consequence of this is that we are less likely to empathize with out-group members. Moreover, we are likely to understand out-group members more mechanically. Simulation involves assimilating the other person to ourselves, and we commonly understand that our own motives, ideas, feelings are changeable, that they are not rigidly fixed.[16] In contrast, we see out-groups as »less complex, less variable, less individuated«.[17]

In this way, the first crucial division in character specification is between us and them, in-group and out-group. This division may be inflected by another division that has consequences for inference and simulation as well. That is the division into characters who are socially

---

[15] For some relevant research, see Mitchell et al.: Thinking, p. 77; Ito et al.: Social, pp. 193, 196; Kunda: Social, pp. 324–325.
[16] See, for example, Holland et al.: Induction, pp. 223–224.
[17] Duckitt: Psychology, p. 81.

normative (i.e., characters who represent social categories and associated norms) and individualistic characters (i.e., characters with idiosyncratic preferences and affiliations, which often run contrary to social norms).[18] Generally, the latter seem more likely to provoke simulation and empathy than the former.

I should note that none of these divisions guarantees either simulation or theory-based inference. Indeed, generally speaking, the greater attention an author devotes to a given character, the more likely it is that the character will provoke simulation and associated empathy – even when that character is an out-group member. In connection with this, I suspect that individualistic characters are not more likely to provoke simulation simply because they are individualistic. Rather, the tendency toward simulation (assuming I am right about this) is due to the greater attention and elaboration commonly given to such characters.

The fundamental divisions in character commonly involve typological categories as well. There are different sorts of category that enter here. Obviously, in the case of in-group/out-group divisions, the first typological categorizations are likely to be based on ideas about group identity, most commonly stereotypes.

Broad ethnic, religious, national, and related categorizations obviously provide some specification of character functions. Suppose Smith wishes to write a heroic narrative and makes the hero a European-American and the enemy an Arab. This will entail certain likely plot developments. For example, based on stereotypes, it may lead to the inclusion of suicide bombing or the use of commercial airliners as weapons. It may lead to a broad characterization of the enemy as ›fanatically‹ religious, thus uncompromising in its commitment to the destruction of the U.S.

Other sorts of typological categorization do not divide along lines of ethnicity and culture *per se*. Instead, they move to a level of abstraction above identity categories, addressing attitudes toward cultural origins and practices. For example, much literature from former British colonies involves a tacit typology of characters defined by their relation to colonial and indigenous cultures. Some characters are mimics, celebrating and (often badly) imitating European practices simply because they are European, rejecting indigenous practices simply because they are not European. Other characters are orthodox, following traditions of the home society in a way that is beneficial for the society and sensitive to changing social conditions. Still other characters are reactionary

---

18 In romantic plots, the first category commonly includes the lovers' forbidding parents or other blocking characters, while the lovers themselves commonly fall into the second category. On this distinction, see Hogan: Mind, pp. 205–217.

traditionalists or fundamentalists, asserting a narrow, rigid, oppressive – and, commonly, inaccurate – form of tradition (often after having been mimics). There are also syncretists, who seek to combine different cultural practices, and so on.[19]

Divisions of this sort may be less simplistic and repetitive, thus more likely to advance distinctive narrative specification. Take Rabindranath Tagore's novel, *Gora*. One plot sequence, a romantic tragi-comedy, makes one lover orthodox, with a strong tendency toward reactionary traditionalism (in response to European colonial denigration of indigenous beliefs), and the other a syncretist. This entails a range of narrative consequences that are intellectually challenging and emotionally effective. It seems unlikely that, other things being equal, a more standard narrative – for example, one in which the lovers came from different castes – would have been equally successful. In any case, it would have been a different story.

On the other hand, even the most fine-grained and culturally illuminating typological categorizations remain limited in their consequences for narrative specification. Stories remain threadbare if they are not particularized beyond typological selection. For such fuller particularization, we need, at the very least, individual traits, distinct from typologies. The obvious way of developing such individual traits is by transferring information about particular people – exempla – who share some narratively relevant category with the character we are trying to develop, including the category defined by the typologically dominant trait – for example, orthodoxy or, to take a trait from psychophysiological typology, melancholy. These particular people, the exempla, may be real or fictional, known directly or only by report. They prominently include ourselves. For example, in forming the character of a melancholic hero in a romantic plot, I will transfer behaviors and propensities from fictional melancholics and lovers, such as Hamlet and Romeo, real people (perhaps including myself) that I would classify as melancholic or in love, and so on.

Such an isolation of individual acts and inclinations tends to foster simulation, and, as such, may make causal sense to readers even when those acts and inclinations are not simply derivable from broad character traits (e.g., ›He did that because he is rash‹), or still less from typological categories (›Arabs are like that‹). Indeed, simulation involves a movement away from group divisions and their differentialist explanations of impulses and actions, toward a more encompassing idea of human motivation. It relies on our sense that people respond with the same sorts of emotions to the same sorts of object or situation. At the same time, it

---

19 For a discussion of these concepts see Hogan: Colonialism, pp. 9–17.

moves toward individualization, for it does not presuppose that we respond in precisely the same way to precisely the same particulars. For example, we assume that people have insecurities about their human attachments, but we do not assume that we all share precisely the same insecurities and, even less, the same attachments.

The preceding reference to insecurity and attachment may seem to suggest that we can give an explicit account of a character's decisions and actions in these cases. That may or may not be the case. In simulation, we primarily experience the character's (or real person's) motivation as comprehensible through our imagination of his or her experiences and feelings. We may be able to articulate specific reasons for this motivation, or we may not. Indeed, in some cases, the discrepancy between our intuitive sense and our explanation of a given character's motives may be obtrusive. Perhaps this is the case with one of the most famous conundrums in the history of criticism – Hamlet's delay in exacting revenge for his father's murder. Critics have elevated Hamlet's delay to one of the great puzzles of literary interpretation. That may mean that we find the contradiction between Hamlet's decision and his action to be incomprehensible. But I doubt it. I doubt that we would find Hamlet so fascinating if we felt that Shakespeare's portrayal of the prince was merely inconsistent or opaque. We should, in that case, see Hamlet's delay as a flaw rather than something to be explained. Our sense that it is explicable suggests that Hamlet's behavior does indeed feel plausible in simulation – even though we cannot articulate an explanation for it. This is not surprising. Again, in simulation we rely on our own experience of motivation, decision, and action. In our own lives, we often make decisions that (like Hamlet) we are unable to follow through. Often we are able to give some sort of explanation for this discrepancy – but not always. In some cases, we are uncertain as to why we did or did not act in a certain way. If asked why, we cannot give an articulate and cogent response.

Indeed, in many cases, even articulate, cogent explanations of our behavior do not really capture our motives and feelings. Explicit explanations abstract from our experiences. They select aspects of the experiences for purposes of causal alignment – I am writing this paper because I have been invited to a conference; Gora wears traditional clothing because he rejects colonialist mimeticism; Hamlet does not commit suicide because he fears hellfire. But these are at best simplifications. Take the first. Clearly, the set of psychological events that give rise to the action of writing this paper is highly complex. For particular purposes, my invitation to the Zentrum für interdisziplinäre Forschung may be the most relevant precedent for the writing, and thus the most relevant cause. However, it is clearly not the only cause of the writing (for example, I could have refused the invitation, however foolish that may have been) – and it is certainly not the sole cause or even an important cause of the particular argument. The general point holds whether I am speaking of my own direct experience of myself or my simulation of someone else.

This discrepancy between an articulated causal account and direct or simulated experience is particularly consequential in the sorts of cases that are crucial to the simulative specification of character – cases of emotion and motivation. One aspect of this merits particular attention. Our emotions and motivations – about ourselves and our actions, and about other people – almost invariably have some degree of ambivalence. In other words, there is almost always some conflict in our feelings. However, our account of these feelings in causal explanations tends to eliminate that ambivalence. For example, I have written about five versions of this paper. My feelings about it, and about my trip to the ZIF are mixed (despite the kind invitation, the friendliness of the organizers, my admiration for the other participants, and so on). I even have ambivalence about the argument itself. I largely believe what I am saying. But I cannot say that I am 100% convinced that the specification of character drives the specification of plot more than the reverse. (I am pretty convinced of this, but not entirely.) Moreover, I am speaking in terms of principles, but I believe these are really more like statistical inclinations, best captured in the operation of connectionist networks – ultimately, brain circuits. (Though in saying this I simultaneously realize that I do not at all wish to reduce narrative development to neuronal circuits and that I find the idea of principles at least practically – and perhaps theoretically – ineliminable.)

All this extends from the real world to character. Indeed, this indicates that ambivalence is likely to be central to our experience of character and narrative more generally. Indeed, I would suggest that ambivalence is inseparable from the purposes of verbal art. This leads to the topic of evaluation principles. Unfortunately, a full treatment of evaluation principles requires a separate essay. Here, I can only sketch a few of the main points.

4 Evaluation Principles

Evaluation principles are simply the principles we use to judge whether or not the work is likely to have the right impact. In verbal art, there are two common sorts of impact that concern authors and readers. One is the thematic point of the work. The other is its emotional force. By ›thematic point‹, I mean any general ideas or attitudes that the author wishes to convey to the reader through the work – more generally, anything that the reader should transfer from the story to the world of his or her ordinary life. Most often, this transfer involves ethical or political/social concerns. Take a simple example – a film about the Iraq war is likely to have a thematic purpose in affecting our attitude toward the war when we leave the theater. I should note, however, that not all themes are self-conscious. Put differently, not all works are didactic, involving clear thematic ideas that we can readily articulate. Indeed, not all authors even have a very clear sense of precisely what point they wish to make. As with so much else, authors commonly evaluate the thematic impact of the work tacitly. They write something, then reread it, judging whether or not it feels right. In ethics and politics, as elsewhere, we may distinguish between self-conscious articulation or theory, on the one hand, and simulation, on the other. In some cases, we make moral judgments by invoking general principles (theories). However, in other cases, we rely on our ›gut‹ (thus simulation). Both enter into the authorial development and readerly experience of stories. Here too the latter tend to be more variable and ambivalent. This returns us to emotional force, for our moral and political concerns – in art and in life – are inseparable from our feelings.

Emotional force is most obviously a matter of enhancing the emotional effect of the work as a whole. However, that overarching concern is qualified by local concerns – such as concerns about sustaining the reader's interest. Moreover, enhancing emotional effect does not necessarily mean producing the strongest emotion. It means, rather, producing the most satisfying emotion – or, in some cases, producing the most appropriate emotion given the thematic purposes of the work. (For example, a film opposing the Iraq war may have the strongest thematic impact if the overall emotional effect of the work is disconcerting, and thus in a sense unsatisfying.) But, given what I have just said, we should expect emotion in either case to be, so to speak, impure, to involve some degree of multiplicity and conflict. In general, then, we might say that the main function of emotive evaluation principles is to manage and orient ambivalence. Certainly, there will be many cases where that ambivalence is minimal. For example, in many romantic tragi-comedies, we just want the lovers to marry; in many heroic tragi-comedies, we just want the evil invader to be repulsed. Nonetheless, here too the operation of the evaluation principles remains a form of shaping ambivalence, even if that shaping involves intensifying one emotion and inhibiting contradictory feelings (which are almost certainly there, even in effervescent comedies and dire melodramas).

I should note that evaluation principles are not, most importantly, general precepts, rules along the lines of those set out by Neo-Classicists. There are undoubtedly some general rules of this sort. Some of these are explicit in creative writing manuals, such as ›Show, don't tell‹. Others are implicit, but easily recognizable, such as ›In developing concrete, perceptual details, draw particularly on properties that are emotionally consequential‹. However, it seems likely that evaluation principles commonly make reference to exempla, rather than precepts. For instance, in evaluating a particular colonial character in a postcolonial novel, a writer might seek to determine if his or her passage has the same careful balance between sympathy and criticism as found in J. M. Coetzee's treatment of the Magistrate in *Waiting for the Barbarians*. In this way, our evaluation principles are more often bound up with shifting configurations of instances than necessary and sufficient conditions, or even schematic rules of thumb.

Here as elsewhere, character is central. We do judge actions moral or immoral, joyous or lamentable, and so forth. However, actions obviously do not occur independent of agents, and the moral praise or blame, as well as the emotion-producing effects of actions, are inseparable from persons. Our ethical and emotional relation to the world is necessarily a relation to people. Our ethical and emotional relation to stories is, then, necessarily a relation to people as well. But is there the same sort of directional orientation in evaluation as there is in developmental imagination? We may qualify our response to an act due to our understanding of the person, but we may also qualify our response to a person due to our understanding of the act. As a result, character may not guide evaluation in the same way it appears to guide narrative specification. On the other hand, our willingness to exculpate a character for apparent crimes and our tendency to experience certain emotions in response to a character's actions and experiences are often inseparable from whether we categorize the character as us or them, and whether we infer or simulate their experiences. In this way, our very understanding of what the relevant events are may be affected by our response to the characters involved. In this way, character may indeed play a guiding role in evaluation – both that of the author and that of readers.[20]

---

20 I should stress once more that the author's own response is itself crucially receptive, for the author necessarily combines the roles of writer (or speaker) and reader (or listener).

5 *Hamlet*

Since the discussion to this point has been fairly general. It is worth considering a particular case in greater detail. In conclusion, then, we might turn again to *Hamlet*. In terms of *prototypes* and initial *alterations*, Shakespeare has chosen to combine two genres – heroic and romantic.[21] In *Hamlet*, Shakespeare has fused the son of the usurped king with the romantic lover (i.e., he has combined these functions into a single character). He has established a parallel between the prince's political dispossession and the lover's separation from his beloved. Since the lover is always melancholic when separated from his beloved, an obvious humor for this character is melancholy.

Once this typological category is established, a number of *specifications* follow. Hamlet's response to his father's death (due to the usurpation) becomes one of intense mourning – not one of, say, righteous anger. Since melancholy tends toward inaction, this leads away from swift revenge toward procrastination. It also suggests the likelihood of suicidal thoughts. Moreover, all this must have made particular literary and biographical exempla salient for Shakespeare. For instance, in developing Hamlet's mourning, Shakespeare almost certainly transferred particular traits from his own mourning for his dead son, Hamnet.

This reference to Shakespeare's own mourning suggests a likely point of transition from mere transfer of properties to broader simulation. Moreover, it suggests just how this simulation could produce the ambivalences that result in Hamlet's inaction. These ambivalences are bound up with the shifting feelings of anger and despair, the fluctuations between manic energy and lethargy, of memory and forgetting – and many more complicated experiences, both simultaneous and sequential – that characterize mourning.

All this helps to indicate how we may find Hamlet's behavior plausible at the level of simulation, but, at best, only partially explicable at the level of overt causal explanation. In relation to this, it also suggests the way that the organization or management of ambivalence might function in this narrative. Mourning, again, gives rise to anger and despair. The bereaved person may simultaneously wish to die – thus forgetting the loss – and to take his or her revenge on a world that caused the bereavement. He or she may also envision an afterlife of possible heavenly union with the beloved

---

21 Again, the heroic plot commonly involves a usurpation of rightful rule in the home society – often by a relative of the rightful ruler – and an external threat to that society. The hero is often exiled by the usurper, but then returns to defeat the external threat and regain his/her rightful position. In one common variant, the usurped ruler dies and his or her role is taken up by a son or daughter.

person – or, due to the commission of a mortal sin, an afterlife of eternal separation. In effect, the play works out these ambivalences, leading to a conclusion that, at least temporarily, may seem almost perfect. All the guilty parties are killed. Claudius in particular is killed when still guilty of mortal sin. While King Hamlet's sins will be burned off in Purgatory, Claudius will suffer eternal punishment. But – and this is why the solution might seem flawless – the final deaths do not lead inexorably to Hamlet's damnation. In the end, he is able to sate his rage without committing cold-blooded murder based on doubtful, ghostly testimony; he is able to fulfill his despairing desire to die without committing suicide. Ultimately, however, the solution is not perfect. Ambivalence remains, or returns. First, we do not know the eternal fate of Cordelia. Second, despite Horatio's invocation of angels bearing him to final rest, even Hamlet seems guilty for the deaths of Rosencrantz and Guildenstern (as well as Polonius). Indeed, that is undoubtedly one reason that the announcement of their deaths directly follows Hamlet's own passing.

This leads us to the thematic concerns of the play. It is, in fact, difficult to say just what the point of all this might be. It faces us very starkly with the absoluteness of death and the irresolvable ambivalence of mourning, the apparent impossibility of working one's way out of complete human loss. It is not a play that suggests to us that good will triumph over evil. It is a play that suggests, rather, that acts of willful evil create situations of moral conflict, where all our moral options are false. In this way, the play displays inexorable cascades of wrong. Perhaps the main thematic aim of the play is simply to present that disconcerting vision of human life, a vision in which the moral valence of human actions is not fully divisible into individual acts, but is diffused in its multiple consequences throughout the society. In any case, the dilemma of that contradictory world, along with its consequences for our own morally diffuse and recalcitrant lives, is revealed to us through the development of a particular character, and thereby the particularization of universal prototypes into his singular story.

In sum, particular stories begin with prototypes and other general structures. These prototypes are developed through alteration principles (including event/explanation reversal, identity concealment, synthesis of prototypes, insertion of motifs, etc.) and specification principles (including typological categorization, trait transfer, and simulation). Developments are continually assessed and selected through ongoing processes of evaluation relative to emotional and thematic goals. Much of this operates crucially through characters. Our imagination ordinarily proceeds by placing particular characters in particular situations in order to envision outcomes. (It does not ordinarily proceed by defining detailed sequences of events, then envisioning what sort of character would produce those events.) Our emotional response and ethical judgment are inseparable from our disposition toward characters – a disposition that often crucially involves the opposition between in-group and out-group categorization and the difference between inference to mental states and simulation of mental states. For almost any significantly developed narrative, particularly any narrative that provokes more than fleeting simulation, our emotional response is likely to be, in some respects, ambivalent. In those cases, the emotional purposes of the work are, at least in part, to organize and direct that ambivalence into an experience that is either intrinsically satisfying or that is best coordinated with the work's thematic purposes.

References

Aristotle: Poetics. In: Aristotle's Theory of Poetry and Fine Art with a Critical Text and Translation of the Poetics. Ed. and trans. S. H. Butcher. 4th edn. New York 1951.

Culpeper, Jonathan / Dan McIntyre: Activity Types and Characterisation in Dramatic Discourse. In this volume.

Duckitt, John H.: The Social Psychology of Prejudice. New York 1992.

Gazzaniga, Michael S.: The Ethical Brain: The Science of our Moral Dilemmas. New York 2005.

Hogan, Patrick Colm: Affective Narratology: The Emotional Structure of Stories. Lincoln, NE forthcoming.

Hogan, Patrick Colm: Colonialism and Cultural Identity: Crises of Tradition in the Anglophone Literatures of India, Africa, and the Caribbean. Albany, NY 2000.

Hogan, Patrick Colm: The Mind and Its Stories: Narrative Universals and Human Emotion. Cambridge 2003.

Hogan, Patrick Colm: Narrative Universals, Heroic Tragi-Comedy, and Shakespeare's Political Ambivalence. In: College Literature 33/1 (2006), pp. 34–66.

Hogan, Patrick Colm: On Interpretation: Meaning and Inference in Law, Psychoanalysis, and Literature. Athens, GA 1996.

Holland, John / Keith Holyoak / Richard Nisbett / Paul Thagard: Induction: Processes of Inference, Learning, and Discovery. Cambridge, MA 1986.

Ito, Tiffany A. / Geoffrey R. Urland / Eve Willadsen-Jensen / Joshua Correll: The Social Neuroscience of Stereotyping and Prejudice: Using Event-Related Brain Potentials to Study Social Perception. In: John T. Cacioppo / Penny S. Visser / Cynthia L. Pickett (Eds.): Social Neuroscience: People Thinking about Thinking People. Cambridge, MA 2006, pp. 189–208.

James, Henry: The Portrait of a Lady. Old Saybrook, CT 2008.

Kunda, Ziva: Social Cognition: Making Sense of People. Cambridge, MA 1999.

Mitchell, Jason P. / Malia F. Mason / C. Neil Macraw / Mahzarin R. Banaji: Thinking about Others: The Neural Substrates of Social Cognition. In: John T. Cacioppo / Penny S. Visser / Cynthia L. Pickett (Eds.): Social Neuroscience: People Thinking about Thinking People. Cambridge, MA 2006, pp. 63–82.

Propp, Vladimir: The Morphology of the Folktale. Transl. by Laurence Scott. Austin, TX 1968.

Rubin, David C.: Memory in Oral Traditions: The Cognitive Psychology of Epic, Ballads, and Counting-out Rhymes. New York 1995.

White, Hayden: Metahistory: The Historical Imagination in Nineteenth-Century Europe. Baltimore, MD 1973.

Wong Kar-Wai (Dir.): In the Mood for Love. Written and produced by Wong Kar-Wai. Directors of Photography: Christopher Doyle and Mark Li Ping-bin. Production Designer, Chief Editor, and Costume Designer: William Chang Suk-ping. Block 2 Pictures, Jet Tone Production, Paradis Films, 2000.

II Characters and Characterisation in Different Media

ALAN PALMER

Social Minds in *Persuasion*

1 Cognitive Frames

Characterisation theory is based on the insight that a reader's construction of a character in a novel is a process that is both frame-driven (top-down in direction) and data-driven (bottom-up). As is now well known, frames (or schemas) are cognitive structures or mental templates that represent generic concepts stored in our memory. They are arrangements of knowledge about objects, people or situations that are used to predict and classify new data. We use frames to simplify reality, organize our knowledge, assist recall, make sense of our current experiences, guide our everyday behaviour and predict likely happenings in the future. By capturing the essence of stereotypical situations such as being in a living room or going out for dinner, frames allow us to use default assumptions about what is likely to happen in those situations. That way, it is only when our assumptions are proved wrong that we have to improvise. Frames are hierarchical arrangements that have slots for variables. Once the most appropriate frame (say, a cat) has been activated, some slots are filled with compulsory values (a cat is an animal), or with default values (a cat has four legs), or are empty until filled with values from the current situation (the cat is black). Frame processing is top-down, in that it guides a selective search for data relevant to the expectations set up by the frame, and also bottom-up, because the data contained in an actual situation will often lead to the modification of the frame, or even the generation of a new frame.

Narrative theorists such as Monika Fludernik (1996), David Herman (1994) and Manfred Jahn (1997) have used frame theory to build on the work of the reader response criticism of Wolfgang Iser and Roman Ingarden in order to illuminate precisely how readers are able to follow narrative texts. They recognised, for example, that story frames are sets of expectations about the internal structure of stories that enable readers or listeners to recognise a text as a narrative. Comprehension of a story means building a representation of the text using the prototypical structural patterns that are stored in memory. We acquire the textual frames relating to our knowledge of genre and other narrative conventions primarily by reading a wide range of stories, and our resulting awareness of the appropriate genre pre-focuses our understanding of and response to a particular text. During the reading process, events in the story are marked as salient and acquire significance because of the expectations defined by frames. In particular, we use frames as part of our literary competence and performance to reconstruct from fictional narratives the storyworlds described in those narratives. They allow readers to fill in the gaps in storyworlds because the appropriate ingredients for extracting the meaning of a sentence in a narrative are often nowhere to be found within that sentence. Schank and Abelson illustrate the point with this example: »The policeman held up his hand and stopped the car«.[1] In understanding this sentence we effortlessly create a driver who steps on a brake in response to seeing the policeman's hand. This sort of gap filling helps readers track the movements of characters and objects through storyworld time and space.

Frame theory considers, for example, how incoming data are put into the relevant slots; the order in which slots are filled; the classification of the information contained in the slots (into, say, rules, events and characters); how stories can be broken down into component parts; the types of causal relations that connect these components; and, importantly, how we repair unfounded assumptions about the direction of the story. As with real-life frames, this is both a top-down and a bottom-up process. It is also dynamic in that, when a reader fills a new slot, changes to existing slots may be required. A reader's attention does not spread equally and evenly through a text, but continually works forwards and backwards to make adjustments to frames. Good novels tend to challenge readers' expectations and thereby force them to abandon established frames in favour of new, refreshed ones. Specifically, frames are essential to the construction of fictional minds. A character frame is established (top-down) on meeting or hearing of a character for the first time, and is then fed (bottom-up) by specific information about the character from the text, and so on. These character stereotypes may come from real-world knowledge or from knowledge of the stereotypes to be found in various literary genres. As more bottom-up information on a particular character is processed, frame refreshment, sub-categorisation or individuation may take place. More radically, frame disruption, de-categorisation, invalidation

---

1   Schank / Abelson: Scripts, p. 9.

of previous inferences, or even a focused search for a new, more adequate character category might occur.

However, it seems to me that this characterisation process has been interpreted up until now in a rather constrained and limiting way. For example, it has been generally assumed that the character frames that are used in the ways described above consist only of cultural and literary stereotypes relating to individual characters such as the rake, the fallen woman, the braggart and so on. The purpose of this essay is to extend in some new and possibly unexpected directions our understanding of character theory by examining some of the very different sorts of cognitive frames that are also used by the reader in the construction of character. This can be done by making use of some of the insights relating to the social nature of cognition that have emerged within social, cognitive and discursive psychology, philosophy of mind and theoretical anthropology. I will describe these developments in the next section and then, in the following sections, apply them to an example character, Anne Elliot, the heroine of Jane Austen's novel *Persuasion* of 1818.

2 Social Minds and Intermental Thought

The aim of deepening and widening characterisation theory in order to provide a richer and fuller account of how readers actually construct fictional characters can be achieved in two stages. The first is to recognise that there is a deep fault line within narratology between the theories relating to characterisation and the theories relating to the representation of consciousness, and that the existence of this fault line has seriously distorted our understanding of fictional mental functioning. Consider a sentence such as this, from Henry James' *Portrait of a Lady*: »Isabel felt some emotion, for she had always thought highly of her grandmother's house«.[2] That is the sort of sentence that readers frequently encounter in fictional texts. It reports a single mental event – Isabel feeling emotion – but, at the same time, it puts this single event into the context of an aspect of Isabel's personality, her character, her self – her whole mind. As readers, we accept this sentence as a whole, as a *gestalt*, as a coherent explanation of the working of Isabel's whole mind. We do not think to ourselves: ›That's a strange sentence – yoking together two completely separate classes of statements‹. However, look at any of the large number of introductions to narrative theory, both old and new, all excellent. What

---

2 James: Portrait, p. 81.

do they have to say about that sentence *as a whole*? Nothing. These volumes typically contain a chapter about the representation of speech and thought and a completely separate chapter about characterisation. As a result, what you find, in effect, is that the first half of the sentence is classified as the representation of consciousness, but the second half of it is classified as characterisation. And, to make the division even deeper, the chapters in these introductions that are devoted to characterisation rarely refer to consciousness, and the chapters on consciousness have almost nothing to say about characterisation. This wholly artificial and arbitrary division completely fails to capture the readers' experience of that completely typical sentence about Isabel's mind.

The second stage is to recognise that the fictional minds belonging to characters in novels do not function in a vacuum. As with real minds, fictional minds are only partially understood if a merely *internalist perspective* is applied to them. Fictional minds, like real minds, are part of extended cognitive networks. We will never understand how these individual fictional minds work if we cut them off from the larger collective minds to which they belong. A large amount of bottom-up data is available in a wide range of fictional texts to demonstrate the truth of this assertion. However, readers have to make use of a number of top-down group frames in place in order to make sense of the data. Characterisation theory will be incomplete until it takes account of the *intermental* aspects of the character construction process. This can be done by adopting an *externalist perspective* on the notion of fictional character. These points will now be developed in detail, and all of the italicised phrases used so far in this paragraph will be explained.

Speaking very broadly, there are two perspectives on the mind: the internalist and the externalist. These two perspectives form more of a continuum than an either/or dichotomy, but the distinction is, in general, a valid one.

– An internalist perspective on the mind stresses those aspects that are inner, introspective, private, solitary, individual, psychological, mysterious, and detached.
– An externalist perspective on the mind stresses those aspects that are outer, active, public, social, behavioural, evident, embodied, and engaged.

The *social mind* and the *public mind* are the synonyms that I will use to describe those aspects of the whole mind that are revealed through the externalist perspective. In what follows, I will attempt to illustrate the importance of social minds in the novel by analysing their functioning in *Persuasion*. I hope to show that it is not possible to understand this novel without an awareness of these minds as they operate within its storyworld.

They are the chief means by which the plot is advanced. If you were to take all of the social thought out of *Persuasion*, very little, I would argue, would be left. So, given the importance of this subject to the study of the novel, it is necessary to find room for it at the centre of characterisation theory. It seems to me that the traditional narratological approach to the representation of fictional character is an internalist one that stresses those aspects that are inner, passive, introspective, and individual. As a result of this undue emphasis on private and solitary thought at the expense of all the other types of mental functioning, the *social* nature of fictional thought has been neglected. But, as the neuroscientist Antonio Damasio suggests, »the study of human consciousness requires both internal and external views«,[3] and so an externalist perspective is required as well, one that stresses the public, social, concrete, and located aspects of mental life in the novel.

An important part of the social mind is our capacity for *intermental thought*, which is joint, group, shared, or collective thought, as opposed to *intramental*, or individual or private thought. It is also known as *socially distributed, situated*, or *extended cognition*, and also as *intersubjectivity*. Intermental thought is a crucially important component of fictional narrative because much of the mental functioning that occurs in novels is done by large organizations, small groups, work colleagues, friends, families, couples, and other intermental units. It could plausibly be argued that a large amount of the subject matter of novels is the formation, development, and breakdown of these intermental systems.[4]

Within the real-mind disciplines of psychology and philosophy there is a good deal of interest in *the mind beyond the skin*: the realization that mental functioning cannot be understood merely by analysing what goes on inside the skull but can only be fully comprehended once it has been seen in its social and physical context. For example, social psychologists routinely use the terms *mind* and *mental action* not only about individuals, but also about groups of people working as intermental units. So, it is appropriate to say of groups that they think or that they remember. As the psychologist James Wertsch puts it, a *dyad* (that is, two people working as a cognitive system) can carry out such functions as problem solving on an intermental plane.[5] You may be asking what is achieved by talking in this way, instead of simply referring to individuals pooling their resources and

---

3   Damasio: Feeling, p. 82.
4   For work by postclassical narrative theorists on distributed cognition, see Margolin: Story, Margolin: Plural, Herman: Stories, and Herman: Regrounding.
5   Wertsch: Voices, p. 27.

working in cooperation together. The advocates of the concept of distributed cognition such as the theoretical anthropologists Gregory Bateson (1972) and Clifford Geertz (1993), the philosophers Andy Clark and David Chalmers (1998) and Daniel Dennett (1996), and the psychologists Edwin Hutchins (1995) and James Wertsch all stress that the purpose of the concept is increased explanatory power. They argue that the way to delineate a cognitive system is to draw the limiting line so that you do not cut out anything which leaves things inexplicable.⁶ For example, Wertsch tells the story of how his daughter lost her shoes and he helped her to remember where she had left them. Wertsch asks: ›Who is doing the remembering here?‹ He is not, because he had no prior knowledge of where they were, and she is not, because she had forgotten where they were. It was the intermental unit formed by the two of them that remembered.⁷

The basis of the approach to fictional texts taken in this essay is *attribution theory* (Palmer 2007): how narrators, characters, and readers attribute states of mind such as emotions, dispositions, and reasons for action to characters and, where appropriate, also to themselves. How do heterodiegetic narrators attribute states of mind to their characters? By what means do homodiegetic narrators attribute states of mind to themselves and also to other characters? And, with regard to the issue of characterisation, how does an attribution of a mental state by a narrator help to build up in the reader a sense of the whole personality of the character who is the subject of that attribution? Attribution theory rests on the concept of *theory of mind*. This is the term used by philosophers and psychologists to describe our awareness of the existence of other minds, our knowledge of how to interpret our own and other people's thought processes, our mind-reading abilities in the real world. Readers of novels have to use their theory of mind in order to try to follow the workings of characters' minds. Otherwise, they will lose the plot. The only way in which the reader can understand a novel is by trying to follow the workings of characters' minds and therefore attributing states of minds to them.⁸ Of particular importance to the concept of the social mind is the fact that this mind reading also involves readers trying to follow characters' attempts to read other characters' minds. A basic level of minimal mind reading is required for characters to understand each other

---

6   Bateson: Steps, p. 465.
7   Sperber / Hirschfeld: Culture, p. cxxiv.
8   For more on theory of mind and the novel, see Palmer: Fictional, and Zunshine: Fiction.

in order to make life possible. At the next level up, characters who know each other well form intermental pairs and small groups. To put the point simply, they are more likely to know what the other is thinking than total strangers will. These small groups will obviously vary greatly in the quantity and quality of their intermental thought. In addition, individuals may be part of larger groups that will also have a tendency to think together on certain issues. In all of these units, large and small, the individuals who belong to them will, of course, frequently think separately as well.[9]

Novels are preoccupied with this balance between public and private thought, intermental and intramental functioning, social and individual minds, and *Persuasion* is no exception. There are frequent references in the text to attributions of mental states, theory of mind and intermental thought. The narrator comments perceptively that »Husbands and wives generally understand when opposition [to the wishes of their spouse] will be vain« (81).[10] The Musgrove daughters know what their mother is thinking: »›My brother‹, whispered one of the girls [to Anne], ›mamma is thinking of poor Richard‹« (91). Anne, who is, as we shall see, generally a very good mind reader, »is ready to do good by entering into [Henrietta's] feelings« (124).

3 Anne Elliot's Social Mind

The central argument of this essay is that readers have to make use of what I call *group frames* in order to make sense of the data that is produced by the attribution of mental states as described above. These group frames may be large, medium or small scale. An example of a large-scale frame is the concept of society. The notion of *the party* that I refer to later is a medium-sized frame. Small-scale frames include married couples, lovers, friends and immediate family. It is the purpose of this essay to show that these three types of group frames are necessary for an understanding of the text of *Persuasion*. In particular, the reader has to place the main character, Anne Elliot, within these frames in order to be able to understand how she functions within the storyworld of the novel. For the rest of this section I will focus on her social mind and thereby establish the large-scale intermental frame. In the following section I will look at

---

9   For an extended treatment of a large intermental unit, see Palmer: Intermental. For an excellent analysis of the small intermental unit of a marriage, see Semino: Blending.
10 Austen: Persuasion. All following references in parenthesis refer to this work.

the medium sized intermental frame that I will refer to as *the party*. Sections 5 and 6 will consider first some of the small intermental frames formed by Anne's relationships with other characters, and then analyse the key intermental unit formed by Anne and Wentworth.

Obviously we bring our real world knowledge to the reading process when we encounter fictional intermental units. The frames that I will be describing entail the default assumption that our theory of mind works better with spouses, friends and immediate family than it does with total strangers. That is to say, we assume that the attributional success rate will be higher than average in such relationships. Sometimes, as we shall see, these default slots are filled; sometimes, when our assumptions are wrong, they are not. When there are misunderstandings, for example, the reader has to reconsider the nature of the relationship and amend the frame. In extreme cases, such as Anne's relationship with her father and older sister, major reconstruction is required. By the end of the novel, Anne almost abandons her family in her eagerness to embrace a new one.

The approach to characterisation taken in this essay assumes that the character of Anne Elliot cannot be seen in isolation. Her mind is public, social and engaged. In Bakhtinian terms, her mind is dialogic, frequently anticipating the views of others, successfully or not, and often judged by others, favourably or not. This inescapability of the social has a profound effect on the value judgements that are made about her mind and the minds of others. For example, Anne is generally judged favourably because she has an elegance of mind and a sweet character »which must have placed her high with any people of real understanding« (37). When Anne is deciding whether or not she likes Mr Elliot, she arrives at this damning judgement: »Mr Elliot was rational, discreet, polished, – but he was not open« (173). This word ›open‹ is an important one within the externalist perspective. For someone like Anne, whose default assumption about others is that their minds should work together to share the benefits of their mental functioning, honesty, good will and openness are vitally important. She likes people whose minds are responsive, spontaneous and generous. Closed minds are for those who favour the internalist perspective. Internalist thinking is solitary, mysterious, and detached, whereas externalist thought is social, evident and engaged, and, for Anne, these are moral choices.

The emphasis in the text on the social nature of cognitive functioning is relentless. In the discussion between Anne and Mr Elliot on what constitutes ›good company‹, this phrase is used seven times in ten lines (162). There are also references on the following page of the text to ›society‹, ›the connexion‹, ›your family‹, ›related‹, ›acquaintance‹, ›the relationship‹, ›acquaintance‹ (again) and ›society‹ (again). All of these terms convey a sense of the context of the large-scale group frame of society within which Anne as an individual and also her smaller scale relationships function. Anne's behaviour is inexplicable without an awareness of the pressures brought to bear on her by the group norms imposed by her society. The following two passages explicitly acknowledge that the social mind is the subject of the novel. Furthermore, they make it clear that Anne is aware that her mind is social:

> Anne had not wanted this visit to Uppercross, to learn that a removal from one set of people to another, though at a distance of only three miles, will often include a total change of conversation, opinion, and idea. [...]. Yet, with all this experience, she believed she must now submit to feel that another lesson, in the art of knowing our own nothingness beyond our own circle, was become necessary for her. (69)

> She acknowledged it to be very fitting, that every little social commonwealth should dictate its own matters of discourse; and hoped, ere long, to become a not unworthy member of the one she was now transplanted into. – With the prospect of spending at least two more months at Uppercross, it was highly incumbent on her to clothe her imagination, her memory, and all her ideas in as much of Uppercross as possible. (70)

These passages, in demonstrating beyond doubt the narrator's awareness of the externalist perspective, may surprise you (as they have surprised me) in spelling out so clearly the practical implications of the theoretical framework described in the previous section.

4 The Party

Despite her frequent longing for solitude, Anne is in fact very rarely alone. When she is not with her father and Elizabeth, she is generally part of a shifting, ever-changing group of people that I shall call *the party*. The composition of the party changes from day to day but the core of it consists of the following characters: Charles and Mary, Mr and Mrs Musgrove, Henrietta and Louisa, Admiral and Mrs Croft, Captain Wentworth, Captain and Mrs Harville, Captain Benwick and Charles Hayter. There are frequent references to Anne's feelings about the workings of the party and her relationship with it: Anne »admired again the sort of necessity which the family-habits seemed to produce, of every thing being to be communicated, and every thing being to be done together, however undesired and inconvenient« (106). »The two families were so continually meeting, so much in the habit of running in and out of each other's house at all hours, that it was rather a surprise to her to find Mary alone« (64). The use of the word ›Uppercross‹ in the two passages quoted in the previous paragraph is a synecdoche for the party. In fact, the identification of the party with Uppercross is frequently made: »Anne thought she left great happiness behind her when they quitted the house« (120); »Scenes had passed in Uppercross, which made it precious« (139); »Anne could not but feel that Uppercross was already quite alive again« (148); and Anne »looked back, with fond regret, to the bustles of Uppercross« (149).

Intermental units often engage in joint decision-making. For example, joint decisions have to be made by the party during the period after Louisa's accident. In the moments immediately following her fall, the party fractures into individuals. An initial decision, what to do with the injured Louisa, is required. However, it is an easy one for the group to make: »That Louisa must remain where she was, however distressing to her friends to be involving the Harvilles in such trouble, did not admit a doubt« (132). (As I explain in Palmer [2005], passive constructions are very common in the presentation of intermental functioning in fictional texts.) Later, more long-term plans are required. This time, the precise membership of the decision making group is specified:

> Charles, Henrietta and Captain Wentworth were the three in consultation, and for a little while it was only an interchange of perplexity and terror [...]. At first, they were capable of nothing more to the purpose than such exclamations [...]. The plan had reached this point [...]. The other two warmly agreed [...]. One thing more and all seemed arranged. (133–134)

Notice that, at first, they are capable only of sharing their emotions. However, they gradually find themselves able to take on the more cognitively oriented functions of short and medium term planning. This small group within the larger party then has second thoughts: »A much better scheme followed and was acted upon« (137). »It was soon determined that they would go« (138). It is clear that this small group is functioning well as a decision making intermental unit. It is decisive but, when flexibility is required, it is sufficiently flexible to change its mind and adopt a better plan.

As with all large groups, questions arise related to individuality and the self. The individual characters that are part of the group may be defined to a greater or lesser extent by their relationship with it. For example, Wentworth becomes the centre of attention within the group. There is »but one opinion of Captain Wentworth, among the Musgroves and their dependencies« (97). Unsurprisingly, thinking of leaving the party to visit his brother, »the attractions of Uppercross induced him to put this off. There was so much of friendliness, and of flattery, and of everything most bewitching in his reception there; the old were so hospitable, the young so agreeable« (97). Despite his partial absorption into the party, he remains a distinct character. By contrast, some of the members of the party such as Mrs Musgrove are difficult to imagine alone, as being an individual or a self apart from the party. At the other end of the scale from Mrs

Musgrove, there are tensions between certain individuals and the group. For example, Benwick's »spirits certainly did not seem fit for the mirth of the party in general« (121). Also, it is notable that, in the description of Louisa's accident, her behaviour is contrasted with the actions of the rest of the group: »All were contented to pass quietly and carefully down the steep flight, excepting Louisa« (129). Significantly, she is punished for her transgression of the group norms, and for taking too seriously Wentworth's passing preference for individuals who are un-persuaded by group pressures.

As is apparent from the references to Uppercross that are quoted above, Anne has ambivalent feelings about what she calls the »domestic hurricane« (149). Sometimes she enjoys it as a marked contrast to the sterility and coldness of her own family; at other times, she wishes to be alone. During the crisis in Bath, when what she really wants is some space, »she gave herself up to the demands of the party, to the needful civilities of the moment« (194), but with clearly marked reluctance. However, at the end of novel, the value to Anne of being part of this intermental unit is heavily underscored by the text. Anne is delightfully happy in being engaged again to Wentworth but one concern remains. Anne has »the consciousness of having no relations to bestow on him which a man of sense could value [...] nothing of respectability, of harmony, of good-will to offer in return for all the worth and all the prompt welcome which met her in his brothers and sisters« (252–253). As I mentioned earlier, Anne virtually abandons her own family and takes up a new, better one. Anne judges these units in ethical terms and is aware that the intermental unit of her own immediate family is of little value compared with the shared humanity and warmth of the party. Our default assumptions regarding the value of a family are questioned and the reader's family frame has to be adjusted.

5 Anne and Smaller Intermental Units

Anne's mind is constantly engaged with other minds and her knowledge of these minds is generally pretty good. »With a great deal of quiet observation, and a knowledge, which she often wished less, of her father's character« (62), Anne generally knows how Sir Walter's mind is going to work. When he and Elizabeth talk to Anne in exaggerated terms about their renewed acquaintance with Mr Elliot, »allowances, large allowances, she knew, must be made for the ideas of those who spoke« (153). Anne's perceptive »quiet observation« is often of the body language of others, in particular of their looks and glances. That Elizabeth and Mrs Clay agree on the merits of Mr Elliot »seemed apparent [to Anne] by a glance or two between them« (154). When Mr Elliot talks to Anne about his apparent suspicions of Mrs Clay, but without mentioning her name, »he looked, as he spoke, to the seat which Mrs Clay had been late occupying, a sufficient explanation of what he particularly meant« (163). Anne immediately knows what he means.[11] Nevertheless, the novel frequently shows that care should be taken with the interpretation of evidence of the apparent mental functioning of others. When Anne confronts Mrs Clay with the fact that she, Anne, saw her talking to Mr Elliot, »It seemed to her [Anne] that there was guilt in Mrs Clay's face as she listened« (232). Anne is right about Mrs Clay's feelings of guilt but wrong about their cause. Anne thinks that Mrs Clay feels guilty because she has been confronted by Mr Elliot about her designs on Sir Walter, whereas she actually behaves in a guilty manner because she thinks her affair with Mr Elliot has been discovered. In another example of half-successful, half-mistaken theory of mind, Mrs Smith says to Anne: »Your countenance perfectly informs me that you were in company last night with the person, whom you think the most agreeable in the world« (210). She is right, but wrong about the identity of the »most agreeable« person. It is not Mr Elliot, as Mrs Smith thinks, but Captain Wentworth. This confusion throws Mrs Smith so completely that she later says: »Now, how I do wish I understood you! How I do wish I knew what you were at!« (203)

One of the major reasons for theory of mind breakdowns is solipsism – the tendency that we all have to forget that other people have minds and that they work differently from ours. Anne is very conscious of this tendency in herself. She has to remind herself that not everyone knows or even cares about her feelings. Most of the time, as shown in the examples given so far, her reminders to herself work. She is usually acutely conscious of other minds and knows that it is sometimes not possible to predict the reactions of others: »She had spoken it; but she trembled when it was done, conscious that her words were listened to, and daring not even to try to observe their effect« (229). But at other times, as Anne herself knows, her tendency to solipsism can get the better of her. On one occasion, Anne thinks that Mrs Croft is talking about Captain Wentworth when she is in fact referring to her other brother, Mr Wentworth. Anne »immediately felt how reasonable it was, that Mrs Croft should be thinking and speaking of Edward, and not of Frederick; and with shame at her own forgetfulness, applied herself to the knowledge of [Edward's] present state, with proper interest« (75). Anne notices immediately that

---

11 For more on the importance of the look, see Palmer: Social.

her ›forgetfulness‹ is of the fact that Mrs Croft's mind works differently from hers. She is understandably so absorbed in Wentworth's coming that she forgets that others will not feel the same way and this causes the misreading of Mrs Croft's mind. Another example of Anne's (admittedly fairly mild) solipsistic tendency is an elaborate set piece that takes up a whole page of text. When Anne is walking in Bath with Lady Russell she sees Captain Wentworth approaching on the other side of the road. During the course of a long paragraph Anne attributes a variety of states of mind to Lady Russell on the assumption that she has seen him and she still disapproves of him. Finally, however, Lady Russell bathetically reveals that all she has been thinking about are curtains! On hearing this, »Anne sighed and blushed and smiled, in pity and disdain, either at her friend or herself« (189).

More generally, the last misunderstanding is indicative of the complexity of the intermental unit formed by the friendship of Anne and Lady Russell. Although Lady Russell is referred to as Anne's »one very intimate friend« (36), the narrator also mentions that, after her refusal of Wentworth, Anne and Lady Russell »knew not each other's opinion, either its constancy or its change« (57). »It was now some years since Anne had begun to learn that she and her excellent friend could sometimes think differently« (160). Indeed, the point is then repeated: »They did not always think alike« (160). However, the friendship is later restored. When Anne discovers Mr Elliot's true nature, she knew that »She must talk to Lady Russell, tell her, consult with her« (218). And, when matters are resolved, »Anne knew that Lady Russell must be suffering some pain in understanding and relinquishing Mr Elliot, and be making some struggles to become truly acquainted with, and do justice to Captain Wentworth« (251). Anne's theory of mind has repaired the intermental unit.

The Croft marriage is an interesting attributional case study. On the one hand, the strongly intermental nature of the relationship between the Admiral and Mrs Croft is frequently emphasised. In Uppercross, »The Admiral and Mrs Croft were generally out of doors together [...] dawdling about in a way not endurable to a third person« (97). In Bath, they »brought with them their country habit of being almost always together [...]. [Anne] delighted to fancy she understood what they might be talking of« (179). Anne responds to them as a couple, not as individuals: The Crofts »were people whom her heart turned to very naturally« (174). While thinking about her earlier engagement to Wentworth, she pays them this heartfelt tribute:

> With the exception, perhaps, of Admiral and Mrs Croft, who seemed particularly attached and happy, (Anne could allow no other exception even among the married couples) there could have been no two hearts so open, no tastes so similar, no feelings so in unison, no countenances so beloved (88).

In addition to her emotional response to them, Anne is also aware that they function as a cognitive unit. She watches the Crofts »with some amusement at their style of driving«, which involves them taking joint decisions on the steering, and »which she imagined no bad representation of the general guidance of their affairs« (114). There is only one occasion on which they are of different minds. When the Admiral warmly praises the Musgrove girls as possible objects of Wentworth's affection, Mrs Croft refers to them »in a tone of calmer praise, such as made Anne suspect that her keener powers might not consider either of them as quite worthy of her brother« (114).

On the other hand, much is also made in the text of the Crofts' regular attributional breakdowns with others. At one point, the Admiral talks to Wentworth »without taking any observation of what he might be interrupting, thinking only of his own thoughts« (92–93). When Anne wishes to be reassured by the Admiral that Wentworth is not grieving over losing Louisa to Captain Benwick, he is not sensitive enough to pick up on her emotional needs and »Anne did not receive the perfect conviction which the Admiral meant to convey« (183). To do him credit, he is sensitive enough to wish to convey the reassurance, but not sufficiently attuned to the workings of other minds to do so successfully. In addition, there is an enjoyably comic example of Mrs Croft's solipsism. She is very insistent to Mrs Musgrove about not referring to Bermuda or the Bahamas as »the West Indies«: »Mrs Musgrove had not a word to say in dissent; she could not accuse herself of having ever called them any thing in the whole course of her life« (94). It is an interesting question whether or not it is a coincidence that the two individuals in the tightest intermental unit in the novel are also amongst the most solipsistic in their relations with others.

6 Anne and Wentworth

The key to the novel is the construction of Wentworth's mind by Anne and by the reader. The central question posed by the text is: What does he now think of her? He appears at first to have no feelings for her and then it becomes slowly apparent that he does still love her. A noticeable feature of the novel is the urgency of the need for accurate mind reading; Anne experiences intense feelings of anguish towards the end of the novel when she is not sure what Wentworth is thinking. Her record is patchy. Sometimes she knows what he is thinking. »When he talked, she heard the same voice, and discerned the same mind« (88–89). And when he talks lightly of being ready to make a foolish match: »He said it, she knew, to be contradicted« (86). At other times she does not know. It is odd that the small intermental unit consisting of Anne and Wentworth is one that does not function particularly well. (It should be said, however, that this is consistent with the default assumptions for the cognitive frame for lovers, in which we assume, for example that the course of true love never runs smooth.)

Generally, as I hope to show below, Anne's knowledge of Wentworth's views on *others* is invariably accurate, but much less so what he is thinking about *her*. When Wentworth is listening to Mrs Musgrove becoming sentimental about her useless son, »there was a momentary expression in Captain Wentworth's face at this speech, a certain glance of his bright eye, and curl of his handsome mouth, which convinced Anne« that she knew what he was thinking, »but it was too transient an indulgence of self-amusement to be detected by any who understood him less than herself« (92). Anne can always discern his views on her family. When Mary makes an excessively snobbish remark to him about the Hayters, she »received no other answer, than an artificial, assenting smile, followed by a contemptuous glance, as he turned away, which Anne perfectly knew the meaning of« (19). And when Anne sees Elizabeth snub Wentworth in the shop in Bath:

> It did not surprise, but it grieved Anne to observe that Elizabeth would not know him. She saw that he saw Elizabeth, that Elizabeth saw him, that there was complete internal recognition on each side; she was convinced that he was ready to be acknowledged as an acquaintance, expecting it, and she had the pain of seeing her sister turn away with unalterable coldness. (186)[12]

Later, when Sir Walter and Elizabeth ostentatiously offer him a visiting card because they know that he will ›look well‹ in their drawing room, Anne »knew him; she saw disdain in his eye« (231).

However, Anne's knowledge of his feelings about her is much patchier. It is fascinating to follow the fluctuations in their relationship in terms of the successes and failures in their theory of mind. At the beginning, Anne lacks any knowledge of his state of mind. Before they meet again, »She would have liked to know how he felt as to such a meeting. Perhaps indifferent, if indifference could exist under such circumstances. He must be either indifferent or unwilling« (83). When she discovers that the latter possibility is the correct one: »Anne understood it. He wished to avoid seeing her« (84); »Anne felt the utter impossibility, from her knowledge of his mind, that he could be unvisited by remembrance any more than

---

[12] For a treatment of this scene as an example of ›deep intersubjectivity‹, see Butte: Subjects, p. 3.

herself« (88); and »She understood him. He could not forgive her, – but he could not be unfeeling« (113). In fact, though, Anne does not understand him; she is unaware of his growing renewed love for her. However, she slowly begins to understand him more and to interpret his behavioural clues correctly. In the scene in Lyme in which Anne, Wentworth and Mr Elliot meet briefly, it seems to Anne that Wentworth sees that Mr Elliot is attracted to her:

> It was evident that the gentleman [...] admired her exceedingly. Captain Wentworth looked round at her instantly in a way which shewed his noticing of it. He gave her a momentary glance, – a glance of brightness, which seemed to say, ›That man is struck with you, – and even I, at this moment, see something like Anne Elliot again‹. (125)

But, even in Bath, her knowledge of his mind is patchy: »He was more obviously struck and confused by the sight of her, than she had ever observed before; he looked quite red [...]. The character of his manner was embarrassment. She could not have called it either cold or friendly, or any thing so certainly as embarrassed« (185). This is another example of partially successful theory of mind. She knows his mind well enough to know that he is embarrassed, but not well enough to know why. However, typically, she knows that she does not know what is troubling him: »She could not understand his present feelings, whether he was really suffering much from disappointment or not; and till that point was settled, she could not be quite herself« (187). Similarly, »Either from the consciousness, however, that his friend had recovered, or from other consciousness, he went no farther« (192). Anne does not know which.

Finally, Anne realises that Wentworth does love her. The point at which she realises it reads like an attribution manual in its analysis of the behavioural clues on which theory of mind rests. For this reason, the passage is worth quoting in full:

> His choice of subjects, his expressions, and still more his manner and look, had been such as she could see in only one light. His opinion of Louisa Musgrove's inferiority, an opinion which he seemed solicitous to give, his wonder at Captain Benwick, his feelings as to a first, strong attachment, – sentences begun which he could not finish – his half averted eyes, and more than half expressive glance, – all, all declared that he had a heart returning to her at least; that anger, resentment, avoidance, were no more; and that they were succeeded, not merely by friendship and regard, but by the tenderness of the past. She could not contemplate the change as implying less. – He must love her. (195)

But a problem remains – his jealousy of Mr Elliot. Anne does not realise this at first: »Anne knew not how to understand him« (239). As above, she knows that something is the matter but does not know for sure what it is: »She saw him not far off. He saw her too; yet he looked grave, and seemed irresolute, and only by very slow degrees came at last near enough to speak to her. She felt that something must be the matter. The change was indubitable« (198). She correctly guesses the reason why: »Jealousy of

Mr Elliot! It was the only intelligible motive« (199). Later, her guess is confirmed: »She had not mistaken him. Jealousy of Mr Elliot had been the retarding weight, the doubt, the torment« (243). In the meantime, the reader is given the only direct access to Wentworth's side of the intermental relationship and, significantly, it is put in theory of mind terms. In his letter to her, he cried out in evident exasperation and suffering, »For you alone I think and plan. – Have you not seen this? Can you fail to have understood my wishes?« (240)

7 Conclusion

Both perspectives on fictional minds, the internalist and the externalist, are required. Nevertheless, within this balance, I have emphasised social minds because they have been neglected up until now by characterisation theory. My intention in quoting so frequently from the novel was to show that these social minds are woven into the fabric of its discourse. I hope that the weight of evidence presented in this essay is sufficient to prove the point. As to whether or not the conclusions reached here regarding the social minds in this novel can also be applied to other novels, more research is required.

In this essay I have argued that we have to be as flexible as possible in considering the types of cognitive frames that are applied by readers in the construction of fictional character. In particular, what I have called group frames have to be put in place in order to understand individual characters. However, I have held back from arguing that there are intermental units in *Persuasion* that can be considered as characters in their own right. Perhaps the Crofts are the most likely candidates, but they are, I think, a marginal case. In Palmer (2005), I argued that the town of Middlemarch is sufficiently well defined to be considered as a character, indeed a major character, in the novel of that name. However, I am not sure that this is the case in *Persuasion*. The position on the existence or otherwise of intermental or group characters will vary from novel to novel.

As I began with examples of some of the large scale group cognitive frames relating to characterisation before going on to discuss medium- and then small-sized frames, I would like to conclude with a passage that brings us full circle by combining all three. The novel ends with Anne and Wentworth together. She is adjusting to her new life, and getting used to how her mind will be working together with other minds, and particularly Wentworth's, in the future. This passage beautifully encapsulates the functioning of Anne's social mind in action by showing her at the centre of an intermental network:

> Mr Elliot was there; she avoided, but she could pity him. [...] Lady Dalrymple and Miss Carteret; they would soon be innoxious cousins to her. She cared not for Mrs Clay, and had nothing to blush for in the public manners of her father and sister. With the Musgroves, there was the happy chat of perfect ease; with Captain Harville the kind-hearted intercourse of brother and sister; with Lady Russell, attempts at conversation, which a delicious consciousness cut short; with Admiral and Mrs Croft, every thing of peculiar cordiality and fervent interest, which the same consciousness sought to conceal; – and with Captain Wentworth, some moments of communication continually occurring, and always the hope of more, and always the knowledge of his being there. (247–248)

References

Austen, Jane: Persuasion [1818]. D. W. Harding (Ed.). Harmondsworth 1965.
Bakhtin, Mikhail: Problems of Dostoevsky's Poetics. Transl. by Caryl Emerson. Manchester 1984.
Bateson, Gregory: Steps to an Ecology of Mind: A Revolutionary Approach to Man's Understanding of Himself. New York 1972.
Butte, George: I Know That You Know That I Know: Narrating Subjects from Moll Flanders to Marnie. Columbus 2004.
Clark, Andy / David J. Chalmers: The Extended Mind. In: Analysis 58 (1998), pp. 7–19.
Damasio, Antonio: The Feeling of What Happens: Body, Emotion and the Making of Consciousness. London 2000.
Dennett, Daniel C.: Kinds of Minds: Towards an Understanding of Consciousness. London 1996.
Fludernik, Monika: Towards a ›Natural‹ Narratology. London 1996.
Geertz, Clifford: The Interpretation of Cultures: Selected Essays. London 1993.
Herman, David: Scripts, Sequences, and Stories: Elements of a Postclassical Narratology. In: PMLA 112/5 (1997), pp. 1046–1059.
Herman, David: Stories as a Tool for Thinking. In: D.H. (Ed.): Narrative Theory and the Cognitive Sciences. Stanford 2003, pp. 163–192.
Herman, David: Regrounding Narratology: The Study of Narratively Organized Systems for Thinking. In: Tom Kindt / Hans-Harald Müller (Eds.): What is Narratology: Questions and Answers Regarding the Status of a Theory. Berlin 2003, pp. 303–332.
Hutchins, Edwin: Cognition in the Wild. Cambridge, MA 1995.
Ingarden, Roman: The Literary Work of Art: An Investigation on the Borderlines of Ontology, Logic, and Theory of Literature. Transl. by George C. Grabowicz. Evanston 1973.
Iser, Wolfgang: The Act of Reading. London 1978.
Jahn, Manfred: Frames, Preferences, and the Reading of Third Person Narratives: Towards a Cognitive Narratology. In: Poetics Today 18/4 (1997), pp. 441–468.
James, Henry: The Portrait of a Lady [1881]. Geoffrey Moore (Ed.). Harmondsworth 1984.
Margolin, Uri: Telling Our Story: On ›We‹ Literary Narratives. In: Language and Literature 5/2 (1996), pp. 115–133.

Margolin, Uri: Telling in the Plural: From Grammar to Ideology. In: Poetics Today 21/3 (2000), pp. 591–618.
Palmer, Alan: Fictional Minds. Lincoln 2004.
Palmer, Alan: Intermental Thought in the Novel: The Middlemarch Mind. In: Style 39/4 (2005), pp. 427–439.
Palmer, Alan: Attribution Theory: Action and Emotion in Dickens and Pynchon. In: Marina Lambrou / Peter Stockwell (Eds.): Contemporary Stylistics. London 2007, pp. 81–92.
Palmer, Alan: Social Minds in Little Dorrit. (Forthcoming).
Schank, Roger C. / Robert P. Abelson: Scripts, Plans, Goals, and Understanding: An Inquiry into Human Knowledge Structures. Hillsdale 1977.
Semino, Elena: Blending and Characters' Mental Functioning in Virginia Woolf's Lappin and Lapinova. In: Language and Literature 15/1 (2006), pp. 55–72.
Sperber, Dan / Lawrence Hirschfeld: Culture, Cognition, and Evolution. In: Robert Wilson / Frank Keil (Eds.): The MIT Encyclopedia of the Cognitive Sciences. Cambridge, MA 1999, pp. cxi-cxxxii.
Wertsch, James V.: Voices of the Mind: A Sociocultural Approach to Mediated Action. Cambridge, MA 1991.
Zunshine, Lisa: Why We Read Fiction: Theory of Mind and the Novel. Columbus 2006.

JONATHAN CULPEPER / DAN MCINTYRE

Activity Types and Characterisation in Dramatic Discourse

1 Introduction

This paper aims to enhance our understanding of how characterisation works in dramatic texts, whether written for the stage or the film screen, and to futher the development of a stylistics of drama. Regarding characterisation, we aim to contribute both to an understanding of how characters are constructed in texts by writers and to how they are conceived by readers. Our approach to characterisation, therefore, involves combining linguistic analysis with insights and models from cognitive science, and might be referred to as cognitive stylistic. It is an approach that has been championed by, notably, Culpeper and Schneider. Regarding the ontology of character, in our view, whilst fictional characters have a passive existence in texts or in people's minds, it is only in the interaction between texts and minds that they attain actual existence. Characters in texts without readers are just patterns of ink on the page; minds without texts (or other media, such as film) are empty of character (or, assuming past exposure to texts, just collections of memories about characters). Regarding the stylistics of drama, we hope to assist in the redress of the quantitative imbalance in work investigating the different literary genres: The quantity of work on drama pales into insignificance compared with work on poetry and prose.[1] Even less work has looked at language and characterisation in plays.[2] It should be noted here that, whilst we keep issues of performance in mind, our focus is on the reading of play-texts.[3]

---

1 See Culpeper / Short / Verdonk: Drama, pp. 3–4, for a discussion as to why this might be.
2 See Culpeper: Language; McIntyre: Plays; Pfister: Drama.
3 A justification of this approach can be found in Short: Performance.

Central to this paper is the notion of ›activity type‹.[4] In a nutshell, an activity type (such as a seminar, a family dinner event, or a birthday party) is a collection of particular speech acts (such as requests, questions and offers) that stand in particular pragmatic relationships to each other and have become a relatively conventionalised whole. Contrary to this, treatments of the language of plays tend to be relatively atomistic in approach;[5] that is to say, they adopt frameworks that treat a specific dimension of the dialogue, or even individual segments of dialogue. Moreover, activity types involve an approach to context that is particularly suited to the dialogue of plays, since this approach involves language determining context rather than the opposite, which is more often the case in traditional pragmatic approaches to context. As far as characterisation is concerned, individual speech acts have an important role, because they embody speakers' intentions and are realized in ways that reflect the speaker's position in social space. Furthermore, activity types have a cognitive dimension and thus play a role in the knowledge-based inferencing that is so important in ›fleshing out‹ our conceptions of characters.

The first part of this paper elaborates the notion of activity type, and concludes with a focus on one specific kind of activity type, the ›interview‹. In the following part, we apply this notion in the analysis of four extracts from plays (or screen-plays). Finally, we consider the implications of what we have discussed and demonstrated in the paper for drama and characterisation.

2 Activity Types

2.1 The Notion of an Activity Type

The pragmatic notion of an activity type is usually credited to Stephen Levinson, though similar notions can be seen in earlier research.[6] Indeed, Levinson himself acknowledges that his work on activity types was inspired by Wittgenstein,[7] where he comments that understanding the

---

4 Levinson: Language.
5 As exemplified in the studies in Culpeper / Short / Verdonk: Drama.
6 E.g. Allwood: Communication.
7 Wittgenstein: Investigations.

meaning of utterances involves knowing the activity within which those utterances play a role.

The notion of activity type, according to Levinson, refers to:

> [...] any culturally recognized activity, whether or not that activity is coextensive with a period of speech or indeed whether any talk takes place in it at all [...] In particular, I take the notion of an activity type to refer to a fuzzy category whose focal members are goal-defined, socially constituted, bounded events with *constraints* on participants, setting, and so on, but above all on the kinds of allowable contributions. Paradigm examples would be teaching, a job interview, a jural interrogation, a football game, a task in a workshop, a dinner party, and so on.[8]

He goes on to say that:

> Because of the strict constraints on contributions to any particular activity, there are corresponding strong expectations about the functions that any utterances at a certain point in the proceedings can be fulfilling.[9]

This has the important consequence that:

> to each and every clearly demarcated activity there is a corresponding set of *inferential schemata*.[10]

> [Activity types] help to determine how what one says will be ›taken‹ – that is, what kinds of inferences will be made from what is said.[11]

As can be seen from these quotations, activity types involve both what interactants do in constituting the activity and the corresponding knowledge one has of that activity. We will examine each of these two sides of activity types in turn.

2.2 The Notion of an Activity Type: The Cognitive Dimension

Despite indicating that every activity type has a ›corresponding set of *inferential schemata*‹, Levinson says nothing more about the cognitive aspect of activity types, except to point out in very general terms the implications for understanding language within particular activity types. Similarly, subsequent researchers have paid little attention to this dimension. But it is a crucial part of how meanings are generated and understood in interaction. Participants use knowledge about a speech activity (e.g. its speech acts, participants, settings, and so on) in interpreting and managing the particular activity they are engaged in. For example, ›how are you?‹ is a

---

8   Levinson: Language, p. 69.
9   Ibid., p. 79.
10 Ibid., p. 72.
11 Ibid., p. 97.

typical phatic question in many circumstances, but this would be an unlikely interpretation in the context of a doctor-patient consultation. Levinson saw activity types as rescuing the more general inferential framework of the ›Cooperative Principle‹,[12] which could not account for the more particular knowledge-based inferences drawn in particular situations. ›Inferential schemata‹ are a mechanism for such knowledge-based inferencing.

Let us explore the notion of schemata a little further. Schema theory is a theory of human knowledge, propounded by cognitive psychologists and researchers from other fields.[13] According to Eysenck and Keane »[t]he term *schema* is used to refer to well integrated chunks of knowledge about the world, events, people, and actions«.[14] Schemata enable us to construct an interpretation that contains more than the information we receive from the text. We can supply, or infer, extra bits of information from our schematic knowledge. If the lack of some particular textually-derived information is preventing the formation of an adequate interpretation, we can simply supply the default value from the relevant schema (i.e. what normally fills that particular slot in the schema network). To use the classic example, a schema for a restaurant contains role slots (e.g. waiters, customers), slots for props (e.g. tables, the menu), and slots for scenes or actions (e.g. entering, ordering, eating). Such a schema would allow us to infer, for example, that the tables have legs (even if they are obscured by the tablecloths), that a chef is cooking the food in the kitchen (even if they cannot be seen), and that we will not be prevented from leaving the restaurant once we have paid the bill. Thus, a schema provides a contextual framework for comprehension. Neisser suggests that »schemata are anticipations, they are the medium by which the past affects the future«.[15] Once activated, a schema gives rise to expectations (i.e. the default values of particular slots).

There are various versions of schema theory, developed in different fields (e.g. cognitive psychology, artificial intelligence) with slightly different emphases and often different labels (e.g. ›schema‹, ›script‹, ›frame‹, ›scenario‹). It is worth noting that the version devised by Schank and Abelson using the label ›script‹ has some particular affinities with activity types. Schank and Abelson describe a script as:

---

12 Grice: Logic.
13 E.g. Bartlett: Psychology; Minsky: Framework; Neisser: Cognition; Rumelhart: Schemata; Schank / Abelson: Inquiry.
14 Eysenck / Keane: Handbook, p. 352.
15 Neisser: Cognition, p. 22.

> A structure that describes appropriate sequences of events in a particular context [...] scripts handle stylised everyday situations [...] [a] script is a predetermined, stereotyped sequence of actions that defined a well-known situation.[16]

This seems to be knowledge about the kind of activity type that Levinson had in mind – a conventionalised bundle of contextualised actions. We will, however, maintain the use of the word *schema*, in recognition of its wider use in cognitive psychology and social cognition.

Schank and Abelson's model was later updated in Schank (1982 and 1999).[17] This is not the place to review those updates. However, we shall briefly note some key points of interest, particularly with regard to how activity types might be linked to the notion of plot. The general thrust of Schank's subsequent work is to propose knowledge structures working at various levels of generality, and in doing so enabled experiences which could not be captured at a more specific level to be captured at a more general level. Scripts are, in fact, at the most specific end of the scale. The next more general level consists of ›scenes‹. We can illustrate this distinction with the notion of an ›interview‹. There are various types of interview, including a ›job interview‹, ›school entrance interview‹, ›police interview‹ and ›news interview‹. Each of these is a particular script; all these scripts are embedded in a more general structure, the interview scene. Scenes include a setting, and instrumental goal and actions, whereas scripts are more focused on just the actions or one set of possible actions within the scene.[18] In our upcoming analyses, we examine the ›interview‹ scene, as we consider both dramatic job interviews and a police interview. Strictly speaking then, this paper is about the interview scene in plays rather than an interview script or activity type. At a more general level than scenes we have ›memory organisation packets‹ (MOPs), and above that ›meta-MOPs‹. MOPs organise other memory structures, such as scenes, into appropriate sequences. They consist of »a set of scenes directed towards the achievement of a goal«.[19] Thus, a possible MOP might be ›getting a job‹, consisting of scenes such as ›searching the newspaper ads‹, ›constructing a CV‹, ›applying for a job‹, ›job interview‹, ›accepting the job‹, and so on. A meta-MOP, as the label hints, organises MOPs. What we are beginning to see here are high-level structures created out of actions and sequences of actions – out of activity types. This is also where we can begin to see a link with plot, as plots are high-level structures created out of actions. Schank introduced one further high-level

---

16 Schank / Abelson: Inquiry, p. 41.
17 Schrank: Memory (1982); Schrank: Memory Revisited (1999).
18 Ibid., p. 86.
19 Ibid., p. 86.

structure, that is, ›thematic organisation points‹ (TOPs). These are designed to highlight the similarities and parallels between different areas of knowledge. In fact, Schank's key example involves similarities between plots. The reason why the plot of *West Side Story* strikes us as similar to that of *Romeo and Juliet* is because they share a TOP, consisting of such features as young lovers with mutual desire to be together despite external opposition, yet coming to a tragic end after a false report of death.

2.3 Activity Types: The Interactional Dimension

How are activity types constituted in interactional terms? Or, to put it another way, what analytical framework does one need to account for the interactional characteristics of an activity type? Levinson himself gives some clues, referring to, for example, ›participants, setting‹ and, most importantly of all, ›allowable contributions‹.[20] He is less explicit about what constitutes a ›contribution‹, but it seems from his analyses that they are conceived of largely in terms of particular speech acts. Subsequent researchers have sought to clarify and detail the ways in which activity types are interactionally constituted. Thomas,[21] for example, provides a list of elements, including:
– The goals of the participants
– Allowable contributions
– The degree to which Gricean maxims are adhered to or are suspended
– The degree to which interpersonal maxims (cf. Leech's Politeness Principle, 1983) are adhered to or are suspended
– Turn-taking and topic control
– The manipulation of pragmatic parameters (e.g. power, social distance)

Clearly, this is a wide-ranging list. This comprehensiveness, coupled with the cognitive dimension, means that activity types accommodate »a wide range of concepts as they operate at different levels of language production and interpretation«, something which Sarangi sees as a particular strength of the activity type.[22] However, the ability to accommodate a wide range of interaction phenomena is double-edged in that one might also see it as something of a weakness: how are we to

---

20 Levinson: Language, p. 96.
21 Thomas: Meaning, pp. 190–192.
22 Sarangi: Activity types, p. 3.

describe one activity type as opposed to another, if what constitutes that activity type can be practically anything?

In fact, Sarangi himself suggests a possible solution, introducing the notion of ›discourse type‹ as a means of characterising the forms of talk occurring within activity types. He defines discourse types as

> specific manifestations of language form in their interactional contexts (e.g., ranging from utterance types such as ›how are you?‹, ›what are we doing here?‹ to the sequential organisation of questions and answers as in a cross-examination, to stylistic features as in promotional talk). While activity type is a means of characterising settings (e.g., a medical consultation, a service encounter, a university seminar), discourse type is a way of characterising forms of talk (e.g., medical history taking, promotional talk, interrogation, troubles telling, etc.).[23]

The key point here is that discourse types refer to *forms* of talk (›stylistic, sequential and structural properties‹) used strategically, whereas activity types also include *contextual* factors (cf. Thomas's list above), which can constrain and affect the interpretation of discourse types. This is not to say that the description of discourse types is necessarily straightforward, not least of all because they have fuzzy edges, and are tricky to label in such a way that they are distinct from activity types. Nevertheless, they are useful. Our analyses of dramatic texts will focus on forms of talk.

Recently, the notion of activity types has enjoyed renewed popularity after several years in the wilderness.[24] The timing of this resurgence parallels a general shift within linguistics of thinking about context. Traditional approaches to context take the view that it is external to the text and relatively stable – it is in some sense ›out there‹. This might be described as the ›outside in‹ approach to context and language; in other words, the analyst looks at how the context shapes the language. But the reverse is also possible. Gumperz's notion of ›contextualization cues‹ are based on this idea. He defines them as »those verbal signs that are indexically associated with specific classes of communicative activity types and thus signal the frame of context for the interpretation of constituent messages«.[25] This might be described as the ›inside out‹ approach to context and language; in other words, the analyst looks at how language is used to shape the context. Of course, in reality meanings are generated through an interaction between both context and language.

---

[23] Ibid., pp. 1–2. See also Fairclough: Language; Fairclough: Awareness; Hasan: Talk, for a related notion.

[24] E.g. Thomas: Meaning, Chapter 7; Allwood: Pragmatics; Sarangi: Activity types; Culpeper / Semino: Speech Acts; Linell / Thunqvist: Framings.

[25] Gumperz: Interviewing, p. 307; see also Gumperz: Discourse; Gumperz: Language; Gumperz: Contextualization.

2.4 The ›Interview‹ Activity Type

Since we are claiming in this paper that the way that characters use language is in part what defines the extracts from the dramatic texts we analyse as interviews, it will be useful first of all to consider what some of the common linguistic structures of this activity type are. Conversation Analysis provides a starting point. Button analyses an interview of a comprehensive school head of department for the position of head of the school's arts faculty, in order to demonstrate what he calls an ›interview orthodoxy‹ which is »constituted in the organization of sequential structures«.[26] Button points out that interviews are, obviously enough, composed of a series of questions and answers, and that answers differ from other classes of utterance (for example, commands and invitations) by exhibiting an awareness on the part of the respondent of the meaning of the prior utterance – i.e. the preceding question. As a result of this, Button explains, »answers are a resource whereby hearers can monitor a speaker's apparent understanding of the question«.[27] Much in the interview is structured around this basic idea of monitoring and assessing the candidate's ability to give satisfactory answers to questions, however those questions might be formulated. Through a series of examples, Button demonstrates some of the defining elements of an interview orthodoxy that arise from his data:

- In everyday conversation, misunderstandings of questions are usually corrected by the questioner at the first available transition relevance place. However, in the job interview transcript that Button analyses, this does not happen.
- In the job interview activity type no provision is made for answers to extend over several turns or for clarification to be requested by the interviewee (cf. everyday conversational behaviour).
- The turns that follow the candidate's answers fulfil one of three functions, all of which preclude the candidate from revising his or her original answer. The three functions are:
  - To signal to the candidate that the questioning is at an end.
  - To ask a further question but one which is unrelated to the topic of the preceding question to which the answer has just been supplied.
  - To provide an assessment of the candidate's answer.

---

26 Button: Answers, p. 214.
27 Ibid., p. 215.

- Of the three types of turn-function listed above, Button notes that only the third allows the candidate the possibility of returning to his/her answer. In practice though, Button shows how, in his data, the interviewer speeds up his speech as he approaches a transition relevance place, in order to prevent the candidate from returning to his answer in order to modify it.
- The candidate's first answer is taken to be absolutely complete and no clarification is asked for.
- The candidate is not allowed any opportunity to revise his/her answer in the light of the interviewer's understanding of it. Consequently the interviewee has no »resource through which he can determine how his answers are being understood«.[28]

These practices, says Button, ›sustain an interview orthodoxy‹ and are consequently elements that we might expect to see in all variations of the interview activity type (i.e. the interview scene).[29] Further defining elements of the interview activity type can be found in the work of Gumperz,[30] though as these refer mostly to prosody we will not consider these here.

In addition to the conversation-analytic sequential practices and contextualization conventions decribed above, we must also consider a wide range of other types of knowledge which feed into the job interview schema. This might include assumptions about the order in which questioning occurs, who is likely to be on the interviewing panel and what they might be dressed like, etc., as well as linguistic assumptions about turn length, register and appropriate propositional content. In cases where these schematic assumptions are not met, or where the sequential practices and contextualization conventions common to the job interview activity type are not apparent, we might expect a foregrounding effect to be generated, with consequences for our interpretation of character.

From the elements discussed above we can extract a general summary of some (but not all) of the conventional linguistic/pragmatic and schematic elements of a job interview activity type in a British cultural context (NB all of these should be seen as prototypical rather than absolute):[31]

---

28 Button: Answers, p. 226.
29 Ibid., p. 227.
30 Gumperz: Interviewing.
31 Strictly speaking, the first and the last items we list are not part of the activity type descriptions in the literature or of descriptions of the formal aspects of activity types (i.e. discourse types). However, activity types must be located in and are indeed

- *Setting.* Usually a formal environment, often connected to the interview (e.g. a job interview would be in the workplace of the applied-for job, a police interview would be at the police station). The interviewer is often positioned behind a desk.
- *Participants and their social roles.* One or more interviewer and usually one interviewee. Adults, formally dressed.
- *Goals.* Interviewee: to secure the job. Interviewer: to appoint the best candidate for the job.
- *Social parameters:* Asymmetric power relations (interviewer possesses institutional power which overrides any other type of power possessed by the interviewee). Usually strangers.
- *Norms of information exchange.*[32] Interviewee/interviewer: information exchanged is relevant to the job and the candidate's suitability for it; Interviewee: the maxims of quantity and quality are relaxed.
- *Politeness norms.* Interviewee: modesty is relaxed.[33]
- *Possible discourse types.* Interviewer: questioning/directing/summarising; interviewee: explaining/justifying/exemplifying/elaborating.
- *Conversation structure.* Interviewee: takes longest turns and most turns. Interviewer: initiates the interaction and controls the topic.
- *Register.* Formal speech, standard dialect.
- *Norms of interpretation.* Interviewee: takes questions and assertions as requests or opportunities for elaboration. Interviewer: takes the management of answers as the focal point of assessment of the candidate's suitability.

We will refer back to these prototypical elements of the interview activity type in the analyses that follow. First, though, let us examine the relationship between activity types and the linguistic and cognitive processes of characterisation.

---

assiciated with particular settings, and so it makes sense to record these too. Also, activity types give rise to particular ways of interpreting behaviours, and it seems reasonable to suppose that these become, over time, a conventional part of the activity type. Both setting and norms of interpretation are in fact features of Hymes's (1972) description of ›speech events‹.

32 Cf. Grice: Logic.
33 Cf. Leech's Politeness Principle in Leech: Principles.

3 Activity Types, Dramatic Texts and Characterisation

A number of researchers have applied speech act theory (Austin 1967; Searle 1969) to dramatic texts, in order to explain how playwrights have deployed speech acts in characterisation and exploited particular speech acts for dramatic effect.[34] Hurst, analysing the characters of Ivy Compton-Burnett's *A Family and a Fortune*, remarks: »[w]e can see how certain personalities gravitate toward certain speech acts«.[35] In fact, the idea that ›certain personalities‹ correlate with certain ›acts‹ is the basic premise behind attribution theories in social psychology.[36] The type of speech act to which a character might gravitate reveals aspects of character because each speech act has contextual implications for character. For a speech act to achieve success, certain ›felicity conditions‹ need to be in place.[37] For example, for a command to be successful, it presumably requires a ›preparatory condition‹ such that the balance of power lies with the speaker;[38] for an apology to be successful, it presumably requires a ›sincerity condition‹ such that the speaker expresses their psychological state of ›sorryness‹.[39] In addition to analysing *what* speech acts characters use, we also need to consider *how* they perform their speech acts. Searle, for example, drew attention to the fact that grammatical sentence types did not always match the illocutionary force traditionally associated with them.[40] For example, ›Pass the salt‹ contains a match between imperative form and requestive force. However, ›Can you pass the salt‹ uses an interrogative form to achieve the requestive force. This is, in Searle's terms, an indirect speech act. Indirect speech acts, depending on context, correlate with the perception of greater politeness,[41] and such perceptions can be taken as evidence of aspects of character, such as social adeptness, weakness or oilyness.[42]

In fact, the link between characterisation and speech acts is fundamental.

---

34 See, for example, Hurst: Speech Acts and Lowe Confessions.
35 Hurst: Speech Acts, p. 356.
36 See Culpeper: Language, Chapter 3, for details.
37 Austin: Words.
38 Searle: Speech Acts.
39 Ibid.; see also McIntyre: Drama, p. 151.
40 Searle: Indirect Speech Acts.
41 Leech: Pragmatics.
42 Culpeper: Language, Chapter 5.

Downes states that

> Characterization essentially involves the manifestation of inner states, desires, motives, intentions, beliefs, through action, including speech acts. We can ask ›why‹ a speaker said what he did and propose an intentional description as an answer.[43]

Speech acts embody speakers' intentions. Graesser et al.,[44] supported by their psychonarratological empirical experiments, emphasise that comprehenders of narratives attempt to understand *why* actions, events and states occur in the text, because that understanding contributes to a kind of higher-level coherence, a deeper understanding. However, speakers' intentions are not written on their sleeves but have to be inferred. There may be formal clues, such as the use of ›sorry‹ for an apology, but speech acts are always sensitive to context. Herein lies the major problem with speech act analyses of literary texts: they lack a theory of context to support the full inference of the speech act. Thus, speech act analyses tend to be rather atomistic, importing contextual features in a rather *ad hoc* way. This is precisely where activity types can make a contribution – showing how speech acts might cohere and how they constitute contexts. By way of example, consider one of Levinson's own illustrations.[45] He argues that in the context of the courtroom many questions can be ›taken‹ as accusations. It is knowledge of the interactional norms of the courtroom activity type that enable one to infer that a question may not be merely a question. A further point to bear in mind is that the ›inside out‹ contextual approach of activity types is entirely suited to play texts. The activity types of play texts create their own contexts.

Furthermore, the parallel schematic aspect of activity types enables the reader to infer much about character, particularly about the character's social role (i.e. their social function within the activity type). Knowing the activity schema, the script, enables the reader to activate expectations about default social roles. For example, a restaurant script may generate expectations not only about the existence of the waiters and chefs, but also more detailed expectations about those roles, such as that they are of a certain age (e.g. not children), of a nationality corresponding with the restaurant, and so on. Such schematic inferences are a crucial part of characterisation.[46] Writers do not write all there is to be known about a character: they mean more than they say. Indeed, often the larger part of our impression of a character is not in the text at all but has been inferred.

---

43 Downes: King Lear, p. 226.
44 Graesser / Singer / Trabasso: Inferences.
45 Levinson: Language.
46 Cf. Culpeper: Language; Scheider: Cognitive Theory.

Toolan refers to this as the ›iceberg‹ phenomenon in characterisation.[47] Schema theory, including scripts, helps explain how that larger chunk below the waterline might be inferred.

4 Exploiting ›Interview‹ Activity Types in Dramatic Texts

4.1 Job Interview Scenes in *Trainspotting*

In this section we focus on two short scenes from John Hodge's screenplay for Danny Boyle's 1996 film *Trainspotting*, based on the best-selling novel by Irvine Welsh. Both scenes are job interviews. The candidates in extracts 1 and 2 are, respectively, Renton and Spud. Both are heroin addicts and have been sent to the interviews by the Department of Employment. Neither have any desire to get a job, preferring to live on unemployment benefit and the profits of petty theft.

Extract 1

INT. INTERVIEW OFFICE. DAY

A Woman and Two Men (1 and 2) are interviewing Renton. His job application form is on the desk in front of them.

1. Man 1	Well, Mr. Renton, I see that you attended the Royal Edinburgh College.
2. Renton	Indeed, yes, those halcyon days.
3. Man 1	One of Edinburgh's finest schools.
4. Renton	Oh, yes, indeed. I look back on my time there with great fondness and affection. The debating society, the first eleven, the soft know of willow on leather –
5. Man 1	I'm an old boy myself, you know?
6. Renton	Oh, really?
7. Man 1	Do you recall the school motto?
8. Renton	Of course, the motto, the motto –
9. Man 1	Strive, hope, believe and conquer.
10. Renton	Exactly. Those very words have been my guiding light in what is, after all, a dark and often hostile world.

---

47 Toolan: Narrative.

Renton looks pious under scrutiny.

11. Man 2	Mr. Renton –
12. Renton	Yes.
13. Man 2	You seem eminently suited to this post but I wonder if you could explain the gaps in your employment record?
14. Renton	Yes, I can. The truth – well, the truth is that I've had a long-standing problem with heroin addiction. I've been known to sniff it, smoke it, swallow it, stick it up my arse and inject it into my veins. I've been trying to combat this addiction, but unless you count social security scams and shoplifting, I haven't had a regular job in years. I feel it's important to mention this.

There is silence.
A paper clip crashes to the floor.

(John Hodge, *Trainspotting: A Screenplay*)

From the outset, extract 1 strongly suggests a job interview activity type. The technical instruction preceding the initial screen direction describes a prototypical formal setting for an interview. The screen direction that follows then supplies specific information about schematic roles (three interviewers) props (desk, job application form) and actions (›interviewing‹). The non-finite progressive participle suggests that the interview is already in progress, so we might reasonably expect that initial formulaic greetings have been dispensed with. Turn 1 contains the classic interview opening gambit. Although having the grammatical structure of a declarative, within this activity type it invites interpretation as an invitation for Renton to elaborate on his time at the Royal Edinburgh College. This utterance also illustrates how Grice's Cooperative Principle is conventionally relaxed in this activity type.[48] The utterance provides no new information (theoretically, they both know that he attended that school); it flouts the Maxim of Quantity. But cooperation is maintained at a deeper level: it triggers the inference that it is not simply an assertion of facts but an invitation for elaboration of those facts. Turn 1 also signal a high degree of formality through the interviewer's use of title plus surname to refer to Renton. Note that the audience may infer at this point that Renton is of fairly high social status, given that he appears to have

---

48 Grice: Logic.

attended a prestigious-sounding school, *Royal Edinburgh College*. Renton begins turn 2 with the affirmative *Indeed*, rather than a simple *yes*, and uses somewhat hyperbolic lexis (›halcyon‹) to signal affiliation. The hyperbole is also apparent in the metaphorical language of turn 10. Renton presumably adopts a relatively sophisticated register to be consistent with his school background. Evidence of his background is also given in turn 4 through his lexical choices from the semantic field of public schools: *the debating society, the first eleven, the soft know of willow on leather*. These lexical contextualization cues are parallel with some of those spoken by the interviewer himself – *finest schools, old boy*; Renton and the interviewer register-match in lexical terms. Indeed, unusually for an interview, the interviewer self-discloses in turn 5, revealing that he is an *old boy* himself. Self-disclosure revealing common ground has the effect of rapidly closing the social distance between participants associated with most interviews. This affiliation is reinforced by the fact that Renton's answers in turns 2, 4 and 10 constitute preferred responses to the adjacency pairs initiated by the interviewer in 1, 3 and 9, thereby increasing the prospect of Renton being seen as suitable for the job. The interviewer's request in turn 13 for more information concerning gaps in Renton's employment record is a normal request in the interview activity type, though the interviewer's mitigation of the potentially face-threatening nature of the question signals a congenial relationship between himself and Renton. Renton promotes a characterisation of himself that closely matches the character of the interviewer. Whether it is a true characterisation is another matter, and perhaps the hyperbole hints that it is not.

However, Renton's final turn (14) subverts this characterisation. Although, in general terms, the register he uses remains schematically appropriate to the interview situation, some lexical choices are foregrounded as a result of their inappropriateness – e.g. the semi-taboo *arse*. Furthermore, Renton's confession to being a heroin addict is at odds with what we would prototypically expect of a job interview situation, as it obviously conflicts with the goal of securing the job. The more usual strategy would be to violate the maxim of quantity or quality (i.e. not mention it or lie).[49] Atypically, Renton, rather than relaxing the maxims of quantity and quality, studiously observes them, thereby forcing a radical reassessment of his character by the interviewer. In general terms, then, Renton's choice of language in extract 1 works to construct the activity type of the job interview, whilst simultaneously promoting a characterisation of himself as educated, charming and suitable for the position.

---

49 Ibid.

Renton then subverts this false characterisation in turn 14 by deviating from the interview activity type. Of course, there is dramatic irony in the fact that the reader/audience is aware – in the light of the early part of the screen-play – that Renton's characterisation of himself is inaccurate. In other words, we understand that the interviewer must recategorise Renton, but our characterisation of him does not change in the same way. For the reader/audience, the pretended characterisation is the trigger for humour, and a major source of humour in the extract is that Renton's linguistic construction of the interview activity type provides the ground against which turn 14 stands out as figural.[50]

Extract 2 also contains many schematic aspects of the interview activity type, but the language of the interviewee belies this and gives rise to a particular characterisation.

Extract 2

INT. OFFICE. DAY

The same office. The same team are interviewing Spud.

1. Spud	No, actually I went to Craignewton but I was worried that you wouldn't have heard of it so I put the Royal Edinburgh College instead, because they're both schools, right, and we're all in this together, and I wanted to put across the general idea rather than the details, yeah? People get all hung up on details, but what's the point? Like which school? Does it matter? Why? When? Where? Or how many O grades did I get? Could be six, could be one, but that's not important. What's important is that I am, right? That I am.
2. Man 1	Mr. Murphy, do you mean that you lied on your application?
3. Spud	Only to get my foot in the door. Showing initiative, right?
4. Man 1	You were referred here by the Department of Employment. There's no need for you to get your ›foot in the door‹, as you put it.
5. Spud	Hey. Right. No problem. Whatever you say, man. You're the man, the governor, the dude in the chair, like. I'm merely here. But obviously I am. Here, that is. I hope I'm

---

50 Cf. Rubin: Figurer.

	not talking too much. I don't usually. I think it's all important though, isn't it?
6. Man 2	Mr. Murphy, what attracts you to the leisure industry?
7. Spud	In a word, pleasure. My pleasure in other people's leisure.
8. Woman	What do you see as your main strengths?
9. Spud	I love people. All people. Even people that no one else loves, I think they're OK, you know. Like Beggars.
10. Woman	Homeless people?
11. Spud	No, not homeless people. Beggars, Francis Begbie – one of my mates. I wouldn't say my best mate, I mean, sometimes the boy goes over the score, like one time when we – me and him – were having a laugh and all of a sudden he's fucking gubbed me in the face, right –
12. Woman	Mr. Murphy, {leaving your friend aside,} do you see yourself as having any weaknesses?
13. Spud	No. Well, yes. I have to admit it: I'm a perfectionist. For me, it's the best or nothing at all. If things go badly, I can't be bothered, but I have a good feeling about this interview. Seems to me like it's gone pretty well. We've touched on a lot of subjects, a lot of things to think about, for all of us.
14. Man 1	Thank you, Mr. Murphy. We'll let you know.
15. Spud	The pleasure was mine. Best interview I've ever been to. Thanks.

Spud crosses the room to shake everyone by the hand and kiss them.

16. Renton (*v.o.*)	Spud had done well. I was proud of him. He fucked up good and proper.

(John Hodge, *Trainspotting: A Screenplay*)

Apart from the schematic roles, actions and props being the same as in extract 1, the sequential and structural properties of the dialogue are such that the discourse type is clearly appropriate for the activity type of the job interview. For example, the question/answer formats follow the convention identified by Button;[51] across turns 6, 7 and 8 the interviewer asks Spud a question, Spud responds and the interviewer asks a second, unrelated question. This demonstrates the prototypical interview

---

51 Button: Answers.

orthodoxy wherein a candidate's first answer is taken to be complete, with no clarification asked for, and a follow-up question is likely to be unrelated to the topic of the previous question. In terms of conversation structure, we also find typical elements of the interview activity type. We expect the longest turns in a conversation to be spoken by the participant who has the most power (whether this be personal, social or institutional power). However, Short points out that prototypical expectations vary according to the activity type in question.[52] The job interview is an example of an activity type wherein our prototypical expectations of turn-length and relative power are subverted, due to the least powerful person, the interviewee, doing most of the talking. Hence, in extract 2, Spud conforms to our expectations of the interview activity type by taking the longest turns; 315 words compared to the collective total of 77 spoken by his interviewers. However, these are the only aspects of Spud's language use that conform to what we might expect of an interview. In other respects he deviates from the pragmatic constraints of the activity type. Unlike Renton, Spud, the interviewee, does not use contextualization cues to promote affiliation, and hence similarity of character, between himself and the interviewers. Moreover, generally Spud's conversational behaviour deviates from the interactional norms of the activity type of a job interview, indicating his unsuitability as a candidate.

He asks questions of the interviewers, something only usually done if directly invited. Moreover, these questions are tag questions, seeking agreement with the sentiments conveyed in the part of the utterance prior to the tag; for example: *I wanted to put across the general idea rather than the details, yeah?* (1), *Showing initiative, right?* (3), *I think it's all important though, isn't it?* (5). This seeking of agreement, whilst normal in informal conversation, is not typical of job interviews. Spud's use of naming conventions to address his interviewers and to refer to others is also abnormal for the interview activity type, and, indeed, the activity type that the *interviewers* are consistent with. While Spud is referred to by the interviewers with title plus surname (*Mr Murphy*), Spud himself address Man 1 simply as *man* (*Whatever you say, man* [5]). He also refers to Francis Begbie by the nickname *Beggars*. A further example of how Spud fails to contribute pragmatically to the construction of a prototypical interview activity type is his excessive observance of Grice's maxims of quantity and quality from the outset of the interview.[53] This is in contrast to the norm of relaxing these maxims in this activity type. For instance, in turn 3 he admits to

---

52 Short: Language, p. 207.
53 Grice: Logic.

having lied on his application form, and in turn 13 he make the unusual admission that *If things go badly, I can't be bothered*. It is also the case that the register that Spud uses is deviant for the activity type, with informalities, slang and taboo language dominating (*I wouldn't say my best mate, I mean, sometimes the boy goes over the score, like one time when we – me and him – were having a laugh and all of a sudden he's fucking gubbed me in the face, right* [11]). With regard to turn 11, it is also the case that Spud's story bears no relevance to the woman's question in turn 8. In this respect Spud's answer does not do what typical interviewee's answers are designed to do; namely, to demonstrate an awareness of the meaning of the interviewer's prior utterance.[54] Further conversational contributions that are at odds with the interview activity type, include Spud's assessments of the interview and his own performance in turn 13 (*I have a good feeling about this interview*) and turn 15 (*Best interview I've ever been to*). Whilst it is the case that modesty is generally relaxed for the interviewee in this activity type, this does not usually extend to uninvited assessments of the interview itself in the hearing of the interviewers, for the simple reason that it is in the power and remit of the interviewers themselves to conduct the interview and assess the interviewee, not the other way round. In fact, in many ways Spud displays behaviour that is typical of someone conducting an interview rather than someone being interviewed. For instance, in turn 13 he attempts a concluding summary of the interview, saying *We've touched on a lot of subjects, a lot of things to think about, for all of us*, using a discourse type more commonly associated with interviewers rather than interviewees.

Spud's conversational behaviour, then, is not in the main what leads us to determine the extract as a job interview. The prototypical interview elements are provided only by the interviewers, whose use of language may be seen as a clear attempt to delineate the interview activity type. For example, turn 6 has a question that is unrelated to Spud's previous turn. Turn 4 provides an assessment of Spud's answer in turn 3 and turn 14 is an attempt to signal the end of the interview. All of these strategies form part of Button's notion of an interview orthodoxy.[55] However, all of them are undermined by Spud's conversational behaviour which does not work to construct the interview activity type. The cumulative effect of Spud's linguistic behaviour not conforming to the interview activity type is to characterise him according to features such as:
  – overly confident (although this confidence is clearly misplaced it is displayed through his willingness to observe the maxims of quantity

---

54 Button: Answers.
55 Ibid.

and quality at all costs, and to add question tags to statements that will more than likely be judged as inappropriate by his interviewers),
- unaware of social conventions (cf. the naming and referring conventions employed by Spud; the politeness conventions regarding modesty),
- inattentive (cf. his failure to pick up on the interviewers' nonplussed reactions – e.g. turn 4 – to his statements), and
- unintelligent (cf. his apparent inability to realise that his linguistic behaviour does not convey the right impression needed to secure the job).

These are some of the characteristics displayed by Spud in extract 2 and likely to be inferred by the interviewers and readers/audience. However, an alternative interpretation is possible, that is, that Spud does not actually want the job and thus he pretends to have the above characteristics, to serve this goal. Renton's speech in turn 16 confirms Spud's linguistic usage is a deliberate ploy to avoid being offered the job (something which may also have implications for the power relations of the interview).

4.2 Police Interview Scene in *One Foot in the Grave*

The extract we will analyse here is from the BBC award-winning comedy series *One Foot in the Grave*, specifically the episode *The Big Sleep* (Series 1, 11/1/90). The series ran during the 1990s over a total of 43 episodes, and attracted critical acclaim, particularly for the scripts penned by David Renwick. The plots revolve around Victor Meldrew, a grumpy (though inadvertently humorous) man dealing with the trials and tribulations of being retired. At the beginning of the episode from which our extract is taken, the female window cleaner claims that she is going to report Victor to the police for indecent exposure whilst she was cleaning the bathroom window (Victor had accidentally exposed himself whilst grappling with a towel in the bath). Later, Victor has just come in from the garden to be told by his wife that there are two men in the living room waiting to speak to him. Victor goes to speak to them.[56]

---

56 This scene is briefly analysed in Culpeper: Language, pp. 97–101.

V = Victor; S1 = dark suited man; S2 = dark suited man.

1.	S1	Victor Meldrew?
2.	V	Yes.
3.	S1	Wondered if we might have a little word with you sir?
4.	V	Oh God.
5.	S2	On the subject of obscene behaviour.
6.	V	Look, it's all very simple really ...
7.	S1	Rather a lot of it going on these days wouldn't you say? ... acts of unbridled filth perpetrated by perverts and sexual deviants who should know better at their age
8.	V	Look. I ... I just got out of the bath and I was just rubbing ... was rubbing ...
9.	S1	How do you think God feels about all this?
10.	V	What?
11.	S1	How do you think the Lord feels about so much sin and wickedness in his holy kingdom on earth?
12.	S2	If we look at Proverbs 6 verse 12 I think we can find the answer. A naughty person a wicked man walketh with a ...
13.	V	You're Jehovah's Witnesses! You're bloody Jehovah's Witnesses! I thought you were policemen.
14.	S1	Oh, we are policemen but on our days off we work for God.
15.	V	Get out!
16.	S1	Let me just read you something sir. In the beginning there was ...
17.	V	Get out of my house!
18.	S1	Sir, we all of us need a moment of soul searching reflection in these iniquitous times ...
19.	V	I know my rights, you can't search my soul without a warrant. Now go on get out of it. Bloody cheek.

(David Renwick, *The Big Sleep*, *One Foot in the Grave*)[57]

---

[57] Despite much searching, we have been unable to find a copy of the script used for this scene. What we provide here is a broad transcription of the scene as played on the video version.

Given that shortly before this scene the audience learns of the threat that Victor will be reported to the police for indecency, it is quite likely that a police-related activity type schema is primed. Research suggests that schemata that have been recently activated are more likely to spring to mind.[58] Indeed, the activity type constructed here appears to be a police interview. Apart from the fact that the two dark-suited individuals readily fills the (plain-clothed) police participant slots of the activity type schema, the opening speech acts (turns 1, 3 and 5), checking the identity of the interviewee and requesting permission to commence the interview on a particular topic, are strongly associated with the police interview. As for how the speech acts are realised, note that the speech act in turn 3 is indirect: it is literally an assertion concerning the speaker's wonderings. Such indirectness might be considered, other things being equal, an indication of politeness, as might be the use of the apparently deferential vocative *sir*. However, politeness on the part of police officers in this activity type is a conventional part of the activity type and cannot be automatically taken to reflect a sincere wish to maintain or enhance social relations with the interactant – it is surface or superficial politeness. Interestingly, politeness theory predicts that more politeness is used by the less powerful to the more.[59] In this case, that general prediction appears not to be supported: the police officers clearly are in a position of power, yet do more linguistic politeness work at the outset of this interaction than Victor. But, of course, this is politeness driven by the activity type, not the participants. Regarding power, the police officers initiate the conversation, ask the questions and control the topic – all contextual cues of power within the interview activity type. Victor treats S1 and S2 in a manner that suggests that he has conceived of them as police officers. He answers their questions and complies with their requests. Moreover, he adopts a tentative style in accounting for his actions, a style which is apparent in his two instances of the minimiser *just*, hesitations and two false starts. Clearly, Victor is playing the appropriate role of interviewee in the police interview activity type.

However, S1's question *How do you think God feels about all this* clashes with the police interview activity type. The fact that this clash also registers with Victor is clear from his response: *What?* Whilst asking questions is perfectly consistent with the police interview activity type, the religious topic is not. This is reinforced by the question *How do you think the Lord feels about so much sin and wickedness in his holy kingdom on earth?* and

---

58 See the references in Fiske / Taylor: Cognition, pp. 145–146.
59 Brown / Levinson: Politeness.

the quotations from the Bible. The idea that this is a police interview activity type can no longer be sustained. Victor realises that the activity type is actually one of religious proselytising, and infers that these are Jehovah's Witnesses, a religious group that is well-known for making door-to-door visits. In fact, the setting is appropriate to proselytising, but not a police interview, as in the UK, although the police may visit suspects, establish their identities and arrest them, questioning takes place in the context of interviews which are usually conducted at the police station. This detail was inconsistent with the earlier police interview interpretation, but was probably drowned out by the weight of evidence in the earlier part of the extract pointing towards a police interview. Victor's linguistic behaviour also quickly changes in accord with the new activity type. He abandons the role forced upon him as a result of the power dynamics of the police interview activity type. He uses commands, makes statements about what the two Jehovah's Witnesses are and are not allowed to do, and evaluates the situation using semi-taboo language. Note that the activity types we see in this abstract, the police interview and the proselytising activity type, share some linguistic and contextual characteristics but differ in others. The focal point of ›obscene behaviour‹ is common to both, as are speech acts of questioning and asserting. As for the differences, the religious aspects are only relevant to proselytising; the initial identity check and the superficial politeness are only relevant to the police interview; the power relationships are diametrically opposite in the two activity types; and so on.

The key point about this extract is it demonstrates how the perception of character is very closely linked to the perception of activity type, particularly with respect to the social role the character is imbued with, and that character recategorisation can be used for humorous effect. It is the switch in activity types that gives rise to a recategorisation of character, from police officer to Jehovah's Witness and from police suspect to potential religious convert. Interestingly, the writer resolves the potential conflict in the fact that S1 and S2 are Jehovah's Witnesses and yet at the beginning of the extract sounded like police officers by providing the information that they are indeed police officers but off duty. This, then, explains ›leakage‹ from the police interview activity type into the proselytising activity type. In the final turn of the extract Victor demonstrates that he is now conscious of the cause of his confusion by blending linguistic elements of the two activity types. His assertion that *you can't search my soul without a warrant* would be an appropriate turn of phrase for the police interview activity type were it not for the word *soul*, which is incongruous and seems more appropriate to the activity type of religious proselytising. Conventionally, we would expect in its place a word such as *house* or *home*, so Victor's use of the word *soul* appears to blend the two activity types together. At the author-to-reader level of discourse structure, this blending of activity types achieves a neat comedic pay-off to the scene.

4.3 Job Interview Scene in *What the Butler Saw* (Act I)

Joe Orton's play *What the Butler Saw* was first performed in March 1969. Considered by some as his best play, it was also his last. It is generally considered a farce, but there are also some obvious elements of social critique. Our extract comes from the very beginning of the play.

A room in a private clinic. Morning.
Doors lead to the wards, the dispensary and the hall.
French windows open on to pleasant gardens and shrubberies.
Sink. Desk. Consulting couch with curtains.

Dr Prentice enters briskly. Geraldine Barclay follows him. She carries a small cardboard box.

1. Prentice   (*turning at the desk*). Take a seat. Is this your first job?
2. Geraldine   (*sitting*). Yes, doctor.

Dr Prentice puts on a pair of spectacles, stares at her. He opens a drawer in the desk, takes out a notebook.

3. Prentice   (*picking up a pencil*). I'm going to ask you a few questions. (*He hands her a notebook and pencil.*) Write them down. In English, please. (*He returns to his desk, sits, smiles.*) Who was your father? Put that at the head of the page.

Geraldine puts the cardboard box she is carrying to one side, crosses her legs, rests the notebook upon her knee and makes a note.

                   And now the reply immediately underneath for quick reference.

4. Geraldine   I've no idea who my father was.

Dr Prentice is perturbed by her reply although he gives no evidence of this. He gives her a kindly smile.

5. Prentice	I'd better be frank, Miss Barclay. I can't employ you if you're in any way miraculous. It would be contrary to established practice. You did have a father?
6. Geraldine	Oh, I'm sure I did. My mother was frugal in her habits, but she'd never economize unwisely.
7. Prentice	If you had a father why can't you produce him?
8. Geraldine	He deserted my mother. Many years ago. She was the victim of an unpleasant attack.
9. Prentice	(*shrewdly*) Was she a nun?
10. Geraldine	No. She was a chambermaid at the Station Hotel.

Dr Prentice frowns, takes off his spectacles and pinches the bridge of his nose.

11. Prentice	Pass that large, leather-bound volume, will you? I must check your story. To safeguard my interests, you understand?

Geraldine lifts the book from the bookcase and takes it to Dr Prentice.

	(*Consulting the index.*) The Station Hotel?
12. Geraldine	Yes.
13. Prentice	(*opening the book, running his finger down the page*). Ah, here we are! It's a building of small architectural merit built for some unknown purpose at the turn of the century. It was converted into a hotel by public subscription. (*He nods, wisely.*) I stayed there once myself as a young man. It has a reputation for luxury which baffles the most undemanding guest. (*He closes the book with a bang and pushes it to one side.*) Your story appears, in the main, to be correct. This admirable volume, of course, omits most of the details. But that is only to be expected in a publication of wide general usage. (*He puts on his spectacles.*) Make a note to the effect that your father is missing. Say nothing of the circumstances. It might influence my final decision.

Geraldine makes a jotting in her notebook. Dr Prentice takes the leatherbound volume to the bookcase.

14. Prentice	Is your mother alive? Or has she too unaccountably vanished? That is a trick question. Be careful – you could lose marks on your final scoring.

(Joe Orton, *What the Butler Saw*)

In this scene, Dr Prentice, a psychiatrist, is interviewing Geraldine Barclay for a job. The physical setting is the clinic. This is consistent with the job interview activity, whereby the work environment is the default value for setting. More precisely we can infer from the stage directions that Prentice must be sitting behind a desk and that Geraldine must be on a chair on the other side of the desk. Again, all this is consistent with expectations generated by the activity type, and also reflects expectations about power. Indeed, the first turns reinforce those expectations: it is the employer, Prentice, who issues an imperative command asking the interviewee to take a seat, and it is he who thereby initiates the interaction, following it with a question, which also controls the topic. In fact, generally, Prentice asks questions, controls the topic and makes commands for the rest of the interview, whilst Geraldine gives answers and complies with the commands. All this, the setting, power relations, questions and answers, commands and topic control, is what one might expect from the activity type of the job interview.

Note that the speech act status of *Take a seat* cannot be inferred from the words and grammar alone. If the utterance had been addressed to a senior member of staff of the clinic who had popped in on a casual visit, the utterance might have counted as an invitation. However, within this activity type, the interviewee has very little option but to sit down, given the power dynamics, and so it counts as a command. Prentice's question, *Is this your first job?*, is typical of the activity type: job experience is a central topic, as it relates closely to the candidate's suitability. Moreover, it is appropriate as an opening gambit, given that the answer to this question will affect subsequent questions. Geraldine's affirmative answer is significant in that it allows the reader to infer that she is inexperienced (and hence possibly vulnerable). Prentice's next sentence is similarly an expected structural part of the job interview activity type. Given Geraldine's inexperience, he indicates what is going to happen next in the interview: *I'm going to ask you a few questions*. Up to this point, the evidence strongly supports the construction of a typical job interview; after this point, things change.

Prentice asks Geraldine to write the questions down. This is not normal practice, and conflicts with the job interview activity type, which normally consists of oral exchanges of questions and answers. However, it is perhaps not inexplicable, as Prentice may be testing her shorthand abilities. However, the following sentence, *In English, please*, is more puzzling. Prentice breaks Grice's maxim of quantity,[60] as it can be readily

---

60 Grice: Logic.

assumed that she will write the questions down in English. Prentice's first question, *Who was your father?*, is not predicted by the activity type: its relevance is not clear. The fact that Geraldine attempts to answer the question rather than question why it was asked, is not unusual, given that the interviewee's role is primarily to answer questions in this activity type rather than ask them, and that her lack of experience might mean that she is prepared to go along with whatever is asked in order to please the interviewer. The stage direction conveys Prentice's reaction: *Dr Prentice is disturbed by her reply although he gives no evidence of this*. Note that this is a peculiar stage direction, as it is not intended as a performance cue (the actor should give ›no evidence‹ of the inner state). In fact, the stage direction is more like a narratorial intervention; more specifically, it is the narratorial report of an internal cognitive state.[61] This allows the reader some insight into the ›inner self‹ of Prentice. It is also possible that the reader may infer that Prentice's reaction is somewhat odd, given that Geraldine's answer can be explained by assuming that she was an orphan or adopted.

Prentice's utterance, *I'd better be frank*, signals a departure from the main business of the activity type, as Prentice pursues the issue of Geraldine's parentage. Prentice's assertion that he could not employ her if she were *in any way miraculous*, allows the inference that he believes that there is a possibility that she was born by miraculous means, otherwise there would have been no need to make the assertion (cf. the maxim of quantity). Of course, one might assume that he is insincere, that he is joking, for example. However, his following text and, more particularly, that of Geraldine does not support this. The reason he gives for not employing a miraculous individual is similarly bizarre, as he does not assert that it is contrary to the laws of nature but to *establish practice*, thereby allowing the reader to infer that Prentice not only thinks miraculous conception is possible (being *contrary* to something presupposes the existence of something else to which it is contrary), but also socially unacceptable. This belief about Prentice is further reinforced by his question, *you did have a father?*, as the question implies doubt about whether this is really the case (in order to uphold the maxim quantity, one would not ask a question about something one already knew for sure). Importantly, Geraldine takes the question as a real question, a question that is sincere. The fact she does so implies that she shares the belief upon which the question was based, that it is possible not to have a natural father. Moreover, this is reinforced in the following sentence where it is implied that dispensing

---

61 Cf. Semino / Short: Corpus.

with a father is a matter of unwise economy rather than an essential part of having a child. The important point is that those characters seem to be sharing the same belief system with respect to how the natural world works, and it is a belief system that conflicts with that of the audience. In addition, both characters seem to have odd value systems attached to their beliefs, Prentice seeing miraculous conception as a social oddity (*contrary to established practice*) and Geraldine seeing it as an optional but wise luxury (*she'd never economise unwisely*).

Turns 7–13 contain further bizarre features, which we shall briefly mention. Turn 7 suggests that Prentice believes that merely having a father automatically means that one knows where he is; the more obvious idea that she is an orphan or her parents are divorced does not occur to him. Clearly, Orton is partly attacking the orthodox views of his time, in which families were considered stable. Prentice's yes/no question in turn 9 implies, via the maxim of relation, that he thinks there is a possibility that Geraldine's mother was a nun. Moreover, the stage direction, *shrewdly*, which reports a mental state, indicates that he thinks that the possibility that she is a nun a clever hypothesis on his part. Of course, the audience does not share this thinking, as there is no obvious connection between being a *victim of an unpleasant attack* and a nun. Prentice's idea that he can verify Geraldine's claims about her parents in a book clashes with the reader's knowledge about what books can contain. Moreover, the fact that he looks up the *Station Hotel* and what he reads out is largely an architectural description, strengthens the clash, as this information is not relevant to an assessment of her claims. His statement that *This admirable volume, of course, omits most of the details* implies (via the scalar implicature conveyed by ›most‹) that some of the details, presumably the relevant details, were actually there in the book. This clashes with what the reader might take to be the case.

Prentice's final turns remind us of the main business of the job interview, namely, a process of selection leading to the employer's final decision. However, whilst the lexis (e.g. *my final decision*) reminds us of this, what he conveys to Geraldine is decidedly odd. He commands her to *say nothing of the circumstances* as it *might influence* his *final decision*; and he warns her to *be careful*, otherwise she could *lose marks*. We know from the job interview activity type that interviewers do not advise interviewees on tactics for securing a job; to do so, would assume that they know who is best for the job already, and so the interview is not a ›real‹ interview. (In fact, the particular absurdity here is that he advises her to withhold information, yet he is the one from whom the information is to be withheld, despite the fact that he knows it already). Nor do they typically alert the candidate to the status of a question (*That is a trick question*). As we pointed out in relation to Button's research,[62] a key feature of the job interview activity type is that questions are not spelt out or clarified: they are thrown at the candidate in order to see how the candidate handles them. Clearly, Prentice has a peculiar conception of the job interview activity type. Geraldine's conception seems to be equally peculiar. Shortly after this extract Prentice asks her to take her clothes off and she obliges, apparently assuming it to be part of the job interview activity type. One could, however, partly rationalise this by remembering that Geraldine has no experience of the job interview. Orton is maybe attacking psychiatrists for abuses of power.

This extract verges towards the theatre of the absurd. The characters seem to share beliefs and value systems that conflict with those of the audience. Of course, it does not require the concept of activity type to understand conflicts with natural laws. However, to fully appreciate how this extract works, including how characterisation works within it, a concept such as activity types is needed. It allows us not only to make characterisation inferences and thus flesh out a character, but also to infer oddities of character. We realise that Prentice, and to a lesser extent Geraldine, have a different conception of how the activity works.

5 Conclusion

We have shown how the notion of activity type is relevant in the stylistic analysis of drama and how it may be employed as a means of further explaining characterisation. We argued that activity types have a pragmatic interactional side and a cognitive side. That this is so accounts for why the notion can feed into both bottom-up and top-down processes of characterisation. An activity type approach provides a means of analysing a verbal construction that generates its own context (an inside out approach), including the characters that are a part of that context. Our analyses show some of the particular consequences for characterisation: particular characterisations can be triggered by activity types; particular characterisations can be foregrounded as a result of deviation from what is expected of an activity type; and particular shifts in characterisation can be achieved through shifts in activity type. Furthermore, blending of activity types can create incongruity that works as a trigger for humour. An activity type approach enables a relatively holistic treatment of drama as discourse, as opposed to the atomistic approach typical of the extant

---

62 Button: Answers.

stylistic analyses of the language of dramatic texts. Moreover, we have demonstrated that the approach can help capture specific dramatic effects, such as humour, absurdity and dramatic irony. It might be noted that our choice of the interview activity type is motivated in part by the fact that it is relatively conventionalised and stable, and thus relatively easy to describe. Chatting with friends or family dinner-table talk are also recognisable speech activities with their own constraints, but they are much more variable.

References

Allwood, Jens: Linguistic Communication as Action and Cooperation. Gothenburg Monographs in Linguistics 2. Göteborg 1976.
Allwood, Jens: An Activity-Based Approach to Pragmatics. In: Harry Bunt / William Black (Eds.): Abduction, Belief and Context in Dialogue: Studies in Computational Pragmatics. Amsterdam 2000, pp. 47–80.
Austin, John Langshaw: How to do Things with Words, Oxford 1962.
Bartlett, Frederick: Remembering: A Study in Experimental and Social Psychology [1932]. Cambridge 1995.
Button, Graham: Answers as Interactional Products: Two Sequential Practices Used in Job Interviews. In: Paul Drew / John Heritage (Eds.): Talk at Work: Interaction in Institutional Settings. Cambridge 1992, pp. 212–231.
Cantor, Nancy / Walter Mischel: Prototypes in Person Perception. In: Leonard Berkowitz (Ed.): Advances in Experimental Social Psychology 12 (1979), pp. 3–52.
Culpeper, Jonathan: Language and Characterisation: People in Plays and other Texts. Harlow, 2001.
Culpeper, Jonathan / Elena Semino: Constructing Witches and Spells: Speech Acts and Activity Types in Early Modern England. In: Journal of Historical Pragmatics 1 (2000), pp. 97–116.
Culpeper, Jonathan / Mick Short / Peter Verdonk (Eds.): Exploring the Language of Drama: From Text to Context. London 1998.
Downes, William: King Lear's Question to his Daughters. In: Willie van Peer (Ed.): The Taming of the Text: Explorations in Language, Literature and Culture. London 1989, pp. 225–257.
Duranti, Alessandro / Charles Goodwin (Eds.): Rethinking Context: Language as an Interactive Phenomenon. Cambridge 1992.
Eysenck, Michael W. / Mark T. Keane: Cognitive Psychology: A Student's Handbook. 4th edn. Hillsdale, NJ 2000.
Fairclough, Norman F.: Language and Power. London 1989.
Fairclough, Norman F.: Critical Language Awareness. London 1992.
Fiske, Susan T. / Shelley E. Taylor: Social Cognition. 2nd edn. New York 1991.
Graesser, Arthur C. / Murray Singer / Tom Trabasso: Constructing Inferences During Narrative Text Comprehension. In: Psychological Review 101 (1994), pp. 371–395.
Grice, H. Paul: Logic and Conversation. In: Paul Cole / Jerry L. Morgan (Eds.): Syntax and Semantics 3: Speech Acts. New York 1975, pp. 41–58.
Gumperz, John: Discourse Strategies. Cambridge 1982.
Gumperz, John: Language and Social Identity. Cambridge 1982.

Gumperz, John: Interviewing in Intercultural Situations. In: Paul Drew / John Heritage (Eds.): Talk at Work: Interaction in Institutional Settings. Cambridge 1992, pp. 302–327.

Gumperz, John: Contextualization and Understanding. In: Alessandro Duranti / Charles Goodwin (Eds.): Rethinking Context: Language as an Interactive Phenomenon. Cambridge 1992, pp. 229–252.

Hasan, Ruqaiya: The Uses of Talk. In: Srikant Sarangi / Malcolm Coulthard (Eds.): Discourse and Social Life. London 2000, pp. 28–47.

Hodge, John: Trainspotting: A Screen Play. London 1996.

Holyoak, Keith J. / Peter C. Gordon: Information Processing and Social Cognition. In: Robert S. Wyer / Thomas K. Srull (Eds.): Handbook of Social Cognition 1. Hillsdale, NJ 1984, pp. 39–70.

Hurst, Mary J.: Speech Acts in Ivy Compton-Burnett's A Family and a Fortune. In: Language and Style 20 (1987), pp. 342–358.

Hymes, Dell: Models of Interaction of Language and Social Life. In: John Gumperz / Dell Hymes (Eds.) Directions in Sociolinguistics: Ethnography of Communication [1967]. New York 1972, pp. 35–75.

Leech, Geoffrey N.: Principles of Pragmatics. London 1983.

Levinson, Stephen C.: Activity Types and Language. In: Paul Drew / John Heritage (Eds.): Talk at Work [1979]. Cambridge 1992, pp. 66–100.

Linell, Per / Daniel P. Thunqvist: Moving In and Out of Framings: Activity Contexts in Talks with Young Unemployed People within a Training Project. In: Journal of Pragmatics 35 (2003), pp. 409–434.

Lowe, Valerie: »Unhappy« Confessions in *The Crucible*. In: Jonathan Culpeper / Mick Short / Peter Verdonk (Eds.): Exploring the Language of Drama: From Text to Context. London 1998, pp. 128–141.

McIntyre, Dan: Point of View in Plays: A Cognitive Stylistic Approach to Viewpoint in Drama and Other Text-types. Amsterdam 2006.

McIntyre, Dan: Point of View in Drama: A Socio-Pragmatic Analysis of Dennis Potter's Brimstone and Treacle. In: Language and Literature 13 (2004), pp. 139–160.

Minsky, Marvin: A Framework for Representing Knowledge. In: Patrick H. Winston (Ed.): The Psychology of Computer Vision. New York 1975, pp. 211–277.

Neisser, Ulric: Cognition / Reality: Principles and Implications of Cognitive Psychology. San Francisco 1976.

Pfister, Manfred: The Theory and Analysis of Drama. Cambridge 1988.

Rosch, Eleanor / Carolyn B. Mervis / Wayne D. Gray / David M. Johnson / Peny Boyes-Braem: Basic Objects in Natural Categories. In: Cognitive Psychology 8 (1976), pp. 382–439.

Rumelhart, David E.: Schemata and the Cognitive System. In: Robert S. Wyer / Thomas K. Srull (Eds.): Handbook of Social Cognition 1. Hillsdale, NJ 1984, pp. 161–188.

Rubin, Edgar: Synsoplevede Figurer. Copenhagen 1915.

Sarangi, Srikant: Activity Types, Discourse Types and Interactional Hybridity: The Case of Genetic Counselling. In: S.S. / Malcolm Coulthard (Eds.): Discourse and Social Life. London 2000, pp. 1–27.

Schank, Roger C.: Dynamic Memory: A Theory of Reminding and Learning in Computers and People. Cambridge 1982.

Schank, Roger C.: Dynamic Memory Revisited. Cambridge 1999.

Schank, Roger C. / Robert P. Abelson: Scripts, Plans, Goals, and Understanding: An Inquiry into Human Knowledge Structures. Hillsdale, NJ 1977.

Schneider, Ralf: Toward a Cognitive Theory of Literary Character: The Dynamics of Mental-Model Construction. In: Style 35 (2001), pp. 607–640.
Searle, John R.: Speech Acts: An Essay in the Philosophy of Language. Cambridge 1969.
Searle, John R.: Indirect Speech Acts. In: Paul Cole / Jerry L. Morgan (Eds.): Syntax and Semantics 3. New York 1975, pp. 59–82.
Short, Mick: Exploring the Language of Poems, Plays and Prose. London 1996.
Short, Mick: From Dramatic Text to Dramatic Performance. In: Jonathan Culpeper / Mick Short / Peter Verdonk (Eds.): Exploring the Language of Drama: From Text to Context. London 1998, pp. 6–17.
Taylor, Shelley E. / Susan J. Fiske / Nancy L. Etcoff / Audrey Ruderman: Categorical Bases of Person Memory and Stereotyping. In: Journal of Personality and Social Psychology 36 (1978), pp. 778–793.
Thomas, Jenny A.: Meaning in Interaction. London 1995.
Toolan, Michael J.: Narrative: A Critical Linguistic Introduction. London 1988.
Wittgenstein, Ludwig: Philosophical Investigations. Transl. by G.E.M. Anscombe. 2nd edn. Oxford 1958.

SIMONE WINKO

On the Constitution of Characters in Poetry

The analysis of characters in literary texts has, for a long time, taken up a position between the poles of practical self-evidence and deficient procedural research: the interpretation of literary texts has always naturally included the examination of the characters involved; however, a convincing and sufficiently complex model of how to identify and define a literary character together with the proper means of analysing it has not been available for a long time. The situation changed in the 1990s, particularly with the research boom inspired by narratology, and there predominantly through the studies by Uri Margolin, Ralf Schneider and Fotis Jannidis.[1] In these contributions, a literary character is understood as the mental model of a human being in a narrated world, created by a reader from information in the text and the reader's world knowledge.[2] The categories for the description of characters – their designation, their construction in the text, etc. – are developed with reference to narrative texts, the examples used to exemplify these deliberations are taken from works in prose. The present contribution seeks to investigate whether these models and their respective categories of description might equally prove their worth with texts of poetry, or whether there is a genre-specific difference that makes the constitution of characters in poetry diverge from that in prose texts:[3] How are characters constructed in poems? Do characters in poems diverge from characters in prose texts and if so wherein? Are there specific means that cannot be found in prose texts?

---

1 Cf. the introduction to this volume; also the historical survey of the different approaches to the literary representation of human beings from pre-modern poetics to the conceptions developed by literary scholarship in the 1980s, in Koch: Menschendarstellung.
2 E.g. Jannidis: Figur, pp. 192f.; Schneider: Grundriß, pp. 349f.
3 I shall not deal with visual poetry whose graphic designs represent visual ›figures‹ that are semantically related to the content of the poems. I am here concerned – roughly speaking – with characters as the textual counterparts of human beings.

These are the questions to be answered. In a first step, the genre-specific or genre-typical features of poetry will have to be examined in order to elucidate the ways in which they may affect the constitution of characters (1). The various means of shaping the characters in poems will then be assembled in a kind of survey (2) and, finally, two exemplary aspects of the constitution of characters will be used to deal with the question how characters might be identified in poems (3). A summary of results will conclude the contribution (4).[4]

1 What Are Genre-Typical Features of Poetry?

The state of the theory of poetry is lamented quite frequently, although with diminishing proper justification. Targets of criticism are insufficiently clarified genre-typological premises, the lack of exchange with recent developments in literary theory, and poor terminological precision.[5] The well-reflected adoption of categories developed in recent international research in narrative theory is seen by some as a possibility of breathing new life into the theory of poetry. Although some of the advocates of this direction are inclined to overestimate the clarity of narratological concepts just as they tend to underestimate the genre-typological consequences of such an adoption,[6] this approach seems to be a viable one as has been demonstrated, for instance, in various contributions by Peter Hühn and Jörg Schönert.[7] As the analysis of characters in the following will proceed from narratological considerations it seems reasonable to pursue this new direction of poetry research.

In order to be able to clarify in what ways poems diverge from narrative texts for which the categories of character analysis have been developed, the genre-specific features of poetry must first be established. It is all too well known that there is no consensus amongst researchers concerning the necessary defining features of poetry. Recently even the apparently consensual feature of verse has come under fire, a feature that has been declared – albeit in the context of differing arguments[8] – to be

---

4 As my field is German studies, all my illustrative examples will come from German-language (lyrical) poetry.
5 E.g. Müller-Zettelmann: Lyrik, p. 131; Wolf: Lyric, pp. 21f.
6 E.g. Müller-Zettelmann: Lyrik, pp. 137, 142f.; cf. however the criticism of obscurities in narratological narrator concepts in: Köppe / Stühring: Pan-Narrator Theories.
7 Cf. Hühn / Schönert: Analyse, esp. pp. 302–305; Hühn / Schönert: Einleitung; with considerations of genre-theoretical consequences Hühn / Schönert: Auswertung, esp. pp. 328ff.; also Müller-Zettelmann: Lyrik.
8 Burdorf: Einführung, p. 20; Lamping: Gedicht, p. 63.

obligatory for poetry or ›lyrical poems‹ by Dieter Burdorf and Dieter Lamping whose suggestions have had a wide influence on lyric theory in the German-speaking area. But this criticism is actually aimed at an even lower level because the requirement of verse implies a concept of text that is inapplicable to Concrete Poetry or visual poetry and thus excludes these varieties from the domain of poetry.[9] Rüdiger Zymner, by contrast, chooses a reception-oriented approach and defines ›poetry‹ as the ›representation of language as the generic display of linguistic mediality and thus as the generic catalyst of aesthetic evidence‹.[10] ›Display of linguistic mediality‹ means a primary mode of reception that may be roughly understood as consisting in the reader's attention being directed towards language by linguistic and formal features,[11] and ›catalyst of aesthetic evidence‹ means a secondary mode of reception that comprises various kinds of hypotheses concerning the construction of meaning. Both modes taken together are distinctive, according to Zymner, and clearly delimit lyrical poetry against other literary kinds. Poetry is, consequently, not specified here with reference to linguistic features; but these features play an ›indirect‹ role in the definition insofar as they can release the two described modes of reception.

However, I need not enter here into the problem of genre definition – an unquestionably important problem. To my mind, it appears to be more productive not to search for an all-encompassing concept of ›poetry‹ but to differentiate concepts of poetry by placing greater emphasis on the historical conventions of production and reception for the specification of concepts of poetry. But it will be enough of a foundation for the following considerations to gather together those features by which different prototypes of poems diverge from narrative texts. I consider it fruitful, however, to include Zymner's reception-oriented perspective because the relevant linguistic features of texts are not meaningful in themselves but become significant for comprehension only in acts of processing.[12] As a consequence, we have to deal not only with the features of a poem but as well with the sequentiality of information processing. Two restrictions must be heeded in the following discussion: the statements about ›typical features‹ of poems apply only to particular groups of poetry; they are, furthermore, formulated relatively ›loosely‹ and would have to be empirically tested and differentiated historically by means of larger corpora. The point of departure might well be the set of

---

9 Vgl. Zymner: Lyrik, pp. 23ff.
10 Zymner: Lyrik, p. 140 (trans. by Alison Rosemary Köck / Wolfram Karl Köck).
11 Due to lack of space, Zymner's comments can only be rendered here in rough outline; for more precise details cf. ibid.: e.g. pp. 97, 111f. and 138.
12 Cf. also Weimar: Text, pp. 110ff.

features that has repeatedly been quoted in various attempts at explaining the genre of ›poetry‹, whose presence is, however, not a necessary condition of the actual occurrence of poetry. Such features are certainly typical of large groups of poems, i.e. characterise at least historical and genre-specific varieties of poetry: brevity, verse, a high degree of textual condensation, songlike qualities (›Sangbarkeit‹), self-reference and reflexivity, grammatical deviations from ordinary language, lack of fictionality, unmediated, ›direct‹ speech situation, the existence of a particular instance called the ›lyric I‹ (›lyrisches Ich‹, ›lyric persona‹) creating a particular closeness between the speaker-I and the author, and finally also the concentration on themes like emotions, moods and sentiments, and reflections about situations or events.[13] Closer examination reveals that only three of the features of this set are suitable for distinguishing poems from narrative texts:

1. Even though there are very long poems and very short prose texts, the *brevity* of poems is generally a conspicuous criterion of distinction.[14] It implies, amongst other things, that poems can communicate less propositionally formulated information than texts in prose.

2. *Verse or metrically bound speech* clearly distinguishes poems from prose. There are two implications: on the one hand, verse increases the amount of communicable information within the limited space available to poems as the schemes of metre and rhyme represent a second kind of information connected with its propositional type. This leads to the feature of condensation. On the other hand, verse can direct the attention of the reader or listener to the language and the form of the texts from which further information may be gleaned. I consider this to be an interpretation of the often-quoted feature of the self-reference of poems, which is non-metaphorical and describes the processing of texts.[15]

3. *Density or condensation* may be specified as the number of items of information in proportion to the amount of text, whereby the different items of information may overlap, i.e. may be gleaned from different levels of the text. High textual density is a characteristic feature of poems although narrative texts can unquestionably also exhibit high density. ›Structural complexity‹ or ›over-structuredness‹ are labels of the same

---

13 Cf. e.g. Wolf: Lyric, pp. 34–31; Burdorf: Einführung, pp. 20f.; Grosse: Lyrik, p. 45.
14 Counterexamples like Albrecht von Haller's »The Alpes« (»Die Alpen«) or Bertolt Brecht's »The Rearing of Millet« (»Die Erziehung der Hirse«) do not refute the assertion that brevity is a prototypical feature of poems. It has to be admitted as a matter of course, however, that the deliberations of this contribution are primarily appropriate for German-language poetry after 1750 and would have to be differentiated historically.
15 Cf. Zymner: Lyrik, p. 140.

feature.[16] Density in poetry is achieved by verse, on the one hand, by the rhetorical means of *elocutio*, on the other, which are both traditionally used in poems – even though with historical and programmatic oscillations. Furthermore, it can arise through the combination of the text of a song with a melody; in this sense, the criterion of songlike quality can be integrated here. Condensation may additionally be achieved by exploiting the semantically usable licence to handle linguistic rules at liberty, e.g. the rules of word formation with regard to neologisms as well as the rules of syntax.[17] This particular feature of a potentially high density of information in a small space corresponds with the thesis of the potential relevance of every feature of the text of a poem in the analytical and interpretative dealing with poems. This thesis possesses the status of a genre convention for poetry.

Criteria that, to me, seem to be unsuited for the delimitation of poetry are the criteria of fictionality, the specific speaker instance, and the thematic specificity of poems. Not all poems are fictional nor are they always non-fictional – something that is equally applicable to narrative texts.[18] The assumption of a particular speaker instance in poems, usually called the ›lyric I‹ (›lyrisches Ich‹), also seems to me unsuitable for the purpose of a fundamental distinction;[19] the pronoun ›I‹ in poems has the same function as in narrative texts.[20] A special case in the history of poetry will be dealt with in section 3. And finally, there can be no doubt that emotions, moods, sentiments and reflections appear frequently in poems but in narrative texts as well, albeit not in comparably high concentration.

As the typical features – in the above-explained understanding –, which distinguish poems from narrative texts, may therefore be named brevity, verse, and the condensation of information.

2 Means of Constituting Characters in Poems

It seems reasonable to investigate the various possibilities of linguistically generating characters in poems on a contrastive basis. The point of departure will be the mechanisms by which linguistic information is placed, and that have been worked out for narrative texts under the aspect

---

16 E.g. Link: Elemente, pp. 92ff.
17 Cf. Grosse: Lyrik, pp. 45, 50.
18 Also Lamping: Gedicht, pp. 108–110; Zipfel: Fiktion, ch. 8.1.1, esp. pp. 303f.; Zymner: Lyrik, p. 11; and others.
19 For criticism of the concept ›lyric I‹ cf. Schönert: Autor; Borkowski / Winko: Gedicht.
20 Cf. Schiedermair: Lyrisches Ich, pp. 89, 123.

of the construction of characters;[21] the question is then whether these can be seen at work in poems as well.

First of all, it must be established more accurately, however, what elements of the fictive world of poems we are actually referring to whenever we speak of ›characters‹. Following a definition by Fotis Jannidis, »Character is a text- or media-based figure in a story world, usually human or human-like«,[22] we shall in the following understand by the concept of ›character‹ human beings or human-like living beings in literary texts, whereby similarity to human beings is established by at least one of the following features: ›intentional action, speech, internal life and [...] external appearance‹.[23] A character arises as ›a linguistically generated conceptual unit‹, i.e. it is constructed through the interplay of the information given by the texts and the knowledge of the world supplied by the reader.[24] With Uri Margolin,[25] characters understood in this way must fulfil two conditions: for one, they must be ascribed ›existence‹ in the poem, i.e. they must be part of the fictive world even though this may, for instance, apply only in a hypothetical or a counterfactual mode. A character must, furthermore, possess at least one clearly identifiable feature (›predication‹). Characters according to this understanding need not be human beings; animals and even inanimate objects may also assume this function in texts. Such a conception of ›character‹ raises the question for ›object poems‹ (›Dinggedichte‹), whether the objects at the centre of these poems are characters or not. Do the archaic torso of Apollo or the blue Hydrangea in Rilke's eponymous poems have the status of characters? This question cannot be answered in a general way for all object-poems but must be carefully examined in every single case. Even though the plant in Rilke's »Blue Hydrangea« (»Blaue Hortensie«) is endowed with anthropomorphic properties it lacks – in contradistinction, for instance, to the rose in Goethe's »Rose in the Heather« (»Heidenröslein«) – a feature like ›intentional action‹ and ›internal life‹ so that the question would have to be negated this case. The torso, however, has been ascribed the property of intentionality at least by one particular interpretative tradition of this poem,[26] and it may therefore be designated a character.

---

21 Cf. for the categories adduced in what follows Jannidis: Figur, chs. 4 and 6; Schneider: Grundriß, ch. 4.
22 Jannidis: Character, p. 14.
23 Jannidis: Figur, pp. 119f (trans. by Alison Rosemary Köck / Wolfram Karl Köck).
24 Cf. ibid.: p. 147. Cf. also Schneider: Grundriß, pp. 80–90; Gerrig / Allbritton: Construction; Culpeper: Character, pp. 335f., 352ff.
25 Cf. Margolin: Characters.
26 See below, section 3.

2.1 Techniques of Character Constitution in Poems

The techniques of character constitution in texts comprise, amongst others, different means of designation and characterisation.

1. *Designation.* The linguistic means employed for designating a character are proper names, noun phrases and pronouns. A frequently used strategy for the generation of a character in prose texts consists in its designation *by means of a proper name.*[27] This kind of designation of a character by means of a name is found considerably less frequently in poetry than in narrative texts. In longer types of narrative poems, particularly in ballads and poems with historical or legend-related themes, this technique is used more frequently than in shorter or non-narrative types. There are distinctions to be drawn here: (i) fictive names, (ii) names of historical, legendary or mythological characters, and (iii) names representing a literary topos, for instance the ›Daphnes‹ and ›Chloes‹ of Anacreontic poetry. All proper names share the function of assembling and tying together the features of characters but they perform this function in different ways. (i) When fictive names are first introduced, only the feature of gender classification is, as a rule, associated with the character they refer to. That Lenore in Bürger's eponymous ballad is a woman or a girl is the only information apparent at the beginning of the text; the properties that distinguish her are only revealed in the course of the text. The attributes of fictive figures depend exclusively on the placement of information in the poem. In contradistinction (ii) the names of historical, legendary or mythological figures immediately conjure up a set of features. Examples are the character Nietzsche in Stefan George's poem »Nietzsche«, Squire von Ribbeck in Theodor Fontane's ballad, the Loreley in Heinrich Heine's or Clemens Brentano's poems, Saint Cecilia in Agnes Miegel's »Santa Cäcilia« or Prometheus in Johann Wolfgang Goethe's prototypical *Sturm-und-Drang* poem. Although only a small number of the attributes semantically associated with the historical personages or mythological figures are explicitly attended to or re-interpreted in the poems – as in the case of Elagabalus in George's »Algabal«-cycle –, the spectrum of potential character attributes is certainly broad here. This holds equally for names that refer to literary characters, for instance ›Ophelia‹ in Georg Heym's eponymous poem, or ›Hamlet‹ whose characteristic attributes of hesitation and reluctance are used in Ferdinand Freiligrath's poem »Hamlet« for describing and assessing the state of Germany. (iii) Names using literary topoi function in a similar way. Employing them, authors again rely on some type of knowledge available to their readers, but this knowledge is

---

27 Cf. Jannidis: Figur, pp. 110f.; Schneider: Grundriß, pp. 75f.

mediated by literature and is not so much directed at the individuality of a character as at its typological properties and functions. Examples are the already mentioned typified names of women in Anacreontic poems. As is well-known, ›Doris‹, ›Daphne‹ or ›Chloe‹ basically designate serene, attractive and lovable women, often scantily dressed and predominantly moving around in idyllic landscapes. The attribute ›natural‹ can be applied to them even if they are placed in a culturally marked setting.

The second group of linguistic expressions for the purpose of character designation are *noun phrases*. In Goethe's »Rose in the Heather« (»Heideröslein«), for instance, the two characters are designated as ›a rosebud‹ (l. 1) and ›the rash boy‹ (l. 15),[28] in his »Erlking« (»Erlkönig«) appears »the father with his child«, in Novalis's »To Tieck« (»An Tieck«) it is »a child«. A distinguishable subgroup of this kind of character designation is formed by designations of type as they appear for instance in folk-song-like Romantic texts, e.g. the cheerful huntsman, the beautiful miller's daughter, or the seductive witch in the work of Joseph v. Eichendorff, Wilhelm Müller or Clemens Brentano. Again the knowledge of the reader about topoi constituted by literature is alluded to by means of such designations. Among these typifying designations may also be collected the personifications of abstract nouns, for instance in Georg Heym's »The War« (»Der Krieg«). The abstract noun used here as a designation has the same function as a typified name: it designates the character and ties together a number of supra-individual properties whose knowledge is presupposed, in the case of »The War« e.g. violence, total destruction and death.

The last group of linguistic means of designation plays a recognisably greater role in poetry than in prose texts: *designation by means of pronouns*. In numerous poems, there are no proper names or designating noun phrases, and the characters are marked exclusively by pronouns. As a rule, personal pronouns are used, especially ›I‹ and ›you‹, but there may also be indefinite pronouns as, for instance, in Hofmannsthal's »Interdependence« (»Manche freilich«), or demonstrative pronouns as in Leo Greiner's Gedicht »Life« (»Leben«), in which the speaker designates other characters only with the pronoun ›this‹, thus calling their identity into question. Pronouns do not communicate any information beyond their pragmatic functions in linguistic communication. The expression ›I‹, for instance, refers only to a speaking instance about whom nothing else is yet known, the expression ›you‹ refers to an addressee who is addressed by a speaking instance. In the linguistic context of a poem, the expression ›I‹ places whatever is represented in perspective and directs the attention of the

---

28 Zeydel: Goethe, p. 33.

reader towards the speaker[29] but does not communicate any further features of this character except that it is capable of speech. This third variant of the designation of characters is therefore semantically the poorest, and the question arises whether pronouns allow for the identification of figures at all. This question leads to the techniques of characterisation.

2. *Characterisation.* The technique of characterisation is understood here very broadly as the tying of information to a character.[30] According to this formal specification, all items of information ascribed to a character in a text contribute to its characterisation, i.e. all kinds of information relating to its external appearance as well as all kinds of information about its mental properties and the situative constellations in which it is located. For narrative texts the differentiation of stable and variable, central and peripheral, essential and accidental, etc. character information plays an important role because it allows for the distinction between characterisations that are ‹characteristic‹ in the narrow sense from characterisations that are irrelevant. For poems, such a differentiation is less informative because due to the brevity of most of these texts; anyway, there is not very much space left for less relevant information or for the development of a character. In other words, the slight character information that is communicated must be ›characteristic‹, which in turn has the consequence that poems frequently contain typified characters. Due to the brevity of the texts, individualisation in the sense of a process in which new features are ascribed to the typified characters[31] therefore plays a less significant role than in narrative texts. For the same reason, the above-stated designations whereby a character is introduced into a poem or that serve the tying together of features may simultaneously function as characterisations. They may even be the only characterising pieces of information available in the text. This applies to the designations by means of proper names and noun phrases but not to the designation by means of pronouns. In the case of pronominal designation at least one further feature must be provided that secures the attribute ›human‹ or ›humanlike‹ to make it possible at all to speak of a character. The information required in this case may be communicated through the ascription of mental states or human actions. Both these possibilities of transforming a pronominally introduced ›object‹ in a poem into a character are used, for example, in Richard Dehmel's poem »Sultry Air« (»Drückende Luft«). Here neither a name nor a description is used to designate the female

---

29 Cf. Schiedermair: Lyrisches Ich, p. 116.
30 Cf. Jannidis: Figur, p. 208.
31 Cf. Schneider: Grundriß, p. 143.

character but merely the pronoun ›she‹. That it is a woman to which the pronoun refers can only be inferred from the first occurrence on the grounds of the references to the activity (piano playing) and the emotional attitude (sadness) ascribed to her.

Even though such brief characterisations, i.e. ascriptions of minimal information, occur with a significantly higher frequency in poems than in prose texts, the categories suggested by research for the description of characterisation may be employed for both genres. The significance of the categories of character portrayal for poems shifts, however, and this will be briefly explained in the following.[32]

Duration indicates how long and therefore also how extensively information ascribed to a character is presented; the duration of the allocation of character information is only ›informative‹ in relation to the length of the whole poem. As this category is measured by reading time, it will tend to be considerably shorter for poems than for narrative texts.

The *amount* of allocated character information in a poem indicates how many different features are ascribed to a character. The minimal option here is that one single feature must be given in order to speak of a character at all.[33] In narrative texts, this minimal amount of character-related information will occur only rarely, in poems, however, as already mentioned, more frequently, for instance in the appeal to fictive addressees about whom not much more is said than that they stand in a particular relationship with the speaker instance. However, it is even less possible in poems than in narratives or novels to infer the relevance of a character in the text from the amount – or the duration – of the character information. Here the feature of information density or condensation takes effect: even a single character feature may turn out to be of particular importance due to the superimposition of other kinds of information of the poem. Therefore, out of genre-specific reasons the weighing of the information in a text plays a stronger role for lyric than for prose. Such weighing may be carried out formally with the help of means subsumed under the categories ›frequency‹ and ›order‹, but also with reference to the content of what is being said. The meaning-related weighing of features may be achieved through the coupling of character information and other information in the poem (›context of information‹ and ›context of characters‹),[34] for example, by combining the character

---

32 Cf. on the following ibid.: pp. 220f. Jannidis quite rightly emphasises that the categories could also be constructed differently.
33 Cf. Margolin: Characters.
34 Ibid.: p. 201.

information with the topic of the poem or with information about the speaker character.

The *frequency* with which the same kind of information is ascribed to a character may be mentioned as the third quantitative element of potential qualitative consequence. For the very reason that poetry, due to its genre specifications, is generally parsimonious with information, the repeated mentioning of the same character feature, possibly in variations, is potentially significant. However, not every repetition in a poem can be directly understood as a straightforward indication of relevance. When character information in songlike texts is communicated in the refrain, for instance, then this repetition is motivated differently, namely by the conventions of the genre, as for instance in Goethe's »Rose in the Heather«, where colour and place are indicated for the rose that is constructed as a character (»Rosebud, little rosebud red, / Rosebud in the heather.« ll. 6f., 13f., 20f.).[35] It must be checked in every individual case whether the character information presented repeatedly in a refrain possesses additional relevance.

The *order* of character information has a qualitative function insofar as it contributes to the weighing of the stated features. Character information may, therefore, gain special significance through rhetorical placement: it may introduce the poem and thus assume a guiding function for the further processing of information, or it may conclude it and thus achieve particular prominence as the last item of information – possibly even by way of a sort of punch line. In contradistinction to narrative texts, poems command the instrument of verse, which provides additional possibilities of accentuating character information, namely by means of conspicuous metrical or rhyme-bound positioning. The scant information about a character will gain weight, for instance, if it is placed in a rhyming position. One of numerous examples is offered by Georg Heym's »The God of the City« (»Der Gott der Stadt«) where – in the original German version – the adjective ›breit‹ (l. 1) ascribed to the principal character is placed in the stressed position at the end of this line, i.e. in the rhyming position, so as to make it more imposing.[36] Its dominance is increased even further by the rhyming combination of ›breit‹ and ›Einsamkeit‹ (l. 3), the attribute of the scattered houses outside the town that are set against the god of the city.

---

35 Zeydel: Goethe, p. 33.
36 Heym: Gedichte, p. 627. An English translation cf. Allen: Life, p. 82: »On a block of houses he spreads his weight. / The winds rest blackly round his brow. / He looks with rage into the distant solitude, / Where the last houses are lost in the land.« (l. 1–4).

The *density* of character information may be understood as the relation between the amount of information about a character and the total amount of information contained in the text. High density occurs in those passages of poems, which present concentrated information about a character, little density if character information is scattered throughout the text. In Hofmannsthal's poem »Interdependence« (»Manche freilich«),[37] for instance, the first two stanzas show high information density with respect to the two groups of characters that are set against each other, whereas the last three stanzas show only little density.

Two categories of character information are of particular significance to poetry: the *context of information* and the *context of characters*. They indicate with what kinds of information the features of a character are interconnected within the poem. As has been mentioned several times, the depiction of characters in poems is generally fairly scant; such relational information is, therefore, of importance because it may at least allow for the derivation of evidence indicative of omitted features that are nevertheless essential for the understanding of the characters. Such kinds of information may belong to the setting of the poem or to the constructed situation; it may also be part of the constellation involving the character in question with other characters. An example of such a way of characterising is given by the characters ›Manche‹ and ›Andere‹ in Hofmannthal's »Interdependence« (»Manche freilich«).[38] It is not clearly stated what groups of human beings are actually referred to, it is only circumscribed and expressed indirectly by images of spaces and situations that are set against each other. Thus, the groups of characters are presented as types and at the same time are described so vaguely that ample room for interpretation remains, which has been extensively exploited by the Hofmannsthal scholarship community.[39]

A good example of the interplay of different means of characterisation is offered by Brentano's »Song of the Spinstress« (»Der Spinnerin Nachtlied«). Striking here is the discrepancy between the amount and the relevance of character information, on the one hand, the proportional relationship between amount and frequency, on the other. Only two items of information are communicated about the character addressed, the ›You‹, in the poem: (i) the character left the ›I‹ some time ago (»That you

---

37 Stork: Poems, p. 37.
38 Hofmannsthal: Werke, p. 26; Stork: Poems, p. 37, translates ›Manche‹ as ›Many men‹, ›Andere‹ as ›Others‹.
39 To mention only two different interpretations: Kayser: Kunstwerk, pp. 311–318; Grimm: Botschaft, pp. 36f.

have left me«, l. 12; »Since you left me«, l. 17);[40] (ii) the character stood in a close relationship with the ›I‹ some time ago (»When we were together«, ll. 4, 9; »How we were together«, l. 20).[41] There is no need to debate the question of whether the ›You‹ represents a character at all because it clearly fulfils the above-stated conditions of the existence of characters: personality, existence and predication. This ›You‹ was at least part of the fictive world in the past and it is ascribed the two quoted features. However, that this character must be identified as an absent lover and that it plays a central role in the poem can only be inferred by reference to other pieces of information in the poem. The decisive factor here is the textual construction of the situation of the female speaker, the distress caused by the loss of the ›You‹ and the hope for a reunion with the help of God. The male gender of the ›You‹ and the identification of the ›close relationship‹ as a relationship of love are never made explicit, these features can only be inferred from the context – with reference, for instance, to the literary tradition of the deserted girl. The relevance of this extremely economical construction of the character of an addressee may be formally enhanced by a quantitative argument not related to the content of the information but to its frequency: it involves the recurrences (ll. 4, 9, 12, 17, 25). Although repetitions of phrases with scant variations characterise the whole poem and although even the moon and the nightingale appear repeatedly as subjects of such repetitions, it is the fictive addressee who turns up most frequently in these variations.

The example demonstrates that it is of the highest importance for poems to assemble all the different types of information in such a way as to enable the image of a character to arise in a text-directed manner. At the same time, it demonstrates that there are cases in which all the *explicit* items of information together still do not suffice to create such an image. The constitution of a character is only possible if the readers supplement all the explicitly given information with their life-world and also literary knowledge about types of situation, patterns of action or typified relations between characters.

---

40 Trans. S.W.; cf. Brentano: Werke, p. 131: »Daß du von mir gefahren«, l. 12; »Seit du von mir gefahren«, l. 17.

41 Trans. S.W.; cf. Brentano: Werke, p. 131: »Da wir zusammen waren«, l. 4; »Als wir zusammen waren«, l. 9; »Wie wir zusammen waren«, l. 20.

2.2 Information about Characters in the Context of Poems

Apart from the techniques of the construction of characters, two further modes of representation must be taken into account that have to do with the integration of character information into the context of the poem: the motivation of the reader, and the relationship betwenn the reader and a character as it is suggested text-internally. Although aspects of both modes may play a role in the portrayal of a character, they will here be dealt with separately because they do not primarily serve the constitution of characters.

1. The investigation of *motivation* may either focus on the function of character information concerning the motivation of the actions in a poem,[42] or it may deal with the question of whether the character information can be considered to be ›motivated‹ wherever it occurs in the poem, i.e. whether these items of information fulfil identifiable functions. In both cases, the investigation will concern the relations between character information and the actions and the events or situations in the poem. In a case of *causal motivation* the property of a character may release an action or provide its reasons or causes; the broken heart of the witch Loreley in Eichendorff's »Conversation in the Wood« (»Waldgespräch«), for instance, motivates her men-murdering behaviour, and the death sentence that is passed by the tyrant in Schiller's ballad »The Hostage« (»Die Bürgschaft«) is causally effected by the love of freedom that made Damon attempt the tyrant's assassination. Character information can hardly contribute to a *final motivation* because this type of motivation is connected with explanatory perspectives involving concepts of destiny or divine providence, and such perspectives allow for a retrospective integration of preceding elements of actions and events after the text has ended. Properties of characters may again be causally incorporated here as, for instance, in Bürger's ballad »Lenore«, where the death of the protagonist is certainly finally motivated but – as indicated by her accusations against God – still stands in a causal relation with a feature of the personality of this character. The third type of motivation, the *motivation by composition*, must be assumed as the ›default position‹, and not only with reference to the total action of a text.[43] All kinds of information in poems tend to be motivated by composition since the thesis of the potential relevance of every single textual feature has the status of a genre convention for poetry.[44] It would be rather bizarre for character

---

42 Cf. the three types of motivation in Martinez: Welten, pp. 27–32.
43 Cf. also Jannidis: Figur, p. 223.
44 See above, section 1, on the feature ›density‹.

information to appear in a poem without any recognisable compositional motivation. Consequently, compositional motivation is of particular relevance for poems simply for genre-specific reasons. However, the fact that actions are not depicted in greater detail and are occasionally rendered in a greatly reduced form does not warrant the conclusion that causal motivation is irrelevant in poetry. Even though causal motivation is not extensively represented in poems, it may still play an important role as presupposed knowledge. Because of the very fact of the parsimonious distribution of explicit information in poetry, the conventionalised assumption that there is a causal connection between an action X and a character property Z, though not mentioned in the text, is used to construct the connection in an implicit way. In Goethe's »Greeting and Farewell« (»Willkommen und Abschied«), for example, the causal chain propelling the action forward remains implicit all the time: the speaker character loves a woman and wants to meet her and therefore gallops through the night. The connection will in all probability be quite clear to every reader because it follows a pattern according to which the topic of the love of the ›I‹ for the ›You‹, which appears only in stanza 3 – and there, again, only as an image – is connected with the apparently unmotivated haste expressed in the first two stanzas.[45]

2. Further light is shed on the construction of a character by the means of specifying the attitude of a reader towards this character. The spectrum of possible *reader attitudes towards a character*, which is only insufficiently labelled as ›identification‹, comprises at least empathy, sympathy, recognition as a role model and aesthetic appreciation.[46] But not the actual attitudes of empirical readers are of importance here; it is the attitudes towards a character as they are suggested to the readers by a poem. Just as there are linguistic resources to establish the psychological condition of a character in a text, there are means by which attitudes of empathy, rejection and admiration may be evoked in the reader. Whether these effects are actually achieved in the end is not a concern of the present debate; the object of investigation is rather the linguistically induced potential. It must be stressed, however, that investigating this potential does not always lead to a better understanding of the poem: there are obviously poems that refrain from unambiguous attributions and do not make use of strategies that evoke sympathy or empathy but construct their characters in a neutral way.

---

45 Zeydel: Goethe, pp. 35ff.
46 Cf. section 12 of the introduction to this book. For an explication of the terms ›perspective‹, ›identification‹ and ›empathy‹ cf. Eder: Figur, ch. 12.2. Eder analyses characters in films but several of his findings apply to literature as well.

The ways and means used to produce certain attitudes towards characters in texts in general and in poems in particular have not yet been sufficiently investigated at all.[47] Among these means are:

(i) different narrative techniques that reduce the distance between the narrator and what is represented and – figuratively speaking – move the reader closer to the narrating instance. Such techniques are, for instance, internal focalisation, techniques of speech rendering, e.g. free indirect discourse, or a scenic mode instead of a narrative mode. The large group of poems with a homodiegetic or an autodiegetic speaker can bring about this very reduction of distance: voice and focalisation can be used so as to create the illusion of an authentic speech situation. This illusion is created through linguistic means, which generate the impression of perspective-dependence and, in this sense, of the ›subjectivity‹ of human perception.[48] The readers are granted an apparently ›direct view‹ of the perception or the reflection of the speaker in this way.

(ii) The second technique comprises various means of emotionalisation. Characters can be represented in such a manner as to make emotional attitudes like compassion, revulsion, joy or anger appear as the appropriate attitudes to be inspired in their recipients. This may happen explicitly as, for instance, in Fontane's ballad »John Maynard«, in which ›love‹ is postulated as the appropriate attitude towards the protagonist. In most cases, however, emotionalisation is brought about by implicit means: when a character is, for instance, connected with a situation that is quite clearly culturally coded as emotional – e.g. distress in a situation of loss – or when it performs an action whose motive is typically assumed to be a strong emotion – e.g. the self-sacrifice out of love, the murder out of jealousy. By alluding to such cultural patterns nameable emotions are evoked, whereas metrical, syntactical or rhetorical means may produce a less specific kind of emotionalisation.[49] Poetry uses possibilities of this kind in greater measure than prose. Although careful checking must establish in every individual case to whom the emotions in a poem are ascribed, emotionalisation as such may be considered to be a strategy to suggest particular attitudes towards characters.

(iii) A third means that cannot be separated distinctly from the second one consists of the text-internal evaluations attached to characters. They shed light on the position taken by a character within the ensemble of all the other figures in the poem and/or ›comment on‹ the properties or

---

47 Cf. e.g. Winko: Gefühle, pp. 143f.; more detailed: Hillebrandt: Verhältnis, ch. 2.
48 Cf. here Müller-Zettelmann: Lyrik, p. 142. On the close relation between the ›perspective‹ of the narrating instance and the representation of other characters, albeit in narrative texts, cf. Roßbach: Figuren, p. 86
49 Cf. in detail Winko: Gefühle, pp. 130–141, 143f.

actions of the character. Here again, explicitly evaluative poems must be distinguished from implicitly evaluative ones. Fontane's already mentioned ballad »John Maynard« leaves no doubt that the unselfish sacrifice of the central character deserves the greatest esteem and that this protagonist may even be attributed a moral model function. But also less explicit indications may render text-internal evaluations clear enough. In Eichendorff's »Conversation in the Wood« (»Waldgespräch«), as already explained above, the manner of action of the Loreley is justified by the account that she has been left by her lover, cannot act in any other way due to her ›broken heart‹, and is therefore doomed to bring disaster on all men. This account does not only serve to explain the manner of action of the character, it has the further function of an implicit commentary because it shifts at least part of the guilt onto the faithless lover. A technique of the implicit evaluation of characters is, therefore, the parallelising or contrasting comparison with actions or characters that have been given an unambiguously positive or negative moral evaluation, independently of whether such an evaluation is culturally accepted or is established within the text. Still other means are the commentary through the direction of actions, e.g. if a character turns out to be wrong at the end, or by linguistic or image-based references to contemporary discourses whose significance is beyond doubt. The use of all these means by poetry is in no way different from the possibilities commanded by narrative texts.

3 The Identification of Characters in Poems

How do we recognise characters in poems, and on what basis do we ascribe attributes to them? This question has only been marginally touched upon so far and will now be dealt with by the example of two problem cases. These problem cases will furthermore lead to questions that are even more fundamental.

3.1 Classification and Interpretation

Normally it does not present any problem to identify an entity in the fictive world as a character, not even in poems with minimal information about characters: a character is usually recognisable as the counterpart of a human being. In some cases, however, it remains unclear whether the textual entity in question is a character or perhaps an inanimate object, and the operations that are required to justify the ascription reveal the mechanisms of the identification of characters. More precisely, they shed light on the relationship between textual analysis and interpretation in the act of the identification of characters.

One of the above-mentioned ›object poems‹ may be used as an example, i.e. Rilke's sonnet »Archaic Torso of Apollo« (»Archaischer Torso Apollos«).[50] Title and beginning of the text make clear that the poem describes an object of art, a statue, and thus the representation of a character, which is, however, not a character itself. First doubts about the object status may arise in verse 4 that ascribes to the torso remnants of a lost ›gaze‹ (›Schauen‹) still recognisable but only as a kind of sheen. Doubts may also be raised by stanza 2 where the formulation »[...] nor through the soft turn / of the loins could this smile easily have passed / into the bright groins where the genitals burned« (ll. 6–8)[51] ascribes the human property of smiling to the apparently fragmentary object. However, this attribution might be part of the tradition to depict objects in an anthropomorphic way without necessarily turning them into characters immediately. In the last line the torso is ascribed the ability to ›see‹ the spectator – in the intentional sense of ›looking at‹ –, and the order how this information is given puts an emphasis on the fact that the statue can actually see: It is communicated in a metrically prominent position in which – in German – three stressed syllables must be spoken one after the other: »[...] denn da ist keine Stelle, / die <u>dich</u> <u>nicht</u> <u>sieht</u>. [...]« (ll. 13f.).[52] Together with the evidence quoted from the preceding stanzas this feature of looking makes it plausible to speak of a character. Furthermore: the last sentence of the sonnet, »You must change your life.«,[53] formulating as it does a surprising appeal for action directed at the spectator may be understood as motivated by the figure of the torso. Although no causal connection will be formulated here, the conclusion seems unavoidable that – if the appeal is not deemed as having no connection at all to the preceding depiction of the torso, i.e. if coherence can be assumed for the poem – there seems to be no alternative to the interpretation that the torso of the god Apollo is the cause of the concluding normative appeal. The character would thus be given the function of a moral instance.

The example demonstrates two things: for one, the classification of an entity in the poem as a character depends on ascriptions of meaning. There are cases in which a relatively complex interpretative act is required

---

50 Cf. MacIntyre: Rilke, 91.
51 »[...] und im leisen Drehen / der Lenden könnte nicht ein Lächeln gehen / zu jener Mitte, die die Zeugung trug.« (ll. 6–8); Rilke: Werke, p. 557.
52 Ibid.; cf. »[...] until there is no place / that does not see you.« (ll. 13f.); MacIntyre: Rilke, p. 91.
53 »Du mußt dein Leben ändern.« (l. 14); Rilke: Werke, p. 557.

in order to make a claim for an object described in a poem to be a character. Furthermore, it becomes clear that the interpretation of the poem is influenced by the hypothesis that the torso is a character: if the torso is an object it is more probable to assume that all the descriptions in the poem including the appeal for action rest on projections of the spectator and must be ascribed to the spectator; if the torso is classified as a character then he can take on the role of an agent and beyond that the function of a moral instance.

3.2 The Speaker as Character

As in narrative texts, the speakers in poems may be constructed as characters, but there are obviously numerous poems in which no character-like speaker instance can be identified.[54] Examples can be found throughout the history of literature and there is no particular need to document them here. Some of these poems are philosophical poems, some deal with religious or poetological reflections; others depict landscapes, evoke certain moods or enclose narratives. Poems with a character-like speaker instance, in their overwhelming majority, have a homodiegetic or an autodiegetic speaker instance. Generally, the speakers of these poems use the first-person singular pronoun, sometimes also its plural form. These speakers may be tagged as characters by a name or a description, often already in the poem's title. »Prometheus« states the identity of the speaker instance just as »Song of the Spinstress« (»Der Spinnerin Nachtlied«), and the speaker in Max Dauthendey's »Autumn of the Blind« (»Der Herbst des Blinden«) is characterised by his most important property, which motivates the plethora of synaesthesias in the poem, already in the title – and only there – as a blind person. In most cases, however, the poems with homodiegetic or autodiegetic speakers lack a character designation. As this applies to the overwhelming majority of poems, the question in which way characters can be identified in these texts gains relevance if merely for quantitative reasons.

The attributes that belong to the ›I‹ as a character are indirectly communicated in these texts, i.e. they must be inferred. Two ways of such

---

54 According to James Phelan in poems ›in which the speaker is not individualized and is not placed in any specific situation‹ ›the speaker's character […] fades back into the image of the implied author‹ (Phelan: Character, pp. 411f.). In my opinion it is not necessary to assume a controversial concept as the implied author to classify the types of speakers in poems; cf. Kindt / Müller: Implied Author. The attempts to adopt a lyric-specific instance of utterance are not plausible as well; see Borkowski / Winko: Gedicht; for a dissenting position cf. Bernhart: Überlegungen, pp. 365–369.

‹inference‹ must be distinguished. In the first place, the character information is extracted from the body of the poem's text. This may be achieved through formal information. As one can understand the utterances of a homodiegetic or an autodiegetic speaker with the contours of a character as the speech of a character, the same categories may be exploited here as with narrative texts. The stylistic specifics of speech may be just as well employed for the identification of this character[55] and the character's ›mind-style‹.[56] Both together may generally be extracted through the same linguistic instruments and resources as are used in prose texts, e.g. choice of words, syntactic structures, modes of argumentation, rhetorical means, etc. In addition, conclusions can be drawn from the selections made by the speaker character: the experiences, actions and situations described or omitted, the internal states topicalised – emotions, moods and sentiments, psychological conflicts, etc. –, all these may reveal the peculiarities of this character.

It would be an idealisation to assume, however, that only features derivable from text-internal information are used by readers to constitute the speaker character. It is quite common practice even amongst expert readers to transfer the gender of the author of a poem to the speaker instance even though the poem may not offer any evidence to justify such an ascription. Such transference, however, is also performed with reference to narrative texts, predominantly with texts that do not contain a narrative instance constructed as a character.[57] The procedure to adduce information about the empirical author in order to lend contours to the speaker character in poems corresponds to the ways of handling non-fictional autobiographical narrative texts. There is a set of poems that actually demands such a far-reaching transference because they are programmatically characterised by a specific relationship between speaker-›I‹ and empirical author: ›poetry of personal experience‹ (›Erlebnislyrik‹). These poems, *per conventionem*, construct the fiction that they express the personal experiences of their authors, their feelings and thoughts in concrete situations, which, however, must have the ability to be generalized.[58] Conditions of such fictions are (i) a conception of individuality tied to historical presuppositions shared by authors and

---

55 Cf. Koch: Menschendarstellung, pp. 188–197.
56 Fowler: Linguistics, pp. 76, 103ff.
57 This assumption is based on my observations and would also have to be tested empirically.
58 Cf. Wünsch: Erlebnislyrik, p. 498. Kaiser: Erlebnisgedicht, p. 141, however, assumes that ›Erlebnisgedichte‹ do not postulate to be based on a real experience; instead, he claims that these poems are »absolute Vergegenwärtigung« and that genuine poetic means are essential for them.

readers, a conception that became possible in the German-speaking area only in the period of the late Enlightenment; (ii) features of content, in particular the topicalisation of internal states (emotions, moods and sentiments) of the speaker-›I‹, and the (framing) presentation of an experience; (iii) the identification of the ›I‹ with the author. This identification can be understood as the result of a sort of contract: the author pretends to be the speaking ›I‹ in the poem, the reader joins the game and identifies the author with the speaker. Readers performing such an identification behave in complete agreement with the convention and are fully justified accordingly to supplement lacking information about the character of the speaker with knowledge they have about the author. Obviously, this procedure is incorrect by the standards of literary scholarship; it may, however, be stated here expressly that it is in conformity with the conventions of the production and the reception of ›poetry of personal experience‹. Conventions of this kind, which direct the textual understanding of those who know and accept them, must be given much more attention by literary scholarship.

4 Summary

It is not surprising that the constitution of characters in poems does not show any essential differences from the constitution of characters in narrative texts. The techniques of the construction of characters in poems seem to be fundamentally the same as in narrative texts, and the reference to mental models does not diverge from what previous investigations of texts in prose have already established as facts. The differences are of a quantitative nature and concern features like verse, density of information and resulting complexity, and the brevity of poems. The feature of verse and its specific mechanisms of metrical binding and rhyming provide a greater number of formal means of weighing the different types of information about characters. Textual density and the associated assumption about the relevance of potentially every single textual feature have the effect that minimal indications on different levels of the texts – phonetic, lexical, syntactic and rhetorical – may be employed to support the construction of characters. It should furthermore have become clear by now that top-down processes of understanding are of particular importance for the construction of characters in poetry. Of crucial relevance here is the feature of brevity: poems frequently contain only very few explicit items of information about characters. The consequence is, amongst other things, that poems depend more on schemata of characters or patterns of established characters and typified situations than texts in prose. This insight involves two aspects: for one, poems must rely to a higher degree on schemata that are brought to the text by the readers for the purpose of understanding, and they must, furthermore, use a greater number of conventional features than texts in prose. This assumption is not meant to deny that prose also employs conventional features; but prose texts simply give their readers more time for the identification of characters and, therefore, have more room to play with variations.

The fact that conventions must play a more important role in poems *qua* genre than in prose is perhaps the most important result of the preceding analysis of the constitution of characters: to guarantee the recognition of a character as a character in an extremely limited space, conventionalised features must be expressed. Typified characters in standard situations are therefore found more frequently in poems than in narrative texts. In these texts more effort is devoted to the ›How‹ – the linguistic presentation and formal variation –, less on the ›What‹. The considerations presented have shown at the same time that considerable research is still needed on the topic ›characters in poetry‹: many of my assertions rest on the impressions of a scholar that has occupied herself intensively with German-language poetry but can unfortunately do no more than just formulate impressions; they would have to be tested with large text corpora in historical sequences. Furthermore, the instruments of analysis would have to be refined – e.g. with reference to the knowledge presuppositions on which poems rely. Rich material is thus available for in-depth studies of the constitution of characters in poetry.

References

Allen, Roy: Literary Life in German Expressionism. Göppingen 1974.
Bernhart, Walter: Überlegungen zur Lyriktheorie aus erzähltheoretischer Sicht. In: Herbert Foltinek / Wolfgang Wiehle / Waldemar Zacharasiewicz (Eds.): Tales and ›their telling difference‹. Zur Theorie der Geschichte der Narrativik. Festschrift zum 70. Geburtstag von Franz K. Stanzel. Heidelberg 1993, pp. 359–375.
Borkowski, Jan / Simone Winko: Wer spricht das Gedicht? Noch einmal zum Begriff ›lyrisches Ich‹ und zu seinen Ersetzungsvorschlägen. In: Hartmut Bleumer / Caroline Emmelius (Eds.): Lyrische Narrationen – narrative Lyrik. Gattungsinterferenzen in der mittelalterlichen Literatur. Berlin / New York 2011 (in print).
Brentano, Clemens: Werke, vol. 1. Ed. by Wolfgang Frühwald / Bernhard Gajek / Friedhelm Kemp. 2nd edn. München 1978.
Burdorf, Dieter: Einführung in die Gedichtanalyse. 2nd edn. Stuttgart 1997.
Culpeper, Jonathan: Inferring Character from Texts. Attribution Theory and Foregrounding Theory. In: Poetics 23 (1996), pp. 335–361.
Eder, Jens: Die Figur im Film. Grundlagen der Figurenanalyse. Marburg 2008.
Fowler, Roger: Linguistics and the Novel. London 1977.

Gerrig, Richard / David W. Allbritton: The Construction of Literary Character. A View from Cognitive Psychology. In: Style 24/3 (1990), pp. 380–391.

Grimm, Reinhold: Bange Botschaft. Zum Verständnis von Hofmannsthals »Manche freilich…«. In: Vom Naturalismus bis zur Jahrhundertmitte. Ed. by Harald Hartung. Stuttgart 1983, pp. 34–42.

Grosse, Siegfried: Lyrik und Linguistik. In: Heidrun Kämper / Hartmut Schmidt (Eds.): Das 20. Jahrhundert. Sprachgeschichte – Zeitgeschichte. Berlin / New York 1998, pp. 43–58.

Heym, Georg: Gedichte 1910–1912. Historisch-kritische Ausgabe aller Texte in genetischer Darstellung. Ed. by Günter Dammann et al., vol. 1. Tübingen 1993, pp. 635–654.

Hillebrandt, Claudia: Zum Verhältnis von literarischer Emotionsdarstellung und emotionaler Leserlenkung. Systematische Überlegungen und historische Beispielanalysen zu Kafka, Perutz und Werfel (PhD.-Thesis. Göttingen, forthcoming).

Hofmannsthal, Hugo v.: Gesammelte Werke, vol. 1: Gedichte, Dramen I, 1891–1898. Ed. by Bernd Schoeller et al. Frankfurt/M. 1979.

Hühn, Peter / Jörg Schönert: Zur narratologischen Analyse von Lyrik. In: Poetica 34 (2002), pp. 287–305.

Hühn, Peter/Jörg Schönert: Einleitung. Theorie und Methodologie narratologischer Lyrik-Analyse. In: P.H. / J.S. / Malte Stein (Eds.): Lyrik und Narratologie. Text-Analysen zu deutschsprachigen Gedichten vom 16. bis zum 20. Jahrhundert. Berlin / New York 2007, pp. 1–18.

Hühn, Peter / Jörg Schönert: Auswertung der Text-Analysen und Schlussfolgerungen zu den Aspekten von Narratologie. Lyrik-Theorie und Lyrik-Analyse. In: P.H. / J.S. / Malte Stein (Eds.): Lyrik und Narratologie. Text-Analysen zu deutschsprachigen Gedichten vom 16. bis zum 20. Jahrhundert. Berlin / New York 2007, pp. 311–333.

Hühn, Peter / Jörg Schönert / Malte Stein: Lyrik und Narratologie. Text-Analysen zu deutschsprachigen Gedichten vom 16. bis zum 20. Jahrhundert. Berlin / New York 2007.

Jannidis, Fotis: Figur und Person. Beiträge zu einer historischen Narratologie. Berlin / New York 2004.

Jannidis, Fotis: Character. In: Handbook of Narratology. Ed. by Peter Hühn / John Pier / Wolf Schmid / Jörg Schönert. Berlin / New York 2009, pp. 14–29.

Kaiser, Gerhard: Was ist ein ›Erlebnisgedicht‹? Johann Wolfgang von Goethe »Es schlug mein Herz…«. In: Augenblicke deutscher Lyrik. Gedichte von Martin Luther bis Paul Celan. Frankfurt/M. 1987, pp. 117–144.

Kayser, Wolfgang: Das sprachliche Kunstwerk. Eine Einführung in die Literaturwissenschaft. 17th edn. Bern / München 1976 (first publ. in 1948).

Kindt, Tom / Hans-Harald Müller: The Implied Author. Concept and Controversy. Berlin / New York 2006.

Koch, Thomas: Literarische Menschendarstellung. Studien zu ihrer Theorie und Praxis. Tübingen 1991.

Köppe, Tilmann / Jan Stühring: Against Pan-Narrator Theories (forthcoming).

Lamping, Dieter: Das lyrische Gedicht. Definitionen zu Theorie und Geschichte der Gattung. Göttingen 1989.

Link, Jürgen: Elemente der Lyrik. In: Helmut Brackert / Jörn Stückrath (Eds.): Literaturwissenschaft. Ein Grundkurs. Reinbek 1992, pp. 86–101.

MacIntyre, C.F.: Rainer Maria Rilke: Fifty Selected Poems with English Translations. Berkeley 1947.

Margolin, Uri: Characters in Literary Narrative. Representation and Signification. In: Semiotica 106 (1995), pp. 373–392.

Martinez, Matias: Doppelte Welten. Struktur und Sinn zweideutigen Erzählens. Göttingen 1996.

Müller-Zettelmann, Eva: Lyrik und Narratologie. In: Vera Nünning / Ansgar Nünning (Eds): Erzähltheorie transgenerisch, intermedial, interdisziplinär. Trier 2002, pp. 129–153.

Phelan, James: Character and Judgement in Narrative and in Lyric. Toward an Understanding of the Audience's Engagement in »The Waves«. In: Style 24/3 (1990), pp. 408–421.

Rilke, Rainer Maria: Sämtliche Werke 1. Gedichte, Erster Teil. Ed. by Rilke-Archiv et al. Frankfurt/M. 1987.

Roßbach, Bruno: Figuren und Figurensysteme in erzählten Welten. In: Claudia Mauelshagen / Jan Seifert (Eds.): Sprache und Text in Theorie und Empirie. Beiträge zur germanistischen Sprachwissenschaft. Stuttgart 2001, pp. 84–97.

Schiedermair, Simone: ›Lyrisches Ich‹ und sprachliches ›ich‹. Literarische Funktionen der Deixis. München 2004.

Schneider, Ralf: Grundriß zur kognitiven Theorie der Figurenrezeption am Beispiel des viktorianischen Romans. Tübingen 2000.

Schönert, Jörg: Empirischer Autor, Impliziter Autor und Lyrisches Ich. In: Fotis Jannidis et al. (Eds.): Rückkehr des Autors. Zur Erneuerung eines umstrittenen Begriffs. Tübingen 1999, pp. 289–294.

Stork, Charles Wharton: The Lyrical Poems of Hugo von Hofmannsthal. Trans. from The German with an Introduction by C. W. S. New Haven et al. 1918.

Weimar, Klaus: Text, Interpretation, Methode. Hermeneutische Klärungen. In: Lutz Danneberg / Friedrich Vollhardt (Eds.): Wie international ist die Literaturwissenschaft? Methoden- und Theoriediskussion in den Literaturwissenschaften. Stuttgart / Weimar 1995, pp. 110–122.

Winko, Simone: Kodierte Gefühle. Zu einer Poetik der Emotionen in lyrischen und poetologischen Texten um 1900. Berlin 2003.

Wolf, Werner: The Lyric: Problems of Definition and a Proposal for Reconceptualisation. In: Eva Müller-Zettelmann / Margarete Rubik (Eds): Theory into Poetry. New Approaches to the Lyric. Amsterdam / New York 2005, pp. 21–56.

Wünsch, Marianne: Erlebnislyrik. In: Harald Fricke / Klaus Weimar et al.. (Eds.): Reallexikon der deutschen Literaturwissenschaft, vol. 1. Berlin / New York 1997, pp. 498–500.

Zipfel, Frank: Fiktion, Fiktivität, Fiktionalität. Analysen zur Fiktion in der Literatur und zum Fiktionsbegriff in der Literaturwissenschaft. Berlin 2001.

Zeydel, Edwin H.: Goethe, the Lyrist. 100 Poems in New Translations Facing the Origins with a Biographical Introduction. Chapel Hill 1955.

Zymner, Rüdiger: Lyrik. Umriss und Begriff. Paderborn 2009.

Murray Smith

Engaging Characters: Further Reflections

When I began working on the thesis that would eventually become the book *Engaging Characters* twenty years ago,[1] the subject of character seemed irredeemably unfashionable in film and literary studies – and that, of course, was part of the attraction. At the time, the theoretical questions connected with fictional characters seemed resolved – or so the reigning structural and post-structural orthodoxies had it. To think that characters had anything to do with actual persons was to fall prey to an illusion. Literary and filmic texts didn't (we were told) refer to or represent things outside them; as an element of such texts, characters could hardly transcend this general condition of representation. Against this backdrop, *Engaging Characters* pursued a critical and a positive agenda. The critical agenda was to take the wind out of the sails of (post-)structuralism, to reveal the numerous logical and empirical problems with a theoretical paradigm that apprentice scholars were being taught as the ›ordinary science‹ of the discipline. Or, more modestly, my agenda in this respect was to assist in this critical project – for although voices sceptical of the orthodoxy were scattered across different disciplines and institutions, they could certainly be heard by those willing to listen.[2] How relevant is this critical agenda today? Certainly the study of film has become more pluralistic, and as the publication of this book and the organization of the symposium which gave rise to it testifies, it is now possible to talk of character, in a more or less traditional sense, without being regarded as naïve or politically retrograde. The legacy of more general (post-)structural hostility towards character, however, is very much alive. Literary critic James Wood recently wrote an essay in the *Guardian* newspaper on the centrality of character to our experience of fiction, and various misappre-

---

1 Smith: Characters.
2 Among the more important ones were Bordwell: Narration; Bordwell: Meaning; Carroll: Movies; Crews: Engagements; Butler: Interpretation; Tallis: Defence.

hensions concerning that centrality.³ The fact that Wood could articulate these views forthrightly is the flip side of the fact that he evidently felt that certain prevailing assumptions about the irrelevance or supposed incoherence of the notion of character still need challenging.

Whatever the continuing relevance of the critical agenda of the book, I am confident of the ongoing importance of its positive agenda – the building of an alternative, naturalistic framework for the understanding of character, and fiction and narrative representation more generally. As an approach, naturalism is characterized by two principles, one substantive and one methodological. Substantively, naturalism regards the human mind, culture and the arts – the traditional subject matter of the human sciences – as central aspects of our evolved, ›species-specific‹ being, rather than phenomena standing outside or opposed to our ›natural‹ being. Following on from this, the methodological stance is that the specialist study of the mind, culture and the arts needs to exploit and situate itself in relation to natural scientific research which bears upon these phenomena. The positive agenda of *Engaging Characters* was not exhausted by this naturalistic agenda, however; the book also sought to open the doors to disciplines, old and new, that might contribute to our understanding of character, including anthropology and, above all, the tradition of analytic philosophy. In drawing together these various threads under the umbrella of naturalism, one other principle was important to me: that the gap between ›folk‹ or everyday talk about characters, and more theoretical reflection upon them, be bridged, if not actually closed. Theoretical discourse serves different purposes to everyday talk, so it is disingenuous to pretend that specialist disciplines can do without jargon and technical terminology altogether. But the active embrace of opaque jargon as an end in itself was and remains one of the most debilitating features of much research in the humanities. It is always worth asking: how does this technical term earn its keep? Theory remains healthy when it lives by the principle of Ockham's razor, positing technical concepts only where it needs to do so; and where the need is justified, by showing how the new concepts go beyond the familiar ones, and how we get from the former to the latter.

Engaging Characters aims to live by this principle (though it does not explicitly articulate it). The book takes the everyday notions of ›character‹ and ›identification‹ as its starting point, building from them but supplementing and revising them, more or less drastically, where necessary. Characters are treated as fictional analogues of human agents, basic constituents of representation embodied in a vast array of specific

---

3   Wood: Life, p. 4; reprinted in Wood: Fiction, pp. 75–106.

modes of characterization and purposes of representation. Characters constitute a major ›entry point‹ into our engagement with narratives: we look for characters (ie. we search for human or human-like agency); we sort major from minor characters;[4] we seek to establish the desires and goals of such characters; and we project and anticipate their destinies.[5] In so engaging with characters, our experience is structured in two primary ways. Narratives shape our experience of characters in terms of our informational *alignment* with them, that is, in terms of the degree to which we are spatially attached, and given subjective access, to them. In addition, our experience of characters is shaped in terms of *allegiance*, that is, in moral and emotional terms, by the manner in which the narrative represents them as (for example) generous or mean, brave or cowardly, diligent or irresponsible (and so on). A film prompts us to feel *for* characters in response to these factors – that is, to feel emotions distinct from but appropriate to the actions and attitudes of the characters. The villain's gleeful sadism, for example, is met with our appalled horror or anger. And prior to either of these processes, narratives must allow us to *recognize* characters, that is, to individuate and re-identify them – a process which is at once a necessary first step and an on-going process. While everyday talk about ›identifying‹ with characters tends to bundle together all three of these phenomena – and in particular typically conflates alignment and allegiance – I argue that the three processes are distinct. Of course they impact on one another, and any analysis of the *structure of sympathy* – the phrase I propose for the systematic interaction of the three processes – of a particular narrative will need to take account of all three. But recognition, alignment and allegiance can only interact because they are distinct from one another.[6]

1 The Mimetic Hypothesis and the Twofoldness of Character

Perhaps the most basic of everyday assumptions about characters is that they are fictional equivalents of real people – just like real people, without actually existing. In other words, a mimetic assumption is built in at ground level in the concept of character. *Engaging Characters* builds on the assumption, rather than rejecting it, but modifies it by thinking in terms of

---

[4] On the significance of the relationship between major and minor characters, see Woloch: One.
[5] Joseph Carroll argues this point from an evolutionary perspective. Carroll: Paradigm, pp. 117–118; see also p. 109 and pp. 133–134.
[6] The relationships among the various elements comprising the structure of sympathy are summarized in the diagram in Smith: Characters, p. 105.

a mimetic *hypothesis* rather than a simple mimetic achievement or fact.[7] That is, characters come into being initially through an imaginative, mimetic act – but they are not *bound* by this initial condition. In fantastic and experimental varieties of fiction, just about every attribute of human existence – physical, psychological, existential – can be stripped away, but perceiving such entities *as* characters still requires the initial frame of the mimetic hypothesis. The one attribute which cannot be removed without decisively removing a character from this framework is *agency*: a fictional entity which lacks the power of actual or potential action dissolves into an aspect of setting.[8] A sequence from the director's cut of Ridley Scott's *Alien* (1979) furnishes an almost literal image of this boundary between character and setting, and the transition of an entity in the fiction from one zone to the other. Fleeing the alien, Ripley (Sigourney Weaver) finds herself in an oddly cave-like space within the spacecraft Nostromo, the mechanical forms of the ship having been transformed by some alien secretion. She then realizes with horror that the organically-textured walls have (former) members of the crew embedded within them, caught in a spider-like trap by the alien, their contorted faces frozen in agony. Most are dead or at least moribund and inert. These figures, while still expressive, are no longer quite characters, but their ghastly residue (fig. 1).

Fig. 1: *Alien* (1979)

Another justification for replacing the mimetic assumption of ordinary discourse with the more circumspect notion of the mimetic hypothesis is

---

7 Butler: Interpretation, p. 7 and pp. 47–59; Smith: Characters, p. 54.
8 For a different perspective stressing the capacity for intention and experience as the most basic attribute of a character, see Eder: Figur, Eder: Figuren, and Eder: Characters.

that it accommodates apparently conflicting intuitions we may have about fictional characters, in a manner unavailable to wholly mimetic or anti-mimetic, post-structuralist approaches. On the one hand, as ordinary discourse constantly betrays, we do think of and respond to characters in many ways as if they were actual persons. We interpret their gestures and expressions; we wonder about their pasts and and futures; we seek their temperaments and abiding attributes, summing these up in terms of ›personality‹, just as we do with friends, relatives, neighbours and colleagues; we judge them in moral and non-moral ways, finding them cruel, kind, wise, irascible, vibrant, generous, fickle – and so on *ad infinitum*. On the other hand, we recognize their artificiality, and their status as constituent parts of those subsuming entities we call ›stories‹. So it is that we happily flip back and forth between references to characters and the stars and performers that embody them – between Scottie Ferguson and Jimmy Stewart in *Vertigo* (1958), Phyllis Dietrichson and Barbara Stanwick in *Double Indemnity* (1944) – as well as thinking about them in terms of the overarching dramatic structures which determine their fates: we guess that things will not end well for Phyllis because we know what usually happens to the *femme fatale* in films of this period and type. The same duality attends the performative and expressive realization of characters. On the one hand, filmmakers and spectators draw upon their real world schemata in, respectively, depicting and understanding characters; on the other, it is always open to filmmakers to depart more or less radically from such familiar and realistic patterns, as we find in many of the films of Jean-Marie Straub and Danièle Huillet, for example.[9]

The mimetic hypothesis also bears some kinship with the view of character emerging from possible world semantics, a tradition that has received some attention in literary theory, but very little in film theory.[10] Philosophers within this tradition have focussed on the ontology of character, noting that we often speak of characters as if they were as real as actual persons, and going on to ask if characters are indeed real, and if so, in what sense. The mimetic hypothesis accords with the view often expressed by such philosophers that characters resemble persons in crucial respects but are not quite ›like ordinary people except for failing to exist‹.[11] On this view, characters are comprised of a ›formal‹ and a ›referential‹ dimension,[12] or ›internal‹ and ›external‹ properties,[13] and the

---

9 See Kelly: Knowledge, Smith: Art, and Smith: Difference.
10 Sellors: Realist is perhaps the only sustained example in film studies. For literary studies, see Doležel: Heterocosmica, Pavel: Fictional, and Ryan: Possible.
11 Dauer: Nature, p. 37.
12 Ibid., p. 36.
13 Reicher: Ontology (in this volume). See also Thomasson: Speaking.

presence of the formal dimension profoundly qualifies the referential dimension, rendering inadequate any simple mimetic account of character. Indeed for Francis Dauer, »fictional characters have an ontological integrity of their own which no imitation theory of art can account for«;[14] and still more radically, for the novelist William Gass, »nothing whatever that is appropriate to persons can be correctly said of« characters.[15]

The mimetic hypothesis is precisely designed to avoid such oversimplification, and to accommodate the formal or external dimension of characters. What is less clear is whether the duality of characters – their constitution through a combination of formal and referential elements – along with a more general disposition towards a realist ontology of character, commits one to the kind of ontology we find in these accounts, in which characters are treated as abstract objects akin to, for example, the concept of a triangle. Nor is it clear whether such an ontology is truly incompatible with the ontological caution and (by implication) ›antirealism‹ of accounts, like Kendall Walton's and my own, which stress the role of the imagination in the creation and appreciation of characters.[16] To hold that characters are real is not necessarily to hold that characters are wandering around in a multiplicity of possible worlds; the reality of characters might be cashed out in several different ways. We surely need a general ontology which is supple and rich enough to credit characters with a kind of reality, but the mimetic hypothesis does not commit us to a naïve realism. A real character is not a real person, any more than a real decoy is a real duck.[17]

This ›twofoldness‹ of our perception of characters – seeing them at once as (more or less realistic) representations of persons and as artifacts in their own right – also enables us to understand fictions which foreground just this duality.[18] Two recent films which exploit this possibility, in complementary fashion, are *Stranger Than Fiction* (2006) and *Infamous* (2006) (one of the two almost simultaneous films about Truman Capote and the writing of *In Cold Blood*).[19] *Stranger Than Fiction* depicts a fictional universe in the process of its creation by a novelist, confronting

---

14 Dauer: Nature, p. 37.
15 Gass quoted in Wood: Life, p. 4.
16 Walton: Mimesis, pp. 385–430.
17 Austin: Sense, Chapter 7, especially pp. 67–68.
18 Richard Wollheim coined the term ›twofoldness‹ to refer to the fact that when we look at pictures, we see a marked or ›differentiated‹, two-dimensional surface, and we see three-dimensional objects ›in‹ that surface; and we see these two facets *at once*. These are »two aspects of a single experience that [...] are distinguishable but also inseparable«. There is a very strong parallel, I contend, in our simultaneous apprehension of the mimetic and artefactual aspects of characters. Wollheim: Painting, p. 46.
19 Capote: Blood.

us with the idea that the inhabitants of this universe become conscious of their situation and seek the autonomy of real human agents. *Infamous*, by contrast, firmly establishes the action in a dramatic world which is not merely realist, but, in outline at least, based on an actual, notorious murder case and its dramatization by Capote in the form of a ›non-fiction novel‹. The film shows Capote (Toby Jones) caught in a dilemma arising from the twofoldness of characterization *misapplied* to the world itself. Capote's growing respect, sympathy and eventual love (as the film depicts it) for one of the murderers, Perry Smith (Daniel Craig), comes into conflict with his desire for what he regards as the dramatically and morally appropriate ending to the story of Smith's life: execution by hanging. We think about, and have desires in relation to, both *characters* and the *narratives* in which they are situated, and these may not always be consistent. We may want Mercutio to survive, but at the same time also want to experience *Romeo and Juliet* as it was written, which necessitates the death of Mercutio. In the context of artistic representation, we can think of this as a paradox.[20] Transferred to real life, the paradox becomes a moral fallacy. In allowing himself to form *narrative* desires in relation to the real Perry Smith, Capote (as depicted in the film) falls into this fallacy. If *Stranger Than Fiction* recalls the metafiction of Pirandello's *Six Characters In Search of An Author*, then, *Infamous* recalls that cautionary tale about the perils of aestheticism, Wilde's *The Picture of Dorian Gray*.[21]

2 Characters, Psychology and the Logic of Situations

These examples remind us that even the most plausible of realist characters lack the autonomy that we ascribe to actual human beings. Characters are representations of personal agents, but have no real agency; if we treat persons as characters, we run the moral risk dramatized by *Infamous*. Hard determinists aside, most of us believe that the pattern of individual human lives is not set out in advance, but arises from a mixture of circumstance, personality, and chance. At another level, though, the parallel between persons and characters reasserts itself. Characters are parts of larger dramatic structures, and lack autonomous agency. Persons possess (more or less) circumscribed autonomy, agency within limits. We are never wholly autonomous, and we tend to overrate the degree of our own autonomy, and especially the autonomy of others. According to one psychological theory, our thinking about the agency of others is

---

[20] Radford: Fear, pp. 76–77; see also Currie: Narrative.
[21] Pirandello: Characters; Wilde: Picture.

consistently skewed by a bias – the ›fundamental attribution error‹ – towards attributing the cause of an action to individual personality traits over situational determinants.²² From this point of view, we have good reason not to underestimate the degree to which human agency is constrained by various kinds of context and structure; and we would do well to consider how this aspect of the world and human psychology manifests itself in the context of fictional and dramatic characterization.

What tools exist that might help us to correct the distortions of the fundamental attribution error? Structuralism must be at the front of the cue here, with its emphasis on the overriding significance of structure at all levels. But as *Engaging Characters* sought to demonstrate, the structural tradition is vitiated by an anti-humanist (and just plain implausible) linguistic determinism, in which both persons and characters tend to be regarded as nothing more than the epiphenomena of language. ›Language speaks us‹ – we do not speak within language, or act by using language as a tool. The medicine of (post-)structuralism thereby kills the patient, entirely negating the significance of agency, personhood, and character, rather than showing how agents are constrained by structure and situational context. Another body of thinking, however, does come to mind as a promising alternative. Beginning in the 1940s, Karl Popper spoke of a ›logic of situations‹, to designate patterns of behaviour which seem to arise consistently given a certain set of elements and an initial set of conditions, irrespective of the variations in personality of the agents involved.²³ Popper's phrase resonates with both the language and methods of many dramatists, who think in terms of the ›dramatic logic‹ of situations rather than merely in terms of characters. »If you were alive at that time it must have been an agonizing choice«, states Ken Loach, in relation to his film *The Wind that Shakes the Barley* (2006), which depicts various phases of the anti-colonial struggle in Ireland in the 1920s. »There were no good people or bad people, all responses to the situation have a logic – that's the terrible dilemma«.²⁴ The potent horror film *Eden Lake* (2008) was conceived by its writer/director James Watkins to confront viewers with a situation in which the most virtuous character in the story performs one of the most heinous acts in a truly dread-inducing scenario. Anticipating an idyllic weekend in a secluded rural location, nursery teacher Jenny (Kelly Reilly) and her boyfriend Steve (Michael Fassbender) are terrorized by a gang of local teenagers. One of the younger members

---

22 Ross / Nisbett: Person; Goldie: Emotions, pp. 160–166, provides an insightful analysis. See also Boyd: Origins, p. 137.
23 Popper: Society, Chapter 14.
24 Quoted in Turan: Barley.

of the gang, Cooper (Thomas Turgoose), breaks ranks and seeks to help Jenny, but in a fit of rage she kills him (fig. 2). Does this action reveal a hitherto unrecognized part of her personality, or is it that the situation furnishes her with no palatable options? The film implies that it is the uniquely extreme situation that drives her to act spontaneously out of fury – an act for which she immediately feels remorse (fig. 3).

Fig. 2 & 3: *Eden Lake* (2008)

The idea here is not that psychological factors (intentions, emotions, motives, personality) can or should be excluded from the explanation of human action, but rather that psychology alone is insufficient. Psychological states arise in and are responses to situations. Situations prompt certain kinds of responses and not others, delimit the possible paths of action, and in this way allow us to measure the ›rationality‹ or otherwise of a response. (A response which seems blind to the nature of the situation is ‹irrational‹ in this sense.)²⁵ Popper's idea accords with research in social psychology demonstrating the power of situational factors over individual choice and action. Consider, for example, *The Lucifer Effect*, Philip Zimbardo's book reflecting on the connections between the Stanford Prison Experiments of the early 1970s, in which he was involved as a young researcher, and the events surrounding prisoner abuse at Abu Ghraib prison in 2004, where he acted as an expert witness. Drawing on the evidence of these episodes and related research, Zimbardo argues that the prison situation predisposes agents occupying particular roles to act in particular ways, irrespective of variations in individual disposition.

The intuitions and assumptions in these cases are explored in *game theory*, the mathematical study of strategy. Game theorists formally model the logic of situations – the Prisoner's Dilemma being the most famous example of such a model. Thus Matt Ridley analyses the story of Puccini's opera *Tosca* in terms of the Prisoner's Dilemma:[26] the choices of the heroine Tosca, and her antagonist, police chief Scarpia, are structured by the situation. Tosca's lover has been condemned to death by Scarpia. He offers her a deal. If she sleeps with him, he will stay the execution. By co-operating with each other and striking a deal, both will gain. Each of them can gain more by reneging on the deal, but at the risk of losing what they gain by sticking to the deal. Thus the dilemma: strike the deal, act in good faith, take the reward; or, strike the deal, and defect in the hope that your antagonist won't do the same, and gain still more. In the opera, both Tosca and Scarpia break the agreement: Tosca stabs Scarpia after he has stayed the execution, but Scarpia has secretly left instructions for the execution to be carried through in any case. Thus neither gains: Scarpia loses his life, and Tosca's lover is executed.

This is as game theory predicts things tend to turn out, in isolated episodes of the dilemma; the temptation to gain additional benefit is too great. The logic of the situation changes dramatically when it recurs repeatedly over time, however. ›The shadow of the future‹ makes defection less attractive, as breaking a bargain is likely to store up distrust, resentment and enmity.[27] Here the gangster drama might prove a fertile example, with the constant trade-offs between individual advantage and collective gain, the endless work to maintain co-operation between rival gangs. What game theory offers is a calculus for the costs and benefits built into particular situations – an abstract and stark representation of

---

25 Popper: Society, p. 97. Popper takes his cue in part from Max Weber, making reference (Popper: Society, p. 324, note 14) to Weber: Aufsätze. The idea is developed in many later writings by Popper.
26 Puccini: Tosca.
27 The phrase is Robert Axelrod's, quoted in Ridley: Origins, p. 73.

situations which characters must navigate, as we follow them in our imaginations. In this way, though the possibility has hardly been considered so far, it may be that game theory, along with the kinds of antecedents I mention here, would enrich our understanding of character and narrative form more generally.[28]

On another level, of course, filmmakers and other narrative artists *exploit* phenomena like the fundamental attribution error, relying on our attributional bias towards personality over situation in developing vivid, complex and (yes!) engaging characters. As David Bordwell notes, »when a character walks into the story world, he or she is characterized by signaling key traits right off the bat«. In *Back to the Future* (1985), for example, »the narration introduces Marty by showing him cranking up the lab's amplifier to overdrive. He strikes a star pose, hits a guitar chord, and is blasted off his feet. He's shaken up but awestruck: ›Whoa. . . Rock and roll‹. We now assume that Marty likes to take risks, that he's committed to his music, that he's a bit preening, and that he can bounce back«.[29] An error-ridden process in ordinary cognition thus becomes a tool of storytelling; a practical vice becomes, so to speak, an aesthetic virtue. And, as Michael Newman has argued with regard to *Welcome to the Dollhouse* (1995), some fictions may invite us to reflect on the very phenomenon itself, by asking us to consider whether a given character's actions arise primarily from temperament or circumstance.[30] Once again we see that there are important asymmetries between characters and persons, even though we must see characters as (if they were) persons if we are to see them as characters at all.[31] A theory of character must account for both the symmetries and asymmetries, and it must recognize both the ordinary heuristic forms of reasoning which form the backdrop to the creation of characters and narratives, and the specialized ways in which such heuristics are exploited by storytellers.

3 More on Morality and Allegiance

I noted above that one of the ways in which we treat characters as if they were persons is in responding to and evaluating them in moral terms. The insistence on the centrality of moral psychology to both the design and reception of narrative in general and film narrative in particular, as well as

---

28 Ridley: Origins, p. 53. See also Flesch: Comeuppance.
29 David Bordwell: Movies.
30 Newman: Characterization. Ramin Bahrani's *Man Push Cart* (2005) raises similar questions.
31 Smith: Engaging, Chapter 1.

using the language of morality to capture this fact, was a feature of *Engaging Characters* that attracted a lot of attention, much of it critical. The book was careful to discuss and describe morality neutrally, as a key ingredient of narrative experience, rather than endorsing any particular set of such values. *Engaging Characters* wants no part of that ›contagion of moralising niceness‹ in which films and novels are criticized or rejected on the grounds that the characters are ›dislikeable‹,[32] or that readers and viewers can't ›identify‹ with them – though it acknowledges and takes seriously the existence of such commonplace responses.

Despite all this caution, in the eyes of some critics the very use of moral language implied a strange throwback to Victorian moral ideals. Hadn't I noticed that we had gone ›beyond good and evil‹? Talk of ›ideology‹ and ideological values is widespread in film and literary studies, but not morality (even though the relationship between ideology and morality must be intimate); indeed, to speak of morality is (sin of sins) to lapse into the language of bourgeois ideology. But I maintain that the boot is on the other foot. Putting it in terms of the naturalized perspective I mention above, morality is a universal, species-specific system of belief and behavioural regulation; and there is increasing evidence of ›proto-morality‹ among other primates.[33] Specific moral doctrines and patterns of belief of course vary between times and places, sometimes startlingly so; as Ridley has written, »to say that the emotions that fuel morality are innate is not to say that they are immutable«.[34] But this is no impediment to moral engagement with narratives expressing moral perspectives distant from our own; all that is necessary for our moral sensibility (or ›module‹, in the language of evolutionary psychology) to be triggered is exposure to a drama of agents of variable moral character interacting in a morally-animated field of action. No human society lacks a moral framework, and, reciprocally, all normally functioning human beings possess a moral dimension to their psychology that connects them to the moral fabric of their society (though the ›connection‹ may take many forms, active and complete endorsement being just one of them). Notwithstanding some of his rhetoric, Nietzsche's ambition was to relativize and ›transvalue‹ the tradition of Christian morality, not to argue that human individuals or society could constitute themselves without any moral system at all.[35] From this point of view, what is parochial is the quaint idea that we denizens of ›late capitalism‹ have transcended morality.

---

32 Wood: Life, p. 4.
33 De Waal: Primates.
34 Ridley: Origins, p. 142.
35 Nietzsche: Anti-Christ.

A more modest criticism of the place accorded to morality in *Engaging Characters* concerns the degree to which moral evaluation plays a role in the allegiances – the sympathetic attachments – that we form with characters. Do we find characters sympathetic always and only because we judge them to be kind, generous, courageous and the like? Several critics have pointed out that we can also form positive emotional attachments to characters on the basis of non-moral attributes – wit, ingenuity, force of personality; the sorts of quality often captured by the notion of ›charisma‹.[36] And as I have recently argued, there are important variations in the nature of moral engagement across modes and genres of narrative.[37] Much comedy seems to depend on what Bergson described as a ›momentary anaesthesia of the heart‹,[38] in which our normal moral and emotional responses are switched off or inverted – where we might, for example, take pleasure in, and find attractive, the charming swindler who outwits the dull but faithful husband.[39] In horror fictions, sometimes our overriding attitude is one of amoral fascination rather than morally-driven evaluation. And in romances, physical beauty and charm may play an important role in guiding our sympathies alongside moral factors. We do not typically fall in love just because we think someone is virtuous, and similarly, in engaging with romantic fictions, we may not form sympathetic allegiances just on the basis of the relative virtuousness of the various characters.

More generally, *Engaging Characters* posits a one-dimensional hierarchy or continuum of moral judgement, ranging from the poles of outright badness to angelic goodness, with a heavily-populated central region where we find more ›graduated‹ cases, ›alloys‹ of virtue and vice. But it may be more accurate to think of a multi-dimensional evaluative *field* in which our judgements operate, in which both moral and non-moral criteria come into play, and where characters may fare well against some criteria and poorly against others. Similarly, if the default mode of sympathetic allegiance implied by *Engaging Characters* involves a largely positive moral evaluation sustained continuously over the course of a film – ›global‹ allegiance – there are many other more intricate patterns of allegiance. These include what I have termed *partial* and *perverse* allegiance. Partial allegiance refers to cases in which we find ourselves sympathetic to some attitudes and actions of a character, but antipathetic to others; perverse allegiance captures those cases where a film seeks to turn around

---

36 Gaut: Review, p. 97; Plantinga: Viewers, pp. 107–118.
37 Smith: Murderer.
38 Bergson: Laughter, p. 11.
39 Jones: Partiality.

aspects of our normal evaluation, eliciting our sympathy for actions and attitudes which, on reflection, we realize we ought not endorse.[40] It is worth stressing here, then, that the concept of allegiance is intended to be used in a neutral, ›unvalenced‹ sense, encompassing the whole range of evaluations, pro and con. That is why the phrase ›sympathetic allegiance‹ is not tautologous; antipathetic and partial allegiances are equally possible.

Notwithstanding all of these qualifications and special cases, I maintain that, even within an expanded evaluative field, moral evaluation functions as our centre of emotional gravity when it comes to the sympathies we form with characters. Brian Boyd writes of the enduring ›power of the goodie-baddie axis‹, and has suggested that our evolutionary history makes us especially sensitive to cheaters, freeloaders, and other types who threaten social cohesion and violate the trust upon which co-operation depends.[41] Back in 1989, Spike Lee thrust moral dilemmas and moral deliberation into the forefront of our experience with *Do the Right Thing* (1989). As I write, one of the hippest and most highly-regarded television dramas ever broadcast, *The Wire* (2002–2008), continues to engross viewers and prompt critical encomiums on a similar basis. Moral matters are absolutely central to the drama of the show and the flow of our sympathies as we engage with it. The climax of the first season of the show focusses on the moral dilemma faced by D'Angelo Barksdale (Larry Gilliard, Jr.), who has come to loathe his drug-running existence. Arrested on drug possession charges, D'Angelo must choose between loyalty to his uncle Avon (Wood Harris) – head of D'Angelo's gang – and honesty, by providing evidence of his uncle's culpability to the police. ›It ain't right‹, mutters D'Angelo angrily to his mother, as she pressures him to take the fall on behalf of his uncle and the Barksdale family as a whole. ›I shoulda done more. But I didn't, man. Fuck, that's on me‹, laments D'Angelo, as he reflects on his failure to stop Avon from ordering the murder of his friend Wallace (fig. 4). Morality may be messily entangled here with self-interest and politics; but it is nevertheless front and centre. Most video games include some sort of gesture towards morality: *Grand Theft Auto IV* (2008) incorporates a ›moral parameter‹, where the central character controlled by the player must decide whether or not to execute characters that they defeat. These decisions go on to affect the options available to the protagonist – or, to put it another way, the decisions affect the attributes that make up this character.

---

40 Smith: Gangsters; Smith: Murderer.
41 Boyd: Origin, pp. 64–65; see also pp. 140–141. Boyd points to evidence from Carroll et al.: Graphing, for the significance of the ›goodie-baddie axis‹.

Fig. 4: *The Wire* (2002–2008)

Even in the supposed moral wasteland of shoot 'em up video games, then, we find some attention to moral psychology. And where amoral or immoral factors do play a role in the positive allegiances we form with certain characters, it is hard to find cases where our allegiance is not conjoined with and consolidated by more conventionally moral responses. Tony Soprano may be an outrageous hedonist and vicious criminal, but he's also a man with a conscience and a genuine sense of responsibility towards his family and close associates. The physical beauty of romantic protagonists is usually conjoined with, and possibly inflected by, some sort of moral goodness; horror films typically rely on our sympathetic attachment to basically good characters in order that we may be fearful for them; and Bergson wrote of the *momentary* anaesthesia of the heart in comedy, not its death or exile.

This insistence on the centrality of moral psychology to the institution of fiction was never meant, however, to preclude political or ideological analysis of films. Robert Stam, nevertheless, writes of my »disastrous substitution of the word ›moral‹ for the word ›ideological‹«, claiming that this gesture »throws out the collective achievements of the Frankfurt School, screen theory, and cultural studies«.⁴² Stam's panicky response reveals that the concept of ›ideology‹ is the dummy in the mouth of

---

42 Stam: Theory, p. 245.

culturalism: threaten to withdraw it or restrict its use and you risk a tantrum. But Stam misrepresents *Engaging Characters*. I don't substitute ›morality‹ for ›ideology‹, in the sense of making the two co-extensive and eschewing the language of ideology altogether. Rather I choose the word ›moral‹ to play an important role in the scheme of character engagement, to describe the evaluative dimension of our interaction with characters. Not all such evaluations are ideologically-driven; and even where they are, they will be typically expressed in moral language (think of George W. Bush's ›axis of evil‹ speech – a clear instance of a political and ideological intervention cast in moral language).

Defined in terms of belief and value systems serving, or at least connected with, the interests and power of social groups, ideology continues to play an important role in the book – in relation, for example, to a variety of Hollywood and Soviet films. And in various essays I have tried to demonstrate how the model presented in *Engaging Characters* enables and opens up new possibilities for the ideological analysis of films, showing how moral judgement feeds into films which reflect explicitly on the injustices of particular social, political and economic regimes, entrenched social prejudices or imbalances of power.[43] Others have developed these possibilities further – Dan Flory in particular has incorporated aspects of the model in an extensive analysis of the racial politics of several strands and cycles of American filmmaking.[44] If we define ideology more loosely – in terms of the beliefs and values expressive of a particular culture or tradition – then ›ideology‹ is even more pervasively acknowledged in the pages of *Engaging Characters*, since the important role of culture is never denied. In short, it's really Stam who's interested in throwing things out. *Engaging Characters* certainly knocks ›ideology‹ off its perch, but it doesn't reject it wholesale.

4 Recognizing Recognition and Alignment

Much, then, has been said about morality and allegiance. But what of recognition and alignment, the other two parameters of the structure of sympathy? One type of alignment structure which has come to the fore since *Engaging Characters* was published, in both filmmaking and in scholarship, is the ›network narrative‹. In such films, which depend on the articulation of numerous parallel lines of action, we are aligned with

---

43 Smith: Realism; Smith: Brechtianism; Smith: Struggle; Smith: Surrealist; Smith: Trainspotting.
44 Flory: Philosophy.

various characters or character groupings, usually in alternating fashion over the course of the work. Network narratives take the principle of cross-cutting and write it large, expanding the number of narrative layers and the possibilities for their intersection.[45] By comparison, recognition – the fundamental business of perceiving and constructing characters – tends to be taken for granted by theorists. It is typically regarded as nothing more than the precursor to the really interesting business, both artistically and theoretically, which (it is thought) takes place exclusively at the levels of alignment and allegiance. Yet a whole string of films have exploited the intricacies of recognition for dramatic effect, including *The Return of Martin Guerre* (1982), *Dead Ringers* (1988), *Suture* (1993), *Lost Highway* (1997), *Fight Club* (1999), *Memento* (2000), *Identity* (2003), *Mulholland Drive* (2001), *I'm Not There* (2007) and *Mad Detective* (2007).[46] There are two basic variations here: films in which a single character is represented by several performers[47], and those in which a single performer represents two or more characters. Thus, the corrupt cop in *Mad Detective* is represented by no less than eight different performers: one for the character as such (Lam Ka-Tung), and a further seven (six male, one female) performers, representing the various facets or ›inner selves‹ of the character, who accompany him like a street gang for much of the film (fig. 5–8). In *The Return of Martin Guerre*, on the other hand, the drama revolves around whether Gérard Depardieu embodies the same character who disappeared from the village several years earlier, or an uncannily similar one. Several of these films were high-profile successes, showing that the play with recognition is not restricted to art house fare like *The Suspended Vocation* (1978) and *That Obscure Object of Desire* (1977) (the principal examples of such experimentation in *Engaging Characters*). And the creation of long-form, ›longitudinal‹ motion picture dramas like *Heimat* (1984, 1992, 2004) encompassing a plot duration of roughly 80 years and a production schedule spread over 20 years, points to the significance and potential complexity of sustaining individual characters over such extended timeframes.

---

45 See Bordwell: Poetics, Chapter 7; Smith: Parallel.
46 On *Lost Highway*, see Romao: Threshold.
47 Cf. the contribution of Johannes Riis in this volume.

Fig. 5

Fig. 6

Fig. 7

Fig. 8

Fig. 5–8: *Mad Detective* (2007): The seven ›inner selves‹ of detective Ko Chi-Wai (fig. 5), each represented by a different performer (fig. 6–8).

On a theoretical level, too, there is unfinished business with recognition. The scheme of *Engaging Characters* implies that the three principal concepts (recognition, alignment, and allegiance) are ordered sequentially – but this is only a half-truth. From the moment we begin to build a character, we become situated in relation to them spatially and psychologically. In other words, the process of alignment begins immediately: we are attached to characters spatially, and given access to their minds, to a greater or lesser degree. And just as importantly, we respond to characters emotionally and morally from the get-go. As Torben Grodal has vigorously argued, our perception of the world and of films is embodied and emotional through and through: »To understand [a] character's situation in depth is to simulate his or her dilemma with eyes, bowels, heart, cognition and muscles«.[48] The point is not that detached and abstract thinking does not or cannot exist, but that embodied and emotionally-laden cognition is the norm rather than the exception. The comprehension of words, categorization and recognition of faces, and perception of actions have all been shown to involve emotional components. So as soon as we see the assassin in Hitchcock's *The Man Who Knew Too Much* (1956) (fig. 9 and 10), we not only individuate him and thereby lay the groundwork for recognition; we also find ourselves with limited access to him both spatially and subjectively, and we are likely to have some sort of aversive affective reaction to his scarred visage and unresponsive demeanor. In sum, although it makes sense conceptually to lay out recognition, alignment and allegiance in that order, in the actual experience of film viewing the three processes work simultaneously and in intertwined fashion.

---

48 Grodal: Visions, p. 196. See also Boyd: Origin, p. 139: ›emotion saturates recognition‹ (Boyd is referring to facial recognition).

Fig. 9 and 10: The Man Who Knew Too Much (1956)

It is also important to acknowledge the significance of recognition even when it is functioning ›under the radar‹ of highly-focussed attention – when it is discreetly enabling us to see characters as continuous agents, rather than drawing attention to itself as in the cases described above. Humans are profoundly social animals. Our social life demands that we monitor allies and foes, remaining vigilant for situations affording opportunities for co-operation as well as those involving competition and conflict; the ability to perceive and cognitively follow causal particulars – this particular person did that specific thing on this particular day – goes hand in hand with such a form of life. One of the mechanisms which binds individuals and communities together is *reciprocal altruism* – you scratch my back, and I'll scratch yours. But the mutual scratching can only take hold if we can reliably recognize, over time, those who have acted well towards us; *reciprocity depends on recognition*. And the flip side of this is our robust capacity for ›cheater detection‹, whereby we keep track of those who fail to reciprocate.[49] Recognition of characters is, then, the echo in the domain of representation of this fundamental human social skill. The richly-developed sense of altruism and ›fair play‹ in humans goes hand in hand with the power of our minds to distinguish and remember individual faces; both the moral and the perceptual capacity far outstrip what we find in any other species. The interdependence of the moral and the perceptual points again to the way in which recognition and allegiance will impact upon one another whenever we engage with characters. Recognition is no

---

49 Ridley: Origins, Chapter 4; Boyd: Origin, pp. 59–61 and p. 141.

mere handmaiden to alignment and allegiance, but an important player in its own right.

5 Imagination, Simulation and Empathy

Alongside its narratological framework – the various character-related structures discerned in films and other narrative forms – *Engaging Characters* posits a psychology of engagement with characters. We have already seen how moral psychology is imporant here; but it is not the whole story. Viewers engage with the structure of sympathy, and its constituent elements of recognition, alignment and allegiance, through two *modes of imagining*. Viewers *acentrally* imagine the action and characters depicted and implied by the narrative when they imagine that such-and-such a character did something in a given setting, when they hold in mind the narrative action as a whole, or as it has unfolded up to a given point. Acentral imagining involves our ›feeling for‹ characters – as implied by the process of allegiance – and for this reason I treat such imagining as cognate with the attitude of ›sympathy‹. For example, to imagine acentrally the plight of Bess in *Breaking the Waves* (1996) is, first of all, to entertain the thought that Bess exists in the world depicted by the film. To the extent that the imagining takes on an emotional character, it will be characterized by an ›external‹ or acentral stance: we recognize her masochistic state of mind, and respond to it with compassion, anger and alarm *for* her; we don't feel her emotions *with* her. Or we might recognize the distaste and displeasure felt by some of the clerical characters in the film towards her, and respond to those characters with disgust or outrage. Insisting on the centrality of *this* kind of imaginative stance represents another important break with much everyday ›storytalk‹, which often implies that we experience narratives wholly or mostly from the (imagined) viewpoint of a particular character. The latter kind of imagining – *central imagining*, or what is often called ›empathy‹, and contrasted with sympathy – does not occupy such a dominant role in our experience of fiction; but it does nevertheless perform a signficant role. Many narratives, I argue, prompt central imagining intermittently, eliciting our empathic engagement with characters either as a means of understanding them (›mindreading‹), or as a means of appreciating their feelings more profoundly where we already understand them (›mindfeeling‹).[50]

Over the last fifteen years or so, there has been a remarkable revival of interest in the concept of empathy. The rehabilitation of empathy within

---

50 Smith: Empathy.

Engaging Characters played its part in this wider revival, though I scarcely saw it at the time. Within film theory, empathy had come to play the role of the degraded contrast to that more rational and critical form of response known as ›alienation‹ or ›distanciation‹. Central to the dramaturgy of Bertolt Brecht, the opposition between empathy and alienation was embraced by a generation of film theorists in the 60s and 70s, becoming an important part of the blend of semiotics, Marxism and psychoanalysis known (within Britain and the US) as ›Screen theory‹.[51] In those alternative traditions of research that *Engaging Characters* drew its inspiration from, however, empathy continued to be treated as a feature of human psychology that warranted dispassionate attention and investigation (rather than, or at least prior to, political or ideological critique). What has really given the study of empathy new momentum, however, is the emergence of *simulation theory*, a theory of our remarkably fluent and speedy ability to ›mindread‹ the thoughts and emotions of others.[52] According to simulation theory, we ›read‹ the thoughts of others by using our minds to model their mental states, running the intentional states of others on our own minds ›off-line‹, feeling our way into their likely mindsets just as many earlier theorists of empathy had proposed. (Empathy had been translated from the German ›Einfühlung‹, literally ›in-feeling‹.) Further momentum has been added to the contemporary debate on simulation and empathy by the discovery of *mirror neurons*, which (at least according to one view) supports simulation theory by providing evidence for simulation and empathy at the neural level. Grodal's case for film viewing as a thoroughly ›embodied‹ activity is in part inspired by the research on mirror neurons.[53]

The arguments in *Engaging Characters* on empathy were flanked by two other interventions, similar in spirit but very different in detail. On the one side, *Engaging Characters* appeared simultaneously with Greg Currie's *Image and Mind: Film, Philosophy, and Cognitive Science*, which placed simulation at the fulcrum of its account of film spectatorship. Although the two books shared a great deal, each of them places simulation and empathy rather differently. For Currie, while simulation is fundamental to the act of engaging with a fiction, empathizing with characters, as a specific form of simulation, plays a rather subordinate role which he terms

---

51 Smith: Brechtianism.
52 For an overview, see Goldman: Minds.
53 See Rizzolatti / Sinigaglia: Mirrors; Iacoboni: People; Grodal: Visions, p. 117. Other recent treatments of empathy in relation to film include Plantinga: Scene; Barratt: Routes; Coplan: Emotions; and Vaage: Seeing.

›secondary imagining‹.⁵⁴ So in this respect Currie's position is in marked contrast to my own. On the other flank, we find the arguments of Noël Carroll on emotional responses to film. *Engaging Characters* is often taken to endorse sympathy over empathy, as part of its polemic against the concept of ›identification‹, and in line with Carroll's critical view of the latter. But *Engaging Characters* articulates a quite different view of empathy to Carroll, who suspects that the concept of empathy is a way of smuggling back ›identification‹ into film theory in another guise.⁵⁵ *Engaging Characters* does not rehabilitate empathy either as the sole successor of identification, or as a competitor with sympathy, but rather seeks to integrate empathic simulation within a broader framework defined by sympathy.⁵⁶ As I now think of it, empathy functions in part as a ›subroutine‹ within the frame of sympathetic engagement. Our basic stance towards characters is not an empathic one in which we experience the fictional world consistently from their imagined perspectives; but through simulation (and related processes, like emotional contagion and mimicry) we flit rapidly in and out of characters empathically, moving with imaginative agility through a variety of perspectives which are then aggregated and interrelated to produce the structure of sympathy – that integrated, dynamic picture of the characters populating the fiction in terms of their moral-emotional appeal.

One of the themes of this essay has been the limitations of ordinary talk about characters. If we want a deep and accurate understanding of the place of character in film and other forms of representation, we cannot expect our folk conceptions, and the resources of ordinary language, to deliver that understanding alone. But neither can we simply ignore the assumptions embedded in folk theory, for sometimes they point us in the right direction, and where they are mistaken, our theory must explain how these errors arise and maintain a grip on our ordinary thinking. Right or wrong, everyday intuitions must provide both the starting point and an ongoing reference point for our theoretical efforts. And the most basic of these intuitions is that those ›virtual people‹ we call characters matter to us, and are an ineliminable part of our imaginative life as it is sustained and nourished by film, literature and the art of storytelling in general. It is

---

54 In ›primary imagining‹, we imagine the contents of storyworld, as these are stated or implied by the narrative text. Empathizing with characters is a ›secondary‹ form of imagining for Currie in the sense that the role of such imagining is to assist the work of primary imagining, where necessary. As I read Currie, empathy thus typically has instrumental, but not intrinsic, value.
55 Carroll: Art, pp. 342–356; Carroll's most recent statement on this subject can be found in Carroll: Philosophy, pp. 147–191.
56 This position is clarified and developed in Smith: Inside, and Smith: Empathy.

that intuition that provides the fundamental warrant for any theory of character.[57]

References

Austin, J. L.: Sense and Sensibilia. Reconstructed from the Manuscript Notes by G. J. Warnock. Oxford 1962.
Barratt, Daniel: Tracing the Routes to Empathy: Association, Simulation, or Appraisal? In: Dan Barratt / Jonathan Frome (Eds.): Film Studies: An International Review 8 (2006), pp. 39–52.
Bergson, Henri: Laughter: An Essay on the Meaning of the Comic. Transl. by Cloudesley Brereton and Fred Rothwell. London 1911.
Bordwell, David: Narration in the Fiction Film. Madison, WI 1985.
Bordwell, David: Making Meaning: Inference and Rhetoric in the Interpretation of Cinema. Cambridge, MA 1989.
Bordwell, David: Observations on Film Art: Minding Movies. (March 5th, 2008) <http://www.davidbordwell.net/blog/?p=2004> (May 27th, 2010).
Bordwell, David: Poetics of Cinema. New York 2008.
Boyd, Brian: On the Origin of Stories: Evolution, Cognition, and Fiction. Cambridge, MA 2009.
Butler, Christopher: Interpretation, Deconstruction, and Ideology: An Introduction to Some Current Issues in Literary Theory. Oxford 1984.
Capote, Truman: In Cold Blood. New York 1966.
Carroll, Joseph: An Evolutionary Paradigm for Literary Study. In: Style 42/2–3 (2008), pp. 103–135.
Carroll, Joseph / Jonathan Gottschall / John A. Johnson / Daniel J. Kruger: Graphing Jane Austen: Human Nature in Canonical British Novels of the Longer Nineteenth Century. <http://www.umsl.edu/~carrolljc/index.htm#Work_in_Progress:> (May 27th, 2010).
Carroll, Noël: Mystifying Movies: Fads and Fallacies in Contemporary Film Theory. New York 1988.
Carroll, Noël: A Philosophy of Mass Art. Oxford 1998.
Carroll, Noël: The Philosophy of Film. Malden, MA 2008.
Coplan, Amy: Catching Characters' Emotions: Emotional Contagion Responses to Narrative Fiction Film. In: Dan Barratt / Jonathan Frome (Eds.): Film Studies: An International Review 8 (2006), pp. 53–67.
Crews, Frederick: Skeptical Engagements. New York 1986.
Currie, Gregory: Image and Mind: Film, Philosophy, and Cognitive Science. Cambridge 1995.
Currie, Gregory: Narrative Desire. In: Carl Plantinga and Greg M. Smith (Eds): Passionate Views: Thinking About Film and Emotion. Baltimore 1999, pp. 183–199.
Dauer, Francis: The Nature of Fictional Characters and the Referential Fallacy. In: The Journal of Aesthetics and Art Criticism 53/1 (1995), pp. 31–38.
De Waal, Frans: Primates and Philosophers: How Morality Evolved. Princeton 2006.

---

57 My thanks to the editors for giving me the opportunity to write this essay, and for their insightful comments and suggestions.

Doležel, Lubomír: Heterocosmica: Fiction and Possible Worlds. Baltimore, MD 1998.
Eder, Jens: Die Figur im Film. Grundlagen der Figurenanalyse. Berlin 2008.
Eder, Jens: Was sind Figuren? Paderborn 2008. (E-book)
Eder, Jens: Understanding Characters. In: Projections 4/1 (2010), pp. 16–40.
Flesch, William: Comeuppance: Costly Signaling, Altruistic Punishment, and Other Biological Components of Fiction. Cambridge, MA 2007.
Flory, Dan: Philosophy, Black Film, Film Noir. University Park, PA 2008.
Gaut, Berys: Review of Engaging Characters, British Journal of Aesthetics 37/1 (1997), pp. 96–97.
Goldie, Peter: The Emotions: A Philosophical Exploration. Oxford 2000.
Goldman, Alvin: Simulating Minds: The Philosophy, Psychology, and Neuroscience of Mindreading. Oxford 2006.
Grodal, Torben: Embodied Visions: Evolution, Emotion, Culture, and Film. Oxford 2009.
Jones, Ward E.: Partiality and Transgressive Comedy: Making Sense of Our Amusement at »His Girl Friday«. In: Ward E. Jones / Samantha Vice (Eds.): Ethics at the Cinema. Oxford 2011 (Forthcoming).
Iacoboni, Marco: Mirroring People: The New Science of How We Connect with Others New York 2008.
Jones, Ward: Transgressive Comedy. In: Ward Jones / Samantha Vice (Eds.): Ethics at the Cinema. Oxford 2011 (Forthcoming).
Kelly, Rory: Knowledge, Emotion, Action: A Sequential Model of Character Motivation and Audience Comprehension. Unpublished conference paper, Society for Cognitive Studies of the Moving Image Annual Conference, University of Copenhagen 2009.
Newman, Michael Z.: Characterization as Social Cognition in »Welcome to the Dollhouse«. In: Dan Barratt / Jonathan Frome (Eds.): Film Studies: An International Review 8 (2006), pp. 53–67.
Nietzsche, Friedrich: Twilight of the Idols/ The Anti-Christ. Transl. by R.J. Hollingdale. London 1990.
Pavel, Thomas: Fictional Worlds. Cambridge, MA 1986.
Pirandello, Luigi: Six Characters in Search of an Author. London 1979.
Plantinga, Carl: The Scene of Empathy and the Human Face on Film. In: Carl Plantinga / Greg M. Smith (Eds.): Passionate Views: Thinking About Film and Emotion. Baltimore 1999, pp. 239–256.
Plantinga, Carl: Moving Viewers: American Film and the Spectator's Experience. Berkeley 2009.
Popper, Karl: The Open Society and its Enemies – The High Tide of Prophecy: Hegel, Marx, and the Aftermath. London 1974.
Radford, Colin: How Can We Be Moved by the Fate of Anna Karenina? In: Proceedings of the Aristotelian Society, Supplementary Volume 49 (1975), pp. 67–80.
Reicher, Maria: The Ontology of Fictional Characters. In this volume.
Ridley, Matt: The Origins of Virtue. London 1997.
Rizzolatti, Giacomo /Corrado Sinigaglia: Mirrors in the Brain – How Our Minds Share Actions and Emotions. Oxford 2008.
Romao, Tico: Beyond the Threshold of Legibility: The Lynchian Aesthetic, Characterisation and Lost Highway. In: Film Studies: An International Review 3 (2002), pp. 59–72.
Ross, Lee / Richard E. Nisbett: The Person and the Situation: Perspectives of Social Psychology. New York 1991.
Ryan, Marie-Laure: Possible Worlds, Artificial Intelligence, and Narrative Theory. Bloomington 1991.

Sellors, C. Paul: A Realist Account of Fiction. In: Film and Philosophy 10 (2006), pp. 51–66.
Smith, Murray: The Influence of Socialist Realism on Soviet Montage. In: The Journal of Ukrainian Studies 19/1 (1994), pp. 45–65.
Smith, Murray: Engaging Characters: Fiction, Emotion, and the Cinema. Oxford 1995.
Smith, Murray: The Logic and Legacy of Brechtianism. In: David Bordwell / Noël Carroll (Eds.): Post-Theory: Reconstructing Film Studies. Madison, WI 1996, pp. 130–148.
Smith, Murray: The Battle of Algiers: Colonial Struggle and Collective Allegiance. In: Iris 24 (Autumn 1997), pp. 105–124.
Smith, Murray: Imagining from the Inside. In: Richard Allen / Murray Smith (Eds.): Film Theory and Philosophy. Oxford 1997, pp. 412–430.
Smith, Murray: Gangsters, Cannibals, Aesthetes; or, Apparently Perverse Allegiances. In: Carl Plantinga / Greg M. Smith (Eds.): Passionate Views: Thinking About Film and Emotion. Baltimore 1999, pp. 217–238.
Smith, Murray: Parallel Lines. In: Jim Hillier (Ed.): American Independent Cinema: A Sight and Sound Reader. London 2001, pp. 155–161.
Smith, Murray: Trainspotting. London 2002.
Smith, Murray: Lars Von Trier, Sentimental Surrealist. In: Mette Hjort / Scott MacKenzie (Eds.): Purity and Provocation: Dogma 95. London 2003, pp. 111–121.
Smith, Murray: Wer hat Angst vor Charles Darwin? Die Filmkunst im Zeitalter der Evolution. In: Matthias Brütsch / Vinzenz Hediger / Ursula von Keitz / Alexandra Schneider / Margrit Tröhler (Eds.): Kinogefühle. Emotionalität und Film. Marburg 2005, pp. 289–312.
Smith, Murray: What Difference Does it Make? Science, Sentiment and Film. In: Projections 2/1 (2008), pp. 60–77.
Smith, Murray: Just What Makes Tony Soprano Such an Appealing, Attractive Murderer? In: Ward E. Jones / Samantha Vice (Eds.): Ethics at the Cinema. Oxford 2011 (Forthcoming).
Smith, Murray: Empathy, Expansionism, and the Extended Mind. In: Amy Coplan / Peter Goldie (Eds.): Empathy: Philosophical and Psychological Perspectives. Oxford 2011 (Forthcoming).
Stam, Robert: Film Theory: An Introduction. Blackwell 2000.
Tallis, Raymond: In: Defence of Realism. London 1988.
Tan, Ed S.: Emotion and the Structure of Narrative Film: Film as an Emotion Machine. Transl. by Barbara Fasting. Mahwah, NJ 1996.
Thomasson, Amie L.: Speaking of Fictional Characters. In: Dialectica 57/2 (2003), pp. 205–223.
Turan, Kenneth: »Barley« Explores Angst of IRA's Early Days. National Public Radio, Morning Edition. (March 16th, 2007) <http://www.npr.org/templates/story/story.php?storyId=8951660> (May 27th, 2010).
Vaage, Margrethe Bruun: Seeing is Feeling. PhD dissertation, University of Oslo 2008.
Walton, Kendall L.: Mimesis as Make Believe: On the Foundations of the Representational Arts. Cambridge, MA 1990.
Weber, Max: Gesammelte Aufsätze zur Wissenschaftslehre. Tübingen 1922.
Wilde, Oscar: The Picture of Dorian Gray. London 1891.
Wollheim, Richard: Painting as an Art. London 1987.
Woloch, Alex: The One vs. the Many: Minor Characters and the Space of the Protagonist in the Novel. Princeton 2003.
Wood, James: A Life of Their Own. In: Guardian, Features and Reviews (Jan 26th 2008), p. 4.

Wood, James: How Fiction Works. London 2009.
Zimbardo, Philip: The Lucifer Effect: How Good People Turn Evil. London 2007.

JOHANNES RIIS

Implications of Paradoxical Film Characters for Our Models and Conceptualizations

1 Introduction

Take your favorite film actor, as an example, and ask yourself this question: Does he or she disappear once the narrative begins and you become immersed in fictional concerns? It seems as though actors do not disappear, and that we may experience emotions directed at fictional events while at the same time appreciating strong performances. Since the early 1910's, actors have played a key role in attracting audiences and, for an equally long time, audiences have been engaged in emotionally gripping narrative events. What is at stake is how best to conceptualize our experience of actors vis-à-vis characters.

Logically, there are two distinct options for solving what is often referred to as the actor/character dualism. The standard option is to assume that actor and character are distinct and separate agents, and that we can only see one of them at a time in the moving picture, or listen to one at a time on the sound track. Not unlike the way we may see either a duck or a rabbit in the famous trick drawing, originally published in *Fliegende Blätter*,[1] we cannot see both actor and character at the same time. The dualist model for actor and character, which I am tempted to call the duck/rabbit model, has been attractive for many film theorists, not least because it accords with a widespread assumption that the moving image, or parts of the image, function as a sign that stands for, in this case, either an actor or a character. I will discuss a version, by Noël Carroll, where he distinguishes between three pictorial levels.

The other option is that actor and character are not separate and distinct but rather different labels for a single agent, the actor. This places

---

1 Fliegende Blätter (Munich, Oct. 23rd, 1892, p. 147). For a discussion of the way in which the drawing became important for discussions in perceptual psychology, see Kihlstrom: Jastrow.

a high value on our awareness that an actor plays and pretends to be another agent, requiring that the spectator sees pretense-beliefs and pretense-desires. According to this hypothesis, the spectator assumes that the moving image and the sound track both allows for watching and listening to an actor in a more or less transparent manner. I will discuss the transparency theory of Kendall Walton, who posits that we are able to look through the photographic medium. The transparency thesis faces problems in accounting for the films, which I will examine here, but I will try to develop an account, which allows for fallibility: that we may experience characters in a way, which we do not believe to be consistent with our empirically grounded beliefs.

In examining actor/character models, I will look at *That Obscure Object of Desire* and *Palindromes*, which both use multiple actors for a single character. Far from the standard film narrative, they offer a means for analyzing various implications. I will distinguish between, on the one hand, conceiving a fictional character as an extension of human agents from everyday experience and, on the other hand, seeing our perception of fictional characters in a film as subject to fallible, perceptual mechanisms, based on Darwinian premises. The two ways of conceiving character and character perception need not be mutually exclusive; this is fortunate since they each explain aspects of our film experience.

2 Decoupling Conchita and Actor

What sets apart my case films from, for example the James Bond series, which has featured different actors as the title character, is that the decoupling of actor and character occurs within a single film.

Luis Buñuel's *That Obscure Object of Desire* (1977) initially obscures the change of actors, as though the purpose is to blind spectators to them. We are aligned with a middle-aged and wealthy widower, Mathieu (played by Fernando Rey), who has fallen in love with Conchita, a young woman from an unprivileged background who still lives with her mother. Conchita is played by both the French actor Carole Bouquet and the Spanish actor Angela Molina, and the changes are difficult to spot up until the point where the actors are placed sufficiently close to each other as to make the visual discontinuity striking. I have tested, informally, my own viewing experience with others. At the point where the two actors are close to one another, without a long scene aligning us with only Mathieu, spectators express their hypothesis that Conchita is played by more than one actor (except, of course, for those spectators who have heard of this trick in advance). The change of actor becomes clear in the bedroom scene, which takes place at Mathieu's country house.

Buñuel's trick makes the most of limitations of spectators' short-term memory. The scenes in which we are aligned with only one party, Mathieu, serve to ›wash‹ away Conchita's specific appearance from short-term memory. Only when Molina and Bouquet are placed close to each other does it become clear that we are looking at distinct actors. What also helps to disguise the changes is that the two actors are framed at a distance and only then, as we are drawn into the action, a close-up ensues. Consider these frame grabs with Mathieu and Conchita, the first two taken from a scene with Carole Bouquet, the next two with Angela Molina in the apartment of Conchita's mother:

Something catches the eye, here a flamenco dance at a distance, and by the time the actor becomes facially identifiable, she has already come to pass as Conchita.[2]

---

2 Although I have not come across anything in the literature to substantiate my speculation, it is possible that Luis Buñuel might have been inspired by perceptual psychologists' experiments with restraints on visual attention. In the 1960's, subjects are exposed to a stimuli for a split-second, within a mask of another picture, called *visual masking*. The first experiments with *change blindness*, whereby subjects fail to detect large changes in a scene, were conducted by George McConkie and his colleagues in the late 1970s, and might have been reported in the press before the final casting of

What are we to make of these changes? Two interpretive strategies for Buñuel's casting are prominent in the literature on *That Obscure Object of Desire*. In the one account, the film makes a rhetorical point on the desired object's substitutability by having two take its place,[3] and in the other, the two women are projections of Mathieu's wish for a woman who is both virginal and lascivious.[4]

The main difference between these two explanations is that the change of actor is motivated either within or outside the fiction. The thesis of Conchita as a projection of split desires attempts to motivate the changes intra-fictionally, by way of Mathieu's mental state. However, the claim that Carole Bouquet represents the virginal woman, and Angela Molina represents the lascivious woman, is inconsistent with a closer look at the film. For example, during the first flirtation in the apartment (see frame grabs above), it is Carole Bouquet's Conchita who first invites him to sit with her on the sofa, and then feeds him chocolate by hand in an erotic manner.

Motivating the changes of actor extra-fictionally seems more plausible. The substitutability thesis places the rhetorical point with someone outside the fiction, for instance Luis Buñuel who wishes to make a claim about male desire. This is consistent with the characters' lack of awareness of the visual discrepancies; at no point does Mathieu, or any other character, reflect on Conchita's changing appearance. Nevertheless, ambiguity may be one of the reasons for casting Conchita in this specific way, she is to appear anything but quickly categorized. Also, it is true that Molina and Bouquet suggest different responses to Mathieu's courting; for example, Bouquet looks more reserved than Molina.

Suppose, instead, that we should explain the use of multiple actors as caused by Luis Buñuel's wish to avoid problems, which the narrative easily invites. One of the accomplishments of having two actors play Conchita is that it adds ambiguity, especially in the first part, since we sense that something is odd. When we later discover that different actors play Conchita, a more profound change occurs in the spectator's relation to Conchita. We keep an eye on who plays Conchita as though we do not want to risk once more overlooking a change. Ronnie Scharfman points out that the film purposefully adds mystery and ambiguity. In one of the final images a woman mends a piece of cloth, which might be viewed as a metaphor for the torn hymen of the wedding night but, as pointed out by

---

That Obscure Object of Desire. More recently, Daniel Levin and associates have demonstrated change blindness with respect to facially distinct agents in moving pictures, analogously to Buñuel's trick. See Levin / Simons: Failure.
3   Scharfman: Deconstruction.
4   Ghillebaert: Double.

Scharfman, »the implications of the image send its would-be decipherers off on another wild goose chase for that never to be obsessed object of their desire: a finite, closed, total meaning«.[5] In keeping an eye on who is appearing in the role, we enter a kind of game-like and playful relation to the film, as though we are rewarded each time we discover another change.

An equally plausible hypothesis might be that the ambiguity and playfulness impede person-directed emotions towards Conchita, thereby leaving the narrative open to our emotional investments. This hypothesis is perhaps better explored by relating it to a more recent film.

3 Decoupling Aviva and Actor

Todd Solondz' *Palindromes* (2004) provides a basis for comparison in relation to which purposes might be served by impeding intense person-directed emotions.

Palindromes takes the use of multiple actors for a single role one step further as a cast of seven actors play the protagonist. From the very beginning, it is clear that there are multiple actors playing the protagonist, Aviva. In the frame grabs below, we can see ›Dawn‹ Aviva (Emani Sledge) explaining to her mom that she really wants to have a baby; ›Judah‹ Aviva (Valerie Shusterov) watching Judah's porn selection; the red-haired ›Henry‹ Aviva (Hannah Freiman) listening to her mother's reasons for choosing to have an abortion; and the obese ›Mama Sunshine‹ Aviva (Sharon Wilkins) who enters the kitchen of a Christian community house:

---

5   Scharfman: Deconstruction, p. 357.

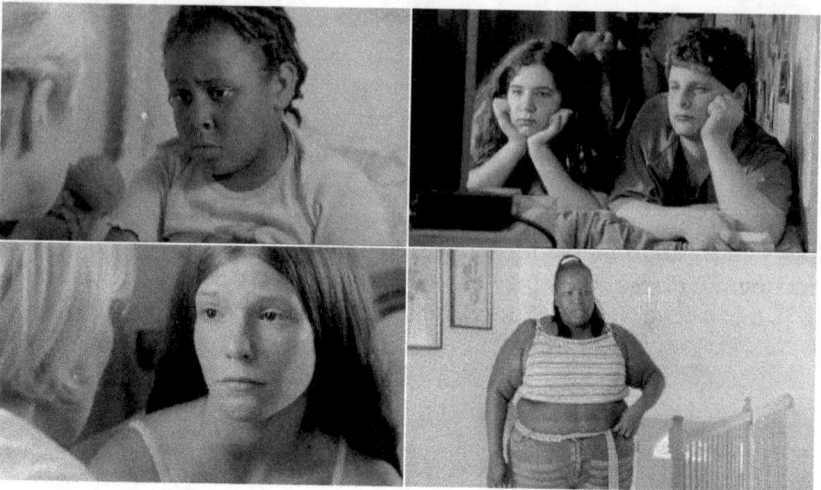

Seven actors play Aviva, and they stand out from each other by means of differences in age, skin color, hair color, body mass, facial features, etc. Each actor appears in her own chapter, which is given a title in accord with the events of that chapter. In contrast to Carole Bouquet and Angela Molina as Conchita, there is no way of mistaking one actor for the other in *Palindromes*.

What holds together the narrative is a journey structure as well as shared vocal patterns by the actors. Each chapter fits almost as a stepping-stone in the story of Aviva's rebellion against overly protective, middle-class parents. After a prologue, the first chapter states her goal (she wants to be a mother); the second brings her part of the way (meeting and having sex with a boy); the third shows the first obstacle (parents persuade her to have an abortion); and the fourth presents her response to the obstacle (running away from home). There are seven chapters with Aviva and when pieced together, they make up the path of the rebellious young Aviva. All seven actors employ a soft and high-pitched voice, and this also serves to give us the impression of a single character. In addition, the lack of response by other characters to her visual changes, most notably by her mother (played by Ellen Barkin), her cousin Mark and two boyfriends, serve to indicate that Aviva is a single character rather than, for example, distinct characters posing as one (the latter, an intrafictional motivation, is further from the film experience than it appears in print).

As the final chapter of *Palindrome* is shared by all seven actors, this not only completes the journey, it also represents a feature of Aviva which transcends her ages and embodiments. The seven actors each take turns in the same date, which culminates in sexual intercourse. This intercourse leaves a somewhat disturbing impression because the actors keep getting younger and younger. When concluded, the first Aviva, played by the young Emani Sledge, proclaims in the very last shot, a close-up, with a triumphant glance at the camera: »I got a feeling that *this* time I'm gonna be a mom!«. The substitution conveys the idea that Aviva has an essence, the desire to give life, which transcends different embodiments.

If we go back to the question of how the spectator is placed emotionally relative to the narrative events, it is clear that intense person-directed emotions such as compassion and anger are avoided. Aviva's abortion; the guilt towards her mother; the pressure which Aviva subjects Bob to, in order to make him commit homicide; the killing of a doctor while he is playing with his children; and the suggestion of paedophilia, are all of a kind which easily evokes intense emotions. Even though we may follow Aviva's journey with genuine interest, intense person-directed emotions are hardly evoked, and I believe that the multiple actors are instrumental in securing a distance to Aviva's predicament and concerns.

Going back to *That Obscure Object of Desire*, we may hypothesize that impeding person-directed emotions serves to avoid misogynism in the portrayal of Conchita. This is an imminent danger due to the repetitious nature of the narrative; Mathieu's approaches and Conchita's rejections, apparently the result of her capricious nature, will easily begin to bore the spectator as there is little development in their relation. *That Obscure Object of Desire* is an adaptation of Pierre Louÿs's *The Woman and the Puppet* (first published in French, 1898), as is Joseph Sternberg's film *The Devil is a Woman* (1935). In Sternberg's version, however, our male protagonist is portrayed as a puppet and Conchita as a manipulative femme fatale (although the performance by Marlene Dietrich suggests that Conchita is animal-like and driven by instincts). We may hypothesize that Buñuel has tried to avoid portraying Conchita as a femme fatale and Mathieu as a puppet even though he retains a narrative of approaches and rejections. First, before we have recognized the changes of actor, multiple actors lend Conchita an air of mystery and ambiguity; second, as we start watching scenes an expectation of actor changes, it allows the spectator to indulge in the additional pleasure of finding a change. Second, once we have realized that Conchita is played by different actors, we may indulge in the pleasure of finding out when the next changes occur.

That emotions are directed at objects is generally agreed upon in emotion psychology. Nico Frijda, a Dutch psychologist, has pointed out that some emotions, for instance anger or fear, are defined by their response, whereas other emotions, such as jealousy or nostalgia, are defined by their objects.⁶ In jealousy, we may respond with anger or sadness, but the underlying concern of someone else enjoying the attention of a loved one remains the same, an instance of jealousy. Following this lead, Ed Tan has distinguished between a general narrative interest directed at the outcome of the narrative and, for example, empathetic emotions such as compassion, admiration and sympathy directed at characters.⁷

In the case of Conchita and Aviva, multiple casting allows the director to downplay intense emotions directed at the characters, such as anger and compassion, and to focus emotions such as curiosity and interest towards broader narrative developments and conflicts. It is plausible that this was aimed for by the directors in order to avoid the problems of a misogynist portrayal and pedophilia and other ›explosive‹ themes, in the portrayal of Conchita and Aviva, respectively.

A kind of *abstraction* may account for the lack of intense, person-directed emotions. Conchita and Aviva are abstract in the sense of not having a specific embodiment but, like other fictional characters, in the additional sense that we cannot look for sources or means of getting to understand them outside of the fiction. Abstraction in the sense of decoupling character from a specific and concrete actor differs from abstraction as the defining property of fictional characters, their lack of a spatiotemporal location.⁸ As they lack a spatiotemporal location outside of the fiction, this means that we cannot conduct a proper investigation of characters; as Conchita and Aviva lack a specific embodiment of an actor, this means that our person-directed emotions are impeded and the object of emotions are to be found in other aspects of the films.

4 Dual Representations or a Transparent, Single Agent

Similar to asking the question of what purpose it serves to decouple character and actor, we might ask what conditions are necessary for the spectator to perceive a human-like character, despite multiple actors.

It is critically important for the narrative that whatever Conchita or Aviva learns in one scene is carried into following scenes, *regardless of whom plays the part*. This is what makes Conchita and Aviva work as single and coherent characters. If we were to compare what Angela Molina's Conchita learns, believes and desires to what Carole Bouquet's Conchita

---

6   Frijda: Emotions, p. 73.
7   Tan: Emotion, p. 177.
8   Thomasson: Fictional.

does, we are likely to suffer from information overload. In the case of Aviva, the spectator has to assume a single set of character beliefs and desires, or the journey structure dissolves into a series of episodes. For instance, motivation would be lacking in the teenager who wants to kill the abortion doctor unless we accept that the character hates the doctor because she has had an abortion and regrets it.

The narrative success of Conchita and Aviva suggests that the dominant conceptualization might be correct: it is best to see actor and character as dual representations. In the standard conceptualization, this means that the spectator will have to decide whether, for instance, a movement in the picture represents the movement of the actor or that of the character. According to Gregory Currie, parts of the picture may function as an easily recognizable sign, which represent either a fictional character or the photographed actor and when parts of the picture move, this represents the movement of either the character or actor.[9] I will discuss an account by Noël Carroll, who tries to solve the issue of actor/character dualism by distinguishing between different kinds of portrayal.

Noël Carroll's theory distinguishes between two kinds of portrayal in the picture.[10] On the one hand, there is a *physical portrayal* of the actor who plays the part and, on the other hand, there is a *nominal portrayal* of the fictional character, the latter relying also on narrative structure, titles, voice-over, etc. In portraying the physical source, due to the photographic process, the picture invariably depicts a type, a member of a general class, and this is what makes the nominal portrayal of a fictional character possible. According to Carroll, »A shot that physically portrays Anthony Perkins in *Psycho* depicts a madman while also, given its place in the context of the story, it nominally portrays Norman Bates«.[11] It is cinematic devices, which »establish that the objects, persons and events ›stand for‹ particular objects, persons and events other than the ones that caused the image«.[12]

The nominal portrayal of Conchita and Aviva occurs, as I have emphasized in my analysis, in large part as the result of cinematic devices such as alignment and framing. The depiction of a young woman who is being courted, functions to portray Conchita regardless of the actor in the photographic source, and this corroborates the dualism of Carroll's theory. However, in the case of *Palindromes*, we arguably recognize several

---

9   Currie: Image, chapter 1 and 2.
10 Carroll: Theorizing.
11 Ibid., p. 47.
12 Ibid.

types, not a single teenager, but a series of types distinguished by hair and skin color, size and weight, age and maturity, etc. Nevertheless, the types of conflicts and events encountered in *Palindromes*, match with the character type, a teenager who wants to have a baby and runs away from home.

Although Carroll's conceptual distinctions are helpful, we might consider another interpretation, in light of some friction. The problem of different teenager types of Aviva and the way in which we keep an eye on actor changes while following Conchita, may explain a comprehensible narrative and a single set of character beliefs and desires, but it does leave certain aspects unaccounted for. The casting is neither idiosyncratic or a preference for the unconventional for its own sake, nor a means for depicting a type, a member of a general class, which leaves each actor substitutions. I have argued that multiple actors offer a means for impeding intense person-directed emotions while presenting a lucid and interesting narrative.

We might hypothesize that spectators follow a film narrative while assuming that they are watching a single agent, an actor who pretends to hold the beliefs and desires that define the narrative, and that this conceptualization is better in explaining not only our awareness of whom is playing Conchita and Aviva, it may also explain the broader phenomenon of star acting. One reason for the importance of stars in cinema might be that spectators watch the film with an assumption that the photographic image and the sound tracks allows them to watch and listen to their favorite actors.

Theories, which stress the uniqueness of the photographic medium, have been the object of severe criticism. Critics have pointed out that André Bazin's claim that we are watching the object of a photographic picture as though we were watching the object itself,[13] has been refuted by, amongst others, Noël Carroll (the theory above is part of a counter-argument to Bazin). However, Bazin's claim has been developed by Kendall Walton who has argued that counter-factual dependence between object and depicted object makes photographs transparent.[14] That is, if the object had behaved in a different way, the picture would have looked different, regardless of the beliefs and desires held by the picture maker. Walton's theory has also been subjected to criticism but, in my view, has not been refuted. This transparency theory by Walton likens photographic pictures to, for instance, pictures from surveillance cameras, which let a

---

13 Bazin: Ontology.
14 Walton: Transparent.

night guard watch several spaces without having to physically move between them.

In the case of Conchita and Aviva, the transparency thesis lets us understand why we intuitively would be suspicious, if anyone claimed that a similar effect could occur in a non-photographic moving picture. Would the visual variations of Aviva and Conchita make any sense in an animated film? In an animation, I suspect we would motivate a similar discontinuity intra-fictionally, for instance as a depiction of Conchita *as* Mathieu experiences her, or we would see a series of distinct characters, seeing for instance Aviva's mother as mistaking different impersonators for her daughter.

What is more, the transparency thesis explains how an actor's earlier roles may feed into current portrayals. For instance, Clint Eastwood's performance in *Dirty Harry* (1971), and specifically in the final scene, where he dares a criminal to pick up his gun (›Go ahead! Make my day!‹), might function as the portrayal against which more recent portrayals are held. Carroll's distinction between two types of portrayal hinges on the depiction of an unspecified type but if an actor plays types which are distinctly different – arguably, Eastwood's gunslinger character in Sergio Leone's westerns does not match Harry Callahan, the contemporary policeman – we *ought* to distinguish between distinct characters regardless of the actor. When we fail to distinguish, I suspect that the reason is that we watch actors on the assumption that actors are the agents of narrative actions, carried out in pretense. Thus in *Dirty Harry*, we see Clint Eastwood pretending to want to kill a criminal with his Magnum, we see Clint Eastwood pretending that he believes the other person has murdered innocent people in the streets of San Francisco. According to this hypothesis, these narrative beliefs and desires are held by an actual agent, the actor, rather than a fictional and non-existent one.

Moreover, we may hypothesize that the dualist model is inadequate in certain respects, even though it does well as general explanation of character consistency in *Palindromes* and *That Obscure Object of Desire*. However, the dualist model can only inadequately account for the way in which, for instance, I recollect the threat and shooting in the final scene of *Dirty Harry,* as carried out by Clint Eastwood. In the case of star actors, the problem is why different characters get conflated since they presumably live in distinct fictional worlds; in the case of Aviva and Conchita, the problem is that the character becomes an abstraction, which is decoupled from a specific embodiment.

5 Empirical Grounding vs. Fallible Agency Perception

For the spectator to perceive a single and coherent character, while also keeping an eye on the different actors in the role, it is critically important that our intuition of a single body for a single mind be given up. I will argue that we may have to acknowledge that the perception of agency is fallible for natural reasons.

An empirically based model for film characters assumes an analogy to everyday experiences with agents when we perceive fictional characters. Consider this list, supplied by Murray Smith in his *Engaging Characters*, of what a human agent is, and is capable of:[15]

(i) a discrete human body, individuated and continuous through time and space
(ii) perceptual activity, including self-awareness
(iii) intentional states, such as beliefs and desires
(iv) emotions
(v) the ability to use and understand a natural language
(vi) the capacity for self-impelled actions and self-interpretation
(vii) the potential for traits, or persisting attributes

We believe that human agents have a discrete and continuous body; yet we also believe that Conchita and Aviva are human agents, in large part because they meet criteria in (ii) to (vii). What makes them paradoxical is the violation of the assumption of (i) a discrete and continuous body.

The paradox may be resolved by introducing an alternative to the experience-based model. The list above is a list of what we *ought* to ask for, if we want a sound and reasonable set of criteria for what should pass as a human agent. Suppose, instead, that perception of agency is fallible and occurs independently of what we believe to be necessary conditions for human agents.

There are good reasons why evolution might have favored fallible perceptual mechanisms. The cognitive anthropologist, Justin Barrett, has suggested that because humans in our ancestral past often faced the risk of being prey, evolutionary pressures selected for the detection of agents even in circumstances where stimuli were poor or inconsistent.[16] It is better to detect an agent and find out that nobody was there, as opposed to overlooking a predator. Errors on the safe side are basically without cost whereas a single error on the wrong side might prove fatal.

Justin Barrett has coined this perceptual and cognitive tendency to err on the safe side *Hypersensitive Agency Detection Device* or, for short, HADD.

---

15 Smith: Engaging, p. 21.
16 Barrett: Why.

In his *Why Would Anyone Believe in God?*, he deploys the HADD as a means to understand why beliefs in spirits and gods are abundant across all cultures. By drawing on another cognitive anthropologist, Pascal Boyer, he applies the theory that supernatural beliefs are dependent on a single violation of what is otherwise a redundant category. In Barrett's discussion of supernatural agents, they must, for example, be like empirical humans in every way but one, which defines the principle of *minimal violation*. For instance, agents must behave as though they are capable of memory, moral emotions, vengefulness, etc., and then violate a basic assumption, for instance, they are invisible or they can immaterialize at will. I suggest that we spell out what might be called Darwinian premises for character perception in this manner:

- Perception of human agents relies on innate perceptual mechanisms, which exist prior to experience
- The relevant mechanisms are fallible, which means that they need not be corrected by beliefs grounded in experience
- Empirically based beliefs on agents may work in accord with fallible and innate perceptual mechanisms

The first proposition is uncontroversial. After all, newborn babies need to get started, and they are better off paying attention to humans rather than inanimate objects. ›To rely on‹ is a relatively weak formulation, which allows for learning through experience, for instance form expectations about social types and their interests (teenagers, single-children, widowers and good-looking young women, etc). The second proposition is controversial. In a strong reading, it suggests that we are misled by our senses when we look at images of performances, and that our beliefs about what we are seeing have little bearing.

In a weak reading, however, the second proposition may have considerable explanatory power in reconciling some of the paradoxes inherent in the actor/character dualism.

First, there is the problem of the transparent, single agent: the strong indication that spectators may watch narratives with star actors, with an assumption that narrative actions are carried out by the actor in pretense. This means that even though we believe characters to be distinct and placed in separate fictional worlds, we may still have expectations concerning the narrative, based on the actor's actions in other films. Even though we believe that fictional agents are distinct, the assumption of a transparent, pretending actor overrules what we believe to be the case, that characters are distinct. Richard Dyer has suggested that when looking at star actors, we look for a selective use of prior roles, or a perfect or problematic fit,[17] and the implication is that we cannot, once we recognize the actor, process the character as though he or she were as distinct as the agents of everyday life.

Second, there is the problem of the actor's performance, whether he or she succeeds in what is aimed for. In a transparent medium, we tend to detect insecurity on the actor's part whereas in an animation, the same would likely pass as indicative of the character's insecurity. Part of an actor's task, at least in mainstream film acting, is to create what actors have referred to as *the illusion of the first time*.[18] Illusion of the first time means that an actor has delivered a line in a manner that makes it appear spontaneous, breathing life into what is otherwise voluntarily executed actions. The illusion of a line as spoken for the first time need not entail a belief that a different agent is suddenly present, that the actor has disappeared. It implies only that narrative intentions and beliefs come to the foreground. Thus, the spectator may not need to discard his or her favorite actor's identity in order to appreciate the illusion of the first time.

The third proposition is implied in the principle of minimal violation and suggests that an empirically based conception of character and one which acknowledges that perceptual mechanisms can be fallible, may work in tandem. One might expect or hope that our empirically based beliefs would send a message equivalent to: ›Stop! Not a possible character! Violation of necessary conditions for the category of human agents!‹ However, a minimal violation such as a single mind/several bodies may work together with the redundancies of social types. Our empirically derived beliefs about a stubborn single-child teenager with overly protective middle-class parents are all brought into play in the portrayal of Aviva and, in a similar vein, our beliefs about an adolescent young woman, and how she might respond to being pursued by a middle-aged, wealthy widower, are cleverly played upon in the portrayal of Conchita. Naturally, these beliefs about social types come to us with experience and recognizing the types in paradoxical characters enables the spectator to assume a single character despite multiple actors.[19]

Film theorists have favored a too narrow conception of fallibility, distinguishing perceptual illusions from epistemic or cognitive illusions.[20] My analysis suggests that a spectator believes that he or she is watching actors in a relatively transparent medium, thereby enabling assumptions from earlier encounters with an actor to be posited on the current role.

---

17 Dyer: Stars, p. 143.
18 This usage was popularized by Gillette: Illusion.
19 Regarding the ways in which we draw on social categories and apply distinctions at different levels, see Eder: Understanding.
20 For these distinctions, see Allen: Projecting; Currie: Image.

This may contradict our empirically grounded beliefs about the distinctness of human agents, but the beliefs concerning actor and transparent medium appear stronger. Mixing features from distinct realms can make for portrayals of greater value and star actors benefit from this, consider for example Stanley Cavell's observation that Humphrey Bogart »means ›the figure created in a given set of films‹«.[21]

What I have referred to as Darwinian premises assume that perceptual and cognitive mechanisms are intertwined, and that they have evolved in order to serve adaptive actions in a historical environment, rather than empirical truth-seeking for its own sake.[22] An example is the preference for errors on the safe side in detecting agents. Similar premises underlie Mark Turner and Gilles Fauconnier's theory on *conceptual blending*, which allows for projecting properties, sequences, relations, etc., from a variety of domains, into a single cognitive field; they show how poetry and literature may play upon this ability.[23] Indeed, Stanley Cavell's impression of Bogart, cited above, may be viewed as a conceptual blend.

6 Conclusion and Implications

My examination of two film narratives with multiple actors for a single character shows that the unconventional casting choice may be viewed as a means for impeding emotional responses, which would too easily be invoked from the narrative. The casting choices cannot be regarded as idiosyncratic choices (unless we first disregard the problems that the themes might have posed).

In order to construct a coherent narrative with a single set of character beliefs and desires, we have to overcome, one way or another, the intuition that a human agent has a single body. The construction of a single set of character beliefs and desires is a matter of fact or else the narrative would lack intelligibility.

In a dualist account, the moving picture depicts either the actor or the character and for this reason, the changing of actors does not pose a particular problem. Since character is always a separate and distinct agent, we simply let information from image and sound feed into the category of a fictional character. In a transparent account the spectator watches the moving picture according to an assumption that a particular actor performs narrative actions in pretense. Thus, spectators may motivate

---

21 Cavell: World, p. 28.
22 In film theory, this perspective was first introduced in Anderson: Reality.
23 Fauconnier / Turner: Way.

Aviva's and Conchita's bodily discontinuities with a change of actor, while continuing to follow the narrative. A transparent account needs additional, theoretical premises, and I have argued that perceptual fallibility is critically important.

To sum up, a single conceptual model is insufficient; we need both of them since the combination allows us a better theoretical grasp of our experience of actors and characters in film narrative. The two models preclude each other in terms of logic but not psychology, and Darwinian premises may account for spectators' simultaneous application of seemingly contradictory models. Dual representations and transparency thesis each have merits and explanatory power.

References

Allen, Richard: Projecting Illusion: Film Spectatorship and the Impression of Reality. New York 1995.

Anderson, Joseph: The Reality of Illusion: An Ecological Approach to Cognitive Film Theory. Carbondale 1996.

Barrett, Justin L.: Why Would Anyone Believe in God? Lanham 2004.

Bazin, André: The Ontology of the Photographic Image. In: Leo Braudy / Marshall Cohen (Eds.): Film Theory and Criticism: Introductory Readings. Oxford 1999, pp. 195–198.

Carroll, Noël: Theorizing the Moving Image. In: Henry Breitrose / William Rothman (Eds.): Cambridge Studies in Film. Cambridge / New York 1996, pp. 45–48.

Cavell, Stanley: The World Viewed: Reflections on the Ontology of Film. Cambridge 1996.

Currie, Gregory: Image and Mind: Film, Philosophy, and Cognitive Science. Cambridge 1995.

Dyer, Richard: Stars. London 1979.

Eder, Jens: Understanding Characters. In: Projections 4/1 (2010), pp. 16–40.

Fauconnier, Gilles / Mark Turner: The Way We Think: Conceptual Blending and the Mind's Hidden Complexities. New York 2002.

Frijda, Nico H.: The Emotions. Cambridge / New York 1986.

Ghillebaert, Francoise: The Double in Buñuel's »That Obscure Object of Desire«. In: Post Script 22/3 (2007), pp. 57–68.

Gillette, William Hooker: The Illusion of the First Time in Acting. In: Toby Cole / Helen Krich Chinoy: Actors on Acting: The Theories, Techniques, and Practices of the Great Actors of All Times as Told in Their Own Words. New York 1970, pp. 564–566.

Kihlstrom, John F.: Joseph Jastrow and His Duck – Or Is It a Rabbit? <http://www.socrates.berkeley.edu/~kihlstrm/JastrowDuck.htm> (June 30th, 2010).

Levin, Daniel T. / Daniel J. Simons: Failure to Detect Changes to Attended Objects in Motion Pictures. In: Psychonomic Bulletin and Review 4 (1997), pp. 501–506.

Scharfman, Ronnie: Deconstruction Goes to the Movies: Buñuel's Cet Obscur Objet Du Désir. In: The French Review 53/3 (1980), pp. 351–358.

Smith, Murray: Engaging Characters: Fiction, Emotion, and the Cinema. Oxford 1995.

Tan, Ed: Emotion and the Structure of Narrative Film: Film as an Emotion Machine. (LEA's Communication Series) New Jersey 1996.

Thomasson, Amie L.: Fictional Characters and Literary Practices. In: British Journal of Aesthetics 43/2 (2003), pp. 138–157.
Walton, Kendall L.: Transparent Pictures. In: Critical Inquiry 11/2 (1984), pp. 246–277.

JÖRG SCHWEINITZ

Stereotypes and the Narratological Analysis of Film Characters

The intellectual discourse on the ›stereotypology‹ of popular media, particularly of feature films, pervaded the entire twentieth century and oscillated between radical critique and renunciation, pragmatic appropriation, and postmodern celebratory revelation. These discourses refer to various concurrent and divergent meanings of ›stereotype‹ in the social sciences, linguistics and literary studies, art history, film and media studies. Thus, various concepts of stereotypes can be brought into play to investigate narrative films, especially film characters deemed to be based on different kinds of stereotypes. Each of these concepts conveys quite different methodological questions.[1]

Social psychology or anthropology linked ›stereotypes‹ particularly to schematized and conventionalized perceptions of the ›Other‹ as well as the ›Self‹ (hetero- and auto-stereotypes). When analyzing film narration, we need to consider how narrative figures interact with, and represent, such beliefs. This has been, and remains, the classic question in film analysis based on social psychology, anthropology, cultural studies, or the analysis of ideology. Pragmatic narratology might also find such a perspective meaningful. Social psychology conceives of ›stereotypes‹ as unsophisticated and fixed mental images of individuals belonging to certain groups. Such conventionalized notions, anchored in everyday cultural awareness, provide important points of reference for the narrative construction of fictional characters. For the experience of reception to work, it matters that a film and its characters, as the key factors of audience participation in the plot, are closely interrelated with everyday beliefs and values.

Apart from that, such referentiality also appears to work in the opposite direction: popular audio-visual narratives actively influence the audience's

---

1 For a comprehensive overview see the first chapter of Schweinitz: Film.

imagination, if only through visually reshaping and rendering the current cognitive schemata concrete, that is, providing a repertoire of evident visible patterns. For instance, Irmela Schneider has observed that the notions held by Germans about Americans (and the members of certain groups in the United States) are to a large extent determined by American television series and their visual representation of figural patterns.[2] The same holds true for feature films – particularly with a view to the pre-television age.

Such findings have prompted progressive attempts to lay open, differentiate, and correct the frequently emphasized reductiveness or distortedness of such conventional notions of the ›Other‹. Even projects like this rest upon the (hoped-for) active repercussion of films on audience disposition. Particularly in the 1970s and 80s, at a time when ideological critique was prevalent, this issue became important not only in film theory and criticism. Committed film-makers, such as Rainer Werner Fassbinder, also made this the aim of their narration. Fassbinder sought to intervene in his audience's social imagination. In *Angst essen Seele auf* (Germany 1973), for instance, he attempted to uncover negative stereotypes, particularly about foreigners and minorities, bring these to public attention, and foreground their superficial, distorted nature. The character of Ali, a North African immigrant, is used to invoke the social stereotype which the film rejects, to sharpen it, and to demonstrate its absurdity through the cinematic staging of marked differences. As a sophisticated and likeable character, Ali affords the audience a powerful experience of the customary stereotype as an instance of impoverished, distorted, and indeed malicious social imagination. Put differently, Fassbinder applies cinematic narration to critique such stereotypes as crystals of false consciousness in the name of reality and humanity. *Angst essen Seele auf* is about the inhuman dynamics of social behaviour guided by ignorant stereotyping, in which almost all its characters are ensnared.

It is not accidental but rather part of the same discourse and sensibility, that in the 1970s and 80s a considerable number of film scholars, like Steve Neale,[3] wrote about the stereotypical images of the ›Other‹ and emphasized how films played with difference and criticized social patterns. Given such interest, it is even less surprising that many film scholars and those studying other narrative media, including Richard Dyer,[4] initially took up the notion of the stereotype as a *socio-psychological* category and linked it fairly directly to film characters. In such contexts,

---

2 Schneider: Theorie.
3 Neale: Story.
4 Dyer: Stereotyping.

the notion of the ›stereotype‹ is for the most part applied to film characters who quite evidently appear to be *narrative* embodiments of stereotypical images of the ›Other‹. For not only do such characters match the stereotypical perceptions of members of certain groups, but they are themselves *narrative*, that is, *aesthetic* constructs (because they are *conventionalized artifacts* reduced to some few conspicuous traits and subject to wholesale intertextual repetition). As Neale observes: »According to this problematic, a stereotype is a stable und repetitive structure of character traits«.[5]

This is where the topic of stereotype also comes into play as a *narrative mode*, or a ›mode of characterization in fiction‹ according to Dyer.[6] It does so not merely in terms of social psychology, but in a broader sense that shows – specifically with a view to narrative – how film characters are involved in the interplay of automatization and conventionalization on the one hand, and schemata and the reduction of complexity on the other. In this spirit Dyer closely examines the two-faced ›dumb blonde stereotype‹,[7] both as an everyday idea and a concrete character pattern of the cinematic-narrative imaginary, established in the 1930s and mainly influenced by American films featuring actresses like Jean Harlow or Marilyn Monroe.

In its attempt to understand stereotype-based perception and thought, social psychology contrasts the precise, unprejudiced, and patient observation of others with the rapid recourse to reduced and distorted conventional images operating as *pre*-judgments and replacing actual observation. It therefore stands to reason that a related, albeit specific antinomy prevails in aesthetic theory, dramaturgy, and narratology. Scholars working in these fields commonly distinguish individual characters from types when discussing narrative figures.

Individual characters only become gradually perceptible as a plot unfolds; they develop through interaction with the course of events and possess an individual and complex intellectual and psychological profile. Umberto Eco makes a similar distinction. Envisaging a character spectrum, he identifies at one end those who attain ›a complete physiognomy [...] which is not merely exterior, but also intellectual and moral‹.[8] With

---

5   Neale: Stereotypes, p. 41.
6   See Dyer: Stereotyping; see further Dyer: Images, esp. pp. 11–18: ›The Role of Stereotypes‹.
7   Dyer thus entitled a documentation for classroom use. See Dyer: Blonde.
8   Eco: Anwendung, p. 169. Eco refers to a special variety of the narrative character, which he calls ›type‹ and contrasts with ›character‹. Please note that this essay is not included in the partial English translation (Apocalyse Postponed) of Eco's *Apocalittici e integrati* (1964). All quotes are trans. by M.K.

reference to Lukács, Eco observes that ideally, such characters can attain an ›intellectual physiognomy‹,⁹ which readers gradually recognize *as the actual goal of the reading process*. Such characters, he argues further, ›never exist prior to the work, but mark its success‹.¹⁰ Narratives of this kind thus attempt to convey to their readers gradually developing, psychologically complex, multi-faceted characters. Such narration and individual characterization can be realized along similar lines in both literature and film.

At the other end of the spectrum, Eco detects schematically reduced characters, immediately recognizable on account of some few distinctive traits. Or as he notes, »[w]hen a person appears on the scene, they are already complete: defined, weighed, and minted«.¹¹ He cites Dumas' d'Artagnan, who lacks psychological complexity and all individual development, as an example. Once introduced, we learn nothing new about d'Artagnan over the course of the plot, beyond the exciting events for which he serves as a vehicle and which he experiences virtually unaffected:

> While his adventures afforded us excellent entertainment, we became aware that the author conveys nothing about him, and that d'Artagnan's adventures by no means determined him. His presence was accidental [...] d'Artagnan serves as a pretext for the staging of events.¹²

Eco's argument prompts two observations. First, operating as a ›pretext‹ for the staging of events, such characters are not really accidental. Rather, their construction is precisely attuned to fulfilling a narrative *function*. That is, time and again, their specific attributes and the narrative programme attached to them enable and convey particular events and narrative procedures. Manfred Pfister has aptly called this the ›action-functional structuring‹ of the character.¹³ Seen thus, d'Artagnan remains indeed unchanged by his adventures: true to his *narrative role*, which is determined from the outset, he is shaped through and through by his function to survive certain adventures. If he has any sense of self-actualization, it consists in the continual actualization of a pre-defined rule.

Secondly, a small set of particularly conspicuous, semantically unequivocal, and stable attributes enhances the poignancy of such characters beyond their characteristic traits by placing counterfigures to them – at times constant, at times alternating, but structurally similar in the latter

---

9   Ibid., p. 171.
10 Ibid., p. 175.
11 Ibid., p. 173.
12 Ibid., p. 177.
13 Pfister: Drama, p. 234.

case. These antagonists are construed along similarly schematic lines. Pitting them against one another renders their characteristics even more apparent than type formation does anyway.¹⁴ Besides, such distinctive traits enable readers and film spectators to readily attribute values and meanings, establish clarity, and thus advance the plot through the conflicts thereby generated.

Incidentally, the (figural) spectrum from individual characters to types as outlined here largely corresponds to E. M. Forster's distinction between ›flat‹ and ›round‹ characters:

> Flat characters were called ›humorous‹ in the seventeenth century, and are sometimes called types. [...] In their purest form, they are constructed round a single idea or quality: when there is more than one factor in them, we get the beginning of the curve towards the round.¹⁵

For round characters ›cannot be summed up in a single phrase‹ and we remember them in connection with the scenes through which they ›passed and as modified by those scenes‹; round characters have ›facets like human beings‹.¹⁶ Finally:

> The test of a round character is whether it is capable of surprising in a convincing way. If it never surprises, it is flat. If it does not convince, it is a flat pretending to be round. It [the round character; J.S.] has the incalculability of life about it – life within the pages of a book.¹⁷

Referring to film, Dyer makes a very similar distinction to that of Forster and Eco, which he describes as opposition between ›novelistic character‹ and ›type‹,¹⁸ and which I adopt here. He explicitly associates the sociopsychological ›stereotype‹ (the mental image of the ›Other‹) with ›type‹ (the figural construct in narrative fiction). Initially, Eco also referred to this second kind of character as a ›type‹ before shifting to ›topos‹. The latter refers beyond the reduced characterization and figural stability existing within a text. It also accentuates the feature of conventionality, or more specifically the intertextual mode of existence. Eco's ›topos‹ thus broadly overlaps with my *narrative sense* of the ›figural stereotype‹ as a conventional artifact:

> As useful and harmless as ›types‹ are, they function as a pattern of the human imagination [...]. We should rather call them *topoi*, that is *places* that can be easily transferred into conventions and used effortlessly. The *topos* as a pattern of the human

---

14 See Asmuth: Dramenanalyse, pp. 96–98.
15 Forster: Novel, p. 67.
16 Ibid., p. 69.
17 Ibid., p. 78.
18 Dyer: Images, p. 13.

imagination is employed excellently where [...] a character recalled takes the place of a compositional act of the imagination; it relieves us [...].¹⁹

While they stand in contrast to *individual characters*, no a priori coincidence between *types* and *figural stereotypes* (or Eco's *topos*) exists. Once established in a text, a type only becomes a narrative *topos* – and thus a figural stereotype in a narrative sense – when it has established itself *as a conventional figural pattern through repetition in the intertextual space of narration*.

Stereotyping a type once developed in a text is thus a second possible step. This *intertextual phase of type formation* brings forth an independent cultural fact, a conventional artifact of narrative imagination. For instance, the screen *vamp* – a type originally aligned through its external traits (particularly costume and make-up, but also habitus) with the tradition of the Italian diva – underwent its original cinematographic conventionalization through repeated performance in a considerable number of silent films. It thus became an established symbol of an audio-visual narrative imagination that maintains close relations with allegory and subsequently inspired a whole array of similar narratives.

Mostly, however, theoretical studies conceive of ›types‹ as fully fledged stereotypes. Scholars happily cite either the stock characters of the Italian *Commedia dell'arte* or the comparable array of seventeenth and eighteenth-century French stage characters as surviving and particularly striking examples.²⁰ Instead of nurturing the futile ambition to reform common usage, I merely wish to suggest that the formation of such fixed ›types‹, which characterizes the intertextual imaginary world of various genres (for instance, the Western or the ›cloak and dagger film‹), is a second, conventionalized phase of type formation, and thus an instance of the *narrative* stereotyping examined here.²¹

This distinction allows us to grasp Stanley Cavell's argument that narration in fully developed popular cinema rests upon types – rather than stereotypes:

> [T]ypes are exactly what carry the forms movies have relied upon. These media created new types; or combinations and ironic reversals of types; but there they were, and stayed.²²

---

19 Eco: Anwendung, pp. 178–179.
20 See Asmuth: Dramenanalyse, p. 88.
21 This is affirmed by etymology. Like ›stereotype‹, ›type‹ also derives from printing language. Originally a ›type‹ was the rectangular block usually of metal, bearing a relief character or so-called ›cliché‹ from which an inked print could be made. See Lausberg: Handbuch, § 901.
22 Cavell: World, p. 33.

Cavell then asks: »Does this mean that movies can never create individuals, only types?«[23] His response is bound to irritate anyone failing to distinguish between types and stereotypes:

> What it means is that this [creating types] is the movies' way of creating individuals: they create *individualities*. For what makes someone a type is not his similarity with other members of that type but his striking separateness from other people.[24]

What Cavell's claim amounts to is that with the advent of its classic phase popular cinema operates less with figural ›stereotypes‹,[25] that is, conventional constructs of *intertextually* repeated character traits and attributes – much like the ready-mades used in naive early silent film. Instead, he argues, it features *individualities*. For Cavell, such *individualities*, created in the individual film (or through a single, popular figure) arise particularly from their accentuated difference, their *striking separateness*, from other characters, particularly their buddies and antagonists but also people from the audience's everyday world. Besides, such reduced complexity and *intra*textual schematization engenders the necessary poignancy. To that extent, such *individualitie*s are not inevitably one and the same as *individual characters* in the above sense, but – as Cavell also observes – *types*, albeit *not* stereotypes.

Cavell's argument seems to underestimate the significance that unambiguous figural stereotypes or so-called ›established types‹,[26] together with more comprehensive conventionalization, have always assumed in the panoply of characters peopling Hollywood genres, particularly as regards the large repertoire of minor characters. Studies on stock characters in Hollywood cinema furnish such evidence, should this be necessary.[27] On the other hand, Cavell's theoretical distinction between *type* and *stereotype* establishes some clarity. For instance, it helps to distinguish between the original invention of a figural type and its later (potential) stereotypization. It also makes for a better description of the differences frequently existing between main and minor characters.

---

23 Ibid.
24 Ibid.
25 Ibid.
26 Perhaps this has to do with the context of Cavell's argument, which adopts a critical stance toward Panofsky's claim that with the rise of the sound film the naive, determined iconography of *established* and visually easily recognisable types loses significance, since the audience no longer needs the explanation contained in the fixed type. Cavell takes up this argument, but objects: »Films have changed, but that is not because we don't need such explanations any longer; it is because we can't accept them«. (Ibid, p. 33.) This doesn't mean that types disappear, but only stereotypes, that is, *intertextually* determined types.
27 Loukides / Fuller: Stars.

As the previous discussion suggests, narrative figural stereotypes are not merely narrative-visual manifestations of normalized mental images of the ›Other‹ which social psychology approaches via the concept of the ›stereotype‹. *Two different aspects of stereotyping* can be distinguished as regards the interrelation of film characters and reality.[28] While these aspects partly come into contact and overlap, they also frequently merge but never wholly absorb one another.

The socio-scientific concept of the stereotype raises various questions (even though such approaches to film characters foreground social science and frequently cultural studies issues). For instance, which sociologically relevant cultural notions of the ›Other‹, of members of particular nations, professional groups, minorities, or other groups belonging to social reality does film represent or influence? Siegfried Kracauer's *National Types as Hollywood Presents Them*,[29] a study undertaken in the 1950s, examines a theme and adopts an approach both of which are characteristic of the interest taken by the social sciences in the representation of such beliefs. This concerns conventional and schematic everyday notions of *the* American, *the* Russian, *the* Turk, *the* African, *the* German – or in other contexts, *the* homosexual, *the* housewife, and so forth. Put differently, this concerns sociologically relevant schematic notions, which, however questionable, *claim a certain validity in the real world and determine attitudes toward such groups*. Such notions can guide practical action and directly affect social interaction, hence making them a preferred subject of both social science and political discourses.

What needs to be set apart here is the *narrative concept of the stereotype*. Primarily, this concerns neither the schematization nor conventionalization of sociologically relevant notions, but rather the *narrative depiction of fictional characters*. The focus thus lies on intertextually recurrent narrative schemata. In *cinematic* narration, these are characterized to a large extent by (audio-)visual concreteness, that is, recurring sensuous traits.

It could be argued that narrative and socio-psychological stereotypes – that is, normalized perceptions of the ›Other‹ – are closely linked. But such interrelation is neither imperative, nor are these two kinds of ›stereotypes‹ by any means congruent. On the one hand, films can take up socio-psychological stereotypes without, however, drawing upon cinematic-narrative ones. Stereotypical notions of the ›Other‹ can affect characterization, of course, but such delineation can be considerably more subtle through narration. Characters as such operate neither as *narrative figural stereotypes* nor as a fixed intertextual type of narration. Characters

---

[28] The same applies to all kinds of fictional narration, not only the cinematic.
[29] Kracauer: Hollywood, pp. 53–72.

who ›playfully sidestep‹ socio-psychological patterns can become ›reindividualized‹ on the surface over the course of narrative presentation. They are by no means rare in cinema.

On the other hand, a whole array of conventionalized intertextual types exists. Such narrative figural stereotypes have little in common with notions of the ›Other‹ associated more immediately with reality, nor do they shape attitudes toward the real world as a result. Instead, spectators consciously perceive and process such stereotypes as conventional patterns of the imagination.

This is possible, I argue, since narrative stereotypes can also take the shape of unequivocally imaginary figural constructs common in a particular genre. Above all, these claim validity within a certain narrative framework, that is, within specific imaginary worlds of narration. They refer precisely *not* (or at best highly indirectly) to the audience's immediate everyday world, and claim no validity in that world. My notion of ›imaginary worlds‹ echoes Wolfgang Iser's triade of ›the real, the fictive, and the imaginary‹.[30] I wish to emphasize that the narrative stereotypes occurring in fictional (and, by implication, cinematic) texts are geared much more frequently toward expressing what Iser calls ›phantasma, projections, and daydreams‹ than striving after a truthful representation of reality.[31] These imaginary worlds crystallize the crossing of boundaries of the imaginary from the diffuse and from the merely individual to the interpersonally structured fact, which comes into its own reality through having become conventional.

The need to distinguish these two concepts of the stereotype becomes particularly urgent when considering highly conventionalized genres like the Western. While the 1930s epic Western declared that its stories were about a real, albeit historical, world, it unmistakably resorted to mythical narration. No later (emphatically!) than the self-reflexive Spaghetti Western did audiences realize that they were party to a ritualized performance, which makes no meaningful reference to any facet of reality, but instead occurs in an utterly conventional, imaginary world. For instance, Sergio Leone's *C'era una volta il West* (Italy/USA 1968) explicitly indulges in parading key stereotypes from a genre-specific repertoire, as regards both characters, their patterns of actions, and various other dimensions of cinematic narration. Leone carries the stereotype mechanism (involving the reduction of complexity together with repetition) – also as regards character delineation – far beyond the limits already adopted during the classic phase of the genre. He thus lays bare

---

30 Iser: Perspektiven, p. 19; Frayling: Westerns, p. 194.
31 Ibid., p 21.

the stereotype mechanism in a self-reflexive manner, and *derealizes* the entire world of action and characters once and for all.

In his study of the Spaghetti Western, Christopher Frayling delineates this procedure and argues that Leone and Bertolucci, his scenarist, purposefully chose

> [...] the most worn-out of stereotypes: the pushy whore, the romantic bandit, the avenger, the killer who is about to become a business man, the industrialist who uses the methods of a bandit. These stereotypes, which, in Leones' and Bertolucci's hands, become fictional ›emblems‹ of a sort, are taken from the dime novel, the Wild West show, the Hollywood film, the pulp magazine, the comic-strip, rather than from American history – parts of a ›fixed terminology‹ or ›code‹ of the fictional genre.[32]

The capitalist thus becomes a flashy type, extremely reduced outwardly and emblematically presented as a cripple harbouring fantasies of omnipotence. Forming part of a cinematic repertoire of stereotypes up to the present, this narrative stereotype recurs throughout film history, such as in the guise of Fritz Lang's banker Haghi (in *Spione*, Germany 1928), Stanley Kubrick's Dr. Strangelove (*Dr. Strangelove, or How I Learned to Stop Worrying and Love the Bomb*, GB 1964), and many other instances, including Barry Sonnenfeld's Dr. Loveless in *Wild Wild West* (USA 1999). This garish character hardly denotes any ›true‹ story, but represents nothing other than an exalted token of an imagination conventionalized long ago – a genre's historical no-man's-land produced by conventionalization.

This example makes evident that while the social sciences define stereotypes as (more or less functional and more or less likeable) constructions of reality which have clear consequences for thought and action in *everyday life*, narratological stereotypes foreground a relatively autonomous construct, which is valid only within fictional worlds, understood as *conventional intertextual worlds of the imagination*. No one would consider Leone's stereotypical characters to have validity beyond the confines of the cinema. Social science studies which somewhat rashly sought to deduce from this *the* ›image of the industrialist‹, prevailing in everyday human imagination and associated with reality, came to nothing since such characters are nothing other than pawns in a ritualised game. Lubomír Doležel, a leading theorist in the field of fictional-worlds theory, in this sense emphasizes ›the sovereignty of fictional worlds‹,[33] and adds: »Mimetic reading, practiced by naïve readers and reinforced by journalistic critics, is one of the most reductive operations of which the human mind is capable: the vast, open, and inviting fictional universe is shrunk to the

---

32 Frayling: Westerns, p. 194.
33 Doležel: Heterocosmica, p. 18.

model of one single world, actual human experience«[34]. Doležel refers to the philosophical framework of possible-worlds semantics.[35] In this sense he gives the definition:

> Fictional worlds of literature [...] are a special kind of possible world, they are aesthetic artifacts constructed, preserved, and circulating in the medium of fictional texts.[36]

In concluding his definition he touches on the second phase of establishing fictional worlds in the interpersonal repertoire of the imaginary. This phase is based on the *intertextual* repetition of central constituents of one of these worlds in a multiple of texts, for example of a genre. Also from this intertextual aspect, Doležel's description of fictional worlds makes sense as ›ensembles of nonactualized possible states of affairs‹.[37]

However, these two kinds of stereotypes – the socio-scientific and the one merely holding true in intertextual fictional worlds, i.e. in the worlds of conventionalized imagination – are not always as easily distinguishable as in the above instances. Distinction is often complicated by the fact that film spectators and readers can hardly ever draw a sharp line between even decidedly imaginary narrative worlds and their imaginary constructions of the real world. After all the latter also comprise a considerable number of imaginary moments (not least determined by media). Besides, both ›kinds‹ of stereotypes often overlap or become intertwined. I therefore referred to *aspects*, which occasionally tend to converge in one and the same character, particularly if this character functions as a stereotype in a narrative sense (or as conventional type) *and* embodies a socially relevant stereotypical notion of the ›Other‹.

The militaristic German, whom Erich von Strohheim, among others, established as a narrative stereotype in American cinema, comes to mind. While following culturally established notions, it engendered a separate narrative template, a type soon conventionalized, a ›mask‹. On account of its latently comical sharpening, its habitus, and some few ostentatiously flaunted attributes, it began to lead its own cinematic life within the conventional sphere of playful imagination. Among others, this independent existence became apparent in that, as a comedy stereotype, the conventional type of narration could oscillate toward the amusing and

---

34 Ibid., p. x
35 Elaborating further, he, however, places value on emphasizing the specific character of fictional worlds in relation to the possible worlds of logic and philosophy, and articulating features ›that are special for the fictional worlds of literature, that is, those features that cannot be derived from the possible worlds model‹ (ibid., p. 16).
36 Ibid., p. 16.
37 Ibid.

almost likeable, although the socio-psychological stereotype upon which it originally rested was distinctly negative.

Being able to obtain this independent existence, based on ›de-realization‹, is typical of narrative figurations once conventionalized. Such independence recurs in the shape of the stereotypical Soviet official – see, for instance, the corresponding characters in Ernst Lubitsch's *Ninotchka* (*Ninotschka*, USA 1939) and Billy Wilder's *One, two, three* (USA 1961) – or the stereotypical psychiatrist – see, among others, Frank Capra's *Mr. Deeds goes to town* (USA 1936), Woody Allen's *Stardust Memories* (USA 1980), and Ethan and Joel Coen's *The Hudsucker Proxy* (USA 1994). Another case in point is the ›drunken journalist‹, as Howard Good's ›biography‹ of this film stereotype shows.[38]

The gradual conventionalizing of a pattern coincides with a tendency toward ›de-realization‹. Thus characters who at first appear as possible representations of reality become puppets in what is an obvious game, to the extent that they become conventional quantities. In this sense, Jurij Lotman, who speaks of an ›aesthetic of identity‹ which is based upon ›model clichés‹,[39] thus remarked on the *comedia dell'arte*:

> The unpitying nature of Italian (and not only Italian) folk theatre is organically connected with its *conventionality*. The audience remembers that these are puppets or maskers on the stage and perceives their death or suffering, beatings or misfortunes, not as the death or suffering of real people, but in a spirit of carnival and ritual. Germi's films would be unbearably cynical if he invited us to see real people in his characters.[40]

If we can neither sharply delineate nor systematize the ramified interactions between these aspects, it nevertheless makes sense to distinguish them. While the socio-psychological concept of the stereotype rests upon social pragmatics, narrative stereotypes are pragmatic quantities of narration and of narrative imagination.

They shape the imaginary and allow it to become ›real‹ as an *open imaginary construct*, that is, a fixed quantity of communication. Stereotypical characters, such as the adventure film's *swashbuckler* or stock Western and science fiction characters, are ›fairy tale figures‹, that is, fixed masks of the imagination. We would be grossly misinterpreting them if we rashly conceived of such characters as ›images of the ›Other« related to reality, or criticized them for falling short of it.[41] Audiences expect such characters to appear solely in an imaginary, intertextually constituted *genre-specific setting*. Within the conventional networks of existing genres, they are

---

38 Good: Journalist.
39 Lotman: Struktur, p. 410.
40 Lotman: Semiotics, p. 22 (my emphasis).
41 Claiming as much doesn't amount to denying any connection with certain conventional notions aimed at immediate reality.

appreciated as sedimentary schemata, as stereotypes of narration, and as ritual quantities. If they were missing therein or subject to fundamental change, this would not only cause irritation but also possibly impair, if not explode, the genre in question. The relationship between such patterns and the audience's everyday world is effectively rather indirect (except for adolescent misconceptions). It is mostly a highly mediated relationship, amounting *in the final instance* to one which *all* imagination entertains with the real world.

Audience expectations as regards genre-specific worlds stem from the fact that as narrative forms figural stereotypes are oriented toward receptive dispositions – and, by implication, toward a desire for the imaginary. Such stereotypes operate neither as realistically understood representations nor as vehicles of immediate real world knowledge, but as personal instances of a repeatable increase in pleasure within a ritualized, self-resembling game continually offered anew by the individual films of a specific genre. It is appropriate to assign these stereotypes serious functions for the kind of narration chosen and its coordination with common cultural dispositions. The successful realization of these functions affords them shape and their form gradually becomes sedimented in the intertext.

Incidentally, such pragmatic thinking proves worthy far beyond the narrative stereotypes of the ›banal‹ genre film. With a view to art history, Ernst Gombrich advocated a similarly pragmatic approach to aesthetic facts, among which he included conventional stylistic forms and means:

> As long as painting is conceived as serving a human purpose, one has a right to discuss the means in relation to these ends.[42]

Gombrich also observed the effect of the ›idea of an ›economy of means‹‹ in classical works.[43] He further asserted that ›the element of a problem solution‹ belongs to art and proceeds through recourse to an array of recurring specific requirements.[44] The narrative figural stereotypes of film, that is, *types conventionalized through repeated use*, can be interpreted as one of the narrative solutions ›found‹ in the cinematic world of characters. They can be considered *pragmatic quantities of a context- and function-bound standardization of narration*, as *recurrent, conventional narrative patterns.*[45]

---

42 Gombrich: Norm, p. 96.
43 Ibid.
44 Ibid., p. 98.
45 Trans. by. Mark Kyburz.

References

Asmuth, Bernhard: Einführung in die Dramenanalyse. Stuttgart 1980.
Cavell, Stanley: The World Viewed: Reflections on the Ontology of Film. Cambridge, MA / London 1979, p. 33.
Doležel, Lubomír: Heterocosmica: Fiction and Possible Worlds. Baltimore 1998, p. 18.
Dyer, Richard: Stereotyping. In: R.D. (Ed.): Gays in Film. London 1977, pp. 27–39.
Dyer, Richard: The Dumb Blonde Stereotype. Documentation for EAS Classroom Materials. London 1979.
Dyer, Richard: The Matter of Images: Essays on Representations. London / New York 1993.
Eco, Umberto: Die praktische Anwendung der literarischen Person. In: U.E. (Ed.): Apokalyptiker und Integrierte. Zur kritischen Kritik der Massenkultur. Frankfurt/M. 1986, pp. 161–186.
Forster, E. M.: Aspects of the Novel. San Diego et al. 1985), p. 67.
Frayling, Christopher: Spaghetti Westerns: Cowboys and Europeans from Karl May to Sergio Leone. London 1981.
Gombrich, Ernst H.: Norm and Form. Studies in the Art of the Renaissance. London 1966.
Good, Howard: The Drunken Journalist. The Biography of a Film Stereotype. Lanham, MD 2000.
Iser, Wolfgang: Das Fiktive und das Imaginäre. Perspektiven literarischer Anthropologie. Frankfurt/M. 1990.
Kracauer, Siegfried: National Types as Hollywood Presents Them. In: Public Opinion Quarterly, 13/1 (1949), pp. 53–72.
Lausberg, Heinrich: Handbuch der literarischen Rhetorik. Eine Grundlegung der Literaturwissenschaft. Munich 1973.
Lotman, Jurij M.: Die Struktur literarischer Texte. Munich 1972.
Lotman, Jurij: Semiotics of Cinema. Ann Arbor 1976 (fist publ. in Russian 1973).
Loukides, Paul / Linda F. Fuller: Beyond the Stars: Stock Characters in American Popular Film. Bowling Green, OH 1990.
Neale, Steve: The Same Old Story: Stereotypes and Difference [1979/80]. In: Manuel Alvarado / Edward Buscombe / Richard Collins (Eds.): The Screen Education Reader: Cinema, Televison, Culture. New York 1993, pp. 41–47.
Pfister, Manfred: Das Drama. Theorie und Analyse. Munich 1977.
Schneider, Irmela: Zur Theorie des Stereotyps. In: Beiträge zur Film- und Fernsehwissenschaft 33/43 (1992), pp. 129–147.
Schweinitz, Jörg: Film und Stereotyp: Eine Herausforderung für das Kino und die Filmtheorie. Zur Geschichte eines Mediendiskurses. Berlin 2006.

CHRISTIAN HUCK / JENS KIEFER / CARSTEN SCHINKO

A ›Bizarre Love Triangle‹
Pop Clips, Figures of Address and the Listening Spectator

> *Every time I think of you*
> *I feel shot right through with a bolt of blue*
> *It's no problem of mine but it's a problem I find*
> *Living a life that I can't leave behind*
>
> New Order, *Bizarre Love Triangle* (1986)

Characters have always been a central element in the study of (narrative) literature and film; what these forms of art have in common is the representation of a diegetic world in which these characters exist. Music, however, is narrative and representational only in a very limited sense,[1] and its diegesis less clearly formed. Characters, in a word, do not exist in music. Pop music, however, (re-)introduces characters – at least in a rudimentary way – by adding words (lyrics) and images (record covers, posters etc.) to music. Music videos, which we will concentrate on in the following, embody this intermedial nature of pop music most perfectly. It is our aim to examine what strange figures appear in this mix of music, words and images.

Music videos are commonly characterized by »nonlinear storytelling, speed-of-sound editing, and the elevation of style over character development«.[2] Consequently, what is made to appear through the three minute-interplay of music, image and text is less a fully-fledged character, but a ›figure‹, a (human) shape or form that is easily recognizable as such, but somewhat empty beyond. For Carol Vernallis, who has presented the most detailed study of music videos to date, ›characters‹ in a music video are most clearly distinguished from those in a feature film by the fact that

---

1 Wolf: Narrativität.
2 Feineman: Introduction, p. 15; cf. Vernallis: Experiencing, pp. 3–26.

whereas »an action of the latter spawns a series of effects that reflect back on him, thereby encouraging him to act again, the impetus in music videos resides episodically in the song or in the way the figures move in concert with the music«.³ What is the figure, then, if it is so different from filmic and literary characters and if it is an effect of music rather than an acting subject?

Instead of analyzing characters in relation to a diegetic world, we are going to concentrate on a feature peculiar to music videos: the figure of a direct address. Music videos generally revolve around a ›me and you‹ configuration,⁴ and while the first-person narrator/speaker has been studied in great detail, the relation to ›you‹ has found only little attention so far. What we will leave aside, then, is the figure (character) as an object of empathy or identification we know from literary and film studies, as well as the various ways authors and directors create characters and their traits; in this regard, the figure in the music video does not differ much from characters in film and music, which have been analysed in some detail already. Similarly, we will neglect the many supporting characters that might appear in a music video as these are merely and bluntly functionalized to highlight the central, performing and addressing figure of a music video⁵ – often by contrast.⁶

Our figure is one that meets the eye, a source of address, a figure that transcends the distinctions between fact and fiction, (real) human being and (fictional) character. This figure is both corporeal and imaginary. While the study of pop music and music videos might have little to add to the intricate ways in which characters are created and received in film and literature, the focus on the ›direct address‹ that is so prevalent in music videos might shed some light on this aspect of characters in film and literature as well. In order to do so, the figure has to be situated at the threshold of image, text and music.

1 The Media Condition of Pop Music and its Embodiment in the Music Video

To understand the specificity of the figure in music videos, we will have to consider the nature of pop music first. Pop is more than just music, even

---

3   Vernallis: Experiencing, p. 17.
4   Cf. Altrogge: Bilder, p. 128.
5   Cf. Vernallis: Experiencing, pp. 54–72.
6   Cf. Peeters: Semiotics.

more than *Music and Lyrics*, as a recent Hollywood production with Hugh Grant and Drew Barrymore defined it. Indeed, as the film itself reveals, pop is much more than just an aural phenomenon, more than mere sound – it is inseparable from its image. Pop music appears (in a phenomenological sense) only as a material event: it is bound to its ›carrier‹ – paradigmatically, it is pressed on vinyl, packaged, distributed, sold and listened to in specific socio-cultural contexts. It is this media-material condition and the parameters it sets for the determinations and possibilities of pop we want to look at in the first part of our text. However, our main focus will be to elaborate the consequences this condition has for (the understanding of) music videos and the function of the figure in these clips.

The media-material manifestation of pop forms the basis for every understanding of pop, as the pop theoretician Diedrich Diederichsen has highlighted. Pop songs are studio products, not simply the work of lyricist and composer, are *not* the *record* of a band performance, but the multilayered result of a complicated production process available as a ›record‹. This result is then, as highlighted above, pressed on vinyl (or burnt on a CD) and becomes – at least before the epoch of the internet – inseparable from the design of its visual-material packaging (cover, inner sleeve, booklet etc.; graphics, photos, typography etc.).[7] As such an audio-visual product, pop can be bought (or stolen) and transported to the locus of consumption: the teenager's bedroom, the subcultural club, the car, etc. It is not simply the message, encoded in the semantics of text and sound, that is important, but also the ›carrier‹ of this message and the embodied modes of consumption it enables. As every pop fan knows, every message comes in a bottle.

This media-material condition of pop has several consequences that are relevant for the question of the figure. Firstly, like movies, pop music does not have a single author as such; every author or speaker has to be created retrospectively. The figure that addresses the listener, consequently, can only be secondary, too. Secondly, pop music is inseparable from its image; even when the visuals accompanying the record are missing, as on the radio, the ›image‹, the ›face‹ of a band or artist ›behind‹ the song is saturated with visual images via concert bills, posters, magazine photo shoots, TV appearances etc. – not to know the image of a pop band has

---

[7] Diederichsen: Gesellschaft, p. 327. It should be evident that this media-material paradigm has changed drastically with the advent of mp3's. In the present paper, however, we are interested in a specific period in which the video clip became the key site of pop's unique form of appellation.

to be considered a rarity. The image, however, remains at the mercy of sound. Thirdly, pop music is (or at least: can be) consumed alone, or with selected friends, individually and in privacy – even though it is a public, mass-mediated good. It is here, in this individual reception, that a pop song comes to life.

Taken together, the conditions of pop music facilitate a strange oscillation between mass mediated image and individual consumption on the one hand, and aurality and visuality on the other. In the following, we will argue that the music video is the perfect embodiment of this media situation. The *figure* of the performer, as we will see, is the knot that ties the different aspects together: s/he is both a public figure and a private interlocutor, both face and voice. This figure, however, comes into being only as a source of address.

Most new media technologies extend the reach of communication, both in numbers of consumers and in the sense of bridging geographical distance. The consequence of such technological abolition of distance is, somewhat paradoxical, often described as a culture of (social) distance: the physical co-presence of those communicating becomes unnecessary and interaction virtually impossible; communication becomes abstract, impersonal, public, alienated and ›distanced‹ – directed, at least potentially, to everyone, everywhere, to a general, rather than a specific addressee.[8] However, as Rudolf Helmstetter has recently emphasized, forms of communication that have been deemed ›popular‹ often work against the grain of this apparent technological determination on a semantic and pragmatic level: they copy forms, styles and themes of private, intimate and direct interactional situations into mass-media produced communications.[9] Consequently, figures of address come to the fore that were unknown to classical rhetoric – in the face-to-face situation on which rhetoric is built direct address is taken for granted.

The popular, one might say, reintroduces communicational forms associated with corporeal closeness into the mass-media culture of distance: popular communication has an air of familiarity, it is affective and personal – without, however, neglecting its mass-media status. Pop music found its own ways to counter the distancing effects of the new, audio-visual mass media of the twentieth century by giving, quite literally, a face and a voice to mass-mediated communications – and by addressing each listener *individually*. While physical closeness to the performer is no longer necessary/possible in the age of radio and record, pop music

---

8 Cf. Zumthor: Mündlichkeit, pp. 248–249.
9 Cf. Helmstetter: Geschmack, p. 54.

reproduces closeness on another level. While the fan is banned from the place of production, intimacies are allowed to leave this place. Alone in the recording studio, bands produce sounds of intimacy that they might not want/be able to produce in the presence of a mass audience of strangers. The new technologies of recording and transmission that gave rise to pop music in the 1950s, indeed, preferred the liveliness and actuality of little imperfections to the idealized beauties of classical Hollywood film.[10]

With these new technologies it became possible to transmit indexical signs of other people's corporeality into the audience's home. Alone in the studio, the pop star speaks to thousands as if to one. On the receiving end, the fan consumes the mass-produced record, a public form of mass communication, privately, individually and alone. The pop record has a double function in the re-individualization of mass communication: it records traces of individuality, audible traces of living, breathing individual subjects, and it makes these traces available for individual consumption. The situation of the (oral) storyteller or traditional folk-singer, always ›talking‹ to a *group* of people, is exchanged for private reception: vociferous declamations are exchanged for intimate whispers. The music video, as we will see, gives the personal, intimate address of the public song a visible, appealing face: other than in the cinema situation, the audience can not merely observe such intimacies, but is addressed intimately and becomes part of an intimate configuration.

The consequence of this intertwining of mass mediated communication and individual consumption in the realm of pop is a doubling of the addresser, who is at the same time the mediated, public figure *and* the physical, ›real‹ individual speaking almost im-mediately to the consumer. Although Madonna can be bought by everyone, it is in *my* bedroom she talks to *me* face-to-face; and although I might *know* – as a cognitively aligned observer – that she is not *actually* talking to me, that she is not actually looking at me, I might still *feel* – as a somatically affected viewer – the warmth and excitement of a personal address.[11] Indeed, as Diederichsen stresses, it is constitutive for pop music that the speakers of pop music are never only fictional characters or authentic, real persons – it is never clear who is speaking in any given moment.[12] And that is what distinguishes music videos from all other forms of audiovisual mass media – and what makes its figures so special.

---

10 Cf. Diederichsen: Gesellschaft, pp. 328–330.
11 For these two modes of reception, see Lowry: Film.
12 Diederichsen: Gesellschaft, p. 330.

Consequently, as we will see, many videos show the performer in both these figurations, as a man from the street and as an otherworldly character. A video by the aptly named band Visage, for example, begins with images of the band as they exit a cab and enter a club; these are then contrasted with images of the singer, dressed and painted as a harlequin, performing the lyrics of the song (fig. 1).

Fig. 1:   Visage – Fade to Grey (1981)

What is most striking about the video is the fact that both incarnations of the figure in the music video are looking directly at the viewer, looking him/her in the eye, meeting his/her gaze. This figure is more than just a plane for projections, but a vis-à-vis demanding positioning: Can you hear me? Don't you want me? Do you really want to hurt me?

Culture Club's *Do You Really Want to Hurt Me?* (1982) is a point in case here. Of course, on the level of the lyrics, the song could be an intimate, autobiographical communication directed to an (ex-)lover of George Alan O'Dowd (the ›real‹ name of Culture Club singer Boy George): ›If it's love you want from me then take it – away‹. Here, the listening spectator is allowed to observe an otherwise private, intimate conversation. On the level of the filmic narration, however, the addressee changes: here, a judge, before which the fictional transgressor (dancing shockingly at a pool) is brought, becomes an internal narratee; the listening spectator becomes part of a public event. Finally, however, a third level, and with it a third addressee, emerges from the address of sound and image: as a popular figure, ›Boy George‹, living a deviant, homo- and/or transsexual life, asks the listening spectator: ›Do you really want to hurt me?‹ Do you really want to penalize apparently abnormal behavior? Do you really want to be part of a society that disciplines and punishes deviant lifestyles? Position yourself! ›Choose my colour, find a star!‹

2 The History of the Music Video and its Theory

Before we continue our own analyses of the role of the figure within the formation of pop music videos, we want to take a short look at the history of the music video and the theoretical debates that have been accompanying these videos. The ›figure‹ has not been granted much importance so far.

Music videos have a long genealogy. Their history reaches from synaesthestic experiments and the performance of songs in the cinema, to the so called ›Soundies‹ made in the 1940s for the Panoram visual jukebox and the Scopitone of the 60s – and finally to promotion clips for bands unwilling or indisposed to tour or appear live in the TV studio.[13] However, the proper birth of the music video as a discrete genre or medium came about with the launch of MTV in 1981: only now the generic forms and techniques were developed that characterize the music video as a TV-phenomenon, only now the popular song became available for private visual consumption. Music videos became a prime vehicle for the promotion of pop and were well funded by the music industry. However, with the rise of internet file-sharing and the demise of the music industry music videos began to disappear from the TV-screens. In our examinations we will concentrate on music videos from the MTV-era, but also consider more recent videos that formally follow these. Whether there might be a new kind of video, or indeed completely new forms of consuming and relating to pop music emerging from the medium of the internet is beyond our scope.[14] Also, we will concentrate on popular videos typical for MTV rather than avant-garde auteur-productions by Spike Jonze, Michel Gondry or Chris Cunningham, which might find their way onto a DVD rather than the TV-screen and consciously break with many of the genre conventions we are interested in here.

The ascent of MTV was coming at a time when a new branch of ›theory‹ came to reign much of the academic world during the eighties and nineties: postmodernism. Post-modern analyses of the music video and MTV soon abounded. John Fiske simply called one of his articles ›MTV: Post-structural Post-modern‹,[15] Briankle G. Chang wrote ›A Hypothesis of

---

13 For a short history of the video clip see Feineman: Introduction.
14 At the moment, YouTube and DVDs have taken over the function of MTV in distributing videos, making them – like CDs – available for consumption at the consumer's choice; the videos themselves, however, might have become cheaper, but mostly still follow similar formulas and conventions; cf. Beebe and Middleton: Introduction.
15 Fiske: MTV.

the Screen: MTV and/as (postmodern) signs‹,¹⁶ Ann Kaplan spoke of ›Feminism/Oedipus/Postmodernism: the Case of MTV‹.¹⁷ Heidi Peeters sums up the claim against MTV in a recent article:

> Music videos often have been characterized as the ultimate medium of the postmodern world. Fast. Empty. Lascivious. At least that is how the majority of the academic and educated world perceives them. Using Frederic Jameson's terms, music videos have been defined as a schizophrenic string of isolated, discontinuous signifiers, failing to link up into a coherent sequence, as a string without a center.[18]

Looking merely at the visuals and the (often lacking) narrative coherence of many music videos, such an interpretation might seem convincing, and as most scholars who attempted an analysis of the music video derived from film and literary studies, an emphasis on visual narration might not come as a surprise. Only slowly, new studies came to integrate other than visual aspects. The musical score, usually highly repetitive in rhythm and melody, for example, often defies the centrifugal powers of the visuals.[19] And although the videos might lack narrative coherence, most of them centre on the presentation of the human body and invite a centripetal, often (heterosexually) sexualized gaze.[20] Another form of coherence appears, if the cultural analyst starts looking beyond the apparently autonomous work the music video never was in the first place. By considering the star system,[21] youth and fan culture, musical traditions and genre conventions, many other elements of the music video give away their apparent obscurity. An adequate examination of the music video, therefore, demands a form of cultural studies that goes beyond (traditional) semiotic analysis and integrates phenomenological, discursive and media-material approaches.

Central to our approach is the fact that amidst the speed of change, often produced by experimental, spectacular forms of editing, and the ambiguity of the images that made MTV (in)famous, the music video places a rock that seems to surpass even the immediacy of the human voice: the personal or direct address of a face-to-face meeting.[22] Although music videos ›come in all sizes, shapes, and colors‹ there are hardly any successful music videos that renounce using this feature.[23] The figure that

---

16 Chang: Hypothesis.
17 Kaplan: Feminism.
18 Peeters: Semiotics.
19 Cf. Goodwin: Dancing, and Björnberg: Relationships.
20 Cf. McDonald: Feeling.
21 Cf. Peeters: Semiotics.
22 Cf. Stockbridge: Music Video.
23 Feineman: Introduction, p. 24.

addresses is so central that it is even indifferent to the constant changes of setting, lighting and camera angle: it survives even the most unconventional forms of editing. Our claim is that no form of mass mediated art has ever spoken to its recipients more directly than the music video – through the figure of address.

›Factual‹ genres, of course, such as news reports, game or other shows feature a direct address as well. Through quizmasters, announcers and ›interviewers‹ they engage in a ›para-social interaction‹ that has been studied since the beginnings of TV.[24] But although these ›persona‹ are roles to be enacted, these roles are essentially *social* roles; what these persona miss is the oscillation between purely fictional character and real-life human that is characteristic for the figure in music videos and pop music in general. While the quizmaster exists before he/she addresses the audience, the figure of the music video is a product of the personal address of the song. Also, and equally important, the quizmaster speaks to his audience in the plural, while the singer addresses a single individual.

The figure we want to concentrate on exists, at least partly, within a fictional world. But while (mainstream) cinema has adopted the heterodiegetic narratee of the novelistic tradition, a number of studies have emphasized that »pop songs are often performed through a direct and/or first-person mode of address, thus breaking with the illusionism of the ›fourth wall‹ of naturalistic cinema and television«.[25] While the actors of a feature film play characters who (apparently) do not know that they are being observed, the pop performer performs for an audience only: there is no point in singing and dancing when no one listens and watches – s/he, literally lives for the music.[26]

3 The Lyrics of the Music Video: Creating Popular Familiarity

Although the audiovisual impression of music videos might be perceived more intensely than the textual, and although some people might not even listen very closely to the lyrics of a song, figures in a video clip are not only composed through their visual appearance and their actions, but are already preconceived on the textual level of a song's lyrics. Of course, lyrics in pop music occur in a variety of different forms from complete

---

24 Cf. Horton and Wohl: Mass Communication.
25 Goodwin: Fatal Distractions, p. 47; cf. Vernallis: Experiencing, pp. 56–57.
26 Exceptions are, of course, avant-garde productions, post-modern comedies and musicals; for modernist productions and musicals see Stockbridge: Music Video; on musicals especially see Mundy: Popular, p. 242 We will return to this later.

narratives to mere utterances of a sentence, an onomatopoetic syllable or the shouting of an unintelligible sound. The degree of ›narrativity‹ of a song's text, in which we are interested here, corresponds with its ability to design a detailed and concrete diegetic world. The world of Trio's famous *Da Da Da* (1982) is quite less detailed and concrete than the world created in The Pogues' *Fairytale of New York* (1987), for example, where the song's title already informs us about the setting.

When compared to the information a reader might extract from a novel it becomes obvious that the possible worlds of pop lyrics – similar to lyrical poetry – tend to be ›undersaturated‹ in terms of information about time, place, the character's appearance and, most importantly, the referents of personal pronouns. Although we get to know the characters' names in, for example, Robert Palmer's *Johnny and Mary* (1980), we learn nothing about their age, whereabouts or biographies. Consequently, Peter Fuchs and Markus Heidingsfelder see a general tendency of pop lyrics towards reduced information as one of its central characteristic features, along with its high degree of self-referentiality and redundancy.[27] The hook, often the only part of a song the listener draws attention to, is especially vague – but all the more memorable: ›da, da, da‹.

However, such reduced informational content is not as strange as it seems: in some situations ›da, da, da‹ and ›I love you‹ make perfect sense. An everyday event where a limited degree of specificity and a general sparsity of information would appear as completely unproblematic is a conversation between two friends. Here, both interlocutors know the persons talked about, because they are familiar with each other's lives, and deictic references are obvious, too, at least in the typical face-to-face meeting of friends. It should be no surprise, then, that the majority of pop lyrics share the language of situated conversations.[28] However, it is one particular element of such conversations that is central to pop lyrics and wholly uncharacteristic for most other forms of mass mediated communications. In his study of lyrics based on fifty chart hits, Tim Murphey has found out that 86% of all songs contained unspecified ›you‹-referents.[29] What is interesting here is not only the fact that the majority of songs refer to a conversational situation by incorporating an addressee in the lyrics, but that the addressee remains unspecified, i. e. that it remains unclear to the listener who precisely is addressed. The addressee is both universal and specific at the same time, it is, indeed, *you*.

---

27 Fuchs & Heidingsfelder: Music, p. 298.
28 Murphey: Lyrics, p. 185.
29 Murphey: Discourse.

The use of the pronoun ›you‹ in narratives has been widely discussed in narratology under the term ›second person narrative‹.³⁰ There are different narrative situations where the pronoun ›you‹ occurs, and not all of these are of course unspecified. Furthermore, not all narratives using this pronoun should be understood as second person narratives, but only those were the addressed ›you‹ functions as an agent in the story. Nevertheless, some narrative texts – e. g. Michel Butor's *La Modification* (1957) – use this communicational device and leave it open whether the ›you‹ is a) a form of narrative self-address, b) referring to a diegetic character/narratee or c) addressing the reader. Similarly, in the music video, »we rarely know whether the singer is singing to us, to a particular hypothetical person, or to himself«.³¹ This ›Protean you‹, as Helmut Bonheim labels it, offers the reader a highly intersubjective mode of reading; however, as a literary technique it remains rare.³²

For the listener of a pop song, on the contrary, the unspecified ›you‹ is the default case, and we argue that many pop songs achieve much of their effect on the listener especially by this form of unspecified address as it invites the listener to feel him-/herself included in a conversation, familiarized and affected. The ›Protean you‹ that enables the listener to conceive him-/herself as the addressee/narratee is central to the popular appeal of pop songs. Through this device, listener and singer, addressee and addresser, are brought closer together: either they are both characters within the diegetic world or they are both part of a ›real‹ conversation. That it remains unclear which it is, or that the listener is oscillating between different positions, is a specific feature of pop. It is part of this ambiguity that listeners can never be sure whether the ›I‹ in the song is meant to be a staged or artistic ›I‹ (a narrative character) or the real ›I‹ (the individual behind the performer), whether the song is meant to be understood fictional or factual. Although there are lots of examples where it becomes quite clear whether the song was meant as factual or fictional communication, the prototypical chart song we are dealing with oscillates between these two poles.

All in all, the lyrics of a prototypical pop song put a heavy emphasis on ›you‹, while the ›I‹ remains a vague presence only. Consider, for example, Mariah Carey's No. 1 hit *Hero* (1993):

---

30 Cf. Fludernik: Second Person.
31 Vernallis: Experiencing Music Video, p. 143.
32 Bonheim: Narration.

There's a hero
If you look inside your heart
You don't have to be afraid
Of what you are
There's an answer
If you reach into your soul
And the sorrow that you know
Will melt away

Chorus
And then a hero comes along
With the strength to carry on
And you cast your fears aside
And you know you can survive
So when you feel like hope is gone
Look inside you and be strong
And you'll finally see the truth
That a hero lies in you

Although the lyrics, the musical accompaniment of piano and strings and Carey's voice and intonation could hardly be more schmaltzy, the aim of the song is clear: it is designed to make the listener feel good about him-/herself, to encourage and invigorate him/her.[33] Those who expect authentic songwriters singing the truth have often criticized that this might be nothing more than a conniving trick to reach into the consumer's pocket. What is important to us here, however, is the fact that the song comes first, and only if the addressee accepts this as an address, an addresser is created: if these words are spoken to me, someone has to utter them.

4 The Moving Image: Between Spectacle and Performance

While the lyrics highlight the act of addressing by emphasizing a ›protean you‹, the moving image gives a face to this address. Indeed, before being anything else, before being a ›character‹ of its own, the figure in the music

---

33 That this schmoozing of the listener might undermine his/her resistance against the economic hardships of late capitalism is a claim against pop music that has been brought forward again and again since Horkheimer and Adorno's famous analysis.

video is the source of an address, comes into being as an addresser first and foremost. Let us look at an example.

In the video to Wham!'s second release *Wham! Rap* (1982) we see and hear George Michael praising the benefits of being on the dole. Strolling along the street while rapping ›I may not have a job, but I have a good time‹ he passes people who seem to be working in everyday professions. In the meantime, the nowadays nearly forgotten second member of Wham!, Andrew Ridgeley, is told off by his assumed parents for not looking for a job. To make sure that Andrew is not foolish enough to listen to their advice, George explains him his philosophy when they meet in the street: ›I'm a soul boy – I'm a dole boy, take pleasure in leisure, I believe in joy!‹ These words are not sung in vain and ›Andrew‹ merrily joins ›George‹ and some female background singers for the chorus: ›Do you enjoy what you do?‹ they ask, looking and pointing at the observer.

Fig. 2: *Wham! – Wham! Rap (1982)*

Although the lyrics leave it open who the addressed ›you‹ is – the singer himself, a fictional character or the listener –, the act of pointing at the camera, and consequently at the absent observer, makes it obvious that the clip is trying to make the viewer part of the communication process. It is not only Andrew who should be elucidated in terms of work ethics, but the viewer him-/herself should be shaken up by the question ›Do you enjoy what you do?‹ Indeed, the song already begins with a popular address: ›Hey everybody!‹ The listening spectator is asked to reflect upon his/her life, and, if necessary, act accordingly – if only by buying a record that promises to be enjoyable.

Having said that ›George‹ is not only communicating with ›Andrew‹ on a diegetic level but with the (real) audience, we might still ask ourselves: ›Why George?‹ Why do we assume that a character from the diegetic world is communicating with us and not the director of the clip. To clarify this point, we have to compare the communicational situation of the music clip with that of a feature film. Although narratologists dealing with filmic communication do not agree whether films have a clearly identifiable enunciator at all, and whether all films have a narrator as a communicating figure, we can still say that viewers usually do not perceive *characters* as the originators of communications but directors, sometimes narrators or the film itself.[34] In classical Hollywood cinema, characters exist only at the mercy of those creating a diegetic world: they know nothing of the ›real‹ world and consequently cannot address anyone in this ›real‹ world. Nevertheless, there are of course many examples in cinema history where diegetic characters address the viewers directly. However, the direct address in comedies and (post-)modernist films are usually asides, which for that moment address the audience, but only very rarely the fictional characters at the same time. In musicals, the viewer stands in for the live audience in the diegetic world. In most of these cases the viewers usually perceive the direct form of address as an attempted transgression of narrative boundaries, as narrative metalepsis.[35] While cinematic conventions mark the character's turn towards his/her audience (if s/he is not the narrator at the same time) as an exception that causes disturbance or in many cases humor, the prototypical music video achieves its central effect by it.

The music video is not perceived as a communication uttered from an extradiegetic position, but by a character from within the diegetic world: the band, or in many cases just the singer, and not the director/producer of a music clip is understood as the source of communication.[36] The main reason for this might be that the viewer regards the imagery of the clip as secondary to the song, and that the song is communicated by the band/singer directly to the audience. Although the pop song and the music video are by no means the work of the singer, he still functions as a point of address, as a ›Zurechnungsinstanz‹,[37] that simulates a direct communication. George Michael is not only a figure in the video, but also becomes the enunciator of the whole communication as which the clip is perceived. Apart from the supposed pre-existence of the song before the

---

34 For different answers to the question of who the narrator of a film is, see for example Gaut: Philosophy, or Chatman: Terms. Bordwell denies that film is understood along a sender-receiver model of communication and treats films as narrations without a narrator; cf. Bordwell: Fiction.
35 For the concept of narrative metalepsis see Genette: Erzählung.
36 Cf. Diedrichsen: Videoclip, p. 73. We should add here that there are of course exceptions, and that auteur videos as e. g. those by Chris Cunningham or Michael Gondry might be treated differently by many people.
37 Cf. Jongmanns: Kommunizieren, p. 71

clip, this effect is achieved by the staging of the singer: we usually see a close up of the singer's face performing the song lip-synchronized, at least during the chorus.

The face of the singer becomes the source of an utterance that is clearly directed at the listening spectator: ›do you enjoy what you do?‹ However, as we learn only little about the figure in the song and the world s/he lives in, the balance of communication is tipped towards the receiver: it is his/her task to make sense of the ambiguous communication, to saturate the ›undersaturated‹ information of a pop song.

The prototypical music clip we are dealing with is usually visually structured according to the song's variation of verse and chorus.[38] While the verse is depicted using narrative elements – a story or at least fragments of a story – the chorus usually presents the band or singer performing.[39] While during the verse George Michael and Andrew Ridgeley might be seen merely as actors playing fictional characters, the chorus points out that the two singing and dancing persons are not only actors but at the same time the real performers themselves. They dance and sing for the viewer as if they were singing and dancing just for him/her, as if they were giving a gig in the viewer's living room. The music clip thereby – not unlike a documentary – attempts to evoke a feeling of ›being there‹: the listening spectator, again, is drawn into the performers' world.[40]

Although the performance during the verses is embedded in (fragments of) a story with characters, the chorus scenes of a clip often aim at resembling a live concert that in the viewer's perception is not fictional – even if the microphones are not plugged in and they perform funny dances. While the verse scenes re-enact intimate conversations (George Michael ›raps‹ in a way close to his ›authentic‹, normal way of conversing), the chorus scenes are highly staged: the performers move from an everyday street scene into an exceptional studio, the everyday images of

---

[38] This sort of the semi-narrative video clip is of course not the only form. There are also videos that only show the singer's performance (as for example in recordings of live concerts), videos that are purely abstract or videos that contain a complete narrative – although the latter two occur only rarely. For a categorization of different clip forms see e.g. Hustwitt: Heaven, or Künzel: Typologie. Altrogge develops a categorization that is based on the degree of the ›naturalness‹ of the musical performance, ranging from a pure performance to a conceptual video without performers. It becomes evident that the different types of music video resemble the different film genres (as in the sense of the German *Gattung*): documentary, (narrative) fiction film and experimental film.

[39] Cf. Diedrichsen, p. 73.

[40] For the narrative situation in documentary films, see Huck / Kiefer: Documentary.

brick and mortar are exchanged for a perfect white background and the conversational tone is exchanged for a chorus in which the individual voice is submerged by the layered chorus. In the end, the music clip is still an artificially created work, but one that makes it difficult, or rather: unnecessary for the listening spectator to differentiate clearly between fact and fiction, everyday life and artificial performance, the intimacy of the voice and the public beauty of the image. The listening spectator is addressed by a very peculiar figure, indeed.

The effect of this oscillation on the listening spectator can be immense. The listening spectator is not simply addressed, as by a real friend, but addressed by a hybrid identity. Unlike a ›real‹ person, the figure is (semantically) charged with imaginary connotations of perfection, completeness and exceptionality, sometimes even otherworldly magic, created in the chorus scenes, which are inscribed on his/her body. These imaginary powers come to exist in the very moment of his/her choreographed, perfectly lighted and post-produced performance. ›I have danced inside your eyes, how can I be real?‹, Boy George asks in *Do You Really Want to Hurt Me?*

However, unlike a completely fictional character, the figure of the music video can transcend the diegetic world and address the listening spectator from within his/her own world. Unlike a real person or a realistically created fictional character, the figure is ›empty‹ enough to be easily charged with imaginary elements – but unlike a literary (fictional) character, the figure is corporeal enough to stand eye-to-eye with the listening spectator and talk to him/her directly: s/he is indeed eye, mouth and make-up only. The above-cited video by Visage highlights this (fig. 3).

 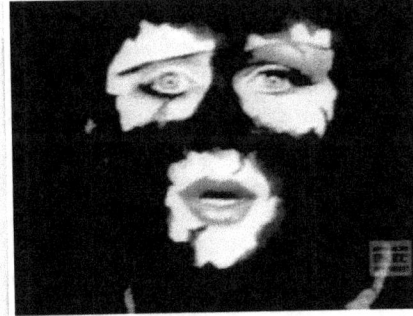

Fig. 3: Visage – Fade to Grey (1981)

As fiction, the video might be seen as a mere spectacle: something to watch from a safe distance for the purpose of entertainment. As a performance of a direct address, transcending the distinction between fact and fiction, however, the moving image can *move* the listening spectator: to tears, to action, to affection. The question is, indeed: ›Do you really want to hurt me? Do you really want to make me cry?‹ And while the figure remains more than flat as a character, as a figure of address it enables the creation of meaning by the listening spectator.

5 The Music of the Video: Somatic Sounds and Mutual Spaces

So far, when listening, we have been listening to words. But, of course, words are not the only, surely not the first, and probably not even the most impressive sound we hear when listening to pop: pop music is first of all *music*, and even words are often used and consumed for their musical qualities first and foremost. And music, as we will see, not only complicates the concept of a ›listening spectator‹, it also makes sure that an address is heard, and felt.

The narratological analysis of texts takes its central paradigms from the realm of the visual, and consequently ›spectating‹ and ›listening to lyrics‹ can be analyzed according to the same categories. Texts have a speaker who takes a specific ›point of view‹, who has a certain (biased) ›perspective‹ on the ›things‹ s/he observes.[41] The addressed is the looked at, and the speaker the observer: ›I‹ and ›you‹ are easily separated, distanced. However, such a neat perspectivism engendering the observation of things, or other observers, evaluating their position in relation to the observed, is hard to maintain once the shift to the sonic is on its way, as »music does not show, but takes us through an experience«.[42]

»No listener can think himself beyond the space of the audible«, Peter Sloterdijk argues, and this subverts the familiar set of (spatial) distinctions:

> The ear does not know a vis-à-vis, it does not produce a frontal view on distant objects, because for the ear ›world‹ or ›things‹ only exist in so far as it is amidst the acoustic event – one could even say, only in so far as it floats in the auditive space or delves into it.[43]

---

41 On the visual bias of narratology see Huck: Senses.
42 Vernallis: Experiencing Music Videos, p. 178.
43 »Kein Hörer kann glauben, am Rand des Hörbaren zu stehen«. »Das Ohr kennt kein Gegenüber, es entwickelt keine frontale Sicht auf fernstehende Objekte, denn es hat ›Welt‹ oder ›Gegenstände‹ nur in dem Maß, wie es inmitten des akustischen Geschehens ist – man könnte auch sagen: sofern es im auditiven Raum schwebt oder taucht.« (Sloterdijk: Musik, p. 52; all quotes are trans. by C.H., J.K., C.S.); cf. Vernallis: Experiencing, p. 44.

A perceptual vis-à-vis gives way to a fuzzier ›Im-Klang-Sein‹ (Sloterdijk). Occupying a perceptual middle-ground, the ear and its listening capability seem to be located somewhere between touching and seeing: the ear can overcome (a certain, limited) distance, but it is still ›in touch‹ with the material resonance of sound waves. Sound encompasses us, disabling in its immersive quality any swift subject-object-relations that – despite their deconstruction – still organize most discussions about images *and* texts.

Music, consequently, can be even more literally ›moving‹ than images. »Music, even if is not translated into corporeal movement, is heard with the body«, Rudi Thiessen writes, reminding us: »Not only the middle ear is a resonating body, but also the abdominal wall, for example«.[44] »Sounds enter«, he adds, »and not only the ear«.[45] Unlike pictures, sonic atmospheres co-emerging with and through sound perception do not place an image in front of a viewer. We can ›enter‹ music while it unfolds, and once we are ›in‹ the song, surrounded by ongoing sonic structures, we might even experience a lack of distinction between self and sound. Music can create a common ground: the distinctions between diegetic and real world, between fictional and real figures, even between addresser and addressed become fuzzy when a listener ›enters‹ a song. Music enables an attachment to the song and a merging of fact and fiction which in turn forms the basis for the demand for positioning the personal address engenders: *if I am ›in‹ the song, ›you‹ is me.*

Music, as the dominating element of music videos, can even transfer its qualities to the other elements of the video: »in music videos, images can work with music by adopting the phenomenological qualities of sound: these images, like sound, come to the fore and fade away, ›stream‹, surround us, and even reverberate within us«.[46] In short, the aural element of the music video undermines any strict distinctions between a real and a fictional world, between the world of the figure in the music video and the world of the listening spectator. All in all, music enhances the feeling of inclusion that the direct address of text and image begin.

The experience of pop music, however, is never fully somatic, but as deeply immersed in semantic negotiations. Moreover, pop fans might forget about the world and their often puberty-ridden bodies during the three minutes of a song; yet after this micro-moratorium has passed the sense of self is rather enhanced. Finally, we should not forget that – while

---

44 »Musik wird, auch wenn sie nicht in körperliche Bewegung übersetzt wird, mit dem Körper gehört«. »Resonanzkörper ist nicht nur das Mittelohr, sondern zum Beispiel auch die Bauchdecke« (Thiessen: Ohren, p. 42).
45 »Töne dringen ein. Nicht nur ins Ohr« (Ibid., pp. 42–43).
46 Vernallis: Experiencing, p. 177.

too much emphasis has been put on pop lyrics in cultural studies – words *do* accompany sounds, and increasingly so.[47] Even if fans at times sing along merely every second line. What we need, finally, is an account of pop music and music videos that does treat the song as its basic unit, a unit that only heuristically can be distinguished into music, lyrics and image.

6 Pop Musical Semiosis

To treat music simply and only as a trigger for a certain atmosphere would run the risk of missing the intricate sonic semiosis of pop songs. What, then, is the nature and function of pop musical signs? What allows us to set them apart from language and/or images? How can we understand the meaning of a pop song that goes beyond the sum of words, image and music? Music critic Ann Powers, noticing the appropriative gestures known of pop fans worldwide, suggests: »Perhaps the real essence of having a song is having it to yourself«.[48] Even more than language and images, pop songs enable the personalization of a public sign: *pop songs create a personal address even before they have a speaker.*

Songs invite mimetic behaviour, imitating not (only) the star, but (also, and especially) the *addressed*. Even though this investment at times does not live up to the words: »As a teen, I did things for my songs – I grew my hair long to be more like the heroine of Bruce Springsteen's ›She's the One‹«, Powers reports.[49] Here, the listening spectator does not want to be like the star, s/he wants to take the place of the loved one. Slightly amending Susan Sontag's famous words, one could argue that pop songs have achieved what she called for: in place of a hermeneutics, we have an erotics of pop – even though it turned out far less benign and is unabashedly profane. »But I still loved it, made my friends shut up while I played it, and felt that somehow, although it was hardly clear how, it spoke for me«.[50] The pop song, here, speaks *for* the listener, because it speaks *to* her: it enables a personal address beyond textual semantics – it is ›my‹ song, speaking just to and for *me*. »My gift is my song and this one's for

---

47 The amount of words used in a pop songs have enormously increased over the last decades (an average of 176 words per chart song in the 1960s against the 436-word-standard in 2007), making the instrumental hit single a thing of an ancient past; cf. Weir: Words.
48 Powers: Love, p. 185.
49 Ibid.
50 Ibid.

you / And you can tell anybody this is your song«, as Elton John famously sung.

What is that ›it‹ speaking here, addressing us? »At its most intense«, Powers reminds us, the power of a song

> can go beyond the private world to feed whole movements. Those moments when songs have emerged as anthems form the soundtrack to our American history of oppression and liberation [...]. Mostly, though, songs exchanged do not travel quite so far. They become part of a personal economy of meaning, shining innocently, like rings bought at the local discount jeweler, their value coming in the giving. Although only in modern times have all songs seemed to be love songs, popular music has functioned as a form of communication between sweethearts for centuries.[51]

Pop songs talk to you as a lover talks to you – a lover, in this case, you hardly know. Indeed, it is only the ›love-like‹ mode of address that produces the figure of the music video as a source of address: the value of the song ›is coming in the giving‹.[52] And only because the song produces the lover can we accept the fickle nature of the pop consumer's love: it is love, and being loved, that we love, not the lover.[53]

How, then, could we assess the semiosis of pop? While it is hard to separate the imagery from the sound and its experience, Powers seems to be on the right track reminding us of an important philosophical contribution. In *Philosophy in a New Key*, published in 1951, Suzanne Langer

> calls music an ›unconsummated symbol‹, and although she is writing about music without words, her phrase applies to pop songs as well, since their words are not only listened to quite inattentively, but usually so oblique or clichéd (or occasionally poetic) that they elide specific meaning.[54]

In Power's reading of Langer, music does not capture and represent particular emotions so much as engender modes of feeling, crude moods – such as ›joy‹, ›anger‹, ›love‹ and other semantic core concepts – which we refine, specify and make our own within the process of reception:

> The listener must form an erotic bond with music for it to have meaning. Listening, linking these sounds and words to memories and unarticulated hopes, she converts songs that naturally belong to no one into personal possessions. But she is also

---

51 Ibid., p. 186.
52 Obviously, this is the point of departure for capitalistic exploitations; music companies, however, can use pop music only because it produces such subject positions, which they might then attempt to make permanent through the star system or other devices.
53 Once again: music companies and ›stars‹ might attempt to monogamize and stabilize such love, but this is a notoriously difficult task.
54 Powers: Love, p. 187.

possessed by it, penetrated, and whenever she hears it next it will arouse a similar set of emotions, even when she doesn't want it to.[55]

In short, the openness of the pop musical sign privileges the individual listener and allows him or her to emotionally assess and access the sound. Not unlike the ›Protean you‹ discussed above, the pop song opens to the listener, demands him or her to specify the relatively unspecific atmosphere, draws him near, affects and consequently moves him/her. Here, the often lamented formulaic nature of popular culture, the repetitive nature of its characters, plots, melodies and images, becomes its greatest asset: each recipient can repeat the same with a difference, because the fact that the general form of a popular song is always already known allows is to be vague enough to become open for individual appropriations; works of high art often show a much greater complexity and attempt to create newness in themselves, leaving less room to make them one's own as they are always and forever owned by the author.

What attracts the listening spectator can be a lyrical line, a specific image or a riff or chord progression. Most often, however, it is the coincidence of all three elements that make a song remarkable and memorable. Most importantly, the conjunction of these three polyvalent levels in the pop song hardly ever complement each other to form a complete whole. Instead,

> pop's artists arrange these half-revelations with profound grace, so that the listener can then complete them. [...] To enter into the circular economy of meaning that gives art its emotional power, a song needs to give you space to make your own conclusions. It needs to need you.[56]

This doubled need, undoubtedly, is enhanced by the fact that the majority of pop songs have been love songs. And these love songs, even though they might be directed to a specific addressee in the real world, or a fictional narratee in the diegetic world, need the listening spectator to come to life. Indeed, the bizarre love triangle becomes a field of mimetic desire: if the narratee's love is needed, the listener's love is needed, too, and if the narratee can love the singer, we can all love the performer and his/her song. And only because the pop song and the music videos find modes of addressing you, the love for the figure in the music video, and with this the figure as such, can come into existence.

---

55 Ibid.
56 Ibid.

7 ›Come on, I'm talking to you‹ (Tears for Fears)

If we return the figure's look/gaze that holds together the video clip, we simultaneously (if unconsciously most of the time) (un-)tie the knot that binds the different levels of performance together. For the eyes that perpetually meet our gaze in video clips belong to pop singers »involved in a *double enactment*: they enact both a star personality (their image) and a song personality, the role that each lyric requires«.[57] Especially during the chorus, the performer's face and body are often disconnected from the narration's diegetic level or series of visual stimuli shown in the background. At other moments, the performer is part of a story unfolding to the song's music that is left surprisingly intact in the vast majority of clips.[58] Often, the figure is both part of a story *and* performing, and thus Frith understands pop's performance as the »art […] to keep both acts in play at once«.[59]

However, it is difficult to talk about the performer without acknowledging the possibility to distinguish the on-stage persona from an assumed ›real‹ person ›behind‹ the performance. Consequently, following Frith's account, Philip Auslander sketches three layers of performance as »the real person (the performer as human being), the performance persona […] and the character (Frith's song personality)«. Not only can all these heuristic levels »be active simultaneously in a given musical performance […], all three levels of personification contribute to the performance's meaning for the audience«.[60] All three levels, also, contribute to the figure that addresses us.

The ›bizarre love triangle‹, then, unfolds between the listening spectator, the fictional narratee or real-life addressee and the figure of the music video, which is itself threefold: real-life person, performer and fictional character. The listening spectator, consequently, competes with the fictional and/or autobiographical ›you‹ as well as all the other ›yous‹ for the affection of the multiple addressing figure: if they can like him/her, we can like him/her, too, if they need him/her, we need him/her, too. Drawn into the triangle by the affective energies of the somatic and the demand/invitation to contribute to pop musical semiosis, to make the song one's own, the addressee is moved enough to be forced

---

57 Frith: Performing, p. 212.
58 Cf. Allan: Musical, p. 4.
59 Frith: Performing, p. 212.
60 Auslander: Performance, p. 6.

to take a stance – if s/he does not want to loose her-/himself, which is also a possible desire.[61]

Consider, finally, the following example of a 2004 R&B hit by Ciara (feat. Petey Pablo), where the media condition of individuated mass reception, the ›protean you‹ of the lyrics, somatic sound and the ›fourth wall‹-breaking direct address come together to form a pop song you can love and make your own. The video begins with a phone conversation between ›Ciara‹ and a friend:

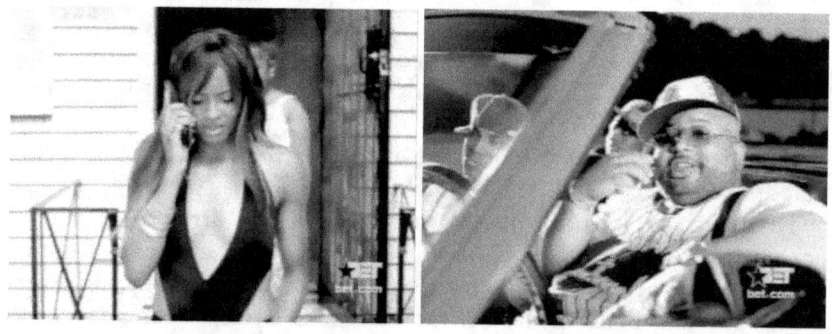

Fig. 4: Ciara (feat. Petey Pablo) – Goodies (2004)

This prologue could be seen as a ›threshold‹ between reality and fiction, introducing the listening spectator to the depicted events and pre-structuring the ensuing experience. The scene is indeed part and not part of the music video: it is obviously part of the video because it marks the beginning of its airing, but it is at the same time not part as the song itself has not yet begun. Here, a (closed) diegetic world is established: the two friends, speaking with their everyday voices, arrange to meet at a car wash; independent of the question whether the scene is meant to be factual (autobiographical) or fictional, or, most likely, a bit of both, the scene adheres to the traditional cinematic convention of the ›fourth wall‹ – no one seems to notice that they are filmed, and observed. The listening spectator remains external to this scene.

However, as soon as the music of the song sets in, the situation changes. Although the diegetic setting is upheld (Ciara is now in the car,

---

61 We are less interested here in the sociological question in how far the ›listening spectator‹ might want to follow, or even imitate the ›star‹, or what a star might be beyond the music video; instead, we are interested in the phenomenological encounter between the music video and the listening spectator, and the media and discursive contexts that inform this encounter.

probably on the way to the car wash), ›Ciara‹ is now clearly a performer addressing the camera; her fellow travelers, however, do not address the camera, and consequently remain within the diegesis. Although her lyrics (›You may look at me and think that I'm just a young girl‹) leave it characteristically open whether she addresses a diegetic narratee (maybe the person she was on the phone with), an autobiographical (ex-) lover (›Petey‹, who raps before Ciara sings, for example) or indeed the listening spectator, the image is less ambiguous. The (camera) position she is looking towards cannot be occupied by a character within the diegetic world; the high angle camera – unusual for feature films, but typical for music videos – highlights this transgression. And even if her words should be addressed to a specific real-life person, the public airing and the openness of the ›pop musical sign‹ offers the position of the addressee to every listening spectator. The listening spectator, indeed, becomes the centre of attention, overshadowing the figures in the video in importance.

Fig. 5: Ciara (feat. Petey Pablo) – Goodies

The music of the song contributes to the destruction of the ›fourth wall‹, too; it quite literally moves the boundaries between diegetic and real world: the bass line of the song regularly shakes the image – the song within the diegetic world comes to affect the tele-audio-visual reproduction at the place of consumption. Like Ciara's hand, the song reaches out into the world of the listening spectator; the music encompasses a mutual world where fact and fiction begin to merge. We might even dance together with the characters.

On the visual level, the video quite obviously invites a classical, heterosexual male gaze, objectifying the depicted women and turning them into ›goodies‹.[62] The chorus, once again set apart from the diegetic

---

62 Cf. Cole: Pornographic.

world of the verse, shows Ciara and other female dancers performing for an imaginary (male) spectator, who, finally, can stand in for, or rather: displace the narratee in the ›love triangle‹. Here, Ciara has changed into a dance ›costume‹ and performs a choreographed routine not in a car or on the street, but on an especially designed, perfectly lighted stage: here, she becomes a ›star‹ whose performance on such a mass mediated stage suggests that she is indeed loved and desired by many, and that the individually addressed listening spectator can (and should) like and love her, too.

Fig. 6:   Ciara (feat. Petey Pablo) – Goodies

The transformation from verse to chorus embodies what Richard Dyer has recognized as the creation of a utopian world through the star: where there was *lack*, there is now *abundance*, where there was *exhaustion* (hanging out at home) there is *energy* (dancing), where there was *fragmentation* (single mother) there is now *solidarity* (dance group), where there was *obscurity* (where are they going?), there is now *transparency* (a party!), where there was *vagueness* (a tentative rap-beat), there is now *intensity* (a driving bass).[63] The figure in the video appears to instigate this utopian world and indeed becomes a star only in this process. From this utopian world, Ciara can see us – and address us. And only within the realm of the music video such a direct address can be attributed to a figure in a (fictional) utopian world.

In the lyrics the image of the easily available, commodified and therefore purchasable ›good‹ is contradicted: »Lookin' for the goodies? / Keep on lookin' cuz they stay in the jar / Oh-oh Oh-oh Oh-oh Oh-oh«. Although the somatics and the imagery of the video might affect the

---

63 Cf. Dyer: Entertainment; Peeters: Semiotics.

listening spectator, ›turn him on‹ and physically move him, the semantics of the lyrics resist a complete appropriation. Even though the song relies on ›you‹ to come to life, the song has a life of its own that can resist the listening spectators appropriative gestures. The figure, a product of the song's mode of address, brought to life by the listening spectator, comes to meet his/her creator – eye to eye.

References

Allan, Blaine: Musical Cinema, Music Video, Music Television. In: Film Quarterly 43/3 (1990), pp. 2–14.
Altrogge, Michael: Wohin mit all' den Zeichen oder: Was hat Madonna mit dem Papst und Pepsi-Cola zu tun? In: Hanns J. Wulf (Ed.): Film- und Fernsehwissenschaftliches Kolloquium, Berlin '89. Münster 1990, pp. 221–234.
Altrogge, Michael: Tönende Bilder. Interdisziplinäre Studie zu Musik und Bildern in Videoclips und ihre Bedeutung für Jugendliche, vol. 2. Berlin 2001.
Auslander, Philip: Performance Analysis and Popular Music: A Manifesto. In: Contemporary Theater Review 14/1 (2004), pp. 1–13.
Björnberg, Alf: Structural Relationships of Music and Images in Music Video. In: Popular Music 13/1 (1994), pp. 51–74.
Bonheim, Helmut: Narration in the Second Person. In: Recherches Anglaises et Americaines 16 (1983), pp. 69–80.
Bordwell, David: Narration in the Fiction Film. London 1985.
Butor, Michel: La Modification. Paris 1957.
Chang, Briankle G.: A Hypothesis of the Screen: MTV and/as (Postmodern) Signs. In: Journal of Communication Inquiry 10/1 (1986), pp. 70–73.
Chatman, Seymour: Coming to Terms: The Rhetoric of Narrative in Fiction and Film. Ithaca 1990.
Cole, Sheri Cathleen: I Am the Eye, You are My Victim. The Pornographic Ideology of Music Video. In: Enculturation: A Journal for Rhetoric, Writing, and Culture 2/2 (1999). <http://enculturation.gmu.edu/2_2/cole/> (Aug. 28th, 2009).
Diederichsen, Diedrich: Allein mit der Gesellschaft. Was kommuniziert Pop-Musik? In: Christian Huck / Carsten Zorn (Eds.): Das Populäre der Gesellschaft. Systemtheorie und Populärkultur. Wiesbaden 2007, pp. 322–334.
Diederichsen, Diedrich: Kunstvideo versus Videoclip: Eine Musik, die ohne Bilder nicht leben kann. In: Ulf Poschardt (Ed.): Look at me, Video. Ostfildern-Ruit 2003, pp. 70–82.
Dyer, Richard: Only Entertainment. London 1992.
Feineman, Neil: Introduction. In: Steven Reiss (Ed.): Thirty Frames per Second: The Visionary Art of the Music Video. New York 2000, pp. 10–29.
Fiske, John: MTV: Post-Structural Post-modern. In: Journal of Communication Inquiry 10/1 (1986), pp. 74–79.
Fludernik, Monika: Second Person Fiction: Narrative You as Addressee and/or Protagonist. In: Arbeiten aus Anglistik und Amerikanistik 18/2 (1993), pp. 217–247.
Fludernik, Monika: Second-Person Narrative as a Test Case for Narratology: The Limits of Realism. In: Style 28/3 (1994), pp. 445–479.
Frith, Simon: Performing Rites. On the Value of Popular Music. Cambridge, MA 1998.

Fuchs, Peter / Makus Heidingsfelder: MUSIC NO MUSIC MUSIC. Zur Unhörbarkeit von Pop. In: Soziale Systeme 10/2 (2004), pp. 292–324.

Gaut, Berys: The Philosophy of the Movies: Cinematic Narration. In: Peter Kivy (Ed.): The Blackwell Guide to Aesthetics. Oxford 2004, pp. 230–253.

Genette, Gérard: Die Erzählung. München 1994.

Goodwin, Andrew: Dancing in the Distraction Factory: Music Television and Popular Culture. Minneapolis 1992.

Goodwin, Andrew: Fatal Distractions: MTV meets Postmodern Theory. In: Simon Frith / Andrew Goodwin / Lawrence Grossberg (Eds.): Sound and Vision: The Music Video Reader. London, New York 1993, pp. 45–66.

Helmstetter, Rudolf: Der Geschmack der Gesellschaft. Die Massenmedien als Apriori des Populären. In: Christian Huck / Carsten Zorn (Eds.): Das Populäre der Gesellschaft. Systemtheorie und Populärkultur. Wiesbaden 2007, pp. 44–72.

Huck, Christian: Coming to Our Senses: Narratology and the Visual. In: Peter Hühn / Wolf Schmidt / Jörg Schönert (Eds.): Modeling Mediacy: Point of View, Perspective, Focalization, Berlin, New York 2009, pp. 201–218.

Huck, Christian / Jens Kiefer: Documentary Films and the Creative Treatment of Actuality. In: Anglistik: International Journal of English Studies 18/2 (2007), pp. 103–120.

Hustwitt, Mark: Sure Feels Like Heaven to Me: Considerations on Promotional Videos. (International Association for the Study of Popular Music Working Paper 6).

Jongmanns, Georg: Kommunizieren und Darstellen. In: montage/av 11/2 (2002), pp. 69–77.

Kaplan, E. Ann: Feminism/Oedipus/Postmodernism: the Case of MTV. In: Peter Brooker / Will Brooker (Eds.): Postmodern After-Images: A Reader in Film, Television and Video. London 1997, pp. 233–247.

Künzel, Werner: Zur Typologie der Videoclips, die Wiederkehr der Oper. In: Wolkenkratzer-Artjournal 6 (1985), pp. 116–119.

Lowry, Stephen: Film – Wahrnehmung – Subjekt. In: montage/av 1/1 (1992), pp. 113–128.

McDonald, Paul: Feeling and Fun: Romance, Dance, and the Performing Male Body in the Take That Videos. In: Sheila Whiteley (Ed.): Sexing the Groove: Popular Music and Gender. New York 1997, pp. 277–294.

Beebe, Roger and Jason Middleton: Introduction. In: Roger Beebe and Jason Middleton (Eds.): Medium Cold: Music Videos from Soundies to Cellphones. Durham 2007, pp. 1–12.

Mundy, John. Popular Music on Screen. Manchester 1999.

Murphey, Tim: The When, Where, and Who of Pop Lyrics: The Listener's Prerogative. In: Popular Music 8/2 (1989), pp. 185–193.

Murphey, Tim: The Discourse of Pop Songs. In: Teachers of English to Speakers of Other Languages Quarterly 26/4 (1992), pp. 770–774.

Peeters, Heidi: The Semiotics of Music Videos: It Must be Written in the Stars. In: *Image & Narrative: Online Magazine of the Visual Narrative* 8 (May 2004). <http://www.imageandnarrative.be/issue08/heidipeeters.htm> (Nov. 1st, 2007).

Powers, Ann: I'll Have to Say I Love You in a Song. In: Karen Kelly / Evelyn McDonnell (Eds.): Stars Don't Stand Still in the Sky: Music and Myth. New York 1999, pp. 183–191.

Schoefield, Dennis. The Second Person: A Point of View. The Function of the Second-Person Pronoun in Narrative Prose Fiction (1998). <http://www.members.westnet.com.au/emmas/2p/thesis/0a.htm> (Feb. 23rd, 2008).

Sloterdijk, Peter: Wo wir sind, wenn wir Musik hören. In: Peter Sloterdijk: Der ästhetische Imperativ. Hamburg: Philo & Philo Fine Arts 2007, pp. 50–82.
Stockbridge, Sally: Music Video: Questions of Performance, Pleasure and Address. In: *Continuum: The Australian Journal of Media and Culture* 172 (1987). <http://wwwmcc.murdoch.edu.au/ReadingRoom/1.2/Stockbridge.html> (Nov 1st, 2007).
Thiessen, Rudi: Mit den Ohren hören, mit dem Körper denken. In: Dietmar Kamper, Christoph Wulf (Eds.): Der andere Körper. Berlin 1984, pp. 41–48.
Vernallis, Carol: Experiencing Music Video: Aesthetics and Cultural Context. New York 2004.
Walton, Kendall: Mimesis as Make-Believe. On the Foundations of the Representational Arts. Cambridge, MA 1993.
Weir, William: Words Words Words. Are Excessive Lyrics Ruining Pop Music? In: Slate Magazine (March 11, 2008) <http://www.slate.com/id/2186341/> (March 15th, 2008).
Wilson, George M.: Elusive Narrators in Film and Literature. In: Philosophical Studies 135/1 (2007), pp. 73–88.
Wolf, Werner: Das Problem der Narrativität in Literatur, Bildender Kunst und Musik: Ein Beitrag zur intermedialen Erzähltheorie. In: Ansgar Nünning / Vera Nünning (Eds.): Erzähltheorie transgenerisch, intermedial, interdisziplinär. Trier 2002, pp. 23–104.
Zumthor, Paul: Mündlichkeit/Oralität. In: Karlheinz Barck (Ed.): Ästhetische Grundbegriffe. Historisches Wörterbuch in sieben Bänden, vol. 4. Stuttgart 2002, pp. 234–256.

Frederick Luis Aldama

Characters in Comic Books

Whether in multiple-protagonist inhabited comic books like those of Los Bros Hernandez, Art Spiegelman's *Maus* or single-protagonist focused comic books like Rhode Montijo's *Pablo's Inferno* or Hergé's *Tintin*, the creating and engaging with character(s) is central to the comic book form. It is not so much the particulars of the plot, but the character's attitudes, actions, and appearance that stay with us long after we close the last page of a comic book.[1]

1 Action, Agency, and Naming

Nothing in the world is off limits to comic book narrative fiction, including character types. They can be as varied as the many shapes, sizes, shades, and personalities that we encounter in our everyday lives. This said, the comic book medium does have certain limitations – and strengths – in its depiction of characters. Unlike novels, for instance, comic books are verbal *and* visual driven media. This necessarily means that their distillation of features of reality – or what Scott McCloud identifes as the process of ›amplification through simplification‹ – depends on the interplay of the visual and the verbal elements of the narrative;[2] their eliciting of the full mental life of characters and action is determined by panel and gutter size and placement as well as degree of presence of the verbal elements, for instance. As Robert C. Harvey states, »when words and pictures blend in mutual dependence to tell a story and thereby

---

1 In addition to remembering characters, we also remember the overall mood of a given comic book – or any narrative fiction for that matter. Again, we do not recall the specifics of events and their respective emotions, but we do recall the mood (depressing or uplifting) that blankets the story.
2 McCloud: Understanding, p. 29.

convey a meaning that neither the verbal nor the visual can achieve alone without the other, then the storyteller is using to the fullest the resources the medium offers him«.³

While there are important differences between how media can represent character, this is not to say that one is better at representing character than the other. Moreover, it changes nothing fundamental about foundational principles of *identity* itself. While comic books use the verbal and visual narrative device to create characters, the cognitive process by which we as reader-viewers identify an entity as a character is cross-medial and foundational. Whether it is novelist and short story author Julio Cortázar's making of his *famas* and *cronopios* (otherworldly creatures) full-blown characters (*Famas y cronopios*), comic book author-artist Carlos Saldaña turning a donkey into a serape-wearing superhero named Burrito (*Burrito*), Brian K. Vaughn infusing a politically astute voice to his anthropomorphic lions in a bombed-out Iraq (*Pride of Baghdad*), or Mark Kalesniko creating a dyspeptic dog anxious about earning a living as a cartoonist (*Alex*), we recognize in all humanlike qualities – agency, intentionality, sense of causality, and movement – and therefore can identify them as characters.

Comic book characters must have agency. As ›agents‹ or ›actors‹ or ›actants‹ they must be capable of self-initiated activities as well as a sense of responsibility for their actions. Let me further clarify. A comic book author who depicts a bacterium that causes another organism like ours to have a digestive problem is not an action with agency; hence, this bacterium would never be read as a character. While it acts, its actions lack the component of agency and responsibility central to the constitution of what we recognize as the basis of character. We recognize agency and responsibility as the basis of identifying character because this is how we also identify the human self; if we were to identify an amoeba as a pathological ›agent‹ for dysentery we would use the word in a technical sense that excludes any attribution of moral responsibility: No amoeba will be condemned in a court of law for causing dysentery. Of course, a comic book author can choose to make a character out of an amoeba, or a donkey, or a lion, or a rock, or anything for that matter, but to do so it has to have agency and responsibility. I think off the cuff here of ›Ivy‹ as Batman's villainous foe and the pile of rocks that become The Thing in *The Fantastic Four*. Moreover, as a short cut for comic book authors to invest these crucial ingredients – self-initiated action, agency, and responsibility – to transform otherwise inanimate objects into character,

---

3   Harvey: Art, p. 4.

they script stories that present ethical dilemmas. (I will return to a discussion of ethics shortly.)

For comic book characters to be involved in self-initiated actions usually means there must be some type of movement in space. This might include the movement of Superman as he flies around the world saving damsels in distress; but it might also find expression in characters that do not physically move but whose actions can cause others to move. An example in film comes readily to mind: the computer ›Hal‹ in Kubrik's *2001 Space Odyssey* is a full blown character. Not because we see Hal move, but because he is capable of self-initiated actions; Hal moves different parts of the space ship that cause others to move – to live or die. This self-initiated action element that identifies character is not only some form of physical negotiation of space, but the movement of a character in time: from birth to death, teenagehood to adulthood, and so on. We see this especially in alternative comics like Los Bros Hernandez's *Love & Rockets* series. And the movement in space (whether rapid-fire as with the panel to panel shifts where Superman is on the ground in one and in the next high above Metropolis) necessarily includes the shifting of perceptions of space. This shift in perception is yet another important ingredient that allows the comic book author – and his or her readers – to identify any given entity as a character.

Of course, this does not mean that all entities transformed into characters are made equal. Some have greater or lesser degrees of agency, action, movement, and perceptual spatial shifts. Characters are made to be simple – and others complex; the more complex the more the character, the more the character's agency (actions and reactions), responsibility, and direction of movement are difficult to pin down.

Giving a name, race, gender, social standing, to a character might distinguish it from another, but it is not until they *act* and *react* that they begin to become interesting and memorable. In the comic book *Shortcomings*, before the story proper begins, Asian American author-artist Adrian Tomine introduces each of the six main characters that fill out his storyworld. Each has a small profile shot of their face and above their name, age, height, birthplace, and occupation. Choosing the name as marker of ethnic identity distinguishes between the different Asian American characters (Japanese, Korean, and so on) that populate the story. However, Tomine overturns the cognitive schema pre-sets of racial identification – Asians as having ›slanted eyes‹ in this case – by not drawing his Asian-identified (by name at the beginning) characters any differently to the white characters. Specifically, they all have the same shaped eyes. And so what becomes memorable about the characters is not so much their ethnic identification – their naming – but that they face the same problems, issues, and ethical dilemmas as the non-Asian identified characters. Here, too, we see the unique interplay of the visual and verbal elements in comic book storytelling that allows for a certain complexity of character that would be less efficiently conveyed in the written-only media of the novel or short story.

2 Author's Selecting In/Out and Reader's Gap Filling

Complex or simple character distinctions aside, no matter how detailed a drawing (photorealist, even) or narrator's detailing of character traits, no comic book story can fill-in all the blanks of character, setting, and event. While the visual element of comic books more efficiently conveys details of character, setting, and event than storytelling media that rely only on the verbal elements (novel, short story, and the like), it still can't include *all* the details. In fact, if it were to do so, it would no longer work as a comic book. One of the distinguishing features of the comic book storytelling medium is its gutter. It is the gutter between the panels – usually a white margin that separates one panel from the next – that allows the reader-viewer to imagine movement; we don't see Superman's flying up above Metropolis as one continuous movement (this would be more akin to film) but rather imagine in the blanks between the panels such movement. Comic books, like all narrative fiction, works according to the principle of relevance (Dan Sperber and Dierdre Wilson). When creating his or her character, the author-artist of comic books imagines an ideal audience at a certain distance to the storyworld that will require more or less information about the character (setting, time, and so on) to be able to imagine fully this character. These details can never be total, so the author-artist must select in (and thus select out) the details that will loosely direct his or her reader-viewers to imagine the character in certain ways, doing certain things, and inhabiting space in certain ways. That is, in the making of the comic book story – its blueprint, say – the author-artist chooses which gaps the reader-viewer will work to fill in to fill out their imagining of the character and his or her world. As Suzanne Keen writes of this process generally when we read narrative fictions: we »create versions of embodied characters out of very few cues, as we project fictional worlds around characters out of sometimes quite minimal data«.[4] Indeed, if the reader-viewer of comic books does not fill in the gaps as directed by comic book blueprint, a very weak characterization or even a mischaracterization results. (This is why with some comic books like those

---

4   Keen: Form, p. 58

of Los Bros Hernandez you have to constantly flip to the back of the book where a series of characters appear drawn and with their name underneath to make sure that you are following the right character and thus not mis-characterizing another.)

In considering what makes a character a *character* in comic books, we have to consider the ways in which it works differently to, say, written-only storytelling media. On a very basic level, given the visual element, we do not need source tags such as ›she said‹ and ›she thought‹. The written-only form of the novel uses a variety of devices – free indirect discourse, interior monologue, psychonarration, and so on. Its deal readers will build an image of a character through statements and descriptive details given by narrators and other characters; readers will infer personality traits through written details of the characters' inter-actions with other characters. In all such cases, the author controls how much information the reader learns about the character; how much of a personality the reader can imagine. Some lean toward the totally opaque and behaviorist depiction of character (Melville's *Bartleby* for example) and others a sense of a near total access to their interiority (Joyce's Penelope chapter in *Ulysses*, for example).[5] The verbal and written narrative form of comic books uses differently configured interplays of the visual (readily reading interior states of mind through visual depictions of outward gesture) and verbal (character's speech, internal musings, and narrator's narration) to create tensions in the reader-viewers identification of character traits.[6]

3 Comic Book Devices

In comic books, the use of visual stock forms (shapes and gestural and physical types, for example) and verbal schemas (third person, first person, interior monologue, or dialogue, for example) cue and trigger in a loosely directed way the reader-viewer's cognitive and emotive responses.[7]

---

[5] Robert Scholes, James Phelan, and Robert Kellogg remind us that no matter the way the narrative fiction asks us to engage with its characters, above all »readers must bring to their consideration of character a versatility of response commensurate with the infinite variety of narrative characterization« (Scholes / Phelan / Kellogg: Narrative, p. 206).

[6] For more on this see my discussion in Aldama: Brain.

[7] No matter the degree of ›realism‹ of a character, whether in comic books (and some like comic book adaptations of films like *Star Wars* or t.v. shows like *Buffy the Vampire Slayer* can be very photo-real) or in written narrative fiction like the novel, no fictional character can match the complex agency and action of people in our everyday lived reality. Our brains perform the same kind of function when we fill in gaps to discern essential traits of fictional character as we do with real people, but whereas in a comic

On a basic level, we do not think ›evil‹ or move with fear when our imagination fills in the blanks when a character appears with a large round head, big eyes, and a small body; this particular distillation of everyday human features recall those little people (toddlers) and thus the image itself comforts.

Even before the character is drawn, however, the comic book author-artist already has a list of character traits in mind: young, old, male, female, Chicano or Anglo, and so on. Comic book author-artists have a good sense of who the character is, what motivates them, and what their goals and dreams are before they even set pencil to paper. Here, too, we see how typically it is the plot that grows from the particular decisions about a given character's traits. (For a more detailed discussion of this creative process, see the interviews collected in the third section of my book, *Your Brain on Latino Comics: From Gus Arriola to Los Bros Hernandez*).

Once the basics are established like age, race, gender, motive (to serve and protect, say), likes and dislikes (a fear of bats, say), and circle of friends and family, then decisions about type of ink, width of line, size and number of panels, and so on, begin to enter the picture. Basic shapes trigger certain schemas – circle (cute, innocent), triangle (sinister, suspicious), square (dependable, solid) – and therefore can create visual shortcuts to identify a given character's personality; the combination of such shapes can indicate a certain interior state of mind: lazy, sullen, active, surprised, at ease, angry, confident. They can also convey action: looking, running, jumping, sliding. Type of clothing, the type of hair style, and other exterior markings (earrings, tattoos, and so on) cue the reader-viewer to read a character's personality in a specific way: prim or sloppy office worker, college student, bad-guy, and so on. As already mentioned, certain combinations of shapes suggestively direct us to infer character's age, but it can also tell us something about the character's worldview. Characters drawn from a three-quarter side-profile angle will be much more emotive than those drawn frontally.[8]

Inferring from shape, angle, gesture, and clothing a character's personality is part of that gap filling process I mentioned above. The author-artist does not have to supply all the details. We automatically add details not given by the text from our experiences of everyday life and from encounters with other fictional characters. Timid people shrink into themselves while loud, aggressive types puff themselves up. Moreover, these devices and their different combinations – say, the varying of line

---

book it is the author-artist directing how we discern a given personality and interior state of mind, in everyday life, we have no such direction.

8   For more on the different devices used in comic books, see Bancroft: Characters.

thickness, the alternating of straight and curved lines, tilts and angles – guide us to identify a character in a loosely directed way. In creating his eponymous character in *La Maggie La Loca* (a series that ran in the *New York Times* in 2006), we see how Jaime Hernandez uses wide and solid inked lines, a subdued palette of browns, yellows, and blues, and the interior monologue device (presented in a sub-panel caption box). The visuals convey a sense of heaviness to the character that casts a shadow over La Maggie's thoughts about herself, her friends, and surroundings. The varied use of devices also infuses a rhythmic and perceptual vitality to comic books. The form and the content are inseparable. An author might set up, say, an interesting character profile, but if there is no variation at the visual level, the story and its character fall flat.

I have up till now used the term author-artist. It is important to point out, however, that often comic books and their characters are the result of many hands and brains working together. (This, by the way, is another important difference to the way most novels are written.) With the titans of the comic book storytelling industry, we see whole armies of creative teams working on a story: writers, artists, inkers, letterers, those who fill-in, and character designers. Even the little guys who belong to the alternative or independent comic book storytelling world might split up the creative work. I think of author Derek McCulloch who teamed up with the artist Shepherd Hendrix to create *Stagger Lee* (2006) or Columbus-based author Dara Naragh who worked with artists from as far away as Brazil to create *Lifelike*. Here it is a joint imaginative effort to define and depict a character's traits. Establishing the degree of realism (or level of simplicity and complexity) of the character and his or her world becomes a collaborative, meeting-of-minds effort; this in turn determines just how the reader-viewer is to be repulsed, sympathize, or deeply empathize with a character.

4 Persistence, Durability, and Continuity of Character's Identity

Character types are relatively stable comic book narrative fictions. While Superman fights many a foe and has a lion's share of anxieties about his identity (to be mortal Clark Kent or to be immortal Superman?), his character traits remain the same. At the visual level, too, Superman's character appears red-capped and spandexed in blue for all eternity. (The post-1990s incarnations of Superman literally tear this stock sartorial wear up, but it's still recognizable and therefore present.) Of course, there are author-artists who choose to create characters who have a wider range of personality traits – and that develop in response to their experiences with the world. Over a twenty-plus year production period, Los Bros Hernandez's *Love & Rockets* series follows a panoply of characters from youth to middle age, for instance. But the characters are fundamentally still recognizable. That is, they do change and even see themselves and the world differently, but they remain at a basic level (name) the same.

This is largely a result of deep cognitive make up. We constantly identify ourselves and others as the same (I am Frederick today and will be Frederick tomorrow) and yet different (on a molecular level I am not today the Frederick I was yesterday). Even though our social contexts constantly alter the way friends and family act, it does not fundamentally alter who they are. My tío Arturo will still be my tío Arturo, today and tomorrow. So, when reading a comic book series like Gilbert Hernandez's *Palomar* with its large cast of Latino characters whose complex layers of interaction take place over years and years, we do not confuse one character for another; if we did, there would be no differences between he characters and therefore no identity to the comic book itself; if all the world is gray, then there is nothing to distinguish between red and black.

Related to this cognitive capacity to identify sameness and difference within characters encountered is the capacity to distinguish between oneself as a reader living and breathing in a world outside the comic book world and those characters that live and breath within the comic book world. While Gilbert Hernandez's characters are deeply compelling, the reader never confuses herself with the identity of the character. Our capacity to distinguish fact from fiction means that when readers identify and even empathize with characters, it is always in an *as if way*.[9] Reader-viewers of comic books never lose sight of the fact that they are not the characters encountered.

Identifying one comic book character as different from another grows out of this epistemological necessity: to be able to identify oneself as ontologically different from the fictional character. This principle of identity begins the moment we are born (in whatever culture) where we are automatically given a name, a social position (son, daughter, etc.), parents (food, clothing, and protection), and a familial matrix made up of others separate from us. All these are basic identity markers. (Other institutional markers include birth certificates, passports, and the like.)

Already the moment we are born we are able to identify ourselves as different from that outside ourselves; if we were not, we wouldn't feed, for example. As our senses develop, we can distinguish more and more ourselves from the world. At the same time, we develop more and more

---

9   See Mellmann: E-Motion. For a discussion of the research of the development in infancy of this capacity to distinguish between fact and fiction see Gopnik: Baby.

solidly a sense of permanence in the world: the parent with disheveled hair in the morning is still the same parent combed and coifed ready for work.

Already, then, as infants we acquire a knowledge of the external world, including a whole series of complex operations such as the acquisition of the category of causality. Along with this is our acquiring of the ability to interpret the action of other human beings; this includes the development of our Theory of Mind capacity (reading the interior states of others from external gestures and body movements generally), even if in a limited way (Lisa Zunshine and Alison Gopnik). This ToM capacity is necessary in our making and consuming of comic book characters. Gesture, posture, and facial expression are, according to Will Eisner, the ›essential ingredients of comic strip art‹.[10] For instance, as Eisner explains, it is the skilled comic book author-artist who must »distill a hundred intermediate movements of which the gesture is comprised into one posture«.[11] Indeed, given the at-once wide ranging and nuanced movements of the face, the author-artist can convey the the reader-viewer the complexity of an individual comic book character's personality. As Eisner remarks, it is the part of the »body that is most individual from the reading of a face, people make daily judments, entrust their money, political future and their emotional relationships«.[12] Most importantly, what is learned here is the category of intentionality. And, also how since birth we learn about ourselves: the notion of self and the notion of the individual as different from other human beings and from the rest of the material, objective world out there.

All of this feeds into our universally shared capacity to identify sameness and difference from a minimal set of identity markers when reading comic books. It is this capacity that allows reader-viewers of comic books to identify the essence of a character – all while revising our understanding of the character as they change through different experiences with the world. If readers don't have something to identify as different from something else – a character with a unique set of traits that differ from another's – then in the best of cases the comic book leaves us non-plussed and in the worst, we simply don't read it. There is an identity that we can point to; an essence that exists. Identity and essence of identity is not, as some would have us believe, fluid or learned. If identity and essence were constructs, then we would not have the cognitive capacity to identify be any stable set of characteristics of a character that make him or her different from another. If our ability to categorize essence were a construction of the mind without anything to do with reality, then there

---

10   Eisner: Comics, p. 100.
11   Ibid., p. 103.
12   Ibid., p. 111.

would be no identity; if there is no identity then there is no agency – and therefore no moral agency. We would not hold fictional characters responsible for their actions just as we would not hold others we cohabitate on this planet with responsible for their actions. If there is no foundation in the person or the individual for ethics, this means that ethics goes to the garbage can and with it goes 99 percent of comic book narrative fiction whose subject matter is to a large extent deals with moral problems and dilemmas.

5 Ethics

With emotions, there are morals – those rules of behavior toward others that each individual internalizes to a greater or lesser degree of consciousness and that shift in time and place. When we read a comic book like Wilfred Santiago's *In My Darkest Hour* that follows the post-9/11 life of Nuyorican Omar and his problems with his own family, his Asian girlfriend's family, and society generally, we are also reading about a social situation with moral dilemmas for this Latino character that's different from yesterday. With moral dilemmas come emotions – the passions – of individual reactions within a social context: a manic-depressive Latino protagonist in Santiago's *In My Darkest Hour* will show his grief privately but not to his Latino, machismo family. While the context might alter the way the emotion is expressed, the basic fundamental emotion is the same whatever your social context.

This is important to keep in mind when we think of comic book authors portray the shaping of rules of behavior and the expression of emotion. If morals are those rules concerning the relationship between individuals that we internalize or consciously reject (during adolescence, typically), the first circle of human interaction – socialization – is the family. It is within this nucleus of the family as social nexus that we internalize and/or reject a series of rules about how to interact with others. This is why family appears so centrally in the lives of comic book characters.

Indeed, an important part of the identity of the implied author-artist entity we form in our minds when reading comic books is achieved by the ethical deductions that we as reader-viewers make about what we are reading; it is the ethical atmosphere that blankets the whole text. If reading a comic book exclusively about romance as with many of the Japanese Manga stories, our image of the implied author-artist might be one with a limited range of emotions, ambitions, and moral dilemmas or one that is complex sufficiently different to the implied reader-viewer. In the former instance, the moral dilemmas are simplified and subordinate to commonplace thinking and feeling with respect to any kind of problems. *In My Darkest Hour* shows just how much command over the verbal and visual elements an author-artist like Santiago has: without realizing it, we slip into an extended flashback that enhances our sense that Omar will escape the prison of his depressed state of mind.

This leads to several conclusions about character in comic books. First, that empathy and ethics play an important role in the making and consuming of comic book character. It also allows us to see just how the neurobiological is integrated with the social in particular, idiosyncratic ways in the author-artist's creating of comic books – and our engaging with them. Second, while we can separate out character as a focus of study in comic books – or any other narrative fiction medium – it is not complex or simple in and of itself; it is complex or simple in relation to all other elements used (point of view temporal shift, duration, etc.) that make up the totality of the fiction. Character at the end of the day is one part of many that make up the gestaltic whole of the comic book.

References

Aldama, Frederick Luis: Your Brain on Latino Comics: From Gus Arriola to Los Bros Hernandez. Austin 2009.
Bancroft, Tom: Creating Characters with Personality: For Film, TV, Animation, Video Games and Graphic Novels. New York 2006.
Eisner, Will: Comics and Sequential Art. Tamarac, FL 1985.
Gopnik, Alison: The Philosophical Baby: What Children's Minds Tell us About Truth, Love, and the Meaning of Life. New York 2009.
Harvey, Robert C.: The Art of the Comic Book: An Aesthetic History. Jackson 1996.
Keen, Suzanne: Narrative Form. New York 2003.
McCloud, Scott: Understanding Comics: The Invisible Art. New York 1994.
Mellmann, Katja: E-Motion: Being Moved by Fiction and Media? Notes on Fictional Worlds, Virtual Contacts and the Reality of Emotions. *PsyArt: An Online Journal* (2002). <http://www.clas.ufl.edu/ipsa/journal/2002_mellmann01.shtml> (June 8th, 2010).
Scholes, Robert / James Phelan/ Robert Kellogg: The Nature of Narrative. New York 2006.
Sperber, Dan / Dierdre Wilson: Relevance: Communication and Cognition. 2nd edn. Oxford 2006.
Zunshine, Lisa: Why We Read Fiction. Theory of Mind and the Novel. Columbus 2006.

HENRIETTE C. VAN VUGT / JOHAN F. HOORN /
ELLY A. KONIJN

Modeling Human-Character Interactions in Virtual Space

1 Introduction

Whereas fictional characters used to restrict themselves to novels, motion pictures, and theater plays, with the rise of computer use, they have recently invaded our work offices and game environments as well, to help us – for better or for worse – or to entertain us, whether successfully or not. Although attempts have been made to understand how people respond to fictional characters, the new media confront us with a new question: to combine the knowledge about characters in the conventional arts and media with the challenge of interacting with a software system that is dressed up like a human and tries to simulate human behavior. Because this is the major difference between interactive digital characters and other fictional characters – it responds to you and you become part of the acting – which makes you feel different than just being a witness. The current chapter is meant to bring together our research over the past years on this topic and to see whether a consistent picture emerges of how humans interact with characters in virtual space.

To have a better understanding of what factors affect user responses in user-character interactions, it seems obvious to start with insights from the field of Human-Computer Interaction (HCI), typically concerned with the understanding of why people use certain technologies and why they ignore others. For a long time, the main focus in HCI was on computers as tools for task performance, just as a carpenter uses a hammer as a tool for making furniture. Microsoft's Office Assistants, for instance, are designed to help us search our directories or to teach us something about computer use. The line of reasoning in HCI was that people evaluate the usefulness of a computer program (e.g., an embodied software agent) mainly through efficiency considerations, to perform a task. Early versions of the influential Technology Acceptance Model (TAM), for example, predicted computer technology acceptance and utilization solely according to the concepts of perceived usefulness and perceived ease of use.[1] In general, aspects of utility and usability, such as learnability, efficiency, and memorability,[2] gained the most attention in HCI. However, HCI scholars and software designers realized that computer program use is not a purely rational, cognitive decision. Extended versions of TAM emphasized user motivation and emotion as mayor components in technology acceptance and use.[3] It appeared necessary to go ›beyond usability‹ to get an understanding of what the total user experience of interacting with computers is about.[4]

Influential in this field of HCI has been the work of Reeves and Nass.[5] Their work demonstrated that people often operate ›mindlessly‹ while interacting with computers.[6] People apply social rules, norms, and expectations to computers, responding to them in a social way, just like they would to real people. »You are very rude! You interrupt our conversation without any real reason. I'll leave you, as you don't wish to talk to me any more« is one of the examples to be found in De Rosis et al.[7] At other times, people are polite to computers or pay them compliments.[8] Impolite computers are deemed offensive, and they are not regarded as technologically deficient, but as socially incompetent.[9] For example, an interface character is not allowed to disappear from the screen without first saying goodbye to its user.[10] People can also be flattered by a computer, even though the flatterer is a piece of communication hardware.[11] As in the real world, interface characters suffer from all kinds of social categorizations, such as ethnicity.[12] If the ethnicity of the interface character is similar to that of the user, characters are more likeable and trusted than when they represent out-group members.[13]

---

1   Davis: Usefulness.
2   E.g., Nielsen: Usability.
3   Venkatesh: Determinants.
4   Preece: Interaction; Shedroff: Experience; Forlizzi: Experience; Garrett: Elements.
5   Reeves / Nass: Media.
6   Cf. Langer: Mind.
7   De Rosis: Agents, p. 6.
8   Reeves: Media, p. 23.
9   Ibid., p. 29.
10 Ibid., p. 33.
11 Ibid., p. 57.
12 Biernat: Categorization.
13 Dryer: Computers; Nass / Moon: Machines.

The phenomenon that systems are seen as independent social actors is known as the Computers as Social Actors (CASA) paradigm.[14] Interestingly, the development of the first intelligent interface character Microsoft's Bob (and friends such as Clippy) was the direct consequence of the Reeves and Nass studies (Figure 1).

Fig. 1: Microsoft's Bob was an attempt to humanize computer interfaces[15]

People thus treat computers not only as tools with which to perform tasks, but also as communication partners with intentions, emotions, personalities, etcetera. Computers are anthropomorphized by their users, that is, they are »described or thought of as having a human form or human attributes«.[16] This has an influence on how well-liked a computer program is that is represented by an interface character. To go ›beyond usability‹, social science theories have enriched models of human-computer interaction with insights from human-human interactions.

---

14 Nass et al.: Computer personalities; Nass et al.: Computers; Reeves / Nass: Media.
15 <http://www.that1blog.blogspot.com/2005_07_01_that1-blog_archive.html> (Dec. 12th, 2007).
16 Merriam-Webster online dictionary <http://www.merriam-webster.com> (June 19th, 2008).

Person perception, interpersonal attraction, and psychological theories of emotion entered the scene to study humans interacting with interface characters.[17]

We too believe that humans use their person-perception skills to interpret and evaluate interface characters. If that is so, then the complex interplay of factors in human-human communication (e.g., looks, ideas, capabilities, the relevance of a person's comments and behavior in a certain context) similarly applies to user responses to interface characters. Yet, since the interface character represents a tool, some other things are important as well. So we must be aware that we are heading for a rather complex theory if we want to understand humans who interact with characters that on the one hand are seen as some sort of personalities and on the other, as tools.

2 Factors that Affect Human-Character Interactions

The factor that received the most attention in interface-character research is realism or epistemics.[18] From a software designer's point of view, the differentiating factor between character interfaces and interfaces that have icons and dialogue boxes is the human or animal-likeness. Obviously, the degree to which the character resembles a real person or animal, in form and behavior,[19] is likely to influence the user. Form realism was subject of investigation in many empirical studies, by comparing realistic and unrealistic outer appearances of interface characters. How much an interface character resembles a real-life person (or animal), intuitively seems to be an important factor that influences the user. Oftentimes, studies that investigated the effects of interface characters on the user focused on realism effects by comparing realistic and unrealistic outer appearances of interface characters. Koda and Maes found that realistic human faces were preferred over cartoon faces in terms of likeability and comfort.[20] On the other hand, Catrambone et al. found that character realism (lifelike versus iconic) had little effect on the perception of an interface character,[21] but user perceptions were strongly influenced by the task. Despite the contradictory findings, Dehn and van Mulken conclude

---

17 Cf. Dryer: Computers; Nass / Moon: Machines.
18 van Vugt et al.: Realism.
19 E.g., Bailenson et al.: Realism.
20 Koda / Maes: Agents.
21 Catrambone et al.: Agents.

that realism is likely to have an important effect on users' responses.[22] Yet, a meta-analysis by Yee and Bailenson indicated that among many published papers,[23] realism was not as influential as expected.

> Human-like representations with higher realism produced more positive social interactions than representations with lower realism; however, this effect was only found when subjective measures were used. Behavioral measures did not reveal a significant difference between representations of low and high realism.[24]

They concluded that ›[...] it appears that the realism of the embodied agent may matter very little‹.[25]

Scholars have argued that next to realism, other agent features are also likely to affect the user. Just like in real-life, human responses are likely to depend on both the way an embodied agent looks (appearance aspects) as well as the things an embodied agent is capable of doing (functional aspects). Indeed, Catrambone et al. sum up a range of agent features such as visual appearance, fidelity, expressiveness, personality, presence, role, initiative, speech quality, and other variables such as gender and competence.[26] Further, Ruttkay et al. distinguish between aspects related to the embodiment (e.g., look, communication modalities), mental aspects (e.g., personality, emotions), and technical issues (e.g., the use of certain programming languages).[27] Finally, Gong et al. created a categorical framework for (static) embodied agents by asking users to categorize pictures of embodied agents into meaningful groups.[28] They identified four dimensions: humanness, graphic details and stylization, good-natured versus bad-natured, and gender. Not surprisingly, the various scholars identified similar dimensions. Surprisingly, however, the categorizations put more emphasis on appearance aspects than on functional aspects, or related aspects such as competence.

It is important to note that although embodied agents can be *designed* to smile, be rude, etcetera, they cannot actually *feel* happy or sad, and they do not actually *have* a rude or extrovert personality.[29] Users will *assign* such qualities to the agents (just as we assign personalities to cars or other objects), but embodied agents do not actually *possess* them. The perceptions that users have are related to design characteristics, though.

---

22 Dehn / van Mulken: Impact.
23 Yee / Bailenson: Meta analysis.
24 Ibid., p. 5.
25 Ibid., p. 6.
26 Catrambone et al.: ECA.
27 Ruttkay et al.: Brows.
28 Gong et al.: Perception.
29 Konijn / van Vugt: Emotions.

For example, an embodied agent using speech may be perceived as more realistic than an embodied agent that is text-based.

It is not just features of the agent (appearance, behavior), but also features related to the user and to the task that may affect user responses to embodied agents. Features of the user include the user's personality, background knowledge, capability, goal, psychological states (e.g., mood), gender, and other variables such as age, and computer experience.[30] One may distinguish between demographic user data (e.g., gender, age, computer skills), psychological data (e.g., personality, cognitive style), and culture (e.g., cultural norms and beliefs).[31] Features of the task include the intent, objectiveness, domain, context, difficulty, timing and duration of the task, as well as consequences of the quality of task performance.[32]

The above studies allow for a systematization of the research on interface characters. They indicate that factors related to the character's outer appearance, as well as factors related to the character's behavior, the user, and the task, all potentially explain user responses. However, to understand the psychological processes that are evoked during human-character interactions, an enumeration of factors does not suffice. We therefore take a more fine-grained perspective in studying user responses to interface characters. We present an integrative model as a conceptual framework to explain user responses to interface characters, which focuses on the psychological processes evoked during human-character interactions. More specifically, the model attempts to explain user engagement with interface characters, the user's intentions to use the character again in the future, as well as user satisfaction, which are all evoked during user-character interactions. Such a systematic integration of factors was missing in literature thus far. The model is user-centered, as it focuses on how users perceive interface characters within a task context. The opposite would be a designer-centered perspective, which may focus on the design of visual life-like appearances, communication modalities, behavior, and emotion modeling. Note that user perceptions might depend on specific design characteristics (e.g., communication modality) and task-context characteristics (e.g., the user's task goal). For example, an interface character using speech may be perceived as more realistic than an interface character with a text balloon. Or, a funny interface character may be perceived as relevant when the user wants to be entertained and irrelevant when the user wants to finish a task efficiently.

---

30 Catrambone et al.: ECA.
31 Ruttkay et al.: Agents.
32 Catrambone et al.: ECA; Ruttkay et al.: Brows.

Instead of starting from scratch, we built upon an existing model that takes a similar perspective in studying human engagement with fictional characters in literature, film, and theatre.[33] This model on Perceiving and Experiencing Fictional Characters (PEFiC) (Figure 2) is based on psychological theories of emotion, interpersonal attraction, and media entertainment. We assume that the process of establishing affective bonds between humans and interface characters bears resemblance to how media users respond to film and TV characters.

3 The PEFiC Model

In analyzing people's experiences towards fictional characters, PEFiC distinguishes between three phases: encode, compare, and respond (Figure 2). Typical factors in the encode phase of character engagement, each modeled with a positive and negative dimension, are ethics (good vs. bad), aesthetics (beautiful vs. ugly), and epistemics or realism (realistic vs. unrealistic). Comparison entails establishing personal relevance and valence towards the character. Similarity between the fictitious character and the self also influences user responses. The response phase, finally, concerns the establishment of engagement, which consists of parallel tendencies to approach and avoid the character. Approach and avoidance are the backbone of the processes of involvement (e.g., empathy, sympathy, challenge) and distance (e.g., antipathy, irritation, boredom), respectively. Konijn and Hoorn and Konijn and Bushman provide evidence that liking a mediated person is best explained by both involvement and distance experiences.[34] Thus, involvement and distance are two distinct experiences that are not the ends of a continuum; they can be experienced at the same time. A user might feel sympathy for a character and at the same time think the character is boring (for example, a virtual news-reader). Last, the PEFiC model states that the trade-off between involvement and distance better explains (dis)liking a character than either involvement or distance alone.[35]

---

33 Hoorn / Konijn: Characters; Konijn / Hoorn: Model.
34 Hoorn / Konijn: Characters; Konijn / Hoorn: Model; Konijn / Bushman: World.
35 Konijn / Hoorn: Model.

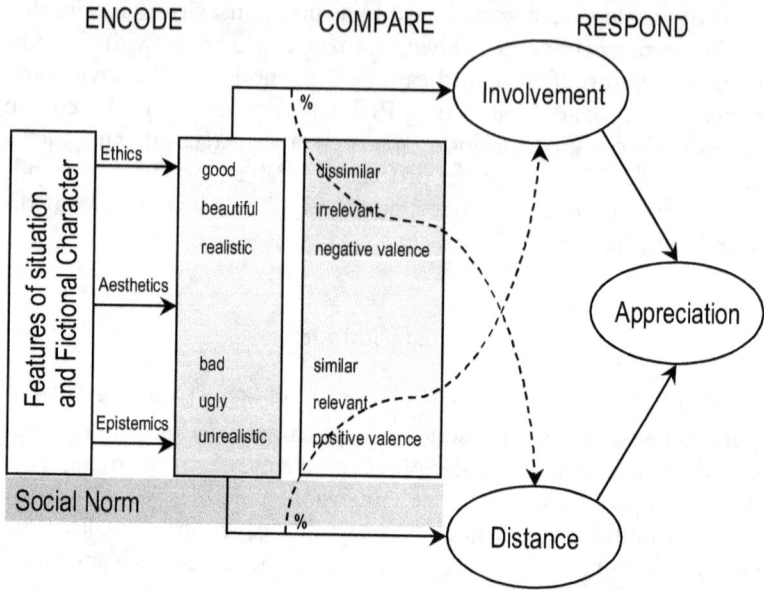

Fig. 2: Perceiving and Experiencing Fictional Characters (PEFiC)[36]

Furthermore, the PEFiC model states that social norms may affect user perceptions and experiences. Norms are social phenomena, and they are propagated among group members through communication.[37] What is considered as ›good‹, ›bad‹, ›beautiful‹, or ›ugly‹ depends to some extent on the prevailing norms in society. Today we are obsessed with the slim body ideal whereas four centuries ago, the round, voluptuous curves would be considered beautiful. Norms may both affect the ›encode‹ factors (e.g., what is perceived as ugly) as well as ›response‹ factors, for example, whether it is allowed to feel engaged with the Bonzi Buddy interface character or not.[38]

4 The I-PEFiC Model

In this section, we explain how we launched the PEFiC model into the interface-character domain.[39] In general, we may conceive of interface

---

36 Ibid.
37 Kincaid: Innovation.
38 Hoorn / van Vugt: Norm.
39 van Vugt et al.: Affordances.

characters in a way similar to fictional characters. When a user encounters an interface character, an engagement process is triggered. However, because users often try to accomplish a task or goal, the engagement process needs to be supplemented with task-related experiences. Unlike film and TV characters, interface characters can be actively interacted with, which has an influence on the user's experience. Probably, this process of interaction pertains to the user's perception of interface characters as tools to accomplish a task. The interaction process explains whether a character is used or not from the actions that can be performed with it and from the usefulness of the actions for the user's task.

Thus, the PEFiC model needed to be adjusted to enrich the engagement during human-character interaction with interface character use. While the engagement process aims to explain the involvement with and distance towards the character, the interaction process aims to explain the intentions to use the character in a task context. Thus, the Interactive PEFiC model (I-PEFiC) integrates two main processes that are evoked during an encounter with an interface character: the engagement process and the interaction process (Figure 3).[40]

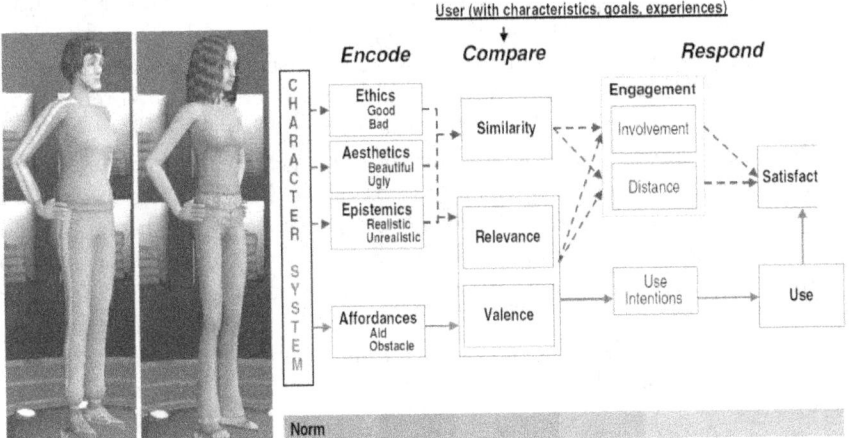

Fig. 3: Two *Sims2* characters serving as input to the I-PEFiC model, which integrates character engagement with use intentions[41]

---

40 Ibid.
41 Ibid.

4.1 User Responses in I-PEFiC

Following the PEFiC model, I-PEFiC claims that engagement with an interface character consists of parallel tendencies to approach (feelings of involvement) and avoid (feelings of distance) the character. A user might feel sympathy for an interface character and at the same time think the character is boring (for example, a virtual news-reader).

The response phase of I-PEFiC concerns intentions to use an interface character, because it is important to understand why users want to use an interface character or not. Use intentions concern the user's decision of whether or not to interact with an interface character. Does a computer user want to use a character again in the future? Would s/he ask for the character's advice in the future? Would s/he want to see the character again on the Internet? Whereas involvement and distance do not concern actual outward behavior, use intentions are tightly connected to actual behavior. In technology-acceptance research, use intentions appeared strong predictors of actual use.[42]

The parallel occurrence of involvement and distance in PEFiC results in a measure of appreciation but in human-computer interaction, user satisfaction is seen as the more important end-goal. Therefore, the ultimate user response in I-PEFiC is user satisfaction, not appreciation. Note that these end-states are related: satisfied users are often happy users. Following the PEFiC way of reasoning, the I-PEFiC model predicts that involvement and distance (together engagement) both nourish user satisfaction. In addition, I-PEFiC predicts that satisfaction with a character not only depends on engagement, but also on the interaction with an interface character during task performance. This argument stems from human-computer interaction literature that indicates that user satisfaction is related to usability and utility aspects of a system during task performance.[43] Hence, user satisfaction is expected to depend on engagement with the interface character as well as on the interaction process.

Affective responses (e.g., involvement, distance, liking, disliking) and behavior (e.g., use intentions, actual use) often go hand in hand. If a user feels involved with and likes an interface character, s/he will use it. However, if a user feels distant to, and dislikes an interface character, s/he will probably not use it. Yet, when a user likes the interface character on a personal level, he or she may still decide not to use it because it is

---

[42] Davis: Usefulness; Venkatesh et al.: Acceptance.
[43] E.g., Gelderman: Relation; Bevan / Macleod: Usability.

inefficient to do so (e.g., in the case of misplaced pro-active behavior of an Office Assistant). Someone may clearly dislike a character but may still use it, because s/he cannot perform a task (e.g., buy online) any other way (e.g., via a product presenter dog).

4.2 The Engagement Process in I-PEFiC

In previous research,[44] we found evidence that the encode factors ethics, aesthetics, and epistemics (or realism) affect the engagement process. Our thought that this should also apply to interface characters was empirically corroborated by a study on the level of realism of virtual museum guides and the level of aesthetics of characters in the *Sims2* game (also Figure 3).[45]

Ethics relates to how people perceive an interface character in terms of being morally good or bad. For example, the purple gorilla Bonzi Buddy supposedly helps you with questions about the Internet, which may be regarded as a ›good‹ feature that is attributed to the character. However, Bonzi is also loathed by many users because he is a cover-up for spyware, which may be deemed a ›bad‹ feature of the character. Certain interface characters comment ironically or even sarcastically on the user's actions (cf. Agneta and Frida),[46] which may be interpreted as being rude. In a study on e-health advisors, we discovered that fat interface characters were judged as more credible and trustworthy than lean characters to give advice on eating healthy, although fat characters were deemed less aesthetic than their lean counterparts.[47] It seemed that participants thought that fat characters had ›more right to speak‹ since fat characters ›know what they are talking about‹ when it comes to loosing weight, thus making them more trustworthy.

Aesthetics concerns the attractiveness of the appearance of the interface character (is she a beauty or an ugly witch?). There are universal standards of beauty (e.g., average face shape and symmetry)[48] that apply to real people. Similar standards apply to interface characters. Ugliness is induced by deviations from the beauty standards, for instance, interface characters having misshapen skulls, showing signs of ›physical‹ decay, or

---

44 Konijn / Hoorn: Model.
45 For the first study cf. van Vugt et al.: Realism; for the second cf. van Vugt et al.: Affordances.
46 Persson: Experience.
47 van Vugt et al.: Characters.
48 See, among others, Johnston / Oliver-Rodriguez: Beauty.

that are judged as being ›fat‹.⁴⁹ A range of studies explored the effects of aesthetics in interfaces.⁵⁰ Tractinsky et al. found that the degree of the system's aesthetics affected post-use perceptions of both aesthetics and usability, whereas, surprisingly, the actual usability had no such effect.⁵¹ In marketing (e.g., advertisements), the importance of aesthetics has also been recognized, which has led to a tradition of manipulating people's experiences to influence consumer (purchasing) behavior.⁵² In I-PEFiC, user perceptions of beauty or ugliness depend on the design of the stimulus as well as ›the eye of the beholder‹.

Epistemics relates to the extent to which the interface character is perceived as a realistic representation of a real life character or as a fantasy figure. Both form and behavioral realism may contribute to perceived realism.⁵³ Behavioral realism of interface characters is concerned with, for example, the character's facial expressions, body and head movements, gestures, eye contact and gaze,⁵⁴ as well as the character's abilities, intelligence, conversational and social behavior.⁵⁵ Form realism is concerned with the outer appearance of the interface character (lifelike vs. fantasy). Form realism is not likely to affect the dynamics of user interactions with an interface character as much as behavioral realism. Form realism can, on the other hand, be important in terms of social identity, and hence engagement with the character. Dryer, for example, contends that visual appearance, in terms of form realism, influences whether an interface character is perceived as agreeable (i.e. involving) or disagreeable (i.e. distancing), which is in line with I-PEFiC.⁵⁶ Many believe that realism is likely to have an important effect on users' responses.⁵⁷ A meta-analysis,⁵⁸ however, indicated that realism is indeed influential, but not as influential as expected.

Similarity, relevance, and valence (Figure 3) are judgments that mediate the effects of the encode factors on engagement. These judgments are based on, and/or evaluated directly after perceiving the three ›encode‹

---

49 van Vugt et al.: Characters, p. 572.
50 Cf. Tractinsky: Aesthetics; Tractinsky et al.: Beautiful; Liu: Dimensions; Norman: Design.
51 Tractinsky et al.: Beautiful.
52 E.g., Sewall: Market; Holbrook / Huber: Dimensions.
53 Bailenson et al.: Effect; Guadagno et al.: Humans.
54 E.g., De Rosis: Mind; Bailenson: Agents; Cassell et al.: Conversation; Cassell / Thórisson: Power.
55 Hayes-Roth: Characters; Dehn / van Mulken: Impact.
56 Dryer: Computers.
57 E.g., Dehn / van Mulken: Impact.
58 Yee / Bailenson: Proteus effect.

factors ethics, aesthetics, and epistemics and impinge upon experiences of involvement and distance. Similarity, relevance, and valence are ›comparison‹ factors that refer to user characteristics and goals. Similarity concerns the commonalities that users perceive between themselves and the character (e.g., both female, similar facial features). Characters that are more similar to the user (e.g., in looks and behavior) are likely to be more involving than dissimilar characters. Bailenson et al. contend that users treat interface characters embodied with their virtual selves fundamentally different from interface characters embodied with virtual others.[59]

Relevance of interface characters is confined to the necessity of completing a computer task; valence to the level of experienced help or obstruction to complete that task successfully. Examples of general goals in human-character interaction are entertainment, efficient task execution, or learning. In an interface character context, valence is concerned with questions such as ›If I use the character, I will have fun‹ versus ›If I use the character, I will waste time‹. Agents that help a user to navigate through a new program are judged as less irritating than agents that give unsolicited opinions on traditional tasks.[60] In the comparison phase of I-PEFiC, the user establishes a level of personal relevance and valence towards the character, which is probably the core of establishing user engagement with interface characters.[61] These factors are intertwined with the task-context in which users find themselves during interaction.

Overlaying the whole of I-PEFiC is the way people apply their norms. In technology acceptance literature,[62] social norm is regarded as a factor that influences system usage. The use of a technology depends on whether that behavior is ›allowed‹ by others, especially peers.

For example, we found empirical evidence that computer-science students experienced different levels of involvement with and distance towards Bonzi Buddy when the norms of the peer group were activated or not, whereas the level of appreciation remained unaffected.[63] Probably, the mild appreciation these students had of Bonzi Buddy (taking a middle position between high distance and low involvement) was put up merely to express a harmless judgment that shielded off what was actually felt inside (i.e. less involvement and more distance than probably allowed); so to ›keep your nose clean‹ as it were. Preparatory activation of the norms of the peer group had a positive effect on the subjectively experienced level

---

59 Bailenson: Agents.
60 Catrambone et al.: Agents.
61 Cf. Konijn / Hoorn: Model.
62 E.g., Venkatesh et al.: Acceptance.
63 Hoorn / van Vugt: Norm.

of involvement as well as of distance. Given the initial low personal involvement, this may be interpreted as a result of group conformity and regression to the average, but in view of the moderate level of estimated group distance, unexpectedly, as rebellion against such group restraints and prejudices as well.

4.3 The Interaction Process in I-PEFiC

The interaction process in I-PEFiC (Figure 3) focuses on the user's perception of interface characters as tools that they can use within a task or goal context. What actions can be performed with the interface character? Are these actions useful for the task? Can positive outcomes (e.g., in terms of efficiency or effectiveness) be expected when using the interface character in the task?

The interaction part of the model is based on affordance theory and technology acceptance theories.[64] The interactive side (i.e. affordances or action possibilities) invokes the intention to use a system or not, which appears to be a strong predictor of actual use.[65] Thus, the interaction process focuses on the user's decision of whether or not to interact with an interface character. The perception of affordances is typical for the interaction process.

4.4 Affordance Theory

The ecological psychologist Gibson was the first to frame affordances as unified relations between the environment and an actor. »The affordances of the environment are what it offers the animal, what it provides or furnishes, either for good or ill«.[66] Affordances can be explained as action possibilities that actors have in the environment. That is, an affordance exists relative to the properties of the environment and the action capabilities of an actor.[67] For example, a chair has the affordance of ›sitting‹, because of its shape, height and carrying capacity. Humans' ability to sit, the length of their legs, and their weight, enables them to sit on the

---

[64] For affordance theory cf. among others Gibson: Approach; Gaver: Affordances; McGrenere / Ho: Affordances. For technology acceptance theories cf. Davis: Usefulness; Venkatesh et al.: Acceptance.
[65] Davis: Usefulness; Venkatesh et al.: Acceptance.
[66] Gibson: Approach, p. 127.
[67] McGrenere / Ho: Affordances.

chair. The concept of affordances is of particular interest in the field of human-computer interaction, which is primarily concerned with studying how properties of computers (the environment) and humans (actors) influence their interaction with each other.

Goals are central in affordance evaluations. It is important to understand that an affordance does not change as the needs and goals of the person change.[68] A chair affords sitting, independent of whether a person wants to sit or not. However, people's actions do depend on the goal context. People typically act within the environment (they use an affordance) because of a goal they want to achieve (for example, doing a calculation, finding something, or having fun). When humans interact with computer systems (such as interface characters), they perceive or ›encode‹ them in terms of action possibilities for goal achievement.

4.4.1 Affordances in I-PEFiC

Affordance theory often differentiates between affordances that are perceptible and affordances that are not perceptible, or hidden.[69] If a person notices that s/he can act in the environment in a certain way, this is called a perceptible affordance. A hidden affordance refers to an action possibility that a person fails to notice or does not understand (for example, because of poor design).

I-PEFiC focuses on user perceptions, in which, obviously, perceptible affordances play a role. Hidden affordances, therefore, fall outside the scope of our model. Like the other encode factors in the I-PEFiC model, affordances have a positive and negative dimension (aid versus obstacle, Figure 3). Affordances perceived as offering help (hence, aids) can be used to increase the likelihood that a desired goal can be reached. They indicate that progress is occurring and evoke intentions to use.[70] This process is further supported by positive outcome expectancies (i.e. positive valence – goals are supported). The side-effect of this process can be the excitement of positive emotions, such as pleasure and pride.[71] However, affordances can also obstruct goal achievement (hence, obstacles), for example, when the user is in a hurry to finish a document and Office Assistant Clippy pops up with a redundant suggestion. Thus, obstacles have the reverse

---

68 McGrenere / Ho: Affordances, interpreting Gibson: Approach.
69 Gaver: Affordances.
70 Peterson: Meaning. For ›technology acceptance theory‹ cf. Venkatesh et al.: Acceptance.
71 Cf. Hoorn / Konijn: Characters.

nature of aids. They indicate that the current path of actions chosen may not lead to goal fulfillment (decreased effectiveness),[72] may prolong goal achievement (decreased efficiency) and/or increase the mental or physical effort required to accomplish a goal. As the technology acceptance theory argues, use intentions are likely to be influenced by efficiency and effectiveness considerations.[73] Hence, obstacles normally invoke negative valence and result in intentions not to use. This process is accompanied by negative emotions (such as anger and disappointment) as a by-product.[74]

5 The Relation Between Performance Effects and Character Effects

We tested I-PEFiC using an experimental design in which 140 secondary school students watched an informative virtual reality demonstration of a tour through an artist's gallery.[75] The tour guide was either a realistic or an unrealistic interface character or no guide was provided (Figure 4). In the realistic condition, the guide was a normally dressed man; in the unrealistic condition, the man had bird features, such as wings, claws, and a beak. The task of the students was to learn as much as possible about the installation of the artwork on show. We wondered whether the presence of a character would affect task performance (e.g., with a guide, I remember more), and we expected that features of the character would affect the engagement with the character (e.g., if the guide wears wings, I feel less involved with the character).

We did not find an effect of character presence on task performance. In addition, although the level of realism designed in the interface character as well as perceived aesthetics contributed to user engagement, these factors did not affect how much participants remembered from the tour. Yet, whether the guide was perceived as relevant for the task or not did affect user engagement. Moreover, for the overall level of satisfaction with the interface character, the combination of user engagement and task performance was a better predictor than either one of the factors alone. Thus, it seemed that factors typical for the character side of I-PEFiC (e.g., realism and aesthetics, see Figure 3) did not affect the performance or task side of the model but that the reverse did occur. The perception of task

---

72 Peterson: Meaning.
73 Davis: Usefulness; Venkatesh et al.: Acceptance.
74 Cf. Hoorn / Konijn: Characters; van Vugt et al.: Affordances.
75 van Vugt et al.: Realism.

relevance was influential for the level of engagement with the interface character.

Fig. 4: Screenshots of the three conditions in which a virtual tour guide explains how to install the artwork *Stone and feather* by Marinus Boezem

We wanted to study the asymmetry in the cross-over of information between the character and system side of I-PEFiC more deeply by systematically manipulating the outer appearance of an interface character as well as the efficiency with which the character could be used as a tool to perform a task. We conducted an experiment using the *Sims2*-game to test the effects of aesthetics (beautiful vs. ugly, as engagement factor) and affordances (help vs. obstacle, as interaction factor) on use intentions, user engagement, and user satisfaction.[76] The beautiful and the ugly looking character are shown in Figure 3. Results of the experiment showed that (1) people tended to use helpful characters more than obstructing characters, (2) user engagement was enhanced by beauty and perceived affordance of the character whereas (3) intentions to use the character

---

76 van Vugt et al.: Affordances.

were not affected by good looks, and (4) the most satisfied users were those that were engaged with the character as well as willing to use it.

Thus, again, the outer appearance of the interface character (here, aesthetics) affected engagement but not intentions to use the character. Instead, again, whether the interface character was helpful or obstructive for task completion (i.e. goal achievement) did affect the level of feeling involved with the character or not. Moreover, for the overall level of satisfaction with the interface character, the combination of user engagement and use intentions was a better predictor than either one of the factors alone.

In a third study,[77] we further studied the asymmetry effect by systematically manipulating the outer appearance of an interface character (facial similar versus facial dissimilar, as engagement factor), as well as the quality of the affordances that could be used in the task (help vs. obstacle, as interaction factor). To manipulate facial similarity, existing character heads were morphed with participant heads resulting in new heads (see Figure 5); participants were not aware of the facial similarity manipulation.

Again, both the outer appearance of the interface character (here, facial similarity) and the affordances of the interface character affected engagement. Unlike in the previous studies, the outer appearance also affected intentions to use the character, but only for men. If an interface character helped male participants complete a task successfully, facial similarity boosted the use intentions. However, if an interface character was incompetent and did not help the male participant successfully complete the task, facial similarity was disadvantageous. Male participants then preferred to use a facial dissimilar character. Furthermore, as in the previous studies, for the overall level of satisfaction with the interface character, the combination of user engagement and use intentions was a better predictor than either one of the factors alone.

---

77 van Vugt et al.: Similarity.

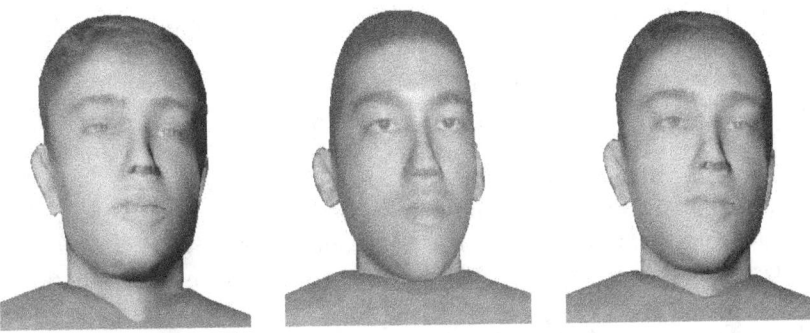

Fig. 5: The manipulation of facial similarity. A character head (left) is morphed with a participant head (middle), resulting in a new head (right)

We also administered two experiments, using so called ›body coaches‹ that provided health advise on food intake and dieting.[78] Users could interact with either slim or heavy-shaped agents, which were either similar or dissimilar to the user's personal body shape. However, despite self-similarity or slimness of the agent's body shape, users felt that the heavier agents were more trustworthy (an aspect of ethics) than their ideally shaped counterparts. This did not only positively affect involvement with the agent but also the willingness to use it – a genuine crossover effect from the character side to the tooling or system side!

The results of the various studies were used to develop the Revised I-PEFiC model, which is depicted in Figure 6. The left box of revised I-PEFiC represents design features of an embodied agent. The model distinguishes between two main categories of agent characteristics. The first category includes ›agent‹ features that deal with the agent's functionality, ›artificial intelligence‹, or ›mental‹ capacity. These features are usually designed by AI programmers. The second category concerns ›embodiment‹ features that graphical designers usually determine. The embodiment of an agent can be designed in different ways, for example, with facial features similar to the user, to be beautiful or ugly, have a slim or heavy body shape, with realistic or unrealistic looks, and other qualities of appearance. The two categories generally are not completely separate from one another. That is, the role of an agent may be presented by both ›agent‹ and ›embodiment‹ features. For example, the embodied agent on the IKEA web site does not only have certain (limited) capacities to help

---

78 van Vugt et al.: When Too Heavy.

online IKEA customers, but is also dressed in yellow and blue like a real-life IKEA employee.[79]

When users interact with an embodied agent, they encode it in terms of 1) affordances, 2) ethics, 3) aesthetics, and 4) realism. The position of the factor in the model is somewhat related to its importance. We found that aesthetics is more important than realism, and affordances and ethics (i.e. trustworthiness) are more important than aesthetics and realism. The relative importance of factors may change, depending on the context.

Users may respond to embodied agents on behavioral, emotional, social, and cognitive (e.g., learning) levels. Of all possible user responses, the revised I-PEFiC model aims to explain involvement and distance (emotional approach and avoidance), use intentions (actual approach and avoidance), and final user satisfaction. Both involvement, distance (together called ›engagement‹), and use intentions are needed to explain satisfaction with the character.[80]

Whereas the interaction with the character (i.e. the affordances) contributes to a level of engagement, the way a character looks has no (realistic, beautiful) or only some (facial similarity) influence on use intentions.[81] You cannot cover up a bad tool by making it look nice. Perhaps this is the answer why Microsoft's Bob turned out to be a disaster.

---

79 <http://www.ikea.com> (Jan. 1st, 2008).
80 van Vugt et al.: Realism; van Vugt et al.: Affordances; van Vugt et al.: Similarity. Cf. Konijn / Hoorn: Model.
81 Ibid.

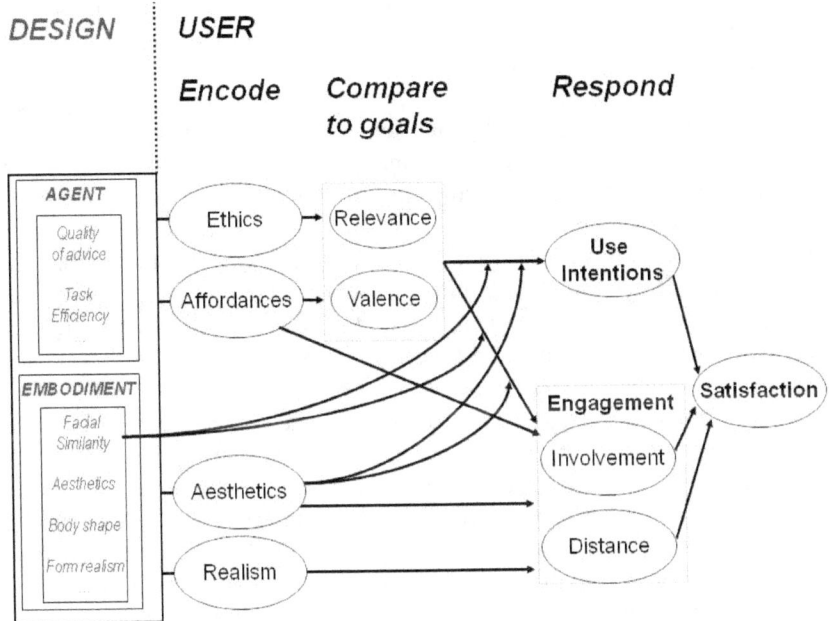

Fig. 6: Revised I-PEFiC[82]

6 Conclusions

Starting from studies of literature, film, and theater, we devised a model (PEFiC) that was capable of explaining engagement with fictional characters by enriching it with insights from emotion and social psychology as well as person perception. This model was then extended with concepts from human-computer interaction, which resulted in the Interactive model of Perceiving and Experiencing Fictional Characters (I-PEFiC). The main results found thus far are that aspects in the execution of (computer) tasks to which the interface character contributes (efficiency, task-relevance) has definite effects on the level of engagement with the character. The other way round, however, does not work that way except for ethical considerations. At least aspects that relate to outer appearance such as aesthetics or form realism do not impact whether people think of interface characters as a useful tool or not. To a degree,

---

82 van Vugt: Agents, p. 165.

facial similarity is an exception, as it may boost and hamper use intentions on an unconscious level.

These findings are consequential for the design of interface characters – whether in office applications, games, or characters in virtual worlds such as *Second Life*. Proper game AI, pro-active behavior that is to the point, and flawless software, greatly contribute to appreciation of and satisfaction with the interface character, not only as a tool but also as a personal companion. For embodied conversational agents, this information is crucial. Development of lip-sync software that enhances the realism effect may be less important than that the agent knows the way conversational rules work in different social settings with people that have different social norms and that it can cope with breaking those rules (e.g., in irony).

If we bring these insights back to conventional media, the first thing we notice is that a reader cannot interact with the novel's protagonist and that the painted portrait does not talk back. However, we should not make the comparison with interactive media from the point of view of the reader or viewer but from the perspective of the creator. Much like a movie or stage director, end-users of an interactive agent create their own little stories and conversations, directing the character as a tool towards a goal. Modern stage acting is quite like that. Gordon points out that in traditional theatre, the actor is an imitator of real life, trying to be the character. In modern theatre, he continues, the actor is an instrument for the stage director to merely *indicate* a character.[83] Brought back to I-PEFiC, a traditional actor offers the director a high degree of realistic performance that in view of the I-PEFiC results does little for engagement (as compared to ethics) and nothing for usefulness. A modern actor, however, performs low on realism, but his or her affordances to indicate a character fosters engagement in the director and the willingness to use the actor for his or her artistic purposes.

The performance of the actor as an instrument to achieve artistic goals will affect the director's level of engagement with the character, whereas a nice make-up or impressive stage setting also may contribute to engagement with the character but will not cover up bad acting. The director's critique of the traditional actor may be, then, that the character is interesting (all hail to the author) in spite of the bad performance. Human-character interactions in liminal space.[84]

---

[83] Gordon: Scenographic, p. 89 and p. 91.
[84] In theatre, liminal space is the back-and-forth between being the actor and being the character.

References

Bailenson, Jeremy N. / Andrew C. Beall / Jim Blascovich / Mike Raimundo / Max Weisbuch: Intelligents Agents Who Wear Your Face: User's Reactions to the Virtual Self. In: Lecture Notes in Artificial Intelligence 2190 (2001), pp. 86–99.

Bailenson, Jeremy N. / Nick Yee / Dan Merget / Ralph Schroeder: The Effect of Behavioral Realism and Form Realism of Real-Time Avatar Faces on Verbal Disclosure, Nonverbal Disclosure, Emotion Recognition, and Copresence in Dyadic Interaction. In: PRESENCE: Teleoperators and Virtual Environments 15/4 (2006), pp. 359–372.

Bevan, Nigel / Miles Macleod: Usability Measurement in Context. In: Behaviour and Information Technology 13 (1994), pp. 132–145.

Biernat, Monica R. / Theresa K. Vescio: Categorization and Stereotyping: Effects of Group Context on Memory and Social Judgment. In: Journal of Experimental Social Psychology 29 (1993), pp. 166–202.

Cassell, Justine / Catherine Pelachaud / Norman I. Badler / Mark Steedman / Brett Achorn / Tripp Becket / Brett Douville / Scott Prevost / Matthew Stone:. Animated Conversation: Rule-Based Generation of Facial Expression, Gesture and Spoken Intonation for Multiple Conversational Agents. In: Proceedings of SIGGRAPH'94 (1994), pp. 413–420.

Cassell, Justine / Kristinn R. Thórisson: The Power of a Nod and a Glance: Envelope vs. Emotional Feedback in Animated Conversational Agents. In: Applied Artificial Intelligence 13/4&5 (1999), pp. 519–538.

Catrambone, Richard / John T. Stasko / Jun Xiao: Anthropomorphic Agents as a User Interface Paradigm: Experimental Findings and a Framework for Research. In: Proceedings of COGSCI 02 (2002), pp. 166–171.

Catrambone, Richard / John T. Stasko / Jun Xiao: ECA as User Interface Paradigm. In: Zsófia Ruttkay/ Catherine Pelachaud (Eds.): Human Interaction Series 7 (2004), pp. 239–270.

Davis, Fred. D.: Perceived Usefulness, Perceived Ease of Use, and User Acceptance of Information Technology. In: MIS Quarterly 13/3 (1989), pp. 319–339.

De Rosis, Fiorella / Addolorata Cavalluzzi / Irene Mazzotta / Nicole Novelli: Can Embodied Conversational Agents Induce Empathy in Users? In: AISB'05 Virtual Social Characters Symposium (2005).

De Rosis, Fiorella / Catherine Pelachaud / Isabella Poggi / Valeria Carofiglio / Berardina De Carolis: From Greta's Mind to her Face: Modelling the Dynamics of Affective States in a Conversational Embodied Agent. In: International Journal of Human-Computer Studies 59/1&2 (2003), pp. 81–118.

Dehn, Doris M. / Suzanne van Mulken: The Impact of Animated Interface Agents: A Review of Empirical Research. In: International Journal of Human-Computer Studies 52/1 (2000), pp. 1–22.

Dryer, D. Christopher: Getting Personal with Computers: How to Design Personalities for Agents. In: Applied Artificial Intelligence 13/3 (1999), pp. 273–295.

Forlizzi, Jodi / Shannon Ford: The Building Blocks of Experience: An Early Framework for Interaction Designers. In: Proceedings of DIS'00 (2000), pp. 419–423.

Garrett, Jess James: The Elements of User Experience: User-Centered Design for the Web. Boston et al. 2002.

Gaver, William W.: Technology Affordances. In: Proceedings of SIGCHI'91 (1991), pp. 79–84.

Gelderman, Maarten: The Relation Between User Satisfaction, Usage of Information Systems and Performance. In: Information & Management 34 (1998), pp. 11–18.

Gibson, James J.: The Ecological Approach to Visual Perception. Boston 1979.

Gong, Li / Carrielynn D. Reinhard / Tingting Lu / Zack Y. Kerr: Perception and Categorization of Computer-Generated Characters. In: International Communication Association 06 (2006) <http://www.allacademic.com//meta/p_mla_apa_research_citation/0/9/1/9/2/pages91921/p91921-1.php> (June 17th, 2010).

Gordon, Robert: The Actor as Scenographic Instrument. In: The Purpose of Playing. Modern Acting Theories in Perspective. Ann Arbor, MI 2009, pp. 89–120.

Guadagno, Rosanna E. / Jim Blascovich / Jeremy N. Bailenson / Cade McCall: Virtual Humans and Persuasion: The Effects of Agency and Behavioural Realism. In: Media Psychology 10 (2007), pp. 1–22.

Hayes-Roth, Barbara: What Makes Characters Seem Life-Like? In: Helmut Prendinger / Mitsuru Ishizuka (Eds.): Life-Like Characters. Tools, Affective Functions and Applications. Berlin 2003, pp. 447–462.

Holbrook, Morris B. / Joel Huber: Separating Perceptual Dimensions From Affective Overtones: An Application to Consumer Aesthetics. In: Journal of Marketing Research 5 (1979), pp. 272–283.

Hoorn, Johan F. / Elly A. Konijn: Perceiving and Experiencing Fictional Characters: An Integrative Account. In: Japanese Psychological Research 45/4 (2003), pp. 221–239.

Hoorn, Johan F. / Henriette C. van Vugt: The Role of Social Norm in User-Engagement and Appreciation of the Web Interface Agent Bonzi Buddy. In: Lecture Notes in Artificial Intelligence 4133 (2006), p. 456.

Johnston, Victor S. / Juan C. Oliver-Rodriguez: Facial Beauty and the Late Positive Component of Event-Related Potentials. In: Journal of Sex Research 34/2 (1997), pp. 188–198.

Kincaid, D. Lawrence: From Innovation to Social Norm: Bounded Normative Influence. In: Journal of Health Communication, 9/1 (2004), pp. 37–57.

Koda, Tomoka / Pattie Maes: Agents With Faces: The Effect of Personification of Agents. In: Proceedings of HCI'96 (1996), pp. 98–103.

Konijn, Elly A. / Brad. J. Bushman: World Leaders as Movie Characters? Perceptions of J.W. Bush, T. Blair, O. Bin Laden, and S. Hussein. In: Media Psychology 9/1 (2007), pp. 157–177.

Konijn, Elly A. / Johan F. Hoorn: Some Like it Bad. Testing a Model for Perceiving and Experiencing Fictional Characters. In: Media Psychology 7/2 (2005), pp. 107–144.

Konijn, E.A. / Henriette C. van Vugt: Emotions in Mediated Interpersonal Communication: Toward Modeling Emotion in Virtual Humans. In: Elly A. Konijn / Martin Tanis / Sonja Utz / Susan Barnes (Eds.): Mediated Interpersonal Communication. New York 2008, pp. 100–130.

Langer, Ellen J.: Matters of Mind: Mindfulness/Mindlessness in Perspective. In: Consciousness and Cognition 1 (1992), pp. 289–305.

Liu, Yili: The Aesthetic and the Ethic Dimensions of Human Factors and Design. In: Ergonomics 46/13&14 (2003), pp. 1293–1305.

McGrenere, Joanna / Wayne Ho: Affordances: Clarifying and Evolving a Cconcept. In: Proceedings of Graphics Interface (2000), pp. 179–186.

Merriam-Webster Online Dictionary: <http://www.merriam-webster.com> (June 19th, 2008).

Nass, Clifford / B. J. Fogg / Youngme Moon: Can Computers be Teammates? In: International Journal of Human-Computer Studies 45/6 (1996), pp. 669–678.

Nass, Clifford / Youngme Moon: Machines and Mindlessness: Social Responses to Computers. In: Journal of Social Issues 56/1 (2000), pp. 81–103.
Nass, Clifford / Youngme Moon / B. J. Fogg / Byron Reeves / D. Christopher Dryer: Can Computer Personalities be Human Personalities? In: International Journal of Human-Computer Studies 43/2 (1995), pp. 223–239.
Nielsen, Jacob: Usability Engineering. San Francisco 1994.
Norman, Donald A.: Emotional Design. Why We Love (or Hate) Everyday Things. New York 2004.
Persson, Per: Agneta & Frida: A Narrative Experience of the Web? In: Proceedings of the AAAI Fall Symposium on Narrative Intelligence (1999), pp. 67–71.
Peterson, Jordan B. The Meaning of Meaning. In: Selected Proceedings on Searching for Meaning in the New Millennium (in press).
Preece, Jennifer / Yvonne Rogers / Helen Sharp: Interaction Design: Beyond Human-Computer Interaction. Chichester / Hoboken, NJ 2002.
Reeves, Byron / Clifford Nass: The Media Equation: How People Treat Computers, Televisions and New Media Like Real People and Places. Cambridge, NY 1996.
Rehm, Matthias / Elisabeth André: Catch Me If You Can – Exploring Lying Agents in Social Settings. In: Proceedings of AAMAS'05 (2005), pp. 937–944.
Ruttkay, Zsófia / Claire Dormann / Han Noot: Embodied Conversational Agents on a Common Ground. A Framework for Design and Evaluation. In: Zsófia Ruttkay / Catherine Pelachaud (Eds.): Human Interaction Series 7 (2004), pp. 27–66.
Sewall, Murphy A.: Market Segmentation Based on Consumer Ratings of Proposed Product Designs. In: Journal of Marketing Research 15 (1978), pp. 557–564.
Shedroff, Nathan: Experience Design. Thousand Oaks, CA 2001.
Tractinsky, Noam: Aesthetics and Apparent Usability: Empirically Assessing Ccultural and Methodological Issues. In: Proceedings of SIGCHI'97 (1997), pp. 115–122.
Tractinsky, Noam / Adi Shoval-Katz / Dror Ikar: What is Beautiful is Usable. In: Interacting with Computers 13/2 (2000), pp. 127–145.
van Vugt, Henriette C. / Johan F. Hoorn / Elly A. Konijn / Athina De Bie Dimitriadou: Affective Affordances: Improving Interface Character Engagement Through Interaction. In: International Journal of Human-Computer Studies 64/9 (2006), pp. 874–888.
van Vugt, Henriette C. / Elly A. Konijn / Johan F. Hoorn / Anton Eliëns / Irene Keur: Realism Is Not All! User Engagement With Task-Related Interface Characters. In: Interacting with Computers 19 (2007), pp. 267–280.
van Vugt, Henriette C. / Elly A. Konijn / Johan F. Hoorn / Jolanda Veldhuis: When Too Heavy is Just Fine: Creating Trustworthy e-Health Advisors. International Journal of Human-Computer Studies, 67/7 (2009), pp. 571–583.
van Vugt, Henriette C. / Jeremy N. Bailenson / Johan F. Hoorn/ Elly A. Konijn: Facial Similarity Shapes User Response to Embodied Agents. In: Transactions of Computer-Human Interaction 17/2/7 (2010), pp. 1–27.
van Vugt, Henriette C.: Embodied Agents From a User's Perspective (2008) Ph.D Dissertation.
Venkatesh, Viswanath: Determinants of Perceived Ease of Use: Integrating Control, Intrinsic Motivation, and Emotion Into the Technology Acceptance Model. In: Information Systems Research 11/4 (2000), pp. 342–365.
Venkatesh, Viswanath / Michael G. Morris / Gordon B. Davis / Fred D. Davis: User Acceptance of Information Technology: Toward a Unified View. In: MIS Quarterly 27/3 (2003), pp. 425–478.

Yee, Nick / Jeremy N. Bailenson: A Meta-Analysis of the Impact of the Inclusion and Realism of Human-Like Faces on User Experiences in Interfaces. Nominated for Best Paper Award in Proceedings of the Conference on Computer-Human Interaction (CHI). April 28th-May 3rd 2007, San Jose CA, pp. 5–6.

III Characters and Their Audiences

RICHARD J. GERRIG

A Moment-by-Moment Perspective on Readers' Experiences of Characters[1]

In the short story *Why I Live at the P.O.*,[2] Eudora Welty introduces a remarkable character called Sister. In the story, Sister functions as a first-person narrator to explain, as the story's title indicates, why she has left her family home to live at the Post Office. With respect to her new address, Sister offers, »But here I am, and here I'll stay. I want the world to know I'm happy«.[3] Sister is an extraordinarily vivid character whose worldview may or may not be credible. Readers will likely differ on the extent to which they believe Sister's accounts of her (possibly) manipulative younger sibling Stella-Rondo. Still, by the end of the story, readers obtain an indelible impression of Sister's sense of her own experiences and why, as a function of those experiences, she has no choice but to live at the P.O.

The goal of this chapter is to explore some of the cognitive processes that underlie readers' moment-by-moment understanding of literary characters. In the first section, I review a general approach that is motivated largely out of the social psychological literature. I suggest that theories in cognitive psychology have generally failed to engage important issues about character that emerge from literary analysis. In the later sections of the chapter, I draw together theoretical constructs that point a way toward enriching cognitive psychological models. To make my

---

[1] This material is based on work supported by National Science Foundation Grant 0325188. I thank David Rapp for his helpful comments on this article. Correspondence concerning this article should be addressed to Richard J. Gerrig, Department of Psychology, Stony Brook University, Stony Brook, NY 11794–2500, USA. E-mail: rgerrig@notes.cc.sunysb.edu.
[2] Welty: Curtain, pp. 89–110.
[3] Ibid., p. 110.

perspective concrete, I focus particular attention on the ways readers assess the relationships between characters' actions and their traits.

1 A Cognitive Perspective on Characters in Fictional Worlds

Several years ago, David Allbritton and I,[4] provided a brief account of readers' construction of character that was motivated from psychological research. Our major assumption was that the processes readers use to encode characters are sampled from the processes they use to encode real-world acquaintances. For example, from Marilynn Brewer's research on impression formation,[5] we borrowed a distinction between *category-based* and *person-based* expectations. This distinction applies to how people generate expectations about individuals' future behavior. I will exemplify this distinction based on the opening paragraph of *Why I Live at the P.O.*, in which Welty provides an opportunity for readers to form their first impression of Sister:

> I was getting along fine with Mama, Papa-Daddy and Uncle Rondo until my sister Stella-Rondo just separated from her husband and came back home again. Mr. Whitaker! Of course I went with Mr. Whitaker first, when he first appeared here in China Grove, taking ›Pose Yourself‹ photos, and Stella-Rondo broke us up. Told him I was one-sided. Bigger on one side than the other, which is a deliberate, calculated falsehood: I'm the same. Stella-Rondo is exactly twelve months to the day younger than I am and for that reason she's spoiled.[6]

As readers make their way through this paragraph, one possibility is that they will begin to assimilate Sister to some social category with which they have prior experience. They might, for example, decide that Sister is representative of a type we could call ›aggrieved older siblings‹. Readers' expectations about Sister's subsequent behavior would very likely be category-based, because those expectations would flow from the norms of that category.[7] Another possibility is that readers would retain a strong sense of Sister as a unique individual who defied easy categorization. In that case, readers' expectations would be person-based because those expectations would flow from the particular information they accumulate about this precise individual.

This distinction – and others Allbritton and I invoked – supplied a useful starting point for a cognitive psychological account of literary

---

4   Gerrig / Allbritton: Construction; see also Gerrig: Experiencing.
5   Brewer: Model.
6   Welty: Curtain, p. 89.
7   Throughout this chapter, I intend ›category‹ to include both common and ad hoc categories (see Barsalou: Categories).

character. Our proposal, however, had two critical limitations. First, it was insufficiently informed by literary analysis of fictional characters. Second, it failed to provide the type of moment-by-moment account that is the hallmark of cognitive psychological theories.

Ralf Schneider has provided a perspective on literary character that overcomes that first limitation. His account successfully captured many of the nuances of literary analyses by focusing on what he terms the »dynamics of mental-model construction«.[8] Schneider drew the concept of mental model from the research literature on text processing.[9] With respect to characters, Schneider suggested that mental models »serve to integrate all pieces of information« where pieces of information might refer to »psychological traits, emotions, and aims of characters«.[10] Schneider articulated the sources of the information readers use to construct mental models by making useful contrasts, for example, between novice and expert readers. He also drew on important literary concepts such as empathy and identification. Schneider imported and expanded the distinction between category-based and person-based expectations to outline how readers' mental models of characters change over time. He articulated a series of processes – categorization, de-categorization, individuation, personalization, and de-personalization – that explain how readers respond as they acquire new information about characters in the course of a narrative.

Although I embrace the major substance of Schneider's theory, it shares the limitation with Gerrig and Allbritton's prior account that it does not specify the types of moment-by-moment mental processes that underlie readers' constructions of literary characters. In this chapter, I offer a greater level of moment-by-moment detail. In doing so, I hope to provide a more precise sense of what it means for readers to encode mental models of characters and to apply those models as a narrative unfolds.

Within cognitive psychology, theories of text processing have largely addressed only very simple aspects of the mental models readers encode for characters. For example, the event indexing model suggests that readers track several narrative dimensions including both characters' identities (e.g., main characters versus scenario-based characters) and characters' goals.[11] This model, however, is silent on the types of issues that are more likely to dominant literary analysis of character. There is no

---

8 Schneider: Theory, p. 607.
9 E.g. Zwaan / Radvansky: Models.
10 Schneider: Theory, p. 610.
11 Magliano et al.: Role; Zwaan et al.: Construction.

discussion, for example, of how readers come to understand the traits from which characters are often constituted or how readers' understanding of characters changes over the course of a narrative. Thus, the event indexing model asserts that readers encode characters' goals but gives no insight into how readers use character information to assess characters' behaviors in pursuit of those goals.

To enlarge the scope of cognitive psychological models of text processing, I import concepts from social psychological theory. However, I filter those ideas through the global perspective I take on narrative processing which is known as *memory-based processing*.[12] A central claim of this perspective is that »the only automatic processes readers bring to bear on text processing are ordinary memory processes«.[13] The perspective contrasts with other approaches to text processing that make claims about special processes that apply only to readers' experiences of texts.[14] I hope to make a persuasive case that readers' construction of literary character draws only on processes that are otherwise necessary for everyday experience.

2 Inferences about Characters

As readers experience the opening paragraph of *Why I Live at the P.O.*, there are many inferences they could encode as part of their discourse representations. However, researchers in psychology have drawn a fundamental distinction between *automatic* inferences – those that arise without the readers' conscious effort – and *controlled* inferences – those that require readers' strategic reflection. Much attention in social psychology has been focused on types of automatic inferences that play a role in impression formation.[15] To demonstrate the relevance of this research to theories of fictional characters, I will focus on the phenomenon of *spontaneous trait inferences*.

Fictional characters are often introduced by their behaviors, rather than by explicit mention of the traits that (potentially) generate those behaviors. For example, among the first information readers obtain about Stella-Rondo is that she stole Mr. Whitaker away from her Sister. This behavior provides a context for some strong inferences about Stella-Rondo's personality. Readers might infer that she is selfish, deceitful, and so on. In

---

12 Gerrig / O'Brien: Scope; McKoon / Ratcliff: Inference.
13 Gerrig / O'Brien: Scope, p. 228.
14 Graesser et al.: Constructing; for reviews see Guéraud / O'Brien: Components.
15 For a review, see Uleman et al.: Inferences.

fact, under appropriate circumstances readers automatically (or spontaneously) encode trait inferences based on characters' behaviors. Consider a project by James Uleman and his colleagues.[16] In their study, participants read sentences of this sort (in the context of one-, three- or four-sentence paragraphs):

> He checked everyone's seat belts before starting off.
>
> Her stories made people laugh so hard they held their sides.
>
> He won first prize in the city-wide high school science fair.[17]

After each sentence, participants had to respond as quickly as possible whether a particular word had appeared in the sentence. For the sentences I just cited, those words were *cautious*, *funny*, and *smart*. The researchers reasoned that, if participants spontaneously encode trait inferences, they should find it relatively difficult to say ›no‹ to these probe words. For comparison, the researchers used participants' performance on control sentences such as ›Everyone started off before checking their seat belts‹ that used the same content words without implying the trait. In fact, when the sentences implied a trait, participants were relatively slow to indicate that the trait words had failed to appear as literal parts of the texts. Results of this sort indicate that readers routinely and unreflectively use characters' behavior to link them to particular categories (e.g., the category of people who are cautious, funny, or smart). Thus, readers often don't have to expend any effort to decide what type of person a character may be.

We have seen so far that readers show great facility in drawing inferences that relate characters to categories. Based on these results, we might be tempted to create a theory about the importance of these inferences or the particular function they provide as readers experience narratives. However, there is no reason to conclude that these inferences are dissimilar from other types of inferences readers encode. From the perspective of memory-based processing, readers automatically encode »two classes of inferences, those based on easily available information and those required for local coherence, are encoded during reading, unless a reader adopts special goals or strategies«.[18] With respect to local coherence, consider this brief excerpt from *Why I Live at the P.O.*:

---

[16] Uleman et al.: Evidence.
[17] For each of the experiments I describe in detail, I provide one or more examples of the stimuli. Note that each experiment, in fact, used roughly 20 to 30 target sentences or stories. Experiments of this sort use multiple participants and multiple stimuli to ensure the generalizability of the results.
[18] McKoon / Ratcliff: Inference, p. 441.

> So the first thing Stella-Rondo did at the table was turn Papa-Daddy against me. ›Papa-Daddy‹, she says. He was trying to cut up his meat.¹⁹

To understand this pair of sentences, readers must infer that ›she‹ refers to ›Stella-Rondo‹ and ›He‹ refers to ›Papa-Daddy‹. It is uncontroversial that readers necessarily encode inferences of this sort. More controversial is the exact implication of the claim that readers only automatically encode inferences based on ›easily available information‹. Critics have been bothered by the impossibility of providing a rigorous account of what will be ›easily available‹.²⁰ However, as supported by empirical data, that's much the point: Different readers bring their own storehouses of background knowledge to bear on their narrative experiences. To the extent that information is readily available for a particular reader at a particular moment, that reader will encode an inference without conscious intervention.

Consider one of the examples for automatic trait inferences I cited earlier. When experimental participants read ›He checked everyone's seat belts before starting off‹ they provided evidence that they had inferred the trait *cautious*. On the memory-based processing view, the reason that Uleman et al. were able to find evidence that participants encoded this inference is because the majority of participants each individually had a sufficient collection of easily available memory traces to yield the inference. Let me reinforce that point with an example from *Why I Live at the P.O.*:

> [A]t 6:30 A.M. the next morning, [Uncle Rondo] threw a whole five-cent package of some unsold one-inch firecrackers from the store as hard as he could into my bedroom and they every one went off. Not one bad one in the string. Anybody else, there'd be one that wouldn't go off.²¹

To understand this passage fully, readers must draw on a good deal of general knowledge: What is a ›one-inch firecracker‹? How many come in a ›five-cent package‹? What does it mean that they come in a ›string‹? Is it, in fact, true that most packages include duds? Some readers will likely have sufficient past experiences so that their memory traces will give rise to automatic answers to these questions as they read the passage. However, given the obscurity of some of these concepts, many readers will have to apply strategic effort. By contrast, the probability is quite high that all readers will have automatic access to memory traces that encode circumstances in which people have responded to unexpected loud noises.

---

19 Welty: Curtain, p. 91.
20 For a review see Gerrig / O'Brien: Scope.
21 Welty: Curtain, p. 102.

Thus, we might expect virtually all readers to encode inferences about how Sister would feel when the last of the firecrackers finally exploded.

This example illustrates the way in which inferences are memory-based: We would expect different readers to encode different inferences as a function of their past experiences. For that reason, it is also an error to imagine that particular functional categories of inferences have special status with respect to text processing. Thus, readers encode spontaneous trait inferences because they have prior experiences that allow them to do so. Readers do not encode those inferences because they are necessary for text comprehension. Still, those inferences have consequences for subsequent text processing: It matters if readers encode an inference that a character is, for example, cautious, funny, or smart. In the next section, I explore how the information readers acquire – either directly from a text or via inferences – has consequences on their explicit and implicit judgments about characters.

3 Readers' Judgments About Characters' Behaviors

In the opening paragraph of *Why I Live at the P.O.*, Sister makes this declaration, »Stella-Rondo is exactly twelve months to the day younger than I am and for that reason she's spoiled«.[22] Assuming that readers accept Sister's trait assessment of her younger sibling as accurate, how might they use the information that Stella-Rondo is spoiled? Let me expand the scope of this question. In Stella-Rondo's case, the text directly provides trait information. As we've just seen, there are many instances in which readers use characters' behavior to infer traits. For example, Sister reports, »There I was over the hot stove, trying to stretch two chickens over five people and a completely unexpected child into the bargain, without one moment's notice«.[23] Readers might encode the trait inference that Sister is filled with self-pity. Once again, we can ask the question of how readers' subsequent experience of the narrative will be affected by that category-based judgment.

Suppose readers believe that Stella-Rondo is spoiled. One possibility is that they would use that information to generate expectations about how she might act in the future. This appears to be the perspective captured by the construct ›category-based expectations‹. The difficulty, however, is that ›being spoiled‹ can give rise to a great diversity of behaviors; it's hard to predict the specifics of how a spoiled person will act in a particular

---

22 Ibid., p. 89.
23 Ibid., p. 90.

situation.²⁴ Anne Maass and her colleagues have captured this intuition in a series of experiments that document what they term the ›induction-deduction asymmetry‹.²⁵ In their research, experimental participants are quite likely to make inductive inferences from behaviors (e.g., ›keeps his or her table untidy‹) to traits (e.g., ›messy‹). The participants were reliably less likely to make deductive inferences from the traits to the behaviors. Maass et al. suggested that this pattern arises from asymmetries in the strengths of memory associations. The link from a behavior to a trait will be strong because of many similar experiences leading to a single trait designation (e.g., the many times in which someone who keeps his or her space untidy is labeled as ›messy‹). However, traits have associations with a wide range of behaviors. This asymmetry provides a poor context for successful prediction. This analysis suggests that readers rarely can use category information to project forward into a text.

Instead, readers' category-based mental models affect the way in which they assimilate new character information as a narrative unfolds. Just after Sister offers the judgment that Stella-Rondo is spoiled, she fills in some of her sibling's history:

> She's always had anything in the world she wanted and then she'd throw it away. Papa-Daddy gave her this gorgeous Add-a-Pearl necklace when she was eight years old and she threw it away playing baseball when she was nine, with only two pearls.²⁶

These behaviors, as Sister represents them, cohere with the judgment that Stella-Rondo is spoiled. In other words, these behaviors seem to be normal behaviors for someone who is spoiled. Daniel Kahneman and Dale Miller originated *norm theory* to explain how people make exactly these sorts of judgment about what seems normal.²⁷ Prior to their account, researchers had most often conceptualized norms as being a source of predictions or expectations. However, Kahneman and Miller suggested that »reasoning flows not only forward, from anticipation and hypothesis to confirmation or revision, but also backward, from the experience to what it reminds us of or makes us think about«.²⁸ That, I argue, is how categories most often function with respect to characters and their actions: Readers make swift, tacit judgments about whether a

---

24 Bortolussi / Dixon: Psychonarratology use Bayesian analysis to provide a formal account of how, for example, information about characters' actions affects readers' trait inferences. The model also describes how readers' mental models for characters change over time.
25 Maass et al.: Asymmetry.
26 Welty: Curtain, p. 89.
27 Kahneman / Miller: Theory.
28 Ibid., p. 137.

character's behavior seems normal in the context of their category-based understanding of the character.

Let's review research evidence that supports this claim. Consider the story written by Edward O'Brien and his colleagues presented in Table 1.[29] In that story, what happens when readers arrive at the sentence, ›Mary ordered a cheeseburger and fries‹? On the view proposed by O'Brien et al., which is consistent with the one I am advocating here, readers' memory processes initiate a search through their text representation. That search provides a context for an implicit assessment of whether an action is ›normal‹ given the prior information. For the story given in Table 1, the text allows readers to construct a category-based model that makes it entirely unsurprising that Mary would order a cheeseburger and fries. However, an alternative version of the text endowed Mary with quite different features:

> This was Mary's favorite restaurant because it had fantastic health food. Mary, a health nut, had been a strict vegetarian for ten years. Her favorite food was cauliflower. Mary was so serious about her diet that she refused to eat anything which was fried or cooked in grease.

O'Brien et al. measured the time it took participants to indicate that they had understood the sentence ›Mary ordered a cheeseburger and fries‹. Participants read the sentence more slowly when Mary's action was inconsistent with the prior characterization than when it was consistent. Thus, the experiment offered evidence that readers are sensitive to what constitutes normal behavior for particular types of characters. When readers experience inconsistencies, text processing is disrupted providing, presumably, a context for them to learn something new about a character (if nothing more than that the character is inconsistent).

In the studies conducted by O'Brien and his colleagues, the texts included overt statements of the categories to which the characters belonged (e.g., Mary was a ›strict vegetarian‹). In a project led by David Rapp,[30] my colleagues and I examined circumstances in which readers' judgments were based on the trait inferences they encode. Consider the story presented in Table 2. Some experimental participants read a version of the story that provided behavioral evidence to support a trait inference. Specifically, when participants read that Albert's shoes were buried under heaps of garbage, we expected them to encode the inference that Albert was *sloppy*. We did not expect that participants who read a version of the story with a control sentence (i.e., ›Albert's friends had suggested meeting outside the pizzeria adjacent to the movie theater.‹) would encode that

---

29 Albrecht / O'Brien: Updating; O'Brien et al.: Updating.
30 Rapp et al., Readers.

inference. As shown in Table 2, the story's second episode provided a context in which Albert could behave in either a sloppy or tidy fashion. By measuring participants' responses to the two possible outcomes, we had an opportunity to determine the extent to which readers' trait-based models swiftly constrain what types of behavior they explicitly or implicitly judge as normal.

We used two measures to demonstrate that readers' narrative experiences are guided by the models they encode for characters. In one experiment, we asked participants to make an explicit judgment about whether a character was likely to perform a particular behavior. For example, we asked participants to respond ›yes‹ or ›no‹ to the statement, ›Albert left the newspaper‹. In a second experiment, we measured participants' reading time on sentences that embodied the alternative outcomes. For the story in Table 2, half of the participants read a trait-consistent outcome: ›Albert ignored the sign and got off the bus. Someone else would come and pick it up‹. Half of the participants read a trait-inconsistent outcome: ›Albert picked up the newspaper to throw away later. He wanted to help keep the bus clean‹.

In our experiments, both measures provided evidence that readers encoded and applied trait-based models. Participants replied ›yes‹ reliably more often to the trait-consistent outcome when they had a prior opportunity to encode a trait model. Participants read the sentences embodying a trait-consistent outcome reliably more quickly when they had a prior opportunity to encode a trait model. Taken together, these measures suggested that trait models wield an influence both when readers have an opportunity to reflect on a text (as indexed by the overt judgments) and as they first understand the text (as indexed by the reading times).

In a final pair of experiments, we explored the specificity of the trait-models readers encoded. Consider the story in Table 2. The claim we wished to support is that readers encode a category-based model of Albert that is focused on his sloppiness. However, with just the data I've reviewed, it's plausible that readers' models would be more general: Albert has negative traits. To rule out the possibility that readers only sort characters into positive vs. negative, we re-arranged our stories to provide second episodes in which a trait had no specific relevance to the situation. Here is that episode for Albert's story:

> Albert was a student attending law school. His classes were taught by professors, judges, and attorneys with backgrounds in business and proprietary law. During one class, a teacher asked a thought-provoking theoretical question. The teacher looked around the class for someone to answer. Albert felt the professor's eyes focus on him.

From our first pair of experiments, we know that readers judge that a *shy* character will avoid the teacher's gaze. If Albert is generally negative (by virtue of being sloppy) but not specifically shy, how do readers assess his behavior? To answer this question, we once again asked participants to respond directly to statements of outcomes (e.g., ›Albert met the teacher's gaze.‹) or to read instantiations of those outcomes (e.g., ›Albert looked directly at the teacher and began giving an answer. He felt confident the class would understand his response.‹). In our experiments, both measures suggested that participants applied specific rather than general trait models. Our readers, apparently, did not assess the normalcy of characters' behavior against the high-level criteria of positive vs. negative. Rather they used specific information about what it means, for example, to be honest, courteous, shy, or sloppy.

The perspective I have developed here embodies the strong assumption that characters are most often the focus of readers' experience of narratives. Before I leave this topic, it's important to note that my claims – and the research results that support them – embody very strong cultural assumptions. In particular, researchers have documented important and consistent cross-cultural differences in the ways that people attend to information. At a global level, Harry Triandis has explicated differences between *individualistic* (mostly Western) cultures that emphasize individuals' needs and *collectivist* (mostly non-Western) cultures that emphasize the needs of the group.[31] This global difference among cultures has important implications for how people conceptualize the *self*. Hazel Markus and Shinobu Kitayama have suggested that people in individualistic cultures most often hold *independent* construals of self:[32]

> Achieving the cultural goal of independence requires construing oneself as an individual whose behavior is organized and made meaningful primarily by reference to one's own internal repertoire of thoughts, feelings, and action, rather than by reference to the thoughts, feelings, and actions of others.[33]

People in collectivist cultures most often hold interdependent construals of self:

> Experiencing interdependence entails seeing oneself as part of an encompassing social relationship and recognizing that one's behavior is determined, contingent on, and, to a large extent organized by what the actor perceives to be the thoughts, feelings, and actions of others in the relationship.[34]

---

31 Triandis: Culture; Triandis: Individualism.
32 Kitayama et al.: Collective; Markus / Kitayama: Culture; Markus et al.: Selfways.
33 Markus / Kitayama: Culture, p. 226.
34 Ibid., p. 227.

These divergent construals of self have a broad range of implications for how people parse up their life experiences. Let me provide an example that has applications to readers' narrative experiences. To study cross-cultural differences in moral judgments, Joan Miller and David Bersoff presented brief scenarios to experimental participants in New Haven, Connecticut, and Mysore, in southern India.[35] In one scenario, a character named Ben needed to travel from Los Angeles to San Francisco for his best friend's wedding ceremony:

> He needed to catch the very next train if he was to be on time for the ceremony, as he had to deliver the wedding rings. However, Ben's wallet was stolen in the train station. He lost all of his money as well as his ticket to San Francisco.

As the story develops, Ben is rebuffed in his attempts to borrow money to buy another ticket. However, fate intervenes:

> While Ben was sitting on a bench trying to decide what to do next, a well-dressed man sitting next to him walked away for a minute. Looking over at where the man had been sitting, Ben noticed that the man had left his coat unattended. Sticking out of the man's coat pocket was a train ticket to San Francisco. Ben knew that he could take the ticket and use it to travel to San Francisco on the next train. He also saw that the man had more than enough money in his coat pocket to buy another train ticket.

After participants read the story, Miller and Bersoff asked them to select one course of action:

1. BEN SHOULD NOT TAKE THE TICKET FROM THE MAN'S COAT POCKET – even though it means not getting to San Francisco in time to deliver the wedding rings to his best friend;
2. BEN SHOULD GO TO SAN FRANCISCO TO DELIVER THE WEDDING RINGS TO HIS BEST FRIEND – even though it means taking the train ticket from the other man's coat pocket.

Participants in the United States disproportionately chose the first option; participants in India disproportionately chose the second option. This result emerges from the greater emphasis on interdependence and mutual assistance in India's collectivist culture. This study, and the cross-cultural analysis that prompted it, suggests that readers who hold interdependent construals of self will have quite different experiences of narratives than readers who hold independent construals of self.

We might expect, for example, that my colleagues and I would fail to replicate our research on readers' trait-based models were we to conduct the studies with participants who hold interdependent construals of the self. Rather than using characters' behavior to infer traits – and applying those traits to understand subsequent behavior – we would expect interdependent readers to look to the narrative situation to understand

---

35 Miller / Bersoff: Culture.

characters' behavior. In fact, it should be possible to devise experiments to demonstrate that interdependent readers encode and apply situation-based models that would do relatively little to structure the experiences of independent readers. The more general conclusion is that, as we develop theories of how readers experience characters in fictional worlds, those theories should be sensitive to potential differences among readers from different cultures.[36]

4 The Dynamics of Readers' Experiences of Fictional Character

My intention for this chapter has been to detail moment-by-moment aspects of readers' experiences of fictional characters. However, I have not yet fulfilled the broader agenda Schneider set for the study of readers' mental models of characters: He notes that »they are successively refined – elaborated, modified or revised – in the reading process«.[37] In this final section, I review research that bears on those successive refinements.

Theorists in cognitive psychology have provided two rather different views on the question of how readers update their mental models of characters. To differentiate the two views, I introduce another version of the story from the research by O'Brien et al. we considered earlier:

> As she was waiting, Mary recalled that this had been her favorite restaurant because it had fantastic health food. Mary recalled that she had been a health nut and a strict vegetarian for about ten years but she wasn't anymore. Back then, her favorite food had been cauliflower. At that time, Mary had been so serious about her diet that she refused to eat anything which was fried or cooked in grease.

After this new material, the story continues in the same fashion as the example in Table 1. Ultimately, Mary orders a cheeseburger and fries. The question is how long it takes readers to assimilate Mary's action to their discourse representation. Two views make different predictions.

On one view,[38] readers maintain fully updated mental models: »Only information that is relevant to the current situation is carried forward in the active portion of the reader's discourse model; information that is not relevant to the current here-and-now is not«.[39] If this view were correct, we would expect readers to have no particular difficulty assimilating the statement ›Mary ordered a cheeseburger and fries‹. The fact that she was a vegetarian in the past should not be active in readers' discourse models.

---

36 See also Nisbett et al.: Culture; Oyserman / Lee: Culture.
37 Schneider: Theory, p. 628.
38 Morrow: Prepositions; Morrow / Greenspan: Situation.
39 O'Brien et al.: Updating, p. 1204.

An alternative view shares the memory-based processing perspective that underlies this chapter. On this view, the information in the sentence ›Mary ordered a cheeseburger and fries‹ cues readers' memory processes to reactivate the information that Mary once was a vegetarian. As such, readers must resolve the inconsistency in the moment. This view claims, in effect, that readers continue to look backwards to earlier portions of the text to ensure that Mary's behavior is normal – given everything they have learned about her.

The data support the claims of the memory-based processing perspective. Participants took longer to read ›Mary ordered a cheeseburger and fries‹ even when the story made it quite plain that her vegetarianism was a thing of the past. O'Brien et al. made other attempts to see if readers would update their mental models to the ›here-and-now‹. For example, one experiment had this as an extra sentence: ›Nevertheless, Mary never stuck to her diet when she dined out with friends because she enjoyed eating meat occasionally‹. This sentence creates a context in which Mary's action is unsurprising. Still, readers took longer to read the statement ›Mary ordered a cheeseburger and fries‹ for this version of the story than they did for the consistent version. These experiments suggest rather strongly that, even if readers encode an updated model of a character, information that contradicts that updated model remains accessible to memory processes and, therefore, continues to wield an influence on readers' moment-by-moment experiences.

David Rapp and Panayiota Kendeou have examined updating processes when new information affects readers' trait inferences.[40] Consider again the story in Table 2. In the research by Rapp et al. that I reviewed earlier, the sentence ›[The shoes] were buried under old candy wrappers, crumpled magazines, and some dirty laundry‹ gave rise to the inference that Albert was sloppy. To study updating, Rapp and Kendeou added a sentence to the story that provided an explanation for the state of Albert's room: ›Albert cared about the condition of his room, but had only moved into the apartment yesterday‹. This additional sentence has the potential to shift readers' attention to the situation, which creates a context in which they might amend their original categorization of Albert as sloppy. Rapp and Kendeou demonstrated that, in the presence of such explanations, participants were considerably less likely to apply trait-models for the characters: Participants were less likely to agree with outcomes that were consistent with a trait inference (e.g., ›Albert ignored the sign and got off the bus.‹); they took longer to read the sentences that embodied those outcomes. Note the contrast to the work by O'Brien et al. who, as we just

---

40 Rapp / Kendeou: Revising.

saw, found that readers continued to respond to an inconsistency between a character's behavior and a trait that was in the character's past. Rapp and Kendeou suggested that the results diverged because of the explicit vs. implicit nature of the trait-based models. Taken together, these projects signal the subtleties that a theory of dynamic aspects of readers' experiences of fictional characters will need to capture.

In his account, Schneider elaborated another important sense in which mental models of characters are successively refined. He reviewed the different ways in which narratives provide information and judgments about characters (e.g., through statements or evaluations by narrators or other characters). We have already seen, for example, how diligently Sister provides evidence that Stella-Rondo is spoiled. In fact, Sister narrates a series of episodes in which her younger sibling outright lies to ruin Sister's standing with her family – which causes her ultimately to decamp for the Post Office. Still, it's hard not to wonder whether Sister's account is wholly accurate. There's something just a bit off about her narration. It seems likely that readers' mental models of both Sister and Stella-Rondo would be affected by the way they filter Sister's narration. Schneider provided a strong form of this claim: »In contrast to interpersonal understanding, the specific literariness of forming impressions of characters results from an additional stage of the narrator's mediation that is hardly ever unbiased«.[41]

I agree with that substance of Schneider's assertion, but do not accept the contrast between ordinary ›interpersonal understanding‹ and the mental processes at work for fictional narratives. People quite often acquire information about other individuals in ways that parallel fictional narration. People's accounts of the same events often differ (i.e., people manifest perspectives in their narration) and people often provide different information when they tell the same story more than once.[42] To the extent that those tellings or retellings provide information about ›characters‹, it seems quite likely that members of the narratives' audience would factor in potential bias of the speaker. Thus, I do not believe that Schneider has made the case for an ›additional stage‹ in the encoding of literary character.

Once, however, we leave aside the contrast to ordinary ›interpersonal understanding‹, Schneider has called attention to a major omission in cognitive psychological theories of text processing: Those theories make no mention of any process of evaluation whereby readers make judgments about the reliability of narrators' worldviews. To develop an account of

---

41 Schneider: Theory, p. 615.
42 Schiffrin: Words.

this evaluation process, it seems prudent to draw upon research on *source credibility* in the context of persuasion. In theories of persuasion, source credibility has figured as an important variable.[43] Researchers have accumulated a diverse set of results that predict how and when people use source information to contextualize new information.

Consider a study by Zakary Tormala and his colleagues.[44] Experimental participants read a persuasive message that argued in favor of phosphate-based laundry detergents. For half of the participants, the source of the message had high credibility: »Participants were told the information came from a government agency that investigates consumer products to help consumers make sound decisions«.[45] For the other half of the participants, the source had low credibility: »Participants were told the information came from a major soap and detergent manufacturer that sells phosphate detergents«.[46] Participants were more persuaded by the message when the source had high credibility. Tormala and his colleagues argued that, when the source information preceded the message, participants engaged in elaborative thought about the message. The credibility of the source (high or low) influenced the valence of their thoughts (favorable or unfavorable).

We might expect readers to respond to Sister in a parallel fashion. To the extent that they view her as a low credibility source, we would imagine that readers would expend effort to elaborate on the information she provides. Those readers, accordingly, might not be persuaded by the case she makes against her family. Their text representations would also include some of the thoughts they generated as they reflected on Sister's information. Of course, there might be readers who find Sister's account completely credible – perhaps readers who view themselves as victims of their spoiled younger siblings. If they read *Why I Live at the P.O.* from the perspective of Sister as a high credibility source, their ultimate mental models for Sister, Stella-Rondo, and the story's other characters will be quite different. More generally, we can see how social psychological research can point the way toward a concrete model of how the ›narrator's mediation‹ affects readers' encoding of characters in fiction.

---

43 For a review, see Pornpitakpan: Persuasiveness.
44 Tormala et al.: Source.
45 Ibid., p. 540.
46 Ibid.

5 Conclusion

The goal of this chapter has been to specify some of the moment-by-moment processes that affect the mental models readers encode for fictional characters. I have focused largely on readers' category-based judgments because the research literature in social and cognitive psychology provides a set of concepts that allowed me to provide a coherent account of those judgments. However, the perspective I have developed can be extended to other aspects of readers' experiences of characters. For example, my colleagues and I have examined how readers respond to the relationship between characters' goals and their actions and how readers encode and apply preferences about the outcomes that befall characters.[47] In each case, we have attempted to redress the narrow treatment of character emblematic of cognitive psychological theories. Ultimately, we need to explain why and how it matters so much when Sister declares near the very end of her story, »I want the world to know I'm happy«.[48]

Tables

Table 1

Sample story from O'Brien, Rizzella, Albrecht, & Halleran (1998)

Today, Mary was meeting a friend for lunch. She arrived early at the restaurant and decided to get a table. After she sat down, she started looking at the menu.
    This was Mary's favorite restaurant because it had fantastic junk food. Mary enjoyed eating anything that was quick and easy to fix. In fact, she ate at McDonald's at least three times a week. Mary never worried about her diet and saw no reason to eat nutritious foods.
    After about ten minutes, Mary's friend arrived. It had been a few months since they had seen each other. Because of this they had a lot to talk about and chatted for over a half hour. Finally, Mary signaled the waiter to come take their orders. Mary checked the menu one more time. She had a hard time deciding what to have for lunch.
    Mary ordered a cheeseburger and fries. She handed the menu back to the waiter. Her friend didn't have as much trouble deciding what she wanted. She ordered, and they began to chat again. They didn't realize there was so much for them to catch up on.

---

47 Egidi / Gerrig: Readers; Rapp / Gerrig: Readers; Rapp / Gerrig: Predilections.
48 Welty: Curtain, p. 110.

Table 2

Sample materials from Rapp, Gerrig, & Prentice (2001)

Albert was listening to the radio. He had finished getting ready to meet his friends at the movies. They were going to see a new comedy that was getting rave reviews.

He pulled a sweater over his head. Then he began to look for his shoes.

Trait continuation: They were buried under old candy wrappers, crumpled magazines, and some dirty laundry.

Control continuation: Albert's friends had suggested meeting outside the pizzeria adjacent to the movie theater.

Albert had to take the bus to the movies. He bought a newspaper to read during the ride to the theater. Albert had finished leafing through the paper when the bus driver announced Albert's stop. Albert put the newspaper on the seat next to him. As he waited for the bus to come to a halt, he noticed a sign asking riders not to leave garbage on the bus.

Trait-consistent outcome: Albert left the newspaper.
Trait-inconsistent outcome: Albert picked up the newspaper.

References

Albrecht, Jason E. / Edward J. O'Brien: Updating a Mental Model: Maintaining Both Local and Global Coherence. In: Journal of Experimental Psychology: Learning, Memory, and Cognition 19 (1993), pp. 1061–1070.

Barsalou, Lawrence W.: Ad Hoc Categories. In: Memory & Cognition 11 (1983), pp. 211–227.

Bortolussi, Marisa / Peter Dixon: Psychonarratology: Foundations for the Empirical Study of Literary Response. Cambridge 2003.

Brewer, Marilynn B.: A Dual Process Model of Impression Formation. In: Thomas K. Srull / Robert S. Wyer, Jr. (Eds.): Advances in Social Cognition 1. Hillsdale, NJ 1988, pp. 1–36.

Egidi, Giovanna / Richard J. Gerrig: Readers' Experiences of Characters' Goals and Actions. In: Journal of Experimental Psychology: Learning, Memory, and Cognition 32 (2006), pp. 1322–1329.

Gerrig, Richard J.: Experiencing Narrative Worlds. New Haven 1993.

Gerrig, Richard J. / David W. Allbritton: The Construction of Literary Character: A View from Cognitive Psychology. In: Style 24 (1990), pp. 380–391.

Gerrig, Richard J. / Edward J. O'Brien.: The Scope of Memory-Based Processing. In: Discourse Processes 39 (2005), pp. 225–242.

Graesser, Arthur C. / Murray Singer / Tom Trabasso: Constructing Inferences During Narrative Text Comprehension. In: Psychological Review 101 (1994), pp. 371–395.

Guéraud, Sabine / Edward J. O'Brien (Eds.): Components of Comprehension: A Convergence Between Memory-Based Processes and Explanation-Based Processes. In: Discourse Processes 39/2&3 (2005), pp. 123–124.

Kahneman, Daniel / Dale T. Miller: Norm Theory: Comparing Reality to its Alternatives. In: Psychological Review 92 (1986), pp. 136–153.

Kitayama, Shinobu / Hazel R. Markus / Cary Lieberman: The Collective Construction of Self-Esteem: Implications for Culture, Self, and Emotion. In: James A. Russell / José-Miguel Fernandez-Dols / Antony S. R. Manstead / J. C. Wellenkamp (Eds.): Everyday Conceptions of Emotion. Dordrecht 1995, pp. 523–550.

Maass, Anne / Mara Cadinu / Mattia Taroni / Margherita Masserini: The Induction-Deduction Asymmetry: Fact or Artifact? In: Social Cognition 24 (2006), pp. 74–109.

Magliano, Jospeh P. / Rolf A. Zwaan / Arthur C. Graesser: The Role of Situational Continuity in Narrative Understanding. In: Herre Van Oostendorp / Susan Goldman (Eds.): The Construction of Mental Representations During Reading. Mahwah, NJ 1999, pp. 219–245.

Markus, Hazel R. / Shinobu Kitayama: Culture and the Self: Implications for Cognition, Emotion, and Motivation. In: Psychological Review 98 (1991), pp. 224–253.

Markus, Hazel R. / Patricia R. Mullally / Shinobu Kitayama: Selfways: Diversity in Modes of Cultural Participation. In: Ulric Neisser / David A. Jopling (Eds.): The Conceptual Self in Context. Cambridge 1997, pp. 13–61.

McKoon, Gail / Roger Ratcliff: Inference During Reading. In: Psychological Review 99 (1992), pp. 440–466.

Miller, Joan G. / David M. Bersoff.: Culture and Moral Judgment: How Are Conflicts Between Justice and Interpersonal Responsibilities Resolved? In: Journal of Personality and Social Psychology 62 (1992), pp. 541–554.

Morrow, Daniel G.: Prepositions and Verb Aspect in Narrative Understanding. In: Journal of Memory and Language 24 (1985), pp. 390–404.

Morrow, Daniel / Steven Greenspan: Situation Models and Information Accessibility. In: Noel E. Sharkey (Ed.): Models of Cognition: A Review of Cognitive Science 1. Norwood, NJ 1989, pp. 53–77.

Nisbett, Richard E. / Kaiping Peng / Incheol Choi / Ara Norenzayan: Culture and Systems of Thought: Holistic Versus Analytic Cognition. In: Psychological Review 108 (2001), pp. 291–310.

O'Brien, Edward J. / Michelle L. Rizzella / Jason E. Albrecht / Jennifer G. Halleran: Updating a Situation Model: A Memory-Based Text Processing View. In: Journal of Experimental Psychology: Learning, Memory, and Cognition 24 (1998), pp. 1200–1210.

Oyserman, Daphna / Spike W. S. Lee: Does Culture Influence What and How We Think? Effects of Priming Individualism and Collectivism. In: Psychological Bulletin 134 (2008), pp. 311–342.

Pornpitakpan, Chanthika: The Persuasiveness of Source Credibility: A Critical Review of Five Decades' Evidence. In: Journal of Applied Social Psychology 34 (2004), pp. 243–281.

Rapp, David N. / Richard J. Gerrig: Readers' Reality-Driven and Plot-Driven Analyses in Narrative Comprehension. In: Memory & Cognition 30 (2002), pp. 779–788.

Rapp, David N. / Richard J. Gerrig: Predilections for Narrative Outcomes: The Impact of Story Contexts and Reader Preferences. In: Journal of Memory and Language 54 (2006), pp. 54–67.

Rapp, David N. / Richard J. Gerrig / Deborah A. Prentice: Readers' Trait-Based Models of Characters in Narrative Comprehension. In: Journal of Memory and Language 45 (2001), pp. 737–750.

Rapp, David N. / Panayiota Kendeou: Revising What Readers Know: Updating Text Representations During Narrative Comprehension. In: Memory & Cognition 35 (2007), pp. 2019–2032.

Schiffrin, Deborah: In Other Words: Variation and Reference in Narrative. Cambridge 2006.

Schneider, Ralf: Toward a Cognitive Theory of Literary Character: The Dynamics of Mental-Model Construction. In: Style 35 (2001), pp. 607–640.
Tormala, Zakary L. / Pablo Briñol / Richard E. Petty: Multiple Roles for Source Credibility Under High Elaboration: It's All in the Timing. In: Social Cognition 25 (2007), pp. 536–552.
Triandis, Harry C.: Culture and Social Behavior. New York 1994.
Triandis, Harry C.: Individualism and Collectivism. Boulder, CO 1995.
Uleman, James S. / Alex Hon / Robert J. Roman / Gordon B. Moskowitz: On-Line Evidence for Spontaneous Trait Inferences at Encoding. In: Personality and Social Psychology Bulletin 22 (1996), pp. 377–394.
Uleman, James S. / S. Adil Saribay: Gonzalez, Celia M.: Spontaneous Inferences, Implicit Impressions, and Implicit Theories. In: Annual Review of Psychology 59 (2008), pp. 329–360.
Welty, Eudora: A Curtain of Green & Other Stories. San Diego 1941.
Zwaan, Rolf A. / Mark C. Langston / Arthur C. Graesser: The Construction of Situation Models in Narrative Comprehension: An Event-Indexing Model. In: Psychological Science 6 (1995), pp. 292–297.
Zwaan, Rolf. A. / Gabriel A. Radvansky: Situation Models in Language Comprehension and Memory. In: Psychological Bulletin 123 (1998), pp. 162–185.

CATHERINE EMMOTT / ANTHONY J. SANFORD /
MARC ALEXANDER

Scenarios, Characters' Roles and Plot Status
Readers' Assumptions and Writers' Manipulations of Assumptions in Narrative Texts

Introduction

Certain types of stories, such as detective, mystery and twist-in-the-tale stories, rely for their plots on readers making assumptions about the role and status of characters, then writers later manipulating readers by reversing these assumptions. In Section 1 we review the psychological and linguistic evidence that shows that assumption-making is a natural part of reading in many narrative situations in order to establish textual coherence. In particular, we draw on the notion of scenarios, part of Sanford and Garrod's Scenario Mapping and Focus model in Psychology.[1] This model explains how readers draw on their general knowledge about everyday situations to make inferences about characters in particular scenarios. We discuss certain linguistic phenomena which are explained by this account, including the interpretation of agentless passives, indefinite and definite noun phrases, and institutional pronouns. We also outline the distinction made in this model between principal characters and scenario-dependent characters, the latter being minor characters who appear in specific roles in specific situations. In the original psychological work, the examples tested were artificially-constructed in the laboratory, but in this article our main aim is to relate the psychological findings to real examples, primarily from fictional narratives, to see how useful these psychological ideas are in the stylistic and narratological analysis of texts. In Sections 2 and 3, we look at how writers manipulate scenario assumptions about characters for rhetorical and plot-specific purposes. In

---

1 Sanford / Garrod: Understanding; Sanford / Garrod: Role; Anderson / Garrod / Sanford: Accessibility.

Section 2, we examine cases where a repair is made shortly after the scenario information is introduced in order to challenge the reader's initial assumptions. Then, in Section 3, we look at how such repairs are managed across two entire short stories and a novel. The psychological theory here provides an explanation of how scenario-dependent information can be used to give low prominence to certain characters, and our stylistic discussion shows how writers subsequently bring these minor characters into greater prominence to provide surprising plot dénouements.

1 Establishing Textual Coherence: The Scenario Mapping and Focus Model

Sanford and Garrod's Scenario Mapping and Focus model is a psychological model of the assumptions readers make as they read.[2] This model explains how general knowledge is organised in the form of *scenarios*, information relevant to typical settings. These scenarios are selectively activated during reading, at each stage being used to make sense of the text which follows, hence controlling the reader's expectations. The Scenario Mapping and Focus model is very similar to schema theory,[3] but the primary difference is that it is a psychological account of how the human mind reads, extensively empirically tested on readers, rather than an artificial intelligence model of how computers can store and access information.

Sanford and Garrod view scenarios as consisting of role *slots* for commonly expected participants in those scenarios.[4] This means that these participants are brought into the reader's mental representation of the text as the scenario is introduced, even if they are not mentioned. So in reading about a restaurant, we would assume a waiter to be there, even if the waiter was not referred to. Where there is no immediate mention, the participant is said to be in *implicit focus*. Conversely, when the participant is mentioned, he or she is held in *explicit focus*. In cases where a participant who has been in implicit focus is later mentioned, the participant is then *mapped* into the relevant role *slot*.

This model explains how readers can understand certain linguistic items and make textual inferences, as follows:

---

2 Ibid.
3 Minsky: Framework; Schank / Abelson: Scripts. For discussions of schema theory in relation to narrative texts see Stockwell: Schema and Emmott / Alexander: Schemata.
4 Sanford / Garrod: Understanding, pp. 91ff.

(i) Inferring participants from agentless passives

Agentless passives, such as the verbs in the following example, can be assumed to have elided agents who are stereotypical participants in the scenario. In Example 1, we include the staff in a holiday resort in our representation of the resort scenario, bringing these staff into implicit focus as the scenario is activated. Since the resort staff are already in implicit focus, there is no need to explicitly mention them at this point.

Example 1

> [In a holiday resort.] Breakfast <u>was laid out</u>, beds <u>changed</u>, tiles <u>mopped</u>, cutlery <u>cleaned</u>, splats of dinner <u>wiped</u> from floors [...][5]

(ii) Assigning roles to unnamed and named characters

When characters are introduced for the first time, we may also map them into scenario role slots. So in Example 2, when we read about a shop, we assume that there will be staff there, bringing these people into implicit focus as the scenario is set up. When there is a subsequent explicit reference to a person performing an action typical of a shop assistant, we can map that explicit reference onto the relevant role slot in the scenario. In the example of a bookstore, below, the female character, referred to by the indefinite noun phrase, can be mapped onto the scenario slot, since she is asking the customer if he needs help. This assumes that the male character who is being addressed by the woman has been mapped onto the customer slot.

Example 2

> The bookstore is small and appealing [...] <u>A young woman in a black sweater</u> asks him if he needs help.[6]

Such assumptions can be challenged. In similar scenarios, in real life and in fiction, we could find out subsequently that the person we thought was a shop assistant was a member of the public offering assistance, or that the main character is a publisher's salesman rather than a customer.

Minor named characters can also be mapped onto scenarios in the same way. In the following example, we can assume that the post office has staff, then map Harry Noonan onto this role.

---

5 Dean: Strangers, p. 107 (our emphasis).
6 Shreve: Where, p. 77 (our emphasis).

Example 3

> It was the most reckless gesture of all, one he regretted the minute he watched <u>Harry Noonan</u> behind the counter at the post office toss it into the Priority Mail bucket.[7]

In this situation it seems highly likely that the person behind the counter handling the mail is employed there.

(iii) Explaining the use of definite noun phrases

In cases where a character is first referred to explicitly with a definite reference, the definite article confirms that the character has been in implicit focus in the scenario and that their role in the scenario is being treated as ›given‹ information. This is the case with the first explicit mention of ›the waiter‹, shown in Example 4 below. Before this the waiter's role was implicit, an assumption about the role of the waiter being needed to make sense of how the brandy arrives.

Example 4

> [In a restaurant.] The brandy he had ordered arrived. [The character thinks about whether his dining partner will show up.] He caught <u>the waiter's</u> eye and asked for another brandy.[8]

(iv) Explaining the use of ›institutional they‹ pronouns

Generally pronouns are used after characters have already been mentioned since pronouns act as shorthand forms for already-introduced individuals. In linguistic terms, they require a previous antecedent noun phrase. However, a certain type of pronoun, the ›institutional they‹, is commonly used without an antecedent. ›Institutional they‹ pronouns generally refer to workers in work-related scenarios. This can be explained by the fact that there is no need for an antecedent since there is already a slot for the characters in the reader's mental representation when the scenario is set up. Hence, a building site would have slots for workmen, with the ›they‹ pronouns being mapped onto this role slot when they occur. Empirical investigations have shown that readers take no significant extra time to interpret an ›institutional they‹ pronoun without an antecedent in contrast to one with an antecedent, showing that institutional characters are implicit in the scenario.[9]

---

[7] Ibid., p. 77 (our emphasis).
[8] Rendell: Going, pp. 172–173 (our emphasis).
[9] Sanford / Filik / Emmott / Morrow: Digging.

Example 5

> This present building was being given the full works – gutted, new drainage system, rewiring. <u>They</u> were taking out the floor in the cellar to lay new drains and also because there seemed to be damp – certainly there was a fousty smell to the place – and its cause needed to be found.[10]

Points (i-iv) above show how scenario assumptions can be used to interpret specific linguistic forms, thereby making sense of narrative texts at the most basic level. Linguists sometimes refer to this as the process of establishing textual coherence, since texts would not read as coherent wholes without the reader making such fundamental assumptions.

Sanford and Garrod's work also has direct relevance to the study of different types of characters in narratives since they make a distinction between *principal characters* and *scenario-dependent characters*.[11] In longer narrative texts, principal characters can often be seen to move through various scenes, adopting different roles in different scenarios. So a particular individual might adopt the role of a student whilst attending a university lecture, then go shopping and adopt the role of a customer, then go to the doctor and adopt the role of a patient, then go home and adopt the role of a flatmate, then go to the theatre and adopt the role of a member of the audience. By contrast, a scenario-dependent character is presented in a narrative as being solely or primarily linked to a particular scenario, such as a waiter in a restaurant. The scenario-dependent character is a minor participant, performing relatively stereotypical actions in the scene, and is not presented as a fully developed personality. We might generally expect little plot involvement, but some stories will make use of scenario-dependent characters at key plot moments (e.g. a courier delivering a plot-significant parcel). This will be discussed further in Section 3(i).

Sanford and Garrod showed empirically that principal characters and scenario-dependent characters have different psychological statuses.[12] When there is an episode shift, such as a scene shift from a hairdresser's salon to a cinema, the experiments showed scenario-dependent characters to be less psychologically prominent and therefore less likely than the principal characters to be referred to by pronouns after the episode boundary. This suggests that the readers assume that principal characters will continue to take part in the action beyond the episode boundary, but that readers generally assume the scenario-dependent characters will be limited to specific roles in specific situations. Moreover, in cases where a

---

10 Rankin: Evidence, pp. 63–64 (our emphasis).
11 Sanford / Garrod: Understanding, pp. 145–153.
12 Ibid., pp. 146–150.

scenario-dependent character is referred to some time after the episode finished (e.g. in the memories of a principal character), Sanford and Garrod suggest that it would be appropriate to use a referring expression which recalls the scenario with it (e.g. ›the usherette at the cinema‹), possibly also with an indicator of the occasion, if there has been a delay (e.g. ›the usherette at the cinema he had visited last week‹).[13] We shall return to this point in Section 3(iii).

Sanford and Garrod's categorisation of characters goes beyond a binary distinction since characters can be made more or less prominent by adding additional descriptive information.[14] They demonstrate this empirically in relation to scenario-dependent characters, such as a ›teenage bus conductor‹ or a ›handsome waiter‹. In all such examples, any additional descriptive information is viewed as attached to the role slot as an *attribute*. Additional attributes foreground scenario-dependent characters in the consciousness of readers, as confirmed by Sanford and Garrod's experiments. The selective addition of attributes to scenario-dependent characters is discussed in Section 3(i-iii) in relation to plot manipulations.

2 Manipulative Rhetorical Strategies: Repairing Scenarios and Scenario Roles

Sanford and Garrod provide a model of the assumptions that readers make about scenarios and characters, as discussed in the previous section. Crucial to their work is the idea that assumptions about participants are made immediately a scenario is encountered. This observation relates not only to the scenario-dependent characters, but also to the principal characters as they adopt roles in particular situations. These assumptions are pragmatic judgements made on the basis of context. As such, they can be repaired if contrary information is encountered. Sanford and Garrod demonstrate this with the following example,[15] discussed in three parts:

Example 6(a), (b) and (c)

(a) John was on his way to school.
     He was terribly worried about the maths lesson.
(b) He thought he might not be able to control the class again today.

---

13 Ibid., p. 146.
14 Ibid., pp. 171–172.
15 Ibid., p. 114.

(c)   It was not a normal part of a janitor's duties.

When presented with (a), the readers in Sanford and Garrod's experiments set up a school scenario and most mapped John onto a schoolboy slot.[16] Although this was the most obvious assumption for the majority of readers, it is not the only possible one since John can, in principle, be anyone associated with a school scenario. When readers then read (b), the extra information caused most readers to change the mapping to assign John to a teacher's role. Then when they read (c), readers encountered the explicit mention of the janitor and were forced to change their assumptions again, assigning John to the role of a janitor acting in an unconventional role. One key aspect of the manipulation in Example 6 is that for such an unusual role, John is *under-specified* in (a) and (b). Roles do not need to be specified when they are the default option, but we would expect much greater specification in this case if the writer was discussing a less obvious option and was not manipulating our assumptions.

Although Example 6 is an example artificially constructed in Sanford and Garrod's psychology laboratory, it nevertheless bears a similarity to real text examples where the writer is being heavily manipulative. Example 7, from a popular science book about the brain, relies on replacing the whole scenario rather than just changing a specific individual's role.

Example 7

> Sarah was lying on her side, eyes shut. Slowly she started to stir, her body making restless, uncoordinated movements as she drifted back into consciousness. Her mouth was dry and she asked for a drink. Julie wiped her mouth with a medicated swab – it would be dangerous to allow someone to take in fluids during surgery. Julie was an anaesthetist; Sarah was lying <u>not in bed</u> but on an operating table. I was watching, for the first time in my life, brain surgery on a conscious patient.[17]

Here the author attempts to create a textual ›garden path‹ effect, where the reader is encouraged to make one interpretation, then this interpretation is withdrawn and the reader is directed down another path, hence possibly prompting a repair.[18] In Example 7, the first three and a half sentences (up to ›medicated swab‹) seem to suggest a hospital ward scene, where we might expect Sarah to be the patient, lying on a bed, with Julie being either a nurse or friend administering care. The details of where Sarah is lying and information about Julie's role are under-specified at this point. Normally, a name is viewed as providing more identifying detail than a

---

16 Ibid., pp. 114–115.
17 Greenfield: Brain, p. 11 (our emphasis).
18 See Jahn: Speak for a discussion of garden paths in narrative texts. Also see Emmott: Narrative regarding narrative repairs.

description, but in this case the use of the name withholds Julie's role and hence delays instantiation of the real scenario. Only at the end of the fourth sentence are we given the details of the actual scenario, ›during surgery‹, with a full explanation at the end of the final sentence that this is brain surgery and emphasis of Sarah's role (›a conscious patient‹). The negation (›not in bed‹) makes explicit that the writer has been hinting at another scenario. Whether or not the reader has actually constructed the ›patient in bed‹ scenario, the rhetorical strategy of assuming a scenario replacement emphasises that the ›surgery on a conscious patient‹ scenario is meant to surprise the reader.[19]

The above example is from a non-fiction text, but the same type of strategy of repair can be used in fictional writing. In fiction, false assumptions can be attributed to a focalizing character, then these assumptions may be repaired when the perspective of a character changes. In the example below, the main character, Inspector Rebus, visits a hospital on police business and observes the following scene through an open door:

Example 8(a)

> [...] <u>a bed</u>, a figure on the bed, staff milling around the various machines [...][20]

Subsequently, Rebus not only identifies the figure as his daughter and realises that she is badly injured, but also repairs his (and our) view of the scenario by negating his initial assumption about the bed:

Example 8(b)

> He was in the room now. They had a mask over her face, feeding her oxygen. Her forehead was cut and bruised, the hair pushed away from it. Her fingers were blistered, the palms scraped raw. <u>The bed she lay on wasn't really a bed</u> but a wide steel trolley.[21]

By this stage, we know that the injured girl is on a trolley because she is about to be taken for a brain scan. The shift in perspective achieved by the negation highlights the sudden shift in the principal character's role from an impartial policeman to an involved relative who notices every detail and is shocked by the severity of the patient's condition.

---

19 This passage is from the opening chapter of an introductory book about the brain, so assumes an implied reader (Iser: Act) who knows little about brain surgery. In fact, brain surgery is often carried out on conscious patients, so this may not be particularly surprising to the informed reader. Regardless, this rhetorical strategy conveys the sense of wonder of the author in relation to this operating technique.
20 Rankin: Garden, p. 18 (our emphasis).
21 Ibid., p. 19 (our emphasis).

This strategy of guiding the assumptions of readers by presenting the wrong assumptions of characters in the story, then counteracting the characters' assumptions, is also seen in Example 9.

Example 9

> Two policemen were sitting at the table. [...]
> You've got good neighbours, the younger one said. [...] The one downstairs. She was the one who phoned.
> Was it a fire? I said. There was no sign of it, no smell.
> The older one laughed. The other one didn't. No, he said. She heard footsteps up here and she knew it wasn't you, she saw you go out, and she didn't hear anyone go up the stairs. He jimmied open your kitchen window.
> I put the shopping basket on the table; then I went and looked at the window, which was open about two feet. The white paint was scratched.
> You could do it with a jackknife, he said. You should get those safety locks. He heard us coming and went back out through the window.
> Did he take anything? I said.
> You'll have to tell us that, said the older one.
> The young one looked uneasy. We don't think he was a burglar, he said. He made himself a cup of Ovaltine. He was just waiting for you, I guess. There was a cup on the table, half full of something light brown. I felt sick: someone I didn't know had been in my kitchen, opening my refrigerator and my cupboards [...] [The older policeman then shows the narrator a length of rope coiled on her bed].[22]

Here, the I-narrator works through two possible scenarios (fire, burglary) both of which are negated by the policemen, replacing these stereotypical scenarios with a more unusual one, the Ovaltine-drinking pervert. The reticence and unease of the police in explaining the real situation highlights the fact that this is perceived by them as odd behaviour and explains the principal character's shocked reaction. Generally, this technique can be used as a way of emphasising the surprising nature of a scenario, since default assumptions are dispensed with first, building up to a scenario which is evaluated as worse than the default scenarios by the characters. The assumption-making of the characters here also pushes the reader towards the stereotypical assumption that the intruder is male, even though there is nothing to suggest that anyone has actually seen the intruder. Although it is not plot-relevant in this particular story, the technique of allowing the characters to assume male gender for the criminal can be used in detective fiction to lead the reader away from suspecting a female criminal.

We have seen that like Sanford and Garrod (Example 6), the authors of Examples 7–9 use under-specification to mislead their readers. One difference is that Sanford and Garrod do not explicitly negate assump-

---

22 Atwood: Bodily Harm, pp. 12–13 (our emphasis).

tions that John is a schoolboy (6(a)) or that he is a school teacher (6(b)), whereas the writers of Examples 7–9 all negate initial role assignments of people or objects. In certain respects, the negation of the roles could be seen to be more manipulative, since the readers are forced to make a repair even if they had not previously made the assumption suggested, adding in the false information to their mental model, then replacing it. The negation can be viewed as a rhetorical device which directs the implied reader,[23] regardless of the reading strategy of the actual reader.

Sometimes a text may prompt readers to assumption-making about a role which is subsequently confirmed by the text, but on other occasions a text may push readers towards a role assignment which is never explicitly stated but without which an episode would make no sense. Example 10 uses both these strategies in representing scenario-dependent characters and the principal character. The background to this example is that the principal character, George, has been in the process of trying on a suit in a department store and has discovered a skin lesion. He reacts with horror and his mind is in the process of running through dreadful future possibilities when a voice breaks into his thoughts, as follows:

Example 10

›Sir ...? Would you mind accompanying me back into the store?‹
A young man of eighteen or thereabouts was staring down at George. He had ginger side-burns and a navy-blue uniform several sizes too large for him.
George realised that he was crouching on the tiled threshold outside the shop.
›Sir ...?‹
George got to his feet. ›I'm terribly sorry.‹
›Would you mind accompanying me ...?‹
George looked down and saw that he was still wearing the suit trousers with the fly undone.
He buttoned it rapidly. ›Of course.‹
He walked back through the doors then made his way between the handbags and the perfumes towards the menswear department with the security guard at his shoulder. ›I appear to have had some kind of turn.‹
›You'll have to discuss that with the manager, I'm afraid, sir.‹
[The security guard takes George to the manager]
›Perhaps we should have a word in my office,‹ said the manager.
A woman appeared carrying George's trousers. ›He left these in the changing room. His wallet's in the pocket.‹
George pressed on. ›I think I had some kind of blackout. I really didn't mean to cause any trouble.‹

---

23 Iser: Act.

[The woman subsequently asks George if he is all right, brings him a cup of tea and suggests calling him a taxi.]²⁴

We would expect competent readers who are utilising a department store scenario to be able to identify the unattributed voice as that of a security guard due to the nature of the request and also the official tone. The subsequent mention of the security guard allows the reader to map this explicit reference to a scenario-dependent character onto the role slot that has already been implicitly set up. By contrast, George's role changes without any subsequent narratorial comment. If the reader is to make any sense of the episode, the assumption has to be made that, in the eyes of other characters, he changes from an ordinary customer to a possible thief, then to a person who has been taken ill. Only if readers make these role assignments can they understand the security guard's insistent requests, ignoring George's claim that he has had ›some kind of turn‹, in contrast with the woman's acceptance that he has had ›some kind of blackout‹ and her subsequent sympathy. The turning-point here is not a negation, but, as in Sanford and Garrod's example in 6(b), information which is incompatible with the assumed role. In this case, it is difficult to imagine a thief leaving his wallet behind in the changing room, so, after the woman has announced this, George's suggested role of an unwell person carries more credibility than the thief role. This example requires the reader to hold a multiple perspective about George's role, since he does not see himself as a thief, although he does seem to be aware (judged by his explanations of his behaviour) of the fact that others temporarily view him in this way.

3 Plot Manipulations and Character Plot Status

Another way in which writers can manipulate our assumptions is to play on our expectations about the plot status of a particular character, i.e. the degree of involvement that a character has in the plot. Such manipulation is common in twist-in-the-tale, mystery and detective stories, where attention can be attracted away from a particular character by placing that character in a scenario-dependent role. Subsequently, the writer can surprise the reader by placing the character in a more central plot role than might have been anticipated (the stereotypical plot twist in detective stories is that ›the butler did it‹, since we are not supposed to suspect the butler). In this section, we examine three different ways in which writers can manipulate scenario-dependency.

---

24 Haddon: Spot, pp. 3–4 (Haddon's omission marks; our emphasis).

(i) Backgrounding and foregrounding a scenario-dependent character

Roald Dahl specialises in plot manipulations in his *Tales of the Unexpected*.[25] In his short story ›Taste‹,[26] which uses a dinner party scenario for its setting, Dahl initially plays down the role of the maid, placing her strictly in a scenario-dependent role, but bringing her into greater prominence later in the story. At the start of the story, the maid is not mentioned at all. She is not included in the initial list of characters (Example 11(a)) and her role in providing the first course is elided since the text does not specify that she serves the food (Example 11(b)).

Examples 11(a) and (b)

(a) There were six of us to dinner that night at Mike Schofield's house in London: Mike and his wife and daughter, my wife and I, and a man called Richard Pratt.[27]

(b) The meal began with a plate of whitebait, fried very crisp in butter, and to go with it there was a Moselle.[28]

After just over a page of description of the dinner party, the maid appears for the first time (Example 12(a) below) so at this point she is in explicit focus and can be mapped onto the scenario of the dinner party. The use of the definite article assumes that she is filling a specific slot in this scenario. No descriptive adjectives are used to provide extra information about her. The actions she performs here and in three other similar passages (12(b)-(d)) are the predictable ones for this scenario-dependent character, all concerning serving food and removing dishes.

Examples 12(a), (b), (c) and (d)

(a) We finished our fish, and <u>the maid</u> came round removing the plates. When she came to Pratt, she saw that he had not yet touched his food, so she hesitated, and Pratt noticed her. He waved her away [...][29]

(b) Soon <u>the maid</u> came forward with the second course. This was a large roast of beef. She placed it on the table in front of Mike who stood up and carved it, cutting the slices very thin, laying them gently on the plates for the maid to take around.[30]

---

25 See Emmott: Reading for a discussion of Dahl's work.
26 Dahl: Taste.
27 Ibid., p. 7.
28 Ibid., p. 8.
29 Ibid., p. 9 (our emphasis).
30 Ibid., p. 9 (our emphasis).

(c) I noticed <u>the maid</u> standing in the background holding a dish of vegetables, wondering whether to come forward with them or not.³¹

(d) I heard <u>the maid</u> put down the dish of vegetables on the sideboard behind me, gently, so as not to disturb the silence.³²

Nothing in the earlier text prepares us for the way in which Dahl suddenly pushes the maid into the spotlight at the climax of the story in Example 13 below. Her role in the plot is crucial because she provides key information which shows that one of the characters, Richard Pratt, has attempted to defraud her employer (Schofield) by cheating in a wine-tasting challenge that has occurred during the dinner party. She has found Pratt's spectacles next to where the wine bottle was stored, explaining how he has managed the supposedly impossible feat of guessing the origin of the extremely rare wine. This example shows the point at which she takes on this plot-crucial role.

Example 13

> Then this happened: <u>the maid, the tiny, erect figure of the maid in her white-and-black uniform</u>, was standing beside Richard Pratt, holding something out in her hand. ›I believe these are yours, sir,‹ she said.
> [The maid hands the spectacles to Pratt who is doubtful about whether they are his. The maid insists that they are.]
> [...] <u>The maid was an elderly woman – nearer seventy than sixty – a faithful family retainer of many years' standing</u>. [The maid places the spectacles on the table and Pratt puts them in his pocket without thanking her.]
> But <u>the maid</u> didn't go away. She remained standing beside and slightly behind Richard Pratt, and there was <u>something so unusual in her manner</u> and in the way she stood, <u>small, motionless and erect</u>, that I for one found myself watching her with sudden apprehension. <u>Her old grey face had a frosty, determined look, the lips were compressed, the little chin was out, and the hands were clasped together tight before her. The curious cap on her head and the flash of white down the front of her uniform made her seem like some tiny, ruffled, white-breasted bird.</u>
> ›You left them in Mr Schofield's study,‹ she said. <u>Her voice was unnaturally, deliberately polite</u>. ›On top of the green filing cabinet in his study, sir, when you happened to go in there by yourself before dinner.‹
> It took a few moments for the full meaning of her words to penetrate [...]³³

Specific features of the text may signal to the reader that this is a significant event. The phrase ›Then this happened‹ is a pre-announcement of the event and may be viewed as stylistically marked. There is also unusual repetition, ›the maid, the tiny, erect figure of the maid‹. The narrator's own reaction (›watching her with sudden apprehension‹) and the

---

31 Ibid., p. 12 (our emphasis).
32 Ibid., pp. 18–19 (our emphasis).
33 Ibid., p. 20 (our emphasis).

maid's odd behaviour (›something so unusual in her manner‹, ›Her voice was unnaturally, deliberately polite‹) signal that something out of the ordinary is happening. The amount of description of the maid at this late stage in the story is also unusual, since earlier references to her have been brief and heavily scenario-dependent. As discussed earlier, Sanford and Garrod's empirical work shows that adding additional description when referring to a scenario-dependent character foregrounds that character in the reader's consciousness.[34] This description also provides a positive evaluation of the maid as ›a faithful family retainer of many years' standing‹, which makes her word carry more weight in its implied accusation of Pratt and also makes her behaviour more plausible in terms of wishing to defend her employer's family.

Looking in hindsight at the references to the maid in Examples 12(a)-(d), there seems to be some strategic placing of these passages. In 12(c) and (d), the maid's presence is mentioned immediately before and after Pratt performs the act of fraudulently guessing the wine's origin, from which we might infer that she was an observer of the episode. A further point about the presentation of Examples 12(a)-(d) is that although the maid and her actions are described in a very stereotypical way, keeping her to a minimal scenario-dependent status, she may be more noticeable to us because of the repeated mentions of her and the fact that the principal focalising characters are aware of her, i.e. Pratt and the narrator noticing her in 12(a) and 12(c), and the narrator hearing her in 12(d). In its original context, the characters' awareness of the maid simply reflects the tension in the room in response to Pratt's behaviour, but in terms of plot development these references to her may make her sufficiently memorable that her sudden foregrounding in 13 is credible. Presumably Dahl does not want us to ask ›What maid?‹ at this point.

(ii) Concealing and revealing a character's additional roles

In the Roald Dahl story in the previous section, the maid becomes plot-prominent, but she is nevertheless still a scenario-dependent character, since at the end of the story she is still simply a maid. Another twist is for a scenario-dependent character to be revealed as having an additional major role or roles in the story, as illustrated by the following Agatha Christie short story, ›The Tuesday Night Club‹.[35] This is a domestic murder mystery which includes a scenario-dependent maid character who is later revealed to have two further roles in the story; she is both the lover of her married employer and the murderess of his wife.

---

34 Sanford / Garrod: Understanding.
35 Christie: Tuesday. For further discussion see Alexander: Cognitive-Linguistic.

As in the Dahl story (Example 11(a)), the maid is not included in the initial character list, only the three principal characters being mentioned and identified:

Example 14

›The facts are very simple. <u>Three people</u> sat down to a supper consisting, amongst other things, of tinned lobster. Later in the night, all three were taken ill, and a doctor was hastily summoned. Two of the people recovered, the third one died.‹
[...]
›And now I must describe <u>the actors in this little drama</u>. I will call the husband and wife Mr and Mrs Jones, and the wife's companion Miss Clark [...]‹[36]

Also, the maid's role in preparing and serving the food is initially elided in the discussion of the meal, in Example 15, as was the case with the maid at the start of the Dahl story (Example 11(b)).[37]

Example 15

›[...]Supper that night had consisted of tinned lobster and salad, trifle and bread and cheese.[...]‹[38]

When the maid first appears in explicit focus, the mention of her is embedded within a discussion of the lobster,[39] which is initially suspected of being the source of the poisoning, but later discounted as a ›red herring‹.

Example 16

›[...]Unfortunately none of the lobster remained – it had all been eaten and the tin thrown away. [The police officer] had interrogated <u>the young maid, Gladys Linch</u>. She <u>was terribly upset, very tearful and agitated</u>, and he found it hard to get her to keep to the point, but she declared again and again that the tin had not been distended in any way and that the lobster had appeared to her in a perfectly good condition.[...]‹[40]

---

36 Ibid., pp. 7–8 (our emphasis).
37 Even after the maid has first been introduced (Example 16), her role in serving the meal is elided and embedded in a point about Mr Jones: »[...] Jones himself had returned from Birmingham just as supper was being brought in to table, so that he would have had no opportunity of doctoring any of the food beforehand.« (Ibid., p. 10.)
38 Ibid.
39 Psychological studies show that embedding can produce ›shallow depth of processing‹, where information is given less attention than if unembedded. (For a summary of this type of work, see Sanford / Sturt: Depth.)
40 Christie: Tuesday, p. 10 (our emphasis).

Some extra attributes of the maid – her youth, distress, and agitation – are provided. These are consistent with her scenario-dependent role in this exceptional situation, a maid being interrogated about possible lethal negligence in preparing food, but there is no suggestion that she has a more prominent role in the story. These extra attributes may nonetheless serve to make her more memorable, in preparation for the dénouement, without, at this stage, taking her beyond her role as maid.

The maid, Gladys Linch, is mentioned again in relation to another item consumed that evening, a bowl of cornflour (an indigestion remedy) which she prepared:

Example 17

> ›After supper on that evening Mr Jones had gone down to the kitchen and had demanded a bowl of cornflour for his wife who had complained of not feeling well. He had waited in the kitchen until <u>Gladys Linch prepared it</u>, and then carried it up to his wife's room himself […]‹[41]

Here Gladys Linch's action is presented as consistent with her scenario-dependent role, as a maid providing food. Although the cornflour is suspected of being poisoned, the suspicion falls on Mr Jones not Linch, and it later transpires that this is another ›red herring‹ since the dead woman did not eat it. At this point, Linch is referred to again, viewed entirely within her normal scenario-dependent role.

Example 18

> ›[…]<u>Gladys is really quite a nice cook</u>. Very few girls nowadays seem to be able to make a bowl of cornflour nicely […]‹[42]

Gladys Linch is not mentioned again until the story's conclusion, where Miss Marple guesses the solution, which is as follows:

Example 19(a) and (b)

(a) ›This story made me think of him at once,‹ said Miss Marple. ›The facts are so very alike, aren't they? I suppose <u>the poor girl</u> has confessed now and that is how you know, Sir Henry.‹
›What <u>girl</u>?‹ said Raymond. ›My dear Aunt, what *are* you talking about?‹
›<u>That poor girl, Gladys Linch</u>, of course – the one who was <u>so terribly agitated</u> when the doctor spoke to her – <u>and well she might be, poor thing</u>. I hope that

---

41 Ibid., p. 11 (our emphasis).
42 Ibid. (our emphasis).

wicked Jones is hanged, I am sure, making <u>that poor girl</u> a murderess. I suppose they will hang her too, <u>poor thing</u>.‹[43]

(b)   ›[...]Jones had got <u>Gladys Linch</u> into trouble, as the saying goes. She was nearly desperate. He wanted his wife out of the way and promised to marry <u>Gladys</u> when his wife was dead. He doctored the hundreds and thousands [poisoned sugar strands placed on the trifle] and gave them to her with instructions how to use them. <u>Gladys Linch</u> died a week ago. Her child died at birth and Jones had deserted her for another woman. When she was dying she confessed the truth.‹[44]

This is the point at which Gladys Linch's other roles are revealed. She is no longer referred to in her scenario-dependent role as ›the maid‹, but described using the repeated phrases ›(poor) girl‹, ›poor thing‹ and her name, as we learn that she is a murderess and was Mr Jones's lover. Possibly the fact that she has previously been named may make it easier to ›upgrade‹ her to a main character at this stage (Dahl's maid, by contrast, remains scenario-dependent and is never named). We learn here that the poisoning was due to the decoration on the trifle, making it more significant that, in Example 15, she was not explicitly mentioned as serving the trifle, but rather was associated, in Examples 16 and 17, with the two items of food that were later discounted as ›red herrings‹.

During the final disclosure, as shown below, Agatha Christie plays on the double roles of the maid, juxtaposing the stereotypical ›little maid‹ with a description which is more suggestive of her role as lover, ›a pretty young girl‹, particularly since Mr Jones has a history of this type of affair (he has had a previous relationship with a local doctor's daughter and has ›a partiality for the society of women‹).[45]

Example 20

›[...] I can't think how on earth you managed to hit upon the truth. I should never have thought of <u>the little maid in the kitchen</u> being connected with the case.‹
›No, dear,‹ said Miss Marple, ›but you don't know as much of life as I do. A man of that Jones's type – coarse and jovial. As soon as I heard there was <u>a pretty young girl in the house</u> I felt sure that he would not have left her alone [...].‹[46]

Agatha Christie's handling of the attributes of the maid is heavily manipulative in this story. The maid's agitation in Example 16 is now re-evaluated in Example 19(a) (›and well she might be‹) as that of a possible murderess. In Example 20 there is a contrast in the presentation of her ›in the kitchen‹ as opposed to ›in the house‹, where she would have been

---

43   Ibid., p. 15 (Christie's italics, our added emphasis).
44   Ibid., p. 16 (our emphasis).
45   Ibid., p. 9.
46   Ibid., p. 16 (our emphasis).

more accessible to Mr Jones. Also, Example 20 provides the first occasion that we learn that the maid was pretty, a description which might have prompted suspicion about the possibility of an affair if presented earlier.

(iii) Concealing and revealing a character's real identity

In the above Agatha Christie story, the maid is both genuinely scenario-dependent, in terms of working as a maid, and also secretly has additional roles as Mr Jones's lover and his wife's murderess. Another possible manipulation is for the scenario-dependent role to be false and for the character to have a different identity as a major character in the story. Louise Welsh uses this technique in her novel *The Cutting Room*.[47] The gardener in a house visited by the narrator is presented first in his scenario-dependent role. He is in the garden helping to clear the possessions of Mr McKindless, the brother of the current owner of the house, Miss McKindless. Mr McKindless has supposedly died recently.

Example 21

> A smell of burning drifted in from the garden. I walked to the door and looked out onto a well tended lawn at the end of which burnt a bonfire. <u>A gnomic gardener</u> jabbed at the flames with a long rake. He caught my stare and raised his free hand in a half-defensive wave, like a man staving off a blow. He lowered his cap over his eyes and fed papers from a black refuse sack into the flames.[48]

The gardener is portrayed here as someone who is no threat to the narrator. By the end of the story, however, the reader will find that the gardener is actually the supposedly dead Mr McKindless, who is the evil controller of a brutal hard core pornography business. The logistical problem for the author of the book is to bring the gardener sufficiently into the forefront of the reader's attention that the reader does not forget about him entirely during the course of the novel, to provide enough information about him to make the real identity credible when it is revealed, but not to alert the reader to his real identity ahead of the dénouement. The descriptive information in Example 21 ('gnomic', 'half-defensive', 'like a man staving off a blow') adds extra attributes which, according to Sanford and Garrod's empirical work, should make the character more memorable than just the phrase 'A gardener' alone. Subsequently, there is an episode in the middle of the book in which the narrator meets the gardener for a second time. When Miss McKindless

---

47 Welsh: Cutting.
48 Ibid., pp. 4–5 (our emphasis).

becomes seriously ill, the narrator visits her in hospital and, whilst there, sees the gardener, who has also been visiting her.

Example 22

> I reached the ward and held the door open for a departing visitor. The shambling figure was vaguely familiar. A shrunken old man, shabby cap pulled low, dark suit that had seen better days – some time around the 1940s, judging from the cut. He was struggling with an old-fashioned cardboard case. It took me a second to place him, then I recognised <u>the gardener glimpsed at the McKindless house on my first visit</u> [...]
> He looked confused and I felt sorry for him, wondered how many friends he had visited in hospital, how many funerals he had attended, each one bringing his own closer. I held out my hand. He gave it a weak shake.
> ›Grieve, Mr Grieve. I did the garden.‹ [...]
> His accent came from another era. A less complicated time.
> [Conversation between the narrator and Grieve, including discussion of Grieve's retirement.]
> He looked well past retirement. Withered and benevolent, almost as old as Miss McKindless.
> ›Aye, though to be honest it's not entirely voluntary.‹
> His tenacity was admirable.
> ›Time to concentrate on your own garden, perhaps?‹
> ›My gardening days are over. I'm retiring in style. There's a wee nest egg coming to me, then I'm away to the sun. This climate's no good for old bones.‹ [...]
> I helped him to a taxi, admiring his strength of character, hoping his nest egg would come through [...]⁴⁹

In certain respects this passage is similar to Dahl's Example 13 since it provides much more detailed information about a scenario-dependent character at a late stage in the story. It does not, however, have any obvious plot-significance when read in context, other than to keep the character in our minds for later.

When introduced here, the form of the reference, ›the gardener glimpsed at the McKindless house on my first visit‹, reflects Sanford and Garrod's predictions that scenario-dependent characters will normally be re-introduced by a specific mention of the originating scenario. We would expect the amount of description and direct discourse in this episode to increase the prominence of the character. The fact that the character is now outside his main scenario is explicable in terms of the story (an employee visiting his employer in hospital), but nevertheless stretches the scenario-dependent role to its limits. The naming of the gardener as Grieve and the personal angle provided by the conversation with the narrator also appears to raise his profile. Unlike Dahl's Example 13, this passage does not have the foregrounding devices that signal plot-

---

49   Ibid., pp. 198–199 (our emphasis).

significance, since the writer is aiming not to alert our suspicions here. Also, the character seems to be exiting from the story at this point, so may not be part of the reader's mentally-represented listing of characters who are likely to reappear again.[50] The author provides the information about age which will make the gardener's real identity plausible (Mr McKindless was old and frail), but the narrator's highly subjective assessment of the gardener (weak but brave) acts as a sleight of hand which detracts attention from any link at this stage with McKindless. Only at the dénouement many pages later (Example 23) is the link made between the evil McKindless and Grieve, in the context of a scene of corruption and the narrator's revulsion at his body.

Example 23

> The body looked small in death. [...] There was a glimpse of entrail, a smell of corruption and decay. [...] [Anne-Marie] trembled towards me. [...] There was a bright flash [from a police photographer's camera] and Mr McKindless, the man I knew as Grieve, was captured for ever.[51]

Overall, this story and the previous stories discussed in this section raise interesting issues that might be used to develop Sanford and Garrod's psychological model in the future. The original model simply assumes that additional attributes increase prominence, but makes no distinction between adding information to make a character more memorable (e.g. in readiness for a surprise ending) and foregrounding/backgrounding the plot-relevance of a character or other related information about a character.

4 Conclusion

The Scenario Mapping and Focus model is a recognised account of text processing in Psychology, since it is based on empirical evidence of how readers form mental representations of situations and make assumptions whilst reading. In this article, our main aim has been to see how this model, originally tested on laboratory-created materials, might be used to explain real narrative examples. We saw in Section 1 that Sanford and Garrod's experiments provide evidence that assumption-making is a natural part of reading. The linguistic features discussed in Section 1 are extremely common. Often the assumptions needed to interpret them will

---

50 See Emmott: Narrative for the notion of a ›central directory‹ of characters.
51 Welsh: Cutting, p. 276.

not play any special rhetorical or plot role, but they will nevertheless allow readers to make sense of narrative texts at a basic level. Writers clearly expect readers to fill in missing information and assign roles to characters.

Generally, the assumptions required are the most obvious ones, but Section 2 showed that writers can deliberately under-specify information about characters for manipulative rhetorical purposes. Sanford and Garrod's empirical testing shows that assumptions are generally made ›up front‹, hence necessitating subsequent repairs in cases where the role of the character is not the most obvious one. Writers of narratives use similar ›garden path‹ strategies and the assumption-making of readers is often guided by the assumption-making of characters and/or explicit negation.

Section 3 explored assumption-making in relation to plot status. We drew on Sanford and Garrod's ideas about the psychological prominence of characters, particularly the notion of scenario-dependency, and we utilised Sanford and Garrod's empirical findings about how additional attributes can raise the prominence of a minor character. The Scenario Mapping and Focus model has not previously been discussed in relation to full-length texts and hence there is a degree of speculation involved in suggesting how laboratory results might apply to such texts. Regardless of how readers actually interpret these texts, the writers in Section 3 do appear to be attempting to manipulate readers' assumptions by strategically backgrounding characters in scenario-dependent roles and providing late information about the attributes of these characters in order to subsequently raise their plot status.

Overall, we have found that Sanford and Garrod's psychological model is useful for explaining textual coherence in real narrative texts and is suggestive about how readers might respond to special manipulative references to characters for rhetorical and plot purposes.[52] The interdisciplinary research in this article shows how these empirically-tested psychological tools can be utilised in Humanities research, and the stylistic and narratological analysis provides fresh ideas about the process of reading by examining narrative texts which are significantly longer and more complex than usual psychology materials.

Acknowledgement

The authors are grateful to the Arts and Humanities Research Council for funding for this work, which was conducted as part of the *STACS* Project

---

[52] See also Emmott / Alexander: Detective for a discussion of reader manipulation in Agatha Christie's *Sparkling Cyanide*.

(Stylistics, Text Analysis and Cognitive Science: Interdisciplinary Perspectives on the Nature of Reading).

References

Alexander, Marc: Cognitive-Linguistic Manipulation and Persuasion in Agatha Christie. University of Glasgow: M.Phil. thesis 2006.

Anderson, Ann / Simon C. Garrod / Anthony J. Sanford: The Accessibility of Pronominal Antecedents as a Function of Episode Shifts. In: The Quarterly Journal of Experimental Psychology 35 (1983), pp. 427–440.

Atwood, Margaret: Bodily Harm. London 1996.

Christie, Agatha: The Tuesday Night Club. In: Agatha Christie: Miss Marple: The Complete Short Stories. London 1997, pp. 3–16.

Dahl, Roald: Taste. In: Roald Dahl: Tales of the Unexpected. Harmondsworth 1979, pp. 7–21.

Dean, Louise: Becoming Strangers. London 2004.

Emmott, Catherine: Narrative Comprehension: A Discourse Perspective. Oxford 1997.

Emmott, Catherine: Reading for Pleasure: A Cognitive Poetic Analysis of »Twists in the Tale« and Other Plot Reversals in Narrative Texts. In: Joanna Gavins / Gerard Steen (Eds.): Cognitive Poetics in Practice. London 2003, pp. 145–159.

Emmott, Catherine / Marc Alexander: Schemata. In: Peter Hühn / John Pier / Wolf Schmid / Jörg Schönert (Eds.): Handbook of Narratology. Berlin 2009, pp. 411–419.

Emmott, Catherine / Marc Alexander: Detective Fiction, Plot Construction, and Reader Manipulation: Rhetorical Control and Cognitive Misdirection in Agatha Christie's *Sparkling Cyanide*. In: Dan McIntyre / Beatrix Busse (Eds.): Language and Style. Basingstoke 2010.

Greenfield, Susan: Brain Story. London 2000.

Haddon, Mark: A Spot of Bother. London 2007.

Iser, Wolfgang: The Act of Reading: A Theory of Aesthetic Response. London 1978.

Jahn, Manfred: Speak, Friend, and Enter: Garden Paths, Artificial Intelligence and Cognitive Narratology. In: David Herman (Ed.): Narratologies. Columbus 1999, pp. 167–194.

Minsky, Marvin: A Framework for Representing Knowledge. In: Patrick H. Winston / Berthold Horn (Eds.): The Psychology of Computer Vision. New York 1975, pp. 211–277.

Rankin, Ian: Concrete Evidence. In: Ian Rankin: A Good Hanging and Other Stories. London 1998, pp. 63–85.

Rankin, Ian: The Hanging Garden. London 1998.

Rendell, Ruth: Going Wrong. London 1990.

Sanford, Anthony J. / Ruth Filik / Catherine Emmott / Lorna I. Morrow: They're Digging up the Road again: The Processing Cost of Institutional They. In: The Quarterly Journal of Experimental Psychology 61/3 (2007), pp. 372–380.

Sanford, Anthony J. / Simon C. Garrod: Understanding Written Language: Explorations in Comprehension beyond the Sentence. Chichester 1981.

Sanford, Anthony, J. / Simon C. Garrod: The Role of Scenario Mapping in Text Comprehension. In: Discourse Processes 26/2–3 (1998), pp. 159–190.

Sanford, Anthony J. / Patrick Sturt: Depth of Processing in Language Comprehension: Not Noticing the Evidence. In: Trends in Cognitive Sciences 6 (2002), pp. 382–386.

Schank, Roger C. / Robert P Abelson: Scripts, Plans, Goals and Understanding: An Enquiry into Human Knowledge Structures. Hillsdale, NJ 1977.
Shreve, Anita: Where or When. London 1993.
Stockwell, Peter: Schema Theory: Stylistic Applications. In: Keith Brown (Ed.): Encyclopedia of Language and Linguistics 11. 2nd edn. Oxford 2006, pp. 68–73.
Welsh, Louise: The Cutting Room. Edinburgh 2002.

Uri Margolin

From Predicates to People like Us
Kinds of Readerly Engagement with Literary Characters

That there are many kinds and degrees of readerly engagement with the worlds projected by works of fiction, and especially with the characters that inhabit them, is a truth universally acknowledged. The literary scholar's task is to define the various kinds of cognitive mechanisms activated when we are thus engaged, relate them to one another according to some general principles (hierarchy, causality, logical priority, sequence) and hopefully come up with a comprehensive map of these activities. Describing one or more kinds of engagement with characters has long been a staple activity of authors, critics, literary scholars, and cognitive and empirical psychologists of all stripes. Two very similar comprehensive maps of these activities have been proposed in recent scholarship by James Phelan and by Jens Eder. Phelan proposes a map consisting of three major kinds of engagement: mimetic, thematic and formal.[1] Eder proposes four such kinds which he terms diegetic, thematic, aesthetic, and pragmatic.[2] In the diegetic mode the character is conceived of as a fictive being, a component of a represented world. In the thematic it functions as a symbol, an individual who stands for or embodies some general concept, abstract theme or idea. In the aesthetic mode the character is an artifact, a constructed object and the main issue involves the ›how‹ aspect, the ways and means by which this character is portrayed or represented. The pragmatic dimension involves the communicative contexts of character creation on the one hand and its reception and use by readers on the other. Notice though that Eder's four dimensions can be reduced to three, in that the diegetic and thematic are both of a semantic nature, involving

---

1   Phelan: People.
2   Eder: Figur.

the ›what‹ side of narrative: hence issues of meaning, truth and reference. The two cannot however be collapsed into each other completely, since statements about characters as individuals in a textually created world can be made both inside this world by narrators and characters and outside it by readers. Claims about the thematic significance of characters on the other hand originate only with agents who are outside the projected world and who treat this world as an artifact. In this essay I am going to set aside the formal or aesthetic dimension and concentrate on the semantic and pragmatic ones. It is precisely in these two areas that analytic philosophers have recently joined the literary group and have come up with some very productive insights regarding the semantic and pragmatic aspects of the activities of the imagination involved in consuming fiction. I will utilize these recent insights, together with a reformulated version of Eder's model and some claims of structuralist literary theory, in order to propose a systematic map of these kinds of engagement.

Surprising as it may seem at first glance, the *fil conducteur* I found most useful for drawing my map comes from medieval philosophy and its distinction of *de sensu, de dicto, de re* and *de se* modes. *De sensu* mode means we are dealing with the senses or meanings of *expressions*. *De dicto* means dealing with the *content or intensions (meanings, senses) of propositions* which in their turn are conveyed by expressions related to one another in some formal logical ways. In the *de re* mode we are concerned with the *truth value* of the claims made by propositions, and with the corresponding *states of affairs and individuals* described by them, hence with references or extensions as well. Finally, in the *de se* mode the *claims, individuals, and states of affairs* projected by the propositions are related to the cogniser's own corresponding mental attitudes, activities and experiences, such as beliefs, desires, and intentions, and to his emotions and actions in the actual world.

1 Characters as Semantic Items

As one can see, the *de sensu* mode is the most basic, but also the minimal one. In it the text is seen as basically a network of lexical features, semantic traits and the like. In Greimassian semantics these would be the semes, classemes, and resultant textual isotopies. Questions of truth and reference or of fictional universes are not part of this mode of engagement, and this minimalist, reductionist way of reading character is of course non mimetic and non illusionist as well. This way of engaging with characters has been advocated by the Russian Formalists and French structuralists of the 60s and 70s. Characters are accordingly nothing but

Mensen van papier,³ bundles of traits or features identified by a tag such as a proper name, pronoun or definite description. We can think of them as a collection of information items compiled from the text by the reader and stored in a common named file. It is indeed Roland Barthes who argued that whenever a collection of adjectives is crossed by a proper name a character is born.⁴ Within Barthes' anti illusionist aesthetics, there is no personnage or reel, only the linguistically created *l'effet personnage* and *l'effet du reel*. Says Barthes (*S/Z* XXVIII):

> When identical semes cross the same proper name several times and seem to affix themselves to it, a *character* is born. Character is a combinatory product which is relatively stable (marked by the repetition of semes) and more or less complex (including traits that are more or less congruent, more or less contradictory). This complexity defines the ›personality‹ of the character. The proper name functions as attractor or magnet of the semes. The literary *figure* is not a combination of semes fixed by a name and has no biography, psychology or time. It is an impersonal, atemporal configuration of symbolic relations.⁵

And in *S/Z* XLI: »A figure is an impersonal network of symbols under a particular proper name. The proper name allows us to substitute a nominal unit for a collection of traits«.⁶

For Mieke Bal, a character is the point of intersection of numerous semantic axes, and different characters in the same text can be compared to one another in a relative contrastive way according to the positions they occupy on shared axes such as wisdom vs. stupidity, courage vs. cowardice, poverty vs. wealth and so on.⁷

The Russian Formalist Boris Tomashevsky treats characters in his textbook as a bundle of motives, or one of the ways in which the overriding themes of the work are embodied or manifested (other ways could be events and situations, settings and so on.). »A work has an overall theme which unites the separate elements of the work and which specifies into a system of motifs«.⁸ »The hero (=character) is a device for grouping and stringing together motifs, a living embodiment of a given collection of motifs«.⁹ Individual destinies are accordingly just particular versions of general problems, such as what makes for happiness in marriage. And the same is true of Alexander Zholkovski, for whom a

---

3   Bal: Mensen.
4   Barthes: S/Z.
5   Ibid., Chapter XXVIII: ›Personnage et figure‹, pp. 174–175; transl. by U.M.
6   Ibid., Chapter XLI: ›Le nom propre‹, p. 197; transl. by U.M.
7   Bal: Mensen.
8   Tomashevsky: Thematics, p. 62.
9   Ibid, pp. 87–88.

character is one of the expressive devices enabling the textual manifestation of a theme.[10] Clearly, this is also the preferred mode of engagement with character for any ideological and allegorical modes of textual processing, where the character is considered as an embodiment, instantiation or exemplification of some abstract quality, as an individual encoding of a universal.

In purely technical terms, one could say that character is conceived of in this context as a collection of abstract predicates, attributes or intensions held together by an individual constant, i.e., a proper name, but with no specific claim being made and no quantification, hence no existence claim. It is like having a bunch of associated nominal phrases but no sentences to go with them.

Within fiction writing itself, this concept of character can be encountered in its most extreme form in works of the French experimental groups Tel Quel and Oulipo. Here narrativity is reduced to sheer textuality, to games of alternative combinations of names and adjectives, or even to playing with alternative versions of the same name (Jabes: Yael, Elya, Aely),[11] with the name being regarded as a purely phonetic or graphic independent unit and not even as a stable label of an information file, let alone as a referring expression, or a unique identifier of an individual entity, the way it functions in representational contexts.

2 Characters as Objects of Thought

In the *de dicto* mode we are basically entertaining in thought, considering, pondering or playing with propositions like ›Sherlock Holmes lived in London‹ or ›Anna Karenina was unhappy in her marriage‹, without asserting or affirming them. We are considering the possibility that such and such might be the case, but do not yet affirm that it is so. In strictly logical terms we are saying ›it is possible that there was an individual called Holmes and that this individual lived in London‹, but that's all. The statement ›Sherlock Holmes lived in London‹ is treated here as an open sentence, a complex expression to which no truth value is attributed, and the singular term ›Sherlock Holmes‹ is not taken to actually designate or refer to some particular individual. We are as yet not making existence claims for any domain with respect to either the general property of living in London or being unhappy in one's marriage or the individual entity

---

10 Zholkovsky: Themes, pp. 275; 278.
11 Jabes: Livre.

(Holmes, Karenina). In traditional terms, we are speaking formally, about propositions, and not materially about states of affairs.

We would certainly agree that all mental engagement with fiction beyond the purely lexical, *de sensu* mode, involves the imagination. According to Alvin Goldman the minimal sense in which consuming fiction involves the imagination is the mental act of supposition: a purely conceptual act in which we are invited to suppose or entertain the hypothesis that P (that there was a man called Holmes and that he lived in London etc.), to play in our mind one particular scenario out of the many conceivable ones.[12] The reader here is precisely the agent who, on the basis of textual information, ponders the potential individuals and states of affairs alluded to in the given text. The proper name of the character is now not a label on a file, but rather an individual constant serving as the subject of predications, and the character himself is now *a conceivable* or possible *individual entity*, textually invoked and sustained, the product of someone else's imagination as encoded in the text we are reading. A useful analogy is that of some person of whom we know second or third hand. We have no direct acquaintance with this individual and are not ready to vouch that he exists or that he is thus and so. All we know is that s/he may exist and be so, based on a given source. A very similar view has been put forth by Pirandello both in *Six Characters in Search of an Author* and in a short story entitled *Character in Distress*. In both of them the initial assumption is that there exists, eternally and independently of any human mind, a vast, possibly infinite collection of properties, general abstract entities expressed by logical predicates. Each particular selection of such properties (property cluster) provides an opening which may be potentially filled by an individual entity, in our case a literary character. In the *de dicto* mode we are accordingly pondering particular such selections and individual fillings or instantiations but without yet claiming that they do exist in some domain. Such possible individual fillings cannot hence be as yet – at least in the case of verbal narratives – objects of any further imaginative levels of engagement such as visualization, sympathy, identification or the like. The text as a whole is at this stage a set of interconnected propositions, and the main issue is not which of them are true and which not, but rather what they logically imply and how they relate to one another logically or formally, especially as regards consistency and implication. For example, if the text says at one point that Holmes lived in London all his life and at another point that he first got there as a teenager, we are at this stage not concerned with which of them

---

12 Goldman: Imagination, p. 41.

is true, since there may not even be any Holmes to begin with. We just notice this (local) internal inconsistency. Coherence and consistency, not correspondence, are the truth criteria employed in this context.

It is interesting to note that a lot of literary interpretation and commentary is or at least can stay on the *de dicto* level. Many interpretative claims need only be guided by the rules of valid inference from text to meta text, with no existence assumptions needed. Thus: In the Holmes stories it says that p, therefore we can infer q. Intertextual comparatist studies are also of this nature, since in them we compare the different versions of say, Faust or Quixote, according to different texts, but without any existence claims or world construction operations, not even within a game of the imagination.

Literary examples of *de dicto* mode of engagement with characters abound in self disclosing narrative from Cervantes to postmodernism. In all such cases, the primary highest level narrator is portrayed as an author in the process of creating or inventing a character, asking himself questions such as what name should I give him/her, should I make him like this or like that, should I make event A and B or rather C and D befall him and so on. The author is thus running in his mind various alternative scenarios without an existential commitment to any of them, in fact reminding us that in the strict sense all fictions are just intensions without extension, scenarios without actualization in the real world. Obviously no mimetic illusion and no fictional world are provided by the *de dicto* mode of textual engagement, but since they involve first order propositions (that is, individual predications) they provide the semantic basis or potential for both illusion and fictional world, once existence and reference claims are added, once we move from the imagining of propositions involving individuals to the imagining of supposedly actual individuals that are (possibly) thus and so.[13]

3 Characters as Existents in Worlds

The *de re* mode of imaginative engagement with fictional characters assumes or posits (Setzung) that there is indeed a domain of verification or a world in which the individuals textually designated by proper names exist and are at least possibly thus and so. The positing in question may in principle be ›serious‹, as when claims about actuality are involved, or ludic, make-believe, purely hypothetical (let us assume *pro tempore/* for the sake

---

13 Alward: Engagement, p. 451.

of the argument that …), as when works of fiction or imagined alternative histories are concerned. Strictly ›one-world‹ philosophers may refuse in principle to engage in any such mental exercises, but in so doing they block any further discussion of a literary work except on the aesthetic level. And this is a heavy price to pay, especially as it runs counter to what millions of readers are doing all the time. If in the *de dicto* we said ›there is possibly in some domain an individual who is designated by the given individual referring expression and who is thus and so‹, now we say *there is* such an individual, and he is possibly thus and so. We are making here a crucial existential jump, in that we are now ready to make an existential commitment, to speak in the material mode of the existence of domains inhabited by the textually named individuals. According to Marie-Laure Ryan,[14] a story is a representation, a mental image, a cognitive construct that concerns certain types of entities and the relations between them. Narrative must be about a world populated by individuated existents. This world must be situated in time and undergo significant transformations. Some of the participants in the events must be intelligent agents who have a mental life and react emotionally to the states of the world. Some of the events must be purposeful actions by these agents, motivated by identifiable goals and plans.[15] In other words, we cannot fully engage with a character until we have in our minds not just propositions, but the mental construct or representation of a world and individuated entities existing in it.

Textual propositions are now not just expressed but affirmed, and are hence true or false with respect to individuals in these domains. Individual constants refer or do not refer, that is, pick out individuals in such a domain or fail to do so, and the truth of propositions is now determined by their correspondence to states of affairs in the domain in question. In Alvin Goldman's terms we are now at the stage of enactment imagination, where sensory data or particulars of time and space are an inseparable part of our imaginative activity, since a world cannot be conceived without such data.[16] According to Goldman, such imaginatively created perception-like states are similar in kind or are facsimiles of states produced by actual perceptual experiences. This is the realm of illusion creating or representational perception of verbal art. One is in fact making the tacit assumptions that the states of affairs referred to by the textual propositions exist *independently* of these propositions, that the text as a

---

14 Ryan: Avatars.
15 Ibid., pp. 7–8.
16 Goldman: Imagination, p. 42.

whole is a true, partially true or false *report* about this domain, and that the characters who are the inhabitants of this domain actually and independently embody at least some of the properties and relations textually attributed to them. The proper names of characters, too, are no longer labels on files: they are fully fledged referring expressions. As readers, we are supposed sometimes to observe in our mind's eye what is happening in the domain in question and on other occasions to be provided with summary reports of events and states in it. While in the *de dicto* mode literary criticism was concerned with comparing the contents of textual claims within a text or between texts, now it undertakes to describe in detail the textually projected domain itself, its governing regularities, the kinds of entities inhabiting it, their properties, relations, mode of action and interaction. Any analysis by a literary scholar regarding the personality, beliefs, intentions, wishes and modes of behaviour of an individual character in one text is of this nature, and analogous descriptions can be undertaken with respect to groups of narratives whose domains share underlying regularities and kinds of entities (realistic novel, science fiction, chivalric romance etc).

The transition from the *de dicto* to the *de re* mode thus enables us to undertake the full range of the operations of concretization described by Ingarden. In the *de dicto* stage we could just draw logically valid inferences from textually given propositions, thereby closing textual information *gaps*. Once we make the existential commitment to individuals in a world, we can proceed to flesh out these individuals much further by ascribing to them numerous additional properties or features which are neither explicitly ascribed to them by textual propositions nor inferable from these propositions, but merely compatible with them. In this way we are able to fill in some of the text's informational *blanks* (Ingarden's Unbestimmtheitsstellen). And such filling in need not be arbitrary, random or unrestricted, as it is normally guided and circumscribed by the textually pertinent model(s) of actuality and/or the relevant type of fictional story world.[17]

How are we to understand such imaginary text-projected domains and a cognitive behaviour with respect to them which grants them, at least temporarily, independent existence? This is the question underlying all theories of fictionality and of fictional worlds, and such a general theory is actually presupposed by any theory about *de re* approaches to fictional characters. Now this is obviously a whole area in philosophy and in literary theory, and what I can do here is only summarise very briefly the

---

17   Ingarden: Kunstwerk, pp. 262–270, esp. 268.

current views on the subject. One extreme view, which we may term the *ontological* view, was espoused by the late philosopher David Lewis in his book *On the Plurality of Worlds*. Based on a complex philosophical argument, he claims that there are in fact many equally actual worlds, not just the one accessible to us.[18] On this view, each work of narrative imagination, insofar as it is by and large consistent, could be conceived of as a partial description of such a world, and we could measure how different from or similar it is to what we consider our world to be. A *logical* approach would liken the creation or positing of a fictional world to the mathematical or logical act of positing or system creation, whereby the mathematician carries out a performative speech act in which he says: let there be a domain D, and let there be in it individuals a, b, c, such that the following properties and relations obtain. A small world is thus freely evoked by the human mind and, once evoked, can be the object of further elaboration. Moreover, both the domain and the elements it contains are open to a variety of interpretations. Interestingly enough, Gerard Genette and Samuel Levin, both primarily literary scholars, have employed this analogy. An *epistemological* approach, influenced by both Lewis and Rescher, has been advocated by Marie-Laure Ryan.[19] Following Lewis, she proposes to understand the term ›actual‹ as an indexical like ›here‹ and ›now‹. ›Actual‹ thus depends on where you are situated. In reading fiction, she says, we imaginatively relocate or recentre ourselves to another world, the one portrayed in the text, and, for the duration of the reading, we make it our base world or textual actual world, the world of fact. In such a world, monsters and angels may be actual existents and claims about them factually true, while university professors may be pure figments of these characters' imaginative activity. The last, and most popular view, is the *pragmatic* one formulated by Kendall Walton and picked up by Gregory Currie and many others.[20] On this view, in going to the theater, watching a feature film or reading a text culturally designated as narrative fiction we engage voluntarily and consciously in a game of pretend or make believe. We thus pretend or make it true for the duration of the reading of *Anna Karenina* that there was indeed a woman thus named, that she had a boy, that she was unhappily married etc. Or we pretend that there are other galaxies in which such and such is the case. Notice that we are NOT making here any ontological commitments that there ARE in any sense or way other universes or that Anna Karenina or any other non-actual

---

18 Lewis: Plurality.
19 Ryan: Worlds.
20 Walton: Mimesis; Currie: Nature.

individual exists in some Meinongian sense. We just pretend or make believe pro tempore that such is the case.

In a recent book entitled *How Ficta Follow Fiction* (2006), the Italian philosopher Alberto Voltolini puts it this way: In order to understand how fictional characters emerge and how we engage with them we must assume three things: a set of properties, which are of course abstract entities; an activity of make believe in which we pretend that there exists in some space-time world an individual who instantiates this set of properties, and an actual-world, man-made artifact (book, movie) or process of story telling which gives rise to this make believe activity on part of the reader.[21] The *de re* mode of engagement with fictional characters cannot be activated without the prior existence of the text or the concurrent activity of story telling. But given this text, it is our choice how to engage: purely *de dicto*, analyzing the content of the propositions the text contains, or *de re*, pretending that these propositions are indeed about independently existing individuals, and then proceeding to a further engagement with these individuals: cognitive, emotive or even behavioural, as we shall see in a moment.

Any illusion-creating and sustaining mode of narration, that is, any mode of narration which presents itself as a factual report, is conducive to a *de re* mode of engagement, regardless of the specific nature of the individual characters projected in it. Conversely, any mode of narration which reminds us that it is just an activity of inventing a world and its inhabitants undermines the game of make believe with respect to the *told*. But, as Walton shrewdly remarks, even here one can still maintain the make believe attitude, at least with respect to the *teller* figure or voice, an individual who is himself a creation of the actual author.[22] So the teller may be unreliable, a chronic liar, a madman, a postmodernist self-cancelling writer figure, but we can still make believe that there is at least such an individual and that what we are reading is indeed a discourse produced by such a character. Never forget that the narrator cum character is as much of a fiction as the individuals he speaks about and is equally amenable to (and in need of) the make believe or pretend mode of reading.

---

21 Voltolini: Fiction, pp. 65–66.
22 Walton: Mimesis, pp. 355–368.

4 Fictional Characters in our Lives

The previous three stages were about how we construe and process a certain object of cognition which is external to us, namely the work world as represented in the text. In the *de se* mode we are concerned with the game world, that is, first with participatory response or *our own experiencing or feelings with respect to the narrated* and second with the real-world impact of the narrated, *our doing* some further *things* in the actual world as a result of our cognitive and emotive encounter with the object called fictional character. In Richard Gerrig's terms, we ask here not how the reader constructs the narrative world, but rather how the narrative world reconstructs the reader.[23] Informally stated, *de se* designates all operations of reader involvement beyond textual comprehension.[24] Purely theoretically, one can distinguish two poles: immersion or intense emotional engagement and close identification with the character on one hand, and pure, distanced observation or contemplation on the other (›sich einlassen‹ and ›sich loesen‹ in Jauss' terms),[25] at times making the game of make believe one's temporary reality and alternately recalling it is only a voluntary game which can be given up at will. As I have just said, at the *de se* stage the focus is on mental activities beyond textual comprehension undertaken by actual human beings with respect to fictional texts and the characters in them. As such, this is the domain of study of psychology, and indeed a huge amount of work has been done by psychologists here. It is also a central area of concern for ESL (= Empirical Study of Literature). I am not an expert in this area, and will therefore report instead on some kinds of *de se* activity distinguished by philosophers, but which may also serve as a useful armature for empirical studies of various kinds. What I am going to present is a logically defined, ascending progression of kinds and degrees of *de se* activity, without claiming that this is also the actual temporal sequence of activities undertaken by any actual reader. It is quite probable that in the act of reading we shift constantly between different stages of engagement, or even engage simultaneously in several of them in different areas of our brain. But this needs to be studied by cognitive psychologists.

Central to the de *re* engagement was imagining that the text is a report of actual events and characters. The *first* de *se* act, the entry level or base

---

[23] Gerrig: Worlds, pp. 11–12.
[24] For a brief overview of the various kinds of reader-character encounter in this context see Jannidis: Character.
[25] Jauss: Identifikation pp. 244; 254.

line so to speak, would accordingly be to imagine that I myself as a participant in the game world am indeed now reading such a report or observing such individuals and events. To use a theater analogy: not only do Hamlet and Claudius exist, but I myself am watching right now their violent confrontation. Now if I am currently reading a report about actual individuals, it makes perfect sense that as a *second* stage I should respond emotionally to them and adopt certain emotive and evaluative attitudes towards them, such as the classical pity and fear, but also concern, caring, feeling for the character, admiration, loathing, sympathy, antipathy and so on. Such affective and evaluative readerly reactions are referred to by psychologists as participatory responses. But no matter how strong my emotions are, there is still a clear separation here between character and reader.

This separation disappears temporarily in the *third stage*, traditionally referred to as identification, but better designated as mental simulation. The difference between the two stages can be elucidated with a simple example: in the second stage I may feel sympathy towards a suffering character and say ›I understand your suffering‹. In the third stage I would feel empathy and say ›your suffering is my suffering‹. In general, simulation means bracketing temporarily one's normal sense inputs and behavioural outputs, one's own beliefs and desires,[26] and adopting or reenacting for the duration of the game of make believe a mental state or activity of the character: emotion, attitude, disposition, belief, intention, wish, goal, etc. But the make-believe/actuality boundary is still preserved in the back of our minds. As Keith Oatley says, we are in the world of the text, but not of it.[27] Simulation means substituting for the duration of the game the character's inner states and feelings for one's own, or simulating someone else's first hand experiences and ways of thinking. Informally it is referred to as putting oneself in the other's shoes, viewing things from the other's perspective, ›sich hineindenken und hineinfuehlen‹ into the other.[28] In the context of fiction reading, mental simulation implies adopting a perceptual, cognitive or affective perspective of a character which may be different from any perspective we have ever had before. According to Oatley, this perspective-taking may enhance our understanding of others in their inwardness and individuality.[29] Character simulation is also the key in some methods of acting as in Stanislavskij's,

---

26 Kieren / Lopes: Imagination, p. 4.
27 Oatley: Taxonomy, p. 61.
28 Coplan: Engagement, pp. 146–147.
29 Oatley: Emotions, pp. 65–66.

who urged his actors to put aside for the duration of the play their own selves and adopt or become their characters instead. Putting oneself in the other's place could thus also be understood as imaginative role taking. One elementary common form of readerly character simulation is focalization, where we are made to perceive (see, hear, taste) things as the character does, a thing most obvious in cinema shots from the character's space-time position and visual acuity.[30] Another example would be when we set aside our own views and judgments and adopt instead those of a personalized narrator.[31] One can generalize in Alvin Goldman's terms that such enactment imagination and empathy lie at the core of our experience of fiction.[32] Miall and Kuiken claim that an extreme form of readerly personal identification with a character, his actions and experiences, may lead to a modification of one's own self understanding and sense of self, ›becoming what one beholds‹.[33] The same view is echoed by Strange,[34] who says:

> Through a process of subjective recentering, fiction invites readers to adopt [in the game of make-believe] perspectives and commitments they would not entertain in their actual world. The further issue is the extent to which perspectives and convictions adopted in the narrative experience are internalized and recruited as grounds for future reasoning, judgment, commitment and action [in the actual world].

Empirical studies have in fact shown that the higher the reader's identification with a character or narrator, the greater the likelihood he will adopt as valid in his life world textual claims made by them even when they conflict with his prior world knowledge.[35]

A fourth stage, straddling the boundary between the make believe world of the other in which we are temporarily immersed and the reader's actual life world, consists of those occasions when events concerning a character in a story and their associated emotions act as cues to recall similar fragments of one's own autobiographical memory of events and emotions, bringing about a reliving of these experiences and emotions.[36] In another essay Oatley speaks of fiction's ability to offer on occasion a ›mimetic parallel‹ to the reader's life,[37] thereby evoking emotion-laden memories, and allowing the reader to relive some patterns of experience. The other's

---

30 For a detailed discussion see Mellmann: Objects (in this volume).
31 Currie: Paradox, p. 72.
32 Goldman: Minds.
33 Miall / Kuiken: Feeling.
34 Strange: Tales, pp. 280–282.
35 Schreier: Textwirkungen, pp. 200–201.
36 Oatley / Gholamain: Emotion, p. 270.
37 Oatley: Emotions, pp. 59; 65.

made up experience overlaps with one's own actual one, and therefore acquires some kind of reality in our own world. But in the context of fiction such reliving of past experience may at the same time make the reader think about the implications of this past experience, thus bringing together experience and its meaning.

The *fifth* and last stage concerns the impact of the engagement with a fictional character on the reader in his actual life world, once the reading act is concluded. What strictly belongs to the make believe sphere is now transferred and applied to the reader's ›Lebenswelt‹. This transfer, or blurring of the make-believe/actual boundary, or life imitating art, may be logically unfounded, yet it is neither rare nor surprising. There are countless examples from literary history of readers adopting the manner of speech, dress, gesture and even whole life style of fictional characters, the most extreme example being the 18th century suicides a la Werther. All didactic fiction with a positive hero is meant to have the reader adopt this fictional character's values and modes of behaviour in his personal and interpersonal life, and already Plato was worried about the undesirable views, attitudes and modes of behaviour readers could pick up from reading the old narratives. Looked at more systematically, there are at least half a dozen areas where such a spillover from fictional to actual may occur. First is the reader's self concept, including sense of self and self understanding, and the construction, formation and transformation of the self and of one's sense of identity. Another area is the affective one, covering the whole range of emotions and attitudes. Next comes the cognitive sphere, where the engagement with the fictional characters may impact one's models of reality, its perception and understanding, especially as regards one's beliefs about the (actual) human psyche, its nature and modes of functioning. In fact, such an engagement may in principle impact one's beliefs and judgments with respect to any phenomena, issues and situations in the actual world. The cognitive psychologist Richard Gerrig has made the very strong claim that we (normally) need to make a conscious effort in order to reject as inapplicable to reality any claims made in a work of fiction. It is thus not Coleridge's ›willing suspension of disbelief‹ that requires a deliberate mental effort,[38] but rather the ›willing construction of disbelief‹. If this is true, then Plato's concern is actually well founded. One's value system, preferences, and evaluation of individuals, situations and events is another area which may be likewise influenced and modified. And the same goes for the agential system: one's grounds for action, expectations, goals and

---

38 Coleridge: Biographia, p.505.

ideals, commitments and processes of decision making. And finally there is of course the sphere of interpersonal or public behaviour, its modes and underlying norms, including a radical change in one's whole way of life.

As in all previous modes of engagement, literature itself embodies this one too, paradigmatically in the life story of Don Quixote whose immersive, identifying and admiring mode of reading of courtly epics makes him totally forget the demarcation between make believe and actual and develop the irresistible desire (and associated intention) to shape his entire behaviour in the here and now on the behavioural norms and goals of his admired heroes. In the Don's story we have in fact the whole spectrum of possible modes of readerly engagement with fictional characters. He begins with the high sounding epithets (predicates) qualifying the heroes of the texts of chivalry he is reading, goes on to the beautifully phrased propositions about them contained in these texts, moves on to a make believe *de re* mode of reception, followed by character admiration and mental simulation, and ends up with the determination to live his life here and now according to the norms and goals of these heroes. The potential splendour *and* misery of engaging with fictional characters, and everything in between, are all there in the story of this paradigmatic, even though himself fictional, reader.

References

Alward, Peter: Leave Me out of It: De Re, but not De Se. Imaginative Engagement With Fiction. In: Journal of Aesthetics and Art Criticism 64/4 (2006), pp. 451–459.

Bal, Mieke: Mensen van Papier: Over Personages in de Literatuur. Assen 1979.

Bal, Mieke: Narratology: Introduction to the Theory of Narrative. 2nd edn. Toronto 1997.

Barthes Roland: S/Z. In: Oeuvres Completes III, ed. by Eric Marty. Paris 2002, pp. 119–341.

Coleridge: Biographia Literaria. In: Hazard Adams / Leroy Searle (Eds.): Critical Theory since Plato. Boston 2005, pp. 501–508.

Conan Doyle, Arthur: Sherlock Holmes: The Complete Novels and Stories, vols. I / II. New York 1986.

Coplan, Amy: Empathetic Engagement with Narrative Fiction. In: Journal of Aesthetics and Art Criticism 62/2 (2004), pp. 141–152.

Currie, Gregory: On the Nature of Fiction. New York 1990.

Currie, Gregory: The Paradox of Caring: Fiction and the Philosophy of Mind. In: Mette Hjort / Sue Laver (Eds.): Emotion and the Arts. New York 1997, pp. 63–77.

Eder, Jens: Die Figur im Film. Marburg 2008.

Gerrig, Richard: Experiencing Narrative Worlds. New Haven 1993.

Goldman, Alvin: Imagination and Simulation in Audience Response to Fiction. In: Shaun Nichols (Ed.): The Architecture of the Imagination. Oxford 2006, pp. 41–56.

Goldman, Alvin: Simulating Minds – The Philosophy, Psychology and Neuroscience of Mind Reading. New York 2006.

Ingarden, Roman: Das literarische Kunstwerk. Halle 1931.

Jabes, Edmond: Le Livre de questions, vols. 4–6: Yael, Elya, Aely. Paris 1967–1972.
Jannidis, Fotis: Character. In: Peter Hühn / John Pier / Wolf Schmid / Jörg Schönert (Eds.): Handbook of Narratology. Berlin 2009.
Jauss, Hans-Robert: Ästhetische Identifikation – Versuch über den literarischen Helden. In: Ästhetische Erfahrung und literarische Hermeneutik. Frankfurt 1982, pp. 244–292.
Kieran, Matthew / Dominic McIver Lopes (Eds.): Imagination, Philosophy and the Arts. London / New York 2003.
Lewis, David K.: On the Plurality of Worlds. Oxford 1986.
Miall, David / Don Kuiken: A Feeling for Fiction: Becoming what We Behold. In: Poetics 30/4 (2002), pp. 221–241.
Mellmann, Katja: Objects of ›Empathy‹. Characters (and Other such Things) as Psycho-Poetic Effects. In this volume.
Oatley, Keith: A Taxonomy of the Emotions of Literary Response and a Theory of Identification in Fictional Narrative. In: Poetics 23 (1994), pp. 53–74.
Oatley, Keith / Mitra Gholomain: Emotion and Identification: Connections between Readers and Fiction. In: Mette Hjort / Sue Laver (Eds.): Emotion and the Arts. New York 1997, pp. 263–282.
Oatley, Keith: Emotions and the Story Worlds of Fiction. In: Timothy C. Brock / Melanie C. Green / Jeffrey J. Strange (Eds.): Narrative Impact: Social and Cognitive Foundations. Mahwah, NJ 2002, pp. 39–69.
Phelan, James: Reading People, Reading Plots. Chicago 1989.
Pirandello, Luigi: A Character in Distress. In: P. M. Pasinetti (Ed.): Great Italian Short Stories. New York 1959, pp. 286–293.
Pirandello, Luigi: Six Characters in Search of an Author. In: Sarah Lawall (Ed.): The Norton Anthology of Western Literature, vol. 2. New York 2006, pp. 1740–1780.
Ryan, Marie-Laure: Possible Worlds, Artificial Intelligence and Narrative Theory. Bloomington 1991.
Ryan, Marie-Laure: Avatars of Story. Minneapolis 2006.
Schreier, Margrit: Textwirkungen. In: Thomas Anz (Ed.): Handbuch Literaturwissenschaft, vol. 1. Stuttgart 2007, pp. 193–202.
Strange, Jeffrey: How Fictional Tales Wag Real-World Beliefs. In: Timothy C. Brock / Melanie C. Green / Jeffrey J. Strange (Eds.): Narrative Impact: Social and Cognitive Foundations. Mahwah, NJ 2002, pp. 263–286.
Tolstoy, Leo: Anna Karenina. New York 2001.
Tomashevsky, Boris: Thematics. In: Lee Lemon / Marion Reis (Eds.) Russian Formalist Criticism: Four Essays. Lincoln 1965, pp. 61–98 (Originally published in Boris Tomashevsky: Teoria Literatury. Leningrad 1925).
Voltolini, Alberto: How Ficta Follow Fiction. Dordrecht 2006.
Walton, Kendall L.: Mimesis as Make-Believe. Cambridge, MA 1990.
Zholkovsky, Alexander: Themes and Texts: Towards a Poetics of Expressiveness. Ithaca / London 1984.

Katja Mellmann

Objects of ›Empathy‹
Characters (and Other Such Things) as Psycho-Poetic Effects

In folk theories of art reception, readers and cinema audiences are said to experience fictional worlds vicariously ›through‹ characters, i.e. they ›identify‹ themselves with them, they partake in their experiences ›empathetically‹. In the first section of my essay, I will argue that it is not character but focalization (point of view) which, on a fundamental level, guides our fictional experience, and I will exemplify several ways that characters (or similar ideas) can then in addition come into play. In the next two sections, I will discuss possible cognitive correlates of both the textual device of focalization and textual clues indicating ›persons‹. The aim is to show that what I call ›psycho-poetic effects‹ (that is, the mental representation of anthropomorphic instances) are best described as by-products of various cognitive programs involved in the reception of narrative fiction. ›Empathy‹, as it is understood in the above mentioned folk theory of art reception, can then be analysed into individual algorithms of social cognition. And it can be differentiated, as is done in the last section, from other phenomena often confused with it, like emotional experience proper and emotional contagion. Also, I refer to the idea that mirror neurons provide the means to empathize with others, literary characters included. My general proposition is to revise and refine those concepts with the help of evolutionary theory and, thus, to hypothesize as cognitive correlates for textual features only programs specific enough to be correlated with a specific adaptive function which they may have performed in the process of human evolution.

1 Focalization – The Door of ›Perception‹

What if there are no characters at all? I start with several passages from the first chapter of Virginia Woolf's novel *Jacob's Room* (1922) in order to show how the imagination of a fictional world can arise independently from the presence of fictional characters, and to discuss various ways the idea of ›character‹, or of character-like entities, might come into play. The textual device I suggest as an alternative to character in explaining imagination processes is as old as the narratological concept of ›perspective‹ or ›point of view‹, though I refer to it in the more specific definition of »a restriction of ›field«‹ as introduced by Gérard Genette.[1] His notion of ›focalization‹ designates the somewhat skeletonized,[2] mere technical fact of ›perception‹ without implicitly suggesting – as ›perspective‹ and ›point of view‹ tended to – that it is *someone's* perception.

In the following text passage Woolf depicts an empty room. There is no character aboard, we are alone with this sight:

> The bareness of Mrs. Pearce's front room was fully displayed at ten o'clock at night when a powerful oil lamp stood on the middle of the table. The harsh light fell on the garden; cut straight across the lawn; lit up a child's bucket and a purple aster and reached the hedge. Mrs. Flanders had left her sewing on the table. There were her large reels of white cotton and her steel spectacles; her needle-case; her brown wool wound round an old postcard. There were the bulrushes and the *Strand* magazines; and the linoleum sandy from the boys' boots. A daddy-long-legs shot from corner to corner and hit the lamp globe. The wind blew straight dashes of rain across the window, which flashed silver as they passed through the light. A single leaf tapped hurriedly, persistently, upon the glass. There was a hurricane out at sea.[3]

The perceiving instance (Genette's ›situated focus‹ or ›focal position‹)[4] is clearly located in the room,[5] so that it can view the ›powerful oil lamp [...] on the middle of the table‹ and the other objects in the room (including the daddy-long-legs) as well as the garden outside the window, and that it

---

1 Genette: Revisited, p. 74.
2 Cf. Genette: Discourse, pp. 189–194; Genette: Revisited, pp. 72–78. As there are various conceptions of that term in post-genettian narrative theory (and as Genette himself was not all consistent), see also Mellmann: Voice, for my preferred understanding of ›focalization‹.
3 Woolf: Jacob's Room, p. 7.
4 Genette: Revisited, p. 74; Genette: Discourse, p. 193. Cf. also O'Neill: Origin, p. 333, who speaks of the »point from which the narrative is perceived as being presented at any given moment«.
5 The notions of ›perceiving instance‹/›uttering instance‹ and ›perceptual situation‹/›situation of utterance‹, were developed in Mellmann: Emotionalisierung, pp. 164–204.

can hear the leaf tapping at the window pane. However, the last sentence makes a small exception.

Theoretically, there are two possible analyses of this sentence, though one of them is more probable to take shape in the mind of a reader: (a) The scope of perception can be said to be widened and displaced out at sea, so that the perceiving instance can *see* that there is a hurricane. (b) Or the sentence can be categorized as a voice-only passage, that is, a comment by the narrator (the ›voice‹ in Genette's terms), simply speaking out of his knowledge (as he does, for instance, when he tells us *how it comes* that there are sewing utilities lying around, and sand on the floor). Option (b) is more likely to represent the understanding of empirical readers, because such a huge shift in imagination as required by (a) would take some time, and one single and short sentence does not really give time enough to fully flesh out the second perceptual situation. A second reason might be, as I will argue below, that we prefer focalizing strategies which mimic natural human movement, and a camera shift out at sea would clearly exceed these limits. So, in order to keep up with the pace of narration and a humanlike scope of experience, it would be easier to stay with the idea of the perceiving instance being in the room and to regard the last sentence as a mere *comment* on the perception of the tapping leaf.

But if we do so, something odd is taking place: For who makes this comment? Obviously, this is the ›voice‹, ergo, the ›narrator‹. But the special thing about this comment is that it is made directly *in response* to a perception. That is, the narrator behaves *as if he himself* is standing in the room (just in the place where the perceiving instance is assumed to be) and commented about *his own* perceptions. The sentence ›There was a hurricane out at sea‹ sounds like a thought someone might have standing there and hearing the leaf tapping at the window. Grammatically, it could even be read as a case of free indirect discourse, albeit there is no character to whom we could ascribe this reflection. Especially by using the deictic phrase ›out at‹, the voice adopts the angle of the perceiving instance. Similarly, the circumstances that ›Mrs. Flanders had left her sewing on the table‹ and that the ›linoleum [was] sandy from the boys' boots‹ are told in a way that makes them sound like the thoughts of somebody who *sees* the sewing lying on the table, the sand on the floor, *and then guesses* that it is Mrs. Flanders' sewing and sand from the boys' boots.

I call this something odd because voice-only passages do not always transfer the narrator into the perceptual situation. Imagine a sentence like: ›The bareness of the front room in Mrs. Pearce's house, which was built in 1891, was fully displayed at ten o'clock at night‹. Again the narrator simply speaks out of his *knowledge* when telling us when the house was built (something which cannot be actually *perceived*). But in this example, the voice-only passage gives *additional* information, which has no close relation to the perceptual situation, and thus evokes the idea of an omniscient narrator external to the fictional world (Genette's ›heterodiegetic narrator‹). In Woolf's original text we have a heterodiegetic narrator too (for none of the characters is identical with the narrator), but what is peculiar is that he often adopts the role of a quasi-homodiegetic narrator by aligning himself with the perceiving instance. This is quite akin to what Franz K. Stanzel called the ›figural narrative situation‹:[6] The impression of a ›figural‹ narrator is brought about by a particular narrative technique involving a tendency toward anthropomorphic focalization (that is, movements of the perceiving instance which mimic, or at least do not exceed, human capabilities of moving) and for a ›subsidiary voice system‹, which means that the voice does not make itself noticeable as a particular person, but rather ties itself down to a mere reflector function, adding no other comments than of the above kind, i.e. closely related to the perceptual situation.[7]

The perceiving instance, as a technical concept, can at heart be understood as kind of a camera (plus microphone, smell, touch and taste recorder). But we often treat it as if it was a personal entity, an incorporeal ›somebody‹ or vicarious ›I‹ witnessing the fictional events (standing in the empty front room of Mrs. Pearce's house, for example). Especially if its spatio-temporal access and its way of moving resembles human capabilities, we tend to imagine a ›figural‹ perceiver. This bias (or, ›fallacy‹) of anthropomorphizing the perceiving instance often entails another bias: to synthesize this ›somebody‹ with any available ›subject‹ in the text. If there is no character, like in the quoted passage,[8] the only available ›subject‹ is that of the narrator, that is, the person we assume – again anthropomorphizing – is behind the ›voice‹ of a narrative. As

---

6   Stanzel: Situations; Stanzel: Theory. For a survey see also Fludernik / Margolin: Introduction.
7   Cf. Mellmann: Voice, pp. 125–129.
8   Or if they are not able to function as perceivers, for example, if they are sleeping: »The little boys in the front bedroom had thrown off their blankets and lay under the sheets. It was hot; rather sticky and steamy. Archer lay spread out, with one arm striking across the pillow. [...] In the other bed by the door Jacob lay asleep, fast asleep, profoundly unconscious« (Woolf: Jacob's Room, p. 9). It would be unreasonable to ascribe the perception that ›it was hot‹, ›sticky and steamy‹, to the boys (although they might feel it even sleeping), so again the narrator has to fill this space.

Bortolussi/Dixon have observed, empirical readers indeed tend to synthesize ›narrator‹ and ›perceiver‹ in their imagination.⁹

Authors exploit these biases by unfolding a versatile back and forth of potential attributions. Here is another example from *Jacob's Room*:

> The rock was one of those tremendously solid brown, or rather black, rocks which emerge from the sand like something primitive. Rough with crinkled limpet shells and sparsely strewn with locks of dry seaweed, a small boy has to stretch his legs far apart, and indeed to feel rather heroic, before he gets to the top.
> But there, on the very top, is a hollow full of water, with a sandy bottom; with a blob of jelly stuck to the side, and some mussels. A fish darts across. The fringe of yellow-brown seaweed flutters, and out pushes an opal-shelled crab – ›Oh, a huge crab‹, Jacob murmured – and begins his journey on weakly legs on the sandy bottom. Now! Jacob plunged his hand. The crab was cool and very light.¹⁰

The quoted passage is separated from its preceding paragraph by an asterisk, indicating kind of a cutaway from the chapter's initial scenery to another place on the beach. Starting with the description of a rock, the passage seems to exhibit a scene again void of characters, and the reader will probably begin with the idea of an anonymous perceiving instance which is installed in front of the rock. However, beginning at the latest with ›But there‹, he will imagine it as a strongly ›figural‹ narrator-perceiver, because the ›But‹ does not make sense except in relation to a psychic entity, to which the perception of the water hollow on the top of the rock would mean a sudden discovery. This anthropomorphization of the perceiving instance is further supported by the switch to present tense, which evokes the imagination of someone really being there. Not before the third paragraph, though, do we understand that this ›someone‹ is Jacob, and that already the considerations of how much ›*a small boy*‹, of all things, ›has to stretch his legs‹ might have been due to this fact. Thus, only retrospectively does the reader become aware that he has been seeing the rock all along ›through Jacob's eyes‹, and that the passage is, in Genette's terms, ›internally focalized‹.

Both examples make clear that, if there was not access to the fictional world independent from characters, texts like the quoted ones would not work. The first one, lacking any characters, would not give rise to any imagination at all. In the second one, Woolf would not be able to suspend

---

9   Bortolussi / Dixon: Psychonarratology, pp. 166–199. Yet I do not follow their conclusion that Genette's distinction of voice and perception therefore »loses […] relevance« (p. 172) as an analytical concept, because how are we to make that important observation (that readers tend to synthesize voice and perception instance) *without* this distinction?
10 Woolf: Jacob's Room, p. 5.

the communication of Jacob's presence until the end of the passage. Only the existence of a textual device called focalization allows her to start as if there were no character, and to make a game out of letting the perceiver become more and more ›figural‹, and finally Jacob.

The fact that ›focalization‹ and ›character‹ are only loosely connected and can combine differently in different cases becomes particularly apparent in the following passage:

> ›Ja-cob! Ja-cob!‹ Archer shouted.
> ›Scarborough‹, Mrs. Flanders wrote on the envelope, and dashed a bold line beneath; it was her native town; the hub of the universe. But a stamp? She ferreted in her bag; then held it up mouth downwards; then fumbled in her lap, all so vigorously that Charles Steele in the Panama hat suspended his paint-brush.
> Like the antennae of some irritable insect it positively trembled. Here was that woman moving – actually going to get up – confound her! He struck the canvas a hasty violet-black dab. For the landscape needed it. It was too pale – greys flowing into lavenders, and one star or a white gull suspended just so – too pale as usual. The critics would say it was too pale, for he was an unknown man exhibiting obscurely, a favourite with his landladies' children, wearing a cross on his watch chain, and much gratified if his landladies liked his pictures – which they often did.[11]

Again the passage begins with an unspecified perceiving instance; Archer's calls could be heard by anyone in this place. Then the perspective slowly becomes that of Mrs. Flanders, with culmination at ›But a stamp?‹, which reflects her looking for a stamp. Afterwards, the text abruptly switches to external focalization (›ferreted in her bag ...‹), which slowly turns into Steele's perception of her, that is, into an internal focalization again. It is most clearly his perception when we reach the exclamation mark (› – confound her!‹), which reflects his emotional reaction to the scene as it appears to him. Finally, the perceiving instance roughly follows the turn of his head to the canvas and, seemingly, glides into his head, depicting his thoughts about his painting and his reputation as an artist. Such a wandering perceiving instance, from one character to another and in and out each time, demonstrates with particular clarity that the focal position is an entity of its own, independent from (albeit casually associating with) characters. However, there are two difficulties which I left out in my analysis.

The first difficulty lies in the interdigitating of internal and external focalization. Similar to the switch from internal to external focalization in ›But a stamp? She ferreted in her bag‹, there are changes of focalization regarding Mr. Steele: The facts that he wears a Panama hat, that he suspends his paint-brush, making it tremble, and that he finally dabs the

---

11 Woolf: Jacob's Room, p. 4.

canvas, are seen from outside. But between these events there is an internally focalized passage about how he sees Mrs. Flanders move and confound herself. This back and forth between internal and external focalization is a technique very common in passages centred on characters,[12] and to lapse into an analysis of the sometimes very dense succession of multiple switches would miss the point. It would seem more reasonable to subsume both techniques under the notion of ›alignment‹, as it was used to describe similar phenomena with films:[13] To ›align‹ a narration with a character means to seemingly walk about and keep close with him, applying internal focalizations (like in point-of-view shots) as well as external ones (like in close-up shots). One aim of alignment can be to provide ›subjective access‹ to a character; and sometimes external focalizations (showing an emotional reaction like that of the trembling paint-brush, for example) serve this purpose better than internal ones. Applying the concept of alignment, I can give a more homogenised description of the quoted passage, saying that it starts with an unspecified perceiving instance, which is then aligned with Mrs. Flanders, and then slowly turns into an alignment with Steele.

The second difficulty is that internal focalizations (like free indirect discourse) are oftentimes ambiguous. For instance, the causal relation which is expressed in ›For the landscape needed it‹ is likely to be understood as a reflection by Steele, because it informs about his motivation to add the black-violet dab; but do we really know that it is his own comprehension of his motives (and not a supposition by the narrator)? The same question applies to the next sentences: ›It was too pale – […] – too pale as usual. The critics would say it was too pale […]‹. Do we know for sure whether these are Mr. Steele's thoughts while gazing at his painting, or rather comments on the part of the narrator? And whose gaze on the picture is it then that is depicted in ›greys flowing into lavenders …‹: Mr. Steele's or that of an anonymous perceiver? And whose knowledge is it when we are told that Steele is an ›unknown man‹ and that the landladies mostly like his pictures: his own or the narrator's knowledge? – If that sounds like (not really false, but) dispensable scepticism, I have achieved my aim. For it would confirm what I want to show: that we automatically yield to the above mentioned biases to

---

[12] Cf. Genette's consideration that internal focalization (as a matter of entire narratives, not of single half sentences) is very rare and »fully realized only in the ›interior monologue‹, or in that borderline work, Robbe-Grillet's *La Jalousie*, where the central character is limited absolutely to – and strictly *inferred* from – his focal position alone« (Genette: Discourse, p. 193).

[13] Smith: Characters, pp. 142–165.

anthropomorphize the perceiving instance and to synthesize it with any available subject in the text, even if the text does not provide sufficient clues to force such interpretation. See as a counter-example another passage:

> [...] for there her pen stuck; her eyes fixed, and tears slowly filled them. The entire bay quivered; the lighthouse wobbled; and she had the illusion that the mast of Mr. Connor's little yacht was bending like a wax candle in the sun.[14]

Here there *is* a reason intrinsic to the text to consider parts of the passage as internally focalized. For only Betty Flanders sees the bay quiver and the light house wobble, as she alone has tears in her eyes. We need to identify *her* as the focal position, because those perceptions cannot be reasonably ascribed to a merely technical perceiving instance (›camera‹), or to the narrator. However, except for such rare cases of unambiguously internal focalization, the association of a focal position with the presence of a character must be regarded as something added by the reader, a *mental construction* which does not have its equivalent in the text. So where does the bias to build such specifying mental constructions come from?

2 Psycho-Poetic (Side-)Effects

My supposition is that the textual device of focalization relies on the same cognitive abilities which are involved in ordinary real-life experience, and that enacting those abilities automatically implies the idea of agency, because real-life experience is first-hand experience, that is, the experience *of someone*. In particular, anthropomorphic focalizations in a way mimic individual experience and thus evoke the idea of someone *who is* experiencing. My second claim will be that social cognition is a highly adaptive and highly rewarding mental occupation and that this is why we are prone to understand characters (or quasi-characters) wherever possible.

These suppositions draw upon an observation made by John Tooby and Leda Cosmides, who wondered why people say so many things in the form of stories, while »there is no extrinsic reason why communicated information needs to be formatted in such a way«. They suggest that »our richest systems for information extraction and learning are designed to operate on our own experience«, because »we evolved not so long ago from organisms whose sole source of (non-innate) information was the individual's own experience«. As a consequence, they consider it

---

14 Woolf: Jacob's Room, p. 3.

»inevitable, now that we can receive information through communication from others, that we should still process it more deeply when we receive it in a form that resembles individual experience [...]. That is, we extract more information from inputs structured in such a form«.[15] I think that the two modes of information gathering mentioned here – social communication and individual experience – correlate perfectly with Genette's concepts of ›voice‹ and ›perception‹:[16] The ›voice‹ aspect of a narrative should involve mainly those cognitive mechanisms which are associated with verbal communication, that is, semiotic faculties, memory, syntax logic, and the like; whereas the ›perception‹ aspect should run a simulation on the perceptual systems of our brains. A focalized depiction of a narrative situation thus should be processed by more or less the same second-order circuits as are involved with processing sensory inputs.

If we assume this is true and that focalized narratives do generate an as-if simulation of first-hand experience on the reader's mind,[17] then the feeling of being in the place oneself and personally witnessing the fictional events would be kind of a natural by-product of the process. This would account for the idea of a vicarious ›I‹, which is somewhat mirrored in the concepts of a ›figural‹ perceiver, an ›invisible witness‹ or ›imaginative spectator‹.[18] – But what about the second bias to associate this figural ›as-if I‹ with a character or, respectively, the narrator?

Tooby and Cosmides, when giving a closer description of what they mean by the story format, list a couple of ›preferences‹:

> People prefer to receive information in the form of stories. Textbooks, which are full of true information, but which typically lack a narrative structure, are almost never read for pleasure. We prefer accounts to have one or more persons from whose perspective we can vicariously experience the unfolding receipt of information, expressed in terms of temporally sequenced events (as experience actually comes to us), with an agent's actions causing and caused by events (as we experience ourselves), in pursuit of intelligible purposes.[19]

---

15 Cosmides / Tooby: Beauty, p. 24.
16 This is my general hypothesis in Mellmann: Voice.
17 Cf. Decety: Empathy, on neural correlates of a spatio-temporal ›sense of agency‹ (p. 257) and a natural bias ›toward self-perspective‹ (p. 258).
18 Cf. Tan: Affect, and Tan: Emotion, for ›invisible witness‹; for ›imaginative spectator‹ cf. Smith: Characters.
19 Cosmides / Tooby: Beauty, p. 24. See also Oatley / Gholamain: Emotions, p. 269: »following a plot requires that actions be understood as steps in plans. [...] the basic modality of the fictional simulation is, therefore, that the actions of the protagonist are run on the planning processor of the reader or audience member. In real-world planning, we have a goal, and we arrange actions as steps in the plan to achieve it. In running a fictional simulation, we allow the text to guide our planning process, to steer

›Preference‹ in an evolutionary logic means something which is sustained by pleasure because it is highly adaptive and the organism shall be motivated to enact the related mechanisms as often as possible.[20] Innate preferences should become manifest by statistical dominance of certain behaviours (compared to others) and/or higher frequency of occurrence than would seem apt for rational means or other reasons. In this sense, the fact that ›[p]eople prefer to receive information in the form of stories‹ may for now pass as commonsensical;[21] yet this is kind of a meta-preference, an across-the-board effect of *several* preferences served by ›narrative structure‹ (including as various features as perspective, sequence, or agency), each of which would need closer examination individually. Note that the analogical structures of narrative texts and real-world experiences are not pleasurable *per se*, but they allow the text to function as kind of a dummy stimulus for several adaptive faculties which, performed in an ›organizational mode‹,[22] may be pleasurable. In order to state a preference for focalized passages over unfocalized ones,[23] and for anthropomorphic focalization over other focalization strategies, it might be sufficient to say that this simply enhances the text's ability to cooperate with the human mind;[24] but to explain why we prefer to ascribe the vision of the painting to Steele rather than to an anonymous perceiver, one has to ask for the reason why this should be more pleasurable than the non-ascribed version.

The answer would be that to regard Steele as the originator of the description of the canvas means to treat this passage as *information about*

---

us through the actions of the narrative. Emotions are then experienced in relation to the goals and plans we have adopted, much as emotions occur in relation to goals in everyday life, happiness with achievements, sadness with losses, anger at frustrations, and so forth«.

20 See Frijda: Pleasure, for a general survey on the psychological concept of pleasure; for an evolutionary perspective on several systems of ›aesthetic preference‹ – i.e. of »motivational systems […] that are designed to find rewarding the kinds of actions and experiences that would have been adaptive for our ancestors« see Cosmides / Tooby: Beauty, pp. 13f.
21 Cf. Frey: Erfahrungshaftigkeit, with preliminary positive results in testing this preference empirically.
22 Cosmides / Tooby: Beauty, p. 16.
23 This preference (like all ›preferences‹ as referred to here) can of course be outrivaled, in a particular case, by another preference; for instance, if the unfocalized passages are employed to flesh out the narrator persona as a social stimulus by interspersing his ironic comments.
24 In the sense of Oatley / Gholamain: Emotions, p. 273, saying that »fiction involves a discourse level and a range of techniques that allow the simulation to run properly on the human mind«.

Steele, that is, as fecund input for social cognition. The popular misbelief that we perceive fictional worlds somewhat ›through‹ characters in my opinion is induced by the fact that we never miss an opportunity to gather social information. A rectified version of that issue would be that we usually perceive fictional worlds directly (as a simulation of first-hand experience, granted by means of focalization), but that, *at the same time*, we use as much information as possible to draw conclusions about the social aspects of the fictional situation – that is, to feed our social cognition systems.

As we have seen, the ›persons from whose perspective we can vicariously experience‹ do not need to be literal persons. On the other hand, passages without any character, like the above quoted examples, occur rather seldom indeed and, typically, in highly modern literature. The ›classical‹ prototype of a story would rather begin with ›Once upon a time there was a king‹ than with ›Once upon a time there was a rock‹; and if it still did so, we would expect to be told immediately after about the role this rock played in some particular people's lives. For, as was rightly claimed, fictional events hardly make sense but in relation to agents.[25] Actually, the very value of narrative and stories seems to be to provide us with complex social models.[26] So, along with many others, I suppose that much of the pleasure we derive from fiction is due to its eliciting our social predispositions (cognitive as well as emotional ones).[27]

Take for instance the detective novel: this ›whodunnit‹ genre is almost exclusively designed to address our capabilities for evaluating people in accordance with the ›good guy‹/›bad guy‹ schema,[28] for mind reading, and ›detecting the cheater‹.[29] The popularity of this genre may be a hint that cognitions of this sort are highly rewarding; and to always be aware of another's intentions, the friendly as well as the hostile ones, should indeed have enhanced the survival and reproductive success of our ancestors. Similar things can be said about other complex social programs such as, for instance, evaluating the hierarchical status of each member of a group,

---

25 Scalise Sugiyama: Narrative, pp. 183–185.
26 Cf. Oatley / Mar: Pre-adaptations.
27 See, for example, Zunshine: Fiction, who connects the study of how texts trigger and exploit our capacity for mindreading with the question of ›why we read fiction‹; further elaborated (and more explicitly drawing on evolutionary aesthetics) in Zunshine: Mind.
28 There is reason to understand this schema as part of a separate mechanism equipped with a separate memory of its own, for even people with completely impaired memory function are able to subliminally recognize someone who has been positive to them (cf. Damasio: Feeling, pp. 43–47).
29 Cf. Cosmides / Tooby: Social reasoning.

which requires permanent attention to their behaviour, memory in order to prepare potential coalitions, continuous reflection on what is good and bad from an ethical standpoint, and so on; another such program is social learning, which involves continuous observation too, and reflection on which behaviours are successful and which are not.[30] Intensely social animals that they are, humans possess plenty of those predispositions to reflect on and react to their social environment, be it real or fictional.[31]

Actually, this is how fictional characters emerge. As William James once said: we do not cry, because we are sorry, but we feel sorry because we cry.[32] Similarly it could be said: we do not cogitate on social facts because we face literary characters, but we figure out personal entities because our social dispositions have been activated. They are triggered by a special kind of information which is appropriate to be used as social information. This is how characters become alive, and ›round‹; we fill them out by thinking about them, driven by our intrinsic interest in other ›members of the group‹ and making use of any available information. When mental processes, of whatever kind (emotional, perceptual, cognitive), thus entail, as mental by-product, the idea of animate beings (like for instance characters, but also ›narrator‹, ›figural perceiver‹, etc.), I speak of ›psycho-poetic effects‹, that is, the effect of ›making psyche‹ by imagining a psychic entity.[33] So what happens exactly when we understand a perceiving instance as an anthropomorphic entity ›walking on two legs‹, rather than a mere technical instance of ›camera‹? And what happens when we equip this anthropomorphic instance with a fully-fledged human psyche, having intentions and feelings?

3 Reverse-Engineering ›Empathy‹

What kind of information is it that is appropriate to be taken as social information? I shall give some suggestions for textual clues possibly corresponding to the releaser schema of particular routines of social cognition;[34] – which also means to dissect the broad popular concept of

---

30 Cf. Eibl: Animal, pp. 194f.
31 Cf. Norris / Cacioppo: I Know, pp. 88f., 90–95.
32 James: Emotion.
33 Mellmann: Emotionalisierung, pp. 99–103.
34 Cf., as a similar attempt, the list of probable sub-mechanisms involved in ›theory of mind‹ which Jannidis: Intention, pp. 191–197, deploys referring to findings from recent developmental psychology and primatology; similar lines of argument in Lauer: Spiegelneuronen.

›empathy‹ into a number of specific adaptations, which together constitute our capacity for empathic experience. This procedure conforms to what is called ›reverse-engineering‹[35] in evolutionary psychology and helps to identify the very entities of a complex design to which we can attribute specific adaptive functions.[36]

For instance, the information that something is moving may belong to one type of socially relevant information, for we have reasons to assume there is a specific cognitive algorithm for distinguishing animate from inanimate objects by self-propelled movement.[37] Think of Steele's trembling paint-brush: As we are not told that his hand would tremble, but his paint-brush itself (›like the antennae of some irritable insect‹!), the paint-brush might momentarily gain qualities of an animate being and thus produce a slightly eerie effect on the reader. Action verbs may represent another type of socially significant triggers, because they indicate someone *doing* something and thus appeals to our ability to infer intentions and goals from animated motion.[38] See for instance phrases like ›A daddy-long-legs shot from corner to corner‹, ›A fish darts across‹, or ›and out pushes an opal-shelled crab‹: Of course semantic memory helps enough to understand that a daddy-long-legs, a fish and a crab are animals, but if they are shown as ›shooting from A to B‹, ›darting across‹, or ›pushing out‹, they gain real life in the imagination of the reader, for he assumes there is kind of an intention in their action. Generally, words indicating intentionality and motivation perform the same function, like for instance the adverbs in ›A single leaf tapped hurriedly, persistently, upon the glass‹.

As you might have noticed, those basic social triggers roughly pertain to what are known as the stylistic devices of ›personification‹ and ›prosopopoeia‹ from classical rhetoric, making it possible to play psycho-

---

35 Tooby / Cosmides: Foundations, p. 61.
36 See also my critique of less strictly ›adaptationist‹ argumentations in the final section of Mellmann: Heuristic. – To give an example from physical evolution: The human hand as a whole is of course highly adaptive (as is ›empathy‹). But if I consider the human hand as ›an adaptation‹, I have to cope with a multitude of potentially adaptive functions (grasping, feeding, waving, beating, picking one's nose …) and will fail to determine both the crucial function for which it was selected and the actually selected entity (for the human hand is not an entirely new design of the human species but the result of many a proto-design appearing throughout animal evolution). A more reasonable method of adaptationist analysis would be to look at one particular feature of the hand, for instance the opposable thumb, and to ask for its particular adaptive value.
37 See Stone: Perspective, pp. 320–322, and the literature reported in Blythe / Todd / Miller: Motion, p. 261, and Zunshine: Strange, pp. 6–14, 15.
38 Cf. Stone: Perspective, pp. 322f., and Blythe / Todd / Miller: Motion.

poetic effects even on inanimate objects or abstract concepts. Comparably, clues of movement and intention can be used to animate an inanimate perceiving instance: If, for instance, the perceiving instance in Mrs. Pearce's empty front room does not only look at the oil lamp on the table, but also at the garden out the window, then again back at the objects lying around in the room and, finally, at the corners where the daddy-long-legs shoots back and forth, it performs kind of a movement of the ›head‹, if not the whole ›body‹, which arouses the imagination of an animate being capable of autonomous movement. Moreover, if the focalization of a text thus performs kind of a zoom, changing from a rather wide scope of perception to the selective depiction of individual spots and details, or the inverse, or if it lingers longer at a place, we might infer from this movement ›behaviour‹ kind of an intention – which we normally ascribe to the ›voice‹ instance (the narrator), but which here aditionally vivifies the perceptual instance, so that it tends to be merged with the narrator in the mind of the reader.

Focalization strategies like zooming or lingering do not only trigger our inference systems for detecting other people's intentions (known as the ›theory of mind‹[39] module), but may also meet our disposition for ›shared intentionality‹ or ›joint attention‹,[40] that is, for directing our attention in accordance with another, which might be a subunit of social learning programs. The sentence ›There was a hurricane out at sea‹, for instance, signals attention to a particular circumstance and invites the reader to follow this selective concentration. This effect often goes along with the use of perception verbs, like if the sentence was: ›One could *hear* the hurricane out at sea‹. Or consider a passage like this one:

---

39 I use this term in the narrow sense of ›theories about another's intentions, beliefs, and desires‹. For a critique of broader conceptions (like, for instance, Sperber's and Wilson's proposition of a ›comprehension module‹) with empiricist arguments see Ermer et al.: Theory; for a comprehensive discussion on ›ToM‹ that convincingly differentiates between several domain-specific sub-mechanisms, including an implicit ›mentalism‹, and domain-general capacities that, among others, also subserve ToM-tasks see Stone: Perspective (especially pp. 319f., 332–337).
40 Cf. Jannidis: Intention, p. 195, Lauer: Spiegelneuronen, p. 148, and Stone: Perspective, pp. 323–329.

> The two women murmured over the spirit-lamp, plotting the eternal conspiracy of hush and clean bottles while the wind raged and gave a sudden wrench at the cheap fastenings.
> Both looked round at the cot. Their lips were pursed. Mrs. Flanders crossed over to the cot.
> ›Asleep?‹ whispered Rebecca, looking at the cot.
> Mrs. Flanders nodded.[41]

We are tempted to follow their look at the cot, even if the pertaining view is not specifically depicted in the text. We even might figure it out on our own instead: Did you imagine a vision of the cot while reading this passage (or even of Mrs. Flanders' view *into* the cot, of the sleeping baby)? If so, you have obeyed the very social algorithm hypothesized here.

The capacities of guessing another's intentions or following another's attention are core components of the meta-capacity to ›understand the other‹, another important sub-program of which surely is the ability to create empathic representations of another's inner states. Empathic mental representations can be induced, for instance, by use of perceptual adjectives. For example, the remark that ›it was hot; rather sticky and steamy‹[42] in the room requires the imagination of a perceiver endowed with a human sensory system and of how these perceptions feel to him. Another source of empathy triggers is the depicting of various emotional display behaviours. When we are told, for example, that Betty Flanders is »pressing her heels rather deeper in the sand«,[43] that she has tears in her eyes, or that Steele's paint-brush is trembling, we may make elaborate guesses about their states of mind. This is more than only inferring intentions or motives, or sharing in somebody's directed attention; it also includes a mental representation of complex sensual data (like feelings and sensations) and of complex cognitive frames (like individual beliefs, a particular set of values and level of information).

The strikingly sensuous quality of empathic representations is what most people first think of when talking about empathy or about experiencing fictional worlds ›through characters‹. And in this view, empathy is often understood as an emotional experience. I do not think that this is correct, and that is why I have to add another section on empathy.[44]

---

41 Woolf: Jacob's Room, p. 8.
42 Cf. note 8.
43 Woolf: Jacob's Room, p. 3.
44 I do not attempt to list and discuss the numerous theories of ›empathy‹ (and ›sympathy‹, ›identification‹, and so on) in literary and, especially, film studies before and after the ›cognitive turn‹ (some of them being more, others less compatible with what I am suggesting in the following section). When, in what follows, I content myself with

4 ›Empathy‹ Revisited

Browsing handbooks of psychological emotion theory, one will rarely find articles on empathy. Publications on empathy are numerous, but, most of the time, without clear affiliation with the domains of emotion research or cognitive sciences; they rather stand alone (or, in the context of developmental psychology) and sometimes tend to reproduce a ›folk theory‹ of empathy, that is, they treat (or rather, celebrate) empathy as a highly valued prosocial endowment for ›sharing‹ the emotions of others. This imprecise notion of empathy has grown particularly virulent after the discovery of ›mirror neurons‹.[45] Vilayanur S. Ramachandran has coined the unfortunate abbreviation term »»empathy neurons‹ or ›Dalai Llama neurons‹« that, »it would seem, dissolve the barrier between self and others«.[46] While it is true that empathic imaginations show an eminently sensuous quality (and thus *resemble* emotional experience) and that this might indeed be due to neural ›mirroring‹ processes (or similar phenomena),[47] there is no worth in metaphors suggesting miraculous fusions of self and other, or a kind of wired connection between them. Actually, it is important to keep in mind the fundamental ›barrier‹ between self and other, because otherwise we would not be able to differentiate between someone *experiencing* an emotion and someone *imagining* that experience.[48] The first may have a mental representation of his feeling too though, and it is quite possible that it closely resembles that one which the latter will elaborate by means of empathy; yet the first will show *both* the elicitation of an emotion program *and* a second-order representation of this process, while the latter shows a mental representation *only* – which, moreover, will have come about very differently and does not result from monitoring processes within the same nervous system. When I, in the following, speak of ›empathy‹, I understand by it »a form of complex psychological inference in which observation, memory, knowledge, and reasoning are combined to yield insights into the thoughts and feelings of another« and to construct a complex mental representation of his state of mind.[49] To

---

arguing against an anonymous ›popular notion‹ of empathy, note that this ›popular notion‹ is not a mere straw man, but has indeed strongly influenced most of the numerous conceptions of ›empathy‹ I have come across both in the humanities and the sciences.
45 See also Batson: Things, and Decety: Empathy, pp. 248–250.
46 Ramachandran: Mirror, par. 15.
47 See note 62.
48 Cf. Heberlein / Adolphs: Neurobiology, p. 46, and Decety: Empathy, pp. 258f.
49 Ickes: Introduction, p. 2; see also Decety: Empathy, pp. 248, 263f.

make more plausible why it does make sense to confine the term that way, I shall explain (a) what *emotional experience,* as opposed to empathic imagination, is, (b) what is understood by ›emotional contagion‹, (c) what role empathic imaginations play in social emotions, and, finally, (d) what it is, probably, that brings about the sensuous quality of empathic imaginations.

(a) To experience an emotion means that, to begin with, an emotion program is triggered. That is, a highly domain-specific situation schema is matched by a stimulus and thus initialises an equally highly domain-specific super-ordinate program of several sub-mechanisms. Those super-ordinate programs were shaped by evolution as ›best-bet responses‹ to statistically reoccurring situations of selective significance. Involved sub-mechanisms include bodily changes as well as cognitive readjustments.[50] The neural second-order monitoring of these processes is what can show up as ›feeling‹ in the experiencing subject's conscious mind.[51]

It is quite possible that two people's emotional experiences closely parallel one another, for instance if both respond to the same stimulus and the respective emotion is a very ›basic‹ one (that is, with a high percentage of ›hard-wired‹ innate sub-mechanisms and a low percentage of individually ›learned‹ elements and modifications). Furthermore, not many but some emotion programs provide another possibility of paralleling two people's feelings by featuring their own ›output‹ of emotional display behaviour also as part of their releasing mechanism, that is, as an additional releaser:[52] for instance, seeing a weeping face may produce the impulse to weep oneself; seeing someone smile may produce the impulse to smile oneself; seeing someone's eyes widen with fear may also spontaneously excite an anxious feeling in the beholder, and so on.

(b) Phenomena of that kind are traditionally known as ›emotional contagion‹. Yet it is important to note that emotional contagion is no general principle, but occurs only with a limited number of emotional behaviours (like, particularly, crying and laughing) and reflexes (for

---

50 This model of emotions follows Cosmides / Tooby: Emotions. Cf. also Scherer: Emotion, and Mellmann: Emotionalisierung, pp. 23–41.
51 Cf. William James' above quoted view on emotions (cf. note 32), or Damasio's distinction of ›emotion‹ – for the objective process of activating and performing an emotion program – and ›feeling‹ – for the sensing of the consequences of the activation as a mental image which can be made conscious (Damasio: Feeling, pp. 37, 55, 79, and passim).
52 The terms of ›releasing mechanism‹ (RM) and ›releaser‹ (key stimulus) are taken from behavioural ecology.

instance, retching and yawning),⁵³ and, which is interesting, in infancy on a larger scale than with adults. It seems that it has been adaptive to attune and synchronize some (but not all) behaviours among group members, and especially to accord some of a child's reactions with those of its adult caregivers, as a still-developing organism may not yet be able to fully asses a situation on its own. Thus, emotional contagion seems to be a specifically adaptive algorithm itself, which applies only to very specific conditions; it cannot account for a general ›transmission‹ of feeling from one individual to another.

Another case of parallel emotional experience is often assumed for some social emotions, especially pity. According to folk psychology, when we cry with pity we cry because of sort of ›sharing‹ the sadness of the pitied person. In terms of films showing close-up shots of a weeping face, I would say that emotional contagion or emotional programs elicited by contextual information (like the one intruduced below) would do to explain the impulse to cry on the part of the spectator; there is no need to claim that he cries with pity. It may be that he *also feels pity*, but the crying response is not very likely to result from this particular emotion. At least it would be hard to confirm this claim from an evolutionary standpoint, for pity as an adaptive prosocial program would be expected to coordinate actions of assistance and shelter,⁵⁴ and bursting out in tears would seem rather dysfunctional in this context. Yet there is another emotional response which applies to ›pitiful‹ stimuli (among others) and which does include the impulse to cry: the response of ›sentiment‹ as it has been described by Ed Tan and Nico Frijda. The sentimental response, according to them, is an archaic capitulation response toward the overwhelming, which can be triggered by »any major resolution in a conflict« involving basic human concerns (like attachment, justice, survival).⁵⁵ That given, it is indeed possible that someone feels like crying when facing the fact that somebody has been done irremediable harm; much the same way as he may cry at two lovers' reunion, the birth of a baby, virtue's triumph, and so on (because ›any major resolution‹ signifies the positive as well as the negative ones). In fine, what appears to be ›crying with pity‹ at first sight, more likely is a compound response,

---

53 For the example of laughing cf. Gervais / Wilson: Laughter, pp. 402f., 413, 415.
54 Cf. Decety: Empathy, pp. 247f., and Mellmann: Emotionalisierung, pp. 125f., on pity as an emotional adaptation resulting from ›inclusive fitness‹.
55 Tan / Frijda: Sentiment, p. 54.

involving further emotion programs beyond pity (or even doing without).⁵⁶

(c) Nevertheless, pity can be said to be an ›empathic‹ emotion, albeit in quite a different sense than in that of emotional transmission. As it is rather difficult to become aware of the fact that someone has been done harm and needs consolation and help (and of what kind) without guessing what he feels like, the emotion of pity somewhat *relies* on empathy. In that way, an empathic imagination is the initial trigger – or at least a crucial sub-mechanism in the emotion episode – of several social emotions. As Tan puts it:

> I refer to emotions as empathic regardless of whether the character's emotions parallel those of the viewers; what matters is that the character's understanding of the situation is relevant for the viewer's emotion. Thus, pity is an empathic emotion, as is schadenfreude, where the viewer's feelings contrast with what is understood to be the character's (negative) appraisal of the situation. However, if the viewers were not aware of that appraisal they would not experience schadenfreude.⁵⁷

In this sense, ›empathy‹ again does not denote any kind of transmission of an individual's emotional experience, but, as said above, ›a form of complex psychological inference‹ on the part of the beholder, here as necessary part of some socially directed emotion programs.⁵⁸

(d) As the foregoing should have made clear, empathy as a component of the capacity to ›understand the other‹ is not per se an emotional experience. Nevertheless, there is something like a ›feeling‹ in empathy, some sensuous quality in imagining another's inner state. We seem to *feel* what it is like to stand in a hot and sticky room, to press one's heels deeper in the sand, to feel sad for certain reasons, and so on. This peculiar feeling might be due to what Antonio Damasio has called the ›as-if-body-loop‹.⁵⁹

Body states are represented in the brain by several neural second-order maps in body-sensing regions. If this process goes its ›normal‹ way, that is, if the representation is the result of signals hailing from the body, Damasio speaks of *direct* simulation, or the ›body-loop‹. Yet it seems that the representation mechanisms can also be activated by cognitive stimulation, that is, by signals coming from »certain brain regions, such as

---

56 Cf. my suggestion to reformulate Lessing's concept of ›weinendes Mitleiden‹ as a combination of a malperformance of the pity program and a subsequently triggered capitulation response in Mellmann: Emotionalisierung, pp. 128–131.
57 Tan: Affect, p. 18f.
58 Cf. note 49.
59 Damasio: Descartes; Damasio: Feeling; Damasio: Spinoza.

the prefrontal/premotor cortices«.[60] This is what he calls *internal* brain simulation, or the ›as-if-body-loop‹, because the somatosensory maps respond only ›as if‹ a sensuous experience had taken place, while there are no actually incoming signals from the body. Damasio considers the as-if-body-loop to be crucial for any process of mental simulation, including empathy. He draws on a study by Ralph Adolph which shows that patients with damage in brain regions concerned with accomplishing »the highest level of integrated mapping of body state« were not able to correctly identify emotional facial expressions.[61] »In the absence of this region«, Damasio suggests,

> it is not possible for the brain to simulate other body states effectively. The brain lacks the playground where variations on the body-state theme can be played. [...] In summary, the body-sensing areas constitute a sort of theater where not only the ›actual‹ body states can be ›performed‹, but varied assortments of ›false‹ body states can be enacted as well, for example, as-if-body states, filtered body states, and so on.[62]

Damasio believes that the as-if-body-loop mechanism draws »on a variant«[63] of the neural mirror system as described by Giacomo Rizzolatti and Vittorio Gallese.[64] And he does right to phrase rather cautiously here, because exactly how the many recent findings in the domain of neural simulation and empathy relate to one another is anything but clear at the moment.[65] ›Mirror neurons‹ is the name of neurons firing not only while performing, but also while observing an action. Note that what was initially observed is the mirroring of *visually* observed (and markedly specific) *motoric* actions.[66] Thus, a macaque's brain mirrors targeted

---

60 Damasio: Spinoza, p. 115.
61 Ibid., p. 117. For the study cf. Adolphs: Role.
62 Ibid., pp. 117f.
63 Ibid., pp. 115f.
64 For two attempts at integrating the discovery of mirror neurons in literary theory see Lauer: Spiegelneuronen, and Salgaro: Stories, both of which in my opinion overstate the significance of mirror neurons in explaining literature; similar, albeit more cautious considerations in Lindenberger: Arts, pp. 15f.
65 Cf. the critical surveys by Heberlein / Adolphs: Neurobiology, and Shamay-Tsoory: Empathic; also, from the humanities, Borg: Mirror, Wübben: Lesen, pp. 34–36, and Koepsell / Spoerhase: Neuroscience.
66 Cf. Rizzolatti / Arbib: Language, p. 188: »The response properties of mirror neurons to visual stimuli can be summarized as follows: mirror neurons do not discharge in response to object presentation; in order to be triggered they require a specific observed action. The majority of them respond selectively when the monkey observes one type of action (such as grasping). Some are highly specific, coding not only the action aim, but also how that action is executed. They fire, for example, during observation of grasping movements, but only when the object is grasped with the index finger and the thumb«.

movements, and subjects who are confronted with pictures of emotional facial expressions activate the respective muscular groups of their own faces. However, Damasio's model of the as-if-body-loop describes a neural mirroring of *cognitive* information about *somatosensory* states. While I think it a plausible supposition that these are quite similar phenomena, I am most sceptical about the inference of a *general principle* of neural mirroring which would suggest an *all-purpose mechanism* mirroring whatever kind of information about whatever kind of another's activity or experience. Indeed, there is some evidence that the mirroring of motoric acts in macaques can also be stimulated cognitively, as the effect is the same when the action is partly hidden or only heard.[67] The more in humans, whose mirror systems respond even to merely mimed actions (without real object, for example).[68] Furthermore, emotion recognition seems to involve »a similar mechanism« as is involved in action recognition:[69] In terms of at least some basic emotions, like for instance disgust, there are findings which indicate that the sight of the corresponding facial expression produces partly the same neural maps as an individual's own experience of that emotion.[70] But these emotional maps still involve different cortical regions than Damasio's body-sensing maps[71] and perhaps are more likely to prepare emotional contagion processes than empathic feelings.[72] – As matters stand, the default hypothesis should be that neural mirroring is an abstraction from many quite specific sub-mechanisms built into specific adaptive programs, rather than a detached all-purpose mechanism. This supposition fits with the observation that the human mirror system responds more eagerly if the observed action has a perceptible goal or intention, and if this goal is a rather biologically ›basic‹ than culturally learned one, like for instance drinking in comparison to

---

67 Gallese / Keysers / Rizzolatti: View, p. 397.
68 Ibid.
69 Ibid., p. 397.
70 Ibid., pp. 399f.; Gervais / Wilson: Laughter, p. 405; Heberlein / Adolphs: Neurobiology, pp. 40–42.
71 Gallese / Keysers / Rizzolatti: View, p. 400, and Rizzolatti / Sinigaglia: Mirrors, pp. 187–189. See also Heberlein / Adolphs: Neurobiology, pp. 42–44.
72 Existing neuroimaging experiments have concentrated on only a handful of affective states, including pain, fear, disgust and, more rarely, anger – all of which are possible instances of emotional contagion. Moreover, the performance of mirror neurons in perspective-taking tasks seems poorer than one would expect if mirror neurons are taken to provide a crucial substrate for empathic imagination (see Pfeifer / Dapretto: Mirror); rather it seems that empathy even works in patients who lack the neural circuits necessary for first-order mirroring (see Danziger / Faillenot / Peyron: Can We).

cleaning.[73] Findings of this kind strongly suggest that neural mirroring circuits always pertain to particular basic behavioural systems,[74] the identification of which should be at least as important as the observation that they involve mirroring processes.[75] Examples of such basic behavioural systems may be the above mentioned ones of mind reading, cheater detection, social learning, social status assessment, and the like.

To come back to literary characters: Programs of social cognition which are likely to be prerequisite to processes of neural mirroring are also likely to be prerequisite to psycho-poetic effects, because their activity, in the first place, identifies socially relevant information as such. Without those programs, textual information about people would remain pallid just as the textual device of focalization would remain pallid without the corresponding cognitive programs of individual experience. Since humans developed the art of storytelling, it is of course hardly surprising that the nature and properties of narratives in a way reproduce and reflect the nature and properties of the human mind. Consequently, the challenge within a perspective of ›cognitive poetics‹ aiming at more than speaking truisms would be to determine the particular mechanisms involved in this relationship. What I tried to show in this paper is that this aim is not achieved by simply replacing traditional aesthetic notions like mimesis, imagination or character with more ›mentalist‹ concepts like imitation, simulation or person schema, or by correlating it with assumed psychological verities like empathy, neural mirroring, or similarly broad concepts; but that the description of the mind probably requires the same grade of differentiation and functional analysis as the description of a text; and that the heuristic question of whether a particular cognitive routine could have evolved as a specifically adaptive algorithm may help us come closer to demounting the too-broad concepts of our intuitive psychological kowledge. It is needless to say that there still remains a lot to be done and that I could only draw a rough sketch of the field.

---

73 Iacoboni et al.: Grasping, p. 533, and Iacoboni: Revolution, pp. 447f.
74 See, as an example, a special mechanism for laughter contagion as proposed by Gervais / Wilson: Laughter, p. 406.
75 Similarly Gervais / Wilson: Laughter, p. 406, arguing that »the neural bases of laughter and yawn contagion should not necessarily be the same« and that »the two behaviors deserve to be evaluated on their own terms and only then compared«.

References

Adolphs, Ralph / Hanna Damasio / Daniel Tranel / Greg Cooper / Antonio R. Damasio: A Role for Somatosensory Cortices in the Visual Recognition of Emotions as Revealed by 3-D Lesion Mapping. In: The Journal of Neuroscience 20 (2000), pp. 2683–2690.

Batson, C. Daniel: These Things Called Empathy. Eight Related but Distinct Phenomena. In: Jean Decety / William John Ickes (Eds.): The Social Neuroscience of Empathy. Cambridge 2009, pp. 3–15.

Blythe, Philip P. / Peter M. Todd / Geoffrey F. Miller (2001): How Motion Reveals Intention. Categorizing Social Interactions. In: Gerd Gigerenzer / P.M.T. / ABC Research Group (Eds.): Simple Heuristics That Make Us Smart. New York / Oxford 1999, pp. 257–285.

Borg, Emma: If Mirror Neurons Are the Answer, What Was the Question? In: Journal of Consciousness Studies 14/8 (2007), pp. 5–19.

Bortulussi, Marisa / Peter Dixon: Psychonarratology. Foundations for the Empirical Study of Literary Response. Cambridge / New York 2003.

Cosmides, Leda / John Tooby: Evolutionary Psychology of the Emotions and Their Relationship to Internal Regulatory Variables. In: Michael Lewis / Jeannette M. Haviland-Jones / Lisa F. Barrett (Eds.): Handbook of Emotions. 3rd edn. New York 2008, pp. 114–137.

Cosmides, Leda / John Tooby: The Cognitive Neuroscience of Social Reasoning. In: Michael S. Gazzaniga (Ed.): The New Cognitive Neurosciences. 2nd edn. Cambridge / London 2000, pp. 1259–1270.

Damasio, Antonio R.: Descartes' Error. Emotion, Reason, and the Human Brain. New York 1994.

Damasio, Antonio R.: The Feeling of What Happens. Body and Emotion in the Making of Consciousness. New York 1999.

Damasio, Antonio R.: Looking for Spinoza. Joy, Sorrow, and the Feeling Brain. Orlando et al. 2003.

Danziger, Nicolas / Isabelle Faillenot / Roland Peyron: Can We Share a Pain We Never Felt? Neural Correlates of Empathy in Patients with Congenital Insensitivity to Pain. In: Neuron 61 (2009), pp. 203–212.

Decety, Jean: A Social Cognitive Neuroscience Model of Human Empathy. In: Eddie Harmon-Jones (Ed.): Social Neuroscience. Integrating Biological and Psychological Explanations of Social Behavior. New York / London 2007, pp. 246–270.

Eibl, Karl: Animal poeta. Bausteine der biologischen Literatur- und Kulturtheorie. Paderborn 2004.

Ermer, Elsa / Scott A. Guerin / Leda Cosmides / John Tooby / Michael B. Miller: Theory of Mind Broad and Narrow. Reasoning about Social Exchange Engages ToM Areas, Precautionary Reasoning Does Not. In: Social Neuroscience 1/3&4 (2006), pp. 196–219.

Fludernik, Monika / Uri Margolin: Introduction. In: Style 38/2 (2004), pp. 148–187.

Frey, Felix: Erfahrungshaftigkeit als Attraktivitätspotential narrativer Formen. In: Carsten Gansel, Dirk Vanderbeke (Eds.): Geschichten erzählen. Evolution und Literatur – Evolution der Literatur. Berlin, New York (forthcoming).

Frijda, Nico H.: The Nature of Pleasure. In: John A. Bargh / Deborah K. Apsley (Eds.): Unraveling the Complexities of Social Life. A Festschrift in Honor of Robert B. Zajonc. Washington 2000, pp. 71–94.

Gallese, Vittorio / Christian Keysers / Giacomo Rizzolatti: A Unifying View of the Basis of Social Cognition. In: Trends in Cognitive Sciences 8/9 (2004), pp. 396–403.

Genette, Gérard: Narrative Discourse. Transl. by Jane E. Lewin. Forew. by Jonathan Culler. Oxford 1986.
Genette, Gérard: Narrative Discourse Revisited. Trans. Jane E. Lewin. Ithaca 1988.
Gervais, Matthew / David Sloan Wilson: The Evolution and Functions of Laughter and Humor. A Synthetic Approach. In: The Quarterly Review of Biology 80/4 (2005), pp. 395–430.
Heberlein, Andrea S. / Ralph Adolphs: Neurobiology of Emotion Recognition. Current Evidence for Shared Substrates. In: Eddie Harmon-Jones (Ed.): Social Neuroscience. Integrating Biological and Psychological Explanations of Social Behavior. New York / London 2007, pp. 31–55.
Iacoboni, Marco / Istvan Molnar-Szakacs / Vittorio Gallese / Giovanni Buccino / John C. Mazziotta / Giacomo Rizzolatti.: Grasping the Intentions of Others with One's Own Mirror Neuron System. In: PLoS Biology 3/3 (2005), pp. 529–535.
Iacoboni, Marco: The Quiet Revolution of Existential Neuroscience. In: Eddie Harmon-Jones (Ed.): Social Neuroscience. Integrating Biological and Psychological Explanations of Social Behavior. New York / London 2007, pp. 439–453.
Ickes, William John: Introduction. In: W.J.I. (Ed.): Empathic Accuracy. New York et al. 1997, pp. 1–16.
James, William: What is an Emotion? In: Mind 9 (1884), pp. 188–205.
Jannidis, Fotis: Zur kommunikativen Intention. Anfänge. In: Karl Eibl / Katja Mellmann / Rüdiger Zymner (Eds.): Im Rücken der Kulturen. Paderborn 2007, pp. 185–204.
Koepsell, Kilian / Carlos Spoerhase: Neuroscience and the Study of Literature. Some Thoughts on the Possibility of Transferring Knowledge. In: Journal of Literary Theory 2/2 (2008), pp. 363–374.
Lauer, Gerhard: Spiegelneuronen. Über den Grund des Wohlgefallens an der Nachahmung. In: Karl Eibl / Katja Mellmann / Rüdiger Zymner (Eds.): Im Rücken der Kulturen. Paderborn 2007, pp. 137–163.
Lindenberger, Herbert: Arts in the Brain; or, What Might Neuroscience Tell Us? In: Frederick Luis Aldama (Ed.): Toward a Cognitive Theory of Narrative Acts. Austin 2010, pp. 13–35.
Mellmann, Katja: Emotionalisierung – Von der Nebenstundenpoesie zum Buch als Freund. Eine emotionspsychologische Analyse der Literatur der Aufklärungsepoche. Paderborn 2006.
Mellmann, Katja: Literatur als emotionale Attrappe. Eine evolutionspsychologische Lösung des ›paradox of fiction‹. In: Uta Klein / K.M. / Steffanie Metzger (Eds.): Heuristiken der Literaturwissenschaft. Disziplinexterne Perspektiven auf Literatur. Paderborn 2006, pp. 145–166.
Mellmann, Katja: Voice and Perception. An Evolutionary Approach to the Basic Functions of Narrative. In: Frederick Luis Aldama (Ed.): Toward a Cognitive Theory of Narrative Acts. Austin 2010, pp. 119–140.
Mellmann, Katja: Evolutionary Psychology as a Heuristic in Literary Studies. In: Simon J. James / Nicholas Saul (Eds.): The Evolution of Literature. Legacies of Darwin in European Cultures. Amsterdam (forthcoming).
Norris, Catherine J. / John T. Cacioppo: I Know How You Feel. Social and Emotional Information Processing in the Brain. In: Eddie Harmon-Jones (Ed.): Social Neuroscience. Integrating Biological and Psychological Explanations of Social Behavior. New York / London 2007, pp. 84–105.
Oatley, Keith / Mitra Gholamain: Emotions and Identification. Connections between Readers and Fiction. In: Mette Hjort / Sue Laver (Eds.): Emotions and the Arts. New York / Oxford 1997, pp. 263–281.

Oatley, Keith / Raymond A. Mar: Evolutionary Pre-adaptation and the Idea of Character in Fiction. In: Journal of Cultural and Evolutionary Psychology 3/2 (2005), pp. 179–194.

O'Neill, Patrick: Points of Origin. On Focalization in Narrative. In: Canadian Review of Comparative Literature 19 (1992), pp. 331–350.

Pfeifer, Jennifer H. / Mirella Dapretto: »Mirror, Mirror, in My Mind«. Empathy, Interpersonal Competence, and the Mirror Neuron System. In: Jean Decety / William John Ickes (Eds.): The Social Neuroscience of Empathy. Cambridge 2009, pp. 183–197.

Ramachandran, Vilayanur S.: Mirror Neurons and the Brain in the Vat. In: Edge, no. 176 (Jan. 12th, 2006).
<http://www.edge.org/3rd_culture/ramachandran06/ramachandran06_index.html.> (May 23rd, 2008).

Rizzolatti, Giacomo / Michael A. Arbib: Language within our Grasp. In: Trends in Neurosciences 21 (1998), pp. 188–194.

Rizzolatti, Giacomo / Corrado Sinigaglia: Mirrors in the Brain. How Our Minds Share Actions and Emotions. Transl. by Frances Anderson. Oxford 2008.

Salgaro, Massimo: Stories without Words. Narratives of the Brain. In: Cognitive Philology 2 (2009).
<http://padis2.uniroma1.it:81/ojs/index.php/cogphil/article/view/3774/3734> (Nov. 1st, 2009).

Scalise Sugiyama, Michelle: Reverse-Engineering Narrative: Evidence of Special Design. In: Jonathan Gottschall / David Sloan Wilson (Eds.): The Literary Animal. Evolution and the Nature of Narrative. Evanston 2005, pp. 177–196.

Scherer, Klaus: Emotion Serves to Decouple Stimulus and Response. In: Paul Ekman / Richard J. Davidson (Eds.): The Nature of Emotion. Fundamental Questions. New York / Oxford 1994, pp. 127–130.

Shamay-Tsoory, Simone G.: Empathic Processing. Its Cognitive and Affective Dimensions and Neuroanatomical Basis. In: Jean Decety / William John Ickes (Eds.): The Social Neuroscience of Empathy. Cambridge 2009, pp. 215–232.

Smith, Murray: Engaging Characters. Fiction, Emotion, and the Cinema. Oxford 1995.

Stanzel, Franz K.: Narrative Situations in the Novel. *Tom Jones, Moby-Dick, The Ambassadors, Ulysses*. Transl. by James P. Pusack. Bloomington / London 1971.

Stanzel, Franz K.: A Theory of Narrative. Transl. by Charlotte Goedsche. With a preface by Paul Hernadi. Cambridge 1984.

Stone, Valerie E.: An Evolutionary Perspective on Domain Specificity in Social Intelligence. In: Eddie Harmon-Jones (Ed.): Social Neuroscience. Integrating Biological and Psychological Explanations of Social Behavior. New York / London 2007, pp. 316–349.

Tan, Ed S.-H.: Film-Induced Affect as a Witness Emotion. In: Poetics 23 (1994), pp. 7–32.

Tan, Ed S.-H.: Emotion and the Structure of Narrative Film. Film as an Emotion Machine. Mahwah 1996.

Tan, Ed S.-H. / Nico S. Frijda: Sentiment in Film Viewing. In: Carl Plantinga / Greg M. Smith (Eds.): Passionate Views. Film, Cognition, and Emotion. Baltimore / London 1999, pp. 48–64.

Tooby, John / Leda Cosmides: Does Beauty Build Adapted Minds? Towards an Evolutionary Theory of Aesthetics, Fiction, and the Arts. In: SubStance. A Review of the Theory and Literary Criticism 30/1&2 (2001) (= Special Issue 94&95: On the Origin of Fictions), pp. 6–27.

Tooby, John / Leda Cosmides: The Psychological Foundations of Culture. In: Jerome H. Barkow / L.C. / J.T. (Eds.): The Adapted Mind. Evolutionary Psychology and the Generation of Culture. New York / Oxford 1992, pp. 19–136.

Woolf, Virginia: Jacob's Room, ed. With an Intr. and Notes by Sue Roe. London et al. 1992.

Wübben, Yvonne: Lesen als Mentalisieren? Neue kognitionswissenschaftliche Ansätze in der Leseforschung. In: Martin Huber / Simone Winko (Eds.): Literatur und Kognition. Bestandsaufnahmen und Perspektiven eines Arbeitsfeldes. Bielefeld 2009, pp. 29–44.

Zunshine, Lisa: Why we Read Fiction. Theory of Mind and the Novel. Columbus 2006.

Zunshine, Lisa: Strange Concepts and the Stories They Make Possible. Cognition, Culture, Narrative. Baltimore 2008.

Zunshine, Lisa: Mind Plus. Sociocognitive Pleasures of Jane Austen's Novels. In: Studies in the Literary Imagination 42/2 (2009) (forthcoming).

DAVID C. GILES

Parasocial Relationships

1 Introduction

> I love Molly. The more I start to think about and analyze the depth of her mothering for her own children and for Harry, the more overwhelmed with emotion I become.[1]

> I don't think Snape has ever said anything untrue, or anything that did not happen or was false, not about anyone. I don't have any doubt about it.[2]

In October 2007 author J.K. Rowling stunned millions of *Harry Potter* fans by suggesting that one of her characters, without any overt indication in the books, might be gay. Arguments raged among fans, some claiming that it had been evident all along, and that Rowling had struck a blow for gay pride, leaving others distraught that their image of Dumbledore, presumably as heterosexual, or asexual at best, had been tarnished forever.

Leaving aside the questionable (or perhaps thrillingly postmodern) act of an author publicly ›outing‹ her own characters and providing spurious ›backstory‹, this act of extra-textual revelation may have served to further reinforce Potter readers' impression that the characters on the page exist as real, tangible people who play a meaningful part in their day-to-day experience. By announcing that Dumbledore is ›really‹ gay, despite any mention or suggestion of sexuality in the novels, Rowling was effectively presenting Dumbledore as an authentic human being with a life beyond the text.

Did Potter fans need Rowling to perform this act of validation? If we study the above quotes, taken from two Harry Potter fan sites, it becomes clear that Dumbledore is not the only ›real‹ entity emerging from the pages of the books. The first fan ›loves‹ the character Molly and is ›overwhelmed‹ by her behaviour; the second claims that Snape is unfailingly

---

1 <http://www.leakylounge.com> (Potter discussion forum, Jan. 14th, 2009).
2 <http://www.chamberofsecrets.com> (Potter discussion forum, Jan. 14th, 2009).

honest, thus opening up a second layer of realism (for what has Snape got to be honest about, other than things that never ›really happened‹?)

These quotes are typical of millions posted on fan sites throughout cyberspace that refer to figures, real and imaginary, who have come to life for the fans involved, where the amount of information, whether factual or fictional, about the figures, have left in people's minds an impression they somehow *know* the figure, just as they know individuals in their immediate social circles. Harry Potter, Prince Harry, Harry Hill... in the imagination of the reader or viewer these distinctions blur. There are just Harries, as real as Harry who lives next door; perhaps more real, since they barely know Harry next door except to see him occasionally putting out his rubbish.

In an urbanised, increasingly alienated society, these imaginary Harries have become our social frame of reference. As James Caughey has argued, any society has a cast of characters that its members are expected to know about — whether spirits, leaders or media figures.[3] Such figures can act as social ›glue‹, to provide common cultural ground among strangers. And it does seem that we spend a good deal of our social interaction time conversing about people we have never met, yet feel that we know. And we spend yet more time privately, consuming media — watching television, listening to the radio, reading newspapers — and reading books and watching films, and surfing the internet. All these activities immerse us in a virtual social network where we come to know faces, voices, bodies, beliefs, opinions, ways of looking at the world, sometimes to a degree of intimacy that might not even be possible with a romantic partner, let alone Harry next door.

This phenomenon — a ›feeling of knowing‹ that comes from media use or cultural activity — is something that most people identify with, at least from an anecdotal point of view. We all seem to have a story about running into someone famous, or at least someone we recognise through the media, who at first strikes us as an old friend or colleague, until a second or so's reflection brings us to the realisation that he or she is someone we have never before actually met in the flesh.

It happened to me once, when I was a student in the leafy Georgian English town of Cheltenham, where the local cricket team, Gloucestershire, play an occasional match at the Boys' college. I saw this portly middle-aged gentleman looking slightly lost at the corner of the street by the college cricket ground one summer evening, and at first took him to be a fellow university lecturer; but I couldn't bring to mind his name, or

---

3   Caughey: Imaginary.

decide whether or not to greet him – standard split-second decisions we all make in social situations of this sort.

Instead he approached me, and asked me in his West Country burr if I knew of a hotel in the vicinity. Suddenly I realised where I knew him from: he was a famous umpire, who had officiated in tests all over the cricketing world, who I had watched on many occasions on television. He had never seen me before in his life. I was a complete stranger to him. And not much help either – I didn't have a clue about local hotels. So there we were, a famous cricket umpire and a budding psychologist with poor local accommodation knowledge. We had a relationship, now, of sorts, but we *had* had, unbeknown to him, a relationship of sorts for many years. I like to describe this kind of one-way relationship as a *parasocial* relationship.

2 Parasocial Interaction: The Research Literature

The concept of parasocial interaction has existed in communication and media studies for several decades. The term was first coined back in the 1950s by sociologist Donald Horton and his psychiatrist co-author Richard Wohl in a paper in a psychiatric journal.[4] The authors were particularly interested in styles of radio broadcasting that had adopted the ›fireside‹ technique of presentation – so-called because the broadcaster's intention was to make the listener feel as if they were at home by the fireside listening to an old friend talking.[5]

During these broadcasts, Horton and Wohl argued, radio listeners become drawn into an illusion of intimacy with the radio persona – whether real or fictional – and may even experience the belief that they are the recipient of a personal address (as intended by the producer). They cited the example of ›The Lonesome Gal‹, a regular broadcast on US network radio in the early 1950s, which featured a young woman with a seductive voice addressing the listener as her lover, inviting ›him‹ to lie down on the couch with her and have ›his‹ hair stroked. Evidently large numbers of lonesome boys were captivated by this broadcast, because thousands of letters subsequently arrived at the radio studio proposing marriage.[6]

The authors were not content to present this as a temporary one-off phenomenon, a quirk solely brought about by the advent of broadcasting.

---

4 Horton / Wohl: Mass.
5 Scannell: Radio, p. 19.
6 Horton / Wohl: Mass, p. 224.

They saw it as symptomatic of fundamental social needs in human beings that had been brought to life by these new media. They explicitly suggested a research programme emerging from their ideas.

> It seems to us that it would be a most rewarding approach to such phenomena if one could, from the viewpoint of an interactional social psychology, learn in detail how these para-social interactions are integrated into the matrix of usual social activity.[7]

In the fifty years that have passed since their paper, however, this research programme is still not forthcoming. The development of the concept of parasocial interaction has undergone periodic bursts without ever really becoming an established topic in communication and media studies: in psychology it is still largely unknown.

Communication research on parasocial phenomena emerged gradually during the 1970s, when an American scholar, Mark Levy, developed a psychometric scale in order to measure the strength of parasocial interaction that existed between television viewers and their local newscasters.[8] He assembled a series of statements about newscasters from comments made in focus groups of local news viewers, for example ›I compare my own ideas with those of newscasters‹, and ›When the newscasters joke around with each other it makes the program easier to watch‹. Then a sample of viewers were asked to rate each statement on a Likert-type scale according to what extent they agreed, or disagreed, with it.

This scale was picked up during the 1980s by a team of researchers at Kent State University and, following a series of publications, turned into an instrument – typically described as the Parasocial Interaction Scale – that could be used to measure ›strength‹ of parasocial interaction.[9] In subsequent research, variants of this scale were used to measure strength of interaction with soap characters, comedians, TV shopping hosts and general television personalities,[10] but few researchers actually oriented their research towards the *topic* of parasocial behaviour. It became just one quantitative ›variable‹ employed in a multivariate study with the aim of predicting scores on another, more important, variable.

More recently, I published a review of the literature on parasocial interaction in an attempt to generate some research that sought to address the limitations in the current literature.[11] Some of my suggestions are slowly being taken on board by other researchers, but it is notable that

---

7   Ibid., p. 229.
8   Levy: Watching.
9   Rubin / Perse / Powell: Audience.
10 Giles: Media, p. 189.
11 Giles: Parasocial.

there is a general reluctance to deal with parasocial interaction in any way other than as a quantitative variable, with researchers unable or unwilling to broaden the concept within scientific psychology, qualitative social science, psychoanalytic theory, or any other academic discipline.

Meanwhile, a related phenomenon has emerged in the psychological literature in the last decade – celebrity worship. Like parasocial interaction, the study of celebrity worship has thus far been chained to the kitchen sink of psychometrics, with the development of a scale – the Celebrity Worship Scale – that first appeared in 2001 and has since inspired over 30 studies,[12] each of them a multivariate study with celebrity worship as a predictor of some other variable of interest. I don't really want to discuss celebrity worship here, because it is a slightly controversial concept in its own right. However, just to clear up a common confusion: parasocial interaction is, occasionally, described as a form of celebrity worship. However, if the concept of parasociality is to be of any use to us at all, it has to be the other way round: celebrity worship is a form, or subset, of the broad and diverse behaviour known as parasocial interaction.

3 Limitations of Research on Parasocial Interaction

Most communication and media scholars agree, I am sure, that the concept of parasocial interaction is undeveloped, and has remained that way simply because nobody has thought up methodologically acceptable ways to develop it. I'm presently working on one, which I will describe at relevant points here, but it's not an easy task, largely because – as I continue to argue – it is really the job of psychology to define the parameters of parasocial behaviour, and psychology seems to have an even bigger problem with the concept.

Let's start by thinking about the parasocial relationship itself. For many psychologists this kind of experience is not strictly speaking a relationship at all, because all relationship theory is founded on the assumption of *reciprocity*. Understandable, because applied psychology – clinical psychology for example – is primarily concerned with the study of dyadic relationships, or specified relationships like families or occupational work groups. Even where interaction is conducted via the internet, we assume reciprocity – if you kept e-mailing someone and never received a single reply you could hardly say that you and that person had a relationship. After all, it could be that the e-mail address does not exist.

---

[12] Maltby et al.: Worshippers.

So the parasocial relationship is not like a social relationship, which is why the term parasocial is used. This, however, leads people to assume that the relationship must be ›imaginary‹, and that the person is experiencing an illusion that the media figure is somehow involved in a relationship with them – rather like the psychiatric syndrome ›erotomania‹ where people believe themselves to be sexually involved with a famous person.[13] This interpretation of parasocial phenomena has alienated many communication and media scholars from the broad concept, leading to charges that it ›pathologises‹ media users. This is, I believe, an over-reaction to a very limited conceptualisation of the phenomenon. For any individual in modern society, parasocial relationships are experienced with many thousands of media figures – real, fictional, perhaps even nonhuman.

To some extent the problems with parasocial interaction arise from the limited way in which the concept has been conceived, and explored, in the literature. Most research involving parasocial phenomena has used the parasocial interaction scale in some form or other, but the parasocial scale usually measures only interaction with one chosen figure (typically ›my favourite soap character‹ or whatever). This may be useful for the purposes of a study with a broad interest in soap (where the researcher might be primarily interested in what motivates viewers to prefer certain characters), but as a global index of an individual's parasocial life, it is of course useless. It could even be argued that it is not much help in understanding how individuals interact with soap characters. It is unlikely that each respondent in the study will only have a meaningful relationship with one character, or that they can even identify one single favourite character (indeed, many studies measuring parasocial interaction fail to gather information about respondents' ›favourite‹ media figures).

Then a great deal of the literature on parasocial interaction defines it in a very narrow fashion. Many researchers use the term to refer to the way that television viewers (invariably television rather than media generally) respond to the presence of a figure on the screen. Some of the items in the parasocial interaction scale seem to invite this interpretation, for example »When I'm watching the newscast, I feel as if I am part of their group«, and »I sometimes make remarks to my favorite newscaster during the newscast«,[14] which suggest that the viewer is responding to the figure as if he or she were another person in the same physical space.

This is where communication research and psychological theory seem to be at odds. A psychologist would, understandably, have little interest in

---

13 Franzini / Grossberg: Eccentric.
14 Rubin / Perse / Powell: Audience, p. 167.

a concept that was restricted to behaviour performed by a television viewer in the act of viewing, unless it had some kind of pathological consequence (hence, I suspect, the objection made by media scholars towards the parasocial concept itself). A communication scholar, being primarily interested in soap per se, might not want to waste time pondering the psychological ramifications of viewer behaviour, or to categorise that behaviour in any wider context.

And yet, a number of researchers have since attempted to expand the measurement of parasocial activity in general by creating new instruments. Philip Auter developed the Audience-Persona Interaction Scale,[15] which includes some similar items to the Rubin Scale but also, importantly, includes items relating to both similarity and wishful identification with the media figure. Brown and Bocarnea have also developed instruments for measuring parasocial interaction and identification, but as separate constructs.[16] Holger Schramm and Tilo Hartmann have developed the PSI-Process Scale,[17] a more theoretically-informed measure of psychological processes that occur during interaction with media figures.

It seems clear that researchers are now expanding the scope of parasocial interaction, but at the same time, making important distinctions between the cognitive, affective, and behavioural processes that take place during the media encounter, and the longer-term psychological processes that influence the development of parasocial relationships with media figures. It is plainly nonsensical to view media figures as temporary phenomena whose existence is only meaningful while they are being watched on the screen. This reductionism stems from ›media effects‹ research where phenomena like ›media violence‹ are treated as experimental stimuli, abstracted from their narrative context and presented in an artificial environment. Media figures enter at multiple levels in our day-to-day lives. A celebrity is watched on TV, heard on radio, read about in newspapers and magazines, interacted with virtually, discussed with peers, and so on.

Hartmann et al. describe the parasocial relationship as »an enduring mental relational schema fueled by parasocial interactions that are conducted during media exposure«.[18] In other words, repeated encounters shape and modify the initial schema over time, particularly in relation to affective evaluations (Do I *like* the figure?). Unusually, these researchers incorporate the possibility that these relationships are not necessarily

---

15 Auter / Palmgreen: Development.
16 Brown / Bocarnea: Celebrity-Persona; Bocarnea/Brown: Celebrity-Persona.
17 Schramm / Hartmann: The PSI-Process.
18 Hartmann / Stuke / Daschmann: Positive, p. 26.

positive, which marks an important break from the long-established focus on ›favourite‹ celebrities, characters, and so on. At what precise point an interaction develops into a relationship, is a question that remains unanswered as yet.

There remains also the problem of measurement. Hartmann et al., in their most recent work on parasocial relationships with racing drivers,[19] used a number of items from existing parasocial scales that captured affective aspects of the relationship. However, the idiographic perspective – focusing on the multiple ›schemas‹ each of us holds in relation to a vast range of media figures – may be harder to capture. Nevertheless, this should not prevent researchers from addressing the question. In personality research, there is a move back towards the idiographic approach:[20] it would be interesting to see if this could be applied to relationship (and parasocial relationship) theory too.

Qualitative researchers might not even see the measurement issue as problematic. After all, who cares about designing instruments and measuring relationship ›strength‹ if you want to fully understand the experience of parasocial interaction, or explore what meanings a broad range of media figures hold for media users? You might also want to broaden the scope of parasocial interaction beyond the experiences of individuals, and explore the way in which media figures are incorporated into the social activities of groups – as discussion material, or points of comparison, yardsticks by which other individuals are judged. All these research questions require the collection of rich qualitative data: they are simply beyond the scope of reliable psychometric scaling.

4 Avenues for Further Exploration of Parasocial Phenomena

The remainder of this chapter will be rather speculative, I'm afraid, but it simply reflects the fact that the research hasn't been done: we are still awaiting serious developments in this field. Nonetheless I will mention, where relevant, ongoing research that is seeking to push some of the boundaries of the parasocial concept.

---

19 Ibid.
20 Cervone: Architecture.

4.1 Parasocial Interaction and the Internet

Developments in parasocial research have been further complicated by the arrival of the internet. It is frustrating that a medium with such a potentially profound impact (as the internet) has appeared before media psychology has really emerged as an academic discipline. Instead of moving swiftly ahead with a set of established theories about the relationship between media and psychology, we have entered the Internet age still speculating about this relationship; meanwhile, a multitude of theories about the Internet have appeared without any reference to traditional media at all. The result: an even greater diversity of research than before.

I have seen, very occasionally, online relationships described as ›parasocial‹. This is of course a misunderstanding of the concept of parasociality (however defined). An online relationship, for example a cyber-romance set in motion via a dating website, consists of two individuals interacting in a reciprocal fashion, sending and receiving emails, texts, or whatever. The only way in which this differs from any other kind of social relationship is that the interaction is not face-to-face. There is actually nothing very new about this kind of interaction. People have been communicating over long distances by letter for centuries, by telephone for decades, without necessarily ever meeting in person. There has always been an identity puzzle to solve (Is the person whose letter I'm reading the same person as in the photo they've inserted?) Of course the internet has made this type of relationship easier to come by, but cyber-relationships are perhaps less interesting and revolutionary than cyber-enthusiasts sometimes make out.

Parasocial relationships, while enjoying a long history, are entirely different. The defining feature of a parasocial relationship is that the communication is all one-way. Of course we can have parasocial interaction online, but if the e-mail I send to my favourite newscaster is responded to by my favourite newscaster, then it is no longer parasocial – it is a relationship like any other, whether ›cyber‹ or *epistolary* (I could have sent my favourite newscaster a letter in 1950 and received a letter in response – the difference is simply one of medium).

But the real issue, now as ever, is whether the response really has emanated from my favourite newscaster rather than a proxy of some sort. Some research in progress on the nature of parasocial interaction online has explored whether fan interaction on fan websites is truly parasocial. It is a good question. Many fan websites have forums in which the celebrity or artist communicates directly with fans. I have heard of fans recounting excitedly the message ›they‹ received from their hero in response to something posted on a message board.

Naturally the technology of the internet has made it easier for celebrities and other media figures to make personal contact with their fans. Once upon a time, Clark Gable (or whoever) could only do this by a) making a personal appearance; or b) sitting down with his PA and signing, or actually typing or handwriting, a pile of letters. Of course a) is still a frequent fan club activity. But I find it hard to imagine b) occurring with any regularity in pre-Internet history.

Today, however, the modern day Clark Gables can log on, from the comfort of their Hollywood mansion, Hawaii hotel suite, or studio lounge, and reply to any number of interesting-looking fan e-mails or forum posts. They don't even need a PA to sift through them. Indeed it may be quite an enjoyable part of modern celebrity life to browse through your cyber-mail and identify quirky or stimulating messages sent by quirky or stimulating fans. Since one of the most irksome features of celebrity is the loss of control over your popularity (inviting interest from unattractive as well as attractive individuals),[21] the Internet is a godsend in this respect.

Where does this leave online parasocial interaction? Undoubtedly it problematises the concept – at least with certain, easily accessible media figures, such as artists, musicians, actors, celebrities. But as I will go on to explain in the next section, these are only a subset of the figures with whom we can have parasocial relationships.

4.2 Parasocial Relationships with Different Types of Media Figure

One of the most important qualities of parasocial interaction, and one of its most fascinating features, is that it pushes the boundaries of logic and rationalism. This of course runs the risk of researchers ›pathologising‹ individuals who have parasocial relationships that are themselves highly illogical (with figures who are dead, fictional, or nonhuman in form). However, on the contrary, I think it is essential that parasocial interaction is *normalised* in the sense that its definition incorporates all these unusual relationships as well as the ones that have been conceptualised in most of the communication research (with ostensibly ›real‹, tangible, and frankly not very interesting figures like newscasters).

In my theoretical 2002 paper I argued that parasocial interaction should be conceptualised as one end of a continuum of *potential encounters* between

---

21 Giles: Illusions.

two individuals.²² At the other end of this continuum I placed a face-to-face encounter between two single individuals – let's say a conventional dinner date. Of course there's nothing remotely ›potential‹ about this encounter. It's undoubtedly happening here and now. The potential is in the outcome of the relationship: for our daters anything is possible – sex, reproduction, eternal union.

Further down the continuum, things become more speculative. The encounter may take place in a much more ambiguous context, such as a lecturer giving a class to 100 students, of which you are just one in the crowd. Not very intimate, but outside the lecture hall it is nonetheless theoretically possible for you to enter into a sexual relationship with the lecturer! Ditto a singer performing live to a concert hall audience. Or the encounter takes place remotely, in which case the actual nature of the individuals involved becomes more important. If your lecturer phones you up then it suddenly becomes much more intimate. If it's your favourite singer on the other end of the phone you really are in luck.

Things only start to get really interesting once we reach the other end of the continuum. Here the remoteness of the encounter is such that intimacy becomes very difficult to conceive: watching your favourite singer on television introduces all manner of doubt as to his or her reality: maybe the performance is recorded, maybe it's someone else masquerading as your favourite singer (although this is, to some extent, applicable to the live performance too), but you are also in a potential audience of millions. Not so intimate.

Then we must consider the role of other figures. Dinner dates, lecturers, singers are all individuals with whom we can – to a greater or lesser extent – consider potential mates, or at least potential friends. But there are a host of media figures for whom this potential is lacking. If your favourite singer is Elvis Presley the chances of him calling you up are slender. James Bond may be your idea of the perfect sexual partner. Harry Potter might seem like your potential best friend. Or Bart or Lisa Simpson. But in each of these cases the potential outcome of your relationship is extremely limited; it is restricted to the parasocial encounter and nothing more.

Bringing fictional and nonhuman figures into the scope of parasocial activity is nothing new – the parasocial interaction scale has been used to measure strength of interaction with soap characters, for example.²³ But the parasocial concept still lacks any theoretical framework to account for their lack of reality status. As the previous section on online interaction

---

22 Giles: Parasocial.
23 Rubin / Perse: Audience.

suggests, this distinction has become more important with the advent of the Internet and the increased potential access to real-life media figures. When Harry Potter replies to a fan post, there is no ambiguity as to his reality status.

The distinction of different levels of parasocial interaction was the cornerstone of my 2002 paper.[24] The model identified three levels: real (newscasters, celebrities, etc), fictional human (soap characters, human protagonists of novels or films), and fictional nonhuman (cartoon or fantasy characters, animals). In recent research I have been attempting to identify differences between parasocial interaction with these figures. It hasn't been easy. The only variable which seems really to identify the different levels is an extreme one: reactions to the envisaged death of the figure. I asked respondents to select ›least favourite‹ figures from each level. While most respondents were happy to see their least favourite fictional nonhuman character meet a messy end, they were less keen to see their least favourite real figure die. However much they might dislike Victoria Beckham, the dislike doesn't really extend to seeing her dead. But for most other parasocial activity, reality status seems (at this stage in the project) to have very little impact.

These findings suggest that parasocial interaction with fictional figures shares a common basis with any other kind of parasocial activity, at least while we are content to maintain the relationship at a parasocial level (and not making strenuous attempts to make contact with the figure, in which case we enter the world of fan activity, which is not quite the same thing).

Recent research on narrative engagement and realism points the way forward for a theoretical framework that ought to underpin much of the future research on parasocial phenomena. Busselle and Bilandzic argue that there are two types of realism that influence our engagement with narratives.[25] One is *external* realism – the degree to which the elements of stories reflect our real world experiences (setting, character, action). The other is *narrative* realism – the plausibility and coherence of the story itself. Through our engagement with this aspect of stories, we are effectively ›transported‹ into narratives to an extent that we lose awareness of the external world.[26]

How does this work in terms of parasocial interaction? The power of narrative realism may be sufficient to overcome the lack of reality status of the media figures – so we respond to fictional characters at the same level as real people. There is plenty of evidence that this happens, and not just

---

24 Giles: Parasocial.
25 Busselle / Bilandzic: Fictionality.
26 Green / Brock / Kaufman: Understanding.

during the act of viewing – for example, soap actors being chastised by members of the public for the moral failings of their characters.[27] Narrative realism may account for the similarity of responses in our own research towards celebrities and cartoon characters.

It might also account for our complex relationships with figures that transcend the media that they appear in. Harry Potter is one: we know him as a literary protagonist and as a film character. The latter representation has of course coloured the former: for many people Potter is indistinguishable from the actor who plays him.

James Bond is an even more complicated example, because not only does he have parallel representations in written fiction and film, he has been represented in film by such a variety of different actors that we have all had, over time, to re-examine our relationship with him (the same applies, albeit largely in a visual context, with the British TV figure Dr Who). Only the narrative is left for us to engage with, and yet we undoubtedly enjoy – to a greater or lesser extent – parasocial relationships with Bond and Potter.

5 Final Thoughts

Ultimately, parasocial interaction is about encountering a figure through a medium and then *treating that figure as if it were another human being*. We don't need to say anything, or ›behave‹ overtly in any particular way, but we need to respond, albeit in a purely cognitive fashion, to the figure as we might respond to a human in an ordinary social encounter. When that figure is a real human being, such as our local newscaster, the response is perhaps logical; when it is a fictional creation, or a nonhuman or dead figure, the response is illogical. But that is not the same as saying it is pathological.

The common framework for all parasocial phenomena should therefore be the narrative context. Parasocial interaction takes place because the figures are encountered in a narrative context that makes a ›humane‹ response a logical one. We cry at the end of a sad film because the narrative has somehow seduced us into treating the characters as real people. We are concerned about the fate of the protagonist in a novel because the narrative has imbued that figure with realistic human qualities which have seduced us into believing in his or her reality. We sympathise with the fate of our favourite member of the Simpson family because the narrative context of the cartoon enables us to make these parallels.

---

27 Tal-Or / Pepirman: Fundamental.

In addition to the persuasive power of narrative we have to consider some potential individual differences. One such possibility is that of anthropomorphism. It is possible that some individuals have a tendency to anthropomorphise more than others – children who are able to bring dolls, teddy bears, puppets and possibly imaginary friends to life (albeit in a well-organised narrative context), adults who can become as attached to pet animals as to humans. This possibility forms part of my current ongoing research programme.

One thing is certain however: the phenomenon of parasocial activity is far more interesting than it has been conceived so far in the academic literature. I hope that in writing this chapter I can stimulate someone, somewhere, to take up some of the themes as a serious research project.

References

Auter, Philip / Philip Palmgreen: Development and Validation of a Parasocial Interaction Measure: The Audience-Persona Interaction Scale. In: Communication Research Reports 17 (2000), pp. 79–89.

Bocarnea, Mihai / William Brown: Celebrity-Persona Interaction Scale. In: Rodney Reynolds / Robert Woods / Jason Baker (Eds.): Handbook of Research on Electronic Surveys and Measurements. Hershey 2007, pp. 309–312.

Brown, William / Mihai Bocarnea: Celebrity-Persona Identification Scale. In: Rodney Reynolds / Robert Woods / Jason Baker (Eds.): Handbook of Research on Electronic Surveys and Measurements. Hershey 2007, pp. 302–305.

Brown, William / Michael Basil / Mihai Bocarnea: Social Influence of an International Celebrity: Responses to the Death of Princess Diana. In: Journal of Communication 53 (2003), pp. 587–605.

Busselle, Rick / Helena Bilandzic: Fictionality and Perceived Realism in Experiencing Stories: A Model of Narrative Comprehension and Engagement. In: Communication Theory 18 (2008), pp. 255–280.

Caughey, James: Imaginary Social Worlds: A Cultural Approach. Lincoln 1984.

Cervone, Daniel: The Architecture of Personality. In: Psychological Review 111 (2004), pp.183–204.

Franzini, Louis / John Grossberg: Eccentric and Bizarre Behaviors. New York 1994.

Giles, David: Illusions of Immortality: A Psychology of Fame and Celebrity. Basingstoke 2000.

Giles, David: Media Psychology. New Jersey 2003.

Giles, David: Parasocial Interaction: A Review of the Literature and a Model for Future Research. In: Media Psychology 4 (2002), pp. 279–305.

Green, Melanie / Timothy Brock / Geoff Kaufman: Understanding Media Enjoyment: The Role of Ttransportation into Narrative Worlds. In: Communication Theory 14 (2004), pp. 311–327.

Hartmann, Tilo / Holger Schramm / Christoph Klimmt: Personenorientierte Medienrezeption: Ein Zwei-Ebenen-Modell parasozialer Interaktionen [Person-orientated Media Reception: A T-Level Model of Parasocial Interaction.]. In: Publizistik 49 (2004), pp. 25–47.

Hartmann, Tilo / Daniela Stuke / Gregor Daschmann: Positive Parasocial Relationships with Drivers Affect Suspense in Racing Sport Spectators. In: Journal of Media Psychology 20 (2008), pp. 24–34.

Horton, Donald / Richard Wohl: Mass Communication and Parasocial Interaction: Observations on Intimacy at a Distance. In: Psychiatry 19 (1956), pp. 215–229.

Levy, Mark: Watching TV News as Para-Social Interaction. In: Journal of Broadcasting 23 (1979), pp. 69–80.

Maltby, John / Lynn McCutcheon / Diane Ashe / James Houran: The Self-Reported Psychological Well-Being of Celebrity Worshippers. In: North American Journal of Psychology 3 (2001), pp.441–452.

Rubin, Alan / Elizabeth Perse: Audience Activity and Soap Opera Involvement: A Uses and Effects Investigation. In: Human Communication Research 14 (1987), pp. 246–268.

Rubin, Alan / Elizabeth Perse / Robert Powell: Loneliness, Parasocial Interaction, and Local Television News Viewing. In: Human Communication Research 12 (1985), pp. 155–180.

Scannell, Paddy: Radio, Television and Modern Life. Oxford 1996.

Schramm, Holger / Hartmann, Tilo: The PSI-Process Scales: A New Measure to Assess the Intensity and Breadth of Parasocial Processes. In: Communications 33 (2008), pp. 385–401.

Tal-Or, Nurit / Papirman, Yael: The Fundamental Attribution Error in Attributing Fictional Figures' Characteristics to the Actors. In: Media Psychology 9 (2007), pp. 331–345.

IV Characters, Culture, Identity

MARGRIT TRÖHLER

Multiple Protagonist Films
A Transcultural Everyday Practice[1]

> *What do such large loose baggy monsters,*
> *with their queer elements of the accidental*
> *and the arbitrary, artistically mean?*
>
> Henry James[2]

Henry James's question refers to novels like William Makepeace Thackeray's *The Newcomes* (1855), Alexandre Dumas's *Les trois mousquetaires* (1844), and Leo Tolstoi's *War and Peace* (1868). The literary scholar Peter Garrett considers James's question to present ›a general challenge to the integrity of the typically large and multifarious nineteenth-century novel‹, especially the Victorian novel.[3] While my essay focuses upon contemporary film, its narrative, media and cultural specificity, and its characters, the *multiplot* has long challenged all the narrative arts. In order to understand how a *multiplot* affects narratives or, more specifically, a narrative organised in terms of a multiple protagonist constellation, we must first revisit the traditional pattern which, at least in Western narrative traditions, has been predominant since the Enlightenment and the development of a modern notion of the subject. To this day, the model of the individual main character has prevailed in literature, the theatre, and film throughout the various historical paradigms in both theory and practice, even though it occurs in contingent variants. Thus, an individual

---

1   An earlier version of this paper was presented at the 2003 SCMS Conference in London. I am grateful to John Orr, Carrie Tarr, Glenn Man, and Samuel Ben Israel for their helpful comments.
2   James, Preface to *The Tragic Muse* (1934), quoted from Garrett: Multiplot, p. 1
3   Ibid. Much the same could be said about French Realism in the second half of the nineteenth century; see Hamon: Le personnel.

(male) hero organises the *character constellation* through a hierarchy of values, vertically so to speak: he stands at the apex of a pyramid or at the centre of a solar system while grouped around him are secondary main characters, actual minor characters, background or ornamental figures, and extras or supernumeraries.[4] As regards the dynamic development of the narration, as seen horizontally, this hero assumes the function of a protagonist who focuses the narrative *upon* himself and his actions, and places them in perspective *through* his world of experience and sometimes explicitly through his perception.[5] Nor does this change *a priori* if the scale of values is turned upside down, as in the modern form of the anti-hero where even a villain or a failure can function as a hero or main character, since the textual mirroring of the crisis of the subject and of social values remains oriented towards the individual.[6] In terms of narrative technique, this prototypical model rests upon a dual basic structure that assigns the narrative engine to two ›roles‹ and organises them in a conflictual or complementary ›pair‹ (Greimas's actantial model speaks of ›sujet‹ and ›anti-sujet‹, which corresponds to Propp's ›hero‹ and ›false hero‹).[7] However, this structure tends towards reduction and closure in a single, unified entity, either through excluding two rivals, or through uniting opposites as a pair of friends, or indeed through merging the pair of lovers in a happy ending – under male dominance.

As regards the *character conception* of the individual hero, that is, of the two-protagonist structure, in realistic texts, this meets the requirements of a psychologically ›round character‹. In contrast to the less important, ›flat characters‹ or ›types‹,[8] this emphasises the singularity and complexity of the individual. Round characters appear as a conglomerate or bundle of ›distinguishing features‹, and they can always spring a surprise.[9] Although embedded in the entire network of figures, as a main protagonist such a character centres the narrative dynamics through his activities or inner conflicts. He also subjects the interaction with the other characters in a given constellation to his development. In its radical formulation, this model seems to apply only to male heroes, since a heroine or female main character appears to shape a character constellation less hierarchically and

---

4   On character terminology, see Tröhler / Taylor: Personnage; on forms of character organisation in fictional worlds, see further Gardies: Récit, pp. 53–68; Doležel: Heterocosmica, pp. 96–112; Eder: Figur, pp. 464–520.
5   Genette: Figures, pp. 183–224; Eder: Figur, pp. 561–646.
6   Vanoye: Scénarios, pp. 46–58; Wulff: Held.
7   Greimas: Actants; Propp: Morphologie.
8   Forster: Aspects, pp. 67–112.
9   Lévi-Strauss: Anthropologie, pp. 162, 170.; Lotman: Struktur, p. 356.

less centripetally from the outset, instead moulding it in more relational terms.

The following criteria thus characterise in *prototypical* and *gradual* terms the narrative dynamics and perception of *individual main characters* or ›pairs‹: such protagonists dominate the (deep) structure of the semantic-logical plot functions (whether considered as ›actants‹, in Greimas's terms, or as ›roles‹ in Propp's). They determine which perspective is placed upon a narrative (thus influencing what spectators are able to see and know), function as social or symbolic nodes in the organisation of the fictional world, and form power centres. They as such often assume heroic status, especially as male characters, thereby activating axiological, moral, or even mythical values. In the case of an argumentative narrative stance, they are thus predestined to appear as the author's mouthpiece (and alter ego). In qualitative and quantitative terms, moreover, they assume a dominant textual, that is, onscreen presence, and attract considerable attention – not only as stage or screen stars who play off their socio-cultural image. Their characters are more strongly elaborated than those of other figures. They function as what is customarily known as a role model. They are the most sympathetic and disliked figures, and bind the emotional perception on the part of both the audience and the other characters.[10] Within the classical-realistic approach, they epitomise the individual psychological conception of an autonomous subject either as an indivisable being whose body and soul are one, or instead as a problematic figure in crisis that has emerged alongside the self-contained subject since modernity.

Obviously, no single main character hardly ever comprises all these various aspects, as modern heroes are not unbroken figures. Some, however, are mutually dependent (for example the morally positive hero and the narrative's main character), while others can be deconstructed without, however, questioning the centering function of one or two protagonists.

Thus, if this dominant pattern of individual main characters favours a dual basic structure and a temporal-causal, psychologically motivated orientation of the narration towards compromise, multiple protagonist constellations by contrast develop *another logic of narration* from the outset. While some of the above factors can become important in the latter constellation – sometimes even only temporarily – and can render obvious the diverse hierarchies between characters, they do not suffice to establish proper main characters or heroes. Decentering forces as such undermine the causal logic of the plot and the conception of the main characters as

---

10 Smith: Engaging; Eder: Figur, pp. 647–706.

motivated by individual psychology. Moreover, the horizontal and vertical interrelation of the individual with the overall constellation becomes foregrounded. Such plural patterns already occur before the birth of the cinema in literature and in the theatre, either as isolated cases or more cumulatively as part of certain trends (various realistic or ideological-militant concerns come to mind) or historical periods (such as the Victorian and nineteenth-century French novel), as well as within certain more favoured genres (comedy, melodrama).[11] Three heuristic dramaturgical patterns can be observed in this respect. First, the *group character*: as a collective entity, this integrates the individual via a central idea more or less stringently into a large and sometimes differentiated assembled character, and structures the narrative through a dynamics tending towards argumentation or demonstration. Secondly, the *character ensemble*: this delineates a heterogeneous group, which develops individual roles and values in a shared polyphonic space and installs a flattened narrative style. Thirdly, the *character mosaic*: no longer constituting an actual group as such, this pattern instead relates characters in an acentric fashion through networks, chain reactions, and other labyrinthine dynamics, sometimes also dispensing with these, so that the characters actually never meet in the fictional world whereas readers and spectators can perceive them as interrelated. While the transitions between these three models are smooth, they remain nevertheless distinct in terms of the individual's relation with the group. Notwithstanding manifold variants and variations, their common feature is that they do not function axiologically (with the exception of the radical form of the collective), but rather typologically or even topographically, since they pursue a shift of emphasis from the temporal to the spatial. Moreover, they are committed less to individual characterisations and binary structured positions than to relational dynamics and a variable narrative perspective. Also, they favour flatness,

---

[11] Besides the above-mentioned novels, see also William Shakespeare's *A Midsommer Night's Dreame* (1595/96), Johann Wolfgang von Goethe's *Die Wahlverwandtschaften* (1809), Honoré de Balzac's *La comédie humaine* (from 1829), Victor Hugo's *Les misérables* (1862), Émile Zola's *Les Rougon-Macquart* (1871–93), Thomas Mann's *Die Buddenbrooks* (1901), Anton Čechov's *Der Kirschgarten*, along the lines of the revolutionary mass theatre from the mid-1910s or John Dos Passos's *Manhattan Transfer* (1925), Gertrude Stein's *The Making of Americans* (1925), Vicki Baum's *Menschen im Hotel* (1929), André Gide's *Les faux-monnayeurs* (1925), André Malraux's *La condition humaine* (1933), as well as thereafter works by Jorge Luis Borges, Julio Cortázar, Dylan Thomas, Wolfgang Koeppen, Irmtraud Morgner, Peter Nichols, Rosetta Loy, Harry Mathews, Irina Liebmann, Dominique Barbéris, Dieter Forte, Ingo Schulze, Kathrin Schmidt, and many others.

flow, the differentiation of values, and the open-ended negotiation of contradictions.

As an alternative to the pattern of the individual hero, these multiple protagonist constellations have also existed since earliest cinema. On the basis of political concerns or aesthetic movements, such diverse, expressly plural dynamics became quite common in feature films and documentaries, for example in the 1920s (for instance, in city symphonies or in Russian Revolution films), after the Second World War (for instance, in the Neorealist *film corale*), or in the 1970s. By no means is the occurrence of such dynamics limited to a national context or the stylistic demands of a certain school. Over the past fifty years, especially postcolonial narratives have reactivated and varied the collective pattern in literature, the theatre, and film, whereas increasingly less use of this particular pattern has been made in the Western world. Even though this ideological model seems to be anchored more obviously in concrete historical and discursive contexts than the other two models are, no single standard implementation has asserted itself. Even though the other two dramaturgies – which are mostly prevalent in the Western world – are contingent upon social and discursive formations, they cannot be reduced wholesale to a questioning of the Western subject that would transfer the modernist experience of ambivalence and postmodern arbitrariness and exchangeability of values.[12] Rather, the various plural dramaturgies and their concrete manifoldness make ever different cultural statements in specific historical, discursive, and intermedia constellations; they circulate synchronically in global narrative contexts and return diachronically in waves, as witnessed recently.

1 Multiple Protagonist Films: A Global Vernacular Practice

Since the late 1980s, so-called Independent Cinema across the world has tended increasingly towards narratives with no single main character. Such ›multiple protagonist films‹ present their many-faceted stories by embedding their characters either in group-dynamic or mosaic-like constellations. Various examples of group-dynamic films come to mind: *Life According to Agfa (Ha Chayim Aply Agfa*, Assi Dayan, Israel 1992), *Bhaji on the Beach* (Gurinder Chada, GB 1993), *À La vie, à la mort* (Robert Guédiguian, F 1995), *Ice Storm* (Ang Lee, USA 1996), *Made in Hong Kong*

---

12 On the interrelation between the notion of the individual subject and the Modernist and Postmodernist paradigms in Western theory formation, see Zima 2000.

(*Xianggang Zhiao*, Fruit Chan, Hong Kong 1997), *Festen* (Thomas Vinterberg, DK 1998), *Flowers of Shanghai (Hai shang hua,* Hou Hsiao-hsien, Taiwan 1998), *The Thin Red Line* (Terrence Malick, Canada/USA 1998) *La Ciénaga* (Lucrecia Martel, Argentina/F/E 2001) or *Elephant* (Gus Van Sant, USA 2003). Mosaic-films include, among others, *Slacker* (Richard Linklater, USA 1991), *Short Cuts* (Robert Altman, USA 1993), *Beijing Bastards (Beijing Zadhong,* Zhang Yuan, China 1993), *71 Fragmente einer Chronologie des Zufalls* and *Code inconnu* (Michael Haneke, A/D 1994; F 2000), *Les Voleurs* (André Téchiné, F 1996), *Magnolia* (Paul Thomas Anderson, USA 2000), *The Circle (Le Dayereh,* Jafar Panahi, Iran/I 2000), *Amores Perros* and *Babel* (Alejandro González Iñárritu, Mexico 1999; F/USA/Mexico 2006). Both types of the multiple protagonist film – group-dynamic as well as mosaic-films, which I will not discuss in detail here – unfold various dramatic compositions within a weakly causal, decentered pattern of narration by establishing through parallelism and simultaneity a spatial, often urban network. Their topological and meandering constructions often present everyday worlds that delineate an open set of value-based, emotional positions through adopting a chronicling, polyfocalised narrative stance. Such films thus produce what I would call an *expressive, ethnographic realism.* Characters and their constellations play a key role in understanding such realism and its genesis.[13]

While such narrative patterns also appear before the 1990s, as mentioned, they have become more frequent in the last fifteen to twenty years. Moreover, it seems legitimate to speak of a transcultural phenomenon, since decentered or acentric modes of representation, and their particular expressive opportunities, emerge at the same time in various places, genres, and formats – and also in other media such as literature, theatre and dance performances, photography, radio plays, and the graphic arts.

Rapid technological development over the past twenty years has affected not only art and everyday life, including how we cope with visuals and the flow of images, but also media carriers and dispositives. Even if single media formats develop their own specific visibilities, stylistic forms, and narrative dynamics, based on their pragmatic conditions and technical possibilities, their forms of address and their structural modes of presentation and of reception tend to come together. While such a tendency to ›media convergence‹ does not describe a new development, it nevertheless seems to have been heightened and in particular accelerated by technological innovation, postmodern pastiche, global circulation, and

---

13 About contemporary tendencies of realism see also Orr: Directions.

the individual appropriation of media productions.¹⁴ Our contingent manner of dealing with images can be understood as a practice that effects the mutual interaction between production and reception, and embeds films in an intermedia context of reciprocal influence or transmission.

Writing about Hollywood cinema of the 1920s and 30s and beyond, Miriam Hansen has established the somewhat paradoxical term ›vernacular modernism‹ and refers to such films as a ›global vernacular‹.¹⁵ She argues that American films and their distinctive national-cultural (and regional) features, which actually defy universalisation, are becoming polymorphous vehicles in concrete pragmatic contexts of sensory appropriation: since American values and views have different meanings in different historical reception situations and cultures, these popular media products are confronted with existing traditional ties, varying aesthetic sensibilities, and various forms of adaptation amid their transcultural circulation. In no other way could Hollywood have otherwise managed to attain, and maintain to this day, its aesthetic and economic hegemony.

Even though the boundaries between Hollywood and Independent productions have become more permeable, and the patterns of the latter rub off on the former (such as in Stephan Gaghan's *Syriana*, USA 2005), transcultural multiple protagonist films and their new realism can definitely not be considered serious economic competition for Hollywood, as little as they can undermine its ›geopolitical aesthetic‹.¹⁶ Put differently, multiple protagonist films are as such *one* form of what can be perceived and expressed at a particular time in a particular culture, proceeding in a »multidirectional flow of aesthetic ideas«, as Ella Shoat and Robert Stam have suggested.¹⁷ However, such independent productions are made in isolation, but across the world – particularly in Europe, Asia, North, and Central America. Various parallel structures exist today that have the features of a ›global vernacular‹ on account of the above mentioned media convergence. Therefore, I would argue that the

---

14 Elsaesser: Cinema.
15 Hansen: Production, pp. 333, 340.
16 Jameson: Aesthetic.
17 Shohat / Stam: Narrativizing, p. 39. Other non-linear dynamics exist alongside strongly present, canonised forms. These alternative forms develop a lower-level expressive ethnographic realism than the multiple protagonist films discussed here, and instead emphasise the structural aspect: they could be called ›meta-cinema‹ and sometimes violently challenge our perceptual conventions of space and time; see, for instance, David Lynch's films, Wong Kar Wai's *2046* (China, France, Germany, Hong Kong 2004), or Christopher Nolan's *Memento* (USA 2000). See Orr: Directions; Orr: Worlds; Cameron: Contingency; Branigan: Plots.

transcultural and transmedia nature of such films and of their specific realism attests to an attention to the everyday, challenging vernacular practice to negotiate an encounter with the social and/or cultural Other. In the course of the ›ethnographic turn‹, whose emergence Hal Foster identifies in artistic production and cultural theory since the late 1980s, such attention to the everyday has also reached the mass media where it flowers differently.[18]

Hence, the new filmic ethnographic realism can be related to fictionalising everyday reportage, reality formats, and family soaps shown on television on the one hand, and the widespread everyday use of (digital) photographic and video cameras and the accessibility and circulation of such images on the Internet on the other. New shooting and editing technology as well as digital imaging and image production now pervade the most diverse media practices. Their straightforward handling, for both professional and private purposes, has also brought forth a new aesthetic sensibility and attitude towards everyday gestures. On the other hand, the particular structural organisation of customary interactive dispositives like computers, the Internet and DVD acts upon feature films and documentaries, promoting a new flexibility in image linking as well as the linking of images with the human voice, music, and language. Such linkage and integration is not in itself narrative; but if we conceive narrative in open terms – that is, in terms of postclassical theory –, we discover new narrative dynamics,[19] which every medium and all media formats configure for their economic, socio-cultural, and aesthetic concerns. In what follows, I discuss such narrative dynamics, which combine a new sensitivity towards the everyday with particular forms of linkage. While I focus on the feature film, these reflections also hold true for more general developments in media.

This essay thus discusses the dynamics of multiple protagonist films and their expressive, ethnographic realism as a vernacular practice. However, it offers no detailed analysis of character constellations, concrete forms of montage, authorial traces, and generic relations.[20] Instead, it opens up a broader view of multiple protagonist films, and suggests how they might be conceived as a transcultural phenomenon. I am particularly interested in two aspects: first, the range of meanings and the palette of emotional positions that these films establish and bring into

---

18 Foster: Real, pp. 171–203.
19 Such new dynamics are adapted and transformed in turn by narratives in film, see e.g. Thanouli: Cinema; Kovács: Things; Smith: Lines. See also footnote 10.
20 Tröhler: Welten.

transnational circulation by devising a narrative iconography of everyday social life; and secondly, the audience activities that these heavily character-centered films imply. Here, I will focus on the potential imaginary activities of cooperative spectators, who embrace the opportunities that an open, polycentric form provides.[21] One of my working assumptions is that while these transnationally circulating films delineate everyday worlds that anchor them in the local and the specific, their body images, social dynamics, and weakly causal narrative forms are nonetheless conceived almost everywhere as everyday life.

2 Images of the Everyday and Analogical Linking

Expressive, ethnographic realism emerges as a two-level, effect-bearing construction: the first level is a *fictional, diegetic* model of everyday life, which is rendered more dynamic and cast into narrative on a second level through an *analogical, associative mode of linkage*. Drawing upon Mikhail Bakhtin's concept of the *Chronotope*, and combining it with a critical reading of Erwin Panofsky's notion of *Iconology* to include the (audio-)visual, I assume that multiple protagonist films project *a fictional image of the everyday*.[22] As a possible world, this *iconographic chronotope* is subject to change through time as well as becoming differently anchored in different cultural contexts. On the level of representation, however, it remains recognisable as a fictional image of the everyday on account of various diegetic elements – and also because similar images circulate worldwide in different media forms. The everyday worlds in multiple protagonist films – Robert Altman's well-known *Short Cuts* may serve as a prototype – do not present heroes, but rather characters whose physical and psychological traits identify them as ordinary people. Based on Raymond Carver's *Selected Stories*, Altman's film features twenty-four characters in Los Angeles, whose lives intersect, some casually, some more lastingly, in a mosaic-like narrative. Each is integrated in a particular environment as well as in the social dynamics of family and friendships. Since no enunciative emphasis is placed on one or two central protagonists, symbolic power and hierarchies become apparent in the confrontation of

---

21 In speaking of ›cooperative spectators‹ here, I do not wish to spotlight the atypical forms of filmic pleasure and the obdurate and aberrant readings that enable spectators to appropriate films to their own ends or for the specific identity construction of socio-cultural groups. See Staiger: Perverse Spectators or Nichols: Film Theory; Ezra / Rowden: Transnational Cinema.
22 Tröhler: Welten, pp. 213–234.

social worlds. These are situated entirely in the ›contingency‹, that is, in the nonsimultaneity of simultaneities, which Bakhtin considered typical of the ›chronotope of meeting‹.[23] Even if these encounters are sometimes not effective, but only perceptible to spectators as co-occurring in the same image or the same diegetic place, they are nevertheless conditioned by the social interrelations of the characters, coincidences, and incidents involved in representing the eventfulness of fictional everyday worlds in a spatial, horizontal mesh. Through their selection of figures and the limits of the network of relations, they represent what is obviously an ordinary social stratum. The narrative perspective coincides with a chronicler's attitude of furnishing a socio-political description of this microcosm.[24] External *focalisation* (in Gérard Genette's sense)[25] depicts the characters of multiple protagonist films as social types inhabiting social roles and located in a polyphonic space. Individual characters attain individuality, psychological depth, and complexity mostly through (often conflict-laden) interaction with other characters. As spectators, we observe their behaviour, errors, and twists and turns. Through their encounters, gestures, and attributes, everyday body images emerge to create a relational dynamics enhanced by an expressive style of acting, which – as so often in Altman's films – stands to one side of character delineation in a somewhat self-reflexive manner. Everything has to be exteriorised (by the actors and the film's aesthetic and structural dynamics), and is carried into a network of interrelated emotions, intentions, and personal histories. Subjectivity arises on the polyphonic, dazzling surface, revealing a character conception that delineates a multi-faceted social and *relational subject* with strong somatic conditioning. As the philosopher Bernhard Waldenfels has shown, such a dialogical conception of the subject arises only in contention, and in conflict, with the Other.[26]

Besides these social dynamics, narration evolves through an alternating, meandering form of montage. This lends support not only to the parallelism (similarities and differences) between the characters in the fictional world, but creates further polyphonic references and relations between the various worlds through aesthetico-plastic moments of image-composition. References and relations, moreover, can be generated by colour relations, movements, the scales of takes, the repetition of gestures, situations, noises, or musical leitmotifs, etc. Notwithstanding the depiction

---

23 Bachtin: Zeit, pp. 23–25; Bakhtin: Time, pp. 98–100.
24 Vanoye: Scénarios, pp. 74–77.
25 Genette: Figures, pp. 206–211; see also Genette: Discours, pp. 48–52.
26 Waldenfels: Stachel, pp. 43–82; see also Zima: Theorie, chap. V.

of the everyday, enunciative activities are very noticeable at both the *expressive* and self-reflective levels. (Fredric Jameson observes that all realisms since modernity attest to the paradoxical quest for self-reflexive authenticity).[27]

Nevertheless, the flow that multiple protagonist films constitute pursues some dominant lines of association, whose absence would prevent narration. And yet these lines – generally tied to and directed by character activities – leave open a complexity of possible connections through a polysemy of images and junctures that differentiates the fictional image of the everyday even further. Even if the overriding plot dynamics appear to be more or less steered and remain more or less open-ended (for example, in Jacques Rivette's films) or closed (for example, in Altman), such associative interrelation, which integrates semantic and formal moments, follows the logical principles of comparison that Barbara Maria Stafford terms ›visual analogy‹. She notes that »most fundamentally, analogy is the vision of ordered relationships articulated as similarity-in-difference. This order is neither facilely affirmative nor purchased at the expense of variety«.[28] She also observes: »This human conjunctive faculty is simultaneously individual and global, specific and general, capable of engendering figures of differentiation and reconciliation«.[29]

Now obviously I am not assuming that this narrative iconography of the everyday is universal: neither are social configurations like families or partnerships, and their conflicts, uniform, transcultural factors, nor is the way in which things are connected and the world made sense of as a result. But the relational, social dynamics that become apparent on the surface of the filmic world provide open constructions, as do the weakly causal, polysemous, and playful dramaturgies of multiple protagonist films taken by themselves. Their expressive, ethnographic realism is at once akin to everyday actions and images of the social Other, as well as aligned with the foreignness of the cultural Other, that is, the recognisable specifics of a socio-politically rooted microcosm.

---

27 Jameson: Signatures, p. 165. Here, I prefer expressivity to self-reflexivity, since my description of expressive ethnographic realism centres on the quasi-phenomenological, world-constituting presence of the audiovisual stream and its affective qualities: film is expression in the first instance and provokes the presentness of media before it means or conveys something – not even on a meta-discursive level, or as Metz puts it: »Le cinéma, comme les arts et parce qu'il en est un, [est] un moyen d'expression beaucoup plus que de communication.« (Metz: Essais, p. 79).
28 Stafford: Analogy, p. 9.
29 Ibid., p. 142.

Analogical linkage connects social and aesthetic moments. We are familiar with such linkage as a structural dynamics from both well-established and more recent everyday practices and current discourses on networks. Various illustrative cases come to mind: the operating principles involved in kinship and friendship affiliations, for instance, or the labyrinthine courses that group conversations take, gameplaying practices, surfing the net, and trying to understand the circulation of information in today's globalised world. I would assume that such familiar associative structures, anchored in a realistic and at the same time self-reflexive everyday world, enables confrontation with the social and cultural Other through the shifts and comparisons involved in the analogical processes brought into play by the ›similarity-in-difference‹ principle.

3 Emotional and Structural Activities of Involvement

I would now like to consider multiple protagonist films in terms of cinema audience activities. Devising a model of audience activity is a complex matter that calls for a flexible theoretical foundation; I will not propose such model here, but merely delineate some salient lines concerning the emotional and structural aspects of spectatorial involvement in multiple protagonist films. While this will amount somewhat to ›bricolage‹, it will undoubtedly leave gaps and even spark controversy.

The analogical thinking that multiple protagonist films evoke as regards their spectators' interpretive opportunities thus connects social and aesthetic moments in a cohesive, audiovisual flux. Or as Stafford suggests: »Perceptually combined information not only avoids the intellectual limitations of linearity but reveals our constant involvement in heterogeneous reasoning«.[30] Moreover, the narrative construction of an audience position shuttles between proximity and distance: on the one hand, the proximity of the chronicle-like presentation of a fictional everyday world in which the characters appear to represent themselves through their body images; on the other, a distance established by the reflexiveness of actor performance, the process of montage, and general filmic expressivity betrays the intrusion and control of an omnipresent enunciative authority. On this level, I would assume that spectators are led into a collage-like process of understanding that operates along the lines of Charles Sanders

---

30 Ibid., p. 144.

Peirce's principle of ›abduction‹:³¹ it gathers the distinct partial worlds into a hypothetical whole, designing the microcosm as an ornamental web, that remains in constant motion and is (time and again) adjusted to the relational web. Notwithstanding the dominant line of association, given by the linear course of narration, spectators are nonetheless required to assume an active role in the signifying process, involving them in observation, recognition, combination, comparison, and evaluation. These activities, in turn, imply two interlocking levels of analogy: first, a semantic-fictional, diegetic level of worldmaking, and secondly, a structural one that concerns analogical linkage. Both attend upon the vernacular aspect of multiple protagonist films and their specific spectatorial engagement.

As regards the first aspect, I draw upon the work of the French social psychologist Denise Jodelet who argues that we summon these activities in what she calls ›social comparison‹.³² To assess ›social objects‹ that unlike material ones primarily elude interpretation in terms of physical, objective criteria (such as form, colour, composition), we compare the appearance, manner, and skills of our fellow human beings with our own self-image – at least in Western cultures. We thus situate ourselves in the social mesh in relation to others. While such comparison reveals small distinctions, it works only with those whom we consider sufficiently similar to ourselves.³³ Obviously, dealing with the everyday characters in the fictional everyday worlds of the cinema or television in a dialogic manner is possible only in an imaginary sense, since social comparison in everyday life always rests upon direct interaction and feedback (which helps explain why we fail to mistake the difference between fiction and reality). I take it that the heightened position of observation in front of the screen – supported by the external focalisation of a chronicling narrative stance – leads spectators to apply similar criteria to compare characters in their relational dynamics. Put differently, we are attracted to some, and repelled by others – according to their social and individual affinities for gendered and/or ethnic identity, age, class, and so forth. Jodelet has also pointed

---

31 ›Abduction‹ occurs in the interplay between intuitive assumption (hypothesis), analysing the individual case (that is, variants), and theory- or model-building in infinite semiosis. Originally devised by Charles Sanders Peirce, the concept has been developed further as a methodological procedure as well as a semiotic and cognitive process, among others by Umberto Eco (Grenzen) and Peter Wuss (Filmanalyse); see also Nöth: Handbuch, pp. 67–70.
32 Jodelet: Le corps, p. 52; here, she makes reference to Louis Festinger's A Theory of social comparison process (1954).
33 Ibid., pp. 43, 52.

out that personal experience as well as social or cultural notions – which also comprise self-images and notions of the body images of others – always enter such emotional and evaluative comparison.³⁴ In film, we might accept that character design influences the appraisal of others as regards their outer appearance, through the casting of actors and the body images they project in their performances as well as through mise-en-scène and other aesthetic factors.

At least in Western societies, it appears that we often deduce a person's values from their appearance; in doing so, we often mistakenly make causal and moralising attributions. Following Léon Beauvois and Nicole Dubois, we could assume on this quasi-phenomenological level of interpreting fictional everyday worlds that audiences attribute significant responsibility to individuals for their behaviour and actions. Such interpretation is based on the illusion of the individual's control and self-determination, and neglects environmental factors.³⁵

In the relational dynamics of multiple protagonist films, however, the strongly interactional narrative dynamics continuously call into question what Hans J. Wulff has termed the ›operations of attribution‹ involved in assessing individuals.³⁶ As the network of relations unfolds, established patterns of perception and explanation are constantly displaced by multi-faceted, social character delineation and by the narrative dynamics dealing with coincidences, incidences, and accidents to provoke encounters or failed rendezvous. Causal attributions of values and the emotions bound up with such attributions are often led astray, laying bare the everyday and the non-comprehension it involves, that is, partial or mistaken understanding.³⁷ On balance, this calls for revising old patterns and drawing new comparisons.

Along these lines, I would argue that spectators can project themselves into an *imaginary circle of friends and acquaintances*. As spectators, we can gradually sympathise with or disapprove of the various members of the group or mosaic constellation. Through the ornamental network of social and aesthetic relations, and the relational distribution of values, where we negotiate an emotional, intellectual, and moral position in respect, for example, of family or group hierarchies, ethnic imputations, and the distribution of gender-related roles and their performances.

---

34 Jodelet: Représentation, p. 127.
35 Beauvois / Dubois: Croyances, pp. 164–169.
36 Wulff: Attribution, pp. 57–59; Wulff draws upon the social psychologist Fritz Heider: »The Psychology of Interpersonal Relations« (1958).
37 Zerbst: Fiktion, p. 59.

In Assi Dayan's *Life According to Agfa*, for instance, the specific narrative perspective introduces us primarily to the core group – the bar staff and regulars, who all bring along their stories to the Tel Aviv-based venue (and who are introduced partly through scenes set in additional locations). We observe several conflictual relationships, among others between Liora, the barkeeper, and her partner, who pretends to tackle drug dealers without compromise, but instead allows himself to be corrupted and moreover deceives Liora. Nevertheless, he regains part of our sympathy when he defends a Palestinian scullion, who is fully integrated into the group, against the abuse of several soldiers who have landed up in the bar by chance. However, this is merely one of several lines in the complex field of emotional relations in which we must continuously adjust our position. Through our narrative and social proximity to the core group, which moreover is focused on and by Liora, we distance ourselves both ideologically and morally not only from the group of soldiers and their commanding officer, but also from the three quarrelsome Arab drug addicts who heat up the conflicts in the bar even more. Although *Life According to Agfa* does not pursue a militant line of argument – as the collective constellation mostly does – and although we establish different or partly even dismissive relations to the members of the heterogeneous core group, we nevertheless become involved not only in the emotional conflicts waged by the various couples, but also in the social and political conflicts, and towards which we must adopt an imaginary stance. We thus exclude the ›rivals‹ of the core group from the circle of friends and acquaintances in which *Life According to Agfa* involves us.

As regards the second, structural aspect of analogical thinking, I wish to return to the above associative dynamics. These serve not only to integrate the characters in social formations, but also establish relations between whatever else is perceived. The relations emerging on the audiovisual surface allow us to link or distinguish atmospheres through colours, camera movements, sounds, music, and finally montage. This concerns loose or vague, often unclear cohesion between heterogeneous elements, fragmentary ideas, expressive nuances, sensuous moments, all inscribed in the audiovisual surface of everyday (fictional) scenes. The fluid nature of these playful dynamics does not follow a centering, vectorising thread, neither in narrative nor argumentative or thematic-descriptive terms. Their plastic-associative logic, which holds together the fictional part-worlds like mosaic stones, arises from the bodily expressiveness of the characters and actors (that is, the acting style), and the particular expressive qualities of a film. Often, the characters themselves function as plastic elements: while they are not conspicuous enough to explode the narrative, they remain nonetheless visible and audible, noticeable on the surface, absorbed by movements and encounters in the everyday, diegetic world, and perceptible as enunciative and self-reflexive creative instances, and so they influence the emotional and haptic reception of the film while indicating new conceptual relationships.

Seen from a critical, rational standpoint, understanding based on analogy – and induction as a procedure common to all empirical sciences – is afforded some degree of validity through confirmation, but never certainty. Predictions, based on the singular and clawing their way from one instance to the next via comparable, provisional conclusions, to account for a certain probability, are not valid as logical deduction and fail to legitimate the assumption of ›lawlikeness‹.[38] However, if we assume that no universal law exists to establish links neither between things nor images, but that coupling and making associations is itself inevitable if one is to find one's bearings in the world and create meaning, these playful forms of expression reveal relational patterns that recall a familiar and yet strange (because mostly not consciously reflected) order; that of the nonverbal and everyday action, which manifests itself in the (culturally specific) fictional world and on the filmic surface; its organisational forms materialise in the media dynamics only to change, and combine to form new statements.

Ideally, this form of integration in fictional, aesthetically designed worlds might even result in spectators examining their own social self-image. Various kinds of cultural practices (including the handling of media images) are part of identity constructions and narrative patterns that have their share in how societies represent themselves and how these societies are perceived by others. Stafford makes a similar point: »How we couple representations in space is the key to understanding selfhood. The activity of linking has an emotional component, fitting our desires to an expanding universe of events in which both self and others are mutually transformed«. Furthermore: »Because it is not preblended, braiding collage obliges us to see ourselves mentally laboring to combine many shifting and conflicting perceptions into a unified representation«.[39]

In any event, I would argue that comparison and integration often enable spectators to engage in more differentiated ways with the social and cultural Other. Not that this amounts to claiming that multiple protagonist films always deal explicitly with the clash of cultures or conflicts with the foreign: they include this in their iconography of the everyday only insofar as the excerpt of the socially anchored microcosm

---

38 Goodman: Riddle, esp. pp. 32–37; see also Goodman: Strictures.
39 Stafford: Analogy, pp. 141–142.

and its depiction of the quotidian permit it. Nonetheless, the emergence of multiple protagonist films in different countries, together with their transnational circulation, offers insight into the fictional design of the everyday in films made, for instance, in Mexico, Israel, China, the USA, or in Europe. These films transport images of the everyday, which are perceived in the entire effort such poetic translation involves. They make sense in transnational terms while remaining shaped by the specific traits of another society's social and political problems, manifesting themselves in the audiovisual design of such films. The transition from the social to the cultural Other is fluid in such everyday worlds, presuming a notion of culture such as that suggested by the ethnopsychoanalyst Mario Erdheim: »Culture is what arises from dealing with the foreign; it represents the outcome of how the assimilation of the foreign changes the local and the self«.[40]

Analogical networking and negotiating value-based, emotional positions offers spectators various ways of integrating themselves in multiple protagonist films, thereby rendering tangible (and enabling) confrontation with the cultural Other. Multiple protagonist films of the 1990s can be conceived as a popular or vernacular cultural practice on a quasi-transnational level. As I mentioned at the beginning, they can be considered part of what Hal Foster calls the ›ethnographic turn‹, in that a narrative and iconographic pragmatic everyday knowledge has arisen together with the worldwide circulation of images of the everyday and the ordinary, the increasing mobility of individuals, and the ever more widespread use of participatory media, such as photographic and video cameras, or the internet, and the technical possibilities they provide. This general tendency towards the ›ethnographisation of society‹ through media has become apparent in multiple protagonist films,[41] particularly in their chronicling attitude (located between participation and observation) and their analogical dynamics of linking which lead to the confrontation of the self and the foreign in the local and the present.[42]

---

40 Erdheim: Das Eigene, p. 734: »Kultur ist das, was in der Auseinandersetzung mit dem Fremden entsteht, sie stellt das Produkt der Veränderung des Eigenen durch die Aufnahme des Fremden dar« (trans. by M.K.).
41 Oester: Le tournant, p. 347.
42 Trans. by Mark Kyburz.

References

Bachtin, Michail M.: Formen der Zeit im Roman. Untersuchungen zur historischen Poetik [1975 for the russian edition; written in 1937–38]. Edward Kowalski / Michael Wegner (Eds.). Frankfurt a.M. 1989. In English: Bakhtin, Mikhail M.: Forms of Time and of the Chronotope in the Novel. In: Michael Holquist (Ed.): The Dialogic Imagination. Four Essays by M. M. Bakhtin. Austin 1981, pp. 84–258.

Beauvois, Léon / Nicole Dubois: Croyances internes, croyances externes. In: Serge Moscovici (Ed.): Psychologie sociale des relations à autrui. Paris 1994, pp. 163–180.

Branigan, Edward: Nearly True: Forking Plots, Forking Interpretations. A Response to David Bordwell's »Film Futures«. In: SubStance 31/1 (2002), pp. 105–114.

Cameron, Allan: Contingency, Order, and the Modular Narrative: 21 Grams and Irreversible. In: The Velvet Light Trap 58 (2006), pp. 65–78.

Doležel, Lubomír: Heterocosmica. Fiction and Possible Worlds. Baltimore / London 1998.

Eco, Umberto: Die Grenzen der Interpretation [1990 for the italian edition]. Munich 1992.

Eder, Jens: Die Figur im Film. Grundlagen der Figurenanalyse. Marburg 2008.

Elsaesser, Thomas: Cinema Futures: Convergence, Divergence, Difference. In: T.E. / Kay Hoffman (Eds.): Cinema Futures: Cain, Abel, or Cable? The Screen Arts in the Digital Age. Amsterdam 1998, pp. 9–26.

Erdheim, Mario: Das Eigene und das Fremde. Über ethnische Identität. In: Psyche 8 (1992), pp. 730–744.

Ezra, Elizabeth / Terry Rowden (Eds.): Transnational Cinema: The Film Reader. London 2006.

Forster, Edward M.: Aspects of the Novel. London 1962 [1927].

Foster, Hal: The Return of the Real. The Avant-Garde at the End of the Century. Cambridge, MA 1996.

Gardies, André: Le récit filmique. Paris 1993.

Garrett, Peter K.: The Victorian Multiplot Novel. Studies in Dialogical Form. New Haven / London 1980.

Genette, Gérard: Figures III. Paris 1972.

Genette, Gérard: Nouveau discours du récit. Paris 1983.

Goodman, Nelson: Seven Strictures on Similiarity. In: Mary Douglas / David Hull (Eds.): How Classification Works. Edinburgh 1992, pp. 13–23.

Goodman, Nelson: The New Riddle of Induction. In: Mary Douglas / David Hull (Eds.): How Classification Works. Edinburgh 1992, pp. 24–41.

Greimas, Algirdas J.: Les actants, les acteurs et les figures. In: Algirdas Julien Greimas: Du sens II. Paris 1981, pp. 49–66.

Hamon, Philippe: Le personnel du roman. Le système des personnages dans les ›Rougon Maquart‹ d'Emile Zola. Genève 1983.

Hansen, Miriam Bratu: The Mass Production of the Senses: Classical Cinema as Vernacular Modernism. In: Christine Gledhill / Linda Williams (Eds.): Reinventing Film Studies. London 2000, pp. 332–350.

Jameson, Fredric: Signatures of the Visible. New York / London 1990.

Jameson, Fredric: The Geopolitical Aesthetic: Cinema and Space in the World System. Bloomington 1995.

Jodelet, Denise: La représentation du corps, ses enjeux privés et sociaux. In: Jacques Hainard / Roland Kaehr (dir.): Le Corps Enjeu. Neuchâtel 1983, pp. 127–141.

Jodelet, Denise: Le corps, la personne et autrui. In: Serge Moscovici (Ed.): Psychologie sociale des relations à autrui. Paris 1994, pp. 41–70.

Kovács, András Bálint: Things that Come After Another. In: Film and Television Studies 5/2 (2007), pp. 157–172.
Lévi-Strauss, Claude: Anthropologie structurale deux. Paris 1973 [1960].
Lotman, Jurij M.: Die Struktur literarischer Texte [1970 for the russian edition]. München 1993.
Metz, Christian: Essais sur la signification au cinéma. Vol. I. Paris 1968.
Nichols, Bill: Film Theory and the Revolt against Master Narratives. In: Christine Gledhill / Linda Williams (Eds.): Reinventing Film Studies. London 2000, pp. 34–52.
Nöth, Winfried: Handbuch der Semiotik. Stuttgart, Weimar 2000.
Oester, Kathrin: Le tournant ethnographique – La production de textes ethnographiques au regard du montage cinématographique. In: Ethnologie Française XXXII/2 (2002), pp. 345–355.
Orr, John: New Directions in European Cinema. In: Elizabeth Ezra (Ed.): European Cinema. Oxford 2004, pp. 299–317.
Orr, John: A Cinema of Parallel Worlds: Lynch and Kieslowski + Inland Empire. In: Film International 7/1 (2009), pp. 28–44.
Propp, Vladimir: Morphologie des Märchens [1928 for the russian edition]. Frankfurt a.M. 1982.
Shohat, Ella / Stam, Robert: Narrativizing Visual Culture: Towards a Polycentric Aesthetics. In: Nicholas Mirzoeff (Ed.): The Visual Culture Reader. London, New York 1998, pp. 37–59.
Smith, Murray: Engaging Characters. Fiction, Emotion, and the Cinema. Oxford 1995.
Smith, Murray: Parallel Lines. In: Jim Hillier (Ed.): American Independent Cinema. London 2000, pp. 155–161.
Stafford, Barbara Maria: Visual Analogy. Consciousness as the Art of Connecting. Cambridge, MA / London 1999.
Staiger, Janet: Perverse Spectators. The Pratices of Film Reception. New York / London 2000.
Thanouli, Eleftheria: Narration in World Cinema: Mapping the Flows of Formal Exchange in the Era of Globalisation. New Cinemas: Journal of Contemporary Film 6/1 (2008), pp. 5–15.
Tröhler, Margrit / Henry M. Taylor: De quelques facettes du personnage humain dans le film de fiction. In : Iris 24 (1997), pp. 33–58.
Tröhler, Margrit: Offene Welten ohne Helden. Plurale Figurenkonstellationen im Film. Marburg 2007.
Vanoye, Francis: Scénarios modèles, modèles de scénarios. Paris 1991.
Waldenfels, Bernhard: Der Stachel des Fremden. Frankfurt a.M. 1990.
Wulff, Hans J.: Held und Antiheld, Prot- und Antagonist: zur Kommunikations- und Texttheorie eines komplizierten Begriffsfeldes. In: Hans Krah / Claus-Michael Ort (Eds.): Weltentwürfe in Literatur und Medien. Phantastische Wirklichkeiten – realistische Imaginationen. Kiel 2002, pp. 431–448.
Wulff, Hans J.: Attribution, Konsistenz, Charakter. Probleme der Wahrnehmung abgebildeter Personen. In: Montage/AV 15/2 (2006), pp. 45–62.
Wuss, Peter: Filmanalyse und Psychologie. Strukturen des Films im Wahrnehmungsprozess. Berlin 1993.
Zerbst, Rainer: Die Fiktion der Realität – Die Realität der Fiktion. Prolegomena zur Grundlegung einer künftigen Romansoziologie, Frankfurt/Main. 1984.
Zima, Peter V.: Die Theorie des Subjekts. Subjektivität und Identität zwischen Moderne und Postmoderne. Tübingen / Basel 2000.

RUTH FLORACK

Ethnic Stereotypes as Elements of Character Formation

1 Probability as Norm

With respect to character and plot formation, poets must consider ›necessity‹ as well as ›probability‹, that is to say: ›that it is necessary or probable that such a person speaks or acts as he does, and that one necessity or probability follows the other‹.[1] This is how Aristotle defines it in his *Poetics*. Throughout the centuries authors of fictional texts have followed his line of thinking in that they have equipped their characters with traits that, they could assume, would be recognised by the audience as probable or at least plausible. It is of special interest to the literary historian exactly where and when the readers or the audience first began refusing to grant such recognizable traits in the formation of characters and plot; both are not necessarily closely linked only with respect to Aristotle. This interests the literary historian because such rejection can be a sign that perceptions and attitudes on the part of the audience have changed and/or that probability and plausibility as standards for fiction have become obsolete. The following focuses on the *unchangeable* rather than the changes. It deals with constant patterns of an ethnic and national sense of belonging which can be evidenced through characters in a text – externally such as in physiognomy and dress – but which is mainly portrayed through patterns of thought; in other words, directly through what the characters say and indirectly through their actions.

References to age, gender and social status help to define a character. But an even stronger indicator than these three is *origin*, which also signifies a spatial affiliation and which only occasionally falls short, as in the case of personification. *Origin* as a character feature has been of special

---

1 Aristotle: Poetics 15 (Trans. in D.A. Russell / M. Winterbottom (Eds.): *Classical Literary Criticism* 1989).

interest recently because it has become a key component in imagological studies within the larger context of cultural studies in intercultural perspectives.²

The following observations pursue this line of research – albeit with certain critical reservations towards those researchers who wish to imply that the authors of this literature, through their ›images‹ of the ›innate‹ and the ›other‹, are the spokespersons for entire populations.³

Whereas Aristotle names the four categories: *age, gender, social status* and *origin* in his *Rhetoric* (as opposed to in his *Poetics*),⁴ Horace expressly advises the poet in ›his‹ *Poetics* on the subject of character creation; he implores him to differentiate and to decide whether the character being introduced »is a god or hero, an old man of ripe years or a hot youth, an influential matron or a hard-working nurse, a travelling merchant or the tiller of a green farm, a Colchian or Assyrian, one nurtured in Thebes or at Argos«.⁵ That said, neither of these two authors of the ancient world pays great attention to content specificities – unlike in the Early Modern Age when the growing knowledge of foreign lands and peoples made various differentiations a necessity. Julius Caesar Scaliger is a case in point; in his influential *Poetics* from the year 1561, he handed authors a catalogue based on poly-historical knowledge for characterizing people of different origins. Under the heading ›Natio sive gens‹ he first offers an oversimplified pattern of attributes. He speaks of the Asians' propensity for luxury, the disloyalty of Africans, the acumen of the Europeans, that mountain dwellers are raucus and that land dwellers, in contrast, tend to be weak and lethargic. He includes in his characterization of the (East) Indians features such as versatile, perceptive and devoted to magic. The

---

2   For an orientation on the current state of research see Beller / Leerssen (Eds.): Imagology.
3   For a critical analysis of comparativistic imagology see Florack: Fremde, pp. 7–32.
4   Here Aristotle demands competence, appropriateness, similarity, and regularity for the formation of the ›character‹ (Aristotle: Poetics 15). See, however – though not only restricted to fictions – the explanations on ›appropriateness‹ of style in his Rhetoric: »[…] to each class and habit there is an appropriate style. I mean class in reference to age – child, man or old man; to sex – man or woman; to country – Lacedaemonian or Thessalian. I call habits those moral states which form a man's character in life…If then anyone uses the language appropriate to each habit, he will represent the character; for the uneducated man will not say the same things in the same way as the educated« (Aristotle: Rhetoric, III).
5   English trans. from *Classical Literary Criticism*, see footnote 1. The Latin original has: »intererit multum, divosne loquatur an heros, / maturusne senex an adhuc florente iuventa / fervidus, et matrona potens an sedula nutrix, / mercatorne vagus cultorne virentis agelli, / Colchus an Assyrius, Thebis nutritus an Argis« (Horaz: Arte 114–118).

Egyptians, on the other hand, are portrayed as cowardly, weak and stupid; the Assyrians, Syrians and Persians as superstitious; and the Swedes, Norwegians, Greenlanders and Goths (!) as coarse. Then he proceeds with even more elaborate lists of characteristics for the English, French, Italians and Spaniards.[6] The Germans, who will be considered as an example here and in the following, are also given a description: »Germani fortes, simplices, animarum prodigi, veri amici, verique hostes«.[7] He lists the written tradition, proverbs and popular sayings as sources for discovering positive and negative character traits which befit the members of the various peoples: »Gentium itaque ac populorum ingenia tum ex historiis tum ex proverbiis atque ex ore vulgi excipienda censeo«.[8] This attributes the same authority to hearsay as to the written text. Both are recognized as bearers of a large expanse of knowledge, which Scaliger demands from the poet. If fictional characters are based on this knowledge, or to put it differently, if they are characterized using the well-known means mentioned, then they appear plausible and probable to the recipient insofar as he is also privy to this knowledge.

This logic is also followed in neoclassical poetics, as for example in La Mesnardière's *Poëtique* (1640), in which he insists on character formation that allows not only the *individual*, but the *typical* to be recognized. In order to portray consistent characters, the poet – and this applies above all to the writer of the high genre of tragedy – needs to know not only the written tradition, but must also familiarize himself with what is common knowledge:

> The poet ought to remember that manners should not only be copied from history and traditional stories, and that he should not depict persons only in the way they are presented in these two sources; but that he needs to pay attention to what comes to everybody's mind in connection with each class, each position and each age.[9]

Here, as in Scaliger, the authority of tradition is complemented through life experiences. With express reference to the law of probability, La Mesnardière imparts to the poet ›a common notion of manners that he needs to attribute to all kinds of persons‹,[10] in which he lists, among other

---

6   See Scaliger: Poetices, p. 102.
7   Ibid.
8   Ibid.
9   »Que le Poëte se ressouuienne que les Mœurs doiuent estre prises, non seulement dans l'Histoire ou dans la Fable receuë, & qu'il doit dépeindre les hommes selon qu'ils sont réprésentez en ces deux Originaux; mais qu'il faut encore obseruer ce que chaque condition, chaque fortune, & chaque âge inspirent ordinairement à chaque espéce de personnes […]« (Mesnardière: Poëtique, p. 119; all quotes are trans. by M.P.).
10 ›Idée généralle des Mœurs qu'il doit attribuer à chaque espéce de gens‹ (Ibid.).

things, epithets which are befitting of social class, gender and origin. He cites Scaliger as his authority and relies in addition on his own experiences. In this way he characterizes the French, Spaniards, Italians, English, Greeks, Egyptians and also Thracians, Moors and Scythians – and naturally the Germans as well: »›The Germans are likely to be rough, faithful, modest, avid eaters, affable, valiant and freedom-loving‹«.[11] He does concede, however, that in individual cases – ›according to the intention of the story‹[12] – a deviation from the pattern of character formation could be necessary; in other words, a humble Spaniard could be just as conceivable as a serious, constant Frenchman, although these attributes would be atypical for the representatives of these ethnic groups. But poetic freedom has its limits: a poet should never make an Asian into a warrior or portray an African as loyal or a Frenchman as coarse – just as a German should never be allowed to appear sensitive.[13] Lists of character traits such as the above which pertain to various ethnic peoples are a common occurrence in poetics, rhetorics and epithet-lexicons in the Early Modern Era.[14] The knowledge gap of the lists of this early era is reflected in the fact that they are more finely differentiated for the politically, economically or culturally important peoples of Europe than for the peoples of more distant, barely known continents. And in the light of this discrepancy in the traditional repertoire of ethnic characteristics, the highly criticized inequality – often called Eurocentrism – in the representation of ›nearer‹ and ›more distant‹ peoples becomes understandable.

In historical reconstructions, the cultural relativity of this catchphrase-like knowledge of ethnic differences in Early Modern Europe can be uncovered in principle; as part of the state-building process, it became more and more bound to national borders. With respect to Europe, however, one should not be rash in differentiating between auto- and heterostereotypes, nor should the ›self‹-images of entire peoples be extrapolated from their images of the ›other‹. What the diachronic and synchronic comparison across language and country borders reveals in reality, is that these attributes of peoples have to do with a somewhat

---

11 »Les Allemans seront sincéres, grossiers, fidelles, modestes, banqueteurs, affables, vaillans, amoureux de la liberté«. (Ibid., p. 123).
12 ›selon l'intention de la Fable‹ (Ibid., p. 123).
13 See ibid., p. 125.
14 In addition, character traits are found in so-called ethnic tables of the early 18th century, upon which the European peoples are depicted in a typical costume and are presented in a catchphrase-like manner with respect to their customs and characteristics. See Stanzel: Europäer, as well as Stanzel: Völkerspiegel.

limited repertoire of characteristics, which in ›self‹ as well as ›other‹ perspectives are in essential agreement with one another. At most, it is the selection of the patterns and their evaluations that are evidence of the author's respective standpoint and of the respective discursive positioning of his text. Since Humanism the intellectual world agreed in substance by which characteristics one could recognize a person's regional or ethnic affiliation. One simply knew, for instance, that physical strength was a characteristic feature of the Germans. The same is true of simplicity and naivety. The traditional Latin epithet ›simplex‹ allows both of these meanings, i.e. either positive or negative connotations depending on the context. So one finds, for example, in French fiction of the 18th century, that the proverbial German ›simplicitas‹ turns into the character either of a simpleton – as in the case of Voltaire's Candide (nomen est omen) who hails from a place in Westphalia with the awkward name of Thunder-ten-tronck – or of an honest soul, a model of modesty – as in the sentimental tale *Pierre. Nouvelle allemande* by Florian. ›Simplicitas‹ on the other hand, in its negative connotation, and imbued with the proverbial combativeness of the Germans, mutates into stupid barbarism and evokes feelings of hatred of the German enemy in propaganda materials and other media of the 19th and 20th centuries.[15]

2 Origin and Climate

More fruitful than the question of the reality content of characteristics such as ›German simple-mindedness‹ is the question of the origin of such patterns. In the case of the Germans, to whom characteristics such as the following are generally attributed: strength, spiritedness, bravery, manual skills, patience, diligence, loyalty and honesty, but also ponderousness in thinking and taking action, raucous behaviour, and a tendency toward excessive drinking,[16] the source is for the most part Tacitus' *Germania*, which, since its rediscovery in the middle of the 15th century, became the most important source of knowledge about the Germans for learned Europeans; this despite the fact that Tacitus had never set foot in Germany and had designed his picture of the Germans as a critical corrective to Roman conditions, and without regard to the obvious fact that the Germans of classical antiquity cannot be equated with the Germans of the Early Modern Era. However, the appeal to ancient

---

15 For more on this see Jeismann: Vaterland, pp. 207–234 and pp. 339–373.
16 See Florack: Deutsche.

sources as authorities in the Early Modern Era is customary even in those areas where the horizon of experience of antiquity clearly lags far behind that of the Early Modern Era. For example, the 17th century South Tyrolean missionary Martino Martini refers to Aristotle – who knew absolutely nothing about China – in his description of the Chinese empire when he attributes to them great intellectual abilities:

> What Aristotle says about the peoples of Asia is proof of the intellect of the Chinese: We Europeans are more manly than the Chinese, and the Chinese surpass us in terms of subtlety. They are clever, sly and very astute and intrepid, and also skilful and diligent.[17]

But Aristotle is referring to the East Mediterranean, which he knew well, when he contrasts the Europeans (NB, the *North Europeans*) with the peoples of Asia in the seventh book of his *Politics*:

> The nations in cold locations, particularly in Europe, are filled with spiritedness, but relatively lacking in thought and art; hence they remain freer, but lack [political] governance...Those in Asia, on the other hand, have souls endowed with thought and art, but lacking in spiritedness; hence they remain ruled and enslaved.[18]

The middle, and hence ideal, position is granted in Aristotle's characterization to the Greeks – that is, to his own culture – because ›the stock of the Greeks shares in both‹, ›for it is both spirited and endowed with thought‹, so that it remains ›free‹ and ›governs itself in the best manner‹.[19]

Through this example some fundamental points become clear: first, there was the conventional appeal to the ancient authors as authorities for the observation and description of foreign lands and peoples even in instances where the authors – due to their lack of knowledge – could provide no information. This is demonstrated by the above quote from Martini's China-Report, which appeared in 1655 in Joan Blaeus' *Novus Atlas Sinensis*, the first truly reliable China atlas in Europe. It remained the most complete description of China until the 19th century. Moreover, in the case of more distant continents, the lack of ancient sources is compensated through other sources, above all the Bible – topoi of paradise, for example, play a not negligible role in expressing the exotic. And yet a second fundamental insight is conveyed through the example from Martini's China-Report. As did Aristotle long before him, Martini

---

17 »Waß die Sineser vor Köpfe seyn / beweist Aristotelis aussag von den Asiatischen Völckern: Wir Europeer sind mannhaffter als die Sineser / und die Sineser übertreffen unß in spitzfündigkeit. Sie sind gescheidreich / verschlagen / und zu unversehenen fällen sehr scharffsinnig und unerschrocken: Auch kunstlich und fleissig [...]« (Martini: Atlas, p. 6).
18 Aristotle: Politics VII 7.
19 Ibid.

uses a rough scheme of extreme oppositions in which the position between the extremes is understood as balanced and ideal. In a historical perspective, this middle position proves to be as much in the nature of a topos as the basic opposition itself.

It is climate theory that offers the theoretical background for this polarizing grid classification of peoples from different origins, which also has its roots in antiquity. Posidonius was one of the first to assume that the environment puts its stamp on people physically as well as psychologically. According to him, courage and cowardice, industriousness or idleness are dependent first and foremost upon the surrounding temperature.[20] Vitruvius developed this idea into a proper system in his treatise *De architectura*, which was rediscovered during the Renaissance and widely received; body size and constitution, in addition to strengths and weaknesses, are directly dependent upon the influence of the sun; where the sun moderately warms the air and the body, these are in a balanced relationship. In distinctively cold or warm regions, however, an imbalance prevails because the humidity in the cold north is not absorbed by the sun; rather, it penetrates into the body, makes it powerfully built, rich in blood and strength, but at the same time leads to a mental sluggishness. In the south, however, it is the reverse: because the sun drives the humidity from the air as well as out of the body, the people there are physically weaker and less courageous, but in exchange mentally agile and acute.[21]

When an interest in cultural differences developed in the periods of the Renaissance and Humanism – and with that a comparison of individual peoples[22] – the influential potency of the theory of the climate's influence on the constitution of people served to explain the observed differences and those that were passed on from generation to generation. In addition to the Greeks, other peoples appear as nothing less than ideal in the favourable central position. According to the theory, Italians, Greeks and Spaniards had an appropriate body size, sufficient strength and quick faculties, and excelled above all other peoples in science and bravery.[23] The French and southern Germans were of average height and weight, peace-loving and friendly. In principle, all inhabitants of moderate countries displayed well-proportioned dispositions and inclinations, possessed good reason and an appreciation of art. In addition, they were stout-hearted and prudent, level-headed and wise in their dealings, and

---

20 Posidonius: Fragments, p. 161.
21 See Vitruvii De Architectura libri decem, liber sextus, I 3f. and I 9f.
22 See Rowe: Renaissance, pp. 8–9.
23 See the statements by the Spanish missionary and South American traveller Las Casas: Apologética, p. 96.

moderate in their pleasure with food and drink.²⁴ In comparison, the north – England, Flanders or Germany – spawned strong, corpulent people because the cold closes the pores.²⁵ The pent up inner warmth causes an active digestion; this in turn results in a large amount of raw nutrients to be absorbed and thus produces a lot of blood and warmth. As a result, the bodily fluids become thick and curdly. The consequence is that those people were hardy, audacious and strong, while at the same time sluggish, simple-minded, and with no ingenuity. The opposite is true in very warm zones, in Asia, for example: because the heat opens the pores and drives the moisture out, the people there had less blood and also less inner warmth. Due to this they tended to be more cowardly, but had more distinct intellectual abilities.²⁶ This contrast is found in Bartolomé de Las Casas' treatise *Apologética Historia* from 1525, whose catalogue-like ethnographical comparison is mentioned here as representative. Numerous other sources confirm the findings, which appear to have been the *grosso modo* consensus among European intellectuals.²⁷

The characteristics of the peoples – as known through tradition – were fitted into this rough and ready scheme and then expanded with striking cultural features which were perceived in the Early Modern Era across nations. As a result, the physical ability of the Germans revealed itself not only in warlike bravado, already known to Tacitus, but also fit the pronounced manual agility in which the people of the Early Modern Era sought an explanation for the epochal inventions of gun powder and printing. Another example are the French: Caesar's description of some Gallic tribes is the ultimate source of their presumed haughtiness, effeminacy, and above all ›levitas‹.²⁸ This concept has been translated into the vernaculars as ›fickleness‹ and ›inconstancy‹, but also as ›superficiality‹ and ›frivolity‹ especially in love. In the Early Modern Era, these traditional ascriptions were supplemented with epithets that result from the development of the centralist, absolutistic court, to which the following also belong: patriotism and love for one's king, sophistication and taste, sociableness, courtesy, gallantry in the social interaction with ladies, but also vanity, braggadoccio and falsehood.²⁹

---

24 Ibid., p. 76.
25 Ibid., p. 96.
26 Ibid., p. 76.
27 See Florack: Deutsche, pp. 32–41.
28 See Caesar: Krieg II 1 and VII 43.
29 See Florack: Deutsche.

3 The Concept of National Character

It is noteworthy that such positive and negative ascriptions – they are, after all, attributes for entire peoples – are not criticized in the Enlightenment period as prejudices. Much more than this, they are considered core elements of *knowledge* which go beyond the climatic, as differences between human beings that are determined by nature. These knowledge segments persist, stubborn and unchanged, that is, as stereotypes, even when people's understanding of human beings changes. For example, Montesquieu is already familiar with the fact that the human body is interconnected through strands of nerves. Based on this knowledge, the traditional doctrine of the temperaments – which is easy to relate to climate theory and which adheres to the notion that temperature influences the bodily fluids, i.e. blood, (yellow and black) bile and phlegm, which then determine the character traits sanguine, choleric, melancholy and phlegmatic – loses explanatory power. Montenesquieu subjugates the new knowledge of the nerves to the old explanatory model of climate theory when he writes in his 1748 treatise, *De l'Esprit des Lois*:

> The nerves, which end in the tissue of our skin, are made of a sheaf of nerves. Ordinarily, it is not the whole nerve that moves, but an infinitely small part of it. In hot countries, where the tissue of the skin is relaxed, the ends of the nerves are open and exposed to the weakest action of the slightest objects. In cold countries, the tissue of the skin is contracted and the papillae compressed. The little bunches are in a way paralyzed; sensation hardly passes to the brain except when it is extremely strong and is of the entire nerve together. But imagination, taste, sensitivity, and vivacity depend on an infinite number of small sensations.[30]

Hence, in spite of new discoveries, he proves what is long-established knowledge: that the northerners possess neither taste nor a sense for subtleties and are dull by nature. For this reason, according to Montesquieu, they prefer strong stimuli such as hunting, war and wine.[31] Thus

---

30 Montesquieu: Laws, pp. 232f. »Les nerfs, qui aboutissent de tous côtés au tissu de notre peau, font chacun un faisceau de nerfs. Ordinairement ce n'est pas tout le nerf qui est remué, c'en est une partie infiniment petite. Dans les pays chauds, où le tissu de la peau est relâché, les bouts des nerfs sont épanouis et exposés à la plus petite action des objets les plus foibles. Dans les pays froids, le tissu de la peau est resserré, et les mamelons comprimés; les petites houppes sont, en quelque façon, paralytiques; la sensation ne passe guère au cerveau que lorsqu'elle est extrêmement forte, et qu'elle est de tout le nerf ensemble. Mais c'est d'un nombre infini de petites sensations que dépendent l'imagination, le goût, la sensibilité, la vivacité« (Montesquieu: Lois, pp. 475f.).

31 Ibid., p. 234; Montesquieu: Lois., p. 477.

their proverbial inclination for drink,[32] stemming from Tacitus, appears from a medical standpoint to be nothing less than a necessity:

> In cold countries, perspiration releases little of the watery part of the blood; it remains in abundance; therefore one can use spirits there without making the blood coagulate. One is full of humors there; alcoholic beverages, which give motion to the blood, are suitable.[33]

When one enquires after the function of the climate-theoretical elements for the line of reasoning of the treatise, *De l'Esprit des Lois*, their potential to enlighten becomes clear: for Montesquieu, the climatically-determined differences between the ethnic peoples represent an essential factor with which to empirically explain the heterogeneity of political laws and societal structures that are determined by space, time and circumstances. Furthermore, they defend against the demands of the church, which was laying claim to universality:

> The question is reduced to this: Whether, in countries placed at a great distance from each other, or whether in different climates, there are the marks of a national spirit. Now that there are such differences, is established by almost the universal consent of writers. As the impressions of this national spirit have a considerable influence on the dispositions of the heart, it cannot be at all questioned that certain dispositions of heart are more frequent in one country than another; and in proof of this, we have also the testimony of an | infinite number of writers in all times and places. [...] the climate may be the physical cause of producing various dispositions of the mind; these dispositions may have an influence on human actions; but how does this give a shock to the throne of him who has created, or to the merits of him who has bought us?[34]

According to the above, there is something like the *nature* of a people which is believed to reveal itself through the appearance and behaviour of those who belong to it. Montesquieu claims that this has been proven by

---

32 See Tacitus: Germania 22.
33 Montesquieu: Laws, p. 239. »Dans les pays froids, la partie aqueuse du sang s'exhale peu par la transpiration; elle reste en grande abondance. On y peut donc user des liqueurs spiritueuses, sans que le sang se coagule. On y est plein d'humeurs; les liqueurs fortes, qui donnent du mouvement au sang, y peuvent être convenables« (Montesquieu: Lois, p. 482).
34 Montesquieu: Defence, pp. 253f. »Toute la question se réduit à savoir si dans des pays éloignés entre eux, si sous des climats différents, il y a des caractères d'esprit nationaux. Or, qu'il y ait de telles différences, cela est établi par l'universalité presque entière des livres qui ont été écrits. Et, comme le caractère de l'esprit influe beaucoup dans la disposition du cœur, on ne saurait encore douter qu'il n'y ait de certaines qualités du cœur plus fréquentes dans un pays que dans un autre; et l'on en a encore pour preuve un nombre infini d'écrivains de tous les lieux et de tous les temps. [...] ce physique du climat peut produire diverses dispositions dans les esprits; ces dispositions peuvent influer sur les actions humaines: cela choque-t-il l'empire de Celui qui a créé, ou les mérites de Celui qui a racheté?« (Montesquieu: Défense, p. 1145).

authors of various epochs and lands. This can be confirmed taking a historical approach: the perception that peoples are collective individuals, each with their own inherent character, that is, their ›national character‹, is indeed a commonplace in the Early Modern Era.[35]

In addition to the authoritative ›perception categories‹ of the time, i.e. social standing and religious denomination, national character also served for centuries as an absolutely ›neutral category of description‹, which only became questionable through ideological monopolization in the context of the nationalism of the 19th and 20th centuries.[36] Today's readers, it has to be admitted, may be alienated by such a hypothesis of collective-individuals in territorial-state borders – especially in the times of growing globalization – because character differences between inhabitants of foreign countries, that is to say, those that are now commonly viewed as historical, i.e. that are determined by social practice, are attributed to the climate in the Early Modern Period. But in the context of the Early Modern Era, this essentialist notion of a national character (or in other words, of the nature or the disposition of a people) stems from an ›increasing readiness‹ to recognize the ›naturalness of people‹ (more especially their ›being determined through sensual factors‹ of a geographical, social-historical nature) and to view as a unity ›man as nature and nature as the milieu of natural man‹.[37] Such an ›initial elementary form of a cultural theory or anthropology‹, which considers culture to be a ›sensually-determined and specifically-situated entity‹,[38] has tended to result in an emancipation from the boundaries of a theocentric world view.

Before the concept of ›culture‹ spread in the second half of the 18th century – *culture* in today's sense of the word, closely connected with the boom of historical philosophy (the term *culture* is derived from the Latin ›cultura‹ in the sense of ›cultivation‹, ›adaptation‹, ›fostering‹ also in the metaphorical sense, so that human activity is accentuated)[39] – the concept of national character served as a rational model for the acquisition, description and explanation of cultural differences. On the basis of this concept of culture, the positive and negative epithets of the peoples that were known through written transmission and observation were recorded in compendiums as collective virtues and vices – and were thus passed

---

35 For information on the French Enlightenment see for example Vyverberg: Human, p. 81.
36 Maurer: Nationalcharakter, pp. 46 and 55.
37 Kondylis: Aufklärung, p. 136.
38 Ibid.
39 On this see Fisch: Zivilisation, p. 707.

down in the atlases of the 17th as well as in the reference works of the 18th century. This is evidenced in the more than sixty-volume work that Johann Heinrich Zedler published around the middle of the 18th century, *Grosses vollständiges Universal-Lexicon Aller Wissenschafften und Künste* [*The Complete Universal Lexicon of the Sciences and the Arts*]. Here one finds a comprehensive article on ›Naturell der Völcker‹, or rather ›Natura populorum‹, which first refers to antiquity (Livy and the Apostle Paul) in order to prove the long tradition of the concept of regional differences between various peoples in ›character and customs‹.[40] He then explains the climate-theory-backed scheme for the broad classification: ›In the same way as it is usual to divide the world‹ – what is meant is essentially the ›world‹ within the borders of the horizon of perception of antiquity, thus Europe and the Mediterranean world – ›according to a three-fold climate into three parts, so also it is customary to arrange peoples according to their disposition into three classes‹: ›of the people from the cold northern lands one is inclined to claim that they have no such swift and alert intelligence and that they are not suited to study‹; they are ›cold-hearted‹ in love , ›otherwise honest, pious and diligent people‹.[41] ›Those who remain in the hot countries of the sun-belt‹ have ›either stupid, or fantastic characters, which the ancient Egyptians can confirm through their example‹; they are also supposedly ›inclined to fornication and lasciviousness‹.[42] Only ›those in the temperate lands‹ – to which Germany is now assigned – are given a more differentiated description, simply ›the most distinguished peoples of Europe‹: in addition to Germans and the Dutch, this group comprises the Spaniards, English, French and Italians. Their supposed collective strengths and weaknesses are presented in a catalogue-like manner. With respect to the Germans one reads, among other things: »One cannot say that they have the best, swiftest and sharpest-witted brains […]. However, what they are lacking by nature they make up for with untiring diligence […]. They are very patient […], and are especially fond of eating and drinking«.[43] What follows then is the unavoidable reference to Tacitus before the passage closes with a sideswipe at the *alamode* fashion – that is, the imitation of French manners in the late 17th and early 18th century: »Apart from that, most Germans, in as far as they do not spoil their manners when in foreign lands, are honest and justice-loving people«.[44]

---

40 Article ›Naturell der Völcker‹, in: Zedler: Lexicon, col. 1246.
41 Ibid., cols. 1246f.
42 Ibid., col. 1247.
43 Ibid., cols. 1247f.
44 Ibid., col. 1248.

Nonetheless, the article from Zedler's *Universal-Lexicon* also documents that climate theory, as the sole explanatory model for cultural differences, came to be perceived as more and more insufficient. He states: »One is accustomed to deducing such differences in character dispositions between nations from natural as well as from moral causes. The natural cause is believed to be the air, which influences character and the circulation of the blood, as well as determines the properties of the disposition of the soul«.[45] On the other hand, ›moral‹ factors also played an important role, such as upbringing.[46] The Jews are mentioned as a good example for this: they are said to be ›dispersed throughout all of the countries, born and raised in all different places‹, but nevertheless are thought to possess as a people, however, ›something particular with respect to their customs that is inherent [...], which noticeably differentiates them from others‹.[47]

Yet, even where the emphasis for describing cultural differences as determined by ›nature‹, that is, where the constant conditions of human ways of life shift to ›customs‹ – or rather, what people customarily *do* in reaction to their environment – the concept of national character stubbornly asserts itself as the explanatory basis for collective peculiarities. David Hume's 1748 essay, *Of National Characters*, may serve to document the above. Hume, in contrast to Montesquieu, is opposed to climate theory. For him it is a result of socialization ›that each nation has a peculiar set of manners, and that some particular qualities are more frequently to be met with among one people than among their neighbours‹:[48]

> Where a number of men are united into one political body, the occasions of their intercourse must be so frequent, for defence, commerce, and government, that, together with the same speech or language, they must acquire a resemblance in their manners, and have a common or national character, as well as a personal one, peculiar to each individual.[49]

Hume opposes the influence of climate and cites the Chinese and, like Zedler, the Jews as examples. In the first case, he argues that it is a centuries-old government that has lead to the fact that ›the *Chinese* have the greatest uniformity of character imaginable‹, although, he claims, air

---

45 Ibid., col. 1250.
46 Ibid., col. 1251.
47 Ibid.
48 Hume: National, p. 244.
49 Ibid., p. 248.

and climate are anything but uniform in China's expansive territorial domain.⁵⁰

The second shows that, ›where any set of men, scattered over distant nations, maintains a close society or communication together, they acquire a similitude of manners‹. From this Hume concludes in an evaluative antithetic generalization, »Thus the *Jews* in *Europe* and the *Armenians* in the east have a peculiar character; and the former are as much noted for fraud, as the latter for probity«.⁵¹ After these historical perspectives on the relationship between cultural difference, the concept of the national character and literature, in what follows a systematic view of the *functions* that ethnic stereotypes may have in fiction will be developed.

4 Ethnic Stereotypes

Fraud, next to greed, is a prevalent negative attribution of Jews which affiliates them with the character of Judas in the New Testament:

> The representative icon of Jewishness became focused in the figure of Judas, who betrayed Christ by kissing him, and took a financial reward for it; thus the notion of greed-driven treason and duplicity was codified into a typical Jewish characteristic.⁵²

This contributes to the feelings of enmity towards the Jews as adversaries and murderers of Christ, which was passed down through the centuries in the Christian tradition; added to this negative image are epithets such as cleverness and shiftiness, which can be traced back to the Jews' marginal social existence in trade and money lending that was forced upon them in the Middle Ages and the Early Modern Era.⁵³ However, in the Modern Era there are also positive attributes for Jews; for example, artistic taste and a distinctive intellectuality.⁵⁴ And already in Scott's *Ivanhoe*, for example, Jews appear as heroic, suffering, persecuted characters with noble morality.⁵⁵ Positive Jewish protagonists also belong to the character-inventory in American books and films of the 20th century:

---

50 Ibid., p. 249.
51 Ibid., p. 250.
52 See Gans / Leerssen: Jews, pp. 202–208 (this also contains further literature), here p. 203.
53 See ibid., pp. 203f.
54 Ibid., p. 205.
55 Ibid.: »Thus the figures of Isaac of York and his daughter Rebecca [...] embody the dignified and heroic endurance of persecution, and a high-minded morality that transcends religious differences«.

> In America, [...] the literary ethnotype has become that of the wily, quick-witted citydweller, good at social banter and street wisdom but with a background of patriarchal and matriarchal family life (Woody Allen, Saul Bellow, Philip Roth, Isaac Bashevis Singer).[56]

The above examples make clear that ethnic attributes made their way into literature as elements of collective, everyday knowledge. These attributes have, by literature and other media, been spread and codified and are still being codified. Occasionally they are also found bundled in a fixed combination of features in fictive characters, which have become an integral, passed-down component part of a character arsenal. An example is offered by Shylock, the avaricious, cruel, and vengeful Jew in Shakespeare's *Merchant of Venice*. It is against the background of this highly influential character of ›the Jew‹ that Lessing's character Nathan develops his potential to enlighten.[57] For, in contrast to Shylock, Nathan is generous to Saladin and he is ready to forego revenge for the cruelty that he has suffered at the hands of Christians.[58] It is exactly this contrast between Shylock and Nathan which underscores the remarkable humanity that Lessing draws attention to with his atypical character. Another example of a type as embodiment of a certain stereotype-combination is the proverbial ›deutsche Michel‹ with his *bonhomie* and righteousness.[59] Of course, Shylock and Michel are connoted differently; the first clearly negatively, the second, in contrast, more probably positively. In both cases, however, an ethnic group is represented in various media and various times through a linguistically – or pictorially – conveyed type that has a fixed combination of characteristics which present an obvious judgement.

Apart from that, ethnic attributions that label characters appear in various combinations and with varying degrees of evaluation: according to context and dependent upon genre guidelines (a topic to which I will return later), a text selects from a heterogeneous repertoire of positive and negative patterns. One could describe these from a literary-scientific perspective as topoi. And the same character features apply to these, which have become formulaic knowledge about character differences between peoples, as to other topoi: a very high degree of familiarity, permanence and multifunctionality. And, like all other topoi, they also

---

56 Ibid., p. 206.
57 For more on the topic of the lingering Shylock type in German-speaking literature after the Holocaust, which at times is only perceptible upon second glance, see for example Klüger: Judenproblem.
58 See Lessing: Nathan, III,7 and IV,7.
59 See Szarota: Michel.

exist in varying degrees in an area of conflict between timeless validity and varying topical adaptations. As topoi for markers of spatial belonging (whereby space is understood in an actual material, as well as social sense, so that it can refer to a country or a district just as well as to a social collective whose speech and customs are shared) they are part of the literary conventions of discourse about cultural difference and their presentation. They can serve in variable combinations and evaluations in the construction of alterity and/or collective identity, depending on whether they deal with attributions that have to do with one's own or with a foreign ethnicity. As a matter of principle, the same will be true for other social patterns – for those, for instance, that apply to social milieus or that mark differences between genders or generations. From a social-psychological standpoint, such character traits, or identity ascriptions of collective entities, are referred to as stereotypes: »Stereotypes are shared beliefs about person attributes, usually personality traits but often also behaviours of a group of people«.[60]

Stereotypes are invariably useful, indeed indispensable. For they serve as a framework which allows the individual to order and comprehend the complexity of his perceived reality, and to come to an understanding about it with others; since they are economical they are used for reference and facilitate communication. The insights that social psychology has brought to our understanding of stereotypes are contrary to our everyday understanding of them; that is to say, that stereotype is generally equated with negative prejudice:

> If stereotypes are considered part of social perception, they should be flexible as well as rigid. Stereotypes are not only lists of attributes that apply to social categories. They function also, and mainly, as theoretical naïve explanations of the world. [...] Stereotypes certainly simplify reality, but they do not necessarily result from intellectual laziness [...]. Stereotypes are a means of shorthand for a vast amount of data, but also a means of extrapolating from a little information. [...] Thus, to the same extent that stereotypes are both flexible and rigid, they simplify past knowledge and create new knowledge.[61]

Granted, stereotypes could certainly be the expression of antipathy and disdain; and they could be incorporated into text and image in such a way that they aim to inflammatorily activate or strengthen a negative image on the part of the reader; it is in this case, and in this case alone, that they are closely associated with prejudice.[62] But whether the application of group-

---

60 Leyens / Yzerbyt: Stereotypes, p. 3.
61 Ibid., p. 204f.
62 Stereotype and prejudice have ›different semantic histories‹: »The concept of stereotype refers primarily to cognitive processes of differentiation and generalization;

specific (including ethnic) stereotypes in individual cases can be viewed as the expression of attitudes, and whether or not they are perceived as such, depends on the respective context in which they are used. In order to examine stereotypes scientifically, one must first analyze their selection – in conjunction with the evaluation that is associated with them in a text – that is to say, in the context of both their production and reception. At the same time, the latter is subject to historical change: the above-mentioned negative Jewish stereotypes can no longer be separated – from today's perspective – from the anti-Semitic stigmatization and ostracism of the Jews in Europe. Rather, they must be viewed in the light of historical responsibility that goes back to the history of the persecution of the Jews, including state-implemented, organized mass murder. But while this ›other‹ religion and culture – established for centuries-long by Christianity as *different* – was precisely not connoted with a ›foreign‹ spatiality, but rather characterized as ›foreign‹ in ›one's own‹ space, the stereotypes that refer to members of foreign countries (as a rule less explicitly connected to evaluative attitudes) serve, at least at first, to designate origin based on the common knowledge of cultural differences, which are in turn understood, as mentioned above, as the expression of national characters.

Depending on the respective context, these stereotypes about a people, which are commonly known at least in Europe, can develop into a regular concept of the enemy if presented in a negative light and with a negative evaluation. Or the opposite can be true: positive characteristics form an ideal image. So, for example, Madame de Staël's well-known book on Germany sketches – in its implicit critique of Napoleonic France – the image of the virtuous, honest, profound and inward-looking German.[63] In the times of the nationalistically-charged wars between the ›arch enemies‹ Germany and France, however, French propaganda depicted the Germans as primarily warmongering barbarians.[64] One finds similar descriptions in French fiction, for example, when characters are explicitly revealed as

---

the concept of prejudice refers primarily to affective processes of debasement. Common to both concepts is that the processes described manifest themselves in judgements about people […] as members of groups […], that they are used by different social groups, and that they are distinguished by notable stability« (Schäfer: Entwicklungslinien, pp. 50f).

63 One finds, in Staël's book, a tendency towards ›profoundness‹ in literature and philosophy in reaction to the blossoming of German literature and philosophy around 1800. It is an example of how the stereotype reservoir occasionally expands in reaction to a special context – though following patterns already in existence; in the case of the Germans, these are e.g. seriousness and thoroughness.

64 See footnote 15; in addition see Leiner: Deutschlandbild, pp. 187–203.

representatives of German culture: Balzac, in his 1848 novel *Le Cousin Pons*, portrays the character of a musician by the name of Schmucke, who is a loyal German and whose stereotype repertoire is accordingly designed as clumsy and clownish, while he is at the same time portrayed as a thoroughly honest, good-natured and self-sacrificing friend of the main character.[65] Maupassant's novella *Mademoiselle Fifi*, on the other hand, published thirty years later, tells of clownish and brutal Prussian officers, whose unsophistication is shown, among other things, during their drinking sessions.[66] The agreement between character portrayal and widespread knowledge about the ›nature‹ of the Germans in both fictional texts refers to verisimilitude as a postulate of Realism in literature. The correspondence between prior knowledge on the part of the reader and character formation makes what is narrated plausible:

> What is important in narrative, [...] is not how characters are, but how their behaviour relates to the audience's expectations concerning them. The predication of action to character, if it is to follow the rule of plausibility, is already pre-inscribed in the character.[67]

The choice of such contrasting professions as musician and soldier, which is important in the case of the extremely different stories by Balzac and Maupassant, determines (under the auspices of Realism) the selection from the familiar ›German‹ national stereotypes for character traits, which manifest themselves through character behaviour and drive the plot forward – in the first case *bonhomie*, devotion and loyalty, and in the second, violence, brutality and ruthlessness.

The familiarity with the ›character‹ of the Germans has a long tradition and is just as ambivalent as for all other peoples because one imagined them as collective individuals with positive and negative character traits (virtues and vices, as they were termed in the Early Modern Era). As was shown above, it was theoretically founded and circulated through the concept of national character, with the selection of patterns depending on the context. Following the traumatic experience of the Franco-Prussian war of 1870–71 in France, it is no wonder that the attributes selected in Maupassant's novella (as well as how they were perceived) are cast in a negative light. This does not mean, however, that the occurrence of ethnical attributes in a text – for instance as elements of character formation – are to be understood as a direct expression of the ›image‹ that an entire society, within its own national borders and at a specific time,

---

65 For the function of this character in Balzac's novel see Florack: Fremde, pp. 169–179.
66 On this see Leiner: Deutschlandbild, pp. 190–192.
67 Leerssen: Mimesis, p. 169.

has formed of a ›foreign‹ people, although such a conclusion has not infrequently been drawn in traditional comparative imagology.[68] This underestimates the stereotypical core of such representations, a core made solid by tradition and transnational spread. In principle, the attitude of the speaker cannot automatically be deduced from the use of a social stereotype in communication, because a distinction must be made between ›knowledge of a cultural stereotype‹ and ›acceptance or endorsement of the stereotype‹: ›although one may have *knowledge of a stereotype*, his or her *personal beliefs* may or may not be congruent with the stereotype‹;[69] this is especially true of literature but also of other media, such as film. And here one sees that the implementation of ethnic- as well as other social stereotypes is subject to its own rules, which to a large extent are determined by the conventions of representation. Some foundational ideas will be summarized in my last section.

5 On the Function of Ethnic Stereotypes in Fiction

Ethnic stereotypes appear (not only in literature) primarily to designate *otherness*, either in persons of foreign origin in a familiar space, or from a foreign space, whose people – endowed with character features from the corresponding stereotype reservoir – can be portrayed as ›typical representatives‹ of this *otherness*, or else distinguished as individuals. When ethnical stereotypes in a non-fictional text are supposed to convey experiences in a foreign place or with the *other*, as is the case in travel reports, they fulfil an orientation- and communication function for the producer as well as for the recipient. Often they are made use of in a structure consisting of comparison and reversal, through which ›the *other*‹ is presented in reference to the ›*self*‹ – that is, as similar with or opposite to that which is well-known.[70] What should be remembered in any case, is that stereotypes in travelogues that show a concern for factual knowledge and a realistic portrayal appear distinctly less frequently than in fictional literature, to which less stringent criteria apply and whose job is after all not necessarily to deal with the transmission of knowledge about the

---

68 As an example of this see Leiner: Deutschlandbild, in addition to Blaicher: Deutschlandbild, or Zacharasiewicz: Deutschlandbild.
69 Devine: Stereotypes, p. 5.
70 For comparison and reversal as fundamental elements of the representation of the *other* since antiquity, see the chapter ›A Rhetoric of Otherness‹, in: Hartog: Mirror, pp. 212–259. Herodotus, however, does not take recourse to national stereotypes.

other.⁷¹ A prominent example of the latter are adventure novels such as those by Karl May.

Fictions seldom document interactions with a foreign culture; as a rule, they serve more to facilitate the processes of understanding within one's own culture. In this case ethnic stereotypes are an efficient, because economical, means through which to call up – in a catchphrase-like manner – the reader's previous knowledge about a foreign country and its people and to entertain or instruct him based on what is known. This can be taken so far that the appearance of a character who is merely labelled as *foreign* can be understood metonymically. In such instances a text introduces a character as foreign in order to develop – narratively or dramatically – character traits and modes of behaviour within the framework of a plot which are generally attributed to the respective foreigners. Because character formation refers back to the familiar national or rather ethnic features, it is possible to deal with a completely different subject in a concise, yet at the same time sensorily graphic manner – for example a conflict about social or moral norms – which has nothing to do directly with the actual foreigner. We see, for example, in selected French narratives of the 17th to 19th centuries, in which ›honest Germans‹ appear as main characters, that the motifs of honesty and loyalty in earlier texts draw attention to a moral lesson while in later texts they convey social criticism.⁷² Neither case has anything to do with Germany or its people.⁷³

It is possible, though far from necessary, that at any given time in a communicative community, certain positive or negative connotations can be combined with the stereotypes; in fact, they are almost activated automatically *through* the stereotypes. Only a literary critic can determine, through careful analysis of the context, whether this is an isolated case or whether it was the norm. But one must keep in mind that such evaluations can change, depending on various factors of reception, such as social status, education, age, and gender of the reader, as well as place, time and means of publication. So it is quite possible that ethnic stereotypes in a

---

71 In this context see also Thomé: Vorbemerkung, pp. 1–7, especially pp. 3–4.
72 See Florack: Fremde, pp. 162–179.
73 Emer O'Sullivan has shown the extent to which the existential theme of ›war‹ in English children's literature of the outgoing 20th century has determined the deployment of characters that are tagged as ›typically‹ German; these characters perform, depending on the context, very different functions. In this connection O'Sullivan speaks of the ›aesthetic potential‹ of the stereotype. (O'Sullivan: National, p. 98.)

text from the 18th century had a different ›charge‹ than the one perceived two hundred fifty years later.[74]

When literary characters (or also characters in other types of fiction) appear as members of a certain people in that they are identified through a combination of corresponding stereotypes considered ›typical‹ for this group, then they *speak* and *behave* according to these typical stereotypes. This means that their positive and negative character traits – unfolded scenically or narratively – correspond with the reader's knowledge about the ›national character‹ of the people they represent. The greater the agreement, the more the character appears one-dimensional and not as a complex ›character‹ with individual traits. And because the traits of a fictive character are developed first and foremost through *behaviour*, one can ascertain, with respect to ethnical and other stereotypes, a fundamentally close connection between character and plot in fiction. Ethnic stereotypes have, therefore, a narrative as well as dramatic potential:

> Since [...] national characterization usually involves the idea of the motivation of behaviour, descriptions of national peculiarities will often gravitate to the register of narrativity – exempla, myths, parables, and jokes, as well as novels or drama.[75]

In this way, for example, ›German‹ awkwardness and the inclination to drink are not only well-suited for jest literature, but also for the stage, preferably comedies. For, according to tradition, characters as types belong more readily in this genre – the character of the comical foreigner is strongly embedded in the Commedia dell'Arte – rather than in tragedy, and coarse vices also have their place in comedy, in the genre, that is, which occupies the lowest position in the system of literary genres.[76]

Since distinctive, easily-recognizable characteristics are generally attributed to entire groups and are subject to exaggeration, ethnic stereotypes often function as a device to expose the comic element, as in

---

74 For the shift in character ascriptions resulting from a change in readership see also Margolin: Characterization, p. 10: »The sets of cultural and generic norms held by readers in different periods and cultures are different. Consequently, the same NA [narrative agent] will be endowed with different mental attributes by different generations of readers« (Margolin's comments do not, however, refer explicitly to ethnic stereotypes).
75 Leerssen: Rhetoric, p. 281.
76 The braggart Capitano of the Commedia dell'Arte is a Spaniard, as is easily recognizable by his costume; originally the character refers satirically to the Spanish occupation of Italy in the 16th century. See Mehnert: Commedia, pp. 113–114. As late a figure as Riccaut de la Marlinière, a relic from the comedy of character, in Lessing's comedy *Minna von Barnhelm* shows some traits of the tradition of the foreign soldier who has only a smattering of the respective foreign language (see for example Hinck: Lustspiel, p. 294).

satire or, to cite a different medium, in caricature, for instance in order to expose the absurdity of positions in intellectual or political debates which are somehow connected to the other culture. This is common knowledge to everyone through popular media, but it is also aesthetically more complex texts that use this potential of stereotypes. Thus Voltaire, in his ›conte philosophique‹ *Candide ou l'optimisme*, allows a simple-minded German to stumble from one disastrous adventure to the next in order to carry Leibniz' idea of theodicy ad absurdum. However, elaborate contextual knowledge is necessary in this case in order to fully decode the reference to ›German‹ above and beyond the character tag. On a superficial level, Candide's ›typically German‹ simple-mindedness does no more than create comical situations that make for an entertaining plot. At the same time, the stereotypically repeated phrase of his teacher Pangloss, that all is for the best in the best of all possible worlds, alludes to Leibniz' teaching of pre-established harmony. The incongruity between Pangloss' comments and Candide's hair-raising experiences seems comical and conveys, as such, Voltaire's mockery of Leibniz. This critique, on the other hand, can be deduced from the ›catastrophe discourse of the 18th century‹ as the expression of the fundamental uncertainty of an optimistic world view in reaction to the devastating earthquake in Lisbon in 1755.[77]

Characters who are patterned as one-dimensional by means of ethnic stereotypes, or rather *types*, not only have a solid place in comedies, satires and instructional literature of various genres, but belong above all in every kind of ›schematic literature‹ and other types of fiction where they are easily recognized by the reader. Here we are reminded again of the economy function of stereotypes, but also of the fact that their occurrence alone is no reliable indicator of prejudicial attitudes towards foreigners in the minds of producers and recipients. It is only in regular inflammatory texts that stereotypes are employed for the purpose of creating an image of the enemy that aims both to repulse and spur the reader's aggression. This is the case, for example, in the poetry of the so-called wars of liberation in 19th century Germany or for Ernst Moritz Arndt's biting antinapoleonic treatise *Spirit of the Times* [*Geist der Zeit*].

Since ethnic stereotypes became a fixed component of the expanding press in the 19th century due to their high functionality – that is, their ability to orient in connection to what is known to be ›universal‹, or more correctly, to that which is known to the widest public – they often appear in aesthetically demanding literature under the auspices of irony.

---

[77] This is the apt title of the essay collection edited by Lauer / Unger: Erdbeben.

This promotes intellectual pleasure above all for educated readers who, after the concept of national character had lost scientific appeal in the outgoing 20th century, view generalizing statements on the nature of peoples as questionable and deem themselves above such generalizations. Of course, the stereotypical attributes are also known to them, otherwise this type of irony would not function. So, for example, Daniel Kehlmann portrays in his novel, *Measuring the World*, the world traveller Alexander von Humboldt as a workaholic, a disciplined scientist whose lack of humour characterizes him as ›typically German‹ – at least in the eyes of his French escort, whose thrill of discovery extends to amorous adventures (this character then is tagged with an ethnic stereotype as well).[78] The fact that the exceptional character of Humboldt appears as a typical German is part of the comic effect of Kehlmann's text. This effect has been described as unusual for German literature by literary critics,[79] as if art in Germany tended *per se* to be more serious and ponderous instead of humorous and light-hearted – proof of the fact that stereotypes remain ineradicable on the level of opinion formation and are in no way banned from elite discourses.

Within the realm of cultural studies, research into ethnic stereotypes in fiction is most promising in those areas where naive hope – to be able to ascertain from positivistically-traced ›images‹ about the *other* the attitudes or even prejudices of entire collectives as producers of these images – has been overcome, and the investigation has begun of the functional value of stereotypes in their narrower and broader context. Taking as my starting point some recent research contributions but without claiming complete coverage, I will discuss in a final section some very promising approaches for interpreting ethnic stereotypes as elements of character formation.

In principle, it is useful to test whether ethnic stereotypes in a text are combined with one or more other superordinate schemes. This is because in literature they often serve to model an opposition which could be, for example, of the social, political or ideological type and be connected to differences in age (generations), gender (male – female) or space (above – below, central – marginal).[80] In this case, ethnic stereotypes – through the characters' appearance, speech and behaviour – can be tagged as similar or

---

[78] See, for example, Kehlmann: Vermessung, p. 111.
[79] To give just one example: Hubert Spiegel writes in his review of Kehlmann: »That one is entertained by this novel in such a subtle, intelligent and witty manner which one has hardly ever experienced before in German-language literature, is […] only one of the many highlights of this remarkable book« (F.A.Z., Oct. 22nd, 2005).
[80] This connects to Leerssen's concept of ›structural patterns‹ (Leerssen: Rhetoric, pp. 271, 275, 278).

opposite via the difference between the characters; they can correlate with other stereotypes (generation-, gender-, social status- or occupation types, for example), so that they contribute to the profiling of contrasting semantic spaces. As a matter of principle, one side or the other of the paired opposites can be connoted either negatively or positively, and the selection and order of the respective positive or negative pattern will turn out accordingly. In this way, the contrast between civilization and barbarism – under altered circumstances – can become its opposite: decadence and instinctiveness. This is a well known phenomenon and stems from the reception history of Rousseauism, not only in France. For example, the proverbial roughness of the Germans (and other peoples of the ›North‹) mutates into an expression of unaffected loyalty and natural kind-heartedness.[81] Similarly, the ›backward‹ peoples overseas become the ›noble savages‹.[82] who serve to be both ›role model and challenge‹ for the Europeans.[83] It would be superfluous to mention that both cases have to do with ethnocentric constructs.[84]

Offering a critical view of Edward Said's book on orientalism, which initially pointed the way,[85] recent literary studies present models for the analysis of stereotypes in discourses, which have proved themselves especially within the realm of Postcolonial Studies. Thus, in her monograph *Stereotype Paradiese* [*Stereotypical Paradises*] Gabriele Dürbeck

---

81 »On the one hand there was the France that was corrupted by a decadent civilization, by luxury and immorality; on the other hand virtuous Germany. In comparison with the noble savage the German had the advantage of some measure of civilization; in comparison with the over-civilized Frenchman he had the advantage of a greater closeness to nature. He was, so to speak, a ›polished‹ ›bon sauvage‹« (Fink: Nachbar, p. 26).

82 »Without a doubt: the cliché of the ›barbarian‹ is closely related to the cliché of the ›noble savage‹, which was to manifest itself especially clearly around the end of the 18th century. A great number of the positive attributes which were to determine the image of the ›noble savage‹ stem directly from what were believed at the time to be the characteristic features of barbarism: simplicity and modesty in this sense are complementary to primitiveness; innocence and impartiality take the place of childish unreasonableness and dullness; idleness is replaced by quiet contentment, lawlessness with natural harmony of existence, and domination by one's physical urges by a carefree zest for life« (Bitterli: Wilde, p. 373).

83 Ibid., p. 367.

84 Bitterli hypothesizes that the interest in ›barbarian‹ and ›noble savage‹ – ›the image of the barbarian turned positive‹ – can be traced back to an ›ethnocentric uneasiness about one's own culture‹; this would hold true for the ›radical questioning of the philosophers of the Enlightenment‹ in the 18th century, as well as for the years ›before and after the First World War‹, in which the ›demise of bourgeois society‹ becomes apparent (Ibid., p. 374).

85 See Said: Orientalism.

examines *Oceanism in German South-Sea Travel Literature* [*Ozeanismus in der deutschen Südseeliteratur*] between the European Restoration and World War I. She develops a multi-levelled approach which takes into account the following: the ›topoi of the other‹, their ›changing functions of portrayal‹, and lastly the ›respective connections, conjunctures and hierarchies of the individual discourses in the field of discourse on Oceanism‹.[86] Through her study Dürbeck is able to demonstrate a ›relative constant repertoire of stereotypes‹ in the genres which she researched (›popular science travel report, memoir literature, magazine and adventure novel‹), but whose use ›varies‹ in ›frequency, connotation and contextualization‹.[87] The findings for the time period under investigation are: ›as long as‹ the ›topos of the earthly paradise‹ in the South Seas ›remains linked to the image of the noble savage it serves to propagate an egalitarian humanism‹.[88] This is the case for example within the discourse of ›Rousseauism‹ (which goes back to the Enlightenment), in which South Sea literature participates: »It comprises the critique of alienation and symptoms of the decline of civilization and, consequently, leads to the exotification of primitive societies«.[89] In the course of the 19th century, however, the topos of the ›noble savage‹ – in the ›context of a religious-moral, Darwinist-racist and/or economic-colonial discourse‹ – fades in favour of the stereotype of the ›uncivilized savage‹, while the ›topos of the earthly paradise‹ lives on. This topos, however, instead of being used to take a critical look at civilization, is, on the contrary, used for propagandistic purposes ›in order for the young and budding German Reich (which, as a colonial power, was a relatively late arrival) to demand its ›place in the sun«.[90]

Dürbeck's observation that character and space formation need not necessarily show corresponding stereotyping is extremely informative (above and beyond the study of South Sea literature) and of fundamental importance for the analysis of ethnic stereotypes as elements of character formation. Indeed, her observation would suggest a fundamental analysis of character formation in its relationship with the construction of space by focusing on the space *within* fiction, as well as on the conception of space (above all in the context of colonialism) that is conveyed *through* such stereotypes. And it is not only where stereotypes are combined and organized to the extent that the disparate, ethnically tagged individual

---

86 Dürbeck: Stereotype, p. 9.
87 Ibid., pp. 340f.
88 Ibid., p. 344.
89 Ibid., pp. 344f.
90 Ibid., p. 345.

characters in various contexts lead back to regular types – as in the case of the North American Indian, where stereotypes become historically effective as perceptible constructs in that they allow the combination of the formation of tradition, the interpretation of the present, and a design for the future;[91] it is not only in such texts that time, in addition to space, plays a constitutive role in understanding the function of ethnic stereotypes in fiction.[92]

References

Aristotle: Poetics (in D.A. Russell and M. Winterbottom (Ed.): Classical Literary Criticism, The World's Classics. Oxford 1989).

Aristotle: The Politics (Translated and with an Introduction, Notes, and Glossary by Carnes Lord. Chicago etc 1984).

Aristotle: Rhetoric (With an English Translation by J.H. Freese. In: The Loeb Classical Library, vol. 193. London et al. 1967).

Beller, Manfred / Joep Leerssen (Eds.): Imagology. The Cultural Construction and Literary Representation of National Characters. A Critical Survey, Amsterdam / New York 2007.

Bitterli, Urs: Die ›Wilden‹ und die ›Zivilisierten‹. Grundzüge einer Geistes- und Kulturgeschichte der europäisch-überseeischen Begegnung. 2nd edn. München 1991.

Blaicher, Günther: Das Deutschlandbild in der englischen Literatur. Darmstadt 1992.

Buchenau, Barbara: *Dreaming America, Ragging the Iroquois: Typecasting in the Atlantic World* [manuscript].

Caesar, C. Iulius: Der Gallische Krieg. Lateinisch-deutsch, ed. by Otto Schönberger. München 1990.

Devine, Patricia G.: Stereotypes and Prejudice: Their Automatic and Controlled Components. In: Journal of Personality and Social Psychology 56 (1989), pp. 5–18.

Dürbeck, Gabriele: Stereotype Paradiese. Ozeanismus in der deutschen Südseeliteratur 1815–1914. Tübingen 2007.

Fink, Gonthier-Louis: Der januskö̈pfige Nachbar. Das französische Deutschlandbild gestern und heute, in: Dietrich Harth (Ed.): Fiktion des Fremden. Erkundung kultureller Grenzen in Literatur und Publizistik. Frankfurt a. M. 1994, pp. 15–82.

Fisch, Jörg: »Zivilisation, Kultur«. In: Otto Brunner / Werner Conze / Reinhart Koselleck (Eds): Geschichtliche Grundbegriffe. Historisches Lexikon zur politisch-sozialen Sprache in Deutschland, vol. 7. Stuttgart 1992, pp. 679–774.

Florack, Ruth: Bekannte Fremde. Zu Herkunft und Funktion nationaler Stereotype in der Literatur. Tübingen 2007.

---

91 Barbara Buchenau investigates an original and very promising link between stereotype research and typology in a religious sense in her analysis of the North American ›Indian‹ as founding figure in her postdoctoral thesis, *Dreaming* (I would like to thank the author for the opportunity to preview her manuscript).

92 Trans. by Michael Pätzold.

Florack, Ruth: Tiefsinnige Deutsche, frivole Franzosen. Nationale Stereotype in deutscher und französischer Literatur. Stuttgart / Weimar 2001.

Gans, Evelien / Joep Leerssen: Article »Jews«. In: Manfred Beller / Joep Leerssen (Eds.): Imagology, pp. 202–208.

Hartog, François: The Mirror of Herodotus. The Representation of the Other in the Writing of History,. Translated by Janet Lloyd. Berkeley et al. 1988.

Hinck, Walter: Das deutsche Lustspiel des 17. und 18. Jahrhunderts und die italienische Komödie. Commedia dell'arte und Théâtre italien, Stuttgart 1965.

Horaz: De arte poetica, translated by Wilhelm Schöne, in: Sämtliche Werke. Lateinisch und deutsch, München 1967, pp. 230–259.

Hume, David: Of National Characters. In: The Philosophical Works. Thomas Hill Green / Thomas Hodge Grose (Eds.), vol. 3. London 1882 (Reprint Aalen 1964), pp. 244–258.

Jeismann, Michael: Das Vaterland der Feinde. Studien zum nationalen Feindbegriff und Selbstverständnis in Deutschland und Frankreich 1792–1918. Stuttgart 1992.

Kehlmann, Daniel: Die Vermessung der Welt. Reinbek bei Hamburg 2006.

Klüger, Ruth: Gibt es ein »Judenproblem« in der deutschen Nachkriegsliteratur? In: R. K.: Katastrophen. Über deutsche Literatur. Göttingen 1994, pp. 9–39.

Kondylis, Panajotis: Die Aufklärung im Rahmen des neuzeitlichen Rationalismus. München 1986.

La Mesnardière, Hippolyte-Jules Pilet de: La Poëtique. Paris 1640 (Reprint Genève 1972).

Las Casas, Bartolomé de: Apologética Historia, ed. by Juan Pérez de Tudela Bueso. In: Obras escogidas, vol. 3. Madrid 1958.

Lauer, Gerhard / Thorsten Unger: Das Erdbeben von Lissabon und der Katastrophendiskurs im 18. Jahrhundert. Göttingen 2008.

Leerssen, Joep: Mimesis and Stereotype. In: Yearbook of European Studies 4 (1991): National Identity – Symbol and Representation, pp. 165–175.

Leerssen, Joep: The Rhetoric of National Character: A Programmatic Survey. In: Poetics Today 21/2 (2000), pp. 267–292.

Leiner, Wolfgang: Das Deutschlandbild in der französischen Literatur. 2nd edn. Darmstadt 1991.

Lessing, Gotthold Ephraim: Nathan der Weise. In: Wilfried Barner et al. (Eds.): Werke und Briefe in 12 Bänden, vol. 9. Frankfurt a. M. 1993, pp. 483–627.

Leyens, Jacques-Philippe / Vincent Yzerbyt / Georges Schadron: Stereotypes and Social Cognition. London et al. 1994.

Margolin, Uri: Characterization in Narrative: Some Theoretical Prolegomena. In: Neophilologus 67 (1983), pp. 1–14.

Martini, Martino: Atlas Deß allereüssersten Asien / Oder Landbeschreibung deß Keyserthumbs Sina. Vorrede an den Leser / in welcher das gantze eüsserste Asien überhaupt beschriben wird. In: Joan Blaeu: Novus Atlas Sinensis. Amsterdam 1655 (Facsimiles of the Edition de luxe from the Herzog August Library in Wolfenbüttel), pp. 6–10.

Maurer, Michael: »Nationalcharakter« in der frühen Neuzeit. Ein mentalitätsgeschichtlicher Versuch. In: Reinhard Blomert / Helmut Kuzmics / Annette Treibel (Eds): Transformationen des Wir-Gefühls. Studien zum nationalen Habitus. Frankfurt a. M. 1993, pp. 45–81.

Mehnert, Henning: Commedia dell'arte. Struktur – Geschichte – Rezeption. Stuttgart 2003.

Montesquieu: Défense de l'Esprit des Lois. In: Roger Caillois (Ed.): Œuvres Complètes, vol. 2. [Paris] 1951, pp. 1121–1168. Translation: Montesquieu: A Defence of The Spirit of Laws. To Which are Added, Some Explanations. In: Montesquieu: The Complete

Works of M. de Montesquieu. Translated From the French. In Four Volumes. London 1777, vol. 4. pp. 219–281.
Montesquieu: De l'Esprit des Lois [1757]. In: Roger Caillois (Ed.): Œuvres Complètes, vol. 2. [Paris] 1951, pp. 225–995. Translation: Montesquieu: The Spirit of the Laws. Trans. and ed. by Anne M. Cohler / Basia Carolyn Miller / Harold Samuel Stone. Cambridge: Cambridge University Press 1989.
»Naturell der Völcker«. In: Zedler, Johann Heinrich: Grosses vollständiges Universal-Lexicon, vol. 23. Leipzig / Halle 1740 (Reprint Graz 1982), cols. 1246–1251.
O'Sullivan, Emer: National stereotypes as literary device. Traditions and uses of stereotypes of Germans in British and the English in German children's literature. In: Harald Husemann (Ed.): As Others See Us. Anglo-German Perceptions. Frankfurt a. M., 1994, pp. 81–98.
Posidonius, vol. 1 In: Ludwig Edelstein / I. G. Kidd (Eds.): The Fragments. 2nd edn. Cambridge 1989.
Rowe, John Howland: The Renaissance Foundations of Anthropology, in: American Anthropologist 67 (1965), pp. 1–20.
Said, Edward W.: Orientalism.Western Conceptions of the Orient, London 1978.
Scaliger, Julius Caesar: Poetices libri septem, a New Facsimile Edition of the Lyon Edition of 1561. Stuttgart 1964.
Schäfer, Bernd: Entwicklungslinien der Stereotypen- und Vorurteilsforschung. In: Bernd Schäfer / Franz Petermann (Eds): Vorurteile und Einstellungen. Sozialpsychologische Beiträge zum Problem sozialer Orientierung. Festschrift für Reinhold Bergler. Köln 1988, pp. 11–65.
Spiegel, Hubert: Review of Kehlmann (F.A.Z., Oct 22nd, 2005).
Stanzel, Franz K.: Europäer. Ein imagologischer Essay. Heidelberg 1997.
Stanzel, Franz K. (Ed.): Europäischer Völkerspiegel. Imagologisch-ethnographische Studien zu den Völkertafeln des frühen 18. Jahrhunderts. Heidelberg 1999.
Szarota, Tomasz: Der deutsche Michel. Die Geschichte eines nationalen Symbols und Autostereotyps. Aus dem Polnischen von Kordula Zentgraf-Zubrzycka, Osnabrück 1998.
Tacitus: Germania. Lateinisch und Deutsch. Translated by Manfred Fuhrmann. Stuttgart 1992.
Thomé, Horst: Vorbemerkung. In: Ruth Florack (Ed.): Nation als Stereotyp. Fremdwahrnehmung und Identität in deutscher und französischer Literatur. Tübingen 2000, pp. 1–7.
Vitruvii De architectura libri decem / Vitruv: Zehn Bücher über Architektur. Transl. by Curt Fensterbusch. Darmstadt 1964.
Vyverberg, Henry: Human Nature, Cultural Diversity, and the French Enlightenment, New York, Oxford 1989.
Zacharasiewicz, Waldemar: Das Deutschlandbild in der amerikanischen Literatur, Darmstadt 1998.

MARION GYMNICH

The Gender(ing) of Fictional Characters

1 Introduction: The Significance of ›Gendering‹ Approaches to Fictional Characters

Gender is beyond doubt one of the central categories operating in the cognitive processes that govern both the perception of human beings and the construction of fictional characters. On the most basic level, this means that readers typically strive to categorize fictional characters consistently as either male or female, even if the textual data on which such a categorization can possibly be based appears to be deficient. Discussions of literary texts such as Jeanette Winterson's *Written on the Body* (1992), where attempts on the part of the reader to categorize the protagonist as male or female remain fruitless right to the end, clearly demonstrate that readers try to construct characters as male or female even if the text does not offer any basis for doing this.[1] In addition, the binary categorization pattern ›male vs. female‹ is typically also used as a starting point for formulating hypotheses regarding a wide range of character-related issues, including identity, emotions, attitudes, values and norms. Since readers tend to assume that there is a straightforward relationship between sex and gender, they are likely to expect characters to act (more or less) in accordance with culturally dominant definitions of masculinity and femininity. The fact that fictional characters are by default categorized as male or female in the reading process as well as the omnipresence of gender-related issues in fictional texts make it desirable for literary and cultural studies to formulate approaches to fictional characters that include the category ›gender‹ in a systematic fashion.

Feminist literary criticism and gender studies have paid much attention to the description and interpretation of literary characters, exploring literary and cultural representations of masculinity and femininity in the

---

1 Cf. Kutzer: Cartography; Quadflieg: Stories.

context of their production and reception. In fact, as feminist narratologist Susan Lanser points out, »[f]eminist critics have tended to be more concerned with characters than with any other aspect of narrative«.[2] This particular interest in literary characters is presumably reflected most clearly in a branch of feminist literary studies which is often referred to as ›Images of Women Criticism‹. Images of Women Criticism, which played an important role in feminist literary criticism in the 1970s and 1980s,[3] regards female characters, in particular those created by male writers, as being predominantly informed by male wishes and anxieties. Gender stereotypes such as the ›witch‹ or the ›femme fatale‹ are read as projections of male anxieties and as containers of male guilt.[4] While Images of Women Criticism sought to draw the readers' attention to the status of literary characters as projections, early feminist literary critics usually were not much interested in *how*, i.e. by means of which textual strategies, characters are constructed within the actual text. In general, feminist literary criticism has tended to focus on matters of content, addressing character-related issues such as the differences between male and female patterns of development, gender and identity, gender roles and sexuality, rather than exploring structural, formal features of literary texts with respect to their impact on the construction of literary characters.

While feminist literary criticism in general has tended to focus on characters and character-related issues, feminist and gender-oriented narratology, which seeks to explore structural features of literary texts, their semanticization and specifically their ideological implications, has largely neglected the analysis of literary characters. Instead of developing gender-conscious models for the conceptualization and analysis of literary characters, feminist narratologists have sought to correct the bias towards the analysis of characters typical of feminist literary criticism by drawing particular attention to the gendering of the level of narrative transmission. Thus, Susan Lanser and Robyn Warhol, who introduced feminist narratology as a distinct branch of narrative theory in their programmatic

---

2 Lanser: Narratology, p. 344. Although scholars working within the fields of feminist literary criticism and gender studies have paid particular attention to character-related issues such as gender-specific patterns of development, gender identity, gender roles and concepts of male and female bodies, issues like the ones just mentioned are of course also explored in a range of other areas of literary and cultural studies, for instance in postcolonial studies.
3 Cf. Cornillon: Images; Bovenschen: Weiblichkeit; Stephan: Bilder; Wittmann: Femme; Würzbach: Forschung; Baader: Frauenbild.
4 Cf. Würzbach: Forschung, p. 141.

texts from the 1980s and early 1990s,[5] propose gender-conscious approaches to the analysis of narrators and narratees, but show little interest in developing criteria for the description of literary characters from a feminist-narratological point of view. In recent years, however, gender-conscious approaches to narrative theory have started to pay more attention to categories such as plot, space, time and characters, trying to bridge the gap between an interest in matters of content and a focus on the structural features of literary texts.[6]

In the following, several steps towards a systematic ›gendering‹ of approaches to fictional characters will be sketched. Firstly, the character concepts that can be identified in various gender-sensitive approaches to literary characters will be examined. In this context it will be argued that cognitive concepts of fictional characters, such as those developed by Grabes, Schneider and Jannidis for instance,[7] constitute an ideal starting point for integrating the notions of characters perpetuated by feminist literary criticism into a theoretical model of fictional characters. Moreover, I will argue that the reconceptualization of sex and gender that has taken place as a result of the ›performative turn‹ within gender studies, which was largely initiated by Judith Butler's influential studies *Gender Trouble* (1990) and *Bodies that Matter* (1993), has to be taken into consideration in approaches to fictional characters. Secondly, the significance of interfigurality for gender-conscious approaches to the analysis of fictional characters will be discussed.[8] Although references to other literary characters may seem to be a comparatively marginal phenomenon, they actually play an important role in the process of contextualizing and historicizing gender concepts in a considerable number of texts. Finally, gender-conscious approaches to the analysis of fictional characters will be discussed with respect to the media-specific nature of the construction and gendering of characters.

---

5 Cf. Lanser: Narratology; Lanser: Shifting; Lanser: Fictions; Warhol: Theory; Warhol: Interventions.
6 Cf. the contributions in Nünning / Nünning (2004), which provide an overview of recent developments within gender-conscious narrative theory.
7 Grabes: Personen; Schneider: Grundriß; Schneider: Theory; Jannidis: Figur.
8 Müller: Interfigurality.

2 Concepts of Fictional Characters in Gender-Conscious Approaches to Literary Studies

The concepts of fictional characters that have been developed and perpetuated in the various gender-conscious approaches to literary studies differ considerably. Given their interest in issues such as gender roles and gender-specific patterns of development it is hardly surprising that feminist literary criticism and gender studies have often drawn upon theories and models developed within sociology and psychology. The widespread practice of falling back on theories and models that were originally proposed to explain *human* behaviour suggests that a ›realistic-mimetic‹ concept of literary characters is privileged (at least implicitly) by many feminist literary critics.[9] In other words, feminist literary criticism tends to regard fictional characters as being constructed on the basis of what one knows about human beings (and specifically about the impact gender has on human behaviour, social structures and human interactions). Starting from this assumption it seems possible to regard fictional characters as representing different ways of coping with a range of gender-related problems; fictional characters, thus, tend to be read, for instance, as victims of patriarchal oppression or as models of female emancipation.

Realistic-mimetic concepts of literary characters have provoked a certain amount of criticism, however. In particular strictly structuralist approaches to the study of literary texts have emphasized that literary characters should not be treated as if they were human beings and, instead, have to be regarded as mere constructs or textual agents, resulting from (inevitably limited) textual information and fulfilling specific roles in the plot.[10] According to structuralist notions of literary characters, attempts to ascribe human attributes and motivations, let alone a ›biography‹, to fictional characters have to be discarded as naïve. Yet reading fictional characters as if they were at least similar to human beings is exactly what both ›average‹ readers and many literary critics seem to be doing in the reading process; literary characters simply appear to be more than a sum of textual information, as Uri Margolin stresses: »Although a

---

9 Cf. Nünning / Nünning: Grundkurs.
10 Vladimir Propp's *Morphology of the Folktale* (1928) is one of the classic texts proposing such a purely structuralist approach to literary characters. Although looking at fictional characters in terms of their functional roles in a particular text promises to provide interesting insights in terms of the representation of masculinities and femininities, feminist literary criticism and gender studies in general have shown little interest in structuralist concepts of characters.

possible individual is evoked or called into existence by a specific originating text, it is not reducible to words«.[11]

Cognitive approaches to the study of literary texts have accounted for readers' intuitive reactions to fictional characters and have argued that it is indeed possible to conceptualize fictional characters as being constructed at least *in analogy to* real persons, despite the fact that they are ultimately of course nothing more than constructions on the part of the reader.[12] The readers draw upon a range of real-world and literary frames in the process of constructing a fictional character in the reading process. These frames include personality theories (real-world frames) as well as the readers' knowledge about character types and character constellations in specific genres, e.g. Gothic fiction or hard-boiled crime fiction (literary frames). Given this premise, it also seems to be legitimate to draw upon sociological and psychological theories in the analysis of fictional characters, as Mieke Bal points out: »It [the character] has no real psyche, personality, ideology, or competence to act, but it does possess characteristics which make psychological and ideological description possible«.[13] As cognitive narratologists have shown, in the process of constructing literary characters readers inevitably project their own (culture-specific and historically variable) knowledge, including assumptions related to the category gender, onto fictional characters. Yet, despite the basic tendency to construct fictional characters in analogy to real persons, the constructions triggered by the textual data may of course still differ significantly in terms of how much they seem to resemble real persons, as Margolin points out:

> It is our intuitive experience as readers that some individuals in narrative are uncannily similar to actual (kinds of) individuals, and we regard them as fully mimetic. Other individuals, such as in science fiction or romance, possess properties, relations or combinations of them which cannot be actualized in the world as we know it. Yet we feel that they still have a representational force, in that they satisfy some minimal criteria for possible or conceivable individuals. In still other cases, especially in modern literature, we feel that the textual data cannot give rise to any possible individual and remain just that: textual potentialities of representation which are not actualized.[14]

One can assume that there is a relatively straightforward correlation between the specific ›representational force‹ of a given literary character and his/her ›marking‹ in terms of sex and gender. If there are ›markers‹

---

11 Margolin: Character, p. 463.
12 Cf., e.g., Grabes: Personen; Koch: Menschendarstellung; Schneider: Grundriß; Schneider: Theory.
13 Bal: Narratology, p. 80.
14 Margolin: Character, p. 461.

which, on the basis of a cultural consensus, allow the readers to categorize a particular character (consistently) as ›male‹ or ›female‹ (name, behavioral patterns, appearance, etc.), the likelihood of a realistic-mimetic reading of this character tends to increase. If such markers are missing, the likelihood of a non-mimetic reading increases. In general, however, as was pointed out above, one can assume that readers ascribe human attributes, including sex and gender, to the ›paper beings‹ they construct in the reading process on the basis of textual information (bottom-up process) and their own literary and real-world frames (top-down process) as long as the textual information does not make it virtually impossible to regard characters as entities resembling human beings.

Ralf Schneider has suggested a model which makes it possible to describe the process of constructing literary characters in the reading process in a more detailed manner by distinguishing between the processes of categorization, individuation, decategorization and personalization.[15] As will be shown in the following, an application of this process-oriented model of the construction of literary characters can also contribute to a systematic gendering of the analysis of literary characters. To begin with, *all* of the aspects of the textual information that can contribute to the process of constructing a character have to be seen in the light of the norms regulating gender roles in a particular cultural and historical context; i.e. the readers' reactions to »descriptions and presentations of a character's traits, verbal and nonverbal behavior, outer appearance, physiognomy and body language made by the narrator, by the character him- or herself or by other characters; [...] the presentation of consciousness and a character's mind-style; and [...] inferred character traits mapped metonymically from the presentation of fictional space to the character« are partially shaped by gender norms, which are part of the readers' real-world frames.[16]

The model of a literary character that is constructed as a result of categorization »will possess a number of well-defined features from which expectations, hypotheses, and inferences as well as explanations concerning that character's behavior can be generated«.[17] More often than not the social or literary categories to which characters are assigned by readers in the reading process involve stereotypical assumptions about gender, as categories such as the ›femme fatale‹, the ›Angel in the House‹ and the ›damsel in distress‹ illustrate. As soon as »subsequent information

---

15 Cf. Schneider: Grundriß; Schneider: Theory.
16 Schneider: Theory, p. 3.
17 Ibid., p. 7.

requires the reader to change some important aspects of the model, though leaving the initial category membership intact, the mental model undergoes some degree of modification and enters into a stage of individuation«.[18] As far as stereotypical notions of femininity and masculinity are concerned, one can assume that they are generally not contradicted or modified substantially in the process of individuation. It is only in the process of decategorization, i.e. in cases where the reader »encounters information that stands in direct opposition to the defining characteristics of the category« that one can expect gender stereotypes to be challenged.[19] If a character initially categorized as an ›Angel in the House‹ all of a sudden displays decidedly ›unangelic‹ traits, the reader is invited to reconsider the category that is undermined in a critical light. Personalization, which, according to Schneider, »is responsible for the more differentiated, more interesting and more effective cognitive and emotional responses in character-reception« and which »can occur whenever the reader does not categorize a character, i.e., when he or she is not able or willing to apply stored structures of knowledge for ad hoc impression formation«,[20] can go a step further than decategorization in the process of challenging gender stereotypes. By presenting characters that cannot easily be put into slots literary texts may contribute to undermining the omnipresence of (gendered) social and literary categories and may allow readings of characters that are ambivalent in terms of gender. Texts that undermine the notion that sex is a stable category (something that will be discussed in more detail below) also tend to privilege personalization. What was said above shows that the process-oriented model of character analysis may, for instance, serve to pick up some of the work done by Images of Women Criticism as well as by feminist literary criticism in general and render the gendered approaches to fictional characters more complex and dynamic by enriching them with cognitive narratological concepts.

Beyond fostering an increasing interest in a range of gender-related issues, feminist literary criticism and in particular gender studies have contributed to a critical revision of the concepts of gender and sex as such, and this critical revision has important implications for the way fictional characters are conceptualized. Feminist criticism in the 1970s and 1980s initiated a revision of the concept of ›gender‹, which has come to be regarded as a social construct, as a set of attributes which is negotiated

---

18 Schneider: Theory, p. 9.
19 Ibid., p. 10.
20 Ibid.

within a specific cultural and historical context. Concepts of femininity and masculinity are now seen as the result of negotiations in a range of discourses including medicine, law and psychology. Literary texts may play an ambivalent role with respect to the cultural negotiation of notions about gender. On the one hand, literary texts may criticize, challenge and subvert traditional concepts of masculinity and femininity, thus fulfilling the function of literature as ›cultural ecology‹.[21] This function can, for example, be ascribed to many feminist literary texts. On the other hand, literary texts may contribute to the construction and perpetuation of gender stereotypes. A case in point is Coventry Patmore's notorious poem »The Angel in the House«, which expresses one of the predominant gender stereotypes of the Victorian Age.

In contrast to gender, ›sex‹ tended to be seen as a stable category in early feminist criticism; while gender was regarded as culturally and historically variable, sex was seen as biologically determined or, in other words, as given. In her studies *Gender Trouble* and *Bodies that Matter* Judith Butler challenges the traditional distinction between the supposedly stable category ›sex‹ on the one hand and the social category ›gender‹ on the other hand, insisting that both sex and gender have to be regarded as being socially constructed in a series of performative acts: »Th[e] production of sex *as* the prediscursive ought to be understood as the effect of the apparatus of cultural construction designated by *gender*«.[22] According to Butler, thus, neither gender nor sex has the status of being given:

> [T]here will be no way to understand ›gender‹ as a cultural construct which is imposed upon the surface of matter, understood either as ›the body‹ or its given sex. Rather, once ›sex‹ itself is understood in its normativity, the materiality of the body will not be thinkable apart from the materialization of that regulatory norm. ›Sex‹ is, thus, not simply what one has, or a static description of what one is: it will be one of the norms by which the ›one‹ becomes viable at all, that which qualifies a body for life within the domain of cultural intelligibility.[23]

Drawing upon the assumption that both sex and gender are generated in a series of performative acts,[24] one can argue that gendered identities have

---

21 Cf. Zapf: Literature; Zapf: Ökologie; Zapf: Dekonstruktion. Zapf regards literature as an ›ecological force‹ which »first and foremost, engages with the cultural systems, categories, forms of consciousness and communication within which we predominantly live and interpret our existence« (Zapf: Literature, p. 85).
22 Butler: Gender, p. 7.
23 Butler: Bodies, p. 2.
24 Cf. Butler: Gender, p. 25: »There is no gender identity behind the expressions of gender; that identity is performatively constituted by the very ›expressions‹ that are said to be its results«.

to be regarded as nothing more than a ›reiteration of norms‹;[25] they are mere ›quotations‹ or ›masquerades‹.[26] The notion of the performative nature of both sex and gender can be staged in literary texts by means of subversive strategies ranging from cross-dressing to mistaken identities and sexual transformations. In fact, fictional characters seem to be an ideal site for exploring the possibilities of constructing even radically different gendered identities and for questioning the notion that sex is a stable category.

Texts such as Virginia Woolf's highly experimental fictional biography *Orlando* (1928), which features a sudden transformation of the protagonist's sex, illustrate that fiction may serve to challenge traditional assumptions about gender and may even question the notion of sex as a stable category. The title character of Woolf's novel, for instance, is first introduced to the readers as a young English nobleman living in the Elizabethan period, whose behaviour, attitudes and career seem to correspond largely to male gender stereotypes.[27] Yet, despite the initial marking of the character as both ›male‹ (sex) and ›masculine‹ (gender), the readers learn at a certain point that the protagonist has undergone a physical transformation and, as a result, is a woman now. In *Orlando* the sexual metamorphosis of the protagonist is mainly a vehicle for drawing the readers' attention to the contrasts between male and female gender roles; nevertheless the fictional text at least *imagines* the possibility of an instability of the category sex – and the social and personal consequences of such an instability. Sarah Kirsch's story »Blitz aus heiterm Himmel« (1975), which also features a literal sexual transformation undergone by the protagonist, in a similar manner highlights the constructed nature of gender and challenges the idea of a ›natural‹ link between sex and gender, thus partially anticipating innovative concepts of sex and gender developed within gender studies since the 1990s.

Beyond the possibility of depicting a sexual metamorphosis on the story level, fictional narratives may also leave the sex of a character unspecified. In Jeanette Winterson's novel *Written on the Body*, for instance, the readers wonder right to the end whether the protagonist is male or female. In this text the narrative situation is the key to making it impossible for the readers to categorize the protagonist as male or female: Due to the fact that the narrator is also the protagonist of the novel, both

---

25 Butler: Bodies, p. 10.
26 Cf. Schabert: Literaturgeschichte, p. 299; Stritzke: Performativität, p. 61.
27 Cf. Young: Object, p. 169: »Orlando runs through standard masculine plots, winning various lovers and high political office«.

the protagonist's name, which might suggest his/her sex, and, more importantly, third-person singular pronouns referring to the protagonist, which are by definition marked male or female in English, can be avoided throughout the text. As M. Daphne Kutzer observes, this strategy can be read as »an attempt at escaping the most central of all pairs, Male and Female, in order to look at the truly human«.[28] To make the readers aware of the ›gap‹ with respect to the information about the protagonist, or rather of their habit of labelling fictional characters as ›male‹ and ›female‹, the text continuously invites the readers to formulate hypotheses about the narrator's sex. *Written on the Body* features a romance plot; yet it soon becomes apparent that the text deals with both heterosexual and homosexual love relationships, which deprives the readers of the possibility of falling back on the norm of heterosexuality in their attempts to draw conclusions regarding the protagonist's sex from either the story or the narrator's comments. Another literary text that, in a very similar fashion, refuses to specify the sex of the narrator and protagonist right to the end is Brigid Brophy's highly experimental novel *In Transit* (1969). In this case, the narrator and protagonist Evelyn Hilary (Pat) O'Rooley, whose first names do *not* specify the character's sex, declares that s/he has simply forgotten her sex as a result of ›sexual amnesia‹, and a substantial part of the (increasingly absurd) plot derives from his/her attempts to find out whether s/he is male or female – a process which involves references to various gender stereotypes and serves to demonstrate that gender roles are nothing but constructions.

While scholars working within the framework of the Anglo-American tradition of feminist literary criticism have often (at least tacitly) assumed that literary characters can be seen in realistic-mimetic terms, as was pointed out above, French feminist critics like Hélène Cixous have propagated a radically different approach to the concept of literary characters. Due to her poststructuralist position, the concept of literary characters in and of itself is highly problematic for Cixous. In her programmatic article »The Character of ›Character«« (1973/74) she in fact rejects the concept of literary characters explicitly, criticizing the implications of this concept as follows: »So long as we do not put aside ›character‹ and everything it implies in terms of illusion and complicity with classical reasoning and the appropriating economy that such reasoning supports, we will remain locked up in the treadmill of reproduction«.[29] According to Cixous, the notion of the literary character

---

28 Kutzer: Cartography, p. 144.
29 Cixous: Character, p. 387.

is nothing more than a myth perpetuated within the ›literary machinery‹,[30] which is bound to reproduce conventional, patriarchal structures of meaning and to bring forth a simplification of the actual complexity that is inherent in the (poststructuralist) notion of the subject:

> A ›character‹ is always in store for the subject along with the chain where everything is coded in advance. ›Character‹ and I.D. card go together in this restricting process of which literary interpretation (by means of the encoding – the laying of the wires for a current – that it effects) becomes the reinforcement and reflection. Now, if ›I‹ – true subject, subject of the unconscious – am what I can be, ›I‹ am always on the run. It is precisely this open, unpredictable, piercing part of the subject, this *infinite* potential to rise up, that the ›concept‹ of ›character‹ excludes in advance.[31]

This rejection of »the ›concept‹ of ›character‹« ultimately results from the poststructuralist notion of the subject as »by definition [...] a non-closed mix of self/s and others«.[32] According to poststructuralist ideas, a subject cannot be conceived of as a coherent entity;[33] yet the concept of the fictional character seems to suggest that there is such coherence and thus the concept should be avoided. Although most scholars interested in gender-conscious approaches to fictional characters would hardly be inclined to follow Cixous' rejection of the concept of fictional characters, one can indeed observe that innovative concepts of literary characters which challenge the readers' construction of fictional characters as coherent, psychologically plausible entities are particularly likely to express subversive qualities, which are conducive to undermining traditional notions of gender roles and sex, as novels such as Woolf's *Orlando* and Brophy's *In Transit*, which were briefly discussed above, illustrate.

3 The Impact of Interfigurality on the Construction of Gender

The construction of literary characters with respect to gender roles may be rendered significantly more complex by means of intertextual references in general and by references to literary characters in other texts (i.e. interfigurality)[34] in particular. Although interfigurality may at first sight appear to be a relatively marginal phenomenon, there are actually a considerable number of literary characters that are intertextually related to

---

30 Ibid., p. 384.
31 Ibid.
32 Cixous: Preface, p. XVII.
33 Cf. Cixous: Preface, p. XVII: »*A subject is at least a thousand people. This is why I never ask myself* ›who am I?‹ (*qui suis-je?*) *I ask myself* ›who are I?‹ (*qui sont je?*)«.
34 Cf. Müller: Interfigurality.

characters in other texts, and, more often than not, these intertextual references turn out to be directly relevant to the construction of gender. Cases in point are the title characters in Henry Fielding's novels *An Apology for the Life of Mrs. Shamela Andrews* (1741) and *The History of the Adventures of Joseph Andrews and of his Friend Mr. Abraham Adams* (1742), which are intertextually related to the protagonist Pamela in Samuel Richardson's eponymous novel. The two novels written by Fielding are critical, and highly ironic, rewritings of Richardson's epistolary novel *Pamela; or, Virtue Rewarded* (1740). The main target of the criticism expressed in Fielding's rewritings is the concept of femininity and in particular the nexus of femininity and moral virtue constructed in Richardson's novel. The title character of *Pamela* embodies an ideal of womanhood which, as the subtitle *Virtue Rewarded* already suggests, is based on virtue and in particular on chastity. Fielding's *Shamela* serves to criticize the exalted model of virtuous/chaste behaviour in Richardson's novel by suggesting that what looks like virtue may actually be nothing more than hypocrisy. This attitude is already expressed very clearly in the subtitle of Fielding's novel, which reads as follows:

> An Apology for the Life of Mrs. Shamela Andrews. In which, the many notorious Falshoods and Misrepresentations of a Book called PAMELA, Are exposed and refuted; and all the matchless Arts of that young Politician, set in a true and just Light.

Fielding's first rewriting of *Pamela*, thus, explicitly questions the gender concepts Richardson evokes, undermining in particular the idealized notion of female chastity. In his second rewriting of Richardson's *Pamela*, Fielding uses the strategy of a gender role reversal to challenge assumptions about gender and gender relations constructed and perpetuated in Richardson's text: Instead of presenting a chaste girl pursued by her lecherous employer, Fielding depicts a female aristocrat trying to seduce her virtuous male servant. Both of Fielding's novels thus challenge gender stereotypes in general and the association of chastity with women in particular. Moreover, they highlight the power of literary texts to propagate and perpetuate stereotypical assumptions about gender by attacking the ›Falshoods and Misrepresentations‹ of the book that is parodied explicitly.

Another text which expresses a criticism of gender stereotypes and their perpetuation in literary texts by means of a reversal of gender roles is Charlotte Lennox' *The Female Quixote or The Adventures of Arabella* (1752). Beyond establishing a specific intertextual link to Cervantes' famous anti-romance *Don Quixote* (1605/15) and replacing its male protagonist by a female main character, Lennox' novel also has to be seen in the wider context of notions about gender roles and heterosexual relations constructed and perpetuated within the genre of the romance since the medieval period. Finally, *The Female Quixote* is also intertextually related to other 18th-century references to Cervantes' classic, for instance Fielding's *Jonathan Andrews*, whose subtitle »Written in Imitation of the Manner of Cervantes, Author of *Don Quijote*« already indicates that this novel is likewise a rewriting of Cervantes' ›master text‹. Intertextual and specifically interfigural references, thus, provide multiple points of reference for an interpretation of Lennox' *The Female Quixote or The Adventures of Arabella* which situate the gender concepts developed within the text in a complex framework of other notions about gender roles and gender relationships and invite the readers to compare the concepts of masculinity and femininity actualized by the texts that are intertextually linked.

As the examples mentioned above have already suggested, intertextual references may contribute to a historical or cultural contextualization of fictional characters which may turn out to be directly relevant to ideas about gender developed within a text: By inviting the readers to compare a particular character to a character from another text and, more often than not, from another period or cultural context, interfigurality may direct the readers' attention towards the cultural and historical variability of gender norms and to changing definitions of masculinity and femininity. In cases where literary characters are intertextually related to others various specifically literary frames may be activated: The knowledge about the gender concepts typical of a particular text and/or a genre (e.g. the romance or the Gothic novel with its stereotypical distribution of gender roles) is triggered by intertextual references and enriches the reading of characters such as Fielding's Shamela and Lennox' Arabella.

The novel *Windward Heights* (*La migration des coeurs*, 1995) by the francophone Caribbean writer Maryse Condé also illustrates that interfigural references may have a significant impact on the construction of fictional characters in terms of gender roles; in addition, this text complicates the intertextual reading of gender by emphasizing the relationship between gender and race. Condé's novel constitutes a postcolonial rewriting of Emily Brontë's classic *Wuthering Heights* (1847) and translates the character constellation and the tragic love story made famous by the Victorian novelist into a Caribbean context. In her dedication »To Emily Brontë Who I hope will approve of this interpretation of her masterpiece. Honour and respect!«, which precedes *Windward Heights*, Condé explicitly refers to Brontë's classic as an inspiration for her novel. The tone of the dedication suggests that the novel is an imaginative reworking of one of the classics of British literature from a postcolonial perspective, but it is definitely not a complete rejection of the European text or its ideological implications. In this respect Condé's novel differs significantly from many other postcolonial rewritings of European classics, such as the various rewritings of William Shakespeare's *The Tempest*, which primarily seek to correct the Eurocentric assumptions inherent in the text they refer to. Given the explicit marking of the intertextual reference to *Wuthering Heights*,[35] the recipients will tend to read the characters developed by Condé on the background of those in Brontë's classic. Thus, for instance, the following passage, in which Razyé, the counterpart of Brontë's Heathcliff, is introduced, is likely to be read on the background of the characterization of Heathcliff, arguably one of the most famous male characters in literary history:

> As usual, Razyé was drinking alone. He was dressed all in black in the French fashion, from his tightly-laced leather boots to his felt hat sewn with a large hem stitch. His skin too was black, that shiny black they call Ashanti, and his hair hung in curls like those of an Indian half-caste, the Bata-Zindien. Nobody could hold the gaze of his languishing eyes, where churned who knows what pain and solitude. His expression was that of a man attending the wake of his own mother. On meeting him, you knew that you had come face to face with a soul that could find no rest, neither day nor night. Melchior could not help comparing him to a spirit of the dead, an *egun*, but an *egun* prevented by an abominable crime from joining the other invisible spirits in the afterlife and who wandered restlessly among the living.[36]

There are several elements in the passage above that seem to echo the depiction of Heathcliff in *Wuthering Heights*, for example the description of the character as someone familiar with ›pain and solitude‹ and as ›a soul that could find no rest‹. Yet the presentation of Razyé is made more complex by the fact that the intertextual echoes apparent in the depiction of the character are modified by references to the specific cultural context in which *Windward Heights* is set. The depiction of the character as resembling ›a soul that could find no rest‹ is re-contextualized by including allusions to the hybrid religions typical of the Caribbean. Moreover, the issue of race plays an important role in the description of Razyé. It is interesting to note that, according to a number of literary critics, the issue of race also informs and complicates the concept of masculinity evoked by the Victorian character. In *Windward Heights* the notion of race is picked up and specified by references that are relevant to the Caribbean context (›that shiny black they call Ashanti, and his hair hung in curls like those of an Indian half-caste, the Bata-Zindien‹). By commenting on the character's racial features in this manner, Condé's text not only renders the depiction

---

35 In addition to the dedication, similarities in terms of the character constellation, the plot and the narrative situation which mark the intertextual reference, even the (first) names of some of the characters are identical in the two novels (e.g. Nelly and Catherine/Cathy). Yet, in contrast to the title of the English translation, the title of the original – *La migration des coeurs* – does not allude to the title of Brontë's novel.
36 Condé: Heights, p. 8.

of Rayzé more complex; it also establishes a dialogue with the Victorian novel, seemingly reacting to one of the possible readings of Heathcliff: The references to Heathcliff's dark skin, hair and eyes, which one encounters throughout Brontë's novel, seem to suggest that the character might be of foreign origin. In her historical contextualization of *Wuthering Heights*, Maja-Lisa von Sneidern argues that the reference to Liverpool, where the foundling Heathcliff is picked up by Mr Earnshaw, can be read as a hidden piece of information about Heathcliff's possible origin. Von Sneidern describes the significance of Liverpool in the eighteenth century, the time when *Wuthering Heights* is set, as follows: »The English city with the most spirited commerce in slaves was Liverpool. At mid-century Liverpool ranked third behind London and Bristol, but by the interbellum period (1763–1776) she had eclipsed her competitors and was the premier slaving port in Britain«.[37] Although Heathcliff is associated with dark hair, eyes and skin, it seems unlikely that he is an African slave. But, as von Sneidern argues, it is at least possible to imagine Heathcliff as »an irregular black, a mongrel, a source of great anxiety for the mid-nineteenth-century Victorian«.[38] The interfigural link between Condé's Rayzé and Brontë's Heathcliff thus serves to complicate the positioning of *both* characters in the gender-race matrix, suggesting a reading of both Rayzé's and Heathcliff's masculinity as being influenced by the history of slavery and the slave trade.

4 Media-Specific Ways of Gendering Fictional Characters

Written texts and audiovisual media differ significantly in terms of the strategies they have at their disposal for creating fictional characters as well as for gendering them and for potentially challenging traditional assumptions about sex and gender. Some critics have argued that it is much more difficult to avoid the marking of a character in terms of sex and gender in audiovisual media than it is to achieve the same effect in literary texts. The main reason for this difference between literary texts and audiovisual media is quite simply that the latter typically *show* the characters, apparently rendering at least certain aspects of the character construct more concrete:

> Oral and visual narratives attach to the body – and hence to performed sex, gender, and sexuality – in overt ways. I think it would be extremely difficult to maintain the kind of

---

37 von Sneidern: Heights, pp. 171f.
38 Ibid., p. 172.

sexual absence that characterizes *Written on the Body* in either a visual or an aural medium.[39]

Due to the fact that characters are generally ›embodied‹ by actors and actresses it is considerably more difficult to present characters whose ambivalence with respect to their gender is convincing in audiovisual media. Even if the performance of sex and gender remains ambiguous on the (big or small) screen, the actor's/actress's sex, which is usually known to the viewers, tends to overwrite the sex/gender created by the performance. Susan Lanser argues that the film based on Woolf's *Orlando* reveals the limits of audiovisual media with respect to presenting ambiguous notions of sex and gender. According to Lanser, the decision to cast actress Tilda Swinton as Orlando has rendered it virtually impossible to see Orlando as a young man right from the start, thus undermining the subversive effect produced by the sexual metamorphosis on the story level.[40] As Lanser points out in the passage quoted above, the performative nature of sex and gender in audiovisual media is not restricted to the visual presentation of the body; voices also play an important role for the performance of sex and gender. After all, voices tend to provoke a categorization of the speaker as either male or female, although the degree to which a voice is perceived as ›typically male‹ or ›typically female‹ may vary considerably. Thus, one can conclude that audiovisual media tend to face significantly more obstacles if they want to portray ambivalence with respect to gender and sex or seek to challenge and subvert the notion that sex is a stable category. Nevertheless audiovisual media, just like literary texts, from time to time challenge and subvert not only traditional gender roles, but also the assumption that there is a stable link between sex and gender. Fictional worlds, being (potentially) exempt from the laws of reality, may contribute to the cultural construction of masculinities and femininities by projecting characters that transcend the gender dichotomy, by developing androgynous, transsexual or fluid concepts of identity and of the human body.

5 Conclusion

Given the fact that the concepts of fictional characters are invariably shaped by culture-specific notions of sex and gender on multiple levels, a

---

39 Cf. Lanser: Poetics, p. 179.
40 Ibid.

comprehensive theory of fictional characters should strive to integrate the categories sex and gender in a systematic fashion. Feminist and gender-conscious narrative theories as well as cognitive approaches to narratology offer an ideal starting point for this endeavour. A comprehensive theory of fictional characters should likewise seek to explore the complex interrelationship between contextual factors informing the construction of sex and gender on the one hand and textual and audiovisual strategies that serve to trigger or undermine the readers'/viewers' notions of femininity and masculinity on the other hand. As was pointed out above, fictional texts may be significantly more radical in their assessment of gender roles and gender concepts than non-fictional ones, potentially even giving rise to utopian or dystopian notions of femininity and masculinity. This should be a sufficient reason for scholars in the field of gender studies to pay attention to the specific dynamics of character construction in fictional (literary and audiovisual) texts.

References

Baader, Renate (Ed.): Das Frauenbild im literarischen Frankreich: Vom Mittelalter bis zur Gegenwart. Darmstadt 1988.
Bal, Mieke: Narratology: Introduction to the Theory of Narrative. Toronto 1985.
Bovenschen, Silvia: Die imaginierte Weiblichkeit: Exemplarische Untersuchungen zu kulturgeschichtlichen und literarischen Präsentationsformen des Weiblichen. Frankfurt/M. 1979.
Butler, Judith: Gender Trouble: Feminism and the Subversion of Identity. New York / London 1990.
Butler, Judith: Bodies That Matter: On the Discursive Limits of ›Sex‹. New York / London 1993.
Cixous, Hélène: The Character of ›Character‹. In: New Literary History 5/2 (1973/74). pp. 383–402.
Cixous, Hélène: Preface. In: Susan Sellers (Ed.): The Hélène Cixous Reader. London et al. 1994. pp. XV-XXII.
Condé, Maryse: Windward Heights [1995]. [La migration des coeurs.] Translated from the French by Richard Philcox. New York 1998.
Cornillon, Susan Koppelman (Ed.): Images of Women in Fiction: Feminist Perspectives. Bowling Green, OH 1972.
Grabes, Herbert: Wie aus Sätzen Personen werden... Über die Erforschung literarischer Figuren. In: Poetica 10/4 (1978), pp. 405–428.
Gymnich, Marion: Entwürfe weiblicher Identität im englischen Frauenroman des 20. Jahrhunderts. Trier 2000.
Gymnich, Marion: Konzepte literarischer Figuren und Figurencharakterisierung. In: Vera Nünning / Ansgar Nünning (Eds.): Erzähltextanalyse und Gender Studies. Stuttgart / Weimar 2004, pp. 122–142.
Jannidis, Fotis: Figur und Person. Beitrag zu einer historischen Narratologie. Berlin / New York 2004.

Koch, Thomas: Literarische Menschendarstellung: Studien zu ihrer Theorie und Praxis. Tübingen 1991.
Kutzer, M. Daphne: The Cartography of Passion: Cixous, Wittig and Winterson. In: Jürgen Kleist / Bruce Butterfield (Eds.): Re-Naming the Landscape. New York 1994, pp. 133–145.
Lanser, Susan Sniader: Toward a Feminist Narratology. In: Style 20/3 (1986), pp. 341–363.
Lanser, Susan Sniader: Shifting the Paradigm: Feminism and Narratology. In: Style 22/1 (1988), pp. 52–60.
Lanser, Susan Sniader: Fictions of Authority: Women Writers and Narrative Voice. Ithaca, NY 1992.
Lanser, Susan Sniader: Sexing Narratology: Toward a Gendered Poetics of Narrative Voice. In: Walter Grünzweig / Andreas Solbach (Eds.): Grenzüberschreitungen: Narratologie im Kontext / Transcending Boundaries: Narratology in Context. Tübingen 1999, pp. 167–183.
Margolin, Uri: The What, the When, and the How of Being a Character in Literary Narratives. In: Style 24/3 (1990), pp. 453–468.
Müller, Wolfgang G.: Interfigurality: A Study on the Interdependence of Literary Figures. In: Heinrich F. Plett (Ed.): Intertextuality. Berlin / New York 1991, pp. 101–121.
Nünning, Vera / Ansgar Nünning: Grundkurs anglistisch-amerikanistische Literaturwissenschaft. Stuttgart 2001.
Nünning, Vera / Ansgar Nünning (Eds.): Erzähltextanalyse und Gender Studies. Stuttgart / Weimar 2004.
Propp, Vladimir: Morphology of the Folktale [1928]. Austin, TX 1968.
Quadflieg, Helga: Feminist Stories Told on Waste Water: Jeanette Winterson's Novels. In: Anglistik & Englischunterricht 60 (1997), pp. 97–111.
Schabert, Ina: Englische Literaturgeschichte des 20. Jahrhunderts: Eine neue Darstellung aus der Sicht der Geschlechterforschung. Stuttgart 2006.
Schneider, Ralf: Grundriß zur kognitiven Theorie der Figurenkonzeption am Beispiel des viktorianischen Romans. Tübingen 2000.
Schneider, Ralf: Toward a Cognitive Theory of Literary Character: The Dynamics of Mental-Model Construction. In: Style 35/4 (2001), pp. 607–640. Quoted from: <http://www.findarticles.com/p/articles/mi_m2342/is_4_35/ai_97114241/print> (June 16th, 2010).
Stephan, Inge: »Bilder und immer wieder Bilder...«: Überlegungen zur Untersuchung von Frauenbildern in männlicher Literatur. In: Inge Stephan / Sigrid Weigel (Eds.). Die verborgene Frau: Sechs Beiträge zu einer feministischen Literaturwissenschaft. Berlin 1983, pp. 15–35.
Stritzke, Nadyne: Subversive literarische Performativität: Die narrative Inszenierung von Geschlechtsidentitäten in englisch- und deutschsprachigen Gegenwartsromanen. PhD Thesis. Justus-Liebig-Universität Gießen 2008.
von Sneidern, Maja-Lisa: Wuthering Heights and the Liverpool Slave Trade. In: English Literary History 62/1 (1995), pp. 171–196.
Warhol, Robyn R.: Toward a Theory of the Engaging Narrator: Earnest Interventions in Gaskell, Stowe, and Eliot. In: Publications of the Modern Language Association 101/5 (1986), pp. 811–818.
Warhol, Robyn R.: Gendered Interventions: Narrative Discourse in the Victorian Novel. New Brunswick, NJ / London 1989.
Wittmann, Livia Z.: Zwischen ›Femme fatale‹ und ›Femme fragile‹ – die Neue Frau? Kritische Bemerkungen zum Frauenbild des literarischen Jugendstils. In: Jahrbuch für Internationale Germanistik 17/2 (1985), pp. 74–110.

Würzbach, Natascha: Feministische Forschung in Literaturwissenschaft und Volkskunde: Neue Fragestellungen und Probleme der Theoriebildung. In: Rainer Wehse / Sigrid Früh (Eds.): Die Frau im Märchen. Kassel 1985, pp. 192–215.

Young, Suzanne: The Unnatural Object of Modernist Aesthetics: Artifice in Woolf's Orlando. In: Elizabeth Jane Harrison / Shirley Peterson (Eds.): Unmanning Modernism: Gendered Re-Readings. Knoxville 1997, pp. 168–187.

Zapf, Hubert: Literature as Cultural Ecology: Notes Towards a Functional Theory of Imaginative Texts with Examples from American Literature. In: Research in Englisch and American Literature 17 (2001), pp. 85–99.

Zapf, Hubert: Literatur als kulturelle Ökologie: Zur kulturellen Funktion imaginativer Texte an Beispielen des amerikanischen Romans. Tübingen 2002.

Zapf, Hubert: Zwischen Dekonstruktion und Regeneration: Literatur als kulturelle Ökologie. In: Hans Vilmar Geppert / H.Z. (Eds.): Theorien der Literatur: Grundlagen und Perspektiven 1. Tübingen 2003, pp. 271–290.

V Transtextual and Transmedial Characters

BRIAN RICHARDSON

Transtextual Characters

1 The Problem

In this paper I will explore the phenomenon and identity of ›transtextual characters‹; or characters that exist in more than one text, and attempt to determine the essential criteria for establishing the persistence of an individual identity across texts. At the most straightforward level, the question is whether it is possible for the same character to appear in two or more works of fiction. Here, narrative theory, authorial sentiment, and common sense converge; virtually no one denies that an author can create a character in one book and then bring him or her back in a sequel, the way Joyce creates Stephen Dedalus in *A Portrait of the Artist as a Young Man* and brings him back (along with several other characters from that book and *Dubliners*) in the pages of *Ulysses*. There are many reasons that contribute to this conclusion. The fictional world is presented as being the same in both works. In the temporally later work, the central character remembers events that took place in the earlier text – he certainly believes himself to be the same being persisting over time and between the volumes that chronicle them. Furthermore, the logic of the mimetic text encourages such continuities. A realist text attempts to reproduce the structure of lived experience, and a key aspect of that experience is its continuity over time. Insofar as a narrative is realistic, it is appropriate for the reader to speculate on the characters' likely attitudes and actions before and after that selected for presentation in the text at hand, formalist cavils about Lady Macbeth's children notwithstanding. When a writer like Balzac, Trollope, or Faulkner returns to the fictional world he has created, there is an implicit assumption that the invented realm will have roughly the same amount of continuity and change as does the actual world on which it attempts to model itself. Possible worlds theory supports such a stance: an author may return to a fictional world he or she has created, whether in a *roman fleuve* like Proust's, the sequel to work, a series of related short stories Hemingway's Nick Adams stories, or novel cycle like Balzac's *La Comédie humaine*. If a character retains its identity from one chapter to another, why would that principle not hold equally from volume to volume, especially since the later work presupposes the continuous existence of the character, as indicated by the original published title of Shakespeare's *The Second part of Henrie the fourth, continuing to his death, and coronation of Henrie the fift?*

Having established this point, a number of related questions immediately present themselves. One is whether a character with the same name as an earlier avatar produced by the same author is always the same individual. We have established that a character may persist from volume to volume; now we ask whether it must? Or does mimetic characterization presuppose some level of consistency that can be abrogated by an author? A case in point is Virginia Woolf's Clarissa Dalloway. There is no reason to deny that the protagonist of the eponymous novel (1925) is the same character as that in the story, *Mrs Dalloway in Bond Street* (1923), as well as the other related stories in which she appears more briefly. But there is another Mrs Dalloway in Woolf's first published novel, *The Voyage Out* (1915). This one has a rather different personality; she is more verbally deft, well-read, and acerbic. There is not an obvious psychological transition that can be brought forth to explain a major change in character. Mark Hussey, in his reference work *Virginia Woolf A to Z*,[1] has two entries for the two Mrs Dalloways and treats them as separate individuals. I believe it makes sense to affirm, as many other Woolf critics have, that the second Mrs Dalloway is a different character who simply happens to share the name of another, nonidentical figure.

This question is equally pressing in the case of Conrad's Charlie Marlow. In a late text, *Chance* (1914), he does not seem to be the same character he was previously in *Youth* (1898), *Heart of Darkness* (1899), or *Lord Jim* (1900). Conrad scholars express considerable differences of opinion on the precise identity of the early and late Marlows. Michael Greaney summarizes these debates:

> Robert Hampson wonders if we are right ›to talk of *Marlow* as if there were a single, consistent character, or should we rather think of four separate Marlows?‹ Is the maudlin raconteur of ›Youth‹ the same person as the flippant sexist of *Chance*? There is no consensus on this question: Jakob Lothe insists that the relationship between the four Marlows is purely nominal, whereas Cedric Watts, ingeniously if unconvincingly, reads the Marlow quartet as a ›vast biographical narrative‹.[2]

---

1 Sternberg: Modes, p. 3.
2 Hussey: Woolf, pp. 66f.

What then are we to do theoretically with such schizophrenic characters? Meir Sternberg argues for a position of ontological separateness. He notes that »the Antony of *Julius Caesar*, the libertine turned demagogue, is altogether incompatible with the monumental figure of *Antony and Cleopatra*, and any reader who attempts to reconcile the two will soon find himself in trouble«,³ and also draws attention to inconsistencies that sometimes occur in different presentations of what ostensibly seems to be the same character, such as the radical change in personality in Faulkner's Henry Armstid or Trollope's Archdeacon Granley, »a hard worldling, a bully and something of a hypocrite in *The Warden*; but when he reappears in *Barchester Towers* his weaknesses are softened«.⁴ While Sternberg seems prepared to treat each work and each character as ontologically independent of any earlier avatar, this seems to be an unnecessarily extreme position that should be reserved only for those rare cases in which an insurmountable contradiction is present. Concerning Armstid, we can agree with Dorothy Tuck who, in her ›Dictionary of Characters‹ in Faulkner's works, states: »the Armstid of *The Hamlet* is clearly a different character from his namesake in the earlier two novels«.⁵

In principle, an author may present two distinct characters under the same name; if someone were to depict a character with attributes incommensurate with what we already know of that character without any explanation for the difference (far beyond the kind of surprising transformations that gifted writers are celebrated for producing), then we may reasonably conclude that it is a separate figure bearing only a nominal relation to the original. We may designate this as an illusory variant; that is, an independent entity misleadingly presented as the same individual. A human being may undergo considerable transformations in his or her personality to the point where we say, ›He is not the person he used to be‹; certain memorable characters are occasionally depicted as moving convincingly from one type of personality to another (»That's he that was Othello«,⁶ Shakespeare's protagonist finally says about himself). Literary creations, however, are not usually allowed the same latitude as figures from life, if only because our sole source for understanding them is the description of their thoughts, emotions, and actions; if these diverge too much without any plausible explanation, we are justified in considering that individual as a separate being. Lastly, when a character has the wrong

---

3   Sternberg: Modes, p. 3.
4   Ibid.
5   Tuck: Handbook, p. 183.
6   Shakespeare: Works, V.ii. 292, p. 1199.

age or is given minor inconsistencies in different volumes, we need to allow for the possibility of correctable authorial error.

2 Different Author, Different Character

The next question we need to consider is whether someone other than the author can extend or alter a character. This is a particularly compelling issue for twentieth century literature as a large number of texts have been rewritten by modernist, postmodern, and postcolonial authors with varying degrees of continuity with the original. I should clarify that I am dealing exclusively here with characters presented as being the same individual as an earlier presentation (e. g. Stephen Dedalus in *A Portrait* and *Ulysses*) and not with later incarnations of similar figures, as Leopold Bloom is a modernized avatar of Homer's Odysseus. The most compelling position on this issue is probably that of Roland Harweg, who, in his discussion of the cases of Richardson's *Pamela* and Fielding's *Shamela*, observes that the latter cannot provide data for the synopsis of the former, and concludes that the

> contents underlying the summaries of fictional texts are the result not of acts of genuine reporting (judgeable as to truth or falsehood) but of creation, and that such products of creation – especially, as in our case, by different authors – are hermetically separated from each other. The creator of a later world is not allowed to intrude into, and thereby modify, a prior work by another author.[7]

According to this theory, we must treat invented characters as parts of invented worlds that can be legitimately modified only by their creator (›Wm. Faulkner, sole owner & proprietor‹ as he notes on the map of his invented territory, Yoknapatawpha County).

We would do well to recall the uncomfortable position of Don Quixote and Sancho Panza at the beginning of the second part of Cervantes' novel as they learn about the strange adventures attributed to them by another author, Avellaneda, who attempted to capitalize on Cervantes' success. Like Sancho, we can say that Avellaneda's portrait is a false one. Cervantes' own sequel to his novel is necessarily more authentic than the imitator's imagined continuation. A fictional work is, I argue, a performative utterance; if the author states that Byron Bunch lives in Jefferson, Mississippi, then he does so by the fact of this utterance, and there is no other evidence, whether fictional or nonfictional, that can contradict this fact. That is, no other author's subsequent account of the origin and

---

7 Harweg: Shamela, p. 296.

career of Byron Bunch can have any bearing on our knowledge of Faulkner's character, just as no consultations of period geographies that show there is no town of Jefferson can add any relevant information to that invented by Faulkner (and the same of course is true of almanacs and histories of Oxford, Mississippi, the real-world model for Faulkner's Jefferson). Cervantes' case is thus the opposite of that of Robin Lippincott, who in his novel, *Mr Dalloway*, records Richard thinking critically about the depictions of himself and Clarissa in the earlier work: that »the latest novel by Mrs. Woolf [...] despite her keenly perceptive mind and – he must admit – considerable descriptive powers, had not captured it all, not all of it, in her novel of two years past«.[8] Lippincott cannot add to our information about Woolf's Mrs and Mr Dalloway, it can only create different characters modeled more or less closely on the originals.

Often, the later avatars move quite far from the originals. Pia Pera's *Lo's Diary* offers a ›corrected‹ version of the events of Nabokov's *Lolita*, based on a journal Lolita is said to have kept. In this work we are told that neither Lolita nor Humbert died, and we get what are said to be the actual versions of names and places fictionalized by Nabokov's Humbert Humbert. He is in fact named Humbert Guibert, Lolita's true name is Dolores Maze (not Haze), her husband is Richard Schlegel rather than Schiller, the town they lived in was called Goatscreek, not Ramsdale, and Charlie, the sexually precocious boy at her camp, was actually a young lesbian girl named Maud. Interestingly, due to legal proceedings brought by Nabokov's estate, the author was required to negotiate permission and turn over a portion of the book's proceeds. Even though Pera's Lolita is a radically different character from Nabokov's, U.S. and British copyright laws still appeared to have jurisdiction over her existence.

These examples, I suggest, corroborate Harweg's principle, though we should note that the principle only works in a single direction: while Pera's novel cannot add to our knowledge of Nabokov's Lolita, one must know Nabokov's text to comprehend Pera's. The working hypothesis is one of minimal departure from the antecedent fictional world, that everything uncorrected in the later text is true and accurate. We may refer to these as variants, that is, recognizable but unauthorized possible continuations or variations of the original figure. We may also note, following Margolin, that the relationship is usually ›one-many‹,[9] though this is not invariably the case, as we will see. Another point that should be discussed is the

---

8   Lippincott: Dalloway, pp. 16f.
9   Margolin: Characters, p. 118.

claim of superior verisimilitude frequently made by or in the later text; this kind of critique goes back to Euripides' *Electra*, who mocks the devices used by Aeschylus' *Electra* to discover that her brother has returned to Argos. Many rewritings, especially postcolonial ones, often claim to correct a variety of ›mistakes‹ or distortions in the motivation of the characters and the forces shaping the fictional world that is being appropriated, as the actions of the character (Pamela) are seen to be in violation with the canons of probability or notions of likely human behavior. To this claim we may respond that the later text may well expose the mimetic failures of the earlier text, but this in itself does not alter an earlier character or its ontological status, it only shows that the character and/or its social setting is not as realistic as it had been presented or assumed to be.

In his book, *Fictional Worlds*, Thomas Pavel offers a different claim about the transportability of a character. Contrasting Shakespeare's Cordelia in *King Lear* with Nahum Tate's later revision of the play, Pavel argues that »Tate has not created a second Cordelia but simply provided Cordelia with a happier destiny«.[10] A look at Tate's play shows this assertion to be false; his Cordelia has a very different character. Unlike Shakespeare's figure, the later version is romantic, somewhat calculating, in love with Edgar, her speech is more direct, and she sets in motion a little plot of deception that the earlier Cordelia would never stoop to. This is clearly not the same character. There is no real issue for narrative or dramatic theory when the characterizations fail to match up, either in the case of the two Cordelias or in Brian Friel's inspired attempt in Afterplay (2002) to dramatize a meeting between two Chekhov characters later in their lives, as Andrei of *The Three Sisters* meets Sonia from *Uncle Vanya*. Unfortunately, the characters don't seem to be plausible continuations of Chekhov's figures; Andrei in particular seems less the hardworking brother of the Chekhov play than an illegitimate descendent of Uncle Vanya.

But let us take up an idealized version of Pavel's challenge: what would we say if the two plays were entirely identical except for the ending? And, in fact, something like this has occurred in the history of the drama: the first German performance of Ibsen's *A Doll's House* was judged to be so incendiary that the ending was changed – and with it, one must conclude, a crucial component of Nora's character. Nor is it enough to dismiss this on the grounds we have just established as being the work of an unauthorized writer: since similar transformations continued to be made

---

10 Pavel: Worlds, p. 34.

when the play was produced, Ibsen wrote his own alternate ending that muted the final, shocking events. Are both of these characters the same Nora Helmer? Once again it seems to me that we must differentiate between two slightly but ultimately different characters; insofar as we are what we do, such a major difference in the life-altering decision strongly suggests a difference in characters.

3 Different Author, Same Character

There are also cases in which different authors can legitimately share the life of a character and extend each other's world, in which an author can ask another to ›Lend Me Your Character‹, as happens in a story of the same name by Dubravka Ugrešić. (In this story, by the way, the author does loan out the character, and is quickly outraged by what the other writer does to the character.) Here the critical consensus is fairly solid: Genette states that ›there is no law that a sequel should be necessarily self-written‹;[11] Margolin argues that logically speaking, the same character may equally appear in a sequel by the original author as in one written by a different author;[12] and Peter Rabinowitz explains that in television and film, there are cases – perhaps, the majority of cases – where the different installments in a series are actually written by different individuals and audiences do not therefore conclude that there is no continuity among the characters.[13]

A number of other examples similarly suggest this can be the case. If the criterion for continuous identity across texts is authorial designation (tempered by consistency and, when appropriate, mimetic fidelity), then authors may equally appoint others to extend their created worlds. The novel, *The Whole Family*, is a single narrative written in episodes by twelve different authors. In almost every case, the characters are self-identical. That characters can endure across and beyond the creation of a single author is further demonstrated by the Vaněk plays, in which four different playwrights wrote short plays about the same central character, Ferdinand Vaněk. After Vaclav Havel wrote the first two plays, fellow playwrights Pavel Kohout, Pavel Landovský, and Jiři Dienstbier constructed their own stories around this character, and did so with the endorsement of Havel.[14]

---

11 Genette: Palimpsests, p. 207.
12 Margolin: Characters, pp. 117–118.
13 Rabinowitz: Series.
14 See Getz-Stankiewiecz: Plays, pp. xv-xxviii and 237–248.

As Kohout recounts, after seeing *Unveiling*, the second of Havel's Vaněk plays, he approached Havel to »ask for permission to use him in recording my own experiences. He not only willingly agreed but also actively endorsed the proposal. Out of this conversation grew the idea for a jointly composed evening of theatrical entertainment«.[15]

Another work suggests that even another critical author can continue to extend the adventures of a character and perhaps even provide a more accurate version than the original author did. In 1696 Colley Cibber wrote a play, *Love's Last Shift*, in which the rakish protagonist, Loveless, abruptly repents at the end of the play and turns into a tender and repentant spouse. John Vanbrugh, unconvinced by the protagonist's conversion, wrote his own sequel, *The Relapse* (1696), in which Loveless' ›true‹ womanizing character returns. After a new set of adventures, he repents and changes his behavior in a better motivated and more convincing manner. The identity of the same characters in both plays is enhanced by the physical presence of the actors representing them: John Verbruggen and Jane Rogers playing the roles of Loveless and Amanda in both plays, while the character of Sir Novelty Fashion (elevated in the sequel to the rank of lord) was portrayed in both by none other than Colley Cibber.

Concerning the authorization of authentic, transtextual characters, the author need not even be the one to make this determination. After Ian Fleming died, Kingsley Amis was hired by his estate to write two additional Bond novels. The publisher of a popular series of detective novels, after the death of the writer, will often commission new works that feature the characteristic detective; as long as these figures maintain the personalities of the original characters, it is not clear to me why anyone would want to dispute the continuous identity of the figure. And in cases where the elaborate construction of a significantly different world is involved, such collaboration is extremely useful, even essential. In 1979, Robert Asprin conceived and edited the *Thieves' World* anthologies, a shared world fantasy series in which numerous authors set related stories and used recurring characters. The new genre of ›Fan Fiction‹, unofficial stories written by admirers of a work or series to add to the adventures of a group of characters, also operates under some of these conditions. In one shared world site, based on H. P. Lovecraft's *Cthulhu Mythos*, both professional and fan contributions have had equally authoritative status for several decades.

We can conclude that an author may continue the depiction of his or her character in other works and may also extend that prerogative to

---

15   Getz-Stankiewiecz: Plays, p. 241.

others (or ›certify‹ it, to use Rabinowitz' term). Again, there are minimal standards of consistency that must be observed. One can imagine a ›bad Vanek‹ composed by a rival of the other authors that travesties the collective character; this would not constitute a continuation of it. William Dean Howells, the instigator of *The Whole Family* and the first delineator of its various characters, was appalled by the transformations the second author, Mary Wilkins Freeman, made in the character of the maiden aunt and sought to suppress her changes. There are also many rogue works that use the setting of *Thieves' World* but which are not accepted as part of its authorized canon.

In genres with weaker mimetic pretensions (low budget television series, Harlequin-type romance novels, operas, etc.), the concept of character is much more limited, and may only have two dimensions; the actor may be portraying little more than a cluster of repeated habits, verbal and facial expressions, and behavioral ticks. Usually, there is no historical memory; detective Columbo doesn't remember getting knocked unconscious 50 times, or that the villain he faces has an identical modus operandi to a very similar villain faced two years ago in viewing time. In such works to say that Mannix of season one is the same character as the Mannix of the third year is not to make a particularly large claim. This is even more true of cartoon characters that have little fixed identity at all, though even here there are limitations: Superman can never become a petty, selfish wastrel, or he would no longer be Superman (unless of course a demented genius concocted, say, a chemical solution that could temporarily alter his personality).

Another issue arises concerning the persistence of the ›same‹ character across genres. In some cases there is no question as to the continuous identity of the character; transmedial or cross-sited narratives demand such continuous identity. In order to follow the characters and plots of such works, viewers are required to track the adventures of the same figures in different media such as books, films, computer games, and web sites. To get the backstory, the other adventures, character profiles, or the next installment, the audience needs to move on to a different medium, as Marc Ruppel explains.[16]

Other cases are more difficult to assess. Even if we start by saying that Shakespeare's Othello is a different character from the much simpler figure in the source story by Geraldo Cinthio, we may ask whether Shakespeare's Othello is the same character in other media transpositions of this work such as the opera by Verdi, the prose version in Lamb's *Tales*

---

16 Ruppel: Traces (Forthcoming).

from Shakespeare, a ballet, a comic book version, a painting? To begin, we need to acknowledge the inability of different media to convey the same degree of narrative complexity; we may therefore conclude that the figure is the same insofar as it reproduces the original character as far as the other medium conventionally allows. Once again, we can find notable cases that fail to reproduce the character adequately. For a musical version of *Don Quixote*, W. H. Auden's libretto was rejected in favor of the sentimental and simplistic text that became *Man of La Mancha*. Auden's version of the protagonist was considerably closer to the original than was the Broadway version, which left out, among other things, most of the irony. The conventions of the sixties Broadway musical included large doses of sentimentality, black-and-white moralism, and plenty of the very romanticism that Cervantes sought to expose. What ensued was the partial elimination of the Don's character. We may conclude that in this case the transposition resulted in the creation of a different, simpler, and doubtless inferior character; not the same individual, but merely a version.

4 Simplified Characters

This principle also extends to other kinds of limited rewritings. Margolin states that »the subtraction or deletion of properties from an original can never engender a version that is incompatible with it, and is often practised in censored versions, versions for children, abridged versions, and the like«.[17] My sense is that there may well be numerous exceptions to this dictum, beginning with the Sherlock Holmes who shoots up cocaine in the works of Conan Doyle. Is this the same individual as the sanitized version in expurgated versions for teenagers or the still more simplified movie characterizations? Insofar as an essential aspect of a character is altered or omitted, I believe we are justified in referring to the new figure as a different being. The further one moves from the original figure the clearer this principle becomes: it is surely true of the most egregious transformations, such as Gene Wilder's comedy, *The Adventures of Sherlock Holmes' Smarter Brother* (1975). It is not enough that a version simply shares some properties with the original; I suggest that most characters have a few essential attributes as well as a cluster of traits that may or may not be included in subsequent presentations. In the case of Holmes, he cannot be merely the mechanical problem solver of the Hollywood adaptations without losing something essential to his being. Among other attributes,

---

17 Margolin: Characters, p. 124.

he must be highly knowledgeable, brilliant in deductive reasoning, he probably has to be English, and I suspect he must be male. Otherwise, he would not be Holmes.

Someone – or, not to beg the question, some*thing* – like James Bond is a more complex and ambiguous case. The books themselves vary quite a bit; the Bond of the second book in the series, *Live and Let Die*, is often a two-dimensional imitation of the psychologically more complex Bond of the first volume, *Casino Royale*. Kingsley Amis has said that »Bond is not what they call a rounded character. He has developed very little over the years«.[18] Amis also notes that the Bond chronology in the novels is falsified so that the character is always the same age; this would seem to be the case of a powerful fixed characterization triumphing over mimetic considerations.[19] After the death of Ian Fleming, Amis and a number of other authors have written new, authorized plots for the character. Films first composed for the screen have gone on to generate their own ›novelizations‹; one organization of James Bond fans does not recognize these as part of its canon. More importantly, in virtually every case the film versions of the books by Fleming alter and suppress Bond's personality and turn him into a cartoon-like character; this is particularly true of the period during which Roger Moore played Bond, as Judith Roof has discussed:

> The literary character James Bond, however, is not coterminous with the cultural Bond figure [...]. Bond has proliferated through culture primarily as the cinematic Bond, a figure who has crackled away from the novelistic, following a new trajectory and chronology whose relation to history is one of updated repetitions.[20]

Recently he has even been altered to eliminate his entrenched male chauvinism. Despite the fact that movie-goers argue over which actor better portrays the ›real‹ Bond, and thus presuppose the continuation of the same character across genres and over time, it seems hard to argue that, in mimetic terms, the Bond of the movies is the same individual as the Bond that appears in the novels by Ian Fleming. For that matter, the Bond of some of the more recent movies is probably not the same as the early cinematic Bond, either. The Bond of the 1954 television dramatization of *Casino Royale* is certainly a different individual (in this piece, he is an American and is called ›Jimmy‹ by the other characters). The Bond of the confused film *Casino Royale* (1967) is in part a deliberate spoof of the character and its franchising: at the beginning an old Bond (David Niven)

---

18 Amis: Dossier, p. 34.
19 Ibid.
20 Roof: Lifestyle, p. 72.

complains about the mediocrity of his successors. By the end of the film, we have been presented with several characters pretending to be James Bond.

But this position threatens to produce its own contradictions: we can agree that the Bond of the film, *Goldfinger*, is rather a cardboard figure with a few recurrent behavioral ticks that does not begin to resemble the considerably more complex character in the novel. But who then is the character in the film who says his name is ›Bond, James Bond‹, battles with the character Oddjob, intrigues with Pussy Galore, is quick on his feet, saves the gold in Fort Knox, and frustrates the evil machinations of Auric Goldfinger? If the events in both film and novel are largely the same, why deny a continuous, transtextual identity to its protagonist, particularly one who was authorized by the character's creator (even though, it may be acknowledged, Fleming didn't especially like Sean Connery in the role of Bond)? This paradox points to the protean nature of character, which many theorists argue has at least two components, including a mimetic and a semiotic aspect: as Joel Weinsheimer notes,[21] characters are both human-like figures and verbal artifacts that satisfy specific functions within a narrative economy.[22] According to the mimetic component of characterization, the two Bonds do not share the same psychological makeup (the action figure of the movie can hardly be said to even have a psychology), so they are different individuals. But according to a semiotic or functional analysis, the actant called Bond performs the same functions in each work, and is therefore the same character. In the light of one aspect of character theory, the Bonds are different; in another, they are the same individual. We may legitimately conclude that the Bond of most of the movies both is and is not the same character as the one in the novels.

Antiquity provides yet another set of possible relations. Most of the narrative materials are already at hand, largely in variable oral forms that preclude the idea of a fixed essence of character or event. We will seek in vain to find an original/copy model; in these cases there is no original to be unearthed. The character pre-exists, but not in a definitive form; all versions are variants. Consequently, one need only refer to the Electra of Aeschylus or that of Sophocles – even as we note that Euripides' versions often stray rather widely from the standard story line (quite egregiously in his depictions of Menelaus and Orestes) and could conceivably be considered what I have called illusory variants.

---

21 Weinsheimer: Theory, p. 195.
22 See also Phelan: Reading; Richardson: Poststructuralism.

Finally we may adduce the cases in which an original version is retrievable but for many purposes, irrelevant. Hector-Neri Castañeda has pointed out that some fictional characters created by individual authors take on additional life as »they undergo a process of culturation, where they finally become common cultural property, such that many or even most participants in the culture do not even know« which text they derive from.²³ This movement away from an individual character to a common name or class concept is indicated in English, Margolin notes in his discussion of this idea, by the use of their use of the indefinite article (›a Don Juan‹).²⁴ These may be considered variants of an original even if the original is unknown to the creators of those variants. And here too, more than one individual may be obscured by a misleading shared name: currently in American popular culture someone who is referred to as ›a Romeo‹ does not resemble Shakespeare's hero but is instead rather something of ›a Don Juan‹. I would call this example another illusory variant.

5 Conclusion

The crucial concepts that emerge from this analysis are self consistency and authorization. Transtextual exemplifications of the same character must be consistent with essential aspects of the original presentation; this is true whether or not the character's creator writes the subsequent work. Someone other than the author may depict the same character in sequels, but only with the authorization of the creator or his or her legitimate proxies. In these cases, the later works will fulfill Harweg's criterion: information from the later works will add to our knowledge of the character. Other figures derived from an original character can be considered variants; one still needs knowledge of the original version to fully comprehend the later one, though the later one cannot provide new information about the original. Finally, two characters presented as the same but given incompatible characterizations should be treated as distinct individuals that share the same name; they can be called illusory variants.

The implications of this analysis up to this point for the theory of character are evident: for a character to be transportable between texts, it must have an independent essence that endures in different situations.

---

23 Castañeda: Fiction, pp. 44f.
24 Margolin: Characters, p. 117.

The mimetic theory of character, or more precisely, the mimetic component of theories of character, which insists on characters as being, at least in part, recognizable representations of human or human-like beings, is validated here. It is also the case that any entity with a recognizable cluster of attributes (e. g. Bugs Bunny) can similarly be considered a character. This is further demonstrated in metafictional texts with dispossessed personages, like Pirandello's *Six Characters in Search of an Author* or intertextual narratives that collect together versions of several characters by different authors, such as Julian Ríos' novel, *Amores que atan o belles lettres* (1995), which devotes a different chapter to a different character in world literature, such as Proust's Albertine, Flaubert's Emma, Nabokov's Lolita, and so on. It is also clear that actantial approaches (variously called semiotic, synthetic, and aesthetic by Weinsheimer, Phelan, and Richardson) are also necessary for a complete theory. Characters are both clusters of human-like attributes and collective functions within narrative economies, even when they move beyond the text that engendered them.

NOTE

I wish to thank Peter Rabinowitz, Matt Kirschenbaum, and Jasmine Lellock for helpful discussions of these texts and issues.

References

Amis, Kingsley: The James Bond Dossier. New York 1966.
Castañeda, Hector-Neri: Fiction and Reality: Their Fundamental Connections. In: Poetics 8 (1979), pp. 31–62.
Genette, Gérard: Palimpsests: Literature in the Second Degree [1982]. Transl. by Channa Newman and Claude Doubinsky. Lincoln, NE 1997.
Goetz-Stankiewiecz, Marketa (Ed.): The Vanek Plays: Four Authors, One Character. Vancouver, BC 1987.
Greaney, Michael: Conrad, Language, and Narrative. Cambridge 2002.
Harweg, Roland: Are Fielding's Shamela and Richardson's Pamela One and the Same Person? A Contribution to the Problem of the Number of Fictive Worlds. In: Style 38 (2004), pp. 290–301.
Hussey, Mark: Virginia Woolf A to Z. Oxford 1995.
Lippincott, Robin: Mr Dalloway. Louisville, KY 1999.
Margolin, Uri: Characters and Their Versions. In: Calin-Andrei Mihailescu / Walid Hamarneh (Eds.): Fiction Updated: Theories of Fictionality, Narratology, and Poetics. Toronto 1996, pp. 113–132.
Pavel, Thomas G.: Fictional Worlds. Cambridge, MA 1986.
Phelan, James: Reading People, Reading Plots: Character, Progression, and the Interpretation of Narrative. Chicago 1989.

Rabinowitz, Peter: »I Never Saw Any of Them Again«: Series, Sequels, and Character Identity. Paper presented at the International Conference on Narrative. Michigan State University, April 2002.

Richardson, Brian: Beyond Poststructuralism: Theory of Character, the Personae of Modern Drama, and the Antinomies of Critical Theory. In: Modern Drama 40 (1997), pp. 86–99.

Roof, Judith: Living the James Bond Lifestyle. In: Edward P. Comentale / Watt Stephen / Skip Willman (Eds.): Ian Fleming and James Bond: The Cultural Politics of 007. Bloomingdale, IN 2005, pp. 71–86.

Ruppell, Marc: Medial Traces: Characters in Cross-Sited Storyworlds (forthcoming).

Shakespeare, William: The Complete Works of Shakespeare. 5th edn., edited by David Bevington. New York 2003.

Sternberg, Meir: Expositional Modes and Temporal Ordering in Fiction. Baltimore 1978.

Tuck, Dorothy: Apollo Handbook to Faulkner. New York 1964.

Weinsheimer, Joel: Theory of Character: Emma. In: Poetics Today 1 (1979), pp. 185–211.

WERNER WUNDERLICH

Cenerentola Risen from the Ashes
From Fairy-Tale Heroine to Opera Figure

1 Figure and Fiction

»You are like a phoenix that rises from the ashes! My eyes have hitherto never been blinded by so lovely a creature«.[1] Such is the surprise displayed by the Royal Adviser, Pernullo, in August von Platen's romantic comedy *The Glass Slipper* (1823) when he comes face-to-face with a certain young woman. She is the daughter of a member of the landed gentry who has previously been repudiated by her father. Pernullo compares the lovely woman who now stands unexpectedly before him with the mythical phoenix that allowed itself to be immolated in order that it might rise rejuvenated from the ashes, ashes that, in concentrated form, contain the powers of the phoenix. The ›lovely creature‹ that has arisen from the ashes not only has a role to play in the aforementioned dramatic context. She also appears in numerous other instances and in such diverse media as literature, opera, ballet, concerts, or film, as well as in various genres such as the novella, fairy-tale, children's books, illustrated volumes, and comics. Since the time of her first appearance in literature in the early 17th century, she continues to be alive today, leading a fictitious existence.

Even though specific details pertaining to the content of the work as well as individual aspects of the plot may long ago have been relegated to obscurity, the central figure has remained in our memory because she has led a life of her own beyond the media of literature, music, and art. Given her appearance as a prototype, her character traits, and the development she experiences in her fictitious world, the figure has come to represent

---

[1] von Platen: Pantoffel, p. 126: »Ein Phönix scheinst du, der dem Aschenhaufen entfliegt! Solch eine liebliche Gestalt hat nie mein altes Auge noch geblendet« (all trans. by W.W.).

certain characteristics, modes of behavior, and life situations, and as such her name has become readily identifiable. The young girl who is both inconspicuous and unnoticed is named after her, as is the unappreciated and unloved, sensitive child, to say nothing of the slovenly maid who is responsible for performing the unsavory and filthy jobs around the house. In literary, theatrical, musical or cinematic adaptations, the figure is represented both directly and indirectly, either through her own comments and actions, as well as through the speeches of other figures with whom she interacts. But the figure also gains a physical, psychic, and social identity as a fictitious individual through the characterization provided by an authorial narrator. As such she embodies virtually exemplary characteristics, and, as such, represents a way of life that holds out the promise of fulfillment and happiness. As an epic figure, she is a narrative component, which, through the text, becomes a living entity in the reader's imagination. As a dramatic figure, she becomes a living entity on the stage and the screen through the role portrayed by an actress, singer, or dancer.

In the course of the historical process, the figure has become the target for certain projections – whether in adaptations or in interpretations – namely, exemplary virtues or worthwhile goals in life. The basic model for the story – a plot that always remains the same – provides the narrative structure. In the course of the historical reception process, that plot was repeatedly modernized and also varied in order to conform to the conditions of presentation and in accordance with the performance principles of the various media and genres. Furthermore, the character, i.e., the basic attributes and traits, the form, i.e., outward appearance and attire, as well as her status within society, i.e., the circumstances of her life and the relationships she enjoys, remain unchanged and basically constitute typical characteristics that can be associated with her person. We are referring here to *Cenerentola*, the name she is called when she appears in literature for the first time.

To be sure, the origins and worldwide dissemination of the figure are to be traced first and foremost to its presence in fairy-tales. The subject-matter contains many associations with everyday reality that allow an identification of the recipients with the figure, independent of their cultural background. True-to-life descriptions of the fate of individuals relate of resentful relatives, degradation, apparently impossible tasks and tests, of being freed from adverse circumstances, well-meaning helpers, marriage, and happiness. Thus, the description of the heroine is not based solely on a single story that has come down to us, and the figure does not appear as the function of a single, fixed plot. She is simultaneously a type of ›collective‹ agent, who can come to embody all sorts of new entities.

Moreover, depending on the interest of the interpreter and what is intended through the depiction of the figure, gender, character, fate, and behavior all may have a key role to play. This applies when it is a matter of imparting – well-nigh as models – binding, moral norms and ethical values as fundamental attitudes; when moral principles, and social rules are to serve as the motivation for basic actions. Given that she is such a figure, Cenerentola, caught between the poles of tradition and change, is constantly subjected to changes in her form as well as in the effect that she may have on others. Thus, an investigation of this figure can contribute to the effort to contend with life's questions and life's plan. She helps us to cope with timeless and ever-recurring conflicts in human existence and has, therefore, become an immortal figure.

2 Name and Plot Type

›Nomen est omen‹ – this Roman saying, according to which one's name may be a harbinger of a fate that could be either good or bad, is applicable to our figure in both senses and in all languages.[2] The name always conveys the same meaning and its function at all times is to delineate the figure as a ›type‹, whether she is known among the Italians as Cenerentola, Cendrillon among the French, Cinderella among the English and Americans, or Aschenputtel in German-speaking areas. These are names that, in themselves, tell us something about the figure, the traits we might associate with her, the way she behaves, as well as the vocation in which she is involved. Moreover, since her name by itself is enough to delineate her clearly and sufficiently, she can be used time and time again without further ado as a type figure that is endowed with stock characteristics.[3] The very variations of the expressive name of the figure point to its remarkable dissemination in different ethnic and national cultures, as well as in diverse regional and local contexts.

As soon as we hear her name, certain images come to mind. It is based on common lemma, and thus it has been incorporated into the vocabulary of any number of languages. One of the etymological roots of the name is to be found in Latin, the other in the Germanic languages. The word *cinis*

---

2 Bartels: Worte, p. 116.
3 Lamping: Name, pp. 41ff.

is used to designate the remains of a fire;⁴ the Gothic *azgô*, an expression for paleness or whiteness, has the symbolic meaning of ›cooled-off cinders‹. From Old High German *ascâ* we get Middle High German *asche* or *esche*, as well as Middle Low German *assce* and the New High German form *Asche* (or, with an Umlaut, *Äsche*).⁵ In accordance with the principle of deriving terms for a person's profession linguistically from the type of work being undertaken, the kitchen boy who tends the fire is called in Latin *cinerarius*. German dialects also employ this rule of word-formation to designate the male personnel who work in a bakery, kitchen, or inn. In the Alemannic linguistic region, there is the *Äscherläppli* (Swiss German *lappi* for a clumsy boy),⁶ and in Low German we find the Mecklenburg form *Aksenpüster* (with the alteration of ›sk‹ to ›ks‹; Low German *pusten* for ›blasen‹ [=›to blow‹]).⁷

Since the Middle Ages, the word *Asche* (cinders) has also been used as a synonym for rubbish, dirt, junk, refuse, filth, or trash. In various languages, the noun used to denote cinders is usually derived from Latin. Conveying a sense of filth and worthlessness, the word is augmented by a diminutive suffix to indicate that we are dealing with members of the female sex. Because of the tasks they perform, these women have been given a name that is degrading and meant to underscore the disdain in which they are held, a word that is intended to be used as a derogatory form of abuse. Thus, from Italian *la cenere* we get ›Cenerentola‹, from the French *la cendre*, ›Cendrillon‹, from the Spanish *la ceniza*, ›Cenicienta‹, from English *cinder*, ›Cinderella‹, from Swedish *aska*, ›Askungen‹, from Serbian *pepeo*, ›pepeljuscha‹ and from the Russian *zolà*, ›Zoluška‹.⁸

In German, this designation of contempt is expressed by a composite noun. Whether or not *Aschenputtel* is based on folk etymology, a combination of the Greek αχυλια (*achylia* = ashes/cinder) and πουττς (*pouttos* = female genitalia/vulva), is questionable. The same holds true for the suggestion that it is meant to designate a woman who sits with her genitalia in the cinders, although in modern Greek, the expression *Achylopouttoura* is used to describe a woman who is constantly by the fire as well as a cat that sits in the ashes of the hearth.⁹

---

4 Georges: Handwörterbuch, cols. 1137f. On Latin and Greek etymology as well as symbolism in religion and folklore, see Brüder Grimm: Wörterbuch, col. 579. Referred below as: DWb1.
5 Etymologisches Wörterbuch, p. 81.
6 Schweizerisches Idiotikon, cols. 1350f.
7 DWb1, col. 579.
8 For further terms in Baltic and Slavic languages see DWb1, col. 581.
9 Wehse: Cinderella, col. 43.

Associated with the noun *Asche* (cinders) is a verbal antecedent that refers to the rummaging or poking about with one's hands in dirt or rubbish. Compound words are used in various German dialects to denote the disdain that is felt towards the filthy handywoman who is of the lowest social standing. In Holstein we find *Aschenpöselken* (from *pöseln* = ›wearily to look for something‹), in Swabia *Aschengrittel* or *Eschengrüdel* (from *grüdeln* = ›to roll around‹), the Upper German form *Aschenbrödel* (from *brodeln* = ›to wallow‹), or *Aschenputtel* (from Hessian *putteln* = ›to roll around by oneself in the dust‹; in the Cologne dialect, a *Puddel* is a filthy person).[10]

The *Deutsches Märchenbuch* (German Book of Fairy-Tales), published in 1857 by Ludwig Bechstein, contains the story of *Aschenpüster*, a daughter who is beloved by her father. After his death she pretends to be a boy, finds shelter in the castle kitchen and is eventually married to the king's son.[11]

The title figure of Ernst Moritz Arndt's fairy-tale *Aschenbrödel* (1843) is also accorded a masculine name. This is Nanthilde, a girl with ›blond curls and rosy-red cheeks‹.[12] She is kept by her stepmother and stepsisters in ›filth and bondage‹ and »called and summoned by no other name than ›ugly, stupid Aschenbrödel‹«.[13] But there are also ›real‹ masculine representatives of the underprivileged kitchen personnel. About 1500, the Strassburg preacher Geiler von Keisersberg refers to a legend of a saint in which a certain *Eschengrüdel* appears as a despised and poorly treated kitchen boy who is serving in a convent.[14] Luther preaches that God is not concerned with outer purity, but with the person who has a pure heart, even if he happens to be »on the outside an aschenbrödel, black with soot and dust from working in the kitchen«.[15] Georg Rollenhagen's foreword to his novel *Froschmeuseler* (1595) makes reference to the »wondrous, domestic tale/of the despised, but pious, Aschenpoessel / and his proud, mocking brothers«.[16]

---

10 DWb1, cols. 581ff.; Bolte-Polívka: Anmerkungen, p. 182f.
11 Bechstein: Märchenbuch.
12 Arndt: Aschenbrödel, p. 286: »blonden Löckchen und rosenroten Wängelein«.
13 Ibid., p. 300: »mit keinem andern Namen genannt und gerufen als ›der hässliche dumme Aschenbrödel‹«.
14 Scherf: Märchenlexikon, p. 43f.
15 DWb1, col. 581: »auswendig ein aschenbrödel, in der küchenschwarz, rustrig und bestoben«.
16 Rollenhagen: Froschmeuseler, p. 22: »wunderbarliche Hausmehrlein / von dem verachten fromen Aschenpoessel / vnd seinen stoltzen spoettischen Bruedern«.

In northeastern Germany, the colloquial term that is occasionally used to describe a fellow who is in charge of carrying out menial tasks in both the house and the farmyard – a rather pathetic, wretched character – is *Aschenpäter* (Low German *paten* for *rühren* [›stir, move‹]). Given the similarity in sounds, he is also called *Aschenpeter*.[17] Of pivotal significance for the name of this figure is the ambiguity of the archaic symbolics associated with its determinative element.[18] *Asche* (cinders) commonly symbolizes earthly transitoriness and death. That is the reason why rituals employ ashes as a sign of death and mourning. In addition, ashes are a sign of humility and misfortune. Thus, Odysseus, while at the court of the Phaeacian king, Alkinoos, pleads for help in his effort to return to his homeland and modestly sits down among the ashes in the hearth (Od. VIII, 153). Sprinkling ashes on one's head is an age-old sign of the most profound dishonor and the greatest ignominy. After Thamar has been raped by her brother Amnon, she sprinkles ashes on her head as a sign of her sorrow and her humiliation (2. Sam 13,19). Ashes are a visible sign of remorse and purification. Lent begins with this gesture as an act of penance. In this context, ashes convey the sense of a ›memento mori‹. In the common, everyday sphere, ashes were used as a cleanser for scrubbing pans, as a medicine for cleaning wounds, and as a cosmetic for skin care. The name of the figure in itself is also a harbinger of a purification process, inasmuch as the bearer of this name arises from the ashes at the conclusion of the process, both in reality and symbolically, a symbol of hope for a new life.

The expressive and typifying name of the heroine serves as a signal for the narrative that describes her fate. As an individual designation and, at the same time, an appellative, it accentuates the plot, so to speak, and awakens expectations with respect to the course and outcome of the story. Even female figures who do not have a name that corresponds to their fate can suffer a typical ›Cinderella existence‹. For example, Princess Kudrun, in the heroic epic of the same name, has to stoke the fire and sweep the ashes with her hair while in captivity. Even the leading figure of one of the most successful plays on the opera stage in the 18th century, Niccolò Piccinni's opera buffa *La Cecchina ossia La buona figliuola* (1760),[19] leads a miserable existence, despite her noble upbringing. She is a despised gardener, a woman who is completely taken advantage of, until she takes

---

17 Brüder Grimm: KHM, p. 38f. See also the Norwegian fairy-tale *The Golden Castle that Hung in the Air* and the remarks in von Beit: Symbolik, pp. 501ff.
18 Biedermann: Symbole, p. 90; Klíma: Asche, cols. 855ff.
19 After the libretto of the same name (1760) by Carlo Goldoni, based on his comedy *Pamela Nubile*, which is in turn based on Samuel Richardson's novel of 1740.

off her apron at the end of the opera and, through her marriage to a marquis, once again rises to become a person of stature.

Regardless of the language used to tell the story of our orphaned maid, she is always accorded the typifying pejorative appellative derived from the word used to describe cinders. She is, at one and the same time, gentle and obedient, diligent and exploited, as well as disdained, but, in the final analysis, she is wonderfully rewarded. This name always lends expression to the degrading living conditions and the unreasonable working conditions of the young girl. It also presents the three-pronged plot structure postulated in narrative type 510A,[20] which can be found throughout the world. This type, together with the narrative cycle that we associate with it, is to be included in the genre Tales of Magic on account of the prevailing ›supernatural adversaries‹, the ›supernatural tasks‹, the ›supernatural helpers‹, the ›magic objects‹, and also the ›supernatural power‹. This holds true, despite the fact that there are to be found forms with clear saga motifs or that even evince the characteristics of a legend.[21] The structure always begins with the degrading and mocking of the heroine by the wicked stepmother and jealous stepsisters, continues with a demonstration of her reliability through her completion of the tasks with which she has been burdened while observing all of the rules and regulations, and culminates in her deliverance by the prince. Archaic narrative motifs such as the benevolent magic practiced by the dead mother or the good fairy, birds as helpers, the culling of lentils and peas from the ashes, attending the festive balls, the prince's search for his bride, the ›shoe test‹ as a ritual for selecting and courting the bride, and, finally, marrying the prince – all of these are long-standing addenda or accessories that can occur in various narrative forms. The figure is thus completely dominated by a stereotypical plot structure. One could even say that, given her name, attributes, and the narrative model, the figure is a typified conveyer of a specific function who, for that reason, is not accorded an individual name. The name of the figure and the plot structure do not leave much room for adaptation. In essence, her character traits have been reduced to the aforementioned virtues and cannot be considered indicative of a psychic individuality. The actions that she intentionally carries out are, after all, an expression of her kind heart, typical of the fairy-tale. Her displays of feeling are confined to a large degree to breaking down in tears and are reactions to external influences such as the death of her mother or being forbidden to leave the house to

---

[20] Uther: Types, pp. 293–295.
[21] See Wehse: Cinderella, cols. 47–49.

attend a ball. The character of the figure, therefore, can be derived solely from her name and the construction of the plot structure.

3 The Type Figure and the Fairy-Tale Figure

›Once upon a time‹ – this is the way all fairy-tales begin that conclude with the assurance that ›they lived happily ever after‹. That is also the way in which this successful fairy-tale begins on the opera stage, a story about a humiliated young girl who is forced to do menial work:

> Long ago there lived a king
> Who grew weary
> Of a lonely, single life.
> All around he sought a wife,
> But there were three who claimed the ring.
> So what then?
> He chose not the rich nor fair,
> But the one nobody knew.
> She was modest, she was simple,
> She was simple, kind and true.[22]

Just the thought of this excellent choice of a woman causes the protagonist, lost in her thoughts and full of hope, to trill: ›*Là là là, li li li, là là là*‹. For no sooner is the song over than the story begins. By its conclusion, two ›rampolli‹, supposedly noble offspring on the father's side, are the ones who end up badly, in comparison to their sister. For the fact is that a *principon* will choose, on his own account, the trilling ›prophetess‹, as the most charming and most kindhearted of the female trio to be his wife. Already one hundred and twenty years earlier, her precursor had been accorded a literary memorial as the personification of female virtue: »The beauty of a woman is an exceptional treasure. Surely no one is happy about taking his leave of the sight of her. But what one calls divine grace has all the more value because it produces even greater marvels«.[23] It is quite fitting to attribute Charles Perrault's ›moralité‹ to his eponymous heroine, a young woman who is incomparably sweet and kind, ›*une jeune fille, mais d'une douceur et d'une bonté sans exemple*‹. Her fate confirms the veracity of that morality. Jacob and Wilhelm Grimm also associate her

---

22 Zedda: Cenerentola, I, 1, no. 1: »Una volta c'era un Re, / Che a star solo s'annoiò, / Cerca, cerca, ritrovò: / Ma il volean sposare in tre. / Cosa fa? / Sprezza il fasto e la beltà. / E alla fin sceglie per se / L'innocenza e la bontà«.

23 Perrault: Cendrillon, p. 143: »La beauté pour le sexe est un rare trésor, / De l'admirer jamais on se lasse; / Mais ce qu'on nomme bonne grâce, / Est sans prix et vaut mieux encore«.

German cousin with the attributes ›*schön, fromm und gut*‹ (›beautiful, pious, and good‹), albeit in contradistinction to the meaning that her name actually conveys. The fairy-tale fate of this French and German fairy-tale teenager has been disseminated throughout the world in about 400 variations,[24] whether in books, illustrated volumes, or stage plays. »This fairy-tale is among the most well known and is told from one end of the world to the other«.[25] This was asserted by the Grimm brothers already in 1812 in the first edition of their *Kinder- und Hausmärchen*. Even though many of the later versions and adaptations of the tale in some ways present varied forms of the heroine and the plot, the focus is always on the degradation of a decent young girl by members of her family, and her magical transformation into the ›*rechten Braut*‹ (›right bride‹) for a king.

In order to determine the place of the title figure and her fate in the Rossini opera within the reception process, I would like to offer at this time an overview of the history of publication history of the literary tradition.

In the first volume of Giambattista Basile's posthumously published collection of tales, *Pentamerone*, we find the novella, *La gatta cenerentola*, contained within the first volume that appeared in 1636. Although his novella organizes the subject matter around the familiar motifs, Basile doubles the family conflict and allows the eponymous figure to be subjected simultaneously to the nastiness of two stepmothers. His heroine, a figure of baroque literature that is informed by the caste system, is a noblewoman, the daughter of a count with the unique name ›Zezolla‹.[26] The name is possibly derived from *zizoleta*, which, in the dialect of the Veneto region, refers to a pretty little girl. As a girl of lower standing, she is humiliated and required to remain by the hearth, and for this reason is called ›*la gatta Cenerentola*‹ (Cindercat). With the aid of a fairy, she is able to dance away the night at three consecutive balls prior to being crowned queen following the obligatory shoe test. With her coronation, she enjoys that which is hers by rights, and is elevated to her predetermined social status. For after all, the person who would set himself in opposition to the stars is a fool: »*Che è pazzo chi contrasta con le stelle*«.[27]

Marie-Catherine d'Aulnoy's *Finette Cendron* from the *Contes de Fées* (1698) is a somewhat verbose tale about three princesses who are abandoned by

---

24 See Diederichs: Märchen, p. 31.
25 Brüder Grimm: KHM, p. 38: »Dies Märchen gehört zu den bekanntesten und wird aller Enden erzählt«.
26 The name Lucretia has also come down to posterity.
27 Basile: Cenerentola, p. 89.

their wicked stepmother. We become acquainted with a kindhearted daughter who is exploited by her family. The youngest of the three, Finette, had repeatedly warned her malicious and arrogant sisters of the impending misfortune. As *Cendron*, this sad girl has to stay at home among the ashes in the hearth when a royal ball is given, until she finds clothes and jewelry in a chest, dresses herself up in them, and conquers the heart of the prince at the ball. The loss of a red satin slipper and the mandatory shoe test are followed by a wedding and a happy ending for all and sundry.

However, the most effective model for subsequent reception proved to be the narrative figure portrayed by Perrault in his fairy-tales. She appears as the heroine in *Cendrillon ou La petite pantoufle de verre* (1697), the beautiful and virtuous daughter of a widowed cavalier. Cendrillon is a member of the family of a ›gentilhomme‹, a nobleman. As such, her humiliation appears all the greater and it is all the more natural that she should be saved by a man of status. In the end, her suffering, her innocence, and her exemplary modesty are appropriately rewarded. The domineering new wife of her father cannot bear the gentle demeanor and kindness of her husband's daughter, given the unbearable nature of her own progeny. Consequently, she assigns the most menial jobs in the house to her stepdaughter. Despite the fact that she is both diligent and modest in her deportment, the kindhearted girl is forced to lead a wretched life. Nonetheless, she always remains well-intentioned towards both humans and animals.

This poor creature does not dare reveal her situation to her father because he is blindly devoted to his second wife. Thus, deeply hurt, the little girl crawls into the corner behind the hearth among the ashes, and for this reason the entire household only calls her by the name *Cendrillon*. Moreover, the younger of her stepsisters even accords her the vulgar term Cucendron (Cinderass), an allusion to her sitting on her bottom in the ashes. She only becomes aware of the full extent of the injustice that she must endure when she is not allowed to attend the prince's ball. By now she has had enough and no longer wishes to remain in the shadows. She gains self-confidence when her mysterious godmother, ›*qui était fée*‹ (›who was a fairy‹), comes to her aid. She conjures up fashionable clothes for her, turns a pumpkin into a golden coach, six mice into white horses, a fat rat into a coachman, and a few lizards into finely-adorned lackeys. Moreover, Cendrillon is also outfitted with glass slippers. Glass was an expensive material and difficult to work with – highly exclusive as an *accessoir de mode*. It also symbolized the fragile nature of fortune. Cendrillon, however, literally totters in her glass slippers fearlessly onward toward her good fortune.[28] She must return home before midnight, for otherwise the entire magic spell will disappear. On the second evening of the ball, Cendrillon almost does not make it home on time. But she does not miss the opportunity to leave the prince a clue as to where she might be found, and in a most ingenious way: »She let fall one of her glass slippers which the Prince picked up solicitously«.[29] There can be no suggestion that Cendrillon simply lost her slipper in her haste to get home. The opposite is the case. Cendrillon intentionally let it fall off at a spot where the prince would be bound to find it and feel obliged to pick it up. He subsequently sends out a call for women to participate in the shoe test, in order to identify the real owner of the slipper, and is quite delighted to choose Cendrillon as his wife. As such, he gives substance to a highly significant idiomatic expression. ›*Trouver chaussure à son pied*‹, with its allusion to the allegory of the lady's shoe as a vulva, basically means ›to find the right woman‹. In the final analysis, Cendrillon finds happiness. In a gesture of reconciliation, Perrault's fairy-tale narrator even allows the stepsisters to participate in the good fortune of the former Cendrillon by arranging their marriages to two ›grand seigneurs‹. Cendrillon, ›*aussi bonne que belle*‹ (›as good as she is beautiful‹) embodies the moral tenet that goodness is always rewarded and that it always does only good, quite naturally in itself an important prerequisite for being rewarded.

In 1812, the Grimm brothers included *Aschenputtel* as (fairy-tale) no. 21 in their *Kinder- und Hausmärchen*. They revised the tale several times. Already by the second edition of 1819, they had eliminated the material taken from Perrault's *Cendrillon* and augmented their version with all sorts of motifs from other popular traditions. This version leaves out the godmother and fairy that are found in Perrault's. On the other hand, it has the good spirit of the mother enter a hazelnut tree and take form as a helpful, white bird or two white doves. The hazel branch that was planted by Aschenputtel on the grave of her mother and which she fertilizes with her tears grows into a magical tree that sprouts clothes. The Grimms have a royal ball given on three nights rather than two. The poetic prince becomes the archaic prince who twice chases after the unknown beauty of the ball, albeit in vain. The first time he believes she has hidden herself in a dove house, which her father, who has been called to the scene, destroys

---

28 Occasionally we come across a reference to ›fur slippers‹, but this can be traced to a misunderstanding by Balzac, who claimed that there was a printing error in Perrault's edition of fairy-tales. He claimed that the slippers were made out of ›vaire‹ (grey fur) and not out of ›verre‹ (glass). See Delarue: Conte populaire, pp. 245–255; 278–280.

29 Perrault: Cendrillon, p. 141: »Elle laissa tomber une de ses pantoufles de verre, que le Prince ramassa bien soigneusement«.

with his ax. But the dove they were looking for was not inside. Once again, he calls on the assistance of her father who, without further ado, fells the tree, symbol of female fertility, with his ax.

The Grimms replace the glass slipper with a golden shoe. As Aschenputtel hastily takes her leave from the ball for the third time, the shoe remains stuck to the steps, which have been covered with pitch as one finds with a bird trap. However, the black pitch eventually turns out to be a stroke of good fortune for Aschenputtel. She is the owner of the second shoe and passes the ›bride test‹ because she has the right shoe size. Even the self-mutilation of the sisters, who cut up their feet because the false shoe is literally too tight for them, is a motif fabricated by the Grimms. These self-inflicted wounds underscore yet again their level of selfishness, greed, and envy. The stepsisters are even willing to endure bodily pain in order to achieve their aim. However, the king's son insists on seeing the ›*kleine verbuttete Aschenputtek*‹ (›filthy, little Aschenputtel‹). The golden slipper fits her to a tee.[30] Needless to say, the fact that the prince is taken with Aschenputtel's dainty, little shoe does not mean that he has a foot or a shoe fetish. The son of the king admires small, female feet because they not only represent an aesthetic ideal, but were also a sign of noble heritage. Even though Aschenputtel, in contrast to her Italian and French cousins, is not of noble lineage, she does have slender feet. Despite the hard, filthy work she is forced to perform, they have not become deformed or disfigured, ugly limbs. Aschenputtel has, so to speak, two good feet, and is on her way to higher things. The Grimms also added the cruel punishment at the end of the fairy-tale. From the second edition of 1819 on, their version redresses deviations from the path of virtue in the relaxed and stylized tone characteristic of the fairy-tale, and exacts severe retaliation on those inflicting the pain. The two white doves that had just cooed from high up in the hazelnut tree to the royal suitor and his bride-to-be »The shoe is not too small, he's bringing the right wife home from the ball«,[31] peck an eye out of each of the wicked sisters: »And thus they were punished for the rest of their lives for their wickedness and falsehood«.[32] They are living proof of the saying: »The fellow blew so long on the cinders until the sparks flew into his eyes«.[33]

---

30 Brüder Grimm: Aschenputtel, p. 127.
31 Ibid.: »Der Schuck [onomatopoetic for ›Schu*h*‹] ist nicht zu klein, die rechte Braut, die führt er heim«.
32 Ibid., p. 128: »Und so waren sie also für ihre Bosheit und Falschheit mit Blindheit auf ihr Lebtag gestraft«.
33 Beyer / Beyer: Sprichwörterlexikon, p. 50: »Man bläst so lange in die Asche, bis einem die Funken in die Augen fliegen«.

Ludwig Bechstein's fairy-tale heroine, contained within his *Deutsches Märchenbuch,* which first appeared in 1845, has the upper-German name *Aschenbrödel*. As the derided stepdaughter of a lower middle-class household who has been banished to the kitchen, she is accorded a much stronger personality through the psychologically understandable reactions she evinces to the malevolence to which she is subjected. She has more childlike features than her counterpart in the Grimms' fairy-tale. On the other hand, she acts in a most goal-oriented way as a clever and thoroughly self-confident young woman when it comes to the matter of a husband. She does not dispense with her ›small, golden shoe‹ on a stairway that has been smeared with pitch, but rather she loses it – as had Cendrillon – by no means ›by accident‹, so that an admiring prince can find it and pick it up.[34]

4 Fairy-Tale Woman and the Role of the Woman

Aschenputtel, as a type figure, corresponds to a bourgeois morality that rewarded diligence and piety, modesty and perseverance, efficiency and honesty. These are the norms of a fictitious fairy-tale time, ›*in der das Wünschen noch geholfen hat*‹, (›where wishing still played a role‹), and while they are in accord with the value system of the Grimm era, they also represent in their *Erziehungsbuch* (›educational primer‹), *Kinder- und Hausmärchen,* timeless claims with respect to feminine role behavior and masculine role expectations. Even though the ›*gute Lehre*‹ (›excellent instruction‹) imparted by the fairy-tales was »not their aim, nor were they invented for such a purpose, but it emanated from them, just like a good fruit is produced by a healthy blossom, without any interference from human beings«.[35] That was what the Grimms had to say about the significance and the benefits of their collection.

Despite all of the humiliation she has to endure, Aschenputtel does not abandon her optimism and her basic kindness. She remains undaunted and courageous. The marvelous turns of fate that she experiences and the indispensable support that she receives from supernatural helpers are to be credited to her basic honesty and demurity. In the final analysis, however, she instinctively knows how she herself can influence fate in

---

34 Bechstein: Aschenbrödel, p. 294.
35 Brüder Grimm: KHM, p. XIIf.: »weder ihr Zweck, noch sind sie darum erfunden, aber es erwächst daraus, wie eine gute Frucht aus einer gesunden Blüthe ohne Zuthun der Menschen«.

order to escape her terrible plight. To be sure, she does not achieve her goal through her own gifts and abilities, but it is rather those aforementioned helpers and magical powers that are decisive in carrying her forward towards the salvation by marriage with the Prince.

Aschenputtel's femininity expresses itself in the charming grace and unpretentious beauty of the young fairy-tale woman that can also be found in illustrated narratives. Certain somewhat kitschy publications with a tendency towards idealization and naivete, as, for example, the *Neuruppiner Bilderbogen* (The Neuruppin Illustrated Chronicle, ca. 1835) or the *Deutsche Bilderbogen* (German Illustrated Chronicle, 1868), added particularly sugar-coated motifs to this image of Aschenputtel. Two of the more prominent scenes that have found their way into art depict Aschenputtel at the hearth, surrounded by birds assisting her with the selection of peas and lentils, or the ›shoe test‹ episode. The best known are Emil Ludwig Grimm's sketch for the *KHM* edition of 1825, Ludwig Richter's drawings for the *KHM* in the definitive edition (1857), Moritz von Schwind's *Aschenbrödel* cycle of oil paintings (1852–54), George Cruikshank's copperplate engraving (1854), Ludwig Pietsch's painting (1858), Gustav Doré's print (1862), Albert Hendschel's woodcut (1863), and Adolf Münzer's Art Nouveau illustration (1905).

In the 20th century, the traditional figure of Aschenputtel became an object onto which were projected a view of the world and an image of humanity that were informed by a variety of sociological and psychological perspectives. Consequently, our fairy-tale heroine came to be interpreted symbolically as a personality with a soul and a subconscious. In this respect, the invented *femina ficta* is treated like a true homo sapiens and the distinction between the fictitious figure and the real person can be eliminated as Lüthi and Bausinger pointed out.[36] However, when social roles and psychic sensibilities are attributed to Aschenputtel with the aim of elucidating personality traits that are molded either by society or by the individual, the distinction between reality and fiction is weakened and this is by no means unproblematic. Behavioral patterns and social denigration in real society can hardly be explained on the basis of fictitious figures. This is particularly the case when sociological or psychological interpretations of problems experienced by real people have previously been applied to invented figures with the aim of using these invented figures to work through such problems.

---

36 Lüthi: Das europäische Volksmärchen, p. 115; Bausinger: Aschenputtel, p. 148f.

The psychologist Hedwig von Beit detected in the Grimms' fairy-tales the oedipal wishes of a premature Lolita,[37] who, in her daydreams, lets her mother die because she desires her father. Torturous feelings of guilt manifested themselves in the stepmother and stepsisters and were overcome when the daughter transferred her feelings of love to a sexual partner of her own age. The latter suppresses fears of castration after having become nervous over the sight of blood in the woman's shoe. The child psychologist Bruno Bettelheim claimed that a child would consider Cinderella's degradation to be punishment, but would also recognize as inherent in the figure and in the plot possibilities for self-emancipation.[38] The sociologist Colette Dowling made the English version of the nickname an integral component of the title of her book *The Cinderella-Complex*.[39] Dowling's guide is intended to shake up those women who are wary of acquiring success and recognition in a profession and who prefer to withdraw into marriage and housework. The man of their dreams is rich and able to give them an appropriate present of high-heel shoes in which they totter toward him to be swept up and carried off in his arms. In this way they internalize their fear of independence, develop an inferiority complex and compensate for it with an existence that revolves around their roles as housewives. The literary Cinderella, however, evinces no Cinderella complex at all, for she does everything she can to escape her miserable and thoroughly wretched situation.

Nowadays, the figure and her story are rarely cited as examples for virtues such as modesty, diligence, and obedience. In all events, Cinderella is recommended for modern-day managers as a sort of exemplary model: the exemplary embodiment of lofty personal virtues such as a willingness to trust others and trustworthiness itself. Nevertheless, Cinderella continues to be parodied in different, even contradictory ways, on the one hand as a ›guide‹ from the realm of depth-psychology, designed to overcome crises, or, on the other, as a socio-utopian model for advancement.[40]

---

37 Beit: Symbolik, pp. 504f., 724ff.
38 Bettelheim: Kinder, pp. 225–265.
39 Dowling: Cinderella-Complex.
40 See Uther: Handbuch, pp. 54f.

5 Adaptations of the Cinderella Figure

It was first and foremost Perrault's fairy-tale that served as the reception model for literary, musical, and cinematic adaptations.[41] The latter are principally concerned with the self-development of the protagonist, and this is viewed as a marvelous realization of her natural destiny. In 1824, August von Platen brought to the stage the ›heroische Komödie‹ (›heroic comedy‹) *Der gläserne Pantoffel* (›The Glass Slipper‹), and substituted Carmosine's evil stepfather for the wicked stepmother. In 1829, Christian Dietrich Grabbe used the subject matter in his fairy-tale comedy, *Aschenbrödel*, intended as a social satire. Baron von Fineterra, who is greatly in debt because of his spendthrift wife, sends his own daughters out to catch affluent husbands so that he can be bailed out. On the other hand, he mistreats his pitiful stepdaughter, Olympia, as though she were a Cinderella figure.

Cinderella has been the subject in dozens of films,[42] beginning already in 1898 with George Albert Smith in England and just one year later with Georges Méliès (who was very much impressed by Massenet's opera) in France. In 1914, Asta Nielsen played the title role in a silent film. Jerry Lewis's slapstick *Cinderfella* appeared in movie theaters in 1959. Hollywood adaptations such as Robert Malenotti's Brooklyn-based *Cinderella* (1984) modernize the ›Cindy‹ plot, whereas Andy Tennant's *Cinderella Story* (1998) is set in a fantastically Dordogne scenery of the 16th century. Several musicals were made based on the Cinderella story, the best known of which is Rodgers and Hammerstein's film from the year 1957. Walt Disney's film *Cinderella*, produced in 1950, remains as popular today as it was almost sixty years ago. It is, probably, the most popular film about Cinderella ever made.

Ben Sharpsteen took Perrault's Cinderella as his starting point and also used some of the motifs to be found in the plot of the Grimm version. Sharpsteen's Cinderella is an American idol. She embodies the American dream of social advancement and success, represents the belief in one's self, in one's own capabilities and one's own resolve, and symbolizes the triumph of good and the reward that comes along with it.

On at least eighty occasions, Cinderella has provided the subject-matter for orchestral music, ballets, and stage shows.[43] Among others, Eugen

---

41 See Peck: Cinderella.
42 See Beck: Movie Guide, p. 55; Internet Movie Database:
   <http://www.imdb.de/find?s=all&q=Cinderella> (Jan. 17th, 2010).
43 Schneider: Lexikon, pp. 172ff.

d'Albert, Marcel Delannoy, Erland von Koch, Selim Palmgren, Henri Pousseur, and Eric Coates have composed small orchestral suites. Since the 18th century, ballet has repeatedly made use of Perrault's fairy-tale on the stage. Louis Antoine Duport used well-known musical selections by Mozart, Nicolas Isouard, and François Adrien Boiledieu for his pantomime ballet *Aschenbrödel* (1813). Andrée Howard's London ballet (1935) used compositions by Carl Maria von Weber. In 1822, Fernando Sor provided the original musical score for François Decombe Albert's London ballet. In 1901, Emil Graeb composed in Berlin a ballet after the *Aschenbrödel* composition by Johann Strauss (the son), in which the prince appears as the owner of a department store. The best known ballet with this theme, a ballet that has remained the most popular to the present day, is Sergej Prokofiev's ballet, opus 87, *Zoluška*, which made its successful premier at the Bolshoi Theater in Moscow in 1946 and continues to be included in the repertoire of the ballet company.

6 The Cinderella of the Opera

However, this fairy-tale heroine celebrated her greatest triumphs on the stage in opera productions. As to the significance of Cinderella herself as an opera figure, we may note that the song that she sings to the accompaniment of music becomes the most important medium for imparting feelings, moods, thoughts, and impressions. Vocal and instrumental music, the pitch of her voice, as well as the role she is assigned, offer additional possibilities, within the framework of the respective plot and given her traits as an adapted type-figure, for a more detailed characterization of Cinderella as an opera figure than is the case with her epic counterpart.

The fairy-tale figure began her stage career in 1759 in Jean-Louis Laruette's one-act opera *Cendrillon* (libretto by Louis Anseaume). Michael Kelly's (Michele Occelli) *Cinderella* followed in 1804. Cinderella celebrated a great triumph in 1810 in Nicolas Isouard's (i.e., Nic[c]olò de Malte) Parisian ›opéra-féerie‹ (›fairy opera‹), *Cendrillon*. With its title figure *Prinzessin Aschenbrödel* or *Äscherling*, this fairy opera remained for many years very popular among the German public.[44] The librettist, Charles Guillaume Étienne, turns the compliant fairy-tale father into a hard-hearted opera stepfather, a widower, who assumes the role of the wicked ›belle-mèr‹. His spoiled daughters are called Thisbé and Clorinde. These mythological

---

44 Etienne / Isouard: Cendrillon.

names constitute ironic allusions to the unrealized love of a beautiful Babylonian woman for Pyramus, a love that ends in tragic death, and the love of a heathen amazon for the crusader Tancredi. The fate of the two women is described in Ovid's *Metamorphosen* (ca. 8 A.D.) and Torquato Tasso's *Gerusalemme liberata* (completed in 1574). The names of the two stepsisters in themselves make it clear that neither will ever be considered a potential spouse for the fairy-tale prince. The wise Alidor, a magician, assumes the role of the fairy-tale-like godmother. He is the mentor of the prince, who is being forced to marry for dynastic reasons. The prince exchanges roles with his stable master, Dandini, so that he can go searching for a bride incognito. Alidor procures a suitable bride for his pupil, while the maliciousness and stupidity of the wicked sisters are revealed through a somewhat contrived comedy of errors.

The music written for the title figure by Isouard – in contrast to the music that is associated with her stepsisters – was remarkably simple and unpretentious. One might say that the ›character‹ of the music corresponds to the basic essence of the protagonist, who introduces herself in the *Allegro non troppo*: »I am modest and submissive and people see me very little, because I am always sitting in a little corner of the fireplace. It is not beautiful but everything seems good to me, that's why they call me little Cinderella«.[45] However, the decision to create a score at this point that was not particularly demanding did not have anything to do with the musical drama per se. Rather, it had to do with the fact that the composer found it necessary to compose the theme song in such a way that it would accommodate the limited vocal range of soprano Alexandrine Saint-Aubin.

Étienne's libretto adapts the epic plot of Perrault's fairy-tale for a dramatic performance on the stage. At the end of the ›introduction‹, Alidor, disguised as a beggar, prophesies to the tormented Cendrillon that heaven will reward her for her good heart. He consequently admonishes her a short time later to take good care of this fortunate gift of nature: »*Conservez bien cette bonté / cet heureux don de la nature*«.[46] The promise that Alidor makes appears several times as a leitmotif and returns in the second finale. After having tried on the white shoe that she had lost earlier, Cendrillon is crowned by her prince as ›*dame aimable*‹, and generously forgives her loathsome sisters. Isouard's *Cendrillon* enjoyed

---

45 Ibid., I, no. 2, Romance, p. 16f.: »Je suis modeste et soumise le monde me voit fort peu, / car je suis toujours assise dans un petit coin du feu. Cette place n'est pas belle mais pour moi tout parat bon, voilà pourquoi l'on m'appelle la petite Cendrillon«.
46 Ibid., I, no. 8, Largo, p. 52.

success throughout all of Europe. However, it was eventually replaced in the repertoires by Rossini's *Cenerentola* and virtually consigned to oblivion. Étienne's libretto was set to music a second time by Daniel Steibelt and performed as *Zoluška* with great success in St. Petersburg in 1810.

Another libretto based on Perrault's fairy-tale was composed by Francesco Fiorini. If Étienne's libretto had avoided the fairy magic to be found in Perrault's tale, Fiorini's opera text, in contrast, once again relies entirely on the effects of the magic opera. In 1814, this opera premiered in Milan as a ›*dramma semiserio*‹ under the title, *Agatina o La virtù premiata*,[47] with music by Stefano Pavesi. The libretto duplicates the typifying name of the original fairy-tale figure, Cendrillon. She appears as an opera figure with the proper name, Agatina, from Greek $\alpha\gamma\alpha\tau\theta o\varsigma$ (›agathos‹), a term that conveys the idea of a ›happy, good-natured‹ person. Cendrillon-Agatina bewitches the prince less through her good character than through her good taste. Thanks to a magic rose, she arrives at the court festival as a fashionable queen of the ball in a coach drawn by two winged dragons. The prince is completely taken with her.

Other operatic works are almost entirely forgotten, namely, the *Cinderella* operas by Emile Jonas (1872) and John Farmer (1882), or the neo-romantic *Aschenbrödel* operas of Ferdinand Langer (1878), Carl Reinecke (1878), Heinrich Schulz-Beuthen (1879), Alban von Hahn (1894), and Leo Blech (1904). Even Ermanno Wolf-Ferrari's *Cenerentola* (libretto by Marie Pezzè-Pascolato) from the year 1900 is only infrequently to be found in repertoires. On the other hand, Jules Massenet's *Cendrillon* (libretto by Henri Cain) from the year 1899 (produced as a ballet film by Roland Petit in 1955 under the title of *The Glass Slipper* with Leslie Caron in the title role) is still very popular in France as a ›Christmas opera‹. A series of *Cinderella* musicals written for Broadway and London from the beginning of the twentieth century on have also disappeared in the interim from the repertoires.

7 Angelina, alias Cenerentola

Up to the present day, Rossini's opera, *Cenerentola,* continues to outshine all of the others by far. Its German adaptations have also contributed to this state of affairs. The most successful, *Angelina,* was produced in 1929 by the Munich conductor and composer Hugo Röhr.[48] Gioacchino

---

47 Fiorini: Agatina.
48 Ferretti / Rossini: Angelina.

Rossini composed the opera in the utmost haste, and for that reason he also fell back on earlier compositions in the process. *La Cenerentola ossia La bontà in trionfo* was completed within twenty-four days for the Roman Teatro Valle, where the premiere took place on January 25th, 1817. The audience greeted it with unbridled enthusiasm. The libretto was written by Jacopo Ferretti. It is a ›*melodramma giocoso*‹, an ›*opera buffa*‹ with the serious motifs of the ›*dramma giocoso*‹ in two acts. Ferretti used Étienne's and Fiorini's opera texts with the entire personnel. In his foreword, *Ai miei cortesi fratelli drammatici*,[49] intended for his ›sympathetic fraternal‹ fellow-dramatists, Ferretti provides the reason for rejecting the magical apparatus of the fairy-tale and his decision to relate a sentimental love story. He refers to his respect for the sophisticated taste of the Roman public, a public that he did not want to entertain with childish nonsense. Ferretti transposed the plot of the fairy-tale into the contemporary Restoration period that was just getting underway. The opera is a satiric, exaggerated commentary on a self-inflated, broken aristocracy, whose foolish class arrogance finds itself confronted by the true nobility of the heart.

Against the contemporary backdrop of the reactionary forces and their authoritarian monarchies, the opera also deals with the moral demands on a just and kind ruler. In the opera, the latter takes on the characteristics of a just king over his people and a kind father of his land. This is already alluded to through his proper name, Ramiro, which, in Spanish, designates an ›honorable‹, high dignitary, as well as the clever, respectively, the highest judge. Just like Fiorini, Ferretti also gave his title heroine a double baptism by likewise according her in addition a proper name that, in itself, conveyed a message: *Angelina*, a truly angel-like being. She is tormented by both her stepfather and her stepsisters, and despite her status as a baroness, she is required to perform the filthiest and lowest jobs for the family, as though she were a servant girl. And the family is not even her own. However, the text and the music make it clear from the outset that this Cenerentola has an astonishingly stable ego, and, as a beautiful soul, is the embodiment of values such as selflessness, gentleness, innocence and compassion. It is, therefore, quite clear from the beginning that she will, after all is said and done, achieve the happiness she so richly deserves.

Significantly, her stepfather, the self-complacent master of the house, is called Don Magnifico, Baron von Fiascone, underscoring the ludicrous contradiction between his demise of status and the pompous claims that he makes within society. He is portrayed as a grotesque, feudal gentleman who has been remarkably unsuccessful. The Baron is not a submissive

---

49 Beghelli / Gallino (Eds.): Rossini, p. 423.

father such as we find in Perrault's tale, but rather a hard-hearted stepfather as in Étienne's libretto. The dim-witted, vain daughters are called Tisbe and Clorinda, just as they are in Etienne's work. In addition, Alidoro, as a quasi protective angel with golden wings, does full justice to his name. In contrast to Isouard's opera, the title role is tailor-made for a coloratura soprano, and it was a role that Rossini had essentially composed for the voice of the celebrated prima donna, Geltrude Righetti Giorgi. None of Rossini's coloratura roles is more demanding or more expressive. In terms of music, the title role offers numerous possibilities for expressing emotions and moods that reflect the transition of the troubled, non-descript wall flower into a young woman in love and the triumphant bride of the prince. Suitable instrumental and vocal forms are used to articulate these emotions and moods at decisive junctures of the plot. The bel canto of the title role is the appropriate medium for the lovely soul of Cenerentola. Her richly embellished solo, the grace notes of the melodic lines, marvelous legati, the rise and fall of the notes, the coloratura, trills, tremolos, runs, jumps, motif sequences (in comparison to the earlier performances that were normally characterized by free improvisation, Rossini had noted everything here) – all of these special characteristics make Cenerentola's musical character irreplaceable. The beautiful sound of the melodies that she intones is a reflection of her genuineness and purity that eclipse everything else. In Ferretti's libretto, the destiny proclaimed by Alidor in Isouard's opera is sung by the title heroine as a canzone. In order to give even greater emphasis to the plot as the realization of that destiny, Rossini replaces in his ›introduzione‹ Cendrillon's entrance song, *Il était un petit homme* (sung to the melody of the children's song, *Compère Guilleri*) with the lyrical D-Minor canzone *Una vola c'era un Re* in an undulating 6/8 time. The ballad-like canzone in the *Andantino*, which tells of a king who chooses from among three sisters the right one for his spouse, anticipates in nuce the plot and its conclusion in the form of an allegory. A prince will select innocence and kindness as his bride. This opening aria is repeated, like a leitmotif, at those junctures where we witness the prophecy fulfilling itself, step by step. At the same time, the simple canzone ›con tono flemmatico‹, a solemn, melancholy melody, characterizes Angelina as the modest, guileless Cenerentola. The melancholy music lets the romantic magic resound that surrounds the title heroine and which accompanies her throughout the opera to its conclusion. She hums her opening aria once again when she brings food to the incarcerated Ramiro. After just a few measures, the two begin a duet, from the composition of the canzone, »Oh, so ardently I gaze / On her eyes, so clear, so bright«,⁵⁰ and precisely at the moment when Cenerentola and the prince experience love at first sight: »She/he is delightful. She/he is enchanting / All my senses now beguiling. / Ah, how sweetly now she's/he's smiling: / All my desire I may hope to gain«.⁵¹ This musical character permits her to be conceived as two persons in one, a dramatic protagonist who is also a vocal virtuoso. On the one hand, Rossini portrays Cenerentola as Aschenputtel through simple melodies, while, on the other hand, Angelina is depicted through an intricate bel canto as the future bride of the fairy prince. In this way, the role that is assumed becomes a dramaturgical instrument for the plot itself. In contrast to her bad-tempered and snobbish stepsisters, Cenerentola has maintained ›*innocenza*‹ (›guilelessness‹), ›*candore*‹ (›purity of soul‹), and ›*bontà*‹ (›kindheartedness‹), and it is these qualities that impress Prince Ramiro. While feigning the role of his manservant, Dandini, the prince is particularly enchanted by the very essence of Cenerentola. Dandini plays his own feigned role as the prince in accordance with his name, which is derived from *danda* (›leading-strings‹). He is, in fact, the ›marionette‹ of his lord.

Cenerentola gives Ramiro a bracelet intended to lead him to her when he sets out searching for her. She is wearing its counterpart on her right wrist. And if Ramiro recognizes her by it and still loves her, she will agree to be his wife. The symbolic shoe test has given way to the typical, realistic plot of a contemporary melodrama: the couple recognize each other again and are brought together. Events then follow in quick succession, underscored by the terrific speed that the music achieves at many spots. Crescendo, forte, presto – the sequence of notes, volume, tempi – work together to produce melodies that are played at breakneck speed, creating an ear-splitting din. The figures on the stage have been overcome by the events and no longer know whether they are coming or going. Storms, ›*tempesta*‹, provide a musical prelude for the highpoint of a plot that is coming to a head. Storms and tempests reflect Angelina's restlessness. They are a harbinger of the impending turbulence and the fact that everything will be clarified in a purified atmosphere.

When, after an accident in the coach, Ramiro and Dandini once again appear at the ruins of Don Magnifico's home, the lovers suddenly recognize each other by the bracelets on their wrists: ›*Siete voi?*‹ Elated over

---

50 Zedda: Cenerentola, I, 4, no. 3: »Un soave no so che in quegl'occhi scintilla«.
51 Ibid.: »Una grazia, un certo incanto / Par che brilli su quel viso. / Quanto caro è quel sorriso! / Scende all'alma e fa sperar«.

this marvelous turn of fate, Angelina forgives her father and her sisters for all the degradation and abuse to which they had subjected her: »Give your hands, and let me now embrace you. / Daughter, companion, and sister, / before you, you see«.[52] The extent of the development of the title figure, and thus the title role, from the simple, opening aria to her final appearance is demonstrated by the highpoint of the opera: Angelina's brilliant closing rondo with its extraordinary coloratura passages in bel canto, which are quite appropriate for her truly royal appearance in the *Maestoso*. The triumphal final aria, »Born to a life that was lonely«,[53] sung in the key of E-Major, represents the full vocal virtuosity of the title figure in its magnificent, flawless tonality. An elegiac tone dominates as Cenerentola reflects back on her fate. The splendid *Cabaletta* that follows in a rapid tempo contains artistic coloratura that give expression to Angelina's greatest happiness and blissful culmination of her love affair. As the subtitle of the opera promised, kindheartedness triumphs over all adversity and nastiness, a point that is made clear in the final chorus: »Long the lane that has no turning / Love and kindness can't go wrong«.[54]

A fundamental means to self-awareness, as well as to an awareness of the ›other‹, is provided by the multitude of figures in literature and opera. The moving story of Cinderella offers such possibilities in abundance. Here we have the tale of a modest and virtuous young woman, unjustly made to suffer and socially despised, who later, as a bride, ascends the social ladder and is consequently viewed as blessed by fortune. However, because we must also consider the venue, perspective, and horizon of the tradition that surrounds this figure in our effort to arrive at a reflected identification and an objective explanation of her person, the present essay has dealt with the representation of typical stations that mark her tradition as well as the depiction of the Cinderella figure that is dependent upon the latter. Unlike any other fairy-tale heroine, this figure, who emanates from a fictitious world, has served in the world of reality as a projection for character and behavioral typologies. She was molded into a figure, who, in her role as a woman, united hopes and opportunities, fears and warnings with respect to psychic sensitivities and social conflicts in the relationship of the sexes to one another.

---

52 Ibid., II, 9, no. 14: »A questo sen volate, / Figlia, sorella, amica, / Tutto trovate in me«.
53 Ibid.: »*Nacqui all'afano*«.
54 Ibid., choir: »Tutto cangia a poco a poco: / Cessa alfin di sospirar. / Di fortuna fosti il gioco; / Incomincia a giubilar«.

References

Primary Sources

Arndt, Ernst Moritz: Aschenbrödel. In: Märchen (Die Fundgrube 53). München 1971, pp. 286–310.
Basile, Giambattista: La gatta cenerentola. In: Alessandra Burani / Ruggero Guarini (Eds.): Il racconto di racconti ovvero Il trattenimento di piccoli. Milan 1994, pp. 81–89.
Bechstein, Ludwig: Aschenpüster mit der Wünschelgerte. In: Walter Scherf (Ed.): Ludwig Bechstein. Sämtliche Märchen. Darmstadt 1985, pp. 477–483.
Bechstein, Ludwig: Aschenbrödel. In: Hans-Jörg Uther (Ed.): Ludwig Bechstein. Märchenbuch. Munich 1997 (Die Märchen der Weltliteratur 1), pp. 292–295.
Beit, Hedwig: Symbolik des Märchens. Versuch einer Deutung. 7th edn. Berne 1986.
Brüder Grimm: Aschenputtel. In: Hans-Jörg Uther (Ed.): Kinder- und Hausmärchen 3. Gesammelt durch die Brüder Grimm. Hildesheim [et al.] 2004 (Jacob Grimm und Wilhelm Grimm. Werke, Abt. III, vol. 45), pp. 120–128.
[Étienne, Charles Guillaume / Niccolò Isouard:] Cendrillon. Opéra féerie en 3 actes. Paroles de M. Etienne. Musique de Nic[c]olò [Isouard]. Partition piano et chant. Paris [o.J.].
Fiorini, Francesco: Agatina o La virtù premiata. Dramma semiserio per musica in due atti. Milan 1814.
Grabbe, Christian Dietrich: Aschenbrödel. Dramatisches Mährchen. [1829 (1835)]. In: Eduard Grisebach (Ed.): Grabbe's Werke 2. Berlin 1902, pp. 397–459.
Homer. Odyssee. Griechisch und deutsch. Übertr. von Anton Weiher. 15th edn. Düsseldorf et. al. 2007.
Madame d'Aulnoy: Finette Cendron. Conte. In: Philippe Hourcade (Ed.): Madame d'Aulnoy. Contes I. Les Contes des Fées. Paris 1997, pp. 363–385.
Perrault, Charles: Cendrillon ou La petite pantoufle de verre. Conte. In: René Hilsum (Ed.): Œuvres de Charles Perrault. Contes de ma mère l'oie. Contes en vers. Histoire, ou contes du temps passé. Paris 1931, pp. 133–143.
von Platen, August: Der gläserne Pantoffel. Eine heroische Komödie in fünf Akten. Oct. 1823. In: Erich Petzet (Ed.): August von Platens sämtliche Werke 7. Leipzig 1910, pp. 101–166.
Rollenhagen, Georg: Froschmeuseler. Ed. by Dietmar Peil. Frankfurt/M. 1989 (BdK 48).
Rossini, Gioacchino: Angelina. Angelina. Komische Oper in 2 Akten. Text von J[acopo] Ferretti. Unter Übers. und Einfügung der Orig.-Secco-Rezitative für die deutsche Bühne umgearb. und neugest. von Hugo Röhr. Berlin [1929].
Zedda, Alberto (Ed.): La Cenerentola, ossia, La Bontà in Trionfo: dramma giocoso in due atti di Jacopo Ferretti; musica di Gioacchino Rossini. Pesaro et al. 1998 (Gioacchino Rossini Works, 1a, 20). English transl. by Arthur Jacobs. In: La Cenerentola (Cinderella). London et al. 1980 (English National Opera Guide 1), pp. 47–93.

Secondary Sources

Bartels, Klaus: Veni vidi vici. Geflügelte Worte aus dem Griechischen und Lateinischen. 9th edn. Darmstadt 1992.
Bausinger, Hermann: Aschenputtel. Zum Problem der Märchensymbolik. In: Zeitschrift für Volkskunde 52 (1955), pp. 144–155.

Beck, Jerry: The Animated Movie Guide. Chicago 2005.
Beghelli, Marco / Nicola Gallino (Eds.): Tutti i libretti di Rossini. Milan 1991.
Bettelheim, Bruno: Kinder brauchen Märchen. Stuttgart 1977.
Beyer, Horst / Anneliese Beyer: Sprichwörterlexikon. München 1985.
Biedermann, Klaus: Knaurs Lexikon der Symbole (Digitale Bibliothek 16) Berlin 2002.
Bleich, Otto: Das Märchen vom Aschenbrödel, vornehmlich in der deutschen Volks- und Kunstdichtung. In: Zeitschrift für vergleichende Literaturgeschichte N.F. 18 (1910), pp. 55–102.
Bolte, Johannes / Georg Polívka: Anmerkungen zu den Kinder- u. Hausmärchen der Brüder Grimm 1. Leipzig 1913, pp. 165–188.
Brèque, Jean-Michel: Sans pantoufle ni fée, mains on sans charmes. In: Rossini, La Cenerentola. Paris 1986 (L'Avant Scène Opéra 85), pp. 4–11.
Brüder Grimm: Deutsches Wörterbuch 1. Reprint. Munich 1984 (dtv 5945).
Brzoska, Matthias: Cendrillon [Isouard]. In: Pipers Enzyklopädie des Musiktheaters 3. Munich et al. 1986, p. 151f.
Cox, Marian Roalfe: Cinderella: 345 Variants of Cinderella, Catskin and Cap o'Rushes. London 1893.
Delarue, Paul: Le conte populaire français 2. Paris 1957.
Diederichs, Ulf: Who's Who im Märchen. Düsseldorf 2006.
Dowling, Colette: The Cinderella-Complex. Women's Hidden Fear of Independence. New York 1981.
Fend, Michael: Cendrillon [Isouard]. In: The New Grove Dictionary of Opera 1. New York 1997, p. 797.
Gossett, Philip: Fairy-Tale and Opera Buffa: The Genre of Rossini's ›La Cenerentola‹. In: La Cenerentola (Cinderella), Rossini. London et al. 1980 (English National Opera Guide 1), pp. 7–16.
Georges, Karl Ernst: Heinrich Georges. Ausführliches Lateinisch-Deutsches Handwörterbuch 1. 9th edn. Reprint. Darmstadt 1998.
Gerhard, Anselm: Cendrillon [Massenet]. In: Pipers Enzyklopädie des Musiktheaters 3. Munich et al. 1986, pp. 766–768.
Hagen, Rolf: Der Einfluss der Perraultschen Contes auf das volkstümliche deutsche Erzählgut. Diss. Göttingen 1954, pp. 54–85.
Henze-Döhring, Sabine: La Cenerentola: Rossini und das phantastische Genre. In: Markus Engelhardt / Wolfgang Witzenmann (Eds.): Convegno Italo-Tedesco ›Mozart, Paisiello, Rossini e l'Opera Buffa‹ (Roma 1993). Laaber 1998 (Analecta musicologica 31), pp. 319–347.
Jannidis, Fotis: Figur und Person. Beitrag zu einer historischen Narratologie. Berlin et al. 2004.
Kant, Marion: Soluschka [Prokofjew]. In: Pipers Enzyklopädie des Musiktheaters 5. Munich et al. 1994, pp. 488–490.
Klíma, Josef R.: Asche. In: Enzyklopädie des Märchens. Handwörterbuch zur historischen und vergleichenden Erzählforschung 1. Berlin et al. 1977, cols. 855–859.
Lamping, Dieter: Der Name in der Erzählung. Zur Poetik des Personennamens. Bonn 1983 (Wuppertaler Schriftenreihe Literatur 21).
Lüthi, Max: Das europäische Volksmärchen. Bern 1947.
Lüthi, Max: Der Aschenputtel-Zyklus. In: Jürgen Janning / Heino Gehrts / Herbert Ossowsk (Eds.): Vom Menschenbild im Märchen. 2nd edn. Kassel 1980 (EMG Schriftenreihe 1), pp. 39–58.
Miller, Norbert: La Cenerentola ossia La bontà in trionfo. [Rossini] In: Pipers Enzyklopädie des Musiktheaters 5. Munich et al. 1994, pp. 398–402.

Milnes, Rodney: Cendrillon [Massenet]. In: The New Grove Dictionary of Opera 1. New York 1997, pp. 797–799.
Nitschke, August: Aschenputtel aus der Sicht der historischen Verhaltensforschung. In: Helmut Brackert (Ed.): Und wenn sie nicht gestorben sind. 2nd edn. Frankfurt/M. 1982 (es 973), pp. 71–88.
Osborne, Richard: La Cenerentola [Rossini]. In: The New Grove Dictionary of Opera 1. New York 1997, pp. 799–801.
Peck, Russell A.: Cinderella Bibliography: <http://www.lib.rochester.edu/camelot/cinder/cin12.htm> (June 07th, 2008).
Pfeiffer, Wolfgang et al. (Eds.): Etymologisches Wörterbuch des Deutschen 1. Berlin 1989.
Pitt, Charles: De la genèse à la création. In: Rossini, La Cenerentola. Paris 1986 (L'Avant Scène Opéra 85), pp. 12–15.
Rooth, Anna Birgitta: The Cinderella Cycle. Lund 1951.
Scherf, Walter: Das Märchenlexikon 1. Munich 1995, pp. 36–46, 151–154, 306–309.
Schneider, Klaus: Lexikon Programmusik. Stoffe und Motive. Kassel et al. 1999, pp. 172–176.
Staub, Friedrich / Ludwig Tobler et. al. (Eds.): Schweizerisches Idiotikon 8. Frauenfeld 1881.
Stier-Somlo, Helene: Das Grimmsche Märchen als Text für Opern und Spiele. Berlin et al. 1926.
Ulanov, Ann / Barry Ulanov: Cinderella and Her Sisters. The Envied and the Envying. Philadelphia 1998.
Uther, Hans-Jörg: The Types of International Folktales. A Classification and Bibliography. Based on the System of Antti Aarne and Stith Thompson. Part 1. Helsinki 2004.
Uther, Hans-Jörg: Handbuch zu den »Kinder- und Hausmärchen« der Brüder Grimm. Entstehung – Wirkung – Interpretation. Berlin et al. 2008, pp. 50–55.
Wehse, Rainer: Cinderella. In: Enzyklopädie des Märchens. 3. Berlin, New York 1981, cols. 39–57.
Wöllner, Hildegunde: Wie aus der Ungeliebten die Auserwählte wird: Aschenputtel. Neu gest. Ausg. Stuttgart 2001.
Wunderer, Rolf: »Der gestiefelte Kater« als Unternehmer. Lehren aus Management und Märchen. Wiesbaden 2008.
Wunderlich, Werner: Figur und Typus. Kleine Phänomenologie des literarischen Personals. In: Versants 37 (2000), pp. 19–68.

Bibliography

JENS EDER / FOTIS JANNIDIS / RALF SCHNEIDER

Characters in Fictional Worlds
A Basic Bibliography

A more comprehensive and occasionally updated version of this bibliography is available at the internet journal *Medienwissenschaft/Hamburg: Berichte und Papiere* <http://www1.uni-hamburg.de/Medien/berichte/index.html>

1 Bibliographies

Garcia Landa, José Angel: Characters in Narrative. In: J.A.G.L.: A Bibliography of Literary Theory, Criticism and Philology.
<http://www.unizar.es/departamentos/filologia_inglesa/garciala/bibliography.html> (Nov. 24th, 2008)

Rosenberg, Brian: Character in Fiction, 1900–1980. In: Bulletin of Bibliography 40 (1983), pp. 200–205.

2 Lexicon Entries on »Character« and Related Concepts

Anz, Thomas: Figuren. In: T.A. (Ed.): Handbuch Literaturwissenschaft. Gegenstände – Konzepte – Institutionen, vol. 1: Gegenstände und Grundbegriffe. Stuttgart / Weimar 2007, pp. 122–127.

Asmuth, Bernhard: Charakter. In: Georg Braungart et al. (Eds.): Reallexikon der deutschen Literaturwissenschaft, vol. 1. Berlin / New York 1997, pp. 297–299.

De Grève, Marcel: Personnage. In: Dictionnaire international des termes littéraires.
<http://www.ditl.info/arttest/art3413.php> (Dec. 7th, 2008).

Eder, Jens: Figur. In: Hans J. Wulff / Theo Bender (Eds.): Lexikon der Filmbegriffe.
<www.lexikon.bender-verlag.de> (July 15th, 2007).

Eder, Jens: Figur; Figurenkonstellation. In: Dieter Burdorf / Christoph Fasbender / Burkhard Moenninghoff (Eds.): Metzler Lexikon Literatur. 3rd edn. Stuttgart / Weimar 2007, pp. 238–239.

Jannidis, Fotis: Figur, literarische. In: Ansgar Nünning (Ed.): Metzler Lexikon Literatur- und Kulturtheorie. Stuttgart, Weimar 1998, p. 149.
Jannidis, Fotis: Character. In: Peter Hühn et al. (Eds.): Handbook of Narratology. Berlin 2009, pp. 14–29.
Margolin, Uri: Character. In: David Herman / Manfred Jahn / Marie-Laure Ryan (Eds.): Routledge Encyclopedia of Narrative Theory. London / New York 2005, pp. 52–57.
Margolin, Uri: Character. In: David Herman (Ed.): The Cambridge Companion to Narrative. Cambridge et al. 2007, pp. 66–79.
Platz-Waury, Elke: Figur. In: Klaus Weimar / Harald Fricke / Klaus Grubmüller / Jan-Dirk Müller (Eds.): Reallexikon der deutschen Literaturwissenschaft, vol. 1. Berlin / New York 1997, pp. 587–589.
Platz-Waury, Elke: Figurenkonstellation. In: Klaus Weimar / Harald Fricke / Klaus Grubmüller / Jan-Dirk Müller (Eds.): Reallexikon der deutschen Literaturwissenschaft, vol. 1. Berlin / New York 1997, pp. 591–593.
Roselt, Jens: Figur. In: Erika Fischer-Lichte / Doris Kolesch / Matthias Warstat (Eds.): Metzler Lexikon Theatertheorie. Stuttgart / Weimar 2005, pp. 104–107.
Wilpert, Gero von: Figur. In: G.v.W.: Sachwörterbuch der Literatur. Stuttgart 1989, p. 298.

3 Character Dictionaries

Calvocoressi, Peter: Who's who in der Bibel. Trans. by Angela Hausner. München 1998.
Choquet, David: 1000 Game Heroes. Köln 2002.
Collectif: Dictionnaire des personnages. Paris 1999.
Diederichs, Ulf: Who's who im Märchen. Düsseldorf 2005.
Fink, Gerhard: Who's who in der antiken Mythologie. München 2004.
Franklin V, Benjamin (Ed.): Dictionary of American Literary Characters. New York 1990.
Freeman, William: Everyman's Dictionary of Fictional Characters. London 1976.
Godin, Seth (Ed.): The Encyclopedia of Fictional People. The Most Important Characters of the 20th Century. New York 1996.
Grant, Michael / John Hazel: Lexikon der antiken Mythen und Gestalten. München 1980.
Horvilleur, Gilles (Ed.): Dictionnaire des personnages du cinéma. Paris 1998.
Karlan, Dan / Allan Lazar / Jeremy Salter: The 101 Most Influential People Who Never Lived: How Characters of Fiction, Myth, Legends, Television, and Movies Have Shaped Our Society, Changed Our Behavior, and Set the Course of History. New York et al. 2006.
Keller, Hiltgart L.: Reclams Lexikon der Heiligen und der biblischen Gestalten. Legende und Darstellung in der bildenden Kunst. 10th edn. Stuttgart 2005.
Leopold, Silke / Robert Maschka: Who's who in der Oper. Wiesbaden 2007.
Laffont, Robert / Valentino Bompiani: Dictionnaire des personnages littéraires et dramatiques de tous les temps et de tous les pays: poésie, théâtre, roman, musique. Paris 1994.
Salzman, Jack / Pamela Wilkinson: Major Characters in American Fiction. New York 1996.
Terrace, Vincent: Television Characters. 1,485 Profiles from 1947 to 2004. Jefferson, NC 2005.
van Rinsum, Annemarie / Wolfgang van Rinsum: Lexikon literarischer Gestalten II. Fremdsprachige Literatur. Stuttgart 1990.

van Rinsum, Annemarie / Wolfgang van Rinsum: Lexikon literarischer Gestalten. 2nd edn. Stuttgart 1993.

4 Trans-medial Theories and Analyses of Characters

4.1 General Publications

Chatman, Seymour: Story: Existents. In: S.C.: Story and Discourse. Narrative Structure in Fiction and Film. Ithaca, NY / London 1978, pp. 96–145.
Friend, Stacie: Fictional Characters. In: Philosophy Compass 2 (2007), pp. 141–156.
Greimas, Algirdas Julien: Les actants, les acteurs et les figures. In: A.J.G.: Du sens II: Essais sémiotiques. Paris 1974, pp.46–66.
Hamon, Philippe: Pour un statut sémiologique du personnage. In: Roland Barthes / Wolfgang Kayser / Wayne C. Booth / Philippe Hamon (Eds.): Poétique du récit. Paris 1977, pp. 115–180.
Heidbrink, Henriette / Rainer Leschke (Eds.): Formen der Figur in Künsten und Medien. Konstanz (forthcoming).
Lavocat, Françoise / Claude Murcia / Régis Salgado (Eds.): La fabrique du personnage. Paris 2007.

4.2 Definition and Ontology

Brock, Stuart: Fictionalism about Fictional Fictional Characters. In: Nous 36 (2002), pp. 1–21.
Crittenden, Charles: Fictional Characters and Logical Completeness. In: Poetics 11 (1982), pp. 331–344.
Currie, Gregory: The Characters of Fiction. In: G.C.: The Nature of Fiction. Cambridge et al. 1990, pp. 127–181.
Doležel, Lubomír: Heterocosmica. Fiction and Possible Worlds. Baltimore, MD / London 1998.
Eaton, Marcia M.: On Being a Character. In: British Journal of Aesthetics 16 (1976), pp. 24–31.
Eder, Jens: Was sind Figuren? Ein Beitrag zur interdisziplinären Fiktionstheorie. Paderborn 2008 (E-Book).
Friend, Stacie: Fictional Characters. In: Philosophy Compass 2/2 (2007), pp. 141–156.
Künne, Wolfgang: Abstrakte Gegenstände. Semantik und Ontologie. Frankfurt/M. 1983.
Lamarque, Peter: Fictional Entities. In: Edward Craig (Ed.): Routledge Encyclopedia of Philosophy. London / New York 1998, pp. 663–666.
Parsons, Terence: A Meinongian Analysis of Fictional Objects. In: Grazer Philosophische Studien 1 (1975), pp. 73–86.
Proudfoot, Diane: Fictional Entities. In: David E. Cooper (Ed.): A Companion to Aesthetics. Oxford / Cambridge, MA 1992, pp. 152–155.
Thomasson, Amie L.: Speaking of Fictional Characters. In: Dialectica 57/2 (2003), pp. 207–226.

van Inwagen, Peter: Creatures of Fiction. In: American Philosphical Quarterly 14 (1977), pp. 299–308.

4.3 Narratology and Semiotics; Characters as Actants

Butte, George: I Know That You Know That I Know: Narrating Subjects from Moll Flanders to Marnie. Columbus 2004.
Carroll, Noël (Ed.): The Aesthetics, Poetics, and Philosophy of Narrative. Malden, MA / Oxford 2009.
Chatman, Seymour: Coming to Terms: The Rhetoric of Narrative in Fiction and Film. Ithaca, NY 1990.
Greimas, Algirdas Julien: Strukturale Semantik. Methodologische Untersuchungen. Braunschweig 1971 (first print ›Sémantique structurale‹. Paris 1966).
Greimas, Algirdas Julien: Die Struktur der Erzählaktanten. In: Jens Ihwe (Ed.): Literaturwissenschaft und Linguistik, vol. 3. Frankfurt/M. 1972, pp. 218–238.
Greimas, Algirdas Julien: Actant and Actor. In: A.J.G. / J. Courtés: Semiotics and Language. An Analytical Dictionary. Bloomington 1982, pp. 5–8.
Reibling, Dylan: »They Only See What They Want to See«. Narrative Strategies in Films with Ontological Revelations. M.A.-Thesis. Montreal 2004.
Ryan, Marie-Laure: Possible Worlds, Artificial Intelligence, and Narrative Theory. Bloomington, IN / Indianapolis, IN 1991.
Ryan, Marie-Laure: Narrative as Virtual Reality. Immersion and Interactivity in Literature and Electronic Media. Baltimore, MD 2001.
Ryan, Marie-Laure: Avatars of Story. Minneapolis, MN 2001.

5 Characters in Film and Television

5.1 Comprehensive Books and Journal Issues

Eder, Jens: Die Figur im Film. Grundlagen der Figurenanalyse. Marburg 2008.
montage av 8/2 (1999). Special issue: Populäre Figuren.
Newman, Michael Z.: Characterization in American Independent Cinema. <http://zigzigger.blogspot.com/2007/05/characterization-in-american.html> (Dec. 5th, 2007).
Schweinitz, Jörg / Margrit Tröhler (Eds.): montage/av 15/2 (2006). Special issue: Figur und Perspektive I.
Schweinitz, Jörg / Margrit Tröhler (Eds.): montage/av 16/1 (2007). Special issue: Figur und Perspektive II.
Smith, Murray: Engaging Characters. Fiction, Emotion, and the Cinema. Oxford 1995.
Tomasi, Dario: Il personaggio. Cinema e racconto. Turin 1988.
Tröhler, Margrit et al. (Eds.): Iris: Revue de Théorie de l'Image et du Son 24 (1997). Special issue: Le personnage au cinéma. The Filmic Character.

5.2 General Surveys (Essays, Book Chapters)

Anderson, Joseph D.: Character. In: J.D.A.: The Reality of Illusion. Carbondale / Edwardsville 1996, pp. 127–143.
Blüher, Dominique: Französische Ansätze zur Analyse der filmischen Figur – André Gardies, Marc Vernet, Nicole Brenez. In: Heinz B. Heller (Ed.): Der Körper im Bild. Schauspielen – Darstellen – Erscheinen. Marburg 1999, pp. 61–70.
Eder, Jens: Filmfiguren: Rezeption und Analyse. In: Thomas Schick / Tobias Ebbrecht (Eds.): Emotion – Empathie – Figur: Spiel-Formen der Filmwahrnehmung. Berlin 2007, pp. 131–149.
Eder, Jens: Understanding Characters. In: Projections 4/1 (2010), pp. 16–40.
Fiske, John: Character Reading. In: J.F.: Television Culture. 9th edn. London / New York 1997, pp. 149–178.
Gardies, André: L'ácteur dans le système textuel du film. In: Francois Baby / André Gaudreault (Eds.): Cinéma et recit. Québec 1980, pp. 77–109.
Livingston, Paisley: Characterization and Fictional Truth in the Cinema. In: David Bordwell / Noël Carroll (Eds.): Post-Theory. Reconstructing Film Studies. Madison, WI / London 1996, pp. 149–174.
Mikos, Lothar: Helden, Versager und andere Typen. Strukturfunktionale Film- und Fernsehanalyse, Teil 7. In: medien praktisch 4 (1998), pp. 48–54.
Mikos, Lothar: Figuren und Akteure. In: L.M.: Film- und Fernsehanalyse. Konstanz 2003.
Phillips, Patrick: Character. In: P.P.: Understanding Film Texts. Meaning and Experience. London 2000, pp. 57–94.
Taylor, Henry M. / Margrit Tröhler: Zu ein paar Facetten der menschlichen Figur im Spielfilm. In: Heinz B. Heller (Ed.): Der Körper im Bild. Schauspielen – Darstellen – Erscheinen. Marburg 1999, pp. 137–151.
Vernet, Marc: Le personnage de film. In: Iris 7 (1986), pp. 81–110.

5.3 General Mimetic Properties of Characters: Body, Psyche, Sociality

Angerer, Marie-Luise / Kathrin Peters (Eds.): Future Bodies. Zur Visualisierung von Körpern in Science und Fiction. Wien 2002.
Aumont, Jacques: Du visage au cinéma. Paris 1992.
Barck, Joanna / Wolfgang Beilenhoff: montage/av 13/1 (2004). Special issue: Das Gesicht im Film / Filmologie und Psychoanalyse. Continued in 13/2 (2004).
Barck, Joanna / Petra Löffler (Eds.): Gesichter des Films. Bielefeld 2005.
Becker, Markus: »Ich bin ein Anderer«. Identitätswechsel im Film. Remscheid 2006.
Buchanan, Judith: »Orgies of Gesticulation?« Pedigree and Performance Codes in Sir Johnston Forbes-Robertson's and Ruggero Ruggeri's Silent Films of Hamlet. In: Shakespeare 2/1 (2006), pp. 24–46.
Centre de recherches de l'UFR d'études anglo-américaines (Ed.): Les bons et les méchants dans le cinéma anglophone: actes du congrès de la SERCIA, Université Paris X Nanterre, Sept. 2001. Nanterre 2005.
Comolli, Annie / Claudine de France (Eds.): Corps filmé, corps filmant. Nanterre 2006.
Dancey, Angela Clair: Before and After. The Makeover in Film and Culture. Ph.D.-Thesis. Columbus, OH 2005.

Davis, Therese: The Face on the Screen. Death, Recognition, and Spectatorship. Bristol 2003.
Dreux, Emmanuel: Les gestes dans le cinéma burlesque. Thèse doctorat (Cinéma et audiovisuel). Vincennes, Saint-Denis 2004.
Fellner, Markus: Psycho Movie. Zur Konstruktion psychischer Störung im Spielfilm. Bielefeld 2006.
Frölich, Margrit / Reinhard Middel / Karsten Visarius (Eds.): No Body Is Perfect. Körperbilder im Kino. Marburg 2002.
Gabbard, Glen / Krin Gabbard: Play It Again, Sigmund. Psychoanalysis and the Classical Hollywood Text. In: Journal of Popular Film and Television 18/1 (1990), pp. 6–17.
Gläser, Helga / Bernhard Groß / Hermann Kappelhoff (Eds.): Blick. Macht. Gesicht. Berlin 2001.
Görtz, Katharina: Die Suche nach der Identität. Erinnerung erzählen im Spielfilm. Remscheid 2007.
Grunert, Andréa: Le corps filmé. Condé-sur-Noireau 2006.
Heath, Stephen: Body, Voice. In: S.H.: Questions of Cinema. London 1981, pp. 176–193.
Heller, Heinz B. / Karl Prümm / Birgit Peulings (Eds.): Der Körper im Bild. Schauspielen – Darstellen – Erscheinen. Marburg 1999.
Helsby, Wendy (Ed.): Understanding Representation. London 2006.
Indick, William: Psycho Thrillers. Cinematic Explorations of the Mysteries of the Mind. Jefferson, NC 2006.
Kraus, Matthias: Der Körper im Bild. GFF-Tagung in Marburg. In: Medienwissenschaft/Rezensionen 4 (1996), pp. 395–399.
Löffler, Petra / Leander Scholz (Eds.): Das Gesicht ist eine starke Organisation. Köln 2004.
MacDougall, David: The Corporeal Image. Film, Ethnography, and the Senses. Princeton, NJ 2006.
Melzer, Patricia: Our Bodies as Our Selves. Body, Subjectivity, and (Virtual) Reality in »The Matrix«. In: P.M.: Alien Constructions. Science Fiction and Feminist Thought. Austin 2006.
Mimoso-Ruiz, Duarte (Ed.): De l'intime à l'altérité: itinéraires. Larbaud, Schnitzler, Woolf, Kubrick, Saura. Toulouse 2005.
Mirzoeff, Nicholas: Bodyscape: Art, Modernity and the Ideal Figure. New York et al. 1995.
Nolan, Amy Lynn: Re-envisioning the Mind-Body Labyrinth. Transformations in the Contemporary Narratives of Stanley Kubrick, Paul Auster, Christopher Nolan and Kathy Acker. Ph.D.-Thesis. East Lansing 2005.
Norden, Martin F. (Ed.): The Changing Face of Evil in Film and Television. Amsterdam / New York 2008.
Peucker, Brigitte: Verkörpernde Bilder. Das Bild des Körpers. Berlin 1999.
Pireyre, Raphaëlle: Un aspect du personnage moderne. Cadre cinématographique et miniaturisation du corps filmique. Mémoire de maîtrise (Cinéma et audiovisuel). Paris 2005.
Pomerance, Murray (Ed.): Bad: Infamy, Darkness, Evil, and Slime on Screen. Albany, NY 2004.
Roselt, Jens: Körperlichkeit. In: Helmut Schanze (Ed.): Metzler Lexikon Medientheorie – Medienwissenschaft. Stuttgart 2002, pp.166–167.
Shaviro, Steven: The Cinematic Body. Minneapolis, MN / London 1993.
Singer, Alina: Wer bin ich? Personale Identität im Film. Stuttgart 2008.

Szaryk, Evelyne: L'esthétique du corps dans l'oeuvre de Claire Denis. M.A.-Thesis. Halifax 2005.
Tan, Ed: Gesichtsausdruck und Emotion in Comic und Film. In: Matthias Brütsch et al. (Eds.): Kinogefühle. Emotionalität und Film. Marburg 2005, pp. 265–289.
The Velvet Light Trap 49 (2002): Beauty Marks.
Tischleder, Bärbel: Body Trouble. Whiteness und das amerikanische Gegenwartskino. Frankfurt/M. 2001.
Williams, Linda: Film Bodies. Gender, Genre, and Excess. In: Film Quarterly 44/4 (1991), pp. 2–13.
Wulff, Hans J.: Konzeptionen der psychischen Krankheit im Film. Ein Beitrag zur »strukturalen Lerngeschichte«. Münster 1985.
Wykes, Maggie / Barrie Gunter: The Media and Body Image: If Looks Could Kill. London / Thousand Oaks, CA 2006.
Zunshine, Lisa: Theory of Mind and Fictions of Embodied Transparency. In: Narrative 16/1 (2008), pp. 65–92.

5.4 Representation by Acting and Stars

Baron, Cynthia / Diane Carson / Frank P. Tomasulo (Eds.): More Than a Method. Trends and Traditions in Contemporary Film Performance. Detroit 2004.
Blank, Richard: Schauspielkunst in Theater und Film. Strasberg, Brecht, Stanislawski. Berlin 2001.
Bleicher, Joan Kristin (Ed.): Komiker, Komödianten, Komödienspieler. St. Augustin 2001.
Dyer, Richard: Heavenly Bodies. Film Stars and Society. London 1987.
Dyer, Richard: Stars. Supplementary Chapter by Paul McDonald. 2nd edn. London 1999.
Faulstich, Werner / Helmut Korte (Eds.): Der Star. Geschichte – Rezeption – Bedeutung (Interdisziplinäre Tagung der DFG zum Starphänomen). München 1997.
Faulstich, Werner / Ricarda Strobel: Die deutschen Fernsehstars, vols. 1–4. Göttingen 1998.
Francis, Terri: Embodied Fictions, Melancholy Migrations. Josephine Baker's Cinematic Celebrity. In: MFS Modern Fiction Studies 51/4 (2005), pp. 824–845.
Gilbert, Tiffany Nicole: Nuclear Diva. Constructing Cinematic Divadom in American Film, 1950–1959. Ph.D.-Thesis. Charlottesville, VA 2005.
Hayward, Susan: Star. In: S.H.: Key Concepts in Cinema Studies. London / New York 1996, pp. 337–348.
Hickethier, Knut (Ed.): Schauspielen und Montage. St. Augustin 1999.
Hickethier, Knut: Das Zucken im Mundwinkel. Schauspielen in den Medien. In: TheaterZeitSchrift 2/2 (1982), pp. 15–31.
Hickethier, Knut: Schauspielen in Film und Fernsehen. In: Kinoschriften. Jahrbuch der Gesellschaft für Filmtheorie. Wien 1990, pp. 45–68.
Hickethier, Knut: Spezialistinnen der kalten Ekstase. Zarah Leander und Magdalena Montezuma. Zum Schauspielen im Film. In: Konstanze Görres-Ohde / Andreas Stuhlmann (Eds.): Reflexionen in Texten – Bilder vom Menschen. Für Horst Ohde. Hamburg 1997, pp. 31–48.
Hickethier, Knut: Der Schauspieler als Produzent. Überlegungen zu einer Theorie des medialen Schauspielens. In: Heinz B. Heller / Karl Prümm / Birgit Peulings (Eds.): Der Körper im Bild: Schauspielen – Darstellen – Erscheinen. Marburg 1999, pp. 9–29.

Hickethier, Knut: Acting und Performance. Angela Winkler. In: Susanne Marschall / Norbert Grob (Eds.): Ladies, Vamps, Companions. Schauspielerinnen im Kino. St. Augustin 2000, pp. 250–267.
Kappelhoff, Hermann: Gestische Emblematik. Fassbinders »Katzelmacher« und Brechts »sozialer Gestus«. In: Knut Hickethier (Ed.): Schauspielen und Montage. St. Augustin 1999, pp. 193–221.
Kiefer, Bernd / Marcus Stiglegger (Eds.): Grenzsituationen spielen. Schauspielkunst im Film. St. Augustin 2004.
Koebner, Thomas (Ed.): Schauspielkunst im Film. St. Augustin 1998.
Krasner, David (Ed.): Method Acting Reconsidered. New York 2000.
Leibowitz, Ed: Playing a Historical Figure, You Can Copy… or Conquer. In: The New York Times, Aug. 6th, 2006.
Lenssen, Claudia (Ed.): Blaue Augen, blauer Fleck. Kino im Wandel von der Diva zum Girlie. Berlin 1997.
Liptay, Fabienne (Ed.): Komödiantinnen. München 2006.
Loukides, Paul / Linda F. Fuller: Beyond the Stars, vol. 1: Stock Characters in American Popular Film. Bowling Green, OH 1990.
Lovell, Alan / Peter Krämer (Eds.): Screen Acting. London / New York 1999.
Lowry, Stephen / Helmut Korte: Der Filmstar: Brigitte Bardot, James Dean, Götz George, Heinz Rühmann, Romy Schneider, Hanna Schygulla und neuere Stars. Stuttgart 2000.
Maltby, Richard: Performance. In: R.M.: Hollywood Cinema. 2nd edn. Malden, MA / Oxford 2003, pp. 368–412.
Marschall, Susanne / Norbert Grob (Eds.): Ladies, Vamps, Companions. Schauspielerinnen im Kino. St. Augustin 2000.
Morawetz, Thomas: Making Faces, Playing God. Identity and the Art of Transformational Makeup. Austin, TX 2001.
Morin, Edgar: Les Stars. Paris 1957.
Naremore, James: Acting in the Cinema. Berkeley / Los Angeles, CA 1988.
Patalas, Enno: Sozialgeschichte der Stars. Hamburg / Frankfurt/M. 1967.
Pearson, Roberta E.: Eloquent Gestures. The Transformation of Performance Style in the Griffith Biograph Films. Berkeley et al. 1992.
Riis, Johannes: Naturalist and Classical Styles in Early Sound Film Acting. In: Cinema Journal 43/3 (2004), pp. 3–17.
Schweinitz, Jörg: »Wenn hinter das Klischee persönliche Energien fahren…« – Jennifer Jason Lee. In: Susanne Marschall / Norbert Grob (Eds.): Ladies, Vamps, Companions. Schauspielerinnen im Kino. St. Augustin 2000, pp. 203–220.
Sternagel, Jörg: Methodische Schauspielkunst und amerikanisches Kino. Berlin 2005.
Wojcik, Pamela Robertson (Ed.): Movie Acting. The Film Reader. New York 2004.

5.5 Character Constellations

Kaplan, Michael Alan: Friendship and Citizenship in the Liberal Imaginary. Ph.D.-Thesis. Evanston, IL / Chicago, IL 2005.
Tröhler, Margrit: Hierarchien und Figurenkonstellationen. In: Britta Hartmann / Eggo Müller (Eds.): 7. Film- und fernsehwissenschaftliches Kolloquium / Potsdam 1994 (Gesellschaft für Theorie & Geschichte audiovisueller Kommunikation e.V.). Berlin 1995, pp. 20–27.

Tröhler, Margrit: Offene Welten ohne Helden. Plurale Figurenkonstellationen im Film. Marburg 2007.
Venus, Jochen: Teamspirit. Zur Morphologie der Gruppenfigur. In: Rainer Leschke / J.V. (Eds.): Spielformen im Spielfilm. Zur Medienmorphologie des Kinos nach der Postmoderne. Bielefeld 2007, pp. 299–327.
Wulff, Hans J.: Das empathische Feld. In: H.J.W. / Jan Sellmer (Eds.): Film und Psychologie – nach der kognitiven Phase? Marburg 2002, pp. 109–121.

5.6 Reception of Characters

Holland, Norman Norwood: Meeting Movies. Madison, NJ 2006.
Keppler, Angela: Interaktion ohne reales Gegenüber. Zur Wahrnehmung medialer Akteure im Fernsehen. In: Peter Vorderer (Ed.): Fernsehen als ›Beziehungskiste‹. Parasoziale Beziehungen und Interaktionen mit TV-Personen. Opladen 1996, pp. 11–24.
Newman, Michael Z.: Characterization as Social Cognition in »Welcome to the Dollhouse«. In: Film Studies. An International Review 8 (2006), pp. 53–67.
Persson, Per: Understanding Cinema. A Psychological Theory of Moving Imagery. Cambridge / New York 2003.
Wulff, Hans J.: Charaktersynthese und Paraperson. Das Rollenverhältnis der gespielten Fiktion. In: Peter Vorderer (Ed.): Fernsehen als ›Beziehungskiste‹. Parasoziale Beziehungen und Interaktionen mit TV-Personen. Opladen 1996, pp. 29–48.
Wulff, Hans J.: Attribution, Konsistenz, Charakter. Probleme der Wahrnehmung abgebildeter Personen. In: montage/av 15/2 (2006), pp. 45–62 (first pub. in French as: La perception des personnages de film. In: Iris. Revue de théorie de l'image et du son 24 (1997), pp. 15–32).

5.7 Identification, Empathy, Emotional Engagement with Characters

Barratt, Daniel: Tracing the Routes to Empathy. Association, Simulation, or Appraisal? In: Film Studies. An International Review 8 (2006), pp. 39–52.
Bartsch, Anne / Jens Eder / Kathrin Fahlenbrach (Eds.): Audiovisuelle Emotionen. Emotionsdarstellung und Emotionsvermittlung durch audiovisuelle Medienangebote. Köln 2007.
Brinckmann, Christine Noll: Empathie mit dem Tier. In: Cinema 42 (1997), pp. 60–69.
Brinckmann, Christine Noll: Somatische Empathie bei Hitchcock. Eine Skizze. In: Heinz B. Heller / Karl Prümm / Birgit Peulings (Eds.): Der Körper im Bild. Schauspielen – Darstellen – Erscheinen. Marburg 1999, pp. 111–120.
Brütsch, Matthias / Vinzenz Hediger / Ursula von Keitz / Alexandra Schneider / Margrit Tröhler (Eds.): Kinogefühle. Emotionalität und Film. Marburg 2005.
Christie, Ian / Michael Grant / Peter Stanfield (Eds.): Film Studies. An International Review 8 (2006). Special issue: Film, Cognition, and Emotion.
Currie, Gregory: The Paradox of Caring. Fiction and the Philosophy of Mind. In: Mette Hjort / Sue Laver (Eds.): Emotion and the Arts. New York 1997, pp. 63–77.
Currie, Gregory: Narrative Desire. In: Carl Plantinga / Greg Smith (Eds.): Passionate Views. Film, Cognition, and Emotion. Baltimore, MD / London 1999, pp. 183–199.

Doane, Mary Ann: The Desire to Desire. London 1987.
Eder, Jens: »Noch einmal mit Gefühl«. Zu Figur und Emotion im Spielfilm. In: Jan Sellmer / Hans J. Wulff (Eds.): Psychologie und Film – nach der kognitiven Phase? Marburg 2002, pp. 93–108.
Eder, Jens: Die Wege der Gefühle. Ein integratives Modell der Anteilnahme an Filmfiguren. In: Matthias Brütsch / Vinzenz Hediger / Ursula von Keitz / Alexandra Schneider / Margrit Tröhler (Eds.): Kinogefühle. Emotion und Film. Marburg 2005, pp. 225–242.
Eder, Jens: Imaginative Nähe zu Figuren. In: montage/av 15/2 (2006), pp. 135–160.
Eder, Jens: Ways of Being Close to Characters. In: Film Studies. An International Review 8 (2006), pp. 68–80.
Eder, Jens: Drei Thesen zur emotionalen Anteilnahme an Figuren. In: Mitteilungen des Deutschen Germanistenverbandes 3/54 (2007), pp. 362–378.
Friedberg, Anne: A Denial of Difference. Theories of Cinematic Identification. In: E. Anne Kaplan (Ed.): Psychoanalysis and Cinema. London / New York 1990, pp. 36–45.
Gaut, Berys: Identification and Emotion in Narrative Film. In: Carl Plantinga / Greg Smith (Eds.): Passionate Views. Film, Cognition, and Emotion. Baltimore, MD / London 1999, pp. 200–216.
Gaut, Berys: On Cinema and Perversion. 1994. <http://www.hanover.edu/philos/film/vol_01/gaut.htm> (Nov. 11th, 2000).
Grodal, Torben: Film, Character Simulation, and Emotion. In: Jörg Frieß / Britta Hartmann / Eggo Müller (Eds.): »Nicht allein das Laufbild auf der Leinwand...« Strukturen des Films als Erlebnispotentiale. Festschrift für Peter Wuss zum 60. Geburtstag. Berlin 2001, pp. 115–128.
Keppler, Angela: Person und Figur. Identifikationsangebote in Fernsehserien. In: montage/av 4/2 (1995), pp. 84–99.
Neill, Alex: Empathy and (Film) Fiction. In: David Bordwell / Noël Carroll (Eds.): Post-Theory. Reconstructing Film Studies. Madison, WI / London 1996, pp. 175–194.
Plantinga, Carl / Greg Smith (Eds.): Passionate Views. Film, Cognition, and Emotion. Baltimore, MD / London 1999.
Plantinga, Carl: Movie Pleasures and the Spectator's Experience. Toward a Cognitive Approach. 1999. <http://www.hanover.edu/philos/film/vol_02/planting.htm> (June 6th, 1999).
Plantinga, Carl: The Scene of Empathy and the Human Face on Film. In: Carl Plantinga / Greg Smith (Eds.): Passionate Views. Film, Cognition, and Emotion. Baltimore, MD / London 1999, pp. 239–255.
Plantinga, Carl: Synästhetische Affekte. Szenarios von Schuld und Scham in Hitchcocks Filmen. In: Anne Bartsch / Jens Eder / Kathrin Fahlenbrach (Eds.): Audiovisuelle Emotionen. Emotionsdarstellung und Emotionsvermittlung durch audiovisuelle Medienangebote. Köln 2007, pp. 350–361.
Rimé, Bernard / Céline Delfosse / Susanna Corsini: Emotional Fascination. Responses to Viewing Pictures of September 11 Attacks. In: Cognition and Emotion 19/6 (2005), pp. 923–932.
Ryssel, Dirk / Hans J. Wulff: Affektsteuerung durch Figuren. In: H.J.W. (Ed.): TV-Movies ›Made in Germany‹. Struktur, Gesellschaftsbild und Kinder-/Jugendschutz. 1. Teil. Historische, inhaltsanalytische und theoretische Studien. Kiel 2000, pp. 236–256.
Schick, Thomas / Tobias Ebbrecht (Eds.): Emotion – Empathie – Figur. Spielformen der Filmwahrnehmung. Berlin 2008.

Schimmack, Ulrich: Attentional Interference Effects of Emotional Pictures. Threat, Negativity, or Arousal? In: Emotion 5/1 (2005), pp. 55–66.
Schirra, Jörg / Stefan Carl-McGrath: Identifikationsformen in Computerspiel und Spielfilm. In: Michael Strübel (Ed.): Film und Krieg. Die Inszenierung von Politik zwischen Apologetik und Apokalypse. Opladen 2002, pp. 149–163.
Smith, Murray: Altered States. Character and Emotional Response in the Cinema. In: Cinema Journal 33/4 (1994), pp. 34–56.
Smith, Murray: Imagining from the Inside. In: Richard Allen / Murray Smith (Eds.): Film Theory and Philosophy. Oxford / New York 1997, pp. 412–430.
Smith, Murray: Gangsters, Cannibals, Aesthetes, or Apparently Perverse Allegiances. In: Carl Plantinga / Greg Smith (Eds.): Passionate Views. Film, Cognition, and Emotion. Baltimore, MD / London 1999, pp. 217–238.
Smith, Murray: Was macht es für einen Unterschied? Wissenschaft, Gefühl und Film. Trans. by Jens Eder. In: Anne Bartsch / Jens Eder / Kathrin Fahlenbrach (Eds.): Audiovisuelle Emotionen. Emotionsdarstellung und Emotionsvermittlung durch audiovisuelle Medienangebote. Köln 2007, pp. 41–61.
Vaage, Margrethe Bruun: Empathy and the Episodic Structure of Engagement in Fiction Film. In: Joseph D. Anderson / Barbara Fisher Anderson (Eds.): Narration and Spectatorship in Moving Images. Newcastle 2007, pp. 186–203.
Vaage, Margrethe Bruun: The Empathic Film Spectator in Analytic Philosophy and Naturalized Phenomenology. In: Film and Philosophy 10 (2006), pp. 21–38.
Van Beneden, Peter: Viewer ›Identification‹ with Characters in Television and Fiction Film. Nov. 1998. <http://www.aber.ac.uk/media/Students/pjv9801.html> (Oct. 24th, 2001).
Wulff, Hans J. / Dirk Ryssel: Affektsteuerung durch Figuren. In: H.J.W. (Ed.): TV-Movies ›Made in Germany‹. Struktur, Gesellschaftsbild und Kinder-/Jugendschutz. 1. Teil. Historische, inhaltsanalytische und theoretische Studien. Kiel 2000, pp. 236–256.
Wulff, Hans J.: Empathie und Filmverstehen. Eine Arbeitsbibliographie. In: Medienwissenschaft / Hamburg. Berichte und Papiere 33 (Feb. 2002). <http://www1.uni-hamburg.de/Medien//berichte/arbeiten/0033_03.html> (Nov 25th, 2008).
Wulff, Hans J.: Empathie als Dimension des Filmverstehens. In: montage/av 12/1 (2003), pp. 136–160.
Wulff, Hans J.: Moral und Empathie im Kino. Vom Moralisieren als einem Element der Rezeption. In: Matthias Brütsch / Vinzenz Hediger / Ursula von Keitz / Alexandra Schneider / Margrit Tröhler (Eds.): Kinogefühle. Emotionalität und Film. Marburg 2005, pp. 377–394.

5.8 (Stereo-)Typification

Dyer, Richard: Stereotyping. In: R.D. (Ed.): Gays in Film. London 1977, pp. 27–39.
Gwózdz, Andrzej: Das Bild des Deutschen im polnischen Nachkriegskino. In: Katrin Berwanger (Ed.): Stereotyp und Geschichtsmythos in Kunst und Sprache. Die Kultur Ostmitteleuropas in Beiträgen zur Potsdamer Tagung, 16.-18. Januar 2003. Frankfurt/M. et al. 2005, pp. 519–532.

Hammer, Tonya R.: Myths, Stereotypes, and Controlling Images in Film. A Feminist Content Analysis of Hollywood's Portrayal of Women's Career Choices. Ph.D.-Thesis. San Antonio, TX 2008.
Hanisch, Michael: »Kann denn Lüge Wahrheit sein?« Stereotypen im polnischen und deutschen Film. Berlin 1995.
Hayward, Susan: Stereotype. In: S.H.: Key Concepts in Cinema Studies. London / New York 1996, pp. 348–353.
Kracauer, Siegfried: National Types as Hollywood Presents Them. In: Public Opinion Quarterly 13/1 (1949), pp. 53–72.
Leab, Daniel J.: From Sambo to Superspade. The Black Experience in Motion Pictures. Boston 1975.
Lester, Paul Martin / Susan Dente Ross (Eds.): Images that Injure. Pictorial Stereotypes in the Media. 2nd edn. Westport, CT / London 2003.
Margolies, Harriet: Stereotypical Strategies. Black Film Aesthetics, Spectator Positioning, and Self-Directed Stereotypes in »Hollywood Shuffle« and »I'm Gonna Git You Sucka«. In: Cinema Journal 38/3 (1999), pp. 50–66.
Neale, Steve: The Same Old Story. Stereotypes and Difference [1979/80]. In: Manuel Alvarado / Edward Buscombe / Richard Collins (Eds.): The Screen Education Reader. Cinema, Televison, Culture. New York 1993, pp. 41–47.
Pleyer, Peter: Nationale und soziale Stereotypen im gegenwärtigen deutschen Spielfilm. Münster 1968.
Schneider, Irmela: Zur Theorie des Stereotyps. In: Beiträge zur Film- und Fernsehwissenschaft 33/43 (1992), pp. 129–147.
Schweinitz, Jörg: Film und Stereotyp. Eine Herausforderung für das Kino und die Filmtheorie. Zur Geschichte eines Mediendiskurses. Berlin 2006.

6 Characters in Literature and Theatre

6.1 Monographs on Character in Literature

Bal, Mieke: Mensen van papier. Over personages in de literatuur. Assen 1979.
Bayley, John: The Characters of Love. A study in the literature of personality. London 1962.
Cartano, Tony / François Coupry / Claude Delarue: Roman. Les personnages. Paris 1982.
Docherty, Thomas: Reading (Absent) Character. Towards a Theory of Characterization in Fiction. Oxford 1983.
Glaudes, Pierre / Yves Reuter: Personnage et histoire littéraire. Toulouse 1991.
Glaudes, Pierre / Yves Reuter: Le personnage. Paris 1998.
Hansen, Per Krogh: Karakterens rolle. Aspekter af en litteraer karakterologi. Holte 2000.
Harvey, William James: Character and the Novel. London 1965.
Hochman, Baruch: Character in Literature. Ithaca, NY / London 1985.
Jannidis, Fotis: Figur und Person. Beitrag zu einer historischen Narratologie. Berlin 2004.
Jouve, Vincent: L'effet-personnage dans le roman. Paris 1992.
Koch, Thomas: Literarische Menschendarstellung. Studien zu ihrer Theorie und Praxis. Tübingen 1991.
Miraux, Jean-Philippe: Le personnage de roman. Genèse, continuité, rupture. Paris 1997.
Montalbetti, Christine (Ed.): Le personnage. Paris 2003.

Nieragden, Göran: Figurendarstellung im Roman. Eine narratologische Systematik am Beispiel von David Lodges »Changing Places« und Ian McEwans »The Child in Time«. Trier 1995.
Paris, Bernard J.: Imagined Human Beings. A Psychological Approach to Character and Conflict in Literature. New York / London 1997.
Phelan, James: Reading People, Reading Plots. Character, Progression, and the Interpretation of Narrative. Chicago, IL / London 1989.
Phelan, James: Living to Tell About It. A Rhetoric and Ethics of Character Narration. Ithaca, NY 2005.
Price, Martin: Forms of Life. Character and Moral Imagination in the Novel. New Haven 1983.
Schneider, Ralf: Grundriss zur kognitiven Theorie der Figurenrezeption am Beispiel des viktorianischen Romans. Tübingen 2000.
Seed, David (Ed.): A Companion to Science Fiction. Malden, MA / Oxford 2005.
Walcutt, Charles Child: Man's Changing Mask. Modes and Methods of Characterization in Fiction. Minneapolis, MN 1966.

6.2 General Surveys (Essays, Book Chapters)

Bortolussi, Marisa / Peter Dixon: Characters and Characterization. In: M.B. / P.D.: Psychonarratology. Foundations for the Empirical Study of Literary Response. Cambridge / New York 2003, pp. 133–163.
Bredin, Hugh: The Displacement of Character in Narrative Theory. In: British Journal of Aesthetics 22/4 (1982), pp. 291–300.
Chatman, Seymour: On the Formalist-Structuralist Theory of Character. In: Journal of Literary Semantics 1 (1972), pp. 57–79.
Cohan, Steven: Figures Beyond the Text. A Theory of Readable Character in the Novel. In: Mark Spilka / Caroline McCracken-Flesher (Eds.): Why the Novel Matters. A Postmodern Perplex. Bloomington, IN 1990, pp. 113–136 (first publ. in: Novel. A Forum on Fiction 17/1 (1983), pp. 5–27).
Ewen, Joseph: The Theory of Character in Narrative Fiction. In: Hasifrut 3 (1971), pp. 1–30.
Fokkema, Aleid: Postmodern Characters. A Study of Characterization in British and American Postmodern Fiction. Amsterdam et al. 1991.
Forster, E. M.: People. In: E.M.F.: Aspects of the Novel. London 1927, pp. 63–112.
Frow, John: Spectacle Binding. On Character. In: Poetics Today 7/2 (1986), pp. 227–249.
Garvey, James: Characterization in Narrative. In: Poetics 7 (1978), pp. 63–78.
Gillie, Christopher: Character in English Literature. London 1967.
Grabes, Herbert: Wie aus Sätzen Personen werden. Über die Erforschung literarischer Figuren. In: Poetica 10 (1978), pp. 405–428.
Hansen, Per Krogh: Figuren. In: Silke Lahn / Jan Christoph Meister: Einführung in die Erzähltextanalyse. Stuttgart / Weimar 2008, pp. 232–246.
Jahn, Manfred: Characters and Characterization. In: M.J.: Narratology. A Guide to the Theory of Narrative. Universität Köln 2005.
Jannidis, Fotis: Zur Erzähltheorie der Figur. Alte Probleme und neue Lösungen. In: Der Deutschunterricht 57/2 (2005), pp. 19–29.

Knapp, John V.: Introduction. Self-Preservation and Self-Transformation. Interdisciplinary Approaches to Literary Character. In: Style 24/3 (1990), pp. 349–364.

Lotman, Jurij M.: Der Begriff der Figur. Von der Spezifik der künstlerischen Welt, Figur und Charakter. In: J.M.L.: Die Struktur literarischer Texte. München 1972, pp. 340–367.

Ludwig, Hans-Werner: Figur und Handlung. In: H.-W.L. (Ed.): Arbeitsbuch Romananalyse. Tübingen 1989, pp. 106–145.

Margolin, Uri: Characterization in Narrative. Some Theoretical Prolegomena. In: Neophilologus 67 (1983), pp. 1–14.

Margolin, Uri: Characters and Their Versions. In: Calin-Andrei Mihailescu / Walid Hamarneh (Eds.): Fiction Updated. Theories of Fictionality, Narratology, and Poetics. Toronto 1996, pp. 113–132.

Margolin, Uri: Characters in Literary Narrative. Representation and Signification. In: Semiotica 106/3&4 (1995), pp. 373–392.

Margolin, Uri: The Doer and the Deed. Action as Basis for Characterization in Narrative. In: Poetics Today 7/2 (1986), pp. 205–225.

Martin, Wallace: The Composition of Character. In: M.W.: Recent Theories of Narrative. Ithaca, NY / London 1986, pp. 116–121.

Mead, Gerald: The Representation of Fictional Character. In: Style 24/3 (1990), pp. 440–452.

Mudrick, Marvin: Character and Event in Fiction. In: Yale Review 50 (1961), pp. 202–218.

Petsch, Robert: Die epischen Figuren. In: R.P.: Wesen und Formen der Erzählkunst. Halle 1934, pp. 117–139.

Petsch, Robert: Die Umwelt der Figuren. In: R.P.: Wesen und Formen der Erzählkunst. Halle 1934, pp. 140–165.

Pfister, Manfred: Personal und Figur. In: M.P.: Das Drama. 6th edn. München 1988, pp. 220–264.

Phelan, James: Character and Judgment in Narrative and in Lyric. Toward an Understanding of the Audience's Engagement in »The Waves«. In: Style 24/3 (1990), pp. 408–421.

Phelan, James: Character, Progression, and the Mimetic-Didactic Distinction. In: Modern Philology 84/3 (1984), pp. 282–299.

Price, Martin: People of the Book. In: Critical Inquiry 1 (1975), pp. 605–622.

Price, Martin: The Logic of Intensity. More on Character. In: Critical Inquiry 2 (1975), pp. 369–79.

Price, Martin: The Other Self. Thoughts about Character in the Novel. In: Maynard Mack / Ian Gregor (Eds.): Imagined Worlds. London 1968, pp. 279–299.

Ransom, John Crowe: Characters and Character. In: American Review 6 (1936), pp. 271–288.

Richardson, Brian: Beyond Poststructuralism. Theory of Character, the Personae of Modern Drama, and the Antinomies of Critical Theory. In: Modern Drama 40 (1997), pp. 86–99.

Rimmon-Kenan, Shlomith: Story: Characters. In: S.R.-K.: Narrative Fiction. Contemporary Poetics. 6th edn. London 1996, pp. 29–42.

Rimmon-Kenan, Shlomith: Text: Characterization. In: S.R.-K.: Narrative Fiction. Contemporary Poetics. 6th edn. London 1996, pp. 59–70.

Rosenberg, Brian: Character in Fiction 1900–1980. In: Bulletin of Bibliography 40/4 (1983), pp. 200–205.

Schlobin, Roger: Character, the Fantastic, and the Failure of Contemporary Literary Theory. 1999. <http://wpl.lib.in.us/roger/CHAR95.html> (July 13th, 1999).
Schneider, Ralf: Toward a Cognitive Theory of Literary Character. The Dynamics of Mental-Model Construction. In: Style 35 (2001), pp. 607–640.
Scholes, Robert / Robert Kellogg: Character in Narrative. In: R.S. / R.K.: The Nature of Narrative. London 1966, pp. 160–206.
Spilka, Mark: Character as a Lost Cause. In: Novel 11 (1978), pp. 197–219.
Stückrath, Jörn: Entwurf eines Kategoriensystems zur Analyse epischer Figuren und Handlungen. Am Beispiel von Sarah Kirschs Erzählung »Blitz aus heiterem Himmel«. In: Bettina Hurrelmann / Maria Kublitz / Brigitte Röttger (Eds.): Man müsste ein Mann sein...? Interpretationen und Kontroversen zu Geschlechtertausch-Geschichten in der Frauenliteratur. Düsseldorf 1987, pp. 83–103.
Stückrath, Jörn: Figur und Handlung. In: Helmut Brackert / J.S. (Eds.): Literaturwissenschaft. Ein Grundkurs. Reinbek 1992, pp. 40–54.
Stückrath, Jörn: Schwierigkeiten beim Beschreiben literarischer Figuren. Ein Versuch strukturalistische und literaturpsychologische Begriffe der Figurenanalyse zu vermitteln. In: Diskussion Deutsch 104 (1988), pp. 356–373.
Stückrath, Jörn: Wovon eigentlich handelt die epische und dramatische Literatur? Kritik und Rekonstruktion der Begriffe ›Figur‹ und ›Geschehen‹. In: Hartmut Eggert / Ulrich Profitlich / Klaus R. Scherpe (Eds.): Geschichte als Literatur. Formen und Grenzen der Repräsentation von Vergangenheit. Stuttgart 1990, pp. 284–295.
Todorov, Tzvetan: Erzählpersonen [1967]. In: T.T.: Poetik der Prosa. Frankfurt/M. 1972, pp. 77–89.
Weinsheimer, Joel: Theory of Character. Emma. In: Poetics Today 1 (1979), pp. 185–211.
Wilson, Robert R.: Approaching a Theory of ›Character‹. In: The Humanities Association Review 27 (1976), pp. 32–46.
Wilson, Robert R.: The Bright Chimera. Character as a Literary Term. In: Critical Inquiry 5 (1979), pp. 725–749.
Zöllner-Weber, Amelie: Formale Repräsentation und Beschreibung von literarischen Figuren. In: Forum Computerphilologie (2006).

6.3 Journal Issues

Harshav, Benjamin (Ed.):. Poetics Today 7/2 (1986). Special issue: Character.
Knapp, John V. (Ed.): Style 24/3 (1990). Special issue: Literary Character.
Cohen, Ralph: New Literary History 5/2 (1974). Special issue: Changing Views of Character.

6.4 Definition and Ontology

Britton, John: A. C. Bradley and Those Children of Lady Macbeth. In: Shakespeare Quarterly 12/3 (1961), pp. 349–351.
Cixous, Hélène: The Character of ›Character‹. In: New Literary History 5 (1974), pp. 383–402.
Cohan, Steven: Figures Beyond the Text. A Theory of Readable Character in the Novel. In: Novel 17/1 (1983), pp. 5–27.

Fisch, Harold: Character as Linguistic Sign. In: New Literary History 21/3 (1990), pp. 593–606.
Gass, William H.: The Concept of Character in Fiction. In: Michael J. Hoffman / Patrick D. Murphy (Eds.): Essentials of the Theory of Fiction. Durham / London 1988, pp. 268–276.
Harweg, Roland: Are Fielding's Shamela and Richardson's Pamela One and the Same Person? A Contribution to the Problem of the Number of Fictive Worlds. In: Style 38 (2004), pp. 290–301.
Knights, Lionel C.: How many Children had Lady Macbeth? An Essay in the Theory and Practice of Shakespeare Criticism [1933]. New York 1973.
Margolin, Uri: The What, the When, and the How of Being a Character in Literary Narrative. In: Style 24/3 (1990), pp. 453–468.
Margolin, Uri: Individuals in Narrative Worlds: An Ontological Perspective. In: Poetics Today 11/4 (1990), pp. 843–871.
Margolin, Uri: The Constitution of Story Worlds: Fictional and/or Otherwise. In: Semiotica 131 (2000), pp. 327–357.
Pickrel, Paul: Character as Nominal. A Sketch for a Theory. In: Novel 22 (1988), pp. 66–85.
Pollard, Dennis E.B.: On Talk ›about‹ Characters. In: British Journal of Aesthetics 16 (1976), pp. 367–369.
Pollard, Dennis E.B.: Characters and Counterparts. In: Journal of Literary Semantics 8 (1978), pp. 71–77.
Suits, David B.: Fictional Characters Are just like Us. In: Philosophy and Literature 18 (1994), pp. 105–108.
Wilkinson, Jennifer: On Being a Fictional Character. Journal of Literary Studies/Tydskrif vir Literatuurwetenskap, 13/3&4 (1997), pp. 317–33.

6.5 General Mimetic Aspects of Characters: Body, Psyche, Sociality

Anz, Thomas: Literatur der Existenz. Literarische Psychopathographie und ihre soziale Bedeutung im Frühexpressionismus. Stuttgart 1977.
Benthien, Claudia: Haut. Literaturgeschichte – Körperbilder – Grenzdiskurse. Reinbek 1999.
Bersani, Leo: A Future for Astyanax. Character and Desire in Literature. Boston 1976.
Groddeck, Wolfgang / Ulrich Stadler (Eds.): Physiognomie und Pathognomie. Zur literarischen Darstellung von Individualität. Festschrift für Karl Pestalozzi zum 65. Geburtstag. Berlin et al. 1994.
Herman, David (Ed.): The Emergence of Mind. Representations of Consciousness in Narrative Discourse in English. Lincoln, NE 2010.
Holland, Norman N.: The Mind and the Book. A Long Look at Psychoanalytic Literary Criticism. 1998. <http://www.clas.ufl.edu/users/nnh/mindbook.htm> (Apr. 18th, 2001).
Jannidis, Fotis: »Individuum est ineffabile«. Zur Veränderung der Individualitätssemantik im 18. Jahrhundert und ihrer Auswirkung auf die Figurenkonzeption im Roman. In: Aufklärung 9/2 (1996), pp. 77–110.

Jannidis, Fotis: Zu anthropologischen Aspekten der Figur. In: Rüdiger Zymner / Manfred Engel (Eds.): Anthropologie der Literatur. Paderborn 2004, pp. 155–172.
Meyer, Richard M.: Lebenswahrheit dichterischer Gestalten. In: R.M.M.: Aufsätze literarhistorischen und biographischen Inhalts, 2 vols. Berlin 1911, pp. 108–148.
Palmer, Alan: Fictional Minds. Lincoln, NE 2004.
Palmer, Alan: Intermental Thought in the Novel. The Middlemarch Mind. In: Style 39/4 (2005), pp. 427–439.

6.6 Literary Techniques of Characterization

Guntli, Markus: Elemente der Charakterisierung von Romanfiguren. Ph.D.-Thesis. Zürich 1981.
Heier, Edmund: The Literary Portrait as a Device of Characterization. In: Neophilologus 60 (1976), pp. 321–333.
Lebowitz, Michael: Creating Characters in a Story-Telling Universe. In: Poetics 13 (1984), pp. 171–194.
Margolin, Uri: Introducing and Sustaining Characters in Literary Narrative. A Set of Conditions. In: Style 21 (1987), pp. 107–124.
Palmer, Alan: The Construction of Fictional Minds. In: Narrative 10/1 (2002), pp. 28–46.
Petruso, Thomas F.: Life Made Real. Characterization in the Novel since Proust and Joyce. Ann Arbor, MI 1991.
Schwarz, Daniel: Character and Characterization. An Inquiry. In: Journal of Narrative Technique 19/1 (1989), pp. 85–105.
Wenger, Christian N.: An Introduction to the Aesthetics of Literary Portraiture. In: Publications of the Modern Language Association of America 50 (1935), pp. 615–629.
Pelling, Christopher B. (Ed.): Characterization and Individuality in Greek Literature. Oxford 1990.

6.7 Proper Names

Birus, Hendrik: Poetische Namengebung. Göttingen 1978.
Birus, Hendrik: Vorschlag zu einer Typologie literarischer Namen. In: Zeitschrift für Literaturwissenschaft und Linguistik 67 (1987), pp. 38–51.
Lamping, Dieter: Der Name in der Erzählung. Zur Poetik des Personennamens. Bonn 1983.
Sanford, A.J. / K. Moar / S.C. Garrod.: Proper Names as Controllers of Discourse Focus. In: Language and Speech 31 (1988), pp. 43–56.
Wolterstorff, Nicholas: Characters and their Names. In: Poetics 8 (1979), pp. 101–127.

6.8 Characters and Narrators

Chatman, Seymour: Characters and Narrators. Filter, Center, Slant, and Interest-Focus. In: Poetics Today 7/2 (1986), pp. 189–204.
Shen, Dan: Unreliability and Characterization. In: Style 23 (2002), pp. 300–311.

6.9 Acting Theory

Brecht, Bertolt: Kurze Beschreibung einer neuen Technik der Schauspielkunst, die einen Verfremdungseffekt hervorbringt. In: B.B.: Gesammelte Werke, vol. 15. Ed. by Elisabeth Hauptmann. Frankfurt/M. 1967, pp. 341–357.
Roselt, Jens (Ed.): Seelen mit Methode. Schauspieltheorien vom Barock bis zum postdramatischen Theater. Berlin 2005.

6.10 Cognitive Reception of Characters

Andringa, Els: Leservoraussetzungen und die Rezeption literarischer Figuren. In: Diskussion Deutsch 19 (1988), pp. 622–644.
Bruder, Gail A. / Janyce Wiebe: Recognizing Subjectivity and Identifying Subjective Characters in Third-Person Fictional Narrative. In: Judith F. Duchan / Gail A. Bruder / Lynne E. Hewitt (Eds.): Deixis in Narrative. A Cognitive Science Perspective. Hillsdale 1995, pp. 341–358.
Culpeper, Jonathan / Elena Semino: Constructing Witches and Spells. Speech Acts and Activity Types in Early Modern England. In: Journal of Historical Pragmatics 1 (2000), pp. 97–116.
Culpeper, Jonathan / Mick Short / Peter Verdonk (Eds.): Exploring the Language of Drama. From Text to Context. London 1998.
Culpeper, Jonathan: Inferring Character from Texts. Attribution Theory and Foregrounding Theory. In: Poetics 23/5 (1996), pp. 335–361.
Culpeper, Jonathan: A Cognitive Approach to Characterization. Katherina in Shakespeare's »The Taming of the Shrew«. In: Language and Literature 9/4 (2000), pp. 291–316.
Culpeper, Jonathan: Language and Characterisation. People in Plays and Other Texts. Harlow 2001.
Culpeper, Jonathan: A Cognitive Stylistic Approach to Characterisation. In: J.C. / E. Semino (Eds.): Cognitive Stylistics. Language and Cognition in Text Analysis. Amsterdam 2002, pp. 251–277.
Graesser, Arthur C. / Cheryl Bowers / Ute J. Bayen / Xiangen Hu: Who Said What? Who Knows What? Tracking Speakers and Knowledge in Narratives. In: Willie van Peer / Seymour Chatman (Eds.): New Perspectives on Narrative Perspective. New York 2001, pp. 255–272.
Graesser, Arthur C. / Cheryl Bowers / B. Olde / K. White / N. Person: Who Knows What? Propagation of Knowledge among Agents in a Literary Story World. In: Poetics 26 (1999), pp. 143–178.
Hillis Miller, J.: Character in the Novel. A ›Real Illusion‹. In: Samuel I. Mintz / Alice Chandler / Christopher Mulvey (Eds.): From Smollet to James. Studies in the Novel and Other Essays Presented to Edgar Johnson. Charlottesville 1981, pp. 277–285.
Hunter, Ian: Reading Character. In: Southern Review 16/2 (1993), pp. 226–243.
Palmer, Alan: Attribution Theory. In: Marina Lambrou / Peter Stockwell (Eds.): Contemporary Stylistics. London 2007, pp. 81–92.
Pollard-Gott, Lucy: Attribution Theory and the Novel. In: Poetics 21 (1993), pp. 499–524.

Rapp, David N. / Richard Gerrig / Deborah A. Prentice: Readers' Trait-Based Models of Characters in Narrative Comprehension. In: Journal of Memory and Language 45 (2001), pp. 737–750.
Schauber, Ellen / Ellen Spolsky: Reader, Language, and Character. In: Bucknell Review 26/1 (1981), pp. 33–51.
Schreiber, Andrew J.: Sign, Seme, and the Psychological Character. Some Thoughts on Roland Barthes' »S/Z« and the Realistic Novel. In: Journal of Narrative Technique 21/3 (1991), pp. 262–273.
Semino, Elena: Blending and Characters' Mental Functioning in Virginia Woolf's »Lappin and Lapinova«. In: Language and Literature 15/1 (2006), pp. 55–72.Van Peer, Willie / Henk Pander Maat: Narrative Perspective and the Interpretation of Characters' Motives. In: Language and Literature 10/3 (2001), pp. 229–241.
Wintermantel, Margret / Ursula Christmann: Textverarbeitung. Empirische Untersuchung zum Verstehen einer Personenbeschreibung. Heidelberg 1983.
Zunshine, Lisa: Theory of Mind and Experimental Representations of Fictional Consciousness. In: Narrative 11/3 (2003), pp. 270–291.
Zunshine, Lisa: Why We Read Fiction. Theory of Mind and the Novel. Columbus 2006.

6.11 Identification, Empathy, Emotional Engagement with Characters

Adler, Günther: Identifikation und Distanzierung bei der Literaturrezeption. In: Weimarer Beiträge 26/2 (1980), pp. 43–72.
Andringa, Els: The Interface between Fiction and Life. Patterns of Identification in Reading Autobiographies. In: Poetics Today 25/2 (2004), pp. 205–240.
Andringa, Els: Wandel der literarischen Identifikation. Eine experimentelle Untersuchung. In: SPIEL – Siegener Periodikum zur Internationalen Empirischen Literaturwissenschaft 3/1 (1984), pp. 27–56.
Anz, Thomas: Literatur und Lust. Glück und Unglück beim Lesen. München 1998.
Coplan, Amy: Empathetic Engagement with Narrative Fiction. In: Journal of Aesthetics and Art Criticism 62/2 (2004), pp. 141–152.
Jauß, Hans Robert: Ästhetische Identifikation – Versuch über den literarischen Helden. In: H.R.J.: Ästhetische Erfahrung und literarische Hermeneutik. Frankfurt/M. 1982, pp. 244–292.
Lees, Francis Noel: Identification and Emotion in the Novel. A Feature of Narrative Method. In: British Journal of Aesthetics 4 (1964), pp. 109–113.
Vermeule, Blakey: Why Do We Care about Literary Characters? Baltimore 2010.

6.12 Poetics, Creative Writing

Aristoteles: Poetik. Trans. and ed. by Manfred Fuhrmann. Stuttgart 1982.
Card, Orson S.: Character and Viewpoint. Cincinnati, OH 1997.
Freytag, Gustav: Die Technik des Dramas [1863]. In: G.F.: Gesammelte Werke, vol. 14. 2nd edn. Leipzig 1896–1897.
Gottsched, Johann Christoph: Versuch einer Critischen Dichtkunst. Leipzig 1730.
Kress, Nancy: Dynamic Characters. Cincinnati 1998.

Lauther, Howard: Creating Characters. A Writer's Reference to the Personality Traits That Bring Fictional People to Life. Jefferson, NC 1998.
Spielhagen, Friedrich: Beiträge zur Theorie und Technik des Romans. Leipzig 1883.

6.13 (Stereo-)Typification

Amossy, Ruth: Stereotypes and Representation in Fiction. In: Poetics Today 5/4 (1984), pp. 689–700.
Beller, Manfred / Leersen, Joeb (eds.): Imagology: The cultural construction and literary representation of national characters. A critical survey. Amsterdam, New York 2007.
Fishelov, David: Types of Character, Characteristics of Types. In: Style 24/3 (1990), pp. 422–439.
Florack, Ruth: Bekannte Fremde. Zu Herkunft und Funktion nationaler Stereotype in der Literatur. Tübingen 2007.
Pickrel, Paul: Flat and Round Characters Reconsidered. In: Journal of Narrative Technique 18/3 (1988), pp. 181–198.
Wunderlich, Werner: Figur und Typus. Kleine Phänomenologie des literarischen Personals. In: Versants 37 (2000), pp. 19–68.

7 Characters in Computer Media

7.1 Books

Baillie-de Byl, Penny: Programming Believable Characters for Computer Games. Hingham 2004.
Klevjer, Rune: What is the Avatar? Fiction and Embodiment in Avatar-Based Singleplayer Computer Games. Ph.D.-Thesis. Bergen 2007.
<http://folk.uib.no/smkrk/docs/RuneKlevjer_What%20is%20the%20Avatar_finalprint.pdf> (Nov. 23rd, 2008).
Manninen, Tony: Rich Interaction Model for Game and Virtual Environment Design. Ph.D.-Thesis. Oulu 2004.
<http://herkules.oulu.fi/isbn9514272544/isbn9514272544.pdf> (Nov. 23rd, 2008).
Sheldon, Lee: Character Development and Storytelling for Games. Boston 2004.

7.2 Essays

Angelini, James R. / Debbie P. C. Goh / Susan Tyler Eastman / Jason A. Rosow / Tyler Dodge / Wenchang Deng / Na Zhou: Prominence of Characters on Television Program Websites. In: Howard Journal of Communications 20/3 (2009), pp. 276–294.
Bailenson, Jeremy N. / A. Beall / J. Blascovich / M. Raimundo / M. Weishbush: Intelligent Agents Who Wear Your Face: User's Reactions to the Virtual Self. In: Lecture Notes in Artificial Intelligence 2190 (2001), pp. 86–99.

Bailenson, Jeremy N. / Nick Yee / Dan Merget / Ralph Schroeder: The Effect of Behavioral Realism and Form Realism of Real-Time Avatar Faces on Verbal Disclosure, Nonverbal Disclosure, Emotion Recognition, and Copresence in Dyadic Interaction. In: Presence: Teleoperators and Virtual Environments 15/4 (2006), pp. 359–372.

Barlett, Christopher / Richard J. Harris: The Impact of Body Emphasizing Video Games on Body Image Concerns in Men and Women. In: Sex Roles 59/7&8 (2008), pp. 586–601.

Behm-Morawitz, Elizabeth / Dana Mastro: The Effects of the Sexualization of Female Video Game Characters on Gender Stereotyping and Female Self-Concept. In: Sex Roles 61/11&12 (2009), pp. 808–823.

Catrambone, Richard / John T. Stasko / Jun Xiao: Anthropomorphic Agents as a User Interface Paradigm. Experimental Findings and a Framework for Research. In: Proceedings of CogSci (2002), pp. 166–171.

De Rosis, Fiorella / Catherine Pelachaud / Isabella Poggi / Valeria Carofiglio / Berardina De Carolis: From Greta's Mind to Her Face. Modelling the Dynamics of Affective States in a Conversational Embodied Agent. In: International Journal of Human-Computer Studies 59/1&2 (2003), pp. 81–118.

Dehn, Doris M. / Suzanne Van Mulken: The Impact of Animated Interface Agents. A Review of Empirical Research. In: International Journal of Human-Computer Studies 52/1 (2000), pp. 1–22.

Dill, Karen E. / Kathryn P. Thill: Video Game Characters and the Socialization of Gender Roles. Young People's Perceptions Mirror Sexist Media Depictions. In: Sex Roles 57/11&12 (2007), pp. 851–864.

Dryer, D. Christopher: Getting Personal with Computers. How to Design Personalities for Agents. In: Applied Artificial Intelligence 13/3 (1999), pp. 273–295.

Duke, D. J. / P. J. Barnard / N. Halper / M. Mellin: Rendering and Affect. In: Computer Graphics Forum 22/3 (2003), pp. 359–368.

Fitzpatrick, Robert / Martin Walsh / Michael Nitsche: Character Data Sets and Parameterized Morality. 2005. <http://www.aestheticsofplay.org/fitzpatrickwalshnitsche.php> (Nov. 24th, 2008).

Gong, Li / Tinting Lu / Carrie Lynn Reinhard / Zack Kerr: Perception and Categorization of Computer-Generated Characters. 2006. <http://www.allacademic.com//meta/p_mla_apa_research_citation/0/9/1/9/2/pages91921/p91921-1.php> (Nov. 23rd, 2008).

Guadagno, Rosanna E. / R. B. Cialdini: Virtual Humans and Persuasion. The Effects of Agency and Behavioral Realism. In: Media Psychology 10 (2007), pp. 1–22.

Hayes-Roth, Barbara: What Makes Characters Seem Life-Like? In: Helmut Prendinger / Mitsuru Ishizuka (Eds.): Life-like Characters. Tools, Affective Functions and Applications. Berlin / New York 2003.

Kennedy, Helen W.: Lara Croft: Feminist Icon or Cyberbimbo? On the Limits of Textual Analysis. In: Game Studies 2/2 (2002). <http://www.gamestudies.org/0202/kennedy/> (Nov. 25th, 2008).

Klevjer, Rune: Gladiator, Worker, Operative. The Hero of the First Person Shooter Adventure. In: Marinka Copier / Joost Raessens (Eds.): Level Up. Digital Games Research Conference 2003 (CD-Rom). Utrecht 2003.

Koda, Tomoka / Pattie Maes: Agents with Faces. The Effect of Personification of Agents. In: Proceedings of HCI'96 (1996), pp. 98–103.

Konijn, E.A. / Henriette C. Van Vugt: Emotions in Mediated Interpersonal Communication. Toward Modeling Emotion in Virtual Humans. In: E.A.K. / Martin Tanis / Sonja Utz / Susan Barnes (Eds.): Mediated Interpersonal Communication. New York 2008.

Lankoski, Petri / Satu Heliö / Inger Ekman: Characters in Computer Games. Toward Understanding Interpretation and Design. Digra Proceedings 2003. <http://www.digra.org/dl/db/05087.10012.pdf> (Dec. 18th, 2008).

MacCallum-Stewart, Esther: »The Street Smarts of a Cartoon Princess«. New Roles for Women in Games. In: Digital Creativity 20/4 (2009), pp. 225–237.

Manninen, Toni / T. Kujanpää: The Value of Virtual Assets – The Role of Game Characters in MMOGs. In: International Journal of Business Science and Applied Management 2/1 (2007), pp. 21–33.

Manninen, Tony: Conceptual, Communicative and Pragmatic Aspects of Interaction Forms – Rich Interaction Model for Collaborative Virtual Environments. In: Proceedings of the 16th International Conference on Computer Animation and Social Agents (2003), pp. 168–174.

Martins, Nicole / Dmitri C. Williams / Kristen Harrison / Rabindra A. Ratan: A Content Analysis of Female Body Imagery in Video Games. In: Sex Roles 61/11&12 (2009), pp. 824–836.

Miller, Monica K. / Alicia Summers: Gender Differences in Video Game Characters' Roles, Appearances, and Attire as Portrayed in Video Game Magazines. In: Sex Roles 57/9&10 (2007), pp. 733–742.

Newman, James: The Myth of the Ergodic Videogame. Some Thoughts on Player-Character Relationships in Videogames. In: Game Studies 2/1 (2002). <http://www.gamestudies.org/0102/newman/> (Nov. 25th, 2008).

Ruttkay, Zsófia / Claire Dormann / Han Noot: Embodied Conversational Agents on a Common Ground. A Framework for Design and Evaluation. In: Zsófia Ruttkay / Catherine Pelachaud (Eds.): From Brows to Trust. Evaluating Embodied Conversational Agents Series. Dordrecht 2004, pp. 27–66.

Schirra, Jörg R. J./ Stefan Carl McGrath: Identifikationsformen in Computerspiel und Spielfilm. In: Michael Strübel (Ed.): Film und Krieg. Die Inszenierung von Politik zwischen Apologetik und Apokalypse. Opladen 2002, pp. 149–163. <ttp://isgwww.cs.uni-magdeburg.de/~schirra/Work/Papers/P01/P01-2/Spiel-Ident.pdf> (Dec. 18th, 2008).

Shaw, David / Nick Barnes / Alan Blair: Creating Characters for Dynamic Stories in Interactive Games. 2001. <users.rsise.anu.edu.au/~davids/docs/Shaw_ADCOG21.doc> (Nov. 25th, 2008).

Thomas, Maureen: Taking a Chance on Losing Yourself in the Game. In: Digital Creativity 20/4 (2009), pp. 253–275.

Van Vugt, Henriette C. / Johan F. Hoorn / Elly A. Konijn / Athina de Bie Dimitriadou: Affective Affordances. Improving Interface Character Engagement through Interaction. In: International Journal of Human-Computer Studies 64/9 (2006), pp. 874–888.

Van Vugt, Henriette C. / Elly A. Konijin / Johan F. Hoorn / I. Keur / A. Eliëns: Realism is not all! User Engagement with Task-Related Interface Characters. In: Interacting with Computers 19 (2007), pp. 267–280.

Van Vugt, Henriette C. / Elly A. Konijin / Johan F. Hoorn / J. Veldhuis: Why Fat Interface Characters are better E-Health Advisors. In: Lecture Notes in Artificial Intelligence 4133 (2006), pp. 1–13.

8 Characters: Approaches from Communication Studies and Media Psychology

8.1 Anthologies

Gumpert, Gary / Robert Cathcart (Eds.): Inter/Media. Interpersonal Communication in a Media World. 3rd edn. New York / Oxford 1986.

8.2 Definition and Ontology

Oatley, Keith / Raymond A. Mar: Evolutionary Pre-Adaptation and the Idea of Character in Fiction. In: Journal of Cultural and Evolutionary Psychology 3/2 (2005), pp. 179–194.

8.3 Cognitive Reception of Characters

Beedie, Christopher / Peter Terry / Andrew Lane: Distinctions Between Emotion and Mood. In: Cognition and Emotion 19/6 (2005), pp. 847–878.

Jesse Chandler / Sara Konrath / Norbert Schwarz: Online and On My Mind. Temporary and Chronic Accessibility Moderate the Influence of Media Figures. In: Media Psychology 12/2 (2009), pp. 210–226.

Egidi, Giovanna / Richard J. Gerrig: Readers' Experiences of Characters' Goals and Actions. In: Journal of Experimental Psychology: Learning, Memory, and Cognition 32/6 (2006), pp. 1322–1329.

Gerrig, Richard J. / David W. Allbritton: The Construction of Literary Character. A View from Cognitive Psychology. In: Style 24/3 (1990), pp. 380–391.

Hoffner, Cynthia / Joanne Cantor: Perceiving and Responding to Mass Media Characters. In: Jennings Bryant / Dolf Zillmann (Eds.): Responding to the Screen. Reception and Reaction Processes. Hillsdale, NJ 1991, pp. 63–102.

Hoorn, Johan F. / Elly A. Konijn: Perceiving and Experiencing Fictional Characters. An Integrative Account. In: Japanese Psychological Research 45/4 (2003), pp. 250–268.

Hoorn, Johan F. / Henriette C. Van Vugt: The Role of Social Norm in User-Engagement and Appreciation of the Web Interface Agent Bonzi Buddy. In: Lecture Notes in Artificial Intelligence 4133 (2006), p. 456.

Izod, John: Active Imagination and the Analysis of Film. In: Journal of Analytical Psychology 45/2 (2000), pp. 267–285.

Konijn, Elly A. / Brad J. Bushman: World Leaders as Movie Characters? Perceptions of George W. Bush, Tony Blair, Osama Bin Laden, and Saddam Hussein. In: Media Psychology 9/1 (2007), pp. 157–177.

Konijn, Elly A. / Johan F. Hoorn: Some Like It Bad. Testing a Model for Perceiving and Experiencing Fictional Characters. In: Media Psychology 7/2 (2005), pp. 107–144.

Lehnen-Beyel, Ilka: Kompetenz ins Gesicht geschrieben. Forscher: Kindliche Züge lassen Politiker weniger kompetent erscheinen und kosten bei Wahlen Punkte. 2005. <http://www.wissenschaft.de/wissen/news/254075.html> (Apr. 10th, 2010).

Little, Anthony C. / Robert P. Burrissa / Benedict Jones / S. Craig Roberts: Facial Appearance Affects Voting Decisions. In: Evolution and Human Behavior 28/1 (2007), pp. 18–27.
Meyrowitz, Joshua: Television and Interpersonal Behavior. Codes of Perception and Response. In: Gary Gumpert / Robert Cathcart (Eds.): Inter/Media. Interpersonal Communication in a Media World. 3rd edn. Oxford / New York 1986, pp. 253–272.
Morrow, D.G.: Prominent Characters and Events Organize Narrative Understanding. In: Journal of Memory and Language 24 (1985), pp. 304–319.
Sanford, Anthony J. / Michael Clegg / Asifa Majid: The Influence of Types of Character on Processing Background Information in Narrative Discourse. In: Memory and Cognition 26/6 (1998), pp. 1323–1329.
Siemer, Matthias: Moods as Multiple-Object Directed and as Objectless Affective States. An Examination of the Dispositional Theory of Moods. In: Cognition and Emotion 19/6 (2005), pp. 815–845.
Skolnick, Deena / Paul Bloom: What Does Batman Think About SpongeBob? Children's Understanding of the Fantasy/Fantasy Distinction. In: Cognition 101/1 (2006), pp. B9–B18.
<http://www.yale.edu/minddevlab/papers/skolnick&bloom%20cognition.pdf> (June 29th, 2010).

8.4 Identification, Empathy, Emotional Engagement with Characters

Bryant, Jennings / Peter Vorderer (Eds.): Psychology of Entertainment. Mahwah 2006.
Bryant, Jennings / Dolf Zillmann (Eds.): Responding to the Screen. Reception and Reaction Processes. Hillsdale 1991.
Cohen, Jonathan: Audience Identification with Media Characters. In: Jennings Bryant / Peter Vorderer (Eds.): Psychology of Entertainment. Mahwah, NJ 2006, pp. 183–198.
Cohen, Jonathan: Audience Identification with Media Characters. Essay on ›Identification‹. University of Haifa 2004 (unpublished).
Frijda, Nico / Dick Schram (Eds.): Poetics 23/1 (1994). Special issue: Emotions and Cultural Products.
Gratch, Jonathan / Stacy Marsella: Lessons from Emotion Psychology for the Design of Lifelike Characters. In: Applied Artificial Intelligence 19/3 (2005), pp. 215–233.
Klesen, Martin: Using Theatrical Concepts for Role-Plays with Educational Agents. In: Applied Artificial Intelligence 19/3 (2005), pp. 413–431.
Oatley, Keith / Mitra Gholamain: Emotions and Identification. Connections between Readers and Fiction. In: Mette Hjort / Sue Laver (Eds.): Emotions and the Arts. New York / Oxford 1997, pp. 263–281.
Oatley, Keith: Emotions and the Story Worlds of Fiction. In: Melanie C. Green / Jeffrey J. Strange / Timothy C. Brock (Eds.): Narrative Impact. Social and Cognitive Foundations. Mahwah, NJ 2002, pp. 39–69.
Paiva, Ana / João Dias / Daniel Sobral / Ruth Aylett / Sarah Woods / Lynne Hall / Carsten Zoll: Learning by Feeling. Evoking Empathy with Synthetic Characters. In: Applied Artificial Intelligence 19/3 (2005), pp. 235–266.
Tan, Ed S.: Emotion and the Structure of Narrative Film. Film as an Emotion Machine. Mahwah, NJ 1996.

Zillmann, Dolf: Empathy. Affect from Bearing Witness to the Emotions of Others. In: D. Z. / Jennings Bryant (Eds.): Responding to the Screen. Reception and Reaction Processes. Hillsdale, NJ 1991, pp. 135–168.

Zillmann, Dolf: Cinematic Creation of Emotion. In: Joseph D. Anderson. / Barbara Fisher-Anderson (Eds.): Moving Image Theory. Ecological Considerations. Carbondale, IL 2005, pp. 164–179.

Oatley, Keith / Mitra Gholamain: Emotions and Identification. Connections between Readers and Fiction. In: Mette Hjort / Sue Laver (Eds.): Emotions and the Arts. New York / Oxford 1997, pp. 263–281.

Oatley, Keith: Emotions and the Story Worlds of Fiction. In: Melanie C. Green / Jeffrey J. Strange / Timothy C. Brock (Eds.): Narrative Impact. Social and Cognitive Foundations. Mahwah, NJ 2002, pp. 39–69.

Paiva, Ana / João Dias / Daniel Sobral / Ruth Aylett / Sarah Woods / Lynne Hall / Carsten Zoll: Learning by Feeling. Evoking Empathy with Synthetic Characters. In: Applied Artificial Intelligence 19/3 (2005), pp. 235–266.

Tan, Ed S.: Emotion and the Structure of Narrative Film. Film as an Emotion Machine. Mahwah, NJ 1996.

Zillmann, Dolf: Empathy. Affect from Bearing Witness to the Emotions of Others. In: D. Z. / Jennings Bryant (Eds.): Responding to the Screen. Reception and Reaction Processes. Hillsdale, NJ 1991, pp. 135–168.

Zillmann, Dolf: Cinematic Creation of Emotion. In: Joseph D. Anderson. / Barbara Fisher-Anderson (Eds.): Moving Image Theory. Ecological Considerations. Carbondale, IL 2005, pp. 164–179.

8.5 Parasocial Interaction

Baeßler, Berit: Medienpersonen als parasoziale Beziehungspartner. Ein theoretischer und empirischer Beitrag zu personazentrierter Rezeption. Baden-Baden 2009.

Cohen, Jonathan / Eyal, Keren: When Good ›Friends‹ Say Goodbye. A Parasocial Breakup Study. Essay zum Thema ›Parasocial Breakup‹. Haifa 2005 (unpublished).

Giles, David C.: Parasocial Interaction. A Review of the Literature and a Model for Future Research. In: Media Psychology 4/3 (2002), pp. 279–304.

Gleich, Uli: Parasoziale Interaktionen und Beziehungen von Fernsehzuschauern mit Personen auf dem Bildschirm. Ein theoretischer und empirischer Beitrag zum Konzept des Aktiven Rezipienten. Landau 1997.

Hartmann, Tilo / Christoph Klimmt / Holger Schramm: Parasocial Interactions and Relationships. In: Jennings Bryant / Peter Vorderer (Eds.): Psychology of Entertainment. Mahwah, NJ 2006, pp. 291–313.

Hartmann, Tilo / Holger Schramm / Christoph Klimmt: Vorbereitende Überlegungen zur theoretischen Modellierung parasozialer Interaktionen im Prozess der Medienrezeption. 2004. <http://www.ijk.hmt-hannover.de/psi/> (Jan. 10th, 2004).

Hippel, Klemens: Parasoziale Interaktion. Bericht und Bibliographie. In: montage/av 1/1 (1992), pp. 135–155.

Horton, Donald / Richard R. Wohl: Mass Communication and Para-Social Interaction. Observation on Intimacy at a Distance [1956]. In: Gary Gumpert / Robert Cathcart (Eds.): Inter/Media. Interpersonal Communication in a Media World. 3rd edn. New York / Oxford 1986, pp. 185–206.

Klimmt, Christoph / Tilo Hartmann / Holger Schramm: Parasocial Interactions and Relationships. In: Jennings Bryant / Peter Vorderer (Eds.): Psychology of Entertainment. Mahwah, NJ 2006, pp. 291–314.

Vorderer, Peter (Ed.): Fernsehen als ›Beziehungskiste‹. Parasoziale Beziehungen und Interaktionen mit TV-Personen. Opladen 1996.

www.ingramcontent.com/pod-product-compliance
Lightning Source LLC
Chambersburg PA
CBHW070746230426
43665CB00017B/2260